the Lyle
official
ANTIQUES
review

All prices quoted in this book are obtained from a variety of auctions in various countries during the twelve months prior to publication and are converted to dollars at the rate of exchange prevalent at the time of sale.

DRAWINGS BY

PETER KNOX
PETER TENCH
GEORGE HOGG
ALISON MORRISON
CARMEN MILIVOYEVICH
ELAINE HARLAND
ROBERT SUTHERLAND
LEN GRAY
CHRIS MANSELL
TOM MACKIE
BRIAN HOLTON

the *Lyle*
official
ANTIQUES
review
1981

COMPILED BY MARGOT RUTHERFORD
EDITED BY TONY CURTIS

The publishers wish to express their sincere thanks
to the following for their kind help and assistance
in the production of this volume:

JANICE MONCRIEFF
MARGARET ANDERSON
BRIAN HOLTON
NICOLA PARK
CHRISTINE BROWN
CARMEN MILIVOYEVICH
MAY MUTCH
ELAINE HARLAND
ANNETTE HOGG

SBN   0-86248-001-9
Copyright © Lyle Publications '80.
Glenmayne, Galashiels, Scotland.

ISBN   0-8256-9686-0
Order Number 450021
Quick Fox,
33 West 60th Street,
New York, N.Y. 10023.

Printed by Apollo Press, Worthing, Sussex, England.
Bound by R. J. Acford, Chichester, Sussex, England.

CONTENTS

Acknowledgements

Abbott's, *The Hill, Wickham Market, Suffolk.*

James Adam & Son, *26 St. Stephen's Green North, Dublin.*

Ader, Picard, Tajan, *12 Rue Favart, Paris 75002.*

Aldridge's, *130-132 Walcot Street, Bath, Avon.*

Alfie's Antique Market, *13-15 Church Street, London.*

Allen & May, *18 Bridge Street, Andover, Hamps.*

Andrew Hilditch & Son, *19 The Square, Sandbach, Cheshire.*

Banks & Silver, *Worcester Street, Kidderminster.*

T. Bannister & Co., *Market Place, Haywards Heath, Sussex.*

Barber's, *12 Shoplatch, Shrewsbury, Salop.*

Barber's Fine Art Auctions, *6 Walton Road, Woking, Surrey.*

Biddle & Webb, *Enfield House, Islington Row, Edgbaston.*

Boardman's, *Clare, Suffolk.*

Messrs. Boisgirard and De Heeckeren, *Paris.*

Bonham's, *Montpelier Galleries, Montpelier Street, London.*

Bonsor Pennington's, *82 Eden Street, Kingston-upon-Thames.*

Brackett's, *27-29 High Street, Tunbridge Wells, Kent.*

Bradley & Vaughan, *59 Perrymount Road, Haywards Heath, Sx.*

British Antique Exporters, *206 London Rd., Burgess Hill, W. Sx.*

E.J. Brooks, *39 Park End Street, Oxford.*

Wm. H. Brown, *33 Watergate, Grantham, Lincs.*

Bruton Knowles & Co., *The Hill, Upton-on-Severn, Worcs.*

Buckell & Ballard, *1a Parsons Street, Banbury, Oxon.*

Buckland & Sons, *7 Blagrave Street, Reading, Berks.*

Bukowskis, *Arsenalsgatan 2, Stockholm.*

Burrows & Day, *39-41 Bank Street, Ashford, Kent.*

Burtenshaws Walker, *66 High Street, Lewes, Suffolk.*

Butler & Hatch Waterman, *86 High Street, Hythe, Kent.*

A.G. Byrne & Co., *Co. Wicklow, Ireland.*

Chancellors & Co., *31 High Street, Ascot, Berks.*

H.C. Chapman & Sons, *North Street, Scarborough, Yorks.*

Christie's, *8 King Street, St. James', London.*

Christie's, *Geneva, Per Agent.*

Christie's New York, *502 Park Avenue, New York.*

Christie'S. Kensington, *85 Old Brompton Road, London.*

Churchman's Auction Galleries, *Church Street, Steyning, W. Sx.*

Clarke Gammon, *45 High Street, Guildford, Surrey.*

Cobern, Entwistle & Co., *21 Houghton Street, Southport.*

Coles, Knapp & Kennedy, *Ross-on-Wye, Herefordshire.*

George Comins & Son, *3 Chequer Lane, Ely.*

Cooper Hirst, *Goldlay House, Parkway, Chelmsford.*

Cubitt & West, *Millmead, Guildford, Surrey.*

Dacre Son & Hartley, *1-5 The Grove, Ilkley, W. Yorks.*

Clifford Dann & Partners, *43 South Street, Eastbourne.*

Alonzo Dawes & Hoddell, *Sixways, Clevedon, Avon.*

Dee & Atkinson, *The Exchange, Driffield, Yorks.*

Dickinson, Davy & Markham, *10 Wrawly Street, Brigg.*

K. Hugh Dodd & Partners, *Chester Street, Mold, Clwyd.*

Robert Dove & Partners, *Dover House, Wolsey Street, Ipswich.*

Robert Dowie, *Leven, Fife.*

Drewatt, Watson & Barton, *22 Market Place, Newbury, Bucks.*

Hy. Duke & Son, *40 South Street, Dorchester, Dorset.*

Eadon, Lockwood & Riddle, *2 St. James' Street, Sheffield.*

J. & R. Edmiston's, *164-166 Bath Street, Glasgow.*

Edwards, Bigwood & Bewlay, *78 Colmore Row, Birmingham.*

Weller Eggar, *74 Castle Street, Farnham, Surrey.*

Elliott & Green, *40 High Street, Lymington.*

R.H. Ellis & Sons, *44-46 High Street, Worthing, Sussex.*

Frank H. Fellows, *Bedford House, 88 Hagley Road, Edgbaston.*

Alan Fitchett & Co., *28 Gloucester Street, Brighton, Sussex.*

John D. Fleming, *Melton House, High St., Dulverton, Somerset.*

John Francis, T. Jones & Sons, *King Street, Carmarthen, Dyfed.*

F. le Gallais, *Bath Street, Jersey, Channel Islands.*

Garrod Turner, *50 St. Nicholas Street, Ipswich, Suffolk.*

P.J. Garwood, *Ludlow, Shropshire.*

Geering & Colyer, *Highgate, Hawkhurst, Kent.*

Stanley Gibbons, *391 Strand, London.*

Rowland Gorringe, *15 North Street, Lewes, Sussex.*

Andrew Grant, *Cookshill, Salwarpe, Droitwich, Worcs.*

Graves, Son & Pilcher, *38 Holland Road, Hove, Sussex.*

Gray's Antique Market, *58 Davies Street, London.*

Gray's Antique Mews, *1-7 Davies Mews, London.*

Green's, *Wantage, Oxon.*

Gribble, Booth & Taylor, *West Street, Axminster, Devon.*

James Harrison, *35 West End, Hebden Bridge, W. Yorks.*

Harrods Auction Galleries, *Arundel Terrace, Barnes, London.*

Heathcote Ball & Co., *47 New Walk, Leicester.*

Hexton & Cheney, *3 Pier Road, Littlehampton, Sussex.*

Hobbs Parker, *9 Tufton Street, Ashford, Kent.*

John Hodbin, *53 High Street, Tenterden, Kent.*

Honiton Galleries, *63 High Street, Honiton.*

Humberts, King & Chasemore, *Magdalene House,*
Magdalene St., Taunton, Somerset.

Hussey's, *Alphinbrook Road, Alphington, Exeter.*

Peter Ineichen, *Zurich.*

Raymond Inman, *35-40 Temple Street, Brighton.*

Jackson-Stops & Staff, *Town Hall, Chipping Camden, Glos.*

Jolly's, *The Auction Rooms, Old King Street, Bath.*

Jordan & Cook, *High Street, Worthing.*

G.A. Key, *Market Place, Aylsham, Norfolk.*

Kings Auction Rooms, *5 Denmark Hill, Camberwell, London.*

G. Knight & Son, *West Street, Midhurst, Sussex.*

Kunsthaus am Museum, *Cologne, Germany.*

Lacy Scott, *3 Hatter Street, Bury St. Edmunds.*

Laidlaw's, *Wakefield, Yorks.*

Lalonde Bros. & Parham, *Station Rd., Weston-Super-Mare, Avon.*

W.H. Lane & Son, *Morrab Road, Penzance, Cornwall.*

Langlois Ltd., *Don Street, Jersey, Channel Islands.*

T.R.G. Lawrence & Son, *19b Market St., Crewkerne, Somerset.*

James & Lister Lea, *11 New Hall Street, Birmingham.*

J.G. Lear & Son, *71 Church Street, Malvern.*

Leys, *Kipdorpvest 46, Antwerp.*

Linden Alcock, *89 Bridge Street, Hereford.*

Locke & England, *1-2 Euston Place, Leamington Spa, Warwicks.*

Loudmer, *Poulain's, Paris.*

R.L. Lowery & Partners, *24 Bridge Street, Northampton.*

Mallams, *26 Grosvenor Street, Cheltenham.*

Mallams, *24 St. Michael's Street, Oxford.*

Manchester Auction Mart, *3-4 Atkinson Street, Manchester.*

Frank R. Marshall & Co., *Marshall House,*
·Church Hill, Knutsford.

Thomas Mawer & Sons, *Lincoln Auction Rooms, Lincoln.*

May, Whetter & Grose, *Cornubia Hall, Par, Cornwall.*

McCartney, Morris & Barker, *25 Corve St., Ludlow, Shropshire.*

Meads of Brighton, *St. Nicholas Road, Brighton.*

Messenger, May & Baverstock, *93 High Street, Godalming.*

John Milne, *9 North Silver Street, Aberdeen.*

Moore, Allen & Innocents, *33 Castle Street, Cirencester, Glos.*

Morphet's, *4-6 Albert Street, Harrogate.*

Morton's, *New Orleans, America.*

Moss, *13 Whitehorse Street, Baldock, Herts.*

Alfred Mossop & Co., *Kelsick Road, Ambleside.*

Neales, *192 Mansfield Road, Nottingham.*

D.M. Nesbit & Co., *7 Clarendon Road, Southsea, Hants.*

Nicholas, *13 Bridge Street, Caversham, Reading.*

Nock Deighton, *52 Whitburn Street, Bridgnorth, Shrops.*

Noton, *High Street, Oakham.*

Nottingham Auction Mart, *Byard Lane, Bridlesmith Gate, Notts.*

Nottinghill Antique Market, *Nottinghill Gate, London.*

Olivers, *23-24 Market Hill, Sudbury, Suffolk.*

Osmond Tricks & Son, *The Auction Rooms, Regent St., Bristol.*

Outhwaite & Litherland, *Kingsway Galls., Fontenoy St., L'pool.*

Palmeira Auction Rooms, *Hove, Sussex.*

Parsons, Welch & Cowell, *129 High Street, Sevenoaks, Kent.*

Peacock, *26 Newnham Street, Bedford.*

Pearsons, *Walcote Chambers, High Street, Winchester.*

Phillips, *7 Blenheim Street, New Bond Street, London.*

Phillips, *New York Gallery.*

Phillips & Jolly, *The Auction Rooms, Old King Street, Bath.*

Phillips Ward-Price, *67 Davenport Road, Toronto, Canada.*

John H. Raby, *St. Mary's Road, Bradford, Yorks.*

Ragg, Travis & Isherwood, *12 Princes Drive, Colwyn Bay, Wales.*

Samuel Rains & Son, *17 Warren Street, Stockport.*

Ernest R. de Rome, *12 New John Street, Westgate, Bradford.*

Russell, Baldwin & Bright, *Ryelands Road, Leominster.*

Shakespear, McTurk & Graham, *17 Wellington Street, Leicester.*

Andrew Sharpe & Partners, *Ilkley, Yorkshire.*

Robert W. Skinner Inc., *Bolton Gallery, Massachusetts, U.S.A.*

Smith-Woolley & Perry, *5 West Terrace, Folkestone.*

Sotheby's, *34-35 New Bond Street, London.*

Sotheby Bearne, *3 Warren Road, Torquay, Devon.*

Sotheby's Belgravia, *19 Motcomb Street, London.*

Sotheby's Hong Kong, *Per Agent.*

Sotheby, King & Chasemore, *Station Road, Pulborough, W. Sx.*

Sotheby's Monaco, *Sporting d'Hiver, Monte Carlo.*

Sotheby's New York, *U.S.A.*

Sotheby's Zurich, *Per Agent.*

Southam & Sons, *Corn Exchange, Kettering, Northants.*

Spear & Sons, *The Hill, Wickham Market, Suffolk.*

Henry Spencer & Sons, *20 The Square, Retford, Notts.*

Spink/Koller, *Zurich.*

Stanilands, *28 Netherhall Road, Doncaster, Yorks.*

Stride's, *Southdown House, St. John's Street, Chichester.*

Swetenham's, *Bold Place, Chester, Cheshire.*

Sworder's Salerooms, *19 North Street, Bishop Stortford.*

Christopher Sykes, *11 Market Place, Woburn, Milton Keynes.*

David Symonds, *High Street, Crediton, Devon.*

Taylor, Son & Creber, *38 North Hill, Plymouth, Devon.*

John E. Tennant, *Old Chapel Saleroom, Market Pl., Richmond.*

Theriault, *Pennsylvania, America.*

Turner Fletcher, *Essex.*

U.T.O., *Auktionen, Lucerne.*

Vernon's of Chichester, *1 Westgate, Chichester.*

Vidler & Co., *Rye Auction Galleries, Rye, Sussex.*

Vincent & Vanderpump, *24 Greyfriars Road, Reading.*

Vost's, *Lower Marney Tower, Colchester, Essex.*

Walker, Barnett & Hills, *Wolverhampton, Staffs.*

Wallis & Wallis, *Regency House, 1 Albion Street, Lewes, Sussex.*

Warner, Sheppard & Wade, *16-18 Halford Street, Leicester.*

Thomas Watson, *27 North Street, Bishops Stortford.*

J.M. Welch & Sons, *The Town Hall, Dunmow, Essex.*

C. Wesley Haslam & Son, *High Street, Rhyl.*

West London Auctions, *Sandringham Mews, London.*

Whitehead's, *34 High Street, Petersfield.*

Peter Wilson, *50 Hospital Street, Nantwich, Cheshire.*

P.F. Windibank, *18 Reigate Road, Dorking, Surrey.*

Richard W. Withington, Inc., *Concord, New Hampshire.*

H.C. Wolton & Son, *The Athenaum, Bury St. Edmunds.*

Woolley & Wallis, *The Castle Auction Mart, Salisbury, Wilts.*

Eldon E. Worral & Co., *Liverpool.*

Worsfolds, *40 Station Road West, Canterbury, Kent.*

ANTIQUES REVIEW

It would be irresponsible to suggest that the past year has been anything but a troubled one for the majority of the antique trade. People have been beleaguered on every side by problems like a strong pound, inflation, recession, lack of consumer spending and ever rising overheads. Talking to dealers all over the country was by and large like meeting old friends at a funeral — but having said all that, it cannot be denied that antique buying and selling can still be profitable if certain guidelines are borne in mind.

So this foreword is not an obituary on the antique trade — rather it is a blueprint for survival brightened up here and there with some very high spots indeed.

It is certain that 1980 will be remembered by many people as the year that gold and silver went mad. Like a bolt from the blue speculators moved in on the bullion trade and prices started on a crazy escalation that was unfortunately to end with several people getting their fingers burned. In September 1979 22 carat gold jumped £4 ($8.50) an ounce in only four days till the price stood at what the market considered the ridiculous level of £125.06 ($271.30) and (£4.29 ($9.27) an ounce for silver). By January the sceptics were shaking

their heads even harder because gold had escalated to £234.70 ($528) an ounce for 22 carat, and sterling silver to £14.30 ($32.20) an ounce. While everybody was getting onto the bandwagon later in the month, Phillips the auctioneers appealed to the Government to try to do something to halt the massive rush to melt down antique silver and other precious metals. Television screens and radio bulletins were full of sad reports of fine quality pieces going to the smelters for quick ready money. Queues formed daily in Hatton Garden with people carrying items which represented another draining away of the antiques heritage. Before long even the smelters stopped coping and called a halt to this new gold rush. But not before many things were lost forever — a regrettable tale.

There is of course a moral in all this. The market proved to be a false one and gold and silver prices had to fall. First of all the smelters had more bullion than they could handle and began to charge a higher premium for their services, then as uncertainty prevailed, the price slide started. Gold and silver dropped daily, till in March the prices were standing at £175.11 ($386) per 22 carat gold ounce and £9.19 ($20.26) per ounce of sterling silver. Gold managed to stay more or less

An early Victorian four-piece tea service, weighing 68oz., sold at Sotheby, King & Chasemore in March for £1,100.

stable at its May price of £173.99 ($402) per ounce, but silver had taken a hammering and it went down as low as £4.88 ($11) at the end of April. The silver market has still not picked itself up and there are many people around who bought when prices were rising and soon found that they held on too long. One piece of belated cheer in all this, however, is that anyone who is in possession of silver which was bought before the crazy market began should find themselves with very attractive items because of the loss of so many pieces to the smelters' furnaces. The moral is, at the moment, hold on to your silver or buy when it is low.

Fortunately the sad tale of silver and gold is not the story of all the anti-

que world. In every part of the country reports have been coming in of small shops going to the wall. Telephone numbers remembered from last year now only give discontinued line signals. Long faces prevail at the bottom end of the market. But there are people who say that this radical pruning was necessary. They remember the times when there were more dealers than goods available and they comfort themselves with the belief that anyone who can hang on through this crisis is sure to have a head start in the future, as well as being able to pick and choose their purchases more easily. From Brighton — the one time antique dealers' paradise — to Edinburgh, many small shops are being vacated. Even in the once safe haven of Kensington Church Street five shops were vacated within a matter of weeks. 1980 was certainly the year of the great thinning out process.

Some of the people forced by rising overheads and falling profits to call a halt to their shop owning days have turned their attention to trade fairs and antique supermarkets but here also there seems to have been rather too much of a good thing going on. It seems as if the great buying public are holding onto their money more than in the past. The antique fair business has been feeling a pinch and perhaps there are too many supermarkets for would-be stall holders to fill them.

Unpalatable as it seems, it is necessary to continue the tale of woe. Not content to plague antique dealers with inflation and rising costs, rents going through the ceiling, petrol always rising and wages having to be increased, the pound sterling decided to flex its muscles and grow strong. This has meant that a pound which stood for a while at $ 2.6 effectively made foreign buying a thing of the past. In the summer while the sun shone, buyers stayed away, particularly the Americans: a dealer on the South Coast said that one very good American customer who used to visit him five times a year only made two visits in twelve months, and even then did not buy anything. The strong pound also meant that the European trade which for so long had been a surefire outlet for almost anything that could vaguely be called old was also in abeyance.

The shippers who built business empires on sending containers to foreign parts were forced to draw back or re-think but again this has not been entirely a bad thing. Many of them have come up with the idea of offering customer inducement. Michael Davis, for example, hit on the scheme of offering space in partly filled containers at very attractive prices and others followed his example — this has meant that people who are still shipping are able to reap some advantages from the embarrassment of their colleagues.

Antique dealers are by nature resourceful people and there is nothing like a troubled situation to bring out the best in them. The trade press is full of business enterprise rising again — attractive rates offered for supermarket stalls, shipping bargains — and not content with that many dealers are 'scouring the world' for things to buy, in the words of one of them. Their track has taken many to the U.S.A. where they are finding that items which do not particularly appeal to the American market can be bought cheaply and shipped back to Britain to show a good profit.

With the recent announcement that more than one and a half million tourists from Britain are expected to visit America by the end of 1980, it might be worth bearing in mind that many portable antiques — small pieces of a decorative nature — and Continental or inlaid furniture make more in Europe at the moment than they do in America. Many dealers have found that a holiday or a visit to America can yield a very nice profit if they are prepared to keep their eyes open for the sort of thing that Americans do not fancy as much as Europeans do.

Occasionally, even very expensive and rare items can be bought in America, like the set of eight English

Sotheby, King & Chasemore sold this fine 19th century Dutch marquetry bureau for £1,500 in July.

chairs dating from around 1739 which London dealers Blairmans bought at Christie's in New York for around one hundred and thirty-two thousand pounds. They bought the chairs for a private client in England. The red lacquer chairs had been made by Giles Grendey for the Duke of Infantando and were part of the furnishing of his castle in Spain before going to America.

The growing trend for purchasing antiques for return to Britain across the Atlantic was also shown by the purchase of a large and important collection of Delftware by the Hampshire County Museum Service from an American West Coast collector.

A new museum is planned for Winchester to open in 1985 and the Delftware will be one of its major exhibits. The collection of Delft belonged to collector James Stevens who originally bought most of it over a period of twenty years from English dealers.

While dealers have been suffering the auction houses have not felt the pinch so badly (though they have not entirely been laughing all the way to the bank). Christie's announced that their profits for the year ending December 31 1979 were £6.2 million. A very healthy sum compared to the £5.6 million they made in 1978. However the 1978 figure represented a thirty-five per cent increase over the previous year while the 1979 figure was only an eleven per cent increase. As far as the London salerooms were concerned in the autumn period it was Christie's who returned the best figures: Sotheby's showed three per cent less in their Bond Street Rooms than they had done in the same period of 1978. Their Belgravia outlet however was up ten per cent to £4.1 million.

Bonham's were up four point two per cent at £4.2 million and Phillips (who do not declare separate figures for London) had a worldwide turnover figure of £30.8 million, an increase of twelve per cent on the previous year's total. Both Sotheby's and Christie's had a worldwide increase of thirty-one per cent. It is very significant that both the big houses made their greatest progress in North America, which shows a rapid growth in the market on that side of the Atlantic.

Figures available from Department of Trade statistics show that the sterling value of Britain's export of antiques in 1979 dropped by four per cent to £123.6 million. Imports also dropped by seventeen per cent to £62.4 million. Exports and imports of fine arts however — fine arts are paintings and sculpture of any age — both increased. Exports were up thirteen per cent to £147.4 million and imports were also up by thirty-six per cent to £201.5 million. It must of course be borne in mind that very often the same picture can appear in both sets of statistics if it is bought in for sale and then re-exported. This gives a picture of Britain as a huge art and antiques market place rather than a country whose own heritage is slowly sold abroad.

America was again top of the league for antiques and art exports from the U.K. but the antiques export market was down one per cent and the art market down seven per cent. France, Japan and Australia all showed an increase in the amounts of antiques exported from Britain — France was up nineteen per cent, Japan up seventeen per cent and Australia up eight per cent. In the art export market Switzerland was up thirty per cent, Holland up a staggering two hundred and forty per cent, Japan up forty-four per cent, Canada up forty-five per cent and Germany up fifteen per cent. Imports of antiques to the U.K. from the U.S.A., Switzerland and Germany were down eighteen per cent, forty-one per cent and ten per cent respectively with Holland showing a thirty-six per cent increase and France a two per cent increase. Art imports from the U.S.A. were up thirty per cent, France up seventy per cent, Germany sixty-seven per cent and Holland another large two hundred and forty per cent rise. Some of the more dramatic rises can be accounted for by the movement of large individual collections. The continuing position of Britain as the international changing house for all this activity is, however, a very cheering sign.

In fact, the world still seems to look to Britain as the antiques headquarters. Dealers who are still flourishing in the export business report that there has been a continued interest from Japanese buyers; Jean Scales, who owns a large furniture warehouse near Tower Bridge, said that Japan is a big buyer of some of her good quality Edwardian and Victorian furniture. Though this does not sound the sort of thing that might go very well with traditional Japanese homes, Mrs. Scales reports that two large customers she has in Japan cannot get enough to satisfy demand — 'Though I must admit they don't buy big items of furniture — more the small pieces which seem on a scale with Japanese culture', she said.

Top: Victorian papier mache work table. (Sotheby, King & Chasemore)   £400
Below: Edwardian mahogany and marquetry serving cabinet. (Sotheby's Belgravia)   £320

A late Ming blue and white bowl with everted rim, 13in. diameter. (Christie's Tokyo) $52,900 £22,800

A Yongzheng pale celadon glazed bowl moulded on the exterior with sprays of peony. (Christie's Tokyo) $17,000 £7,370

The Far East has also been the scene for interest from London based auction houses. Christie's held a series of sales in Tokyo in February and that was a very big breakthrough for them: previously it was not possible, because of local legislation, for outside auctioneers to conduct sales in Japan. The Christie's move followed that of Sotheby's who a few months before managed to make an agreement with a large Japanese department store, Seibu, where Sotheby's catalogues for worldwide sales would be available in the store and bids could be taken on behalf of the auctioneers. Spinks too plan to operate in Japan and the opening of this market can only provide a boost for the antique trade.

Although the trade has had its black patches throughout the year, there have also been one or two areas of great interest and keen buying, especially in furniture of the 1920's and '30's period. The French in particular have shown keen interest in this sort of thing and Sotheby Parke Bernet in Monaco jumped on the bandwagon when they held three sales in one day in May at the Sporting D'Hiver in Monte Carlo. Even the auctioneers were surprised by the prices some of the items made. One of the sales was of the contents of the Paris flat of designer Eileen Gray who was born in Eire but went to live and work in Paris in 1907. Miss Gray died there in 1976 and her niece decided to sell the contents of her flat, much of which had been designed by Miss Gray herself. Because of the rarity of some of the lots it was particularly difficult for estimates to be given. One of them, a five-fold lacquer screen made 110,000 French francs. Even more spectacular and unexpected prices were made at another sale on the same day of Modernist furniture

A five-fold lacquer screen by Eileen Gray sold by Sotheby's in Monaco for 110,000 French francs.

from the palace of the Maharajah of Indore in India. The Maharajah's Palace was designed by Eckhart Muthesius, between 1930 and 1933, and at the same time the furniture was also commissioned from several famous designers. A pair of red leather armchairs designed by Muthesius himself sold for 180,000 French francs; a bed made of chrome metal tubes sold for 230,000 francs; another in aluminium and chrome made the highest price in the sale, 560,000 francs.

A 1930's tubular chrome bed belonging to the Maharajah of Indore, sold by Sotheby's in Monaco for 230,000 French francs.

This magnificent aluminium and chrome bed made 560,000 French francs at Sotheby's, Monaco, the highest price in the sale.

This interest in Modernist furniture on the Continent is also reflected in the very high prices being recorded now for good quality Art Deco, particularly bronzes, and glass by Daum, Galle and Lalique.

A small Galle cameo glass vase. (Sotheby, King & Chasemore) £200

In fact Art Deco, and to a lesser extent Art Nouveau, is still one of the strongest areas of the antique market. But to make good prices and hold their value, the items have to be of good quality. The time when any old Deco tat could sell has passed and buyers have become very much more selective. There is still a good deal of Deco around however, particularly in jewellery, where the prices are continually rising.

In fact, one of the great guidelines for surviving the slump is always to concentrate on quality. Every dealer has stressed that and in an address to members of B.A.D.A., Mr. Julian Agnew recently said 'the party is over' . . . . . adding, 'Probably we had it too easy. The collectors who bought unwisely, the dealers who paid too much and the auctioneers who over-promoted had their sins washed away by the rising tide of inflation.' He felt however that in the end this may not be a bad thing because

A bronze and ivory figure of a dancing girl by Joe Descomps, 1920, sold by Sotheby, King & Chasemore for £400.

there would be a revulsion against buying purely for 'investment', and this might lead to a sorting out of the goods.

This is exactly what appears to have been happening since then. Dealers all stress that they are still selling better quality pieces (and portable items — buyers from abroad often want to avoid heavy shipping costs so they buy something they can carry themselves).

'It is becoming increasingly difficult to sell repaired or damaged pieces,' said one South Coast dealer, 'What people want are first class pieces in excellent clean condition. We are still doing very well with good quality Victorian and Edwardian oak and mahogany furniture that people can live with.'

Another London dealer, Nick Bell, who owns a warehouse in Notting Hill Gate, said that his stall holders who are still making a living specialise in good quality household furniture.

'This is a residential area where flats change hands frequently,' he said, 'People still buy furniture that is good and they want to keep all their lives. They will also buy items that they might see reproduced and they either find that they can get it cheaper from a dealer or that it has just that little something special that makes them prefer it to the modern example.'

In general it seems that the 'tat' market is fairly static. People just do not have the spare money to spend on something that may not hold its price. In spite of that, however, there will always be collectors and there are always areas for them to specialise in. One area that has been quietly growing through the years is cameras. Now 1930's and even '40's cameras are making good money and they can certainly be seen as

A set of six Victorian walnut balloon back chairs. (Sotheby, King & Chasemore)
£580

A 1938 Swiss Compass II miniature camera. (Sotheby's Belgravia) **£380**

A 1930's Soho tropical reflex camera. (Sotheby's Belgravia) **£950**

At the same sale Lincoln's bearskin top hat made four thousand nine hundred and fifty pounds.

Any interesting item associated with a historical character like Lincoln, of course, will always find an interested buyer, but there are other items as well which cannot fail to make money. Much interest has been shown in recent years in animal skins — tiger skin rugs, polar bear rugs. A good tiger skin mounted on felt with a ferocious set of well-preserved teeth should make at least four hundred pounds in auction today. The price is perhaps protected by the fact that tigers are also protected now and no more skins will be preserved for the future.

A Continental polyphon sold with 22 discs. (Sotheby, King & Chasemore) **£1,400**

an investment. Opera and field glasses, especially those from around the time of the first world war, are also highly regarded. Recently Sotheby's in New York sold a pair of opera glasses belonging to Abraham Lincoln for eleven thousand pounds — the price was perhaps explained by the tale that he had been carrying them when he was assassinated.

The antique world keeps throwing up its interesting and humorous items — old gramophones have a strong following. A Columbia Regal Junior gramophone from around 1914 sold for five hundred and fifty pounds at

An American Wurlitzer 700 78 rpm jukebox, in a cabinet by Paul Fuller, circa 1939, 4ft. high. (Sotheby's Belgravia) £1,600

Christie's in South Kensington recently and at the same sale a de luxe New Melba gramophone sold for one thousand two hundred pounds. Music boxes too always have keen interest shown in them even when in need of repair, and fun items like pianolas, especially if they come with a good collection of rolls, are continually making very healthy prices. Perhaps all this shows a longing to return to the Victorian days of home entertainment.

Buyers are always well advised to put their minds to building up a collection if they want to end up with a money making asset. Collections of early motoring artefacts or items from early flying history which have sold recently have more than repaid the original investment. A good collection of course has to be built up with love. Here again the old advice holds good — only buy something that you like and not just because you think you will be able to sell it again at a profit.

In the field of china the very finest and rarest items are still making large prices. A large rush of interest has recently been shown in Cantonese ware. Belleek china, which has always been sought after by a few specialist collectors, has also gained a great deal of popularity recently with rapid growths of collectors' clubs in the United States. At a sale held in Slane Castle, Eire, recently, bids for Belleek items were taken from customers as far away as California and Hong Kong, and a modest little Belleek jampot went for over two hundred pounds.

Another area of the market which has boomed in the past year is fans. A year ago it would have been possible to buy even the very finest fan

A Belleek beehive shaped pot and cover sold for over £200 at Sotheby's Slane Castle sale.

for around fifty pounds. Today however prices have trebled and quadrupled and interest has been greatly whetted by a special sale of fans held at Bonham's in the spring. Again there have always been fan 'fans' but publicity about the subject and one or two new books about fans have sparked off a wider and more general interest — and consequently a rise in prices.

At Edinburgh, Phillips also held a successful sale of some thirty fans in the summer. This seems to be the time to buy fans before the prices rise too high because it is still possible to get some very good examples for under one hundred pounds.

If fans have a connotation with a bygone and romantic age, another area of the collecting world reminds buyers of their childhood. Dolls never lose their value, especially good French or German bebes, but the market has widened to include 1930 Chad Valley examples that many buyers living today can remember handling in their own nurseries. Toys seem to be on an ever increasing spiral . . . especially tin plate toys which seem to be a sure fire recipe for financial success, especially if they are in an unchipped condition. Children's games too are selling well — and even more adult games like seaside 'What the Butler Saw' machines and jukeboxes from the 1940's and the early '50's. Look out too for 1950 and '60 type toy robots — they might well be the collector's items of the future. The sort with eyes that light up as they stride about the floor are very highly prized indeed.

Bryan's 'Hidden Treasure' penny in the slot amusement machine.(Sotheby, King & Chasemore) £48

A collection of German bisque headed dolls sold for a total of £420 at Sotheby Bearne.

A very scarce set of six Hornby model cars.(Sotheby, King & Chasemore) £1,460

Clothes as antique items are always wanted. This is an area of the market that does very well in days of poverty — buyers will pay highly for examples of dresses, coats and shoes from the 1920's, 1930's and 1940's that can still be worn and look smart.

Also sought after are clothes which have belonged to celebrities — film stars and notables of almost any sort. Bonham's had a sale recently of clothes belonging to such recent and short lived luminaries as Katy Boyle and Anthea Redfern — remember Anthea? More serious, however, are lovely clothes from the past — some dating back for centuries, others only to the earlier years of the twentieth century. Buyers are also keen to buy old Chinese robes, lace, furs and good quality old fashioned luggage and handbags, especially in crocodile.

In fact the spectrum of the antique trade is as wide as life itself. Like life it has its ups and downs, but pessimism is not entirely called for when surveying the state of the market. There are still lovely and rare things to be bought; there are still people eager to acquire them; there are still real lovers of beauty who would rather eat fish fingers off a fine china plate than a fillet steak off chipped earthenware. The best advice, given by all the most resilient dealers and collectors, is to ignore the gloom and pessimism and to go on buying and looking for what you like. If you like it and can afford it, the thing to do is to buy it. Investing in something worthwhile, especially when it gives you pleasure, is never a mistake.

LIZ TAYLOR

THE REVISED CHINESE SPELLING SYSTEM

The Chinese writing system differs from our own Roman alphabet in that it is not a phonetic system. There is thus no simple one-to-one correspondence between equivalent letters and transcription has until recently been done according to several different systems. In the West, the most familiar is the Wade-Giles romanisation, through which we know almost all the basic trade terms. It has, however, several shortcomings, such as the confusing use of the apostrophe to show aspiration.

For some thirty years now, the system known as "Pinyin" has been in general use in the People's Republic of China. It has the merits of phonetic accuracy and simplicity, and has been used in the academic world for some time. No doubt as a result of closer East-West contact, the English-speaking media have recently adopted Pinyin, and, as from 1979-80, so too have the major auction houses.

As it seems likely that Pinyin will continue in use as the only acceptable system of transcribing Chinese terms, we have used it throughout this book.

The table below shows the main phonetic changes (Pinyin is in italics)

INITIALS

P	–	*B*
TS	–	*Z*
CH	–	*J**
T'	–	*T*
CH'	–	*CH**
K	–	*G*
SS	–	*S*
HS	–	*X*
TZ'	–	*C*

T	–	*D*
CH	–	*ZH**
P'	–	*P*
TS'	–	*C*
CH'	–	*Q**
TZ	–	*Z*
J	–	*R*
K'	–	*K*
SZ	–	*S*

FINALS*

IH	–	*I*		IEH	–	*IE*
UEI	–	*UI*		U	–	*U*
UAN	–	*UAN*		U	–	*I*
IEN	–	*IAN*		UNG	–	*ONG*
UEH	–	*UE*		UN	–	*UN*
YEN	–	*YAN*				

*eg.

chih	–	*zhi*		chi	–	*ji*
ch'ih	–	*chi*		ch'i	–	*qi*
chu	–	*zhu*		chu	–	*ju*
ch'u	–	*chu*		ch'u	–	*qu*

EXAMPLES

anhua	an hua	*feicui*	fei ts'ui
jia	chia	*Fujian*	Fukien
jiao	chiao	*he*	ho
Jian	Chien	*Hehe Erxian*	Ho-ho Erh Hsien
zhi	chih	*Henan*	Honan
chilong	Ch'ih Lung	*Xiwangmu*	Hsi Wang Mu
qilin	ch'i-lin	*Yixing*	I Hsing
jue	chueh	*Ru*	Ju
Jun	Chun	*ruyi*	ju-i
fahua	fa hua	*gu*	ku

Guandi	**Kuan Ti**	*Budai*	**Pu Tai**
guang	kuang	*Sancai*	**San ts'ai**
Guangdong	**Kuang Tung**	*Shoulao*	**Shou Lao**
Guan	**Kuan**	*taotie*	**t'ao-t'ieh**
Guanyin	**Kuan Yin**	*ding*	ting
gui	kuei	*dou*	tou
kui	k'uei	*doucai*	**tou ts'ai**
Guyuexuan	**Ku Yueh Hsuan**	*Caishen*	**Ts'ai Shen**
lehan	lohan	*cong*	ts'ung
leiwen	lei-wen	*Cizhou*	**Tz'u chou**
lingzhi	ling chih	*wucai*	**wu ts'ai**
Longquan	**Lung-ch'uan**	*yanyan*	yen-yen
meiping	mei-p'ing	*yingqing*	**ying ch'ing**
Baxian	**Pa Hsien**	*Yue*	**Yueh**
bi	pi		

CHINESE DYNASTIES

Shang	**1766-1123BC**		*5 Dynasties*	**907-960**
Zhou	**1122-249BC**	**(Chou)**	*Liao*	**907-1125**
Warring States	**403-221BC**		*Song*	**960-1279** (Sung)
Qin	**221-207BC**	**(Ch'in)**	*Jin*	**1115-1234** (Chin)
Han	**206BC-AD220**		*Yuan*	**1260-1368**
6 Dynasties	**317-589**		*Ming*	**1368-1644**
Sui	**590-618**		*Qing*	**1644-1911** (Ch'ing)
Tang	**618-906**	**(T'ang)**		

REIGN PERIODS

MING

Hongwu	**1368-1398**	*Chenghua*	**1465-1487**
Jianwen	**1399-1402**	*Hongzhi*	**1488-1505**
Yongle	**1403-1424**	*Zhengde*	**1506-1521**
Hongxi	**1425**	*Jiajing*	**1522-1566**
Xuande	**1426-1435**	*Longqing*	**1567-1572**
Zhengtong	**1436-1449**	*Wanli*	**1573-1620**
Jingtai	**1450-1456**	*Taichang*	**1620**
Tianshun	**1457-1464**	*Tianqi*	**1621-1627**
		Chongzheng	**1628-1644**

QING

Shunzhi	**1644-1662**	*Daoguang*	**1821-1850**
Kangxi	**1662-1722**	*Xianfeng*	**1851-1861**
Yongzheng	**1723-1735**	*Tongzhi*	**1862-1874**
Qianlong	**1736-1795**	*Guangxu*	**1875-1908**
Jiali	**1796-1820**	*Xuantong*	**1908-1911**

32

OOLA BOOLA ANTIQUES
AT TOWER BRIDGE

166 TOWER BRIDGE ROAD
LONDON, S.E.1.

01 403-0794 (Warehouse)
01 693-5050 (Home)

10,000 SQUARE FEET WAREHOUSE

WITHIN TWO MINUTES WALKING DISTANCE
OF BERMONDSEY MARKET

We stock large quantities of good quality Victorian and Edwardian furniture, also shipping furniture. Our Warehouse is very large, 10,000 square feet (926 square metres) on 3 floors where the furniture is displayed so that it can be easily seen. Also we have a restoration unit for our customers. Ample parking and good loading facilities. Open Monday – Friday 9 a.m.–5.30 p.m. with late night Thursday until 7 p.m., and early opening on Friday morning at 8 a.m., OR BY APPOINTMENT.

We look forward to welcoming you to Oola Boola Antiques at Tower Bridge. WE ALSO, OF COURSE, BUY ANTIQUES AND OFFER THE HIGHEST PRICES POSSIBLE.

BRITISH ANTIQUE EXPORTERS LTD

WHOLESALERS EXPORTERS PACKERS SHIPPERS

HEAD OFFICE: QUEEN ELIZABETH AVENUE, BURGESS HILL, WEST SUSSEX, RH15 9RX ENGLAND

TELEX 87688

CABLES BRITISHANTIQUES BURGESS HILL

TELEPHONE BURGESS HILL (04446) 45577

To: Auctioneers,wholesalers and
retailers of antique furniture,
porcelain and decorative items.

Dear Sirs,
We offer the most comprehensive service available in the U.K.
As wholesale exporters, we sell 20ft. and 40ft. container-loads of
antique furniture, porcelain and decorative items of the Georgian
Victorian, Edwardian and 1930's periods. Our buyers are strategically
placed throughout the U.K. in order to take full advantage of
regional pricing. You can purchase a container from us for as little
as £5,000. This would be filled with mostly 1870 to 1920's furniture
and chinaware; you could expect to pay approximately £7,000 to
£10,000 for a quality shipment of Georgian, and Victorian furniture
and porcelain. Our terms are £500 deposit, the balance at time
of arrival of the container. If the merchandise should not be to
your liking, for any reason whatsoever, we offer you your money
back in full, less one-way freight.
If you wish to visit the U.K. yourself and purchase individually
from your own sources, we will collect,pack and ship your
merchandise with speed and efficiency within 5 days. Our rates
are competitive and our packing is the finest available anywhere
in the world. Our courier- finder service is second to none and we
have knowledgeable couriers who are equipped with a car and the
knowledge of where the best buys are.

If your business is buying English antiques, we are your contact.
We assure you of our best attention at all times.

Yours faithfully
BRITISH ANTIQUE EXPORTERS LTD.

N. Lefton
Chairman and Managing Director.

DIRECTORS N. LEFTON (Chairman & Managing),   P.V. LEFTON, G. LEFTON, THE RT. HON. THE VISCOUNT EXMOUTH, A. FIELD, MSC FBOA DCLP FSMC FAAO, D.W. GILBERT
REGISTERED OFFICE: BURGESS HILL   REGISTERED NO 893406 ENGLAND
THE CHASE MANHATTAN BANK, N.A., 410 PARK AVENUE, NEW YORK
BANKERS: NATIONAL WESTMINSTER BANK LTD. 155 NORTH STREET, BRIGHTON, SUSSEX

THERE ARE A GREAT MANY ANTIQUE SHIPPERS IN BRITAIN

but few, if any, who are as quality conscious as Norman Lefton, Chairman and Managing Director of British Antique Exporters Ltd. of Burgess Hill, Nr. Brighton, Sussex. Eighteen years' experience of shipping goods to all parts of the globe have confirmed his original belief that the way to build clients' confidence in his services is to supply them only with goods which are in first class saleable condition. To this end, he employs a staff of over 50, from highly skilled, antique restorers, polishers and packers to representative buyers and executives. Through their knowledgeable hands passes each piece of furniture before it

BRITISH ANTIQUE EXPORTERS LTD

QUEEN ELIZABETH AVENUE   Member of L.A.P.A.D.A.
BURGESS HILL
WEST SUSSEX, RH15 9RX, ENGLAND
Telex 87688
Cables BRITISH ANTIQUES BURGESS HILL
Telephone BURGESS HILL (04446) 45577

leaves the B.A.E. warehouses, ensuring that the overseas buyer will only receive the best and most saleable merchandise for their particular market. This attention to detail is obvious on a visit to the Burgess Hill warehouses where potential customers can view what must be the most varied assortment of Georgian, Victorian, Edwardian and 1930's furniture in the UK. One cannot fail to be impressed by, not only the varied range of merchandise but also the fact that each piece is in showroom condition awaiting shipment. As one would expect, packing is considered somewhat of an art at B.A.E. and David Gilbert, the director in charge of the works, ensures that each piece will reach its final destination in the condition a customer would wish. B.A.E. set a very high standard and, as a further means of improving each container load David Gilbert, who also deals with customer/container liaison, invites each customer to return detailed information on the saleability of each piece in the container thereby ensuring successful future shipments. This feedback of information is the all important factor which guarantees the profitability of future containers. "By this method" Mr. Lefton explains, "we have established that an average £7000 container will immediately it is unpacked at its final destination realise in the region of £10000 to £14000 for our clients selling the goods on a quick wholesale turnover basis". When visiting the warehouses various container loads can be seen in the course of completion. The intending buyer can then judge for himself which type of container load would best be suited to his market. Initial enquiries are dealt with by Suzanne Seear and Diana Hammond who both ensure that the documentation is correct in all its detail. They guarantee the container a smooth passage until its final destination.

BRITISH ANTIQUE EXPORTERS LTD

QUEEN ELIZABETH AVENUE   Member of L.A.P.A.D.A.
BURGESS HILL
WEST SUSSEX, RH15 9RX, ENGLAND
Telex 87688
Cables BRITISH ANTIQUES BURGESS HILL
Telephone BURGESS HILL (04446) 45577

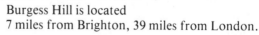

Burgess Hill is located
7 miles from Brighton, 39 miles from London.

In an average 20-foot container B.A.E. put approximately 150 to 200 pieces carefully selected to suit the particular destination. There are always at least 10 outstanding or unusual items in each shipment, but every piece included looks as though it has something special about it.

Based at Burgess Hill 7 miles from Brighton and on a direct rail link with London 39 miles (only 40 minutes journey) the Company is ideally situated to ship containers to all parts of the world. The showrooms, restoration and packing departments are open to overseas buyers and no visit to purchase antiques for re-sale in other countries is complete without a visit to their Burgess Hill premises where a welcome is always found.

BRITISH ANTIQUE EXPORTERS LTD

QUEEN ELIZABETH AVENUE   Member of L.A.P.A.D.A.
BURGESS HILL
WEST SUSSEX, RH15 9RX, ENGLAND
Telex 87688
Cables BRITISH ANTIQUES BURGESS HILL

Telephone BURGESS HILL (04446) 45577

WANTED

SPECTACULAR SHIPPING PIECES

We are looking for The Unusual, The Outrageous,
The High Quality, The Spectacular pieces of Shipping Furniture
from Desks, Hall Stands, Washstands, Clocks, Cabinets to
Wardrobes.
**We will pay
maximum possible prices**
to obtain The Unusual.

BRITISH ANTIQUE EXPORTERS LTD

QUEEN ELIZABETH AVENUE   Member of L.A.P.A.D.A.
BURGESS HILL
WEST SUSSEX, RH15 9RX, ENGLAND
Telex 87688
Cables BRITISH ANTIQUES BURGESS HILL
Telephone BURGESS HILL (04446) 45577

43

A selection of antiques

Georgian Mahogany Bureau bookcase

Victorian Card Table

1920 Queen Anne High-backed Chair

Georgian Mahogany Chest of Drawers

Edwardian Oak Bureau

Victorian Duchess Marble-top Wash Stand

Victorian Windsor Chair

American Wooton Desk

Victorian Walnut Queen Anne High-backed Chair

from a container load

Victorian Mahogany
Cylinder Desk

Georgian Mahogany
Tall-Boy

1920 Barley-Twist
Chair

Bracket Clock

Victorian
Twin Pedestal Desk

Victorian
Cylindrical
Pot Cupboard

Victorian
Mahogany
Torchere

Victorian
Carved Oak Hall-stand

Victorian Walnut Marble Top and
Mirrored- back Credenza

There are many pitfalls...

awaiting the novice and experienced buyer alike in the Antique world. The biggest question mark in the mind of the potential container buyer must be "How will they know what to send me and will the quality be right?" In an attempt to answer these and other questions, here follows a typical question and answer session with David Gilbert, the Director in charge of the works:

BUYER:
"How many items will I get for my money?"

DG:
"A typical 20 foot container will have 120 pieces of furniture and approximately 50 pieces of china-ware packed in it. We can regulate the price of the container with the quantity of small items; the higher the value of the shipment, the higher the number of small pieces. Of course the type and style of furniture, for example period Georgian, Victorian or Edwardian, also regulates the price."

BUYER:
"What type of merchandise will you send me?"

DG:
"We have researched all our markets very thoroughly and know the right merchandise to send to any particular country or region in that country. We also take into consideration the type of outlet e.g. auction,

wholesale or retail. We consider the strong preferences for different woods in different areas. We personally visit all our markets several times a year to keep pace with the trends."

BUYER:
"Will we get the bargains?"

DG:
"In the mind of any prospective buyer is the thought that he or she will find the true bargains hidden away in the small forgotten corners of some dusty Antique Shop. It is our Company policy to pass on the benefit of any bargain buying to our client."

BUYER:
"With your overheads, etc., how can you send these things to me at a competitive price?"

DG:
"Our very great purchasing power enables us to buy goods at substantially less than the individual person; this means that we are able

to buy, collect and pack the item for substantially less than the shop price."

BUYER:
"Will everything be in good condition and will it arrive undamaged?"

DG:
"We are very proud of the superb condition of all the merchandise leaving our factory. We employ the finest craftsmen to restore each piece into first class saleable condition before departure. We also pack to the highest standards thus ensuring that all items arrive safely."

BUYER:
"What guarantee do I have that you will do a good job for me?"

DG:
"The ultimate guarantee. We are so confident of our ability to provide the right goods at the right price that we offer a full refund, if for any reason you are not satisfied with the shipment."

BUYER:
"This all sounds very satisfactory, how do we do business?"

DG:
"Unlike most Companies, we do not require pre-payment for our containers. When you place your order with us, we require a deposit of £500 and the balance is payable when the container arrives at its destination."

BRITISH ANTIQUE EXPORTERS LTD

QUEEN ELIZABETH AVENUE Member of L.A.P.A.D.A.
BURGESS HILL
WEST SUSSEX, RH15 9RX, ENGLAND
Telex 87688
Cables BRITISH ANTIQUES BURGESS HILL
Telephone BURGESS HILL (04446) 45577

48

14th century Nottingham alabaster panel of the Assumption of the Virgin, 42cm. high. (Christie's) $12,530 £5,800

Mid 15th century Malines alabaster pieta, 32cm. high. (Christie's) $6,910 £3,200

14th century Nottingham alabaster panel of the Nativity, 42cm. high. (Christie's) $12,530 £5,800

Early 17th century Flemish alabaster group of Hercules slaying the Nemean lion, 71.5cm. high. (Christie's) $2,300 £1,000

Coloured alabaster bust of a young woman in a square necked dress, circa 1890, 14½in. tall. (Sotheby's Belgravia) $360 £160

Egyptian alabaster alabastron of typical form, circa 100B.C., 12½in. high. (Sotheby's) $3,300 £1,500

14th century Nottingham alabaster panel, 42cm. high, showing the Coronation of The Virgin. (Christie's) $17,280 £8,000

Chinese alabaster head of Guan Yin, 14in. high. (Phillips) $515 £230

15th century Nottingham alabaster fragment of the Coronation of The Virgin, 20cm. high. (Christie's) $2,810 £1,300

Large Egyptian alabaster jar, early Dynastic Period, 11½in. high. (Sotheby's) $1,060 £460

Early 20th century gilt metal, wood and alabaster frame with naughty photograph, 21.2cm. high. (Sotheby's Belgravia) $275 £120

Egyptian alabaster cylindrical jar with rounded rim, 9¾in. high, Dynasty II. (Christie's) $885 £400

Victorian silver mounted table snuff mull. (Christie's & Edmiston) $2,035 £900

Leopard skin rug, mounted on felt backcloth, 72in. long, nose to tail tip. (Sotheby's Belgravia)
$900 £400

Cased stuffed fish, labelled 'Thames Trout', dated 1883. (Bermondsey Auctions) $75 £35

One of a pair of stuffed curlews. (Phillips) $55 £25

Victorian cased set of birds amid foliage. (Phillips) $85 £40

One of a pair of stuffed puffins. (Phillips) $45 £20

Stuffed raven on stand. (Phillips) $35 £15

Tiger skin rug, mounted on felt with oilskin backing, 91in. long. (Sotheby's Belgravia) $495 £220

Stuffed crow on a branch-like perch. (Phillips) $45 £20

Pacific Island turtle shell mask. (Woolley & Wallis)
$2,150 £1,000

Case of stuffed birds. (Phillips)
$70 £30

Stuffed young male lion mounted on papier mache rock. (Phillips) $1,195 £550

Large Scottish silver and gilt metal mounted ram's head snuff mull by R. & H. B. Kirkwood, Edinburgh, 1885, 24in. long. (Sotheby's Belgravia) $2,025 £900

Unusual stuffed and mounted cayman, 37in. long. (Sotheby's Belgravia) $200 £90

Stuffed magpie. (Alfie's Antique Market) $30 £15

Tiger skin rug with glass eyes and chipped teeth, 121½in. long. (Sotheby's Belgravia) $630 £280

One of a pair of beaded and quilted buffalo hooves. (Phillips) $3,840 £1,700

White-tailed sea eagle and chick in glass case, 36in. high. (Sotheby's Belgravia) $270 £120

Life-size owl in case. (Gray's Antique Mews) $140 £60

Lion skin rug, of a male African lion with snarling head, 120in. long. (Sotheby's Belgravia) $785 £350

Stuffed barn owl. (Alfie's Antique Market) $105 £45

One of a pair of English shell decorations, with glass domes, circa 1880, 23in. high. (Sotheby's Belgravia) $325 £150

One of two cases of butterfly specimens. (Phillips) $20 £10

Huge mounted head of an Indian water buffalo. (Spear & Sons) $215 £100

BAROMETERS

Late 19th century aneroid barometer on a spelter figure of an eagle, 18in. high. (Sotheby's Belgravia) $250 £110

Rosewood banjo barometer with white enamel dial, circa 1850, 40in. high.(Sotheby's Belgravia) $400 £180

Fine Louis XV kingwood and tulipwood cartel barometer, 42in. high, with painted face. (Christie's) $37,400 £17,000

George III style rosewood barometer by Ciceri Pini & Co., Edinburgh. (Phillips) $325 £140

19th century barometer by F. Amadio, London, 38in. high. (Parsons, Welch & Cowell) $460 £210

Fine large clock wheel barometer by I. W. Hancock, Yeovil, 48in. high. (Christie's) $1,590 £710

Mahogany wheel clock barometer by Pastorelli, London, 47in. high. (Christie's) $1,300 £580

Sheraton period barometer, dial inscribed M. Salamon, Oxford, 38in. high. (Parsons, Welch & Cowell) $485 £220

19th century mahogany banjo barometer with silvered dial and a timepiece above, 112cm. high. (Sotheby King & Chasemore) $1,020 £475

Early 18th century walnut stick barometer, 46in. high. (Christie's) $1,790 £800

Late Georgian mahogany wheel clock barometer, signed Leonardo Camberwell No. 460, 46in. high. (Christie's) $900 £400

18th century mahogany stick barometer by Ed. Nairne, London, 37in. high. (Christie's) $1,525 £680

52

George III style mahogany barometer by B. Corji, Aberdeen. (Phillips) $392 £170

Mahogany cased wheel or banjo barometer, circa 1830, 37½in. high. (Christopher Sykes) $450 £195

Late 18th century mahogany wheel barometer. (Bradley & Vaughan) $775 £340

Mahogany cased wheel or banjo barometer, circa 1820, by G. Balsary, 39½in. high. (Christopher Sykes) $658 £285

18th century mahogany wall stick barometer, circa 1790, 38¾in. high. (Christopher Sykes) $824 £365

Brass and steel gimballed stick barometer on a mahogany plaque. (Phillips) $277 £120

Queen Anne walnut stick barometer with domed pediment. (Phillips) $1,339 £580

George III style mahogany stick barometer by Jas. Cork, Glasgow. (Phillips) $924 £400

Early 19th century barometer by C.A. Canti and Son, London, 38in. high. (Parsons, Welch & Cowell) $440 £200

18th century mahogany wall stick barometer with brass dial, 38¾in. high. (Christopher Sykes) $843 £365

Early Victorian wheel or banjo barometer, circa 1850, in walnut case, 40in. long. (Christopher Sykes) $565 £245

Very rare mid 19th century barometer in cast iron case, 24½in. high. (Christopher Sykes) $381 £165

BAROMETERS

English brass lighthouse, combining clock and barometer. (Sotheby Bearne) $450 £200

George III mahogany stick barometer by D. Fagoli, 38in. high. (Olivers) $1,175 £520

Antique wheel or banjo barometer in pinewood case, circa 1860, 37in. high. (Christopher Sykes) $372 £165

George III mahogany cased stick barometer, circa 1790, 37in. high. (Christopher Sykes) $553 £245

19th century barometer with silvered dial in rosewood banjo case. (Hobbs Parker) $304 £150

Mid 19th century mahogany stick barometer by B. Martin, London, 90cm. high. (Sotheby King & Chasemore) $1,252 £580

Early 19th century barometer and thermometer by Taylor & Son, London, 38in. long. (Hy. Duke & Son) $317 £155

Early 17th century barometer in mahogany case. (W. H. Lane & Son) $871 £425

George III rosewood stick barometer by L. Casella & Co. (Olivers) $723 £320

Early Victorian wheel or banjo barometer, circa 1850, 40in. high. (Christopher Sykes) $553 £245

George III mahogany stick barometer, circa 1790, 37in. high. (Christopher Sykes) $553 £245

Wheel barometer in rosewood case, circa 1830, 43in. high. (Christopher Sykes) $621 £275

Rare stick barometer in herringbone walnut with boxwood stringing, circa 1760, 38in. high. (Christopher Sykes)　$791　£350

18th century angle barometer in case of banded and inlaid mahogany, inscribed David Fosell, Hinckly. (Graves, Son & Pilcher)　$2,376　£1,100

18th century mahogany stick barometer with three brass finials. (W. H. Lane & Son)　$972　£450

Mid 19th century walnut veneered banjo wheel barometer, signed Stopani, Aberdeen, 95cm. high. (Sotheby King & Chasemore)　$592　£260

19th century stick barometer by J. Pasini, Dorchester, 36in. high. (Hy. Duke & Son)　$533　£260

Ship's barometer by Cox of Devonport. (Sotheby Bearne)　$1,512　£700

Victorian Admiral Fitzroy barometer in glazed mahogany case, 35in. long. (Hy. Duke & Son)　$164　£80

19th century stick barometer with engraved ivory scale in rosewood case, 36in. long. (Hy. Duke & Son)　$328　£160

Admiral Fitzroy barometer by Negretti and Zambra in carved oak case. (Hobbs Parker)　$822　£405

Rosewood cased wheel barometer circa 1840, by Callaghan, Preston, 40½in. high. (Christopher Sykes)　$418　£185

George III mahogany stick barometer by George Adams of Fleet Street. (Sotheby King & Chasemore)　$832　£410

Charles II marquetry stick barometer. (Boardman's)　$7,344　£3,400

Green patinated bronze figure of Eve by Rodin, 1881, 68in. high. (Sotheby's Monaco) $198,090 £92,135

Bronze lamp signed E. Marioton, entitled Fascinator, 1880's, 74cm. high. (Sotheby's Belgravia) $665 £300

'Aeroplane' depicting the God of Aviation in spelter on ebonised plinth. (Phillips) $216 £100

Art Deco green patinated bronze table lamp. (Phillips) $455 £203

18th century Japanese bronze Buddha, 96cm. high. (Leys, Antwerp) $3,290 £1,550

Pair of late 19th century bronze figures by Moreau, 23in. high. (Christie's S. Kensington) $2,270 £1,050

Gilt bronze figure of a torch bearer by Agathon Leonard. (Christie's N. York) $8,500 £3,935

Bronze and ivory figure of a young woman on onyx base, 34.5cm. high. (King & Chasemore)$990 £440

Bronze figure of a 'Boy Bather', 45cm. high. (Phillips) $1,085 £480

Gilt bronze figural lamp by Raoul Larche, 46cm. high. (Phillips) $19,440 £9,000

Egyptian bronze figure of Osiris wearing an atef crown, dating from the Ptolemaic period. (Christie's) $1,505 £700

Bronze candlestick, with Doric column stem on circular moulded base, 8¼in. (Robert W. Skinner Inc.) $675 £315

A late 19th century Yamamoto inlaid bronze vase, 23cm. high. (Sotheby's Belgravia) $920 £400

Preiss bronze and ivory figure of a girl in trousers, 1930's, 24.5cm. high. (Sotheby's Belgravia) $2,847 £1,300

One of a pair of mid 18th century Chippendale bell metal andirons, 20in. high. (Robert W. Skinner Inc.) $1,000 £440

Spelter figure of a schoolboy by Aug. Moreau. (Alfie's Antique Market) $102 £45

A pair of late 19th century Seiya bronze figures, 26cm. high. (Sotheby's Belgravia) $600 £260

A good and large late 19th century Miyao parcel gilt bronze group of a Samurai warrior, 55cm. high. (Sotheby's Belgravia) $14,250 £6,200

One of a pair of Tiffany Studios gilt bronze candlesticks, circa 1900, 24cm. high. (Sotheby's Belgravia) $985 £450

Bronze and ivory figure of a dancing girl, inscribed Joe Descomps, 43cm. high. (Sotheby King & Chasemore) $924 £400

One of a pair of Tiffany Studios silvered bronze candleholders, circa 1900, 40cm. high. (Sotheby's Belgravia) $1,355 £620

Art Deco bronze figure of a nymph, 35cm. high, base incised Le Faquays. (Sotheby King & Chasemore) $438 £190

Amusing E. David bronze mask pendant, circa 1925, 5cm. wide. (Sotheby's Belgravia)
$440 £190

Late 17th century bell metal bowl of flared circular form, 26cm. diam. (Sotheby King & Chasemore)
$360 £160

Good Gurschner bronze vase, 18cm. high, circa 1910. (Sotheby's Belgravia) $395 £180

One of a pair of Directoire style ormolu and dyed agate cassolettes, 55cm. high. (Sotheby King & Chasemore)
$735 £340

Theodore Riviere bronze group of a man and woman, circa 1900, 32cm. high. (Sotheby's Belgravia)
$1,530 £700

Art Nouveau bronze candelabra, designed by Georges de Feure, circa 1900, 33cm. high. (Sotheby's Belgravia)
$1,380 £600

One of a pair of bronze faun candlesticks. (Nicholas) $880 £380

One of a pair of Japanese bronze Samurai. (Phillips) $30,000 £13,000

4th/3rd century B.C. Etruscan figure in bronze of Herakles, 2¾in. high. (Christie's) $330 £150

Early 16th century Venetian bronze processional cross, 48.5cm. high. (Christie's) $600 £280

Hagenauer ebonised wood and bronze gondola, circa 1910-20, 44.75cm. wide. (Sotheby's Belgravia) $220 £100

L. Kann gilt bronze mug with cylindrical body, 10cm. high, circa 1900. (Sotheby's Belgravia) $240 £110

Large pair of bronze Venetian door knockers. (Gray's Antique Mews) $420 £185

'Louis XVI' gilt bronze fender, 1870's, 60¼in. wide. (Sotheby's Belgravia) $625 £300

Gurschner bronze vase, circa 1910, of oval section and flared rim. (Sotheby's Belgravia) $920 £420

Japanese bronze eagle. (Stride's) $5,310 £2,300

Art Deco French spelter figure on tri-coloured marble base. (Alfie's Antique Market) $295 £130

One of a pair of patinated bronze Hagenauer book-ends, 20th century, 16.5cm. high. (Sotheby's Belgravia) $615 £280

Benin bronze figure of a temple guard, 19cm. high. (Phillips) $150 £65

Pair of Marley style bronze horses, each with a running youth, 19cm. high. (Phillips) $185 £80

Roman bronze from the 1st or 2nd century A.D. 18½in. high. (Christie's) $30,400 £14,000

One of a pair of Qing dynasty bronze censers cast as standing geese, 14in. high. (Christie's) $1,440 £650

Art Nouveau gilt bronze dish by A. Vibert, circa 1900, 15.5cm. high. (Sotheby's Belgravia) $480 £220

19th century Russian bronze group, inscribed and stamped 1878, 16in. high. (Phillips) $2,360 £1,045

BRONZE

Mid 19th century rococo gilt bronze candlestick, one of a pair, 12¼in. high. (Sotheby's Belgravia) $1,000 £480

Bronze tripod, circa 1830-40, 10in. high. (Gray's Antique Mews) $192 £85

One of a pair of mid 19th century gilt bronze candelabra, 28½in. high. (Sotheby's Belgravia) $1,289 £620

Late 19th century bronze figure of a woman, 1890, 53cm. high. (Sotheby King & Chasemore) $690 £320

One of a pair of gilt bronze and champleve candelabra, circa 1870, 27in. high. (Sotheby's Belgravia) $3,120 £1,500

Patinated bronze figure of a naked girl, Art Deco style by K. Perl, 39cm. high. (Sotheby King & Chasemore) $669 £310

One of a pair of Second Empire bronze candelabra, circa 1860, 28in. high. (Sotheby's Belgravia) $1,248 £600

Large gilt bronze and ivory figure, probably by Duvernet, 19in. high. (Christie's S. Kensington) $1,188 £550

Bronze figure of a labourer, signed Aime Jules Dalou, circa 1905, 113cm. high. (Sotheby's Belgravia) $10,800 £5,000

One of a pair of ormolu three-branch candelabra, 15in. high, circa 1870. (Sotheby's Belgravia) $540 £260

One of a pair of bronze male figures, 52cm. high. (Sotheby King & Chasemore) $1,060 £490

One of a pair of Second Empire bronze and gilt bronze candelabra, 29in. high, 1850's. (Sotheby's Belgravia) $915 £440

BRONZE

One of a pair of bronze urns, circa 1880, 22¾in. high. (Sotheby's Belgravia) $520 £250

Bronze group of three musicians, 33cm. high. (Sotheby Humberts) $410 £190

Bronze figure of a man, signed R. Kaesbach, 43cm. high. (Sotheby Humberts) $432 £200

2nd/3rd century A.D. bronze applique with Medusa head design, Roman. (Stanley Gibbons Currency Ltd.) $750 £365

18th century Japanese Edo archer in patinated bronze. (Leys, Antwerp) $1,380 £640

One of a pair of gilt bronze candelabra, 27in. high, 1870's. (Sotheby's Belgravia) $936 £450

1930's Art Deco dancing figure on a stepped base. (Alfie's Antique Market) $103 £48

One of a pair of late 19th century gilt bronze candelabra, 24in. high, on white marble socles. (Sotheby's Belgravia) $832 £400

One of a pair of gilt bronze ormolu and porcelain urns, 15in. high, 1870's. (Sotheby's Belgravia) $811 £390

Italian bronze figure of a drunken Silenus, circa 1700, 12½in. wide. (Sotheby's) $868 £400

One of a large pair of cast iron and gilt bronze ewers, circa 1880, 40½in. high. (Sotheby's Belgravia) $1,665 £800

Pair of large 'Egyptian' bronze and parcel gilt figures by Emile Louis Picault, 1870's. (Sotheby's Belgravia) $14,040 £6,500

BRONZE

Fine 19th century animalia bronze figure of a gun dog with game, 12in. long. (Shakespear, McTurk & Graham) $604 £280

3rd/6th century A.D. Sassanian bronze horse, 6¾in. long. (Christie's) $43,200 £20,000

Saxon bronze model cannon with moulded muzzle, 18th/19th century, 21in. high. (Sotheby's) $4,162 £1,850

Roman hollow-cast bronze bust of Dionysius.(Christie's) $30,240 £14,000

19th century bronze study of a youth entitled 'Florentine Singer, by P. Dubois, 1865. (Sotheby King & Chasemore) $1,775 £790

Late 19th century bronze group, 13in. high. (Vost's) $717 £350

Bronze and ivory figure of The Egyptian Dancer by J. R. Colinet, 12in. high. (Christie's S. Kensington) $1,414 £700

Pair of 19th century bronzes by A. Carrier, 77cm. and 64cm. high. (Sotheby King & Chasemore) $3,375 £1,500

Gilt bronze figure of Zhen Wu, 1587, Chinese, 63.5cm. high. (Sotheby's) $11,650 £5,400

Bronze and ivory figure of Hamlet on onyx base, 26.5cm. high. (King & Chasemore) $315 £140

Bronze group of a huntsman, horse and two hounds, 19½in. high. (Heathcote Ball & Co.) $5,616 £2,600

Figure in coloured bronze and ivory by Chiparus, 20cm. high. (Leys, Antwerp) $1,660 £770

French bronze of Derby winner Macaroni, by P. J. Mene. (Sotheby's Belgravia) $12,960 £6,000

Bronze hollow-cast Egyptian cat from the 26th Dynasty, 9in. high. (Christie's) $17,280 £8,000

Silvered French bronze, circa 1850. (Alfie's Antique Market) $202 £100

One of a pair of miniature bronze urns. (Shakespear, McTurk & Graham) $60 £28

19th century Japanese bronze gong with enamelled decoration, 42in. diam. (D. M. Nesbit & Co.) $1,800 £800

Fine 19th century bronze figure of a snarling lion, 48in. long, by Elkington. (Phillips) $6,177 £2,860

Fine Japanese bronze koro and cover. (Russell, Baldwin & Bright) $9,936 £4,600

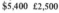

Fine bronze figure of a racehorse and jockey, 18in. high. (Heathcote Ball & Co.) $5,400 £2,500

One of a pair of 19th century bronze incense burners. (Alfie's Antique Market) $213 £95

Third millenium B.C. Anatolian bronze cart and oxen, 8½in. long. (Christie's) $4,752 £2,200

Bronze and ivory figure of The Culotte Dress by F. Preiss, 13in. high. (Christie's S. Kensington) $2,590 £1,200

Large bronze elephant, Meiji period, 39.5cm. long. (Christie's) $900 £400

Dominique Alonzo bronze figure of a man on horseback. (Christie's S. Kensington) $3,240 £1,500

Bronze study of a medieval guardsman by A. L. Leveel, 1947, 70cm. high. (Sotheby King & Chasemore) $945 £420

Spelter group on marble base, circa 1925, 16in. high. (Gray's Antique Market) $675 £300

19th century bronze figure 'The Musical Fawn', 12in. high. (Shakespear, McTurk & Graham) $324 £150

19th century bronze figure by Cugnot, 94cm. high. (Sotheby King & Chasemore) $1,305 £580

Fine pair of late French Empire bronze figures by E. Barrias, 13in. high. (Eadon, Lockwood & Riddle) $777 £360

French cast Smoking Boy bust, circa 1900-1910. (Alfie's Antique Market) $168 £75

Late 19th century Oriental bronze candlestick. (Alfie's Antique Market) $168 £75

BRONZE

'La Coquette', bronze figure, 34½in. high. (Christie's S. Kensington) $2,700 £1,250

Pair of bronze figures of Centaurs, 49cm. high. (Sotheby King & Chasemore) $4,060 £2,000

Bronze figure of a dancer by Franz von Stuck, circa 1897. (Kunsthaus am Museum, Cologne) $9,595 £4,750

Fine Japanese bronze koro and cover with finial missing, 5½in. high, on ivory stand. (Russell, Baldwin & Bright)$9,935 £4,600

Statue of a javelin thrower, signed, 15in. high. (Nottinghill Antique Market) $130 £55

11th century B.C. ritual bronze Ding. (Boisgirard & de Heeckeren) $65,000 £30,000

Early 20th century bronze 'The Iron Age', by Hamo Thorneycroft, 14½in. high. (Vost's) $902 £440

Bronze mortar with pestle, circa 1684. (Leys, Antwerp) $1,385 £640

Late 19th century bronze fawn, after the Roman original. (Alfie's Antique Market) $1,134 £525

Bronze of Pierre de Wissant, by Rodin, 1889, 32¼in. high. (Sotheby's Monaco) $193,000 £85,400

Pair of spelter figures as original lamps, signed Ch. Levy, 2ft.9in. high. (Alfie's Antique Market) $1,210 £600

One of a set of three bronze harpies, Etruscan, 3rd century B.C. (Stanley Gibbons Currency Ltd.) $380 £185

Silvered bronze figure,
1930's. (Nottinghill
Antique Market)
$258 £115

Fine pair of 19th century bronze Marley
horses with trainers, 58cm. high. (Sotheby
King & Chasemore) $1,035 £460

Bronze statue of W. G. Grace
by James Butler, No. 1 of a
limited edition of 250.
(Phillips) $675 £300

Pair of large spelter figures
of Juno and Minerva, circa
1870. (Alfie's Antique
Market) $101 £45

Gilt bronze sledge, circa 1880, 16in. wide.
(Sotheby's Belgravia) $885 £400

Bronze model of a woun-
ded centaur by Franz
von Stuck. (Christie's)
$4,320 £2,000

'La Coquette', a bronze
figure of a girl.
(Christie's S. Kensington)
$2,537 £1,250

Bronze and ivory Colinet Valkyrie off towards
the unknown. (Bonham's) $7,775 £3,600

Late 4th century B.C.
bronze of Hercules,
5in. high, slightly dam-
aged. (Spink/Koller)
$48,816 £22,600

Egyptian bronze figure of
a cat's head, 4½in. high.
(Sotheby's) $10,750 £5,000

Pair of bronzes by Francois Duquesnoy
'Apollo and Cupid' and 'Mercury and
Cupid', over 2ft. high. (Christie's)
$90,720 £42,000

Mid 19th century bronze group
of Una and the Lion, signed G.
Geefs, 43.2cm. high. (Christie's
S. Kensington) $2,925 £1,300

Early 20th century bronze vase, details bronzed, silvered and gilt. (Sotheby's Belgravia)
$325 £150

French bronze group of a lion attacking a horse, circa 1600, 20.5cm. wide. (Christie's)
$3,456 £1,600

Late 16th century Venetian bronze door-knocker, 28cm. high, with iron hinge. (Christie's)
$11,664 £5,400

Early 18th century Dutch bronze statuette of a peasant, 15cm. high. (Christie's) $2,376 £1,100

German bronze group of two putti playing pick-a-back, 11.3cm. high. (Christie's) $604 £280

Late 19th century bronze falcon on wooden post, 69cm. high. (Sotheby's Belgravia)$1,844 £850

One of a pair of 17th century Venetian bronze andirons, 72.5cm. high. (Christie's)
$3,456 £1,600

Large 20th century bronze figure of a fisherman, 50cm. high. (Sotheby's Belgravia)
$759 £350

Ormolu candelabrum, signed Henry Dasson, late 1870's, 25½in. high. (Sotheby's Belgravia)
$1,040 £500

Obriol parcel gilt bronze Art Nouveau inkstand and pen tray, circa 1900, 25cm. wide. (Sotheby's Belgravia)$613 £240

Second Empire ormolu torchere, 1850's, 46in. high. (Sotheby's Belgravia) $915 £440

Large late 19th century bronze incense burner and cover, 100cm. high, with wood stand. (Sotheby's Belgravia)
$2,495 £1,150

Good Breche Violette
and ormolu urn, circa
1860, signed Robert
Sculpteur, 27in. high.
(Sotheby's Belgravia)
$3,952 £1,900

Bronze jardiniere with Art
Nouveau features, 30cm.
high. (Phillips) $146 £65

One of a pair of late
19th century bronze
incense burners and
covers, 44cm. high.
(Sotheby's Belgravia)
$303 £140

George I English bronze
mortar, 3½in. high,
circa 1720. (Christopher
Sykes) $85 £38

Late 19th century
bronze vase, cover
and stand, 147.5cm.
high. (Sotheby's
Belgravia)
$1,300 £600

Tiffany four-branch bronze
candelabrum, 12¼in. high.
(Robert W. Skinner Inc.)
$550 £250

Late 19th century Japan-
ese bronze model of a
hawk on a tree stump,
45cm. high. (Sotheby
King & Chasemore)
$949 £420

Bronze figure of a hunter,
42cm. high, restraining a
dog. (Phillips) $723 £320

Solid bronze coat-of-arms,
circa 1840, 6½in. high.
(Christopher Sykes)
$108 £48

Chinese bronze figure of
Guanyin, 9½in. high.
(Christopher Sykes)
$85 £40

Regency period two-colour
bronze letter-rack to stand
on a writing desk. (Christopher Sykes) $110 £50

Large 20th century
bronze peasant
woman, 48cm. high,
black patination.
(Sotheby's Belgravia)
$672 £310

BRONZE

18th century Bengali bronze pan box set of eight hinged boxes on a tripod, 8in. high. (Christie's) $650 £280

15th century Mamluk oval shaped bronze repousse foodbox and cover, 45cm. long. (Christie's) $2,310 £1,000

One of a pair of 19th century Qajar cast metal figures of seated dogs, damascened with foliate designs, 20cm. high. (Christie's) $2,310 £1,000

19th century French bronze bust of Raphael, signed A. Cartier. (Christie's) $170 £75

Lalique bronze medallion, 6cm. diam., circa 1900. (Sotheby's Belgravia) $655 £300

Chinese bronze figure of Guanyin, late Ming or early Qing dynasty, on wood stand, 25cm. high. (Christie's) $510 £220

15th/16th century South Indian bronze figure of a Deva standing in slight Abhanga, 43.5cm. high. (Christie's) $2,310 £1,000

A pair of 19th century bronze elephants, 44cm. long. (Phillips) $360 £160

12th century Nagapattinam figure of the Buddha on a large rectangular waisted plinth, 19.5cm. high. (Christie's) $1,110 £480

15th/16th century Northern Thai bronze figure of the Buddha, 54cm. high. (Christie's) $2,195 £950

Early Islamic bronze globular jug, probably Persian, 7th/8th century, 20cm. high. (Christie's) $460 £200

15th/16th century Tibetan gilt bronze group of a Dharmapala in Yab Yum, trampling a prostrate figure, 18.5cm. high. (Christie's) $2,770 £1,200

17th century bronze candle snuffer, marked with heart and cross, 6½in. (Robert W. Skinner Inc.) $85 £40

14th century Timurid bronze repousse candlestick base, 7cm. high.(Christie's) $185 £80

18th century Sino-Tibetan gilt bronze figure of a wrathful deity, 29.5cm. long. (Christie's) $1,500 £650

Seljuk bronze globular bucket with looped handle, Khurrasan, 12th/13th century, 20cm. diam. (Christie's) $5,775 £2,500

Mid 19th century bronze incense burner and cover, 51cm. high. (Sotheby's Belgravia) $460 £200

14th/15th century Tibetan bronze figure of Padmasambhava, with dedicatory inscription round base, 25.5cm. high. (Christie's) $810 £350

19th century French pigmented bronze bust of a young girl, signed G. Samuel. (Christie's) $1,265 £550

A bronze and ivory group of a musician and dancer by Laurent Hely, 54.5cm. wide. (Christie's) $3,500 £1,600

Late 19th century Oriental bronze jardiniere, 53cm. high. (Sotheby's Belgravia) $370 £160

16th/17th century Tibetan gilt bronze figure of Amitayus seated in Dhyanasana, 11.5cm. high. (Christie's) $415 £180

One of a pair of bronze and ormolu chenets, each with a putto leaning forward, 12½in. wide, circa 1880. (Sotheby's Belgravia) $630 £280

15th/16th century Central Thai bronze figure of the Buddha, 64cm. high. (Christie's) $3,235 £1,400

BRONZE

One of a set of four spelter carytid wall lights, circa 1890, 41in. high. (Sotheby's Belgravia) $3,205 £1,450

Jean d'Aire, nude figure standing, 80in. high, circa 1886, by Rodin. (Sotheby's Monaco) $253,655 £117,980

18th century Sino-Tibetan gilt bronze figure of Sadaksari seated in Dhyanasana, 17cm. high. (Christie's) $925 £400

Spelter figure of a woman, signed August Moreau, circa 1900, 17in. high. (Sotheby's Belgravia) $1,105 £500

One of a set of four bronze and gilt bronze wall lights, circa 1880, 20in. high. (Sotheby's Belgravia) $3,205 £1,450

A bronze figure of a school-girl by D. H. Chiparus, 18.5cm. high. (Christie's) $915 £420

One of a pair of large spelter and porcelain ewers with a winged beast handle, 30in. high, circa 1880. (Sotheby's Belgravia) $475 £210

A bronze and ivory figure of a girl by D. H. Chiparus, 31.5cm. high. (Christie's) $3,000 £1,400

One of a pair of Venetian 'Renaissance' bronze torcheres, circa 1870, 48in. high. (Sotheby's Belgravia) $2,035 £920

Gilt bronze and Sevres candelabra, circa 1880, 23in. high. (Sotheby's Belgravia) $730 £330

Pair of bronze candelabra of a satyr and a putto, circa 1880, on white marble socles, 17¾in. high. (Sotheby's Belgravia) $840 £380

Fine 15th century Vijay-anagar bronze figure of a Deva standing in Abhanga, 39.5cm. high. (Christie's) $2,770 £1,200

One of a pair of Barbed-
ienne bronze candelabra,
signed, circa 1870, 26in.
high. (Sotheby's
Belgravia) $330 £150

16th century Tibetan gilt
bronze figure of Syamatara
seated in Lalitasana, 27cm.
high. (Christie's)
                $1,850 £800

Bronze and ivory group of
a young couple, circa
1890, signed P. Tereszczuk,
12½in. high. (Sotheby's
Belgravia) $550 £250

Early 20th century German
bronze group of two lovers,
signed F. Lepcke, 28cm.
(Christie's) $1,610 £700

Important French bronze
statuette of a Roman trumpeter, signed J. L. Gerome,
1889, 95cm. high. (Christie's)
        $69,000 £30,000

A bronze figure of an
athlete by P. Le Faguays,
73cm. high. (Christie's)
        $3,500 £1,600

Late 17th century bronze
candlestick with tapered
stem, 10in. (Robert W.
Skinner Inc.) $450 £210

A bronze and ivory figure
of a nude girl by F. Preiss,
14.5cm. high. (Christie's)
        $2,000 £900

Preiss bronze and ivory
figure of a golfer,
24cm. high, 1930's.
(Sotheby's Belgravia)
        $2,630 £1,200

Pair of spelter figures of
Roman soldiers, 20in. high,
circa 1880. (Sotheby's Belgravia) $265 £120

One of a pair of gilt bronze
candlesticks, mid 19th century, 11½in. high.
(Sotheby's Belgravia)
        $665 £300

One of a pair of gilt bronze
candelabra, bases cast with
roses and foliage, circa
1870. (Sotheby's Belgravia)
        $200 £90

BUCKETS AND HODS

Early Victorian copper helmet-shaped coal scuttle. (Alfie's Antique Market) $112 £52

Victorian portable lavatory by R. Wiss, London, in copper with a blue and white china bowl, 15in. high. (Sotheby Bearne) $155 £70

Metal and brass inlaid coal box, 1876 by H. Loveridge & Co. (Alfie's Antique Market) $135 £60

George III mahogany peat bucket with circular lid, circa 1765, 1ft. 6in. high. (Sotheby's) $2,160 £1,000

Copper coal scuttle with shovel. (Hexton & Cheney) $155 £72

Unusual Victorian parlour coal box, 26in. high, with mirrored lid and ceramic handles. (James Harrison) $205 £100

Art Deco copper/brass coal bin with brass shovel, 16in. high. (Alfie's Antique Market) $105 £40

Victorian copper coal scuttle. (Alfie's Antique Market) $102 £45

George III mahogany brass bound plate bucket with swing over brass handle, 37cm. high. (Phillips) $925 £400

George III mahogany circular bucket, bound in brass, 37cm. high. (Phillips) $1,040 £450

Copper coal helmet with swing over handle. (Phillips) $36 £16

George III mahogany and brass bound plate bucket, 12¼in. high. (Christie's S. Kensington) $1,080 £500

Anglo-Indian ivory veneered work-box with gadrooned domed lid, 11¾in. wide. (Christie's) $675 £300

Late 18th century Anglo-Indian ivory inlaid hardwood toilet box, 17¼in. wide. (Christie's) $1,455 £650

Early 19th century Anglo-Indian ivory and ebony veneered games box, 18in. wide. (Christie's) $900 £400

Mid 18th century Dutch Colonial writing box with fitted interior, 2ft.1½in. long. (Sotheby's) $915 £400

Mid 19th century red boulle encrier, lid opening to reveal letter compartments. (Sotheby's Belgravia) $700 £310

Mid 17th century English leather document case with hinged lid, 16½in. wide. (Christie's) $1,375 £600

Louis Philippe ormolu mounted faded tulipwood casket with Sevres pattern plaque, 16½in. wide.(Christie's) $1,400 £620

Burr chestnut games compendium for chess, backgammon, bezique and cribbage, circa 1860. (Sotheby's Belgravia) $870 £380

Early 19th century Chinese export black and gold lacquer toilet mirror base, 19½in. wide. (Christie's) $450 £200

One of three George III lignum vitae spice grinders each in three parts, with screw-on lids. (Sotheby's) $1,320 £580

A pair of mid Georgian mahogany cutlery boxes with brass handles, 9¾in. wide. (Christie's) $1,275 £550

Superb rectangular Kobako, signed Seishu, with mother-of-pearl, ivory and hardstone design. (Phillips) $13,330 £6,200

CADDIES AND BOXES

Neapolitan tortoiseshell case for counters, 7½in. wide, circa 1725-50. (Sotheby's) $25,920 £12,000

Miniature carved wood Scandinavian butter box, 4in. long. (Christopher Sykes) $85 £38

Upright walnut desk tidy with opening front, 37cm. high. (Phillips) $35 £16

13th century Limoges reliquary casket of champleve enamel on copper. (Spink/Koller) $190,000 £88,000

Rare 18th century Italian carved, painted and gilt wood ballot box in two parts, 17¾in. high. (Sotheby's) $1,025 £450

Mid 19th century coromandelwood tea caddy, 38cm. wide. (Phillips) $270 £120

Tokelau Islands oval wood box with flat lid, 11¾in. wide, with plaited coir cord handle. (Sotheby's) $1,260 £580

Late 16th century small Namban lacquer reliquary of domed coffin form, Momoyama period. (Sotheby King & Chasemore) $670 £310

Victorian coromandelwood combined toilet case and writing box with silver mounted bottles, 34cm. wide. (Sotheby King & Chasemore) $540 £250

Viennese enamel mounted rectangular miniature casket. (Christie's S. Kensington) $1,025 £450

Pair of Pontypool urns and covers, 13in. high. (Christie's S. Kensington) $1,035 £820

19th century rosewood travelling drinks cabinet. (J. M. Welch & Son) $455 £210

Mid 19th century scarlet boulle tantalus with fitted interior, 13½in. wide. (Christie's S. Kensington) $1,080 £500

Italian ebony and engraved ivory box, circa 1860, 18½in. wide. (Sotheby's Belgravia) $840 £380

Silver mounted Shibayama spice casket, 5 x 5in. (Langlois) $3,240 £1,500

Chinese carved ivory needle-work box, with fitted interior. (Eadon, Lockwood & Riddle) $3,455 £1,550

Royal Worcester pierced silk box and cover. (Sotheby's Belgravia) $3,025 £1,400

Late 18th century Russian walrus ivory casket, from the Kholmorgory region, 19.2cm. wide. (Sotheby's) $640 £280

One of a fine pair of mahogany knife boxes with inlaid conch shells. (British Antique Exporters) $1,125 £500

Gilt wood casket with five Limoges plaques, attributed to Pierre Reymond. (Christie's) $15,120 £7,000

George III mahogany knife box with boxwood string inlay fitted with twenty-three knives and forks. (Christie's S. Kensington) $480 £210

Maori wood presents box showing a crouching figure with box on back, 7in. high. (Sotheby's) $5,640 £2,600

Pair of late Victorian mahogany urn-shaped decanter boxes, 31in. high. (Christie's S. Kensington) $1,835 £850

Early 19th century mahogany and brass bound decanter case, 22cm. wide. (Sotheby King & Chasemore) $700 £325

George III mahogany tea caddy, front inlaid with satinwood conch shell motif, 7½in. wide, circa 1790. (Sotheby King & Chasemore) $169 £75

Regency rosewood lady's box, circa 1830, 11in. wide. (Christopher Sykes) $192 £85

Enamelled silver rectangular cigarette box, London, 1944, 15.5cm. long. (Sotheby's Belgravia) $716 £310

Chippendale period mahogany tea caddy, circa 1770, with brass handle, 11in. long. (Christopher Sykes) $192 £85

Rioro nuri two-tier jubako, upper fitted as a suzuribako and lower part as a kowasibako. (Christie's S. Kensington) $293 £130

Sheraton mahogany tea caddy, circa 1800, 12in. long. (Christopher Sykes) $149 £66

Model of a terrestrial globe in the form of a string box, 4¼in. high, circa 1890. (Christopher Sykes) $192 £85

Edwardian optometrist's outfit with lenses, rules, test cards and ophthalmoscope. (Alfie's Antique Market) $226 £100

Snuff box in the form of an Oriental slipper, circa 1780, 3½in. long. (Christopher Sykes) $63 £28

WMF electroplated metal casket with hinged top, circa 1900, 24.25cm. wide. (Sotheby's Belgravia) $175 £80

Farmhouse salt box, circa 1780, 10¾in. high. (Christopher Sykes) $101 £45

Regency tea caddy, inlaid with brass and mother-of-pearl floral design. (Gray's Antique Mews) $370 £165

19th century tortoiseshell sewing box. (Vost's) $307 £150

Victorian papier mache trinket box with floral decoration. (Phillips) $69 £30

Victorian burr walnut writing slope with brass mounts, 1ft.2in. wide, circa 1880. (Sotheby King & Chasemore) $1,039 £460

John Paul Cooper galuchat box and cover, circa 1900, 9.3cm. wide. (Sotheby's Belgravia) $240 £110

Coachbuilder's tool chest and contents, tools bearing the stamp of John Hartley, circa 1839. (Christie's S. Kensington) $3,164 £1,400

Bavarian brass and amboyna jewel coffer, circa 1900, 34cm. wide. (Sotheby's Belgravia) $1,201 £520

Victorian coromandelwood and brass tantalus with three bottles, 12in. wide.(Gray's Antique Mews) $620 £275

18th century American mahogany pipe box with wall attachment, 16½in. high. (Robert W. Skinner Inc.) $1,400 £600

Indo-Portuguese inlaid box, 18th century, 21in. long. (Robert W. Skinner Inc.) $450 £200

Unusual fruitwood tea caddy, circa 1830, 10½in. wide, with rosewood lidded tea containers. (Christopher Sykes) $192 £85

19th century Japanese lacquer cigar case, 5in. wide. (Christopher Sykes) $192 £85

Sheraton period tea caddy, circa 1800, 7in. wide, in mahogany with ebony stringing. (Christopher Sykes) $146 £65

CADDIES AND BOXES

Good Alphonse Giroux miniature casket, circa 1850, 16in. wide. (Sotheby's Belgravia) $3,224 £1,550

Early 19th century Persian pen box in papier mache, 9¼in. long. (Christopher Sykes) $271 £120

Small Japanese lacquer kobako of the Meiji period, 17cm. wide. (Sotheby King & Chasemore) $604 £280

Upper Rhine pine casket, front with roundels, circa 1500, 11in. wide. (Sotheby's) $1,435 £650

Late 16th/early 17th century Nuremberg steel casket, 11.5cm. wide. (Christie's) $3,456 £1,600

Mid 19th century Japanese lacquer box and cover, 43.5cm. wide. (Sotheby King & Chasemore) $1,136 £560

18th century Portuguese padoukwood cutlery box. (Christie's) $1,180 £520

18th century Indo-Portuguese bible box in teak and ebony, 18½in. long. (Robert W. Skinner Inc.) $350 £160

15th century French gilt copper Chrismatory, on raised base, 5½in. wide. (Sotheby's) $1,880 £850

Lacquer okimono stand on four cabriole feet, 30cm. wide. (Sotheby King & Chasemore) $1,017 £450

17th century German casket, decorated with ivory and mother-of-pearl, 12½in. wide. (Robert W. Skinner Inc.) $1,500 £725

French tortoiseshell and ormolu mounted casket. (Christie's S. Kensington) $972 £450

18th century Japanese round lacquered box in wood with pewter frames, 3in. diam. (Robert W. Skinner Inc.) $275 £125

Art Nouveau glove box, circa 1890, of finely grained red leather, 13½in. long. (Christopher Sykes) $85 £38

Toleware circular spice cabinet, circa 1835, 6¼in. diam. (Christopher Sykes) $63 £28

Gentleman's blue enamelled travelling toilet case. (Alfie's Antique Market) $499 £220

19th century Persian papier mache scribe's pen box, 12in. long. (Christopher Sykes) $600 £265

Late 17th century Dutch East Indies tortoiseshell and silver mounted casket, 7¾in. long. (Sotheby's) $2,061 £950

18th century French silvered and gilt metal casket covered with ajoure tortoiseshell panels, 15cm. high.(Christie's) $8,208 £3,800

Victorian Chinese ivory cricket box, circa 1840, 3½in. wide. (Christopher Sykes) $80 £35

Mid 18th century inkstand in kingwood and tulipwood, mounted in ormolu, 14in. wide. (Sotheby's Monaco) $13,300 £6,500

Mid 17th century Dutch or French walnut casket, 11¾in. long, inlaid with mother-of-pearl. (Sotheby's) $1,655 £750

Early 20th century leather writing folder and stationery box with silver coloured metal mounts. (Sotheby's Belgravia) $270 £130

Small 18th century oyster veneered walnut deed box. (Watson) $1,687 £750

CADDIES AND BOXES

19th century Tunbridgeware tea caddy with floral inlay. (D. M. Nesbit & Co.) $315 £140

Georgian mahogany tea caddy. (Nottinghill Antique Market) $260 £115

Box made from a coco-de-mer and carved to resemble a peacock. (Alfie's Antique Market) $205 £95

One of a pair of George III satinwood cutlery boxes, 1ft. 3in. high, circa 1785. (Sotheby's) $2,050 £950

George III mahogany and satinwood tea caddy, circa 1780. (Sotheby's) $300 £140

19th century homeopathic medicine chest with twenty four glass bottles, circa 1870, 9in. long. (Christopher Sykes) $399 £185

Sheraton period tea caddy in inlaid partridgewood, 9½in. high. (Neales) $545 £270

Late 19th century oak cased games compendium, 35cm. wide. (Phillips) $285 £140

George III satinwood cutlery urn, 28in. high, circa 1785. (Sotheby's) $972 £450

Mid 17th century needlework casket. (Christie's S. Kensington) $7,105 £3,500

Tunbridgeware writing slope with oval reserve. (D. M. Nesbit & Co.) $120 £55

Rare Charles II needlework and micre casket, circa 1660. (Sotheby's) $3,145 £1,550

Carved oak letter box, circa 1860.
(Alfie's Antique Market)$120 £55

19th century French tortoiseshell and
ormolu mounted bombe basket, 14¾in.
wide. (Christie's S. Kensington)
$970 £450

William IV rosewood tea
caddy with mother-of-pearl
inlay, 15in. wide. (Hobbs
Parker) $345 £170

19th century tortoiseshell
tea caddy. (Vost's)
$369 £180

Oak spoon rack in three layers, 30cm. wide.
(Phillips) $125 £60

Edwardian picnic basket with
copper spirit kettle. (Alfie's
Antique Market) $120 £55

One of a pair of George III
mahogany cutlery urns, 2ft.
4in. high, circa 1790.
(Sotheby's) $2,590 £1,200

Fine set of four knife boxes. (Phillips)
$1,710 £790

Late Victorian mahogany and
floral marquetry stationery
box, 13¼in. high. (Christie's
S. Kensington) $450 £200

Burr-walnut tea caddy, circa 1830,
15½in. wide. (Alfie's Antique
Market) $190 £95

Antique carved oak bible box.
(J. M. Welch & Son) $455 £210

Victorian papier mache sewing
box. (Vost's) $295 £145

CADDIES AND BOXES

Bavarian brass and walnut jewel coffer, circa 1900, 30.8cm. wide. (Sotheby's Belgravia) $744 £340

George III harewood and satinwood marquetry tea caddy, circa 1770. (Sotheby's) $320 £140

Edwardian cigarette box made from silver plated brass. (Gray's Antique Mews) $250 £250

Finely carved Oriental needlework box, fitted with compartments and ivory tools. (Eadon, Lockwood & Riddle) $3,580 £1,550

Victorian rosewood and mother-of-pearl dressing box complete with silver plated accessories. (Gray's Antique Mews) $364 £160

Regency rosewood tea caddy of casket form, 35cm. wide. (Phillips) $46 £20

One of a pair of 'George III' mahogany knife urns with gadrooned lids, circa 1880. (Sotheby's Belgravia) $1,150 £500

Early Victorian cribbage board made from ebony and mother-of-pearl, circa 1840, 12¼in. long. (Christopher Sykes) $146 £65

George III mahogany knife box, top with silver crest mount, 34cm. high. (Phillips) $196 £85

English apothecary's chest in mahogany, 1830-40, 10½in. high. (Sotheby's Belgravia) $525 £240

English A. S. Maw & Sons portable medical cabinet, circa 1863, 6½in. high. (Sotheby's Belgravia) $655 £300

Victorian rosewood stationery box with brass fittings. (Phillips) $110 £48

Sheraton tea caddy in mahogany and partridgewood, 5in. high. (Gray's Antique Mews) $136 £60

Ornate, plated on brass, box, lined in velvet. (Alfie's Antique Market) $115 £50

Sheraton tea caddy in mahogany and partridgewood, 6¼in. high. (Gray's Antique Mews)$160 £70

Regency rosewood tea caddy, with mother-of-pearl inlaid lid, 35cm. wide. (Phillips) $87 £38

Edwardian writing box in light oak, circa 1905, 16in. wide. (Gray's Antique Mews)$275 £120

Pair of Georgian mahogany knife boxes. (Bradley & Vaughan) $1,687 £740

Cribbage board of solid mahogany, standing on brass feet, circa 1800. (Christopher Sykes) $85 £38

Antique mahogany apothecary's medicine chest, circa 1830, 9½in. wide, with brass hinged handle. (Christopher Sykes) $365 £160

Regency rosewood tea caddy with bombe front, 37cm. wide. (Phillips) $115 £50

George III mahogany knife box. (Phillips) $12, £55

Victorian oak cased tantalus with cut glass decanters. (Bradley & Vaughan) $638 £280

Late 18th century Sheraton period cutlery urn. (Locke & England) $1,368 £600

Fine Sands and Hunter Exhibition tailboard camera, circa 1883, 8½in. wide. (Sotheby's Belgravia) $560 £250

'Stereo Hawkeye' folding camera by Blair Camera Co., model No.2. (Sotheby Humberts) $195 £90

Ticka watch pocket camera in original box, by Houghton's, London, circa 1906. (H. C. Chapman & Son) $290 £130

Unusual mahogany reflex camera, circa 1920's, 9 x 12cm. (Sotheby's Belgravia) $675 £300

English 15 x 15in. studio camera on tripod stand, circa 1880. (Sotheby's Belgravia) $435 £190

Rare Ernemann ernoflex folding reflex camera, German, circa 1925. (Sotheby's Belgravia) $900 £400

Century No.2 studio portrait camera on base. (Ronald Garwood) $930 £410

English Sanderson hand-and-stand tropical camera, 3¼in. x 4¼in., with lenses, circa 1910. (Sotheby's Belgravia) $505 £220

Good German full-plate studio camera by Staeble, Munich, with lenses, circa 1880. (Sotheby's Belgravia) $980 £450

'The Una', quarter plate camera by James A. Sinclair. (Sotheby's Belgravia) $1,250 £550

Rare Negretti and Zambra small wet-plate camera, circa 1860, 3¼in. square. (Sotheby's Belgravia) $1,125 £500

Early English dry-plate tailboard camera, circa 1870's, 8in. wide. (Sotheby's Belgravia) $545 £240

Gentleman's malacca, Wedgwood and silver walking stick with ivory handle, 34¼in. long. (Christopher Sykes) $170 £75

French green silk parasol with frosted quartz fox mask knop. (Heathcote Ball & Co.) $495 £230

Victorian walking stick with snuff box handle, maker's initials E.N. 1887. (Christie's S. Kensington) $540 £240

Rare Chelsea cane handle in the form of a girl's head, 2¾in. high. (Olivers) $2,375 £1,050

Brigg lady's umbrella, bamboo shaft with gold mounted tortoiseshell handle, 1905, 93.5cm. long. (Sotheby's Belgravia) $320 £140

English gold and malacca walking cane, circa 1765-1770, 130.5cm. long. (Sotheby's) $1,060 £480

Unusual walking stick handle of naturally formed blackthorn, 12in. long. (Christopher Sykes) $25 £12

Early 20th century French walking cane, gold-coloured rose diamond and sapphire set handle on bamboo shaft. (Sotheby's Belgravia) $645 £280

Large night stick or constable's truncheon of turned oak, 21in. long. (Christopher Sykes) $175 £78

Ben Akiba miniature walking stick camera. (Christie's S. Kensington) $7,685 £3,400

18th century malacca staff with ivory pommel and tapering shaft, 56in. high. (Christie's) $675 £300

Art Nouveau gold mounted parasol handle, French, circa 1900. (Sotheby's Belgravia) $875 £380

English gold topped walking cane, circa 1780, 97.5cm. long. (Sotheby's) $135 £60

William IV silver topped walking cane by John Linnit, London, 1831, 40in. long. (Sotheby's) $2,485 £1,150

English gold, enamel and malacca walking cane, circa 1775, 107cm. long. (Sotheby's) $705 £320

Bent cane walking stick handle, 9in. long. (Christopher Sykes) $25 £11

Lalique glass car mascot in the form of rearing horses, 1920's, 11cm. high. (Sotheby's Belgravia) $1,860 £850

Glass motor car mascot by Lalique, 9.7cm. high. (Phillips) $170 £80

Frosted glass model of an eagle, 15.2cm. high. (Phillips) $69 £32

Lalique glass car mascot 'Spirit of the Wind', 1930's, 25.5cm. long. (Sotheby's Belgravia) $4,160 £1,800

Lalique glass hawk car mascot, 19cm. high, circa 1930. (Sotheby's Belgravia) $1,535 £700

Fine solid brass car mascot, circa 1925, 4¾in. high. (Christopher Sykes) $130 £58

'Bruno' standing bear car mascot in chromium plated brass, 11.2cm. high. (Phillips) $60 £28

'Pegasus' silvered bronze car mascot by Asprey, London, 16.7cm. high. (Phillips) $520 £240

Car mascot modelled as Cupid in chromium plated brass, 20cm. high. (Phillips) $140 £65

Vauxhall car mascot in burnished brass, 8.8cm. high. (Phillips) $140 £65

Silver plated stag's head car mascot in brass, 13.7cm. high. (Phillips) $64 £30

Lalique glass car mascot 'The Archer', moulded in intaglio, 12.5cm. high. (Sotheby King & Chasemore) $560 £260

'The Archer', a Lalique glass car mascot, 1930's, 13cm. high. (Sotheby's Belgravia) $1,270 £550

Nickel plated bronze car mascot 'The Bowler', 16cm. high. (Phillips) $162 £75

'Spirit of the Wind' glass car mascot by Lalique, 19.5cm. long. (Phillips) $1,620 £750

'Vulcan' Edwardian brass car mascot, 18.8cm. high. (Phillips) $97 £45

A pair of gilded wood angels with arms outstretched. (Worsfolds) $225 £100

North American Indian wooden rattle. (Stride's) $7,850 £3,400

Early 19th century Dutch carved oak carriage foot-warmer with brass handle, 9¼in. wide. (Christie's) $780 £340

Hardwood Polynesian ceremonial mace with ritual carvings. (Worsfolds) $1,360 £600

One of a pair of North German oak panels, 14in. high. (Sotheby's) $545 £240

Mid 17th century Flemish baroque fruitwood carving of The Virgin Mary, 8¾in. high. (Sotheby's) $500 £220

One of a pair of 18th century mahogany candlesticks, 39cm. high. (Phillips) $105 £45

Qing dynasty bamboo tripod cylindrical vase, slightly damaged, 11¾in. high. (Christie's) $445 £200

Qing dynasty bamboo cylindrical brush pot, 6½in. high. (Christie's) $335 £150

Two from a set of six important Liegeois walnut bas-reliefs by Simon Cognoulle, circa 1740. (Christie's) $118,800 £55,000

Jokwe wood carving of a seated territorial chief, 14½in. high. (Christie's) $140,400 £65,000

One of a pair of late 17th century patinated pine naiads, 33in. wide. (Christie's S. Kensington) $2,485 £1,150

Late 16th century Italian polychrome wood figure of a Dominican friar, 96cm. high. (Christie's) $2,810 £1,300

CARVED WOOD

13th century Gothic polychrome wood group of the Virgin and Child, 59cm. high. (Christie's)
$3,672 £1,700

One of a pair of 17th/18th century turned wood candlesticks, 14.5cm. high. (Christie's)
$1,296 £600

Late 13th century Italian figure of an angel, 75cm. high. (Christie's)
$8,640 £4,000

Early 19th century Chinese gold lacquer figure on an ebonised and gilt base, 23in. high. (Phillips)
$1,125 £500

Two German carved wood figures of saints, late 17th/early 18th century. (Bonham's) $1,035 £480

16th century Spanish polychrome wood group of the Virgin and Child with St. Anne, 60cm. high. (Christie's)
$4,968 £2,300

Early 17th century Hispano-Flemish oak relief of the Sacrifice of Isaac, 20in. high. (Sotheby's) $1,258 £580

Early 17th century Flemish boxwood statue of Bellona, 16½in. high. (Sotheby's)
$1,260 £580

Venetian carved wood and composition figure of a blackamoor, 6ft. 8in. high. (D. M. Nesbit & Co.) $2,268 £1,050

Austrian carved wood figure of a musician, circa 1880, 66in. high. (Sotheby's Belgravia)
$1,352 £650

12th century Burgundian carving in limewood of a crucifix figure, 43¼in. high.(Sotheby's)
$474,600 £210,000

Mid 16th century French fruitwood statuette of the Virgin and Child, 29.5cm. high.(Christie's) $4,105 £1,900

Important 17th century German fruitwood statuette of Adam, 28cm. high. (Sotheby's) $34,560 £16,000

Early 17th century Spanish carved wood figure of St. James, 55in. high.· (Sotheby's) $1,560 £720

Late 16th century Flemish polychrome limewood statuette of the Virgin and Child, 37.5cm. high. (Christie's)$10,370 £4,800

Early 16th century Spanish polychrome wooden group of the Flight into Egypt, 42cm. high. (Christie's) $3,024 £1,400

Pair of carved limewood and painted figures of the Seasons, 84in. high. (Christie's S. Kensington) $9,000 £4,000

Flemish oak relief carving of Saint Hubert, circa 1500, 34 x 35½in. (Phillips) $21,000 £10,500

One of a pair of modern painted wood blackamoors, 60½in. high, now fitted for electricity.(Sotheby's Belgravia) $1,455 £700

Mid 17th century Dutch walnut bust of a bishop-saint, 12¾in. high. (Sotheby's) $434 £200

One of a pair of late 17th century Italian wood angels, 43in. high, both lacking wings. (Sotheby's)$2,390 £1,100

Early 16th century polychrome limewood statuette of St. Mary Magdalene, 52.5cm. high. (Christie's) $14,040 £6,500

Maori hardwood club. (McCartney, Morris & Barker) $950 £440

Interesting carved wood Chinese figure of a seated god, 19in. high. (Butler & Hatch Waterman) $226 £105

Italian carved wood Jester's head, circa 1860. (Alfie's Antique Market) $292 £130

Azande wood figure of a man. (Christie's) $4,466 £2,200

Maori carved canoe prow. (Bonham's) $2,052 £950

19th century carved wood 'Bateka'. (J. M. Welch & Son) $315 £146

Carved walnut figure of a bargee, 36in. high. (Phillips) $1,319 £650

Italian carved wood figure of a herald with a fanfare trumpet, 50in. high. (Phillips) $1,220 £600

Senufo wood rhythm pounder. (Sotheby's) $205,200 £95,000

Carved oak combined mantelpiece and overmantel, 70in. wide. (Butler & Hatch Waterman) $670 £310

Austrian carved walnut umbrella stand, 81in. high, 1870's. (Sotheby's Belgravia) $1,622 £780

Rare Maori carved wood over-door. (Phillips) $23,230 £11,500

African funerary mask in heavily carved wood. (Manchester Auction Mart) $4,850 £2,400

Pair of finely carved walnut cherub scrolls, mid 19th century, 35½in. high. (Christopher Sykes) $776 £345

Baroque polychrome wood coat-of-arms, 85cm. high. (Christie's) $970 £420

One of a pair of antique yew-wood adjustable table candlesticks, 10in. high. (Whiteheads) $771 £380

19th century Chinese rosewood carving, 14in. high. (Nottinghill Auction Market) $200 £90

Dogon wood female figure. (Sotheby's) $58,320 £27,000

Egyptian New Kingdom wood Royal Ushabti figure of Ramesses IX, 13½in. (Sotheby's) $9,900 £4,500

African Mende female wood figure from South-Central Sierra Leone. (Christie's) $5,185 £2,400

Easter Island wood figure. (Christie's) $27,000 £12,000

Mid 18th century cricket bat, 105cm. long. (Phillips) $1,305 £580

Azande wooden figure of a mother and child. (Christie's) $8,526 £4,200

Carved wood New Ireland figure. (Christie's) $3,888 £1,800

Stern board carving, circa 1900, 59in. wide. (Robert W. Skinner Inc.) $1,900 £830

Beechwood butter marker, circa 1840, 4½in. diam. (Christopher Sykes) $79 £35

Carved wood decoy teal duck, 12in. long, with glass eyes. (Christopher Sykes) $153 £68

Fine mid 19th century Italian ship's figurehead from The Benvolio. (Alfie's Antique Market) $2,147 £950

Japanese portrait sculpture, late Kamakura period, lacquered in red, brown and cream. (Ader, Picard, Tajan) $54,360 £25,285

Early 16th century South German boxwood carving of St. Christopher, 22in. high. (Phillips) $9,900 £4,500

Two American 19th century wooden flagons, 10in. and 9½in. high. (Robert W. Skinner Inc.) $450 £200

One of a pair of George III mahogany and brass candlesticks, circa 1790, 13½in. high. (Sotheby's) $775 £340

Shield-shaped family horse coach panel, circa 1840, 17½in. wide. (Christopher Sykes) $192 £85

19th century human face mask of the Senufo tribe, 13½in. high. (Christopher Sykes) $644 £285

16th century Spanish polychrome oak processional head, 34cm. high. (Christie's) $1,800 £780

Late 17th century Dutch ciborium in turned and lacquered wood with gilt brass mounts, 12in. high. (Robert W. Skinner Inc.) $400 £180

Carved wooden decoy mallard
duck, 13½in. long. (Christopher
Sykes) $151 £67

Sycamore wood butter marker, circa
1830, 5in. diam. (Christopher Sykes)
                              $85 £38

Carved wood and gilded eagle,
circa 1810, 18½in. wide.
(Christopher Sykes)$108 £48

18th century Bali carved wood
buffalo and figure, 20in. high.
(Robert W. Skinner Inc.)
                    $500 £225

Early 19th century pinewood bowl,
possibly American, 15in. diam.
(Christopher Sykes) $146 £65

One of a pair of 19th century
carved wood models of stags,
8in. high. (Christopher Sykes)
                    $198 £88

Good Toleware polished chamberstick, circa 1840, 2½in. high,
by H. F. & Co. (Christopher
Sykes) $63 £28

Chemist's boxwood bottle holder
with screw-on domed lid, circa 1860,
6in. high. (Christopher Sykes)$40 £18

Olivewood Scandinavian carved
jug, with carved pattern, 4¼in.
high, circa 1860. (Christopher
Sykes) $63 £28

Early 16th century Flemish
pieta in carved oak, 16¼in.
high. (Robert W. Skinner Inc.)
               $2,900 £1,300

Rare mask from the South Eastern
Congo of the Jokwe tribe, sold with
tight fitting costume, 55in. high.
(Christopher Sykes) $847 £375

20th century American wooden
horse's head mounted on a wall
plaque, 20in. high. (Robert W.
Skinner Inc.) $350 £150

19th century lignum vitae tobacco jar, 8½in. high. (Olivers) $158 £70

17th century Spanish rectangular poly-chrome gilt wood relief of Christ in the Garden of Gethsemane, 84cm. wide. (Christie's) $1,620 £750

18th/19th century bamboo brush pot, slightly damaged, 6½in. high. (Christie's) $1,000 £450

Mid 17th century Flemish fruitwood statuette of the Immaculate Conception, 20cm. high. (Christie's) $3,888 £1,800

Late 15th century Spanish polychrome walnut relief of St. Jerome, 63cm. high. (Christie's) $10,370 £4,800

Large Oriental carved wood group, 93cm. high, circa 1900. (Sotheby's Belgravia) $737 £340

Late 15th century Spanish poly-chrome walnut group of the Last Supper, 33cm. high. (Christie's) $5,400 £2,500

Late 15th century Flemish or German polychrome group, 31.5cm. high. (Christie's) $3,240 £1,500

Spanish polychrome and gilt wood relief, circa 1600, 23½in. wide. (Sotheby's)$1,520 £700

Fine George III stripped pine chimney-piece with later top, 88½in. wide. (Christie's) $2,320 £1,000

One of a pair of good 17th century Flemish carved oak panels, 35 x 26cm. (Christie's) $1,265 £550

Unusual lacquered wood fig-ure of a wrestler, circa 1900, 38cm. high. (Sotheby's Belgravia) $435 £200

One of a pair of North German oak reliefs of St. Augustine, mid 17th century, 14¼in. high. (Sotheby's) $955 £440

Mid 16th century Spanish polychrome and gilt softwood lunette relief of The Annunciation, 100cm. wide. (Christie's) $5,400 £2,500

Boxwood domed top bottle holder, circa 1860, 3in. high. (Christopher Sykes) $31 £14

Spanish seated polychrome figure of the Ecce Homo, 17in. high, circa 1600. (Sotheby's) $2,060 £950

One of a pair of Austrian wood panels, circa 1700, 14½in. high. (Sotheby's) $1,085 £500

Large polychrome wood figure of St. Francis, circa 1700, 48in. high. (Sotheby's) $1,690 £780

Late 15th century Flemish polychrome oak wood group, 37.5cm. high. (Christie's) $10,800 £5,000

Early 16th century Spanish polychrome wooden group of the Meeting at the Golden Gate, 44.5cm. high.(Christie's) $5,500 £2,500

16th century Spanish polychrome wood relief of the Circumcision, 22¾in. high. (Sotheby's) $2,280 £1,050

Mid 15th century Umbrian polychrome and gilt poplarwood pieta, 42.5cm. high. (Christie's) $4,320 £2,000

English limewood relief of Queen Tomyris with the head of Cyrus, circa 1670, 59cm. long.(Christie's) $14,040 £6,500

Early 16th century Flemish polychrome oak figure of a knight on horseback, 42.3cm. high. (Christie's) $12,960 £6,000

Dutch six-branch chandelier, circa 1700, 20in. spread. (Christopher Sykes) $1,520 £675

Daum glass and wrought-iron chandelier, circa 1925, 62.5cm. wide. (Sotheby's Belgravia) $655 £300

Modern gilt bronze chandelier, 34in. wide. (Sotheby's Belgravia) $770 £370

Opaque glass chandelier with eight slender twisted flowering stems, circa 1900, 28in. high. (Sotheby's Belgravia) $550 £250

Cut glass and gilt bronze hanging lamp, fitted for electricity, circa 1900, 38½in. high. (Sotheby's Belgravia) $2,495 £1,200

Gilt metal and Meissen porcelain four-light chandelier, 19th century, 29in. high. (Christie's) $2,750 £1,250

Regency bronze and ormolu chandelier with quadruple chain suspension, 36in. wide. (Christie's) $1,570 £680

Unusual leaded glass chandelier with pulley pull-down mechanism, 52½in. high. (Robert W. Skinner Inc.) $3,500 £1,590

Dutch brass six-light chandelier. (Christie's S. Kensington) $590 £260

Rare Dutch seven-light sabbath lamp by Hendrik Dauw, 1783, 116oz., 32in. high. (Christie's) $60,480 £28,000

Early 19th century tin Argand-type chandelier, 35in. high. (Robert W. Skinner Inc.) $400 £185

Dresden nine-light chandelier, 81cm. high. (Christie's) $2,965 £1,300

A Rockwood oviform vase mounted in silver as a ewer, 21cm. high. (Christie's) $2,000 £900

A Theodore Deck large circular wall plaque, 59cm. diam. (Christie's) $1,750 £800

A Van Briggle Pottery Co. oviform vase of shaped outline, 26.5cm. high. (Christie's) $260 £120

ARITA

17th century Japanese Arita blue and white lidded porcelain jar, 13in. high. (McCartney, Morris & Barker) $3,635 £1,800

One of a pair of Arita Imari vases. (Harrods Auction Galleries) $13,110 £5,800

Fine 18th century Arita blue and white hexagonal lobed bowl with floral design, Fuku mark, 21.2cm. diam. (Sotheby's) $875 £380

One of a pair of Japanese Arita style porcelain vases, 4ft. high. (Allen & May) $2,808 £1,300

Japanese Arita dish painted with flowers and foliage in underglaze blue. (H. Spencer & Son) $2,810 £1,250

Late 19th century Japanese Arita vase of exaggerated baluster body, 54.5cm. high. (Sotheby's Belgravia) $520 £240

BAYREUTH

Fine and rare Bayreuth Hausmaler bowl, 18.5cm. diam., circa 1740. (Sotheby's) $26,040 £12,000

Bayreuth Hausmaler teabowl and saucer, circa 1740. (Sotheby's) $3,472 £1,600

Du Paquier Bayreuth Hausmaler teabowl, 15cm. diam., circa 1740. (Sotheby's) $13,020 £6,000

BELLARMINE

Antique brown glazed stoneware Bellarmine jug, 13in. high. (Geering & Colyer) $710 £350

Late 16th/early 17th century Bellarmine jug, slightly damaged. (Sotheby Bearne) $785 £390

Early 17th century Frenchen stoneware Bellarmine jug, 25cm. high. (Sotheby King & Chasemore) $560 £260

17th century German Bellarmine type stoneware handled jug, with English silver mounts, 9½in. high. (Robert W. Skinner Inc.) $500 £225

17th century saltglazed stoneware Bellarmine jug, 22cm. high. (Sotheby King & Chasemore) $505 £250

17th century German stoneware handled jug, 8½in. high. (Robert W. Skinner Inc.) $500 £225

BELLEEK

Good Belleek basket with latticework and basketwork body, circa 1870, 22cm. wide. (Phillips) $300 £140

Unusual Belleek bust of a young woman, circa 1860, 11in. high. (Sotheby's Belgravia) $390 £180

One of a pair of Belleek pitchers with scrolled handles and applied floral decoration. (Robert W. Skinner Inc.) $425 £190

Lenox Belleek classic form vase, 16½in. high. (Robert W. Skinner Inc.) $275 £125

Belleek tea kettle on stand, (Christie's S. Kensington) $2,485 £1,100

Belleek centrepiece, 12in. high, circa 1927-41. (Sotheby's Belgravia) $260 £120

A Berlin plaque painted with St. Cecilia, late 19th century. (Sotheby's Belgravia) $950 £420

A mid 18th century Berlin dish of chamfered square form, 27cm. across. (Sotheby's Belgravia) $590 £260

One of a pair of Berlin white and gold two-handled campana vases with bronze profile of Carl Johann XIV, 31cm. high. (Christie's) $2,735 £1,200

Berlin plate decorated with scenes of St. Stephen's Church, Vienna. (Christie's S. Kensington) $1,405 £650

A Berlin Art Deco part tea service designed by Theo Schmus-Baudiss. (Christie's) $2,600 £1,200

19th century Berlin circular tureen and cover, 12in. diam. (Sotheby Humberts)$775 £360

BOTTGER

Bottger stoneware teapot.(Phillips) $67,500 £30,000

Rare Bottger double-handled beaker and saucer, circa 1720-25.   (Sotheby's) $5,640 £2,600

Rare Augsburg-decorated Bottger pagoda figure, circa 1720, 8.3cm. high. (Sotheby's) $10,415 £4,800

Rare Augsburg-decorated Bottger pagoda figure of a Chinaman, circa 1720-25, 10.5cm. high. (Sotheby's) $22,785 £10,500

Rare Bottger/early Meissen teapot and cover, 11cm. high, circa 1730. (Sotheby's) $8,245 £3,800

Very rare Bottger jug and cover, circa 1720. (Sotheby's) $17,280 £8,000

Rare Bow sucrier and cover,
circa 1755, 3½in. high.
(Sotheby's) $328 £150

Rare Bow miniature teapot and
cover, 2¾in. high, circa 1760.
(Sotheby's) $832 £380

Rare early Bow rose water
bowl, 3in. high, circa
1751-53. (Sotheby's)
               $481 £220

Bow porcelain vase and
cover, circa 1750, 13in.
high. (Phillips)
        $3,255 £1,500

Bow blue and white cider jug,
circa 1754, 8¼in. high.
(Sotheby's) $219 £100

Early Bow bell-shaped
mug, circa 1751-53,
3½in. high. (Sotheby's)
          $700 £320

Rare Bow figure of a putto
in disguise, circa 1760, 5in.
high. (Sotheby's)
        $569 £260

Rare and amusing Bow teapot and cover,
circa 1754-56, 5¼in. high. (Sotheby's)
                $700 £320

Bow figure representing Autumn,
circa 1765, 26cm. high.
(Sotheby King & Chasemore)
                $492 £240

A Bow figure of Autumn,
7in. high, circa 1765.
(Sotheby's) $585 £260

A pair of Bow figures of dancers,
6in. high, 1755-60. (Sotheby's)
          $1,800 £800

A Bow figure of a sports-
man, 6in. high, circa
1765. (Sotheby's)
          $585 £260

Bow figure of a seated
nun with book, repaired,
circa 1755, 14.5cm.
high. (Christie's)
$864 £400

Bow triple shell salt, 18cm. wide,
circa 1760, slightly restored.
(Christie's) $345 £160

Bell-shaped mug from
the Bow porcelain
factory. (Phillips)
$1,036 £480

Bow bell-shaped mug with
loop handle, circa 1755,
9cm. high. (Christie's)
$364 £160

Bow plate in Chelsea style, circa
1760, 23cm. diam. (Christie's)
$456 £200

Rare Bow figure of a gold-
finch, 3¾in. high, circa
1758-62. (Sotheby's)
$525 £240

Bow figure of a 'New
Dancer', circa 1760-
62, 7in. high.
(Sotheby's)
$416 £190

Pair of Bow candlesticks, figures of 'New Dancers',
circa 1765, 8¾in. and 9½in. high. (Sotheby's)
$1,204 £550

Bow figure of a flower
girl, 7in. high, circa
1758-62. (Sotheby's)
$744 £340

Rare Bow figure of a Turk,
circa 1756, 7¼in. high.
(Sotheby's) $1,861 £850

Rare pair of Bow white glazed figures,
10¼in. high. (Olivers)
$3,503 £1,550

Bow figure of a Turkish
lady, circa 1756, 6½in.
high. (Sotheby's)
$1,138 £520

101

One of a pair of Bristol delft powdered manganese ground dishes, circa 1745, 30cm. diam. (Christie's) $1,620 £750

Bristol delft shallow dish, circa 1760, 31cm. diam. (Christie's) $800 £350

One of a pair of Bristol delft blue and white lobed plates, circa 1760, 22.5cm. diam. (Christie's) $300 £140

Bristol delft blue and white flower-brick, circa 1760, slightly chipped, 16cm. high. (Christie's)$390 £180

Bristol delft polychrome tile, circa 1760, 13cm. square, slightly chipped. (Christie's) $235 £110

Bristol delft flower-brick, circa 1740, 6in. wide. (Sotheby's) $830 £380

Bristol delft plate, circa 1720, with crowing cockerel. (Sotheby's) $1,080 £500

Bristol delft polychrome blue dash portrait charger, circa 1710, 34cm. diam. (Christie's) $4,580 £2,000

Bristol delft polychrome blue dash charger, circa 1700, 33.5cm. diam. (Christie's) $2,750 £1,200

Bristol delft polychrome dish, circa 1760, 34.5cm. diam. (Christie's) $365 £160

Pair of Bristol delft Royalist portrait plates, circa 1710, 22.5cm. diam. (Christie's) $10,990 £4,800

Bristol delft polychrome dish decorated with bamboo and shrubs, circa 1740, 33.5cm. diam. (Christie's) $550 £240

Carter, Stabler & Adams Poole pottery vase, circa 1930, 9¾in. high. (Sotheby's Belgravia) $55 £25

Unusual British dish impressed Linthorpe, dated 1879-99, 12in. diam. (Sotheby's Belgravia) $345 £150

One of a pair of unusual Charlotte Rhead vases. (Alfie's Antique Market) $45 £20

Rare British commemorative polychrome posset pot and cover, 1668, 21cm. high. (Sotheby's) $9,200 £4,200

Newcastle pearlware cow group, circa 1800, 12.5cm. wide. (Christie's) $550 £240

Wrotham slipware inscribed and dated tyg by Henry Ifield, 13cm. high, 1644. (Christie's) $7,330 £3,200

Pearlware tea caddy of canted rectangular form, 13cm. high, circa 1860. (Phillips) $215 £100

19th century pair of white clay figures. (Gray's Antique Mews) $955 £420

Carter, Stabler & Adams Poole pottery vase, circa 1930, 10¾in. high. (Sotheby's Belgravia) $250 £110

Victorian jug and basin set. (Phillips) $50 £20

Martha Gunn Toby jug, circa 1790, 28cm. high. (Christie's) $915 £400

Burmantofts dish, circa 1885, 16in. diam. (Sotheby's Belgravia) $340 £150

BRITISH

Vine leaf sweetmeat dish, 5in. long. (Andrew Grant) $95 £44

Clarice Cliff biscuit barrel and cake plate. (Alfie's Antique Market) $165 £75

Large oblong basket with pierced trellis sides and paired lug handles, 16in. long. (Andrew Grant) $1,382 £640

Victorian flower patterned biscuit barrel and stand. (Alfie's Antique Market) $48 £24

Part of a seven-piece Stevenson & Hancock part dessert service, circa 1918-30. (Sotheby's Belgravia) $865 £400

One of a pair of porcelain baluster vases, 12½in. high, circa 1900. (Sotheby's Belgravia) $582 £280

English tin glazed earthenware candlestick, circa 1660, 24.6cm. high. (Sotheby's) $12,375 £5,500

English delft blue dash charger portraying King William III, 13¾in. diam. (Sotheby's) $3,075 £1,500

Large T. C. Brown-Westhead, Moore & Co. majolica vase, 24in. high, circa 1870. (Sotheby's Belgravia) $410 £190

One of two hen tureens, 24cm. and 21.5cm. wide. (Phillips) $43 £20

One of a pair of plates, circa 1820, 8½in. diam. (Sotheby's Belgravia) $302 £140

Pair of lawn tennis figures, coloured bisque, circa 1895, 26cm. tall. (Phillips) $810 £360

One of a pair of porcelain figures of spaniels, 5cm. high, circa 1845. (Sotheby King & Chasemore) $153 £75

Mid 19th century blue and white meat dish showing a cricket match, 50cm. wide. (Phillips) $990 £440

William Brownfield saltglaze jug, 1868, decorated with vine leaves. (Alfie's Antique Market) $59 £27.50

Late 16th/early 17th century stove tile showing Emperor Rudolph II, 11in. high. (Whiteheads) $1,583 £780

Large hand-painted Stilton cheese dish. (Alfie's Antique Market) $118 £55

Small English delftware cistern and cover, 1644, 14in. high, probably by Christian Wilhelm. (Sotheby's) $3,456 £1,600

Earthenware figure of Robert Burns by Pittendrigh McGilvery. (Phillips) $164 £80

Set of Victorian glazed tiles depicting a maltster, now made into a coffee table top. (Spear & Sons) $263 £130

Late 14th century English medieval baluster jug, 19cm. high, slightly chipped. (Christie's) $324 £150

Blue dash charger, late 17th century, painted with tulips, 13¼in. diam. (Sotheby's) $3,280 £1,600

A pair of early English candlesticks in the form of a man and a lady. (Worsfolds) $900 £400

One of a pair of plant pots, 16.5cm. diam. (Phillips) $82 £38

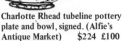

Wemyss-ware bowl, circa 1900, 9½in. diam. (Sotheby's Belgravia) $216 £100

Charlotte Rhead tubeline pottery plate and bowl, signed. (Alfie's Antique Market) $224 £100

Pair of 19th century Noddy figures. (Alfie's Antique Market) $117 £52

Dunmore plant pot with two ring handles, 27.5cm. high. (Phillips) $75 £35

Early 19th century English porcelain cabaret set. (Woolley & Wallis) $1,130 £500

Rare and attractive brown salt-glaze stoneware charger, probably Nottingham, 18th century. (Phillips) $450 £200

Small Wemyss conserve pot and cover, painted with cherries, 7.5cm. high, with matching stand. (Phillips) $90 £40

18th century English delft charger, 20in. diam. (Robert W. Skinner Inc.) $450 £200

Blue and white platter by Andrew Stevenson, circa 1820. (Alfie's Antique Market) $130 £58

Part of a forty-eight piece Clarice Cliff dinner service, 1930's. (Sotheby's Belgravia) $613 £280

Set of five Art Nouveau tiles by Sherwin and Cotton, circa 1900. (Alfie's Antique Market) $78 £30

One of a pair of mid 18th century blue and white delft plates, 12¾in. diam., from the De Claeuw factory. (Sotheby Humberts) $1,080 £500

Elers redware coffee cup and saucer, circa 1760. (Christie's) $216 £100

Part of a twenty-four piece Davenport dessert service, 1870's. (Sotheby's Belgravia) $1,512 £700

Sam Haile slipware vase, circa 1946, 11in. high. (Sotheby's Belgravia) $499 £230

One of a pair of moulded blue and white vine leaf sweetmeat dishes, 5½in. long. (Andrew Grant) $77 £36

Cetem-ware black ground toilet set of nine pieces. (Phillips) $67 £30

Clarice Cliff cockerel teapot. (Nottinghill Antique Market) $281 £125

Wemyss-ware moulded jug, circa 1910, 8in. high. (Sotheby's Belgravia) $259 £120

Part of a sixteen-piece E. J. D. Bodley dessert service, dated for 1877. (Sotheby's Belgravia) $302 £140

Carltonware vase, circa 1900, 18in. high, in perfect condition. (Alfie's Antique Market) $280 £130

Wileman & Co. character teapot and cover, depicting Joseph Chamberlain. (Sotheby's Belgravia) $195 £90

Part of a Powell, Bishop & Stonier dessert service, circa 1880. (Alfie's Antique Market) $175 £75

Amusing Cumnock pottery hen salt crock, 1872, 29.5cm. high. (Phillips) $205 £95

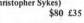

Unusual covered vegetable dish in rich blue copper lustre, circa 1850, 0¼in. diam.(Christopher Sykes) $65 £20

Potted char dish, 5in. wide, circa 1820, enamelled in cerise, turquoise and green. (Christopher Sykes) $80 £35

Mid 19th century Jackfield pottery cow creamer jug, circa 1840, 5¼in. high. (Christopher Sykes) $80 £35

Unusual Pilkington's Royal Lancastrian plate, 12¾in. diam., dated for 1906. (Sotheby's Belgravia) $565 £260

Antique copper lustre cream jug, circa 1835, 3⅜in. high. (Christopher Sykes) $105 £45

Medium blue jasper ware drum shaped base, impressed Adams, 5in. high, Tunstall, England. (Christopher Sykes) $80 £35

Enoch Wood figure of a parrot with brown breast and beak, circa 1785, 22.5cm. high. (Christie's) $3,435 £1,500

Pair of Art Deco style bisque figures of tennis players, circa 1920, each 8cm. high. (Sotheby's Belgravia) $205 £95

Shelton porcelain bell-shaped mug with double scroll handle, 11cm. high, circa 1780. (Christie's) $365 £160

Brown transfer printed child's milk jug, circa 1860, 2¾in. high. (Christopher Sykes) $40 £18

Large pottery charger, inscribed 'La Fontaine', 61cm. diam. (Sotheby King & Chasemore) $530 £260

Crackle glazed ceramic group, 1932, 28cm. wide, from a model by S. Nicholson Babb. (Sotheby's Belgravia) $615 £280

One of a pair of red pottery sweetmeat moulds in the form of chickens, circa 1850, 4½in. long. (Christopher Sykes) $34 £15

Wemyss cone shaped vase with four ring handles, 13cm. high. (Phillips) $80 £40

Part of a Clarice Cliff dinner service of twenty-five pieces, 1930's. (Sotheby's Belgravia) $830 £380

Silver lustre jug, circa 1815, slightly chipped. (Christopher Sykes) $195 £85

Saltglaze stoneware Cyder dispensing jar, 18in. high, with pewter spigot. (Christopher Sykes) $64 £28

Child's plate with the heading 'Pilgrim's Progress', circa 1845, 7¼in. diam. (Christopher Sykes) $57 £25

Imposing Robinson and Leadbeater Parian bust of Queen Victoria, 17in. high. (Sotheby's Belgravia) $250 £110

Victorian decorated toilet set. (Phillips) $92 £40

Rozenburg pottery vase with twin loop handles, circa 1900, 26.5cm. high. (Sotheby's Belgravia) $480 £220

Small Pilkington's Royal Lancastrian ovoid jar and cover, 1926, 12cm. high. (Phillips) $160 £75

Two of four various Toby jugs, 22cm.-25cm. high. (Phillips) $140 £65

One of two Parianware busts by C. Delpech. (Worsfolds) $390 £190

Michael Cardew stoneware bowl, 14in. diam., 1960's. (Sotheby's Belgravia) $715 £330

Swansea lobed oval crested dish, 26.5cm. wide, 1815-1822. (Christie's) $205 £95

Michael Cardew stoneware bowl with tapering foot rim, 1960's, 7¾in. diam. (Sotheby's Belgravia) $250 £115

Michael Cardew large slipware dish, circa 1930, 16½in. diam.(Sotheby's Belgravia) $910 £420

Part of a Copeland's Spode seventeen-piece dessert service. (Sotheby's Belgravia) $680 £300

Victorian brown glazed pottery cheese dish. (Alfie's Antique Market) $124 £55

A Swansea plate, probably painted by Henry Morris, 8in. diam., 1813-22. (Sotheby's) $425 £190

A Caughley cylindrical mug printed in blue, 6in. high, circa 1780. (Sotheby's) $425 £190

Blue and white transfer printed Caughley bowl, 7½in. diam. (G. E. Sworder & Sons) $2,635 £1,220

Rare Toby jug 'General Sir Douglas Haig', circa 1917. (Christopher Sykes)$650 £285

Swansea shaped rectangular dish painted in the manner of William Pollard, 28.5cm. wide, 1815-1822. (Christie's) $648 £300

Porcelain figure of a black cat, circa 1840, 5cm. high. (Sotheby King & Chasemore) $265 £130

Early 19th century Canton
porcelain dish painted in
famille rose. (Sotheby
King & Chasemore)
$1,210 £590

A Canton jardiniere and stand, 22.5cm.
high, circa 1880. (Sotheby's Belgravia)
$600 £260

Early 19th century Canton bowl
painted with reserves of figures
on terraces, 39cm. diam.
(Sotheby's Belgravia)
$1,150 £500

Part of a mid 19th century Canton coffee set of six pieces.
(Sotheby's Belgravia)
$480 £210

Cantonese oval floral basket
and stand, Jiaqing. (Christie's
S. Kensington) $970 £480

Canton dish, typically painted
and gilt, 35cm. diam., circa
1870. (Sotheby's Belgravia)
$280 £130

19th century Canton tall
jar. (Moore, Allen &
Innocents) $1,620 £750

Part of a ninety-six piece Cantonese
dinner service. (Cubitt & West)
$16,385 £7,250

One of a pair of 19th century
Canton double gourd vases,
41.3cm. high. (Sotheby's
Belgravia) $1,600 £700

Late 19th century Canton
globular jar and cover, 9in.
high. (Sotheby Humberts)
$240 £110

Cantonese earthenware fish tank, 20in.
diam. (James Harrison) $340 £150

Mid 19th century Canton
jardiniere and stand, 12¾in.
high, slightly cracked.
(Sotheby Humberts)
$205 £95

One of a pair of Canton hexagonal jardinieres, circa 1840, 7in. high. (Sotheby Humberts) $410 £190

One of a pair of Canton vases, circa 1870, 43.5cm. high, neck with Buddhist lions. (Sotheby's Belgravia)$911 £420

One of a pair of Canton stools, 18in. high. (Cober, Entwistle & Co.) $1,922 £890

One of a pair of late 19th century turquoise-ground Canton vases, 35.5cm. high, with Buddhist lion handles. (Sotheby's Belgravia) $651 £300

One of a pair of late 19th century Canton vases. (Sotheby Humberts) $4,752 £2,200

Canton vase with rouleau body, fitted for electricity, circa 1880, 57cm. high. (Sotheby's Belgravia) $282 £130

One of a pair of mid 19th century Canton vases with gilt Buddhist lion handles, 45cm. high. (Sotheby's Belgravia) $1,085 £500

One of a pair of large Canton vases, circa 1880, 66cm. high. (Sotheby's Belgravia) $1,519 £700

Cantonese polychrome vase with ovoid body, 18in. high. (D. M. Nesbit & Co.) $162 £75

One of a pair of early 19th century famille rose Canton vases, 25in. high. (Heathcote Ball & Co.) $4,428 £2,050

Mid 19th century Canton vase and cover, with pear-shaped body, 68cm. high. (Sotheby's Belgravia) $737 £340

One of a pair of Canton famille rose vases, mid 19th century, 35cm. high. (Sotheby King & Chasemore) $1,080 £500

Late 19th century Canton hexagonal vase, 41cm. high. (Sotheby's Belgravia) $238 £110

One of a pair of squat bodied Canton vases, circa 1880, 22.5cm. high. (Sotheby's Belgravia) $368 £170

Large famille verte Canton single vase. (Phillips) $2,250 £1,000

One of a pair of Canton garden seats, 1870's, 47.5cm. high, with hexagonal bodies. (Sotheby's Belgravia) $3,906 £1,800

One of a pair of late 19th century Canton vases, 46.5cm. high, with Buddhist lion handles. (Sotheby's Belgravia) $694 £320

One of a pair of late 19th century Canton vases, 62cm. high. (Sotheby's Belgravia) $1,128 £520

Mid 19th century Canton celadon ground vase of baluster form, 62.5cm. high. (Sotheby's Belgravia) $911 £420

One of a pair of late 19th century Canton vases, 45cm. high. (Sotheby's Belgravia) $651 £300

One of a pair of early 19th century Canton vases, 25in. high. (Heathcote Ball & Co,) $4,428 £2,050

One of two similar Canton vases of Gu form, circa 1870, 40cm. high. (Sotheby's Belgravia) $1,128 £520

Late 19th century Canton vase with Buddhist lion handles, 61.3cm. high. (Sotheby's Belgravia) $781 £360

One of a pair of Canton vases, circa 1870's, 36cm. high. (Sotheby's Belgravia) $693 £320

Rare Chelsea white glazed
figure of a bird on a tree
trunk, 3¾in. high. (Olivers)
$1,715 £760

An attractive Chelsea petal-
mounted teapot and cover,
6in. high, 1752-56.
(Sotheby's) $1,320 £600

Mid 18th century Chelsea cabbage
leaf bowl. (Sotheby's)$3,045 £1,500

Chelsea fable decorated plate.
(Christie's) $10,370 £4,800

One of a pair of rare Chelsea claret
ground bough pots, 24.5cm. high.
(Sotheby King & Chasemore)
$730 £360

A Chelsea 'Japan' pattern dish
with lobed rim, 9¾in. diam.,
circa 1752. (Sotheby's)
$810 £360

A rare Chelsea saucer painted with
flowers and insects, circa 1749-52.
(Sotheby's) $685 £300

Chelsea polychrome crayfish
salt, 5in. wide. (Olivers)
$1,040 £460

One of a pair of Chelsea oval two-
handled dishes, circa 1755, 28cm.
wide. (Christie's) $910 £400

Rare Chelsea 'scolopendrium'
teabowl and saucer, circa 1749-
52. (Sotheby's) $2,410 £1,100

Chelsea studio pottery
figure by Charles Vyse,
'The Cineraria Boy',
1923, 10½in. high.
(Geering & Colyer)
$535 £260

Chelsea pale yellow ground may
blossom ecuelle, stand and cover,
circa 1765. (Christie's)
$2,280 £1,000

Chelsea figure of a cow, circa 1755, 11cm. wide, slightly damaged. (Christie's)
$1,730 £800

Rare and attractive Chelsea fluted teabowl, circa 1752-56. (Sotheby's) $2,160 £1,000

A rare pair of Chelsea partridge tureens and covers. (Sotheby's)
$5,685 £2,800

Chelsea porcelain plate, circa 1752, 9in. diam., painted with the fable 'The Lion that was Sick'. (Sotheby's)
$4,920 £2,400

Attractive Chelsea fluted teabowl and saucer painted in Kakiemon palette, 1749-52. (Sotheby's) $3,500 £1,600

An attractive Chelsea saucer painted in a pale Kakiemon style, 1749-52.(Sotheby's)
$900 £400

Chelsea studio pottery figure of 'The Balloon Woman', 1922, by Charles Vyse, 8¾in. high. (Geering & Colyer)
$490 £240

A pair of Chelsea sporting figures, the gentleman leaning on a gun, his companion with a dead bird, 9in. high, circa 1765. (Sotheby's)$765 £340

Chelsea seal in the form of a parrot on a mould inscribed 'Discret en Amour'. (Sotheby's) $890 £440

Chelsea leaf dish, circa 1758, 28cm. wide. (Christie's)
$160 £75

A Chelsea 'silver shape' dish with brown edged wavy rim, 11½in. wide, 1752-54. (Sotheby's)
$475 £210

One of a pair of Chelsea two-handled dishes, circa 1755. (Christie's) $925 £400

115

Chinese Jian Yao Temmoku
teabowl, 12.5cm. diam.
(Sotheby King & Chasemore)
$1,695 £750

Chinese Jizhou teabowl with
brown glaze, 11.5cm. diam.
(Sotheby King & Chasemore)
$900 £400

Chinese white glazed jar from
the Song dynasty, 10.5cm.
high. (Sotheby King &
Chasemore) $450 £200

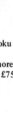

Tang dynasty glazed
pottery figure of an
attendant, 8½in.
high. (Sotheby's)
$545 £240

Chinese 'orange Fitzhugh-pattern' export
oval dish, 16¾in. wide. (Christie's)
$920 £400

One of a pair of unusual
Chinese yellow ground
vases with lids, circa
1870. (Gray's Antique
Mews) $2,700 £1,200

Chinese export baluster
vase painted in iron red,
14in. high. (Christie's)
$690 £300

18th/19th century blanc-de-chine
group of a lady and a scholar,
7¼in. wide. (Christie's)
$1,150 £500

18th century Chinese apple-
green glazed pear-shaped
vase, 5¾in. high. (Christie's)
$275 £120

Late 19th century Chinese
celadon ground vase,
62.4cm. high. (Sotheby's
Belgravia) $520 £240

One of a pair of Yingqing shallow
conical dishes with petal-shaped
borders, 5in. diam. (Christie's)
$505 £220

White porcelain blanc-de-
chine squatting Guanyin.
(Leys, Antwerp)
$5,180 £2,400

Blanc-de-chine teapot, moulded with twigs and leaves. (Graves, Son & Pilcher) $3,025 £1,400

18th century Chinese export charger, 12½in. diam., slightly damaged. (Robert W. Skinner Inc.) $175 £75

18th century Chinese turquoise glazed water dropper, 3¼in. wide. (Christie's) $505 £220

Mid 19th century Chinese blue and white water filter, 37cm. high. (Sotheby's Belgravia) $370 £170

Early 19th century Chinese blue and white moon flask, 46cm. high. (Sotheby's Belgravia) $500 £230

One of a pair of late 19th century Chinese blue and white quintil vases, 25cm. high. (Sotheby's Belgravia) $390 £180

18th/19th century blanc-de-chine figure of an immortal seated on a throne, 10¼in. high. (Christie's) $1,060 £460

Chinese blue and white tureen, stand and cover. (Sotheby's) $1,185 £520

Early 20th century Chinese blue and white figure of a warrior, 122cm. high. (Sotheby's Belgravia) $3,255 £1,500

18th century Chinese porcelain blue and white Yanyan vase, 17¾in. high. (Geering & Colyer) $1,165 £575

18th century Chinese Export porcelain documentary punchbowl. (Phillips) $4,040 £2,000

One of a pair of Chinese export porcelain temple jars, 18in. high. (Robert W. Skinner Inc.) $650 £285

COALBROOKDALE

One of a pair of Coalbrookdale vases, 1820's, 8in. high. (Sotheby's Belgravia) $475 £220

Coalbrookdale seated Parian figure of The Duke of Wellington, 26cm. wide. (Christie's) $661 £290

One of a pair of Coalbrookdale vases, circa 1840, 14in. high. (Sotheby's Belgravia) $540 £250

COALPORT

Coalport three-handled loving cup, 25.5cm. high, circa 1900. (Phillips) $205 £95

One of eight Coalport plates, 24cm. diam., circa 1850. (Phillips) $345 £160

One of a pair of Coalport vases, decorated with fruit. (H. Spencer & Sons) $7,006 £3,100

Part of an eighteen-piece Coalport tea service, circa 1900. (Sotheby's Belgravia) $520 £240

One of a pair of rectangular Coalport plaques, 13½in. wide, 1820-30, one cracked. (Sotheby's) $1,300 £580

One of a pair of Coalport bucket-shaped ice pails, covers and Derby liners, circa 1810, 29.5cm. high. (Christie's) $2,160 £1,000

Coalport goblet, circa 1830, 13cm. high. (Sotheby King & Chasemore) $296 £130

Coalport 'jewelled' garniture of three vases and covers, circa 1900. (Sotheby's Belgravia) $1,310 £580

One of a pair of wine coolers and covers, probably Coalport, 11½in. tall, early 19th century. (Sotheby's) $1,400 £620

Copeland/Spode tureens and dish, circa 1850. (Nottinghill Antique Market) $281 £125

One of a pair of Copeland & Garrett Japan pattern New Stone plates, 21.5cm. diam. (Phillips) $70 £30

Copeland & Garrett cup and saucer in mint condition, circa 1833-47. (Gray's Antique Mews) $170 £75

Rare Copeland commemorative tyg, circa 1902, 6in. high. (Sotheby's Belgravia) $1,060 £480

Part of a Copeland tea and coffee service of eighty-two pieces, circa 1900. (Sotheby's Belgravia) $565 £250

Copeland & Garrett figure of Narcissus by John Gibson, 1846, 31cm. high. (Christie's) $800 £350

COPER

Hans Coper stoneware vase, 3¾in. diam., 1960's. (Sotheby's Belgravia) $1,193 £550

Part of an unusual stoneware coffee set by Lucie Rie and Hans Coper, 1950's. (Sotheby's Belgravia) $910 £420

Hans Coper spherical stoneware vase, 1960's, 8½in. high. (Sotheby's Belgravia) $1,844 £850

A stoneware vase by Hans Coper, the flattened bowl with slightly swelling sides, 16cm. high. (Christie's) $900 £420

A stoneware candlestick by Hans Coper covered overall in a matt black glaze, 11.5cm. high. (Christie's) $825 £380

Good black Hans Coper stoneware vase, circa 1970, 8in. high. (Sotheby's Belgravia)$2,280 £1,050

119

18th century delft blue and white baluster shaped vase, 7½in. high. (Geering & Colyer) $110 £50

Rare 18th century English delft plate, 9in. diam. (Christopher Sykes) $290 £125

Pair of Dutch Delft Oriental figures, early 18th century, 6½in. high. (Sotheby's) $5,400 £2,500

18th century blue and white delft saucer dish, 8in. diam., circa 1740. (Christopher Sykes) $80 £35

Fine Dutch Delft tea kettle and cover, 25cm. high. (Phillips) $970 £450

18th century Dutch Delft charger with wide rim, 13¼in. diam. (Robert W. Skinner Inc.) $375 £165

Late 18th century Dutch Delft blue and white circular dish, 35cm. diam. (Sotheby Humberts) $235 £110

One of a pair of Dutch Delft nine-tiered tulip vases, circa 1690, 5ft.3in. high. (Christie's) $112,750 £55,000

One of a pair of Bristol delft polychrome farmhouse plates, circa 1740, 22.5cm. diam. (Christie's) $2,520 £1,100

Dutch Delft lobed octagonal polychrome punch bowl, 28.5cm. diam. (Phillips) $160 £75

One of a pair of old delft dog ornaments. (Weller Eggar) $1,160 £515

One of a very rare pair of English delft flower-bricks, circa 1750, 6¼in. long. (Sotheby King & Chasemore) $3,240 £1,500

Large de Morgan vase, slightly damaged, 19½in. high, 1882-88. (Sotheby's Belgravia) $1,560 £720

Unusual de Morgan lustre tile, 9in. square, circa 1888-1897. (Sotheby's Belgravia) $300 £140

A de Morgan vase with ovoid body, 11½in. high, circa 1882-88. (Sotheby's Belgravia) $735 £340

William de Morgan bowl decorated by F. Passanger. (McCartney, Morris & Barker) $607 £270

A de Morgan tile panel circa 1880, 16¼in. wide. (Sotheby's Belgravia) $735 £340

William de Morgan saucer lustre dish, Fulham period, 36cm. diam. (Sotheby King & Chasemore) $855 £380

A de Morgan ewer, circa 1885, 14½in. high. (Sotheby's Belgravia) $735 £340

William de Morgan lustre plate decorated by Charles Passanger, circa 1898-1907. (Sotheby's Belgravia) $1,400 £650

A de Morgan lustre vase decorated by Joe Juster, 27.5cm. high. (Christie's) $390 £180

William de Morgan lustre bottle vase, 17cm. high. (Phillips) $151 £70

Three de Morgan rectangular tiles decorated in the Isnik style, 61cm. long. (Christie's) $150 £70

A de Morgan copper lustre goblet, 10.5cm. high. (Christie's) $110 £50

Royal Crown Derby miniature coal scuttle, dated for 1915, 3¼in. high. (Sotheby's Belgravia) $150 £70

Early 19th century Derby porcelain chamber candlestick complete with snuffer, 4¾in. diam. (Christopher Sykes) $110 £48

Royal Crown Derby miniature teapot and cover, 3¼in. high, dated for 1908. (Sotheby's Belgravia) $205 £95

Fine pair of 20th century Royal Crown Derby circular vegetable tureens, covers and stands, 25cm. high. (Sotheby King & Chasemore) $1,065 £520

Set of six Derby Imari pattern coffee cans and saucers, silver holders, circa 1920. (Alfie's Antique Market) $505 £250

Rare Derby figure of a spaniel, circa 1765, 8cm. long. (Sotheby King & Chasemore) $715 £350

One of a pair of Derby salmon pink ground two-handled campana-shaped vases, circa 1815, 32.5cm. high. (Christie's) $3,460 £1,600

Set of four Derby biscuit figures of the Seasons, 25cm. high. (Sotheby King & Chasemore) $1,320 £650

Crown Derby ewer decorated in Imari colours, 26.5cm. high. (Phillips) $175 £80

Two early Derby figures of a gallant and his companion, 7in. high, 1755-57. (Sotheby's) $475 £210

A Derby teabowl and saucer of octagonal shape, 1750-55. (Sotheby's) $475 £210

Derby 'Tithe Pig' group by Stevenson and Hancock, circa 1865, 22cm. high. (Phillips) $325 £160

Royal Crown Derby minia-
ture tea kettle and cover,
dated for 1908, 3in. high.
(Sotheby's Belgravia)
$215 £100

A pair of superbly gilded Derby sweetmeat comports. (Alfie's Antique Market)
$640 £295

Derby teapot and stand,
circa 1810. (Gray's
Antique Mews)
$250 £110

One of two Derby coffee cans and
saucers painted with 'Japan' patterns. (Phillips) $85 £40

Derby 'dry-edge' figure of a
ram, 4¾in. wide, circa 1750-
54. (Sotheby's) $615 £280

One of a pair of Derby ice pails,
complete with covers and hinges.
(Phillips) $1,555 £720

'One of a pair of Derby flared
flower pots and stands, circa
1815, 19cm. high. (Christie's)
$915 £400

Rare pair of Derby busts of 'The Laughing and
Crying Philosophers', late 18th century, 6in.
high. (Sotheby's) $700 £320

One of a pair of Royal Crown
Derby dark blue ground vases
and covers, dated for 1898,
8¼in. high. (Sotheby's
Belgravia) $2,590 £1,200

Rare Derby figure of Winter,
4½in. high, circa 1755-58.
(Sotheby's) $920 £420

Early 19th century Bloor Derby veilleuse in
three parts, 22.5cm. high. (Phillips) $410 £190

A Derby group modelled to
show a seated woman and a
young boy, 8in. high, circa
1790. (Sotheby's)
$675 £300

Small Derby leaf-moulded sauceboat, painted in puce camaieu
and gilt, circa 1760, 5in.
(Sotheby's) $380 £170

Two Derby figures of a shepherd and
shepherdess playing bagpipes and
mandoline, 1765-75, 7½in. high.
(Sotheby's) $1,315 £600

Derby kingfisher centrepiece
with two tiers of three shells,
circa 1760, 21.5cm. wide.
(Christie's) $905 £420

Derby figure of Mars wearing gilt cuirass over yellow
tunic, on mound base,
circa 1760-65, 6¾in.
(Sotheby's) $450 £200

Pair of Derby named view plates, circa 1815,
22.5cm. diam. (Christie's) $955 £420

Samson 'Derby' Falstaff
figure in enamelled coat,
22cm. high. (Phillips)
                $162 £75

Bloor Derby scent sprink-
ler, circa 1830, 9cm. high.
(Sotheby King & Chasemore)
        $670 £310

Part of an early 19th century Derby
sixteen-piece dessert service, gilt
and painted. (Sotheby's) $810 £360

Part of a Derby thirty-six piece
dessert service, circa 1820-40.
(Sotheby's Belgravia)
                $2,080 £920

Derby dessert plate, 1787,
8¾in. diam. (Neales)
                $820 £380

A pair of Samson Hancock Derby
figures of a boy and girl, circa
1880, 16.8cm. high. (Sotheby's
Belgravia) $385 £170

One of a pair of Derby
plates, late 18th century.
(Sotheby's) $425 £190

Royal Doulton coffee set in box, circa 1930. (Alfie's Antique Market) $190 £89

A Doulton mice group by George Tinworth and John Broad, dated 1886, 12.5cm. high. (Christie's) $1,300 £600

Unusual Royal Doulton 'Dickens' jug, circa 1936, 10½in. high. (Sotheby's Belgravia) $360 £160

One of a pair of Royal Doulton vases by Emma Shute, 21cm. high. (Christie's) $260 £120

One of a pair of Doulton oviform vases decorated by Hannah Barlow, 17cm. high. (Christie's) $480 £220

Royal Doulton figure of 'Pierrette', 1925, 7in. high. (Sotheby's Belgravia) $495 £220

A Doulton moon flask decorated by Frank A. Butler, 33cm. high. (Christie's) $480 £220

One of a pair of Doulton gilt metal mounted candlesticks by Frank A. Butler. (Christie's) $260 £120

One of a pair of Doulton slender oviform vases decorated by Hannah Barlow and Eliza Simmance, 24.5cm. high. (Christie's) $610 £280

Royal Doulton figure of 'The Parson's Daughter' after a design by H. Titensor, 1929, 25.5cm. (Sotheby's Belgravia) $250 £110

Pair of Doulton oviform vases by Mary Mitchell, dated 1881, 23cm. high. (Christie's) $700 £320

A Doulton oviform vase decorated by Hannah Barlow and Emily E. Stormer, 25.5cm. high. (Christie's) $285 £130

125

DOULTON

Late 19th century Doulton Carrara jug with globular body, 7in. high. (Sotheby's Belgravia) $340 £150

Doulton Lambeth 'cricketana' vase by George Tinworth, 1880, 39cm. high. (Phillips)
$4,750 £2,200

Royal Doulton 'Chang' vase by Charles Noke and Harry Nixon, 6¼in. high, circa 1930. (Sotheby's Belgravia) $385 £170

One of a pair of Doulton stoneware bottle vases, 26cm. high. (Phillips) $110 £50

Royal Doulton figure 'August', modelled by F. G. Doughty. (Phillips) $60 £30

Doulton stoneware silver mounted cycling jug and two beakers, circa 1900. (Vernon's) $330 £160

Royal Doulton figure 'The Paisley Shawl'. (Phillips) $150 £70

Doulton stoneware jug decorated by George Tinworth, 9½in. high, circa 1875. (Sotheby's Belgravia) $435 £190

George Tinworth terracotta figure of 'The Jester', circa 1897, 12½in. high. (Sotheby's Belgravia) $870 £400

One of a pair of Royal Doulton vases, circa 1891-1920. (Alfie's Antique Market) $100 £45

Large Royal Doulton stoneware vase with tapering cylindrical body, dated for 1902, 17¾in. high. (Sotheby's Belgravia) $730 £320

Doulton stoneware jug, circa 1895, 9in. high. (Sotheby's Belgravia) $590 £260

Royal Doulton 'Butterfly', signed, 6¼in. high. (McCartney, Morris & Barker) $495 £220

Large Doulton vase, circa 1902-1912, 17½in. high. (Sotheby's Belgravia) $1,510 £700

Doulton Lambeth vase decorated by Florence Barlow, 14¾in. high, 1886. (Sotheby's Belgravia) $410 £180

Royal Doulton Sung vase, circa 1920, 9¾in. high. (Sotheby's Belgravia) $475 £220

Unusual Doulton stoneware vase, dated 1879, 6¾in. high. (Sotheby's Belgravia) $260 £120

Large Royal Doulton vase painted by D. Dewsberry, 17¼in. high. (Sotheby's Belgravia) $1,080 £500

Rare George Tinworth frog group, circa 1870, 5in. high. (Sotheby's Belgravia) $1,300 £600

One of a pair of Doulton Lambethware vases. (Alfred Mossop & Co.) $250 £115

Two Royal Doulton mask jugs 'Auld Mac' and 'Gondolier'. (Phillips) $110 £50

Royal Doulton figure 'June', modelled by F. G. Doughty, of a boy with a dog. (Phillips) $50 £25

One of a pair of Doulton stoneware vases, dated 1888, 18½in. high. (Sotheby's Belgravia) $590 £260

Doulton stoneware jardiniere and stand, circa 1895, 30½in. high. (Sotheby's Belgravia) $640 £280

Victorian Doulton jardiniere stand with floral decoration. (Vernon's) $125 £55

One of a pair of Doulton 'Faience' vases, circa 1900-20, 13½in. high.(Sotheby's Belgravia) $735 £340

Doulton stoneware vase by Eliza Simmance, 10¾in. high, dated 1881. (Sotheby's Belgravia) $650 £300

Large Royal Doulton Sung vase, 15¼in. high, circa 1930. (Sotheby's Belgravia) $2,965 £1,300

Doulton stoneware jug, dated 1877, 8¾in. high. (Sotheby's Belgravia) $590 £260

Unusual Doulton stoneware jug, circa 1895, 9in. high, decorated by Florence Barlow. (Sotheby's Belgravia) $385 £170

'Pussy' a rare early Doulton figure. (Phillips) $1,468 £680

Mark V. Marshall Doulton vase in stoneware modelled as a rabbit, 1880's, 8in. wide. (Sotheby's Belgravia) $651 £300

Royal Doulton earthenware jardiniere, 12½in. diam. (Sotheby's Belgravia) $302 £140

Large Royal Doulton Sung vase, 1923, 15¾in. high, by Arthur Eaton and Cecil J. Noke, signed. (Sotheby's Belgravia) $4,557 £2,100

One of a pair of Doulton stoneware candlesticks, 7¼in. high, dated 1879. (Sotheby's Belgravia) $455 £210

One of an unusual pair of Doulton stoneware vases by Mark V. Marshall, 15¼in. high, dated for 1906. (Sotheby's Belgravia) $911 £420

Royal Doulton Sung vase and cover by Noke and Fred Moore, 6½in. high, circa 1930. (Sotheby's Belgravia) $520 £240

Doulton stoneware footed bowl, 1880's, 9¾in. high, slightly chipped. (Sotheby's Belgravia) $455 £210

Royal Doulton figure of 'Hermina', 6½in. high, circa 1934-38. (Sotheby's Belgravia) $432 £200

Doulton Slater's patent stoneware water filter, cover and liner, circa 1890, 14in. high. (Sotheby's Belgravia) $325 £150

Royal Doulton wall mask of St. Agnes, 1930-34, 11in. high. (Sotheby's Belgravia) $412 £190

Doulton stoneware jug by Hannah Barlow, 9½in. high, dated 1874. (Sotheby's Belgravia) $629 £290

Doulton stoneware cylindrical mug decorated by Florence Barlow, with silver rim.(Christie's S. Kensington) $388 £180

Late 19th century Doulton stoneware jardiniere by Mark V. Marshall, 21in. diam. (Olivers) $519 £230

Doulton jardiniere, circa 1891. (Alfie's Antique Market) $75 £35

Royal Doulton stoneware vase, circa 1905, 16in. high, decorated by Mark V. Marshall. (Sotheby's Belgravia)$781 £360

Royal Doulton figure of a stalking Bengal tiger, 15¼in. long. (Robert W. Skinner Inc.) $375 £170

Mark V. Marshall Doulton stoneware monster vase, 1880's, 9¾in. high. (Sotheby's Belgravia) $520 £240

One of a pair of Royal Doulton vases, decorated by Hannah Barlow. (H. Spencer & Sons) $518 £240

Royal Doulton 'Shakespeare jug, 1930's, 10½in. high. (Sotheby's Belgravia)$172 £80

Large Doulton blue and white vase, circa 1900, 21¾in high. (Sotheby's Belgravia)$172 £80

Doulton stoneware oil lamp, dated 1883, 26½in. high, decorated by Edith Lupton and Francis Lee. (Sotheby's Belgravia) $781 £360

Pair of Doulton vases by Hannah Barlow, circa 1890, 15in. high. (Manchester Auction Mart) $791 £390

Royal Doulton figure 'The Orange Lady', 21.5cm. high. (Phillips) $129 £60

129

Late 19th century Eckert & Co. Dresden group of a lady and gentleman at cards, 22.8cm. high. (Sotheby's Belgravia) $590 £260

Part of an A. Lamm Dresden-decorated C. M. Hutschenreuther supper set of thirty-one pieces, circa 1910. (Sotheby's Belgravia) $765 £350

Part of an early 20th century Dresden coffee service of forty-three pieces. (Sotheby's Belgravia) $725 £320

One of a pair of 20th century Dresden four-light candelabra, 49.5cm. high.(Sotheby's Belgravia) $635 £280

Dresden style flower encrusted five-light chandelier, 48.5cm. high. (Sotheby Humberts) $435 £200

Dresden nine-light chandelier, 81cm. high. (Christie's) $2,965 £1,300

Continental Dresden style figure of a tennis player, circa 1900, 11.5cm. high. (Sotheby's Belgravia) $175 £80

Late 19th century Dresden mirror frame, 67cm. high. (Sotheby's Belgravia) $820 £360

19th century Dresden style group of Venus and Cupid, 32cm. high. (Sotheby Humberts) $185 £85

19th century Dresden centre-piece. (Bradley & Vaughan) $1,070 £470

A large pair of Dresden figures of a gentleman playing bagpipes and his companion with a hurdy-gurdy, 47cm. high. (Sotheby's Belgravia) $1,150 £500

Dresden comport pierced and gilt with leaves, 25in. high. (Neales) $1,130 £500

Red earthenware globular flagon, probably West African, 20cm. high. (Phillips) $45 £20

One of a pair of white tin glazed earthenware seated hounds, 35in. high. (Dacre, Son & Hartley)
$520 £240

Earthenware teapot with pewter lid, circa 1870. (Alfie's Antique Market) $65 £30

One of a pair of earthenware vases, circa 1870, 24.5cm. high. (Sotheby's Belgravia)
$585 £270

Austrian glazed earthenware vase, circa 1910, 20.5cm. high. (Sotheby's Belgravia) $285 £130

One of a pair of unusual earthenware vases, circa 1880, 36.8cm. high, on jardiniere style stands. (Sotheby's Belgravia)$605 £280

Large Carrier Belleuse earthenware jardiniere, circa 1900, 38.5cm. high. (Sotheby's Belgravia) $1,140 £520

Late 19th century earthenware incense burner and cover, 13.5cm. high. (Sotheby's Belgravia)
$780 £360

One of a pair of acanthus leaf and scroll terracotta shelf brackets, 12½in. high, circa 1840. (Christopher Sykes) $110 £50

EDO

Early Edo period pottery chaire with ivory cover, 7cm. high. (Sotheby King & Chasemore)
$450 £200

Early Edo period seto chaire with ivory cover, 5.5cm. high. (Sotheby King & Chasemore)
$360 £160

Mid Edo period Tamba 'moxa' chaire with ivory lid, 11cm. high. (Sotheby King & Chasemore) $1,400 £620

131

EUROPEAN

Brown glazed Portuguese pottery bull, 16in. long. (Abbott) $135 £60

18th century Spanish pottery charger, 17½in. diam. (Robert W. Skinner Inc.) $150 £70

Sculptured porcelain figure of Lucifer fighting the Serpent, circa 1860. (Alfie's Antique Market) $275 £120

Large Continental pottery figure, circa 1870. (Christopher Sykes) $355 £165

Hochst tea caddy and cover possibly painted by Heinrich Usinger, circa 1770, 14cm. high. (Sotheby's) $3,100 £1,400

An Austrian glazed earthenware jardiniere and stand, circa 1905. (Sotheby's Belgravia) $1,020 £450

Fine quality lady figure, signed Schoop. (Alfie's Antique Market) $415 £185

Late 16th century pottery dish from Isnik, Turkey, 10¼in. diam.(Sotheby's) $18,000 £8,000

One of a pair of Austrian porcelain vases, circa 1890, 11½in. high. (Christopher Sykes) $155 £70

FAMILLE NOIRE

Famille noire tapering square vase, 20¾in. high. (Christie's) $875 £380

One of a pair of large Chinese famille noire pear-shaped vases painted with dignitaries and immortals, 21¾in. high. (Sotheby's) $3,330 £1,500

Mid 19th century famille noire vase with waisted neck, 53.5cm. high. (Sotheby's Belgravia) $20 £10

Qianlong famille rose 'pseudo tobacco leaf' leaf-shaped sauceboat, 7½in. wide. (Christie's) $800 £360

A late 19th century famille rose jardiniere, 26cm. high. (Sotheby's Belgravia) $1,100 £480

Famille rose oval tureen and cover with coronet handle to lid, 21cm. wide. (May, Whetter & Grose) $690 £320

Late 19th century yellow ground famille rose moon flask, 58.7cm. high. (Sotheby's Belgravia) $1,520 £700

Large famille rose jar and domed cover with double lion mask handles, 13in. diam. (Christie's) $1,555 £700

Famille rose vase of Ku form, circa 1870, 39cm. high. (Sotheby's Belgravia) $370 £170

One of a pair of famille rose vases, possibly Daoguang reign, 1821-1850, 21.8cm. high. (Sotheby's Belgravia) $345 £160

Qianlong famille rose tobacco leaf oval dish with wavy rim, 14½in. wide. (Christie's) $1,100 £500

One of a pair of late 19th century famille rose vases, 43.5cm. high, incised seal mark. (Sotheby's Belgravia) $1,345 £620

Late 19th century famille rose vase and cover, 46.8cm. high. (Sotheby's Belgravia) $605 £280

Mid 19th century well painted famille rose screen with carved hardwood stand, 55cm. high. (Sotheby's Belgravia) $520 £240

Early Qianlong famille rose porcelain vase, 25cm. high. (Sotheby King & Chasemore) $295 £130

FAMILLE ROSE

Mid 19th century famille rose jardiniere, 31.2cm. diam. (Sotheby's Belgravia) $735 £340

Famille rose globular teapot and shallow domed cover, 7¼in. wide. (Christie's) $360 £160

Mid 19th century famille rose jardiniere, 31.8cm. diam. (Sotheby's Belgravia) $870 £400

One of a pair of late 19th century famille rose jars and covers with wood stands, 24cm. high. (Sotheby's Belgravia) $1,085 £500

One of a pair of late 19th century famille rose vases of flared hexagonal body, 41.8cm. high. (Sotheby's Belgravia) $1,100 £480

Famille rose jar and cover, incised mark, circa 1900, 29cm. high. (Sotheby's Belgravia) $130 £60

One of a pair of late 19th century famille rose vases on wood stands, 33cm. high. (Sotheby's Belgravia) $565 £260

Pair of famille rose figures of seated sages, late Qianlong, 8¾in. high. (Christie's) $460 £200

One of a pair of mid 19th century famille rose vases and covers, 28.5cm. high. (Sotheby's Belgravia) $180 £80

One of a pair of late 19th century famille rose vases, 59.7cm. high. (Sotheby's Belgravia) $1,735 £800

One of a pair of famille rose saucer dishes, probably Yongzheng, 6in. diam. (Christie's) $805 £350

Late 19th century famille rose vase with false gadroon borders, 59.7cm. high. (Sotheby's Belgravia) $150 £70

Mid 19th century famille verte jardiniere, 40cm. high. (Sotheby's Belgravia) $975 £450

A famille verte compressed globular bowl with lion mask handles, 15cm. diam. (Christie's) $265 £120

One of two late 19th century famille verte jardinieres, 19cm. high.(Sotheby's Belgravia) $260 £120

Late 19th century famille verte vase and cover with baluster body, 43cm. high. (Sotheby's Belgravia) $565 £260

A mid 19th century famille verte vase and cover, 43.5cm. high, with baluster body. (Sotheby's Belgravia) $325 £150

One of a pair of late 19th century famille verte vases and covers, 41cm. high. (Sotheby's Belgravia) $520 £240

One of a pair of mid 19th century famille verte vases, 30.5cm. high. (Sotheby's Belgravia) $650 £240

Pair of famille verte figures of boys on water buffalo, 18th century, 8¾in. long. (Christie's)$1,105 £480

Trumpet shaped famille verte vase, circa 1870, 46.5cm. high. (Sotheby's Belgravia) $345 £160

One of a pair of late 19th century powder blue ground famille verte vases, 45cm. high. (Sotheby's Belgravia) $1,375 £600

18th century famille verte baluster vase, minor neck repair, 14in. high. (Christie's) $1,000 £450

One of a pair of mid 19th century famille verte vases, of Gu form, 61cm. high. (Sotheby's Belgravia) $1,520 £700

135

One of a pair of Jacob Petit urn shaped porcelain wine coolers, 12in. high. (Parsons, Welch & Cowell) $605 £270

Large Fath pottery group of two girls, 1920's, 33cm. wide, stamped 'Made in France'. (Sotheby's Belgravia) $160 £70

Large Rene Buthaud pottery vase, circa 1925, 45cm. high. (Sotheby's Belgravia) $2,885 £1,250

One of a pair of 19th century French ormolu porcelain lamp bases. (Nottinghill Antique Market) $560 £250

Limoges fish service of twelve plates, a sauceboat and salmon dish, circa 1910. (Sotheby's Belgravia) $795 £350

Galle glazed Faience figure of a rabbit, 1880's, 20cm. wide. (Sotheby's Belgravia) $350 £160

Rare faience cistern, 18th century, 40.5cm. high. (Sotheby King & Chasemore) $1,120 £550

A pair of late 19th century French coloured biscuit figures of lovers, 36cm. high. (Sotheby's Belgravia) $860 £380

A large French earthenware figure of Venus after Falconet, late 19th century, 77cm. high. (Sotheby's Belgravia) $320 £140

Marseilles Faience deep dish, slightly chipped, 31cm. diam., circa 1770. (Sotheby King & Chasemore) $785 £340

A pair of French bisque figures of Spanish dancers, 44cm. high. (Sotheby Humberts) $1,035 £480

Vincennes porcelain covered supper dish, circa 1755, 8¼in. wide. (Christie's Geneva) $4,345 £1,965

Unusual teabowl and saucer with Hausmaler decoration, circa 1730. (Sotheby's) $1,345 £620

Part of an 18th century Furstenburg tea service. (Vost's) $12,300 £6,000

German bonbonniere in the form of a pug dog. (Bonham's) $410 £200

One of a pair of Nymphenberg cabinet cups and saucers, 9cm. high, circa 1830-40. (Sotheby King & Chasemore) $1,155 £500

Pair of 19th century German figures of Beau and Maid, 18in. high. (Hobbs Parker)$150 £75

Mid 12th century Rhenish censer cover by Godefroid, 10.5cm. diam.(Sotheby's) $76,500 £34,000

Late 16th century Siegberg stoneware jar with coat-of-arms of Nassau. (Leys, Antwerp) $895 £415

Rare set of four Niderville figures of Summer and Autumn, 13cm. high. (Sotheby King & Chasemore) $3,045 £1,500

A Frankenthal figure of a fruit seller, 14cm. high, 1759-62. (Christie's) $1,250 £550

Hochst teapot and cover, circa 1765-70, 10.2cm. high. (Sotheby's) $1,350 £600

Mid 18th century German beaker inset with coins. (Christie's) $1,820 £900

Fine and rare Du Paquier teapot and cover, 10.5cm. high, circa 1740. (Sotheby's) $23,870 £11,000

Late 19th century Goss model of
Izaak Walton's Cottage, 3½in.
wide. (Sotheby's Belgravia)
$486 £220

Early 20th century Goss
model of Grinlow Tower,
3¼in. high. (Sotheby's
Belgravia) $121 £55

Goss model of a polar bear. (Christie's
S. Kensington) $475 £220

HAN

Rare green glazed Han dynasty
flask of mottled yellowish-
green colour, 15.6cm. high.
(Sotheby's H.K.)
$14,160 £6,510

Han dynasty L-shaped
model of a farm.
(Sotheby's)
$13,130 £6,500

Han dynasty unglazed grey
pottery broad oviform jar
with two flower head
handles 5½in. diam.
(Christie's) $71 £32

ITALIAN

One of a pair of 18th century
Savona cisterns and covers,
52cm. high. (Sotheby King
& Chasemore)
$6,006 £2,600

Italian Faenza dish, dated 1537,
47cm. diam. (Christie's)
$67,500 £30,000

One of a pair of majolica
ewer jugs, 19in. high.
(Honiton Galleries)
$94 £42

Castel Durante majolica dish,
1532, 17¾in. diam.
(Sotheby's) $28,700 £14,000

Rare Italianate porcelain vase
and cover, 18th century.
(Sotheby King & Chasemore)
$470 £230

Large Italian majolica platter,
circa 1750, 14¾in. diam.
(Christopher Sykes)
$173 £75

One of a pair of Doccia blue
and white moutardieres,
11.5cm. high, circa 1760.
(Christie's) $595 £260

Mid 19th century majolica
jardiniere and stand, 22¼in.
diam. (Sotheby's Belgravia)
$561 £260

One of two matching
Sicilian majolica jars,
10in. high. (Geering
& Colyer)
$1,080 £480

Early 17th century Man-
ganese glazed tyg, Cister-
cian type ware, 21cm.
high. (Sotheby King &
Chasemore) $129 £60

18th century Italian pottery tile,
painted in polychrome enamels,
11½in. high. (Robert W. Skinner
Inc.) $325 £150

19th century Italian three-
part architectural garden
ornament, 42in. high.
(Robert W. Skinner Inc.)
$450 £200

Sicilian majolica bottle, 24cm.
high. (Sotheby King & Chasemore) $585 £270

Italian polychrome terracotta
bust of Pope Leo X, early 16th
century, 37.5cm. high.
(Christie's) $3,024 £1,400

17th century Caltagirone
albarello, 32cm. high.
(Sothèby King & Chasemore)
$691 £320

One of a pair of mid 19th century
majolica vases with flared lips and
double floral handles, 22in. high.
(T. Bannister & Co.) $105 £50

Urbino istoriato dish, painted by
Francesco Xanto Avelli. (Christie's)
$34,510 £17,000

19th century white porce-
lain Naples figure, 10¾in.
high, signed. (Alfie's
Antique Market)
$146 £65

19th century Japanese
Imari bowl. (May,
Whetter & Grose)
$252 £125

Imari jardiniere in the
form of a tied bag, circa
1870, 30.5cm. diam.
(Sotheby's Belgravia)
$564 £260

Large Imari punchbowl,
cracked, circa 1700,
14½in. diam. (Sotheby
Humberts) $864 £400

Mid 19th century fluted Imari
dish with central medallion of a
vase of peonies, 46.5cm. diam.
(Sotheby's Belgravia)$520 £240

Mid 19th century Imari
porcelain vase, Japanese.
(Sotheby King & Chase-
more) $345 £160

Large late 19th century
Imari dish, 56cm. diam.
(Sotheby's Belgravia)
$499 £230

One of a pair of mid 19th
century Imari vases and
covers, 56cm. high.
(Sotheby's Belgravia)
$1,345 £620

Early 18th century Japanese Imari
porcelain bowl and cover in underglaze blue, 7½in. wide. (Sotheby's
Zurich) $26,136 £12,750

One of a pair of late 19th
century Imari vases with
lobed and flared bodies,
37cm. high. (Sotheby's
Belgravia) $781 £360

Large Imari dish painted in
typical palette, 47cm. diam.,
circa 1870. (Sotheby's
Belgravia) $260 £120

Japanese Imari porce-
lain vase, late 17th
century, 50cm. high.
(Sotheby King &
Chasemore)$691 £320

One of a pair of late 19th
century Imari plates,
63.5cm. diam., painted
seal mark. (Sotheby's
Belgravia)$1,085 £500

Small late 19th century
Imari seated pug dog,
5in. long. (Christie's S.
Kensington) $225 £100

Late 19th century Imari jardiniere with U-shaped body,
24.2cm. high. (Sotheby's
Belgravia) $455 £210

One of a pair of Imari
vases of baluster shape,
18in. high. (Russell,
Baldwin & Bright)
$1,123 £520

Mid 19th century fluted Imari
dish, 46.5cm. diam., with basket of flowers in centre.
(Sotheby's Belgravia)
$477 £220

Late 19th century Imari
vase with panels of The
Three Friends, 53cm.
high. (Sotheby's Belgravia)
$390 £180

One of a set of six late 19th
century Imari plates, 24.6cm.
diam. (Sotheby's Belgravia)
$325 £150

One of a pair of late 19th
century Imari oviform
vases, 30½in. high.
(Buckell & Ballard)
$1,900 £880

Late 17th century green
ground Imari wine ewer,
15.5cm. high. (Sotheby
King & Chasemore)
$2,260 £1,000

Large late 19th century
Imari vase, 47.5cm. high,
with flared body and
waisted neck. (Sotheby's
Belgravia) $607 £280

Late 19th century Imari
dish with pierced rim,
41.5cm. diam., painted
Fuku seal. (Sotheby's
Belgravia) $325 £150

One of two 19th century
Japanese Imari vases, one
with cracked rim, 24½in.
high. (Manchester Auction
Mart) $1,730 £800

One of a pair of late 19th
century Imari dishes,
47cm. diam. (Sotheby's
Belgravia) $1,128 £520

141

Japanese earthenware bowl, circa 1900, 16cm. diam., with enamelled interior. (Sotheby's Belgravia) $345 £160

Japanese whisky set with five bowls. (Alfie's Antique Market) $320 £140

19th century Japanese tureen and cover in the form of a roosting crane, 26.5cm. wide. (Sotheby's Belgravia) $780 £360

Japanese Komai inlaid vase, circa 1900, signed Kyoto Ju Komai Sei. (Sotheby King & Chasemore) $1,580 £700

One of a pair of very large late 19th century Japanese vases with frilled flared rim, 125cm. high.(Sotheby's Belgravia) $3,475 £1,600

Japanese plique a jour vase with gold wire framed enamel decoration. (Phillips & Jolly's) $875 £380

One of a pair of large Japanese blue and white vases. (Sotheby's Belgravia) $5,850 £2,600

One of a pair of Japanese earthenware plates, 23.8cm. diam., circa 1870. (Sotheby's Belgravia) $735 £340

An Oriental earthenware bottle vase with tall flared neck, 56cm. high, circa 1880. (Sotheby's Belgravia) $670 £290

Large late 19th century Japanese vase and cover, 66cm. high. (Sotheby's Belgravia) $870 £400

Mid 19th century Tomonobu earthenware koro and cover, 20cm. high. (Sotheby King & Chasemore) $820 £380

One of a pair of Japanese vases, circa 1900, 40cm. high, with fluted and barbed rim. (Sotheby's Belgravia)$695 £320

A Nisshutso Shokai Koro and cover, painted with panels of courtesans in a garden, 6.8cm. high, circa 1900. (Sotheby's Belgravia) $620 £270

A stoneware flared vase by Shoji Hamada, 19.5cm. high. (Christie's)
$565 £260

Mid 19th century Japanese blue and white porcelain dish, 14½in. diam. (Christopher Sykes) $110 £48

One of a pair of Taizan vases painted and gilt with finches flying amongst exotic flowers, 37cm. high, circa 1880. (Sotheby's Belgravia)
$740 £320

A stoneware shallow circular dish by Shoji Hamada, 34cm. diam. (Christie's) $435 £200

One of a pair of Otsuta earthenware vases, painted and gilt with courtesans, 25cm. high, circa 1900. (Sotheby's Belgravia)
$920 £400

A Ryozan earthenware dish enamelled and gilt with child acrobats, 15.5cm. high, circa 1900. (Sotheby's Belgravia) $740 £320

A mid 19th century Hododa moon flask, 19.5cm. high. (Sotheby's Belgravia)
$195 £85

A stoneware circular dish by Shoji Hamada, 32cm. diam. (Christie's) $3,900 £1,800

A Senzan earthenware vase with ovoid body and flared foot, 30.3cm. high, circa 1900. (Sotheby's Belgravia) $300 £130

An Oshima jardiniere, brightly enamelled with peacocks, 25.5cm. high, circa 1900. (Sotheby's Belgravia) $250 £110

Hirado blue and white ewer and cover modelled as a seated boy holding a dog. (Christie's S. Kensington) $965 £450

JONES

Large George Jones majolica jardiniere, 18½in. high, dated for 1877. (Sotheby's Belgravia) $520 £240

Vase by George Jones & Sons, circa 1900, 11½in. high. (Alfie's Antique Market) $65 £28

Boxed coffee set by George Jones, circa 1891. (Alfie's Antique Market) $145 £70

KAKIEMON

One of a pair of porcelain octagonal Kakiemon dishes, 5½in. diam. (Gray's Antique Mews) $1,835 £850

One of a pair of late 17th century blue and white Arita vases in Kakiemon style, 8in. high. (Gray's Antique Mews) $2,585 £1,150

Kakiemon decagonal dish of late 17th century date. (Sotheby's) $9,225 £4,500

KANGXI

Kangxi period blue and white conical bowl with foliate rim, decorated with romantic figures. (Christie's) $1,050 £480

Kangxi period copper red and underglaze blue censer of bombe form, 6½in. diam. (Sotheby's) $925 £420

Kangxi lemon yellow glazed bowl with slightly everted bowl, 5¾in. diam. (Christie's) $920 £400

Late Kangxi period blue and white saucer dish painted with Shou medallions inside and cranes outside, 6½in. diam.(Christie's)$1,200 £550

Rare Kangxi period carved vase of archaic bronze form with rich turquoise glaze, 9¼in. high. (Sotheby's) $1,320 £600

Kangxi period blue and white dish of saucer shape, decorated with lotus blossoms and Tibetan characters, Chenghua mark, 5¾in. (Sotheby's) $330 £150

Kangxi blue and white bowl, 14.5cm. diam. (Sotheby King & Chasemore) $540 £250

Kangxi famille verte dish with floral decoration. (Peter Wilson) $980 £480

Kangxi blue and white bowl, 19.5cm. diam. (Sotheby King & Chasemore) $760 £350

Late 19th century Kangxi blue and white ginger jar, 29.5cm. high. (Sotheby's Belgravia) $110 £50

One of a pair of Chinese Kangxi plates, circa 1662-1722. (Gray's Antique Mews) $540 £240

Very rare large European subject famille verte Kangxi vase. (Sotheby's) $21,565 £9,500

Kangxi Yanyan vase, 44.5cm. high. (Sotheby King & Chasemore) $865 £400

Pair of Kangxi period famille verte Buddhistic lion joss stick holders, 20.5cm. high. (Sotheby King & Chasemore) $345 £170

One of a pair of famille verte Kangxi vases. (Sotheby's) $12,960 £6,000

Kangxi porcelain two-handled cylindrical vase in blue and white, 6¼in. high. (Geering & Colyer) $490 £240

Chinese famille verte dish of the Kangxi period, 16in. long. (Gray's Antique Mews) $1,300 £600

Late 19th century Kangxi powder blue ground famille verte jar and cover, 33cm. high. (Sotheby's Belgravia) $390 £180

One of a pair of Kangxi period small blue and white bowls decorated with the Eight Trigrams, 12.2cm. wide. (Sotheby's Hong Kong) $9,100 £4,185

Brinjal shallow bowl under mustard yellow glaze, cracked, Kangxi, 8½in. diam. (Christie's) $835 £380

Fine small Kangxi period blue and white bowl with floral decoration 13,2cm. diam. (Sotheby's Hong Kong) $3,845 £1,770

Kangxi famille verte porcelain plate, 23cm. diam. (Sotheby King & Chasemore) $410 £190

Late 17th century Chinese porcelain peachbloom bottle of the Kangxi reign, 8in. high. (Sotheby's Hong Kong) $45,610 £22,250

Fine large Kangxi sancai biscuit dish with design of pomegranates and aubergines, 24.8cm. diam. (Sotheby's Hong Kong) $20,230 £9,300

Very rare Turkish market Wucai bottle in Iznik palette, Kangxi, 23.1cm. (Sotheby's) $1,470 £680

One of a set of four Kangxi famille verte plates. (Phillips) $9,505 £4,400

Kangxi blue and white beehive-shaped teapot and cover with rectangular arch handle, 6½in. high. (Christie's) $570 £260

One of a pair of Kangxi famille verte figures of Buddhistic lions, 8in. high. (Christie's) $615 £280

Famille verte biscuite group of the Laughing Twins, Kangxi period, 5½in. high. (Christie's) $420 £200

Large baluster shaped Doucai Meiping, painted with a dragon and phoenix among peonies, late Kangxi/early Yongzheng, 18¾in. (Sotheby's Hong Kong) $22,255 £10,230

A good late 19th century Kinkozan plate well painted by Seizan, 20.6cm. high. (Sotheby's Belgravia)
$1,150 £500

A large Kinkozan vase enamelled and gilt with finches amongst peonies, 53.5cm. high, circa 1880. (Sotheby's Belgravia)
$1,265 £550

Japanese Kinkozan bowl, circa 1870. (Sotheby's Belgravia) $400 £185

KOREAN

Yi dynasty Korean blue and white jar, 8.5cm. high. (Sotheby's) $500 £220

Rare Korean celadon bottle of barrel form, early Yi dynasty, 7¾in. long. (Sotheby's) $660 £300

Korean Yi dynasty blue and white globular vase painted with peony sprays. (Christie's) $700 £320

Rare Korean blue and white dragon jar of baluster form, 17th/18th century, 16¼in. high. (Sotheby's)$14,330 £6,500

Korean Koryo dynasty celadon bowl with moulded floral decoration, 6¼in. diam. (Sotheby's) $2,100 £950

Korean Yi dynasty blue and white globular vase, chipped, 12¾in. high. (Christie's)
$3,270 £1,500

Korean Yi dynasty blue and white globular jar, cracked, 8½in. diam. (Christie's) $480 £220

18th century Korean blue and white bottle vase, 25cm. high. (Sotheby King & Chasemore)
$2,485 £1,100

Korean inlaid celadon bowl from the Koryo dynasty, 18cm. diam. (Sotheby King & Chasemore)
$540 £240

KUTANI

Ko-Kutani Japanese bottle in many colours, 8in. high, circa 1650-75. (Sotheby's) $9,720 £4,500

Japanese Kutani plate, 14in. diam. (J. M. Welch & Son) $270 £125

One of a pair of late 19th century Kutani vases, 33.5cm. high. (Sotheby's Belgravia)$520 £240

Very large late 19th century Kutani vase, 92cm. high. (Sotheby's Belgravia) $4,340 £2,000

19th century Japanese Kutani figure of a man holding a fan, 17in. high. (Robert W. Skinner Inc.)$1,500 £680

One of a pair of Watano Kutani vases with panels of warriors, 37.5cm. high, circa 1870. (Sotheby's Belgravia)$500 £220

One of a pair of late 19th century Kutani vases with arch handles, 32.7cm. high. (Sotheby's Belgravia)$455 £210

Japanese Kutani plate, 14in. diam. (J. M. Welch & Son) $270 £125

One of a pair of large Yoshidaya Kutani vases, 47cm. high, late 19th century. (Sotheby's Belgravia) $575 £250

A Kutani washing set comprising a bowl, jug and two boxes, circa 1900. (Sotheby's Belgravia) $460 £200

One of a pair of Kutani vases painted by Setsuzan, 52cm. high, circa 1880. (Sotheby's Belgravia) $1,650 £720

A Kutani vase and cover, a young sake tester modelled on one side, 27cm. high, late 18th century. (Sotheby's Belgravia) $530 £230

148

One of a pair of late 19th century spherical vases on squat feet, 22cm. (Sotheby's Belgravia) $685 £300

One of a pair of Kutani vases painted with flowers and birds, circa 1900, 33cm. high. (Sotheby's Belgravia)$685 £300

One of a pair of Kitayama Kutani ovoid vases painted with courtesans, signed, circa 1900.(Sotheby's Belgravia) $455 £200

LAMBETH

Early 18th century Lambeth delft drug jar, 11.5cm. high. (Sotheby King & Chasemore) $510 £220

Lambeth delft polychrome charger, circa 1780, 34cm. diam. (Phillips) $235 £110

Lambeth delft blue and white cylindrical jug, circa 1780, 18.5cm. high. (Christie's) $1,145 £500

Lambeth delft flower-brick, circa 1760, 15cm. wide. (Sotheby King & Chasemore) $345 £160

A pair of Lambeth delft blue and white cylindrical drug jars, circa 1720, 12.5cm. high. (Christie's) $1,125 £520

Lambeth delft flower-brick painted in cobalt blue, 15.5cm. wide, circa 1760. (Sotheby King & Chasemore)$325 £150

Mid 18th century Lambeth polychrome delft plate, 33.3cm. diam. (Sotheby King & Chasemore) $455 £210

Early 18th century Lambeth delft globular jar, 5¼in. diam. (Sotheby's)$3,490 £1,600

Early dated Lambeth delft 'marriage' plate, 1688, 8¼in. diam. (Sotheby's) $2,190 £1,000

Bernard Leach stoneware bowl, circa 1950, 10¾in. diam. (Sotheby's Belgravia) $540 £250

Bernard Leach stoneware vase with flattened ovoid body, 1950's, 4in. high. (Sotheby's Belgravia) $800 £370

Bernard Leach stoneware bowl in mottled grey glaze, 6¾in. diam., 1930's. (Sotheby's Belgravia) $345 £160

Bernard Leach large vase of square section, 1960's, 14in. high. (Sotheby's Belgravia) $650 £300

Bernard Leach stoneware 'Pilgrim dish, 1960's, 12½in. diam. (Sotheby's Belgravia) $1,735 £800

Bernard Leach large jug with lobed ovoid body, 1930's, 17¾in. high. (Sotheby's Belgravia) $2,170 £1,000

Bernard Leach stoneware bottle vase, 1960's, 7¾in. high. (Sotheby's Belgravia) $760 £350

Bernard Leach stoneware bowl covered overall in a celadon glaze, 1930's, 7in. diam. (Sotheby's Belgravia) $540 £250

Bernard Leach stoneware bottle, circa 1970, 9in. high, of fluted pear form. (Sotheby's Belgravia) $1,845 £850

Bernard Leach rectangular stoneware bottle vase, circa 1965, 8in. high. (Sotheby's Belgravia) $1,735 £800

Bernard Leach stoneware vase, 1930's, 3½in. high. (Sotheby's Belgravia) $410 £190

Bernard Leach stoneware bottle vase, circa 1965, 8in. high. (Sotheby's Belgravia) $2,170 £1,000

Late 18th century Leeds type creamware figure of a young girl, 6¾in. high. (Olivers) $190 £85

A figure of a Leeds pearlware stallion, 16¼in. high, circa 1790. (Sotheby's) $14,000 £6,200

Leeds creamware figure of Charity, circa 1770, 20.5cm. high. (Christie's) $915 £400

LIMOGES

13th century Limoges head of a crozier, showing the stoning of St. Stephen. (Spink/Koller) $123,120 £57,000

Limoges plaque painted in polychrome enamels, 36cm. wide. (Sotheby King & Chasemore) $410 £200

Limoges enamelled vase by Camille Faure, circa 1930, 17.5cm. high. (Sotheby's Belgravia) $1,200 £520

LIVERPOOL

Liverpool delft blue and white oviform vase, circa 1765, 19cm. high. (Christie's) $775 £360

Liverpool blue and white bowl printed with chinoiserie figure scenes, 19cm. diam., circa 1775-85. (Phillips) $95 £45

One of three 18th century Liverpool delft plates by Fazackerley. (Sotheby King & Chasemore) $9,000 £4,000

Large Liverpool delft polychrome baluster vase and domed cover, circa 1760, 49.5cm. high. (Christie's) $1,620 £750

Rare Liverpool delft 'Veilleuse', circa 1770, 12in. high. (Sotheby's) $1,925 £880

Liverpool vase of inverted baluster shape, circa 1750-60, 11¼in. high. (Sotheby's) $415 £190

London delft white bleeding bowl, circa 1690, 18cm. wide, slightly chipped. (Christie's) $645 £300

London delft vase in the form of a cat, 16cm. high, circa 1675. (Christie's) $7,775 £3,600

Rare London or Liverpool delft sauceboat, circa 1760, 8½in. wide. (Sotheby's) $1,970 £900

Rare London delft 'Union' plate, circa 1708-14, 9in. diam. (Sotheby's) $3,615 £1,650

Rare dated London delft puzzle jug, 6¾in. high, 1729. (Sotheby's) $3,840 £1,700

London or Wincanton delft saucer dish, circa 1740, 8¼in. diam. (Sotheby's) $440 £200

London delft polychrome Royalist portrait charger, circa 1690, 35cm. diam. (Christie's) $1,715 £750

London or Liverpool delft wall pocket, circa 1740-50, 8in. high. (Sotheby's) $460 £210

Good late 17th century London delft 'tulip' charger, 13¼in. diam. (Sotheby's) $1,315 £600

LONGTON HALL

18th century Longton Hall figure of a ram, 3¼in. high. (Olivers) $475 £210

Rare Longton Hall 'oak leaf' dish, circa 1754-57, 8½in. wide. (Sotheby's) $2,300 £1,050

One of a pair of Longton Hall figures of seated nuns, chipped, circa 1775. (Christie's) $710 £330

Lowestoft blue and white butterboat moulded with arcaded panels, 4¼in. wide. (Sotheby's) $430 £200

Rare Lowestoft figure of a swan, 2½in. high. (Olivers) $1,445 £640

Lowestoft blue and white candlestick. (Phillips) $1,685 £780

Rare Lowestoft inscribed mug. (Sotheby's) $5,400 £2,500

Attractive miniature Lowestoft teabowl and saucer in underglaze blue, circa 1760-65. (Sotheby's) $590 £270

Lowestoft figure of a pug dog, 3½in. high. (Olivers) $880 £390

Lowestoft blue and white creamboat, circa 1775, 13cm. wide. (Phillips) $95 £45

Rare Lowestoft saucer painted with Oriental figures, circa 1785, 4¾in. diam. (Sotheby's) $685 £300

Rare Lowestoft figure of a cat, 2¼in. high. (Olivers) $1,150 £510

LUSTRE

Rare Sunderland lustre pitcher, 1817, 8in. high. (Christopher Sykes) $255 £110

Part of a floral teaset in pink lustre of thirty-one pieces, circa 1860. (Phillips) $40 £19

Transfer decorated jug with semi-lustre glaze, circa 1870. (Alfie's Antique Market) $35 £18

A Martinware spoon warmer modelled as a grotesque sea monster, 12cm. high. (Christie's) $740 £340

Martinware grotesque dish, 11in. wide, dated 3-84. (Sotheby's Belgravia) $1,260 £580

A Martinware shaped square vase, 1904, 12.5cm. high. (Christie's) $325 £150

Martin Brothers imp musician, cracked and chipped, circa 1900, 4¾in. high. (Sotheby's Belgravia) $130 £60

A Martinware jug of gourd shape, 16.5cm. high. (Christie's) $175 £80

Martin Brothers bird, dated 9-1898, 9½in. high, on fixed wooden stand. (Sotheby's Belgravia) $1,060 £500

One of a pair of large Martin Brothers vases, 21in. high, dated 17.7.82. (Sotheby's Belgravia) $1,195 £550

A Martinware tobacco jar and cover modelled as a standing grotesque bird, 1903, 23cm. high. (Christie's) $2,400 £1,100

Martinware brown jar with detachable head, 1894, 11¾in. high. (Woolley & Wallis) $6,930 £3,000

Large Martin Brothers bird, 13½in. high, 9-1898. (Sotheby's Belgravia) $2,170 £1,000

Two Martinware figures, 1888, 6¾in. and 7in. high. (Woolley & Wallis) $3,350 £1,450

Martin Brothers bird, dated 1913, 6in. high. (Sotheby's Belgravia) $1,740 £800

154

Martin Brothers imp musician, circa 1900, 3½in. high. (Sotheby's Belgravia) $260 £120

Martinware toad with detachable head, 1895, 10¼in. high. (Woolley & Wallis)
$2,540 £1,100

Martin Brothers imp musician, circa 1900, 3½in. high. (Sotheby's Belgravia) $370 £170

MASON'S

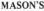

Mason's ironstone mug, circa 1823. (Alfie's Antique Market)
$280 £125

Part of a Mason's ironstone dinner and dessert service of sixty-two pieces, 1813-15. (Sotheby's)
$2,350 £1,050

One of a pair of Mason's ironstone jars and covers. (Phillips) $1,470 £680

Large pair of Mason's ironstone vases and covers with hexagonal bodies, 32in. high, circa 1820-30. (Sotheby's)
$1,530 £700

Part of a Mason's 'Japan' ironstone dinner service of fifty-five pieces, circa 1815-20. (Sotheby King & Chasemore)
$1,960 £850

Unmarked Mason vase and cover, circa 1840. (Alfie's Antique Market) $150 £75

Mazarine blue Mason jug, circa 1820. (Alfie's Antique Market)
$270 £120

One of a pair of Mason's ironstone campana shaped flower vases and ewers, 10in. wide, circa 1815. (Sotheby Humberts) $605 £280

Slightly damaged Mason's pot pourri vase in mazarine blue, circa 1820. (Alfie's Antique Market) $205 £95

Meissen oval sugar box and cover, circa 1730, 14.5cm. diam. (Phillips)
$4,725 £2,100

Meissen dish in porcelain decorated in colours and gold, circa 1735, 36.8cm. diam. (Sotheby's) $27,120 £12,000

Early Meissen sugar bowl and cover, circa 1723, 8.5cm. wide. (Sotheby's) $3,689 £1,700

Meissen tea caddy with hexagonal body, circa 1730, 10.5cm. high. (Sotheby's)
$3,038 £1,400

Meissen porcelain ewer and basin painted by C. F. Harold, circa 1740, ewer 8¾in. high. (Christie's) $17,360 £8,000

Rare Meissen milk jug and cover with silver mounts, 15.5cm. high, circa 1735. (Sotheby's)
$27,125 £12,500

Early 18th century Meissen porcelain 'The Crinoline Group', circa 1736, 5¾in. high. (Christie's)
$36,480 £16,000

A pair of mid 19th century Meissen cruets, covers and fitted stand, 22.5cm. high. (Sotheby's Belgravia)
$635 £280

Part of a ninety-four piece Meissen 'fabeltiere' dinner service, circa 1740. (Christie's)
$185,920 £87,000

One of a pair of 19th century Meissen vases, 13in. high. (Russell, Baldwin & Bright)
$1,728 £800

Late 19th century Meissen cockerel teapot and cover, 21cm. high. (Sotheby's Belgravia) $1,250 £550

Early 18th century Meissen yellow coffee pot, 9¾in. high. (Christie's)
$2,821 £1,300

Rare and fine Meissen bowl, 20.3cm. diam., circa 1725-30. (Sotheby's) $8,680 £4,000

Meissen bowl sparsely decorated with trailing sprays of flowers, circa 1730, 16.8cm. diam. (Sotheby's) $1,844 £850

Meissen bowl, decorated with panels of chinoiserie figures, circa 1725, 17.5cm. diam. (Sotheby's) $2,061 £950

Meissen Kakiemon style decorated dish. (Phillips) $1,385 £600

Meissen porcelain milk jug by Johann Ehrenfried Stadler, circa 1730, 6½in. high. (Phillips) $10,800 £4,800

Rare early Meissen bowl and cover with chinoiserie panels, circa 1725-39, 17cm. diam. (Sotheby's) $6,510 £3,000

Meissen figure of a Turkish musician, circa 1750. (Bonham's) $1,512 £700

A large, late 19th century, Meissen group of Count Bruth's tailor, 43cm. high. (Sotheby's Belgravia) $3,000 £1,300

Rare early Meissen coffee pot and cover of pear-shape, circa 1725, 25cm. high. (Sotheby's) $13,020 £6,000

Early 18th century Meissen stoneware tankard by Bottger, 9½in. high. (Christie's) $9,765 £4,500

A very rare Meissen 'Japonnaise' teapot and cover, circa 1875. (Sotheby's Belgravia) $1,200 £520

Meissen beaker decorated in famille verte style, circa 1730. (Sotheby's) $1,085 £500

157

Fine Meissen leaf-shaped dish, circa 1730, 8.6cm. wide. (Sotheby's)
$1,844 £850

Early Meissen bowl and cover, 10cm. high, circa 1730. (Sotheby's)
$2,170 £1,000

Meissen fluted tea-bowl, circa 1730, decorated with man and woman. (Sotheby's)
$2,387 £1,100

One of three 18th century Meissen soup plates. (Phillips)
$1,462 £650

Kaendler modelled Meissen figure of a Freemason. (Christie's)
$11,880 £5,500

Late Meissen plate painted with panels of lovers. (Christie's S. Kensington)
$181 £90

One of a pair of early Meissen teabowls and saucers decorated with plants and hedges, circa 1730. (Sotheby's)
$5,210 £2,400

Meissen chocolate pot and cover of a cylindrical shape, 16cm. high, circa 1740.(Sotheby's)
$1,150 £530

Early Meissen bowl, cover and stand, circa 1725-30, 14cm. high. (Sotheby's)
$30,380 £14,000

Meissen double-handled beaker, circa 1735, 7.5cm. high. (Sotheby's)
$1,627 £750

One of a pair of Meissen sea-swallows, circa 1748, 21cm. high. (Christie's)
$42,760 £19,000

Early Meissen saucer dish, circa 1725-30, 24.5cm. diam. (Sotheby's)
$6,076 £2,800

18th century Hausmalerei 'Goldchinesen' Meissen beaker. (Sotheby King & Chasemore) $1,685 £820

One of a pair of Meissen plates, 23.7cm. diam., circa 1740. (Sotheby's) $2,387 £1,100

Attractive early Meissen double-handled beaker, 7.6cm. high, circa 1720. (Sotheby's) $1,844 £850

Miniature Meissen teapot and cover gilded at Augsburg, circa 1730, 7.5cm. high. (Sotheby's) $1,845 £850

Rare early Meissen coffee pot and cover, 23.5cm. high, circa 1725. (Sotheby's) $4,340 £2,000

Unmarked Meissen figure of a parrot, painted in brilliant enamels, circa 1820, 5¾in. high. (Christopher Sykes) $219 £95

One of a pair of Meissen teabowls and saucers, circa 1730. (Sotheby's) $5,425 £2,500

Early Meissen teapot and cover of pear-shape, circa 1725, 14cm. high. (Sotheby's) $9,765 £4,500

Small Meissen jar and cover, circa 1730-35, 7.5cm. high, with artichoke knop and silver mount. (Sotheby's) $868 £400

Meissen plate with well-known 'gelber Lowe' pattern, circa 1735, 23cm. diam.(Sotheby's) $1,085 £500

Meissen table candelabrum, emblematic of Autumn, 80cm. high. (Sotheby King & Chasemore) $3,565 £1,650

Meissen saucer with shaped and moulded rim, circa 1730. (Sotheby's) $1,844 £850

Mettlach stein with porcelain, lid inset with pewter thumblift, 14in. high. (Robert W. Skinner Inc.) $1,150 £520

One of a pair of German Mettlach jardinieres, 23in. wide, signed Warth. (H. Spencer & Son) $4,210 £1,950

Half litre Mettlach stein with incised polychrome decoration, 8¼in. high. (Robert W. Skinner Inc.) $1,050 £477

Half litre Mettlach stein with incised polychrome gambling scene, 9½in. high. (Robert W. Skinner Inc.) $475 £215

A late 19th century Mettlach stoneware stein decorated after C. Warth, 22.5cm. high. (Sotheby's Belgravia) $430 £190

Five litre Mettlach flagon with embossed pewter lid and thumblift, 20in. high. (Robert W. Skinner Inc.) $1,600 £717

MING

One of a pair of late Ming blue and white saucer dishes, 7¾in. diam. (Christie's) $621 £270

16th/17th century late Ming celadon tripod broad bucket shaped censer, 10½in. diam. (Christie's) $299 £130

Early Ming dynasty Zhejiang celadon dish, 32.5cm. diam. (Sotheby's) $545 £240

Late Ming dynasty blue and white Swatow dish, 41.9cm. diam. (Sotheby's) $570 £250

Ming blue and white moon flask. (Sotheby's) $100,000 £50,000

Ming white glazed saucer dish incised with a large peony spray, 16th century, 12¼in. diam. (Sotheby's) $575 £250

Late 16th/early 17th century Ming white glazed bowl with white biscuit dragon handles, 4¼in. wide. (Christie's) $244 £110

Brown glazed Martaban storage jar, Ming dynasty, 59.5cm. high. (Sotheby King & Chasemore) $324 £160

Late Ming blue and white dish, 14½in. diam. (Phillips) $807 £374

Unusual Ming dynasty celadon group, 9in. high. (Sotheby's) $1,550 £680

Two late 17th century Ming blue and white saucer dishes with foliate rims, 5¼in. diam. (Christie's) $355 £160

Blue and white porcelain moon flask from the early Ming dynasty of the 15th century, 9½in. high. (Sotheby's Hong Kong) $95,165 £46,422

South Chinese Ming dynasty green glazed lobed broad globular kendi, 6in. wide. (Christie's) $333 £150

Fluted early Ming dynasty Zhejiang celadon dish, 26cm. diam. (Sotheby's) $590 £260

Early 16th century Ming polychrome wine jar, 27cm. high. (Phillips) $145,960 £68,500

Early Ming dynasty celadon dish, 31cm. diam. (Sotheby's) $570 £250

Ming dynasty green glazed ridgetile figure of a Kylon, 36cm. high, on wood stand. (Sotheby's) $798 £350

Early Ming dynasty Zhejiang celadon dish, green glazed, 33.7cm. diam. (Sotheby's) $865 £380

One of twelve Minton pottery tiles decorated with classical scenes. (Phillips) $115 £55

One of a pair of Minton oval plaques, dated for 1887, 12½in. wide. (Sotheby's Belgravia) $1,295 £600

Fine Minton cup and saucer, circa 1870. (Alfie's Antique Market) $80 £35

Minton pottery charger, painted by Emile Lessore, 58cm. diam. (Sotheby King & Chasemore) $485 £240

Minton shaped rectangular tray with pierced borders, 37cm. wide. (Christie's) $125 £55

Minton earthenware wall plaque, 15½in. diam., dated 1883. (Sotheby's Belgravia) $325 £150

One of a pair of Minton 'Sevres' pink ground vases with exaggerated ovoid body, circa 1835-40, 28.6cm. high. (Sotheby's Belgravia) $655 £290

Minton reticulated teacup and saucer, impressed marks. (Christie's) $250 £110

Minton pate-sur-pate elongated shield-shaped vase and cover, signed by A. Birks, circa 1906, 37.2cm. high. (Sotheby's Belgravia) $1,360 £600

One of a pair of Minton shield-shaped vases and covers, circa 1860, 16½in. high. (Sotheby's Belgravia) $1,600 £700

A pair of large square earthenware vases in Minton Secessionist taste, circa 1905, 17¾in. high. (Sotheby's Belgravia) $410 £180

Minton Parian figure of Diana impressed with ermine mark, No. 297, 35.5cm. high. (Christie's) $325 £140

Minton Secessionist jardiniere, 1908, 14½in. diam. (Sotheby's Belgravia) $520 £240

19th century English Minton parian-ware group of a boy on a dolphin, 23cm. high. (Christie's) $390 £180

Four tiles from a set of twelve by Minton, designed by Moyr Smith, circa 1875. (Alfie's Antique Market) $335 £150

Large Minton Art Nouveau vase, dated for 1906, 47.5cm. high. (Sotheby's Belgravia) $415 £190

Pair of large Minton earthenware wall plaques, dated for 1872, 19in. diam. (Sotheby's Belgravia) $1,480 £650

Minton Parian figure of Clorinda modelled by John Bell, signed and dated 1848, 34cm. high. (Christie's) $190 £80

One of a pair of Minton earthenware plaques, dated 1878, 15¼in. diam. (Sotheby's Belgravia) $1,370 £600

One of a pair of Minton potiches by H. Boullemier. (Peter Wilson) $570 £250

A plate from a nineteen-piece Minton dessert service, dated for 1869. (Sotheby's Belgravia) $325 £150

One of a pair of Minton Japanese style vases painted in white enamel on a turquoise ground, circa 1880, 24.8cm. (Sotheby's Belgravia) $815 £360

Pair of Minton table salts of a young gallant and his girl, 7¼in. high, circa 1870. (Christopher Sykes) $290 £125

Unusual Minton majolica Toby jug, dated for 1865, 11½in. high. (Sotheby's Belgravia) $410 £190

163

Moorcroft biscuit barrel and cover, 6¾in. high, circa 1905. (Sotheby's Belgravia) $500 £230

Unusual Moorcroft 'Hazledene' bowl, circa 1925, 5½in. diam. (Sotheby's Belgravia) $455 £210

Rare Moorcroft loving cup, circa 1900, with three blue glazed loop handles, 10in. high. (Sotheby's Belgravia) $410 £180

One of a pair of Moorcroft Florianware vases with tapering bodies, 8in. high, circa 1898. (Sotheby's Belgravia) $870 £400

Rare Moorcroft Florianware vase, dated 1899, 16in. high.(Sotheby's Belgravia) $910 £420

One of a pair of Moorcroft Florianware vases, circa 1900, 8¾in. high. (Sotheby's Belgravia) $475 £220

Moorcroft Florianware vase, circa 1900, 7¾in. high. (Sotheby's Belgravia) $280 £130

Unusual Moorcroft Macintyre jardiniere, circa 1900, 7in. high. (Sotheby's Belgravia) $590 £260

Moorcroft Florianware vase, circa 1900, 7½in. high. (Sotheby's Belgravia) $300 £140

Moorcroft vase with flaring cylindrical body, circa 1918, 12½in. high. (Sotheby's Belgravia) $325 £150

Moorcroft powder blue ground vase, dated 1915, 16in. high. (Sotheby's Belgravia)$295 £130

Moorcroft vase with baluster body, circa 1935, 9¼in. high. (Sotheby's Belgravia) $550 £240

Moorcroft Florianware vase with flaring neck, 5¼in. high, circa 1903. (Sotheby's Belgravia) $275 £120

Moorcroft slip-trailed flower bowl, 5¼in. diam., circa 1898, on wood stand. (Sotheby's Belgravia) $240 £110

Moorcroft 'Hazledene' vase, circa 1925, 8½in. high. (Sotheby's Belgravia) $540 £250

Moorcroft Florianware jug, circa 1900, 8in. high. (Sotheby's Belgravia) $585 £270

Part of an eleven-piece Moorcroft coffee service in 'Hazledene' pattern. (Sotheby King & Chasemore) $900 £420

Moorcroft Florianware vase with squat body and tall neck, 7in. high, circa 1900. (Sotheby's Belgravia) $370 £170

Moorcroft bowl, 9in. diam., circa 1901-1913. (Sotheby's Belgravia) $385 £170

Moorcroft pewter mounted vase of trumpet shape, 6½in. high, circa 1925. (Sotheby's Belgravia) $200 £90

Moorcroft flambe vase, coloured in mustard, turquoise and red, circa 1930, 10in. high. (Sotheby's Belgravia) $340 £150

Moorcroft vase, dated 1914, 6¼in. high. (Sotheby's Belgravia) $500 £220

Moorcroft vase decorated in blue, green and purple. (West London Auctions) $725 £320

Moorcroft vase, decorated in blue, green and purple. (West London Auctions $880 £390

MURRAY

Early William Staite Murray stoneware vase, 1923, 8½in. high. (Sotheby's Belgravia) $695 £320

William Staite Murray stoneware bowl, circa 1930, 5½in. diam. (Sotheby's Belgravia) $540 £250

A stoneware oviform vase by William Staite Murray, 21.5cm. high. (Christie's) $240 £110

William Staite Murray vase with ovoid body, circa 1930, 12¼in. high. (Sotheby's Belgravia) $475 £220

A stoneware flared bowl by William Staite Murray, 21cm. diam. (Christie's) $200 £95

William Staite Murray stoneware vase, circa 1930, 19½in. high. (Sotheby's Belgravia) $650 £300

NANTGARW

Fine Nantgarw plate decorated with five carnations, 24cm. diam., circa 1817. (Sotheby King & Chasemore) $530 £230

Nantgarw 'London decorated' sucrier and cover, 4in. high, circa 1817-20. (Sotheby's) $2,190 £1,000

Nantgarw plate, circa 1820, 25cm. diam., impressed mark. (Christie's) $1,510 £700

NEWHALL

Teapot from a Newhall forty-two piece tea service, circa 1820-30. (Sotheby's) $525 £240

Part of a twenty-five piece Newhall teaset, circa 1800. (Phillips) $1,125 £500

Newhall shaped helmet jug with pink border on the Inner rim, circa 1790. (Vernon's) $115 £50

Ban Chiang grey pottery bowl with flaring rim, 2nd/1st millenium B.C., 16½in. diam. (Christie's) $760 £350

Blanc-de-chine teapot, moulded with twigs and leaves. (Graves, Son & Pilcher) $3,025 £1,400

15th century Annamese polychrome foliate circular box and cover, 3¼in. diam. (Christie's) $1,115 £480

Mid 16th century blue and white porcelain dish, 26cm. diam. (Sotheby King & Chasemore) $340 £150

One of a pair of Oriental earthenware vases, 15cm. high, late 19th century. (Sotheby's Belgravia) $550 £240

Late 18th century Imari charger. (Clevedon Salerooms)$760 £330

Late 19th century Hichozan Shinpo vase, 49.5cm. high, with pierced neck. (Sotheby's Belgravia) $280 £130

16th century blue and white dish, 35cm. diam. (Sotheby's)$320 £140

A large Tomimura Arita vase, painted with panels of officials, 92cm. high, late 19th century.(Sotheby's Belgravia) $2,650 £1,150

Ban Chiang grey pottery jar with globular body and flared neck, 2nd/1st millenium B.C., 12in. high. (Christie's) $870 £400

Annamese polychrome storage jar. (Sotheby's) $56,560 £28,000

Late 17th century blue and white globular kendi with metal spout tip, 9in. high. (Christie's) $460 £200

Late 19th century blue and white dish with foliate scroll border, 54.7cm. diam. (Sotheby's Belgravia) $434 £200

Mid 16th century Isnik pottery stemmed dish, 12in. diam. (Sotheby's) $14,040 £6,500

Oriental porcelain charger, 24in. diam. (Vidler & Co.) $184 £90

One of a pair of Nankin style blue and white porcelain vases, 10¾in. high. (D. M. Nesbit & Co.) $604 £280

Late 16th century blue and white Near Eastern ewer, 23cm. high. (Sotheby's) $387 £170

Oriental export porcelain chocolate pot, late 18th century, 10in. high. (Robert W. Skinner Inc.) $650 £285

Celadon vase, circa 1870. (Alfie's Antique Market) $452 £200

Mid 17th century transitional jar, 27cm. high. (Sotheby King & Chasemore) $1,620 £750

One of two similar blue, white and iron red Oriental plates, 11in. diam. (Vidler & Co.) $164 £80

Chinese moon flask, Yongle period, 24.1cm. high, with underglaze blue decoration. (Sotheby's Hong Kong) $135,000 £60,000

Large transitional blue and white jar of baluster form, 15in. high. (Sotheby's) $1,230 £540

One of a pair of late 19th century underglaze blue and copper red vases, 65.5cm. high. (Sotheby's Belgravia) $1,519 £700

One of two large circular dishes, 14¾in. diam. (Heathcote Ball & Co.) $842 £390

Oriental tureen, stand and cover, 12in. wide. (Heathcote Ball & Co.) $864 £400

Longquan celadon dish of saucer shape on wood stand, 6½in. diam. (Sotheby's) $453 £190

One of a pair of 18th century famille jaune vases with lids. (Leys, Antwerp)$1,500 £700

Unusual 16th century blue and white bottle of Near Eastern inspiration, 29.5cm. high. (Sotheby's) $912 £400

Wanli blue and white pear-shaped bottle, 27cm. high. (Sotheby's) $456 £200

Large late 19th century enamelled dish, 59.2cm. diam. (Sotheby's Belgravia) $651 £300

Late 19th century blue and white vase. (Sotheby's Belgravia) $1,080 £500

Kraak porcelain dish Wanli period, circa 1600, 11in. diam. (Gray's Antique Mews) $765 £340

Late 19th century unusual triple gourd vase, 45.5cm. high. (Sotheby's Belgravia)$477 £220

15th century brown glazed jar of thickly potted baluster form, 15in. high. (Sotheby's) $433 £190

One of a pair of late 19th century blue and white vases and covers, 46.5cm. high. (Sotheby's Belgravia) $325 £150

A Paris biscuit figure 'Abaignee', 21.6cm. high, circa 1870. (Sotheby's Belgravia) $225 £100

A large late 19th century Paris plaque painted with a gallant and two female companions, 50cm. diam. (Sotheby's Belgravia) $795 £350

An unusual emerald green ground Paris inkstand, circa 1850. (Sotheby's Belgravia) $385 £170

A pair of Paris 'Chelsea' bocaye figures of a shepherd and shepherdess, 25cm. high, circa 1900. (Sotheby's Belgravia) $820 £360

Late 19th century Paris bleu celeste ground gilt metal mounted ovoid vase, 34cm. high.(Sotheby's Belgravia) $320 £140

A pair of Paris 'Derby' figures of a musician and his companion, 20cm. high, late 19th century. (Sotheby's Belgravia) $475 £210

One of a large pair of Paris vases, 49.5cm. high, mid 19th century. (Sotheby's Belgravia) $7,950 £3,500

Attractive Paris part solitaire set, painted with peasants. (Sotheby King & Chasemore) $485 £240

An unusual gilt metal mounted Paris vase and cover, 29cm. high, circa 1890. (Sotheby's Belgravia) $225 £100

A good Paris plaque painted by Aimee Lachassaigne, dated 1834. (Sotheby's Belgravia) $1,600 £700

A pair of St. Denis Paris gilt ground vases, 32cm. high, circa 1880. (Sotheby's Belgravia) $545 £240

One of a pair of Feuillet decorated Paris cups and saucers, circa 1840. (Sotheby's Belgravia) $430 £190

PERSIAN

18th century Persian blue and white baluster scent bottle, 7½in. high. (Andrew Grant) $260 £120

Persian dish 12th/13th century, made in Rayy, 9½in. diam. (Phillips) $690 £320

PERSIAN

Early 18th century blue and white hookah, probably Persian, 8½in. high. (Andrew Grant) $1,080 £500

PILKINGTON

Large Pilkington's Royal Lancastrian lustre vase, 18¾in. high, dated for 1910. (Sotheby's Belgravia) $1,825 £800

Pilkington's lustre vase with shouldered barrel body, circa 1907, 8in. high. (Sotheby's Belgravia) $340 £150

Pilkington's lustre vase with inverted pear form body, 14½in. high, dated for 1906. (Sotheby's Belgravia) $180 £80

PRATTWARE

A Prattware tea caddy depicting George III, 6¼in. high, 1780-90. (Sotheby's) $675 £300

Rare Prattware Toby Jug, circa 1780-90, 10in. high. (Sotheby's) $540 £240

Rare Prattware pottery plate depicting 'The Two Anglers', circa 1850, 9½in. diam. (Christopher Sykes) $110 £45

Prattware figure of 'Charity' on moulded plinth, 9½in. high. (Phillips) $285 £130

Rare Prattware decorated punchbowl. (Phillips) $1,855 £815

One of a pair of Prattware 'malachite' flasks.(Phillips) $345 £160

Rare pot lid, circa 1855, 'The First Appeal', first issue. (Gray's Antique Mews) $605 £280

Rare coloured pot lid 'The Matador', by Meyer, 1850. (Phillips) $1,730 £800

'A Fix', a large lid with white surround, framed. (Sotheby's Belgravia) $55 £25

Medium lid 'The Battle of the Nile'. (Sotheby's Belgravia) $65 £30

Medium lid 'Osborne House, Isle of Wight', framed. (Phillips) $235 £110

Large pot lid 'Tria Juncta Uno', printed retailer's mark for Robert Feast, framed.(Sotheby's Belgravia) $285 £130

Rare large pot lid, 'The Sea Eagle', 1920's. (Sotheby's Belgravia) $330 £150

'Floral', an uncommon rectangular lid with gilt line border and base. (Sotheby's Belgravia) $200 £90

Medium pot lid 'The Rivals', framed. (Sotheby's Belgravia) $120 £55

Rare medium lid with base 'Floral', in good condition. (Sotheby's Belgravia) $440 £200

'Injury', a medium lid with registration mark, framed, slight rim flakes. (Sotheby's Belgravia) $60 £30

Rare pot lid 'Great Exhibition of 1851'. (Phillips) $595 £275

Extra small pot lid 'Volunteers', framed in good condition. (Phillips) $380 £175

Rare lid 'Strathfield Say', framed, in good condition. (Phillips) $500 £230

Extra small pot lid 'Old Jack', framed. (Phillips) $475 £220

Blue and white porcelain potato ring, Qianlong, 8½in. diam. (Vernons) $110 £50

A pair of Qianlong period export porcelain seated hounds. (Christie's) $4,750 £2,200

Qianlong exportware blue and white bowl, 36cm. diam. (Sotheby King & Chasemore) $690 £320

Qianlong cloisonne incense burner and cover. (Sotheby King & Chasemore) $820 £380

Qianlong famille rose dish, 38.5cm. diam., painted with fenced garden. (Sotheby King & Chasemore) $405 £180

One of a pair of mid 19th century Qianlong blue and white vases, 49.5cm. high. (Sotheby's Belgravia) $1,845 £850

Large blue and white Qianlong foot bath. (Bonham's) $2,160 £1,000

Broad globular teapot and cover of early Qianlong date, 8½in. wide. (Christie's) $285 £130

18th century Qianlong export armorial salt, one of a pair. (Graves, Son & Pilcher) $1,080 £500

Slightly damaged brindled Qianlong hound, 6in. high. (Sotheby Bearne) $1,120 £520

Part of a Qianlong nine-piece dessert service. (Phillips) $1,570 £725

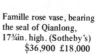

Famille rose vase, bearing the seal of Qianlong, 17¾in. high. (Sotheby's) $36,900 £18,000

Lucie Rie porcelain bowl of
wide conical form, 8in. diam.,
1960's. (Sotheby's Belgravia)
$195 £90

A porcelain bowl by Lucie Rie of
wide conical form, 23.5cm. diam.
(Christie's) $435 £200

Lucie Rie porcelain bowl of
conical form, 1960's, 8½in.
diam. (Sotheby's Belgravia)
$455 £210

A stoneware vase by Lucie Rie,
covered in cream grey glaze,
30cm. high. (Christie's)
$700 £320

A porcelain vase by Lucie Rie, the
oviform body covered in a metallic
black gold glaze, 25cm. high.
(Christie's) $370 £170

A stoneware vase by Lucie Rie,
of inverted baluster form, 40cm.
high. (Christie's) $785 £360

ROCKINGHAM

Rockingham scent bottle and
stopper with tall neck, circa
1831-42, 16.5cm. high.
(Christie's) $435 £190

A Rockingham style part tea and coffee
service of forty-five pieces, circa 1830.
(Sotheby's) $850 £380

Rockingham scent bottle and
stopper, moulded and coloured
with trailing flowers, 15.5cm.
high, circa 1831-42. (Christie's)
$340 £150

ROYAL COPENHAGEN

A Royal Copenhagen porcelain
vase of double gourd shape,
21cm. high. (Christie's)$610 £280

A Royal Copenhagen porcelain
oviform vase and cover designed
by Ch. Thomasen, 21cm. high.
(Christie's) $1,150 £520

Large and rare Royal Copenhagen
group of St. Paul slaying the Lie,
circa 1925, 24½in. high.
(Sotheby's Belgravia)$1,185 £520

A Royal Dux group of a young boy riding a white horse, 34cm. high, circa 1910. (Sotheby's Belgravia) $475 £210

Large pair of Royal Dux figures of a Shepherdess and Shepherd, 79cm. high. (Sotheby King & Chasemore) $1,740 £850

Large Royal Dux group of The Blacksmith and his Family, 49.5cm. high.(Phillips)$205 £95

RUSKIN

Ruskin high-fired bowl and stand, 1926, 7¾in. diam. (Sotheby's Belgravia) $455 £210

Ruskin high-fired vase with trumpet neck, 1909, 15in. high. (Sotheby's Belgravia) $910 £420

Ruskin flambe saucer, mottled in raspberry and pale pink, 1927, 14.5cm. diam. (Phillips) $30 £14

A Ruskin high-fired slender oviform vase with spreading foot, 31.5cm. tall. (Christie's) $960 £440

Ruskin high-fired two-handled vase, 14in. high, dated 1914. (Sotheby's Belgravia)$540 £250

Ruskin vase, dated 1909, 10½in. high. (Sotheby's Belgravia) $685 £300

Ruskin high-fired vase with baluster body, dated 1914, 15in. high. (Sotheby's Belgravia) $585 £270

Ruskin high-fired vase with ovoid body, dated 1924, 11in. high. (Sotheby's Belgravia) $275 £120

Ruskin high-fired vase, circa 1904-20, 11½in. high. (Sotheby's Belgravia) $1,005 £440

A Samson two-handled oval tureen with domed cover, 37cm. wide. (Christie's) $600 £270

Meissen style gaming box and cover painted with the four suits of cards, 17cm. wide. (Christie's) $400 £180

Samson two-handled flared jardiniere painted with floral swags, 26cm. wide. (Christie's) $90 £40

A famille rose flattened head shaped ewer with high domed cover, 36cm. high. (Christie's) $925 £420

A Samson figure of a Freemason after a model by J. J. Kaendler, 28.5cm. high. (Christie's) $625 £280

Samson ormolu mounted baluster pot pourri vase and cover, 28cm. high.(Christie's) $290 £130

German musical group of three ladies before a standing courtier, 32.5cm. long. (Christie's) $350 £160

Meissen style figure of a water bird, 25cm. high. (Christie's) $155 £70

Samson white and gold kavette shaped pierced centre dish, 46cm. high. (Christie's) $380 £170

Pair of Samson parrots on tree-stumps, repaired, 42cm. high. (Christie's) $750 £350

German group of two women enticing a third into bed with a gentleman kneeling beside, 43.5cm. high. (Christie's) $1,050 £480

Samson 'Derby' Falstaff figure wearing a blue and gilt decorated coat, 20cm. high. (Phillips) $103 £48

A famille verte flaring deep bowl painted on the exterior, 34.5cm. diam. (Christie's) $880 £400

Samson 'Derby' 'Mansion House' dwarf, 17.5cm. high. (Phillips) $130 £60

A Samson globular octangular teapot and cover, 18cm. wide. (Christie's) $290 £130

A Samson silver mounted oviform jar and cover, 18cm. high. (Christie's) $225 £100

A pair of Samson figures of a pug dog and a bitch, 15cm. high. (Christie's) $1,000 £450

Sevres style chocolate cup, cover and stand painted with entwined flowering foliage. (Christie's)$330 £150

Samson shaped oval two-handled yellow ground Monteith bowl, 30.5cm. wide. (Christie's) $250 £110

A Samson pear-shaped coffee pot with domed cover, 21cm. tall. (Christie's) $290 £130

Samson baked quatrefoil dish painted in the Kakiemon palette, 24cm. wide. (Christie's) $310 £140

A Samson figure of Lucinda from the Italian comedy series, 19.5cm. high. (Christie's) $290 £130

Samson group of the Levee du Roi of five figures, 38cm. wide. (Christie's) $625 £280

A Samson Wucai style baluster vase with shallow domed cover, 42cm. high. (Christie's) $490 £220

One of a pair of Satsuma vases of broad squat shape. (Christie's S. Kensington) $1,036 £480

Satsuma bowl and cover, 5in. diam. (D. M. Nesbit & Co.) $325 £150

19th century Satsuma decorated teapot, 7½in. high. (J. M. Welch & Son) $390 £180

Globular Satsuma koro and cover, 33cm. high, circa 1870. (Sotheby's Belgravia) $607 £280

Satsuma plate, circa 1880, 10in. diam. (Gray's Antique Market) $855 £380

One of a pair of late 19th century Satsuma vases, 37cm. high. (Sotheby's Belgravia) $737 £340

A Ryozan Satsuma vase painted with travellers in a bleak snowy landscape, 24cm. high, late 19th century. (Sotheby's Belgravia) $1,265 £550

Satsuma vase and stand. (Sotheby's Belgravia) $21,315 £10,500

An attractive Satsuma double gourd vase, painted with fans, 13.5cm. high, mid 19th century. (Sotheby's Belgravia) $1,330 £580

Satsuma vase, circa 1900, 45cm. high, painted with ladies in a landscape. (Sotheby's Belgravia) $607 £280

Satsuma circular dish with girl attending fabrics suspended on a line from a tree, 9¾in. diam. (D. M. Nesbit & Co.) $365 £170

A pair of tall decorative Satsuma vases, 18in. high on shaded green ground. (Butler & Hatch Waterman) $185 £85

Mid 19th century Satsuma Shi-Shi, 20cm. high. (Sotheby's Belgravia) $607 £280

Mid 19th century Satsuma earthenware bowl, 14.5cm. diam. (Sotheby King & Chasemore) $768 £340

Mid 19th century Satsuma elephant lying down with head turned, 14cm. long. (Sotheby's Belgravia) $660 £290

Mid 19th century Japanese Satsuma earthenware caddy and cover, 13.5cm. high. (Sotheby King & Chasemore) $1,038 £460

Satsuma circular dish with mother and two children watching kittens at play, 11¼in. diam. (D. M. Nesbit & Co.) $540 £250

Mid 19th century Satsuma koro, painted in thick enamels, 27.5cm. high, with floret handles. (Sotheby's Belgravia) $1,302 £600

One of a pair of Satsuma vases painted with birds flying amongst exotic plants, 23.8cm. high, circa 1900. (Sotheby's Belgravia) $370 £160

One of a pair of Meikozan Satsuma vases painted with panels of arhats and courtesans, 32cm. high, circa 1900. (Sotheby's Belgravia) $920 £400

Late 19th century Satsuma koro and cover, 33cm. high, with Shi-Shi knop. (Sotheby's Belgravia) $303 £140

One of a pair of late 19th century Satsuma vases, enamelled and gilt with figures in discussion, 24cm. high. (Sotheby's Belgravia) $390 £180

Satsuma circular dish with two females talking by a flowering bush, 9¾in. diam. (D. M. Nesbit & Co.) $390 £180

One of a pair of Satsuma cylindrical vases, 10in. high. (D. M. Nesbit & Co.) $390 £180

179

Sevres porcelain shaped oblong dish, 1763, 29.5cm. wide. (Christie's) $1,095 £500

Sevres apple-green ground pear-shaped milk jug on three branch feet, 1768, 12.5cm. high. (Christie's) $550 £250

A late 19th century Sevres gilt bronze mounted oval dish. (Sotheby's Belgravia)$635 £280

A Sevres biscuit bust of Marie Antoinette, 34cm. high, late 19th century. (Sotheby's Belgravia) $225 £100

Sevres porcelain apple-green ground teapot and cover, 1768, 18.5cm. wide. (Christie's) $765 £350

An unusual 18th century Sevres bleu de roi ewer, 25.2cm. high. (Sotheby's Belgravia) $340 £150

One of a pair of Sevres pattern ormolu mounted two-handled oviform vases, 37cm. high. (Christie's) $865 £380

One of a pair of Sevres porcelain plates, 1790, 23.5cm. diam. (Christie's) $920 £420

19th century Sevres gilt metal mounted rose pompadour ground pot pourri vase and cover, 29cm. high.(Sotheby's Belgravia) $900 £400

One of a pair of Sevres soft paste cache pots painted with rustic lovers, late 19th century. (Sotheby's Belgravia)$570 £250

Sevres pattern ormolu mounted bleu nouveau oval casket, 32cm. wide, on four paw feet.(Christie's) $1,710 £750

18th century Vincennes Sevres portrait of Louis XV. (Alfie's Antique Market) $685 £300

A late 19th century Sevres bleu celeste ground bowl, 24.6cm. diam. (Sotheby's Belgravia) $340 £150

Sevres porcelain coffee cup and saucer, 1759. (Christie's)$700 £320

Sevres pattern ormolu mounted inkstand, dated 1770, 33cm. wide. (Christie's) $1,480 £650

A Sevres cabinet plate painted by D. Ceniers, late 19th century, 24cm. diam. (Sotheby's Belgravia)$225 £100

Sevres apple-green ground sugar bowl and cover, 1768, 11.5cm. high. (Christie's) $480 £220

One of a pair of Sevres porcelain soupplates, marked Land DR, circa 1785, 23.5cm. diam. (Christie's) $240 £110

A Sevres hard paste cup and saucer, circa 1870. (Sotheby's Belgravia) $295 £130

One of a pair of Sevres blue and gilt porcelain wall plaques in ormolu frames. (Vidler & Co.) $615 £300

One of six Sevres porcelain soup plates, circa 1770, 24cm. diam. (Christie's) $615 £280

One of a pair of large Sevres pattern turquoise ground oviform vases and covers, 86cm. high. (Christie's) $3,190 £1,400

A late 19th century Sevres solitaire, each piece painted with a portrait of Louis XVI or Marie Antoinette. (Sotheby's Belgravia) $525 £230

A Sevres two-handled cup and cover, 16.5cm. high, late 19th century. (Sotheby's Belgravia) $570 £250

181

19th century Sitzendorf candelabra. (Alfie's Antique Market)
$618 £275

Late 19th century Sitzendorf clockcase, 38cm. high. (Sotheby's Belgravia)
$635 £280

Sitzendorf table centre-piece with pierced basket, 29cm. high. (Phillips) $172 £80

SPODE

Spode miniature chamber candlestick, circa 1825, 7cm. diam. (Sotheby King & Chasemore)
$840 £410

Spode ewer-shaped jug and stand, 9cm. high, circa 1825. (Sotheby King & Chasemore) $780 £380

Part of a Spode pearlware part dessert service painted in green and gilt, circa 1820. (Christie's) $870 £380

Spode blue ground oviform vase with gilt scroll handles, circa 1820, 18cm. hjgh. (Christie's) $685 £300

Spode armorial soup plate with central coat-of-arms, circa 1815, 23.5cm. diam. (Christie's)
$195 £85

Spode pink ground oviform vase with loop handles, circa 1820, 18.5cm. high. (Christie's) $605 £280

Part of a one hundred and seventy-four piece Spode 'Imperial' pattern part dinner service. (Sotheby Humberts)
$4,750 £2,200

One of a pair of Spode pink ground spill-vases, 11.5cm. high, circa 1820. (Christie's) $215 £100

Part of a thirty-eight piece Spode bone china tea and coffee service, circa 1820. (Phillips) $140 £65

Staffordshire silver lustre jug transfer-printed in black with the Molyneux/Cribb fight, circa 1810, 14.5cm. high. (Sotheby's Belgravia) $370 £170

Staffordshire figure of William O'Brien, circa 1848, 7¼in. high. (Sotheby's Belgravia) $618 £280

Large Staffordshire pottery P. Sherry dispensing barrel, circa 1850, 14½in. high. (Christopher Sykes) $219 £95

Rare Staffordshire jug commemorating Queen Victoria's Coronation, circa 1838, 5in. high. (Sotheby's Belgravia) $550 £250

Staffordshire pottery figure of a gentleman on horseback, circa 1840, 12¼in. high. (Christopher Sykes) $173 £75

Staffordshire group of horse and foal, circa 1855, 12in. high. (Christopher Sykes) $196 £85

Rare Staffordshire pottery group of France, England and Turkey, circa 1855, 11½in. high. (Christopher Sykes) $225 £100

Unusual World War I Toby jug entitled 'Push and Go', Staffordshire, circa 1917, 10½in. high. (Christopher Sykes) $660 £285

Rare Staffordshire equestrian figure of Queen Alexandra, 12in. high. (Christopher Sykes) $290 £125

Pair of Staffordshire portrait figures of a French sailor and his girl, circa 1854, 10¼in. high. (Sotheby's Belgravia) $187 £85

Rare Staffordshire figure 'Bloomers' from the Alpha factory, circa 1851, 9½in. high. (Sotheby's Belgravia) $265 £120

Pair of Staffordshire groups of Queen Victoria with the Princess Royal and Prince Albert with the Prince of Wales, circa 1843. (Sotheby's Belgravia) $510 £230

Staffordshire figure of Christ in the Garden of Gethsemane, 8½in. high, impressed title 'Christ's Agony'. (Phillips) $190 £90

Part of a nine-piece Staffordshire azure ground dessert service, circa 1860. (Sotheby's Belgravia) $475 £220

Late 18th/early 19th century Staffordshire 'bear' coffee pot and cover, 6¾in. high. (Sotheby's) $305 £150

Large Staffordshire porcelain model of a sheep, circa 1850, 7in. high. (Christopher Sykes) $150 £65

Staffordshire saltglaze figure of an athlete, circa 1760, 10.5cm. wide. (Christie's) $730 £320

Staffordshire Prussian General, circa 1850, 12in. high. (Christopher Sykes) $170 £75

Staffordshire pearlware inscribed and dated oval plaque, 18cm. high. (Christie's) $570 £250

One of a pair of Staffordshire saltglaze figures of court ladies, circa 1750, 8.5cm. high. (Christie's) $1,375 £600

Staffordshire pearlware inscribed and dated oval portrait plaque of Joseph Lownds, 1811, 18.5cm. high. (Christie's) $595 £260

One of a pair of Staffordshire saltglaze hawks. (Christie's) $14,690 £6,500

Staffordshire saltglaze commemorative dish, circa 1760, 36.5cm. diam. (Christie's) $365 £160

Early Victorian Staffordshire Toby jug. (Alfie's Antique Market) $100 £45

Staffordshire 'Peace', circa 1860, 15in. high. (Christopher Sykes) $650 £285

Part of a mid 19th century Staffordshire 'stone china' dessert service of forty-eight pieces. (Sotheby's Belgravia) $775 £360

South Staffordshire enamel shoe bonbonniere. (Bonham's) $280 £130

Staffordshire saltglaze commemorative teapot and cover, circa 1757, 19cm. wide. (Christie's) $1,030 £450

Staffordshire square based figure named 'Hope', circa 1810, 7½in. high. (Christopher Sykes) $175 £75

Staffordshire saltglaze depressed globular teapot and cover, circa 1755, 16cm. wide. (Christie's) $865 £400

Staffordshire figure saltglaze teapot and cover in the form of a squirrel, circa 1755, 15.5cm. high. (Christie's) $2,175 £950

Staffordshire saltglaze square teapot stand, circa 1755, 14cm. square. (Christie's) $300 £140

Staffordshire mare and foal, circa 1855. (Christopher Sykes) $170 £75

Staffordshire coloured saltglaze figure of Harlequin, circa 1755, 12cm. high. (Christie's) $1,600 £700

An 18th century Staffordshire slipware baking dish, 14½in. diam. (Sotheby's) $1,250 £550

Staffordshire saltglaze commemorative mug with grooved loop handle, circa 1740, 12cm. high. (Christie's) $2,175 £950

185

Staffordshire saltglaze agateware figure of a seated cat, 12.5cm. high, circa 1755. (Christie's) $820 £380

Staffordshire mauve coloured pastille burner, 11cm. high, circa 1840. (Sotheby King & Chasemore) $389 £190

Staffordshire saltglaze pear-shaped milk jug, circa 1755, 8.5cm. high. (Christie's) $129 £60

Cottage pastille burner, 11cm. high, circa 1840. (Sotheby King & Chasemore) $390 £190

Staffordshire figure 'Bloomers', showing a young girl in that fashion. (Christie's S. Kensington) $259 £120

Rare Staffordshire figure of Rev. C. H. Spurgeon. (Christie's S. Kensington) $1,036 £480

Staffordshire saltglaze agateware figure of a lady, 14cm. high, circa 1745. (Christie's) $1,123 £520

One of a pair of mid 19th century Staffordshire pot pourri vases and covers, 17¼in. high. (Sotheby's Belgravia) $345 £160

One of three Staffordshire black basalt vases, late 19th century, 35cm. high. (Phillips) $82 £38

Staffordshire figure of Sir Walter Scott and 'Maid', 15in. high. (Phillips) $123 £57

Rare Staffordshire pottery bust of a man, possibly Cobbett, 19cm. high. (Sotheby King & Chasemore) $324 £150

Early Staffordshire figure of a shepherdess, circa 1800, 13.5cm. high. (Phillips) $60 £28

Staffordshire figure of Wellington, 13in. high. (Christie's S. Kensington) $450 £200

Staffordshire saltglaze lobed oval two-handled tureen and cover, 27cm. wide, circa 1760. (Christie's) $475 £220

Staffordshire cottage pastille burner, 12in. high. (Phillips) $95 £44

Staffordshire cottage with adjoining byre and two lambs, 8in. high. (Phillips) $166 £77

Pre-Victorian Staffordshire figure of Moses, 11in. high, with bocage base. (Phillips) $205 £95

Staffordshire saltglaze wall-pocket, 23cm. high, circa 1760. (Christie's) $648 £300

Staffordshire figure of General Sir George Brown, titled, 13in. high. (Phillips) $153 £71

Staffordshire group of The Victory, modelled as an English sailor and a Turkish and French soldier. (Christie's S. Kensington) $1,947 £950

Staffordshire saltglaze globular bottle, circa 1755, 23cm. high. (Christie's) $280 £130

Staffordshire coloured saltglaze figure of a hawk. (Christie's) $14,040 £6,500

Staffordshire portrait bust of George Washington, 21cm. high. (Sotheby King & Chasemore) $560 £260

Rare Staffordshire figure of a fox, 11cm. high, circa 1825. (Sotheby King & Chasemore) $285 £140

187

STONEWARE

Quimper Art Deco decorated stoneware vase, 1920's, 18cm. high. (Sotheby's Belgravia) $306 £140

A stoneware dish by Poh Chap Yeap, painted in colours, 35cm. diam. (Christie's) $185 £85

Large Lachenal stoneware vase, circa 1900, 32cm. high. (Sotheby's Belgravia) $394 £180

Victorian Gothic castle candleholder of glazed stoneware, 11½in. high. (Robert W. Skinner Inc.) $230 £105

A stoneware oviform vase by Charles Vyse, 1931, 26.5cm. high. (Christie's) $220 £100

Biscuit coloured stoneware spirit barrel with brass tap, circa 1860, 13¼in. high. (Christopher Sykes) $80 £35

TERRACOTTA

Etruscan terracotta 'plastic vase' in the form of an ape, early 6th century B.C., 3¾in. high. (Sotheby's) $570 £260

Mid 16th century Italian terracotta modello of a river god, 10in. high. (Sotheby's) $800 £350

5th century B.C. Sicilian terracotta vase in the form of a Siren, 4¼in. high. (Sotheby's) $770 £350

Terracotta plaque by Martin Bros., showing the interior of the Southall Pottery. (Woolley & Wallis) $1,339 £580

Late 18th century French terracotta bust by Pajou, 18in. high. (Gray's Antique Mews) $501 £220

Pair of terracotta jardinieres, circa 1880. (Alfie's Antique Market) $311 £135

Mid 19th century Vienna plate. (Alfie's Antique Market) $342 £150

A Vienna equestrian figure of a sportswoman in a black tricorn hat, 9cm. high, circa 1765. (Christie's) $1,250 £550

A Vienna slender beaker and saucer with chinoiserie figures, circa 1745. (Christie's) $2,750 £1,200

One of a pair of Vienna style vases and covers of ovoid shape, 29cm. high.(Phillips) $150 £70

Vienna pattern plate signed Killman. (Christie's S. Kensington) $129 £60

One of a pair of late 19th century Vienna vases and covers painted by A. Heer, 21cm. high. (Sotheby's Belgravia) $320 £140

An Ernst Teichert Vienna plate painted by Worojner, 24.3cm. high, late 19th century. (Sotheby's Belgravia) $295 £130

A Vienna group of an old man and a young girl, 13cm. high, circa 1765. (Christie's) $1,000 £450

One of a pair of Vienna wall plaques each painted by R. Ulma, 31.5cm. diam., circa 1900. (Sotheby's Belgravia) $1,020 £450

WALFORD

20th century James Walford stoneware model of a head of a shoebill, 7¼in. high. (Sotheby's Belgravia) $250 £110

James Walford stoneware nude, 1950's, 11in. high. (Sotheby's Belgravia) $59 £26

20th century James Walford stoneware model of a hippopotamus head, 6¾in. wide. (Sotheby's Belgravia) $148 £65

Wedgwood Fairyland
lustre bowl. (Christie's
S. Kensington)
$1,530 £680

Wedgwood Fairyland lustre bowl,
21cm. diam., with printed mark.
(Sotheby King & Chasemore)
$585 £260

Wedgwood Fairyland
lustre octagonal bowl,
23cm. wide, circa
1928. (Sotheby Bearne)
$1,300 £600

Wedgwood 'moonlight
lustre' inverted baluster
shaped urn with lid, 20in.
high. (Andrew Grant)
$2,480 £1,210

Wedgwood creamware teapot and
cover, circa 1770, 5½in. high.
(Sotheby's) $830 £280

One of a pair of Wedgwood
Fairyland candlemas lustre
vases and covers, 1920's,
8½in. high. (Sotheby's
Belgravia) $1,300 £600

Wedgwood blue and white
jasper circular medallion,
6cm. diam., dated 1789.
(Christie's) $560 £260

Late 18th century Wedgwood
black basalt bust of Mercury,
18¼in. high. (Sotheby's)
$415 £190

Wedgwood soup plate,
circa 1825, Blue Claude
pattern. (Gray's
Antique Mews)
$50 £23

Blue jasper Wedgwood
cheese dish, circa 1870.
(Alfie's Antique Market)
$135 £60

Set of three Wedgwood black basalt
spill vases, circa 1830. (Alfie's
Antique Market) $200 £90

Wedgwood dark blue
jasper jardiniere, 18cm.
high. (May, Whetter &
Grose) $120 £56

Wedgwood Fairyland lustre bowl, 11in. diam., 1920's, restored. (Sotheby's Belgravia) $540 £250

Wedgwood Fairyland lustre dish, 5½in. diam. (Christie's S. Kensington) $415 £180

Wedgwood Fairyland octagonal lustre bowl, 9in. diam., 1920's. (Sotheby's Belgravia) $1,300 £600

Wedgwood dark blue jasper jug with rope twist handle, 22cm. high. (May, Whetter & Grose) $77 £36

Wedgwood creamware cruet with five containers, circa 1810, 17cm. wide. (Christie's) $690 £320

Wedgwood creamware cylindrical mug, circa 1765, 12cm. high, transfer-printed in black. (Christie's) $540 £250

Mid 19th century Wedgwood black basalt bust of Homer, 14¾in. high. (Sotheby's Belgravia) $650 £300

Pair of Wedgwood creamware oviform vases, painted by Emile Lessore, 34.5cm. high, dated for 1861. (Christie's) $1,620 £750

Mid 19th century Wedgwood black basalt bust of Lord Byron, 15¼in. high. (Sotheby's Belgravia) $520 £240

Wedgwood 'trial' copy of the Portland vase, circa 1791, 10¾in. high. (Sotheby's) $9,850 £4,500

Wedgwood Fairyland lustre plate, 1920's, 10¾in. diam. (Sotheby's Belgravia) $1,200 £550

Wedgwood blue and white jasper silver mounted circular scent bottle and opaline glass stopper, circa 1795, 7.5cm. high. (Christie's) $345 £160

Rare Wedgwood lustre bowl of 'Daventry' form, circa 1929, 13in. diam.(Sotheby's Belgravia) $1,580 £700

Wedgwood Whieldon teapot and cover moulded with fruits and foliage, circa 1760-65, 5¼in. high. (Sotheby's) $335 £150

Early 19th century Wedgwood black basalt bowl, circa 1820, 8¼in. diam. (Christopher Sykes) $125 £55

Mid 19th century Wedgwood black jasper-dip Portland vase, 7in. high. (Sotheby's Belgravia) $250 £110

Wedgwood blue jasper medallion modelled in white relief with Shakespeare, 4in. high, circa 1780. (Sotheby's) $180 £80

An early 19th century Wedgwood 'Rosso Antico' wine cooler of barrel shape, 9in. high. (Sotheby's) $585 £260

Unusual Wedgwood Fairyland coral and bronze lustre 'candlemas' vase, 10½in. high, 1920's. (Sotheby's Belgravia) $1,355 £600

Part of a Wedgwood dinner and dessert service of one hundred and one pieces, circa 1835. (Sotheby's) $3,600 £1,600

Early 19th century Wedgwood 'encaustic' vase, 15in. high. (Sotheby's) $1,900 £850

A Wedgwood Whieldon cornucopia wall-pocket probably modelled by Wm. Greatbatch, 8¼in. high, 1760-65. (Sotheby's) $225 £100

Pair of Wedgwood blue jasper candlesticks, 19th century, 6¼in. high. (Christopher Sykes) $160 £70

Wedgwood pottery milk jug, circa 1860, 6½in. high. (Christopher Sykes) $110 £50

Wedgwood caneware chamber candlestick with loop ring handle, circa 1810. (Christie's) $229 £100

Wedgwood caneware octagonal teapot and cover, circa 1790, 21cm. wide. (Christie's) $972 £450

Wedgwood caneware cylindrical basket, circa 1810, 10.5cm. wide. (Christie's) $206 £90

Wedgwood black basalt 'encaustic' decorated two-handled campana vase, circa 1810, 23cm. high. (Christie's) $960 £420

Wedgwood biscuit barrel. (Alfie's Antique Market) $110 £48

Wedgwood black basalt globular two-handled pot pourri vase, lid and pierced cover, circa 1815, 295.cm. high. (Christie's) $915 £400

One of a pair of Wedgwood three colour jasper barber vases and stoppers, 1867, 26cm. high. (Christie's) $1,099 £480

Set of three Wedgwood dark blue jasper graduated jugs. (May, Whetter & Grose) $135 £60

Wedgwood caneware mug with loop basketwork handle, circa 1800, 8.5cm. high. (Christie's) $229 £100

Late 16th century Westerwald stoneware vase with pewter lid. (Leys, Antwerp) $1,385 £640

Early 18th century Westerwald salt cellar with saltglaze, 17cm. high. (Leys, Antwerp) $760 £350

Early 18th century Westerwald saltglaze stoneware jug, 25cm. high. (Sotheby King & Chasemore) $342 £150

193

Whieldon pew figure modelled as a lady in crinoline, circa 1750, 11.5cm. wide. (Christie's) $2,975 £1,300

Whieldon square tea caddy, circa 1760, 12.5cm. high. (Christie's)$650 £300

Whieldon globular teapot and cover, circa 1760, 19cm. wide. (Christie's) $1,605 £700

Whieldon figure of a Turk in grey-green turban and coat, circa 1760, 14.5cm. high. (Christie's) $1,715 £750

Whieldon group of embracing lovers in green, brown and yellow glazes, circa 1750, 12cm. wide. (Christie's) $3,200 £1,400

Whieldon figure of a standing Turk, circa 1760, 14cm. high (Christie's) $1,490 £650

Whieldon green glazed rectangular tea caddy, circa 1760, 11.5cm. high. (Christie's) $570 £250

Whieldon figure of a standing lion, circa 1760, 20cm. wide.(Christie's) $5,040 £2,200

One of a pair of Whieldon cornucopias modelled as a female mask, circa 1760, 31cm. high. (Christie's) $1,375 £600

Whieldon conical coffee pot and domed cover, circa 1760, 23cm. high. (Christie's) $3,665 £1,600

Pair of Whieldon figures of A Turk and his Companion, circa 1760, 18.5cm. high. (Christie's) $3,780 £1,650

Whieldon hot milk jug and cover, circa 1750, 15.5cm. high. (Christie's)$960 £420

Ralph Wood figure of a youth in green breeches, circa 1775, 17.5cm. high. (Christie's) **$735 £320**

Ralph Wood triple spill-vase, circa 1785, 27cm. high.   (Christie's) **$495 £230**

Ralph Wood triple spill-vase, 23cm. high, circa 1785. (Christie's) **$520 £240**

Ralph Wood figure of Jupiter with an eagle at his feet, circa 1775, 26.5cm. high.(Christie's) **$1,145 £500**

Ralph Wood group of St. George and The Dragon, circa 1775, 28cm. high.(Christie's) **$800 £350**

Ralph Wood figure of Admiral van Tromp drawing his sword, circa 1775, 26.5cm. high.(Christie's) **$960 £420**

Ralph Wood fair hebe jug, circa 1788, 24.5cm. high, slightly chipped.(Christie's) **$605 £280**

Ralph Wood figure of a cockerel with brown comb and wattle, circa 1780, 19cm. high. (Christie's)**$1,145 £500**

Ralph Wood Toby jug in dark brown tricorn hat, circa 1785, 24.5cm. high. (Christie's) **$1,420 £620**

Ralph Wood Toby jug with grey hat, blue jacket and yellow waistcoat, circa 1785, 26cm. high. (Christie's) **$505 £220**

Ralph Wood figure of a mounted officer, circa 1775, 14cm. wide. (Christie's) **$2,750 £1,200**

An inscribed and dated Ralph Wood jug of large size, modelled by Jean Voyez, 9½in. high, 1788. (Sotheby's)**$990 £440**

195

Dr. Wall Worcester scale blue tureen with cover, saucer stand and a ladle. (Graves, Son & Pilcher) $4,212 £1,950

Graingers Worcester white porcelain part teaset of thirteen pieces. (Phillips)$30 £15

Late Victorian Royal Worcester porcelain tyg showing a cricket scene. (Geering & Colyer) $5,900 £2,600

Royal Worcester figure of a soldier, circa 1916, 5½in. high. (Sotheby's Belgravia) $151 £70

Unusual pair of Royal Worcester earthenware figures of 'Joy' and 'Sorrow', circa 1880, 10¼in. high. (Sotheby's Belgravia) $410 £190

Royal Worcester figure of a youth, dated 1883, 25.5cm. high. (Sotheby King & Chasemore) $390 £180

Set of six Royal Worcester silver mounted ashtrays, 1931, each 2¾in. diam. (Sotheby's Belgravia) $540 £250

One of a pair of Worcester Dr. Wall Blind Earl circular plates, 19cm. diam., circa 1770. (Christie's) $561 £260

Royal Worcester figure of Percheron stallion, 1965, 9½in. long. (Sotheby's Belgravia) $604 £280

One of a pair of Royal Worcester pierced vases, 11in. high, 1886. (Sotheby's Belgravia)$194 £90

Unusual glazed earthenware Royal Worcester figures, circa 1880, 16¾in. high. (Sotheby's Belgravia)$561 £260

Royal Worcester vase and cover, dated for 1901. (Alfie's Antique Market) $429 £190

Royal Worcester teacup and saucer.
(R. H. Ellis & Sons) $47 £21

One of a pair of first period
blue scale Worcester vases
and covers, 1760's. (Bonham's)
$6,075 £2,700

Royal Worcester porcelain figure of
an Aberdeen Angus bull by Doris
Linder, 1960's, 9½in. high.
(Christie's & Edmiston's)
$1,232 £560

One of a pair of Worcester wall-
pockets, circa 1755, 24cm. high.
(Sotheby King & Chasemore)
$2,035 £900

Pair of Royal Worcester figures 'Salt
and Pepper', 7¼in. high, dated for
1893. (Sotheby's Belgravia)
$475 £220

Kerr & Binns Worcester vase,
7in. high, dated 1858.
(Sotheby's Belgravia)
$388 £180

Royal Worcester model of
'Arkle', 9¾in. long, 1967.
(Sotheby's Belgravia)
$1,296 £600

One of a pair of Flight, Barr & Barr
claret ground plates, circa 1820,
22.5cm. diam. (Christie's) $259 £120

One of a pair of Worcester dark
blue ground moon flasks, circa
1880, 7in. high. (Sotheby's Belgravia) $648 £300

One of six Flight, Barr & Barr
dessert plates, circa 1820, 22.5cm.
diam. (Christie's) $583 £270

Worcester vase decorated in Oriental
style, circa 1874. (Alfie's Antique
Market) $214 £95

Worcester 'blind earl' plate moulded
in relief with rose sprays, circa 1765,
7½in. diam. (Sotheby's)
$1,050 £480

197

Worcester punchbowl, circa 1760, enamelled in polychrome, 9in. diam. (Shakespear, McTurk & Graham) $205 £95

Dr. Wall Worcester teapot, 6in. high, with scale blue base. (Graves, Son & Pilcher) $1,552 £720

One of a set of three Worcester shaped pickle dishes, 5in. wide. (Andrew Grant) $86 £40

One of a pair of Worcester candlesticks, circa 1760, 10¼in. high. (Christie's) $31,320 £14,500

19th century Barr, Flight & Barr soup tureen, cover and stand from a dinner service of forty-two pieces. (Garrod Turner) $14,220 £7,040

Lidded vase by Locke & Co., Worcester, on square pierced base, 13in. high. (Andrew Grant) $164 £80

Small Royal Worcester posy vase by H. Stinton, 5in. high. (Andrew Grant) $410 £200

Rare Royal Worcester scent flask, 5in. high. (McCartney, Morris & Barker) $260 £120

Locke & Co. pierced moon flask with blue and gilt decoration. (Andrew Grant) $225 £110

Locke & Co. pierced work vase, impressed with peach and gilt. (Andrew Grant) $410 £200

Part of a Royal Worcester sixteen-piece fish service. (Sotheby Bearne) $1,685 £780

Royal Worcester figure of a young girl on a tree stump, 10in. high. (Andrew Grant) $410 £200

One of a set of three 18th century Worcester oval baskets, 11in. wide, two repaired. (Andrew Grant) $280 £130

Royal Worcester bowl by Ricketts. (Christie's S. Kensington) $303 £150

One of a pair of 18th century Worcester sauceboats, 8in. long. (Andrew Grant) $334 £155

One of a pair of Royal Worcester vases, decorated by R. Sebright. (Samuel Rains & Son) $2,270 £1,050

A pair of Royal Worcester vases, painted by Harry Stinton. (Samuel Rains & Son) $2,160 £1,000

Royal Worcester vase with lid signed Sedgley, circa 1920, 18in. high. (Gray's Antique Mews) $695 £310

One of a pair of Royal Worcester vases, signed J. Stinton, 7in. high. (Andrew Grant) $1,271 £620

Part of a Barr, Flight & Barr one hundred and ten-piece armorial dessert, tea and coffee service. (Phillips) $1,545 £715

One of a pair of first period blue scale Worcester vases and covers, 1760's. (Bonham's) $6,075 £2,700

Chamberlain Worcester vase and cover of baluster shape, 46cm. high. (Sotheby King & Chasemore) $205 £100

Fine and rare Worcester blue and white chestnut basket, cover and ladle, circa 1770, 4½in. diam. (Sotheby's) $2,740 £1,250

One of a pair of pierced vases by Locke & Co., Worcester, 10½in. high. (Andrew Grant) $615 £300

Royal Worcester porcelain
two-handled vase. (McCartney,
Morris & Barker) $290 £125

Chamberlain Worcester card tray
with painted centre. (Phillips
New York) $1,500 £665

Royal Worcester porcelain vase.
(McCartney, Morris & Barker)
              $195 £85

Large Royal Worcester vase and cover,
dated for 1892, 11¼in. high.(Sotheby's
Belgravia) $1,040 £460

A Worcester fluted coffee cup
and saucer, 1765-70.(Sotheby's)
              $585 £260

Royal Worcester vase with ovoid body,
dated for 1913, 8in. high. (Sotheby's
Belgravia) $1,085 £480

Royal Worcester pot pourri
bowl and cover, dated for
1912, 10in. high. (Sotheby's
Belgravia) $630 £280

Pair of Royal Worcester 'sugar sifter'
figures, circa 1880, 7in. high.
(Sotheby's Belgravia) $385 £170

Royal Worcester pot pourri vase,
liner and cover, 12¾in. high,
dated for 1902.(Sotheby's Belgravia) $1,130 £500

Early Worcester vase of thistle
shape, 6¼in. high, circa 1756-58.
(Sotheby's) $3,720 £1,700

A rare Worcester 'Japan' pattern plate,
9in. diameter, circa 1770. (Sotheby's)
              $1,000 £450

A Worcester cylindrical mug
printed with a foxhunting
scene, 4¾in. high, circa 1770.
(Sotheby's) $675 £300

A Worcester blue and white teapot and cover, 5½in. tall, 1765-70. (Sotheby's) $585 £260

Barr, Flight & Barr Worcester campana-shaped vase, 18cm. high. (Sotheby King & Chasemore) $290 £130

A good Worcester rice bowl and cover, 4¾in. high, circa 1770. (Sotheby's) $1,125 £500

Royal Worcester figure of a Grecian water carrier, 1933, 20¼in. high. (Sotheby's Belgravia) $520 £240

One of a pair of Worcester chocolate cups and saucers, circa 1775.(Sotheby's) $1,050 £460

One of a set of six Royal Worcester coffee cups and saucers, dated for 1923. (Sotheby's Belgravia) $1,580 £700

Royal Worcester 'new three-claw spill-vase', 6in. high, circa 1868. (Sotheby's Belgravia) $180 £80

Fine Worcester wet mustard pot, cover and spoon, 3½in. high, circa 1770. (Sotheby's) $875 £400

Royal Worcester figure of a Chinaman, 7in. high, dated for 1881. (Sotheby's Belgravia) $315 £140

An early Worcester cream jug with a Long Eliza figure, 3¼in. high, 1753-55. (Sotheby's) $2,250 £1,000

A fine Worcester plate with fluted rim, 7½in. across, 1765-70. (Sotheby's) $1,000 £440

An attractive early Worcester jug of inverted baluster shape, 7in. high, 1754-56. (Sotheby's) $1,400 £620

WUCAI

Wucai transitional period jar, circa 1650, 10½in. high. (Gray's Antique Mews) $720 £320

One of a pair of Ming dynasty Wucai saucer-dishes painted with The Three Friends of Winter, 5¾in. diam. (Christie's) $740 £340

Wucai porcelain vase in underglaze blue, 23.5cm. high. (Sotheby King & Chasemore) $1,220 £540

YONGZHENG

Blue and yellow Chinese porcelain bowl, Yongzheng, 10¼in. diam. (Sotheby's) $11,880 £5,500

Yongzheng or early Qianlong famille rose square vase on short feet, 5in. high. (Christie's) $285 £130

One of a pair of Yongzheng famille rose soup plates, 8¾in. diam. (Christie's) $400 £180

YORKSHIRE

Pair of Yorkshire cream-ware standing figures of officers, circa 1780, 18cm. high.(Christie's) $780 £340

Pair of Yorkshire groups, circa 1785, 15cm. wide. (Christie's) $1,715 £750

Late 18th century Yorkshire 'squat' Toby jug, with carya-tid handle, 7¾in. high. (Sotheby's) $990 £440

YUAN

Yuan dynasty Jun Yao type saucer-dish with petal shaped rim, 5in. diam. (Christie's) $310 £140

Chinese porcelain vase of the Yuan dynasty with pale blue glaze, 28.6cm. high. (Sotheby's)$157,500 £70,000

Moulded Yingqing Yuan dynasty dish with shallow sides, 18cm. diam. (Sotheby's) $275 £120

Carved walnut bracket clock with dial regulation, circa 1880.(Alfie's Antique Market)
$440 £195

Ebonised striking bracket clock, 12in. high. (Christie's) $1,530 £680

Regency ebonised striking bracket clock, signed Moncas, Liverpool, 18½in. high. (Christie's) $1,215 £540

George III bracket clock by J. Warne, London, in mahogany case, 1ft.8in. high.(Sotheby King & Chasemore) $5,830 £2,700

Mid 18th century fruitwood striking bracket clock, signed Thos. West, London. (Christie's) $1,685 £750

Regency mahogany striking bracket clock by Panchaud & Cumming, London, 16in. high. (Christie's) $1,800 £800

George III ebonised quarter striking bracket clock, by J. Tregent, London, 17¼in. high. (Christie's) $5,850 £2,600

George II lacquered striking bracket clock by Thos. Hunter, London. (Christie's) $2,925 £1,300

Late George III striking bracket clock by Thos. Sutton, Maidstone, 15in. high. (Christie's) $2,925 £1,300

Mid Georgian ebonised fruitwood striking bracket clock by Thos. Martin, London, 17in. high. (Christie's) $2,700 £1,200

Walnut striking bracket clock by Robt. Sadler, London, 14½in. high. (Christie's) $2,360 £1,050

Mahogany striking bracket clock by John Wilcox, 19in. high. (Christie's) $5,175 £2,300

203

BRACKET CLOCKS

Late 19th century ebonised bracket clock by Hurt & Sons, Birmingham, 19in. high. (Phillips)$1,475 £680

Small rare olivewood basket-top bracket timepiece by Nathaniel Hodges.(Sotheby's) $17,280 £8,000

Mahogany bracket clock with inlaid stringing. (Alfie's Antique Market) $223 £110

Continental ebonised bracket clock by Joseph Keipmuller, 15in. high. (Heathcote Ball & Co.) $1,685 £780

Elaborate bracket clock by William Vale, London, 36in. high, in padoukwood case. (Sotheby King & Chasemore) $10,800 £5,000

18th century eight-day walnut bracket clock by Lagisse et Fils, London. (H. Spencer & Sons) $6,156 £2,700

Fine late 18th century bracket clock by Hare, London, 43cm. high. (Sotheby King & Chasemore) $5,076 £2,350

George III ebonised bracket clock by Edward Lister, 19in. high. (Christie's S. Kensington) $3,300 £1,500

George III ebonised bracket clock by William Edwards, London, 21in. high. (Phillips) $2,257 £1,045

Mahogany bracket clock by Robert Harding, London, 1ft.10in. high. (Sotheby's)$3,450 £1,500

18th century bracket clock by Lancaster & Son. (W. H. Lane & Son) $1,566 £725

Early 18th century bracket clock by Henry Clarkson, Wolverhampton, in ebonised pearwood case, 19in. high. (Sotheby King & Chasemore)$4,536 £2,100

204

Ebony veneered bracket clock by Samuel Barkley and Thomas Colley, London, 1751-54, 35.5cm. high. (Christie's)
$25,056 £11,600

Early 19th century ebonised lancet top bracket clock by Grant, London. (Heathcote Ball & Co.)
$1,252 £580

Mid 18th century eight-day bracket clock by John Ellicott, London, 42cm. high. (Sotheby King & Chasemore)
$8,664 £3,800

Late George III period mahogany cased domed top bracket clock, 16¾in. high, by Dwerrihouse Carter & Son, London. (Geering & Colyer)
$4,500 £2,000

English Regency bracket clock in mahogany case, 20in. high. (Vernon's)
$1,425 £650

Late 18th century mahogany cased bracket clock by Fran. Zagnani, London, 24in. high. (Sotheby King & Chasemore)
$3,672 £1,700

George II bracket clock in ebony case by John Gordon, London, 17¾in. high. (Olivers)
$5,198 £2,300

Mid 18th century ebonised bracket clock by J. Thwaites, London. (Heathcote Ball & Co.)
$3,024 £1,400

19th century bracket clock in a mahogany case by George Sharpe. (Hobbs Parker)
$1,583 £780

George III tortoise-shell veneered musical bracket clock. (Bonham's)
$9,720 £4,500

Mid 17th century bracket clock in an ebony veneered case by Pieter Visbagh, 10in. high. (Graves, Son & Pilcher) $16,564 £8,200

Late 18th century musical bracket clock by Robert Ward, London, 61cm. high. (Sotheby Bearne)
$6,264 £2,900

BRACKET CLOCKS

Important late 18th century mahogany quarter repeating bracket clock by William Dutton, 14in. high. (Jackson-Stops & Staff) $7,560 £3,500

Large mid 18th century ebonised bracket clock, 20½in. high, with silvered dial.(Boardman's) $1,475 £680

Bracket clock by Joseph Knibb, London, 1685, in ebony case, 31cm. high. (Sotheby's) $25,990 £11,500

George II ebonised striking bracket clock, 22in. high. (Christie's) $2,135 £950

Mahogany bracket clock, signed Sam. Watson, London, 19in. high. (Sotheby's) $2,070 £900

Red lacquered chiming bracket clock by McCabe, London, 22in. high. (Christie's) $4,500 £2,000

George III mahogany bracket clock by Richard Webster, London, 18½in. high. (Sotheby's) $1,760 £1,200

Late 18th century Irish bracket clock in mahogany case, on ball feet. (British Antique Exporters) $1,820 £810

Gilt brass night and day clock, dial in marquetry case, by Ed. East. (Christie's) $4,930 £2,200

Early 19th century mahogany musical bracket clock by J. & S. Farr, Bristol, 25in. high. (Sotheby's) $5,520 £2,400

18th century walnut cased bracket clock with silvered dial, date ring, 21in. high. (Parsons, Welch & Cowell) $1,475 £725

Fine ebonised bracket clock with ormolu fittings. (West London Auctions) $1,400 £650

Ebonised timepiece bracket clock, signed 'Hannah Jones ye Widdow of Henry Jones, London', 15½in. high. (Christie's) $7,170 £3,200

Early 18th century ebony striking bracket clock by Martin Jackson, London, 14¼in. high. (Christie's) $5,600 £2,500

Ebonised striking bracket clock, circa 1700, by E. Fletcher, 14½in. high. (Christie's) $4,145 £1,850

William IV mahogany bracket clock, dial inscribed Taylor & Son, Bristol, 19in. high.(Parsons, Welch & Cowell) $1,150 £510

Early 19th century bracket clock by J. Harper, London, (Vernon's) $1,180 £525

19th century ebonised bracket clock by Hill, Edinburgh. (Phillips) $1,663 £720

Mahogany bracket clock, dial signed Whytock & Sons, Dundee, circa 1890, 22in. high. (Sotheby's Belgravia) $810 £360

Brass and oak bracket clock with silvered dial, circa 1870, 23in. high. (Sotheby's Belgravia) $1,980 £880

Darkened mahogany striking bracket clock by J. Drabble, London, 16in. high. (Christie's) $2,465 £1,100

Early ebonised basket-top quarter repeating bracket clock by William Cattell, circa 1685, 14½in. high. (Sotheby's) $9,200 £4,000

Ebonised bracket clock by Charles Gretton, circa 1700, 13½in. high. (Sotheby's) $5,290 £2,300

Basket-top quarter repeating bracket clock by Daniel Quare, circa 1695, 14in. (Sotheby's) $24,150 £10,500

CARRIAGE CLOCKS

French striking carriage clock in gorge case with lever escapement and push repeat. (Phillips) $1,170 £515

Fine quality carriage clock with alarm, circa 1895. (Gray's Antique Mews) $1,810 £800

Brass cased gong striking carriage clock, dial signed Pedler, 7½in. high. (D. M. Nesbit & Co.) $495 £230

Gilt metal carriage clock by Shreve Crump & Low, Boston, 6in. high. (Sotheby Humberts) $650 £300

French repeater carriage clock.(Honiton Galleries) $860 £380

Small gilt metal quarter striking carriage clock by Chas. Frodsham, Paris, 4¼in. high. (Christie's) $1,800 £800

Gilt metal quarter striking carriage clock, 5¾in. high. (Christie's) $1,485 £660

English gilt metal carriage timepiece by Viner & Co., London, 4½in. high.(Christie's) $2,070 £925

Gilt metal striking carriage clock, 6in. high. (Christie's) $1,350 £600

Silver mounted carriage clock set with transparent ruby ground glass, maker's mark WW/WW, London, 1894.(Sotheby's Belgravia) $650 £290

Edwardian gilt brass and painted porcelain carriage clock. (Sotheby's Belgravia) $2,700 £1,250

Enamel mounted alarm carriage clock, case decorated with cloisonne scrollwork in red, blue and yellow. (Sotheby's)$3,220 £1,400

Brass grande sonnerie striking carriage clock, 5½in. high.(Christie's) $1,800 £800

Liberty & Co. 'Cymric' silver and enamel travelling clock, 1903, 15.2cm. high. (Sotheby's Belgravia) $3,066 £1,400

Gilt metal striking carriage clock by Drocourt, 6in. high. (Christie's) $1,530 £680

Liberty & Co. 'Cymric' silver and enamel clock, Birmingham, 1904, 8cm. high. (Sotheby's Belgravia) $875 £400

Brass and enamelled grande sonnerie striking carriage clock by Drocourt, 6in. high. (Christie's)
$4,160 £1,850

Brass striking carriage clock, 5¾in. high. (Christie's)
$1,530 £680

Gilt brass gong repeating carriage clock with painted porcelain side panels, 8in. high. (D. M. Nesbit & Co.)
$1,100 £510

French clock with brass overlay on ebony, 1880, eight-day movement. (Gray's Antique Mews)
$565 £250

Victorian silver carriage clock. (Alfie's Antique Market)
$450 £200

Brass striking carriage clock with movement by Bolviller, Paris, 5½in. high. (Christie's) $990 £440

French carriage clock in baroque brass case with silvered dial. (Robert W. Skinner Inc.)
$900 £410

Gilt metal oval brass striking carriage clock by Drocourt, 5½in. high. (Christie's)
$2,025 £900

19th century repeating alarm carriage clock, 19cm. high. (Woolley & Wallis) $1,010 £450

French brass carriage clock in an Anglaise Riche case with porcelain side panels. (Gray's Antique Mews)
$1,835 £850

Late 19th century carriage clock by Nicole Nielson & Co., in silver case, 11.5cm. high. (Christie's)
$108,000 £48,000

Unusual carriage timepiece by Thwaites & Reed, London, 5¾in. high. (Sotheby's)
$3,680 £1,600

19th century petite sonnerie carriage clock by Joseph Berrolla, Paris. (Vost's) $1,370 £670

Late 19th century French brass carriage clock, 7½in. high. (Olivers) $610 £270

Gilt metal quarter striking carriage clock, 6in. high. (Christie's)
$1,530 £680

Gilt metal striking carriage clock, 4¾in. high. (Christie's) $1,800 £800

CARRIAGE CLOCKS

Swiss silver gilt and enamel miniature carriage clock, 2¼in. high. (Christie's) $2,530 £1,100

Grande sonnerie carriage clock by Glading & Co., Brighton, 7in. high. (Sotheby's) $2,530 £1,100

Swiss silver gilt and enamel miniature carriage clock with oval mother-of-pearl dial, 2½in. high.(Christie's) $2,070 £900

Silver gilt and enamel miniature carriage clock in diamond set case, 3in. high. (Christie's) $3,680 £1,600

Small gilt metal striking carriage clock, 4¼in. high. (Christie's) $1,530 £680

Swiss silver gilt and enamel miniature carriage clock in the manner of Cartier, 2¼in. high. (Christie's) $3,680 £1,600

Grande sonnerie carriage clock by Charles Frodsham, London, circa 1917, 12cm. high. (Bonham's) $38,250 £17,000

Swiss silver gilt and enamel miniature carriage clock, 2½in. high. (Christie's) $2,415 £1,050

Early French gilt metal pendule de voyage, dial signed Dubois, Paris, circa 1780, 7½in. high. (Christie's) $9,200 £4,000

Small ebony veneered carriage clock by Vulliamy, London, circa 1840, 6½in. high. (Sotheby's) $14,950 £6,500

Late 19th century gilt brass alarm carriage clock, probably by Brune, 7in. high. (Sotheby's Belgravia) $740 £380

19th century ormolu cased repeater carriage clock. (Bradley & Vaughan) $2,050 £900

Silver gilt and enamel miniature carriage clock with ivory dial, 2½in. high. (Christie's) $2,760 £1,200

Gilt metal and enamel striking carriage clock in travelling case, 7in. high. (Christie's) $2,760 £1,200

A grande sonnerie carriage clock by Nicole Nielson & Co., London, circa 1900, 15cm. high. (Christie's) $44,800 £20,000

Good polychrome enamel mounted alarm carriage clock by Leroy et Fils, Paris, 5¾in. high. (Sotheby's) $3,220 £1,400

Small polychrome enamel mounted carriage time-piece, 3¾in. high. (Sotheby's)$1,550 £675

Gilt metal petite sonnerie striking carriage clock by Leroy, 4¼in. high. (Christie's)$2,115 £920

Fine eight-day carriage clock by Mappin & Webb, Paris, 6in. high.(Christopher Sykes) $700 £325

Quarter striking alarm carriage clock by C. H. Toutouze, Paris, 5½in. high. (Sotheby's) $1,955 £850

Swiss silver gilt and enamel miniature carriage clock on rose quartz feet, 2¼in. high. (Christie's) $3,105 £1,350

Silver gilt and enamel miniature desk carriage clock with flared case decorated with scenes of the four seasons, 2¾in. square. (Christie's) $3,105 £1,350

Swiss silver gilt miniature enamel carriage clock, the sides with enamel roundels of ladies, 2¼in. high. (Christie's)$2,070 £900

Rare brass four dial timepiece carriage clock, 6in. high. (Christie's) $1,680 £750

Unusual Biedermeier grande sonnerie alarm travelling clock, 9in. high.(Sotheby's) $4,370 £1,900

Enamel mounted grande sonnerie alarm clock, 7in. high. (Sotheby's) $3,900 £1,700

Gilt metal porcelain mounted striking carriage clock, 7¾in: high. (Christie's) $2,025 £900

French grande sonnerie striking alarm calendar carriage clock by Drocourt, Paris. (Bonham's) $8,665 £3,800

Fine late 19th century French carriage clock with ivory coloured enamel dial, 10¾in. high. (Sotheby King & Chasemore) $5,060 £2,200

Late 19th century French brass carriage clock with grande sonnerie eight-day movement, 26cm. high. (Sotheby King & Chasemore) $4,730 £2,200

Silver gilt and enamel miniature carriage clock with mother-of-pearl dial, on green agate base, 2½in. high. (Christie's) $2,760 £1,200

Gilt metal grande sonnerie striking carriage clock by A. Margaine, 6¾in. high. (Christie's) $2,530 £1,100

211

Fine Christofle cloisonne enamel clock garniture, 1874, clock 16¼in. high. (Sotheby's Belgravia) $4,160 £2,000

Gilt brass and porcelain clock garniture, circa 1900, clock 16½in. high. (Sotheby's Belgravia) $1,250 £600

Gilt bronze and marble clock garniture, clock 26in. high, circa 1900. (Sotheby's Belgravia) $1,770 £850

Unusual gilt and patinated bronze clock garniture, inscribed Japy Freres, circa 1900, 13½in. high. (Sotheby's Belgravia) $935 £450

Ormolu bronze and marble clock garniture by Briscard a Paris, 1870's, clock 18in. high. (Sotheby's Belgravia) $1,205 £580

19th century French style clock garniture. (Phillips) $554 £240

A Berlin clock garniture, the white enamel dial enclosed in a rococo case, 25.5cm. high, 1849-70. (Sotheby's Belgravia) $1,140 £500

Late 19th century garniture of blue glass, clock by J. Leemans, Brussels. (May Whetter & Grose) $995 £460

Gilt bronze and champleve clock garniture, circa 1890, clock 10¾in. high. (Sotheby's Belgravia) $1,245 £580

Gilt bronze and champleve enamel clock garniture, circa 1890, clock 12in. high. (Sotheby's Belgravia) $1,290 £600

Gilt bronze and Dresden porcelain clock garniture, circa 1880, clock 14in. high. (Sotheby's Belgravia) $1,330 £620

Mid 19th century French ormolu exhibition clock set, clock 20in. high. (Lacy Scott) $1,865 £920

Gilt bronze and Sevres clock garniture, dial with Roman numerals, circa 1880. (Sotheby's Belgravia) $1,290 £600

Good patinated spelter composed clock garniture, stamped Le Message par J. Castellamare, circa 1890, clock 19in. high. (Sotheby's Belgravia) $965 £450

Cloisonne and ormolu clock set, circa 1870. (Gray's Antique Mews) $1,865 £825

Ormolu and porcelain composed clock garniture, 1880's, clock 16in. high. (Sotheby's Belgravia) $2,080 £1,000

213

Late 19th century bronze and red and black marble clock garniture, clock 10½in. high. (Sotheby's Belgravia) $645 £300

Gilt bronze and porcelain composed clock garniture, dial inscribed Hry. Marc, Paris, circa 1890. (Sotheby's Belgravia) $1,180 £550

Gilt bronze and jewelled Sevres porcelain clock garniture, circa 1880. (Sotheby's Belgravia) $1,350 £600

Gilt bronze and jewelled Sevres composed clock garniture. (Sotheby's Belgravia) $1,575 £700

Brass and electrotype clock garniture, circa 1870. (Sotheby's Belgravia) $1,350 £600

Gilt bronze clock garniture, clock in the form of an owl, circa 1890. (Sotheby's Belgravia) $1,800 £800

Composed gilt bronze champleve enamel and painted opalescent glass clock garniture, circa 1880. (Sotheby's Belgravia) $4,500 £2,000

Gilt bronze and Sevres porcelain clock garniture, circa 1890, clock 16in. high. (Sotheby's Belgravia) $1,125 £500

French Sevres and gilt brass garniture de cheminee.
(Bradley & Vaughan) $2,375 £1,100

Gilt spelter and Sevres porcelain clock garniture, clock
17in. high, circa 1880. (Sotheby's Belgravia)$855 £380

Gilt bronze and Sevres clock garniture, circa 1880.
(Sotheby's Belgravia) $1,800 £800

Lacquered brass and polychrome enamel clock garniture
with Arabic numerals, clock 18½in. high, circa 1900.
(Sotheby's Belgravia) $1,615 £750

Ormolu and marble clock garniture, circa 1900, dial
signed Camerden and Foster, New York, Made in
France. (Sotheby's Belgravia) $1,395 £620

Early 20th century French gilt spelter and Paris porcelain clock garniture, clock 15½in. high. (Sotheby's
Belgravia) $785 £350

Ormolu and jewelled Sevres porcelain clock garniture,
circa 1880, clock 20½in. high. (Sotheby's Belgravia)
          $6,450 £3,000

Gilt bronze and porcelain clock garniture on gilt wood
bases, circa 1900. (Sotheby's Belgravia) $815 £380

215

Georgian oak longcase clock by John Wainwright, Wellingborough, 6ft.7in. high. (Shakespear, McTurk & Graham)$1,900 £880

Mid 18th century longcase clock in mahogany case, 250cm. high. (Sotheby King & Chasemore) $3,825 £1,700

George III inlaid mahogany longcase clock by W. Yeadon. (Neales) $3,150 £1,400

Oak longcase clock by William Jackson, London. (Phillips) $3,150 £1,400

Mahogany longcase clock by John Hamilton, Glasgow. (Andrew Grant) $2,727 £1,340

18th century Continental longcase clock with brass dial, 6ft. long.(Shakespear, McTurk & Graham) $918 £425

Early Victorian mahogany longcase clock by John Monk, Bolton. (Geering & Colyer) $1,350 £625

Mahogany longcase clock by Hugh Gordon, Aberdeen, 93in. high. (Phillips) $2,700 £1,200

Walnut and marquetry longcase clock by Wm. Garfoot, London, circa 1710. (Vost's) $11,480 £5,600

Fine 18th century walnut and inlaid eight-day longcase clock by B. Fieldhouse. (Smith-Woolley & Perry) $5,076 £2,350

Oak, mahogany and boxwood strung longcase clock by Barwise, London, 93in. high. (Vidler & Co.) $738 £360

Oak and mahogany inlaid longcase clock by Frederick Garrett, Lutterworth, 7ft. high. (Shakespear, McTurk & Graham) $777 £360

Late 18th century long-
case clock by S. Lang-
ford, Ludlow, in maho-
gany case. (Russell,
Baldwin & Bright)
$3,240 £1,500

Mahogany longcase regu-
lator, dated 1904. (D.
M. Nesbit & Co.
$1,998 £925

Early 19th century
mahogany cased long-
case clock, 84in. high.
(Lacy Scott)
$1,015 £500

Regency longcase clock
with brass dial by N.
Barwise, London.
(Worsfolds)
$5,740 £2,800

George III mahogany
eight-day striking clock
by Francis Perigal, 8ft.
2in. high. (Woolley &
Wallis) $5,832 £2,700

Late 18th century oak
longcase clock by A.
Dickie, Edinburgh.
(Hobbs Parker)
$1,603 £790

Georgian mahogany
longcase clock by
Harrison, Liverpool.
(C. Wesley Haslam &
Son)
$4,806 £2,225

George III mahogany
longcase clock by
Caleb Pitt, Frome,
86in. high. (Christie's
S. Kensington)
$4,275 £1,900

Small longcase clock in
a walnut marquetry
case by John Wise, circa
1680, 6ft.8in. high.
(Sotheby's)
$10,250 £5,000

Well patinated maho-
gany longcase clock
with domed hood.
(Phillips) $779 £380

George II longcase
clock. (H. Spencer
& Sons)
$4,535 £2,100

Early 18th century mar-
quetry longcase clock by
John Finch, London.
(Phillips)
$11,232 £5,200

George IV mahogany long-
case regulation clock by
Sherbourne, Aberdare.
(Coles, Knapp & Kennedy)
$1,835 £850

Fine George II chinoi-
serie lacquered long-
case clock. (Phillips)
$21,600 £10,000

Longcase clock in oak
case, circa 1800. (J. M.
Welch & Son)
$1,080 £500

George III longcase
clock by Jas. Cameron,
Dundee. (Phillips)
$415 £180

Edwardian longcase
clock in carved maho-
gany case, 8ft.3in.
high. (McCartney,
Morris & Barker)
$4,520 £2,000

18th century provincial
red lacquer longcase
clock by Edward Stevens,
Boston, 80in. high.
(Boardman's)
$1,600 £740

Oak longcase clock by
L. B. Hayes, Stamford,
6ft.1in. high. (Shake-
spear, McTurk &
Graham) $735 £340

18th century Dutch wal-
nut marquetry longcase
clock by Hendrik Borias,
91in. high. (Olivers)
$7,345 £3,250

Early 19th century maho-
gany longcase clock by
Daniel Brown, Glasgow,
7ft.3in. high. (Messenger
May & Baverstock)
$1,690 £750

Edwardian mahogany
and inlaid longcase clock
striking on tubular bells,
105in. high. (Christie's S.
Kensington)
$4,840 £2,200

18th century Dutch long-
case clock by Gerrit
Kolmer in walnut case,
96in. high. (Robert W.
Skinner Inc.)
$8,000 £3,635

French provincial long-
case clock with elabo-
rate brass pendulum.
(Vernon's)
$2,020 £875

Longcase clock with glazed door. (Eldon E. Worrall)
$6,700 £2,900

Mid 19th century mahogany drum head longcase clock by J. Jeffrey. (Phillips) $600 £260

18th century mahogany longcase clock, 90¾in. high, with brass dial. (Olivers)$2,215 £980

18th century mahogany longcase clock by Jn. Manby, Skipton, 89in. high. (Olivers)
$995 £440

Longcase clock in oak and walnut by S. H. Smith, Leicester. (Honiton Galleries)
$1,490 £660

Oak longcase clock by H. White, Cheapside, with brass and silvered dial. (Worsfolds)
$2,940 £1,300

18th century longcase clock in black lacquered and painted case, by James Ferrey. (Messenger May & Baverstock)
$1,810 £800

Early 18th century walnut longcase clock by George Neale, London, 8ft.9in. high. (Geering & Colyer)
$3,375 £1,500

18th century Belgian longcase clock in oak. (Leys, Antwerp)
$3,800 £1,760

18th century mahogany longcase clock by Matthew and Thos. Dutton. (Locke & England)
$19,435 £8,600

Symphonium 'Sublime Harmony' musical longcase clock. (Christie's S. Kensington) $8,545 £3,700

Early 18th century walnut marquetry longcase clock, 84in. high. (Olivers)$9,490 £4,200

219

GRANDFATHER CLOCKS

Fine late Victorian mahogany longcase clock 107in. high. (Christie's S. Kensington) $6,265 £2,900

George III mahogany longcase clock by Thos. Hughes, London, 8ft. 2in. high. (Christie's) $2,250 £1,000

Late George III mahogany longcase clock by Frodsham & Son, Kensington, 8ft.4in. high. (Christie's) $4,275 £1,900

Small marquetry longcase clock by Benjamin Wright, London, 6ft.6in. high. (Sotheby's) $6,440 £2,800

Early 18th century marquetry walnut longcase clock by T. Bridge. (J. Francis, T. Jones & Sons) $6,300 £2,800

Oak longcase clock by Corless Stockwell. (R. H. Ellis) $2,375 £1,050

French month-going timepiece longcase regulator in mahogany case, 82in. high. (Christie's) $5,650 £2,500

18th century eight-day clock in a carved oak case. (Sotheby Bearne) $1,350 £600

Oak grandfather clock by J. McKerrow. (Alfred Mossop & Co.) $1,035 £480

Late George II cream and apple green lacquered longcase clock, 2.53m. high, circa 1740, by Isaac Nickals. (Phillips) $22,600 £10,000

Late 17th century marquetry longcase clock by Ed. Norton, Warwick, 6ft.9in. high. (Christie's) $6,750 £3,000

18th century mahogany longcase clock by Thomas Wiggan, Bristol. (Alonzo Dawes & Hoddell) $3,995 £1,850

Oak dead-beat longcase clock with brass dial, circa 1855, 92in. high. (Sotheby's Belgravia) $2,810 £1,250

George III mahogany longcase clock by John Thompson, London 7ft.6in. high. (Christie's) $3,920 £1,750

Burr elmwood longcase clock by Wm. Sellers, London, 7ft. 1in. high. (Sotheby's) $5,875 £2,800

Walnut marquetry longcase clock by Fra. Coulton in St. Anns, circa 1690, 8ft.5in. high. (Sotheby's) $8,135 £3,600

Late Georgian mahogany longcase clock by Reynolds, Oxford, 7ft.3in. high. (Christie's) $1,075 £480

Burr walnut longcase clock by Joseph Tipp, London, 7ft.4in. high. (Sotheby's) $4,295 £1,900

George II red japanned longcase clock by John Lister, London, 8ft.2in. high. (Sotheby's) $3,165 £1,400

'George IV' mahogany longcase clock, circa 1825, 97in. high. (Sotheby's Belgravia) $1,170 £520

Walnut marquetry longcase clock by Chas. James Crisp, Bristol, 7ft.4in. high. (Sotheby's) $4,745 £2,100

'William IV' mahogany longcase clock, circa 1835, 97in. high, with rosewood inlaid door. (Sotheby's Belgravia) $1,460 £650

George III mahogany longcase clock by John Powell, London, 7ft. high. (Christie's) $3,360 £1,500

Mid 19th century mahogany longcase clock, 92½in. high. (Sotheby's Belgravia) $1,170 £520

Early 19th century mahogany longcase clock, dial signed J. N. O. Green, Barnstaple, 82in. high. (Sotheby's Belgravia) $1,350 £600

Victorian mahogany longcase regulator with panelled plinth, 6ft.4½in. high. (Christie's)$7,200 £3,200

Early longcase clock by A. Fromanteel, London, 6ft. 3in. high. (Christie's) $18,000 £8,000

George II walnut provincial longcase clock, dial signed E. Greatrex, Birmingham, 7ft.3in. high. (Christie's)$2,585 £1,150

Scottish mahogany longcase clock by L. Dalgleish and A. Dickie, Edinburgh, 7ft.6in. high. (Christie's)$4,035 £1,800

Mahogany longcase regulator, silvered dial signed E. H. Suggate, London, 6ft.2in. high. (Christie's) $6,750 £3,000

Marquetry longcase clock by J. Windmills, London, late 17th century, 7ft. 8½in. high. (Christie's) $9,000 £4,000

George II walnut longcase clock, signed Foster, London, 7ft. 5in. high. (Christie's) $3,375 £1,500

Late 17th/early 18th century walnut and marquetry longcase clock. (Parsons, Welch & Cowell) $5,750 £2,500

Georgian oak longcase clock in plain case, 6ft. 8in. high. (Christie's) $3,375 £1,500

Charles II walnut and parquetry longcase clock by William Clement, London, 6ft.7in. high. (Christie's) $7,650 £3,400

Mid Georgian mahogany longcase clock by N. Blondell, Guernsey, 9ft. high. (Christie's) $4,050 £1,800

Unusual painted mahogany musical calendar longcase clock, 8ft. 10in. high. (Sotheby's) $8,280 £3,600

Georgian oak and mahogany longcase clock by Nathaniel Brown, Manchester, 7ft.2in. high. (Christie's) $4,275 £1,900

George III mahogany longcase clock on bracket feet, signed Isaac Hurley, London, 7ft.8in. high. (Christie's) $4,725 £2,100

Satinwood longcase clock, signed O. Vali, London, 80in. high, 1860-80. (Sotheby's Belgravia) $4,500 £2,000

Boulle longcase clock in waisted arched case, mid 19th century, 81½in. high. (Sotheby's Belgravia) $7,740 £3,600

Mahogany longcase clock by Barker of Wigan, 8ft. 1in. high. (Christie's) $4,050 £1,800

Mid Georgian green lacquered longcase clock with chinoiserie decoration, by S. Harris, 8ft.8in. high. (Christie's) $4,590 £2,050

George III mahogany longcase clock by Wm. Franklin, London, 7ft. 3in. high. (Sotheby's) $4,370 £1,900

Figured and inlaid mahogany longcase clock by John Halliwell, 92in. high. (Christopher Sykes) $3,115 £1,450

Unusual late 19th century French colonial hardwood bracket clock, 36in. high. (Phillips) $870 £385

George I burr walnut month longcase clock by Daniel Delander, 6ft. 11in. high.(Sotheby's) $8,050 £3,500

Scottish George III mahogany longcase clock by J. Houden, Edinburgh, 6ft. 10in. high. (Sotheby's) $3,680 £1,600

LANTERN CLOCKS

17th century brass lantern clock by Tho. Wheeler, 13in. high. (Robert W. Skinner Inc.) $2,700 £1,227

Cromwellian brass lantern clock with thirty-hour movement. (Palmeira Auction Rooms) $2,925 £1,300

Miniature brass lantern clock, 7½in. high. (Vost's) $2,050 £1,000

Brass lantern clock by Stephen Levitt, circa 1690. (J. M. Welch & Son) $3,670 £1,700

English brass miniature lantern clock, unsigned, 9¾in. high. (Christie's) $6,750 £3,000

Small alarm lantern timepiece by Joseph Knibb, London, 7in. high, sold with a wooden bracket. (Sotheby's) $6,780 £3,000

17th century brass lantern clock, by John Stakes, Dartford, 16in. high. (Graves, Son & Pilcher) $2,160 £1,000

Early 18th century brass lantern clock by John Draper, London, 14½in. high. (Alonzo Dawes & Hoddell) $3,300 £1,500

Lantern clock, dial signed Edward Stanton, London, 15in. high. (Sotheby's) $4,050 £1,800

Late 17th century brass lantern clock. (Phillips) $2,415 £1,050

Lantern clock with 6½in. dial by T. Budgen, Reigate, 16in. high. (Sotheby's) $1,840 £800

19th century brass cased lantern clock after Richard Raiment, Bury, 23¼in. high. (Phillips) $1,100 £550

Patinated metal and glass clock, 38cm. high, 1930's. (Sotheby's Belgravia) $615 £280

Lalique frosted glass clock, 16cm. high, circa 1920. (Sotheby's Belgravia) $765 £350

Mid 19th century gilt and patinated bronze mantel clock, 18in. high. (Sotheby's) $705 £340

Early 19th century French ormolu mantel clock, 16in. high. (Vincent & Vanderpump) $3,520 £1,600

Fine bronze and ormolu mantel clock with Sevres panel. (Vernon's) $1,500 £650

19th century gilt cased French striking mantel clock, inset with porcelain panels. (D. M. Nesbit & Co.) $475 £210

Alarm day and night clock by John Hilderson, London, 1ft.9¼in. high. (Sotheby's) $39,000 £18,000

Bronze clock showing a group of athletes, circa 1900, with modern movement. (Sotheby's Belgravia) $65 £30

Fine Louis XVI ormolu mantel clock, signed Bouchet du Roy a Paris, 22in. high. (Christie's) $26,400 £12,000

Late 19th century brass cased mantel clock with enamel dial. (Phillips) $370 £160

19th century French ormolu mantel clock. (Bradley & Vaughan) $1,550 £680

Austrian F. Kunz musical mantel clock with two-air cylinder movement, circa 1880, 1ft.5in. high. (Sotheby's Belgravia)$800 £350

225

Gilt bronze mantel clock with polychrome enamel dial, 19½in. high, circa 1890. (Sotheby's Belgravia) $1,289 £620

19th century French mantel clock by J. Marti et Cie., 32cm. high, with glass dome. (Sotheby Humberts) $388 £180

Carved beechwood mantel clock, 23in. high, circa 1910. (Sotheby's Belgravia) $499 £240

Pink Sevres porcelain mantel clock, 1860's, 15¾in. high. (Sotheby's Belgravia) $852 £410

19th century lyre clock in porcelain case, movement by Kinable. (Phillips) $5,684 £2,800

Ormolu and marble mantel clock, circa 1870, 19in. high, dial signed Daniere a Paris. (Sotheby's Belgravia) $1,913 £920

Boulle mantel clock with enamel numerals, 1880's, 13½in. high. (Sotheby's Belgravia) $915 £440

Mid Victorian mantelpiece clock in brass and bronze mounted case. (Lacy Scott) $588 £290

Good ormolu malachite and lapis part clock garniture, circa 1860, stamped Bourdin, Paris. (Sotheby's Belgravia) $1,664 £800

White marble and gilt metal mantel clock, dial signed Lemerle-Charpentier, Paris, 1870's, 25½in. high. (Sotheby's Belgravia) $1,497 £720

Gilt bronze and porcelain mantel timepiece by Heuret Horloger du Roy, 16in. high, 1870's. (Sotheby's Belgravia) $873 £420

Gilt and patinated bronze and marble mantel clock, circa 1840, 23in. high. (Sotheby's Belgravia) $707 £340

Fine ormolu mantel clock in rococo case, 1870's, 26½in. high. (Sotheby's Belgravia)$1,622 £780

Liberty & Co. 'Tudric' pewter and enamel clock, circa 1905, 25.5cm. high. (Sotheby's Belgravia) $416 £190

Gilt bronze and porcelain mantel clock signed Levy Freres a Paris, circa 1870, 13¾in. high. (Sotheby's Belgravia) $956 £460

Regency period mahogany cased mantel clock, 13in. high. (Christopher Sykes) $1,026 £475

Mid 19th century boulle mantel clock by J. Marti et Cie, 17¼in. high. (Sotheby's) $388 £180

Modern gilt bronze and porcelain mantel clock, 18in. high, in lyre-shaped case. (Sotheby's Belgravia) $1,144 £550

Seth Thomas glass and brass mantel clock with enamel floral motif. (Robert W. Skinner Inc.)$1,150 £520

19th century Dutch Delft clock with brass works, 18½in. high. (Robert W. Skinner Inc.) $600 £270

Bronze and ormolu 'Renaissance' mantel clock, circa 1870, 25½in. high. (Sotheby's Belgravia) $873 £420

Bronze and ormolu mantel clock, 12in. high, circa 1860-80. (Sotheby's Belgravia) $998 £480

Bronze patinated and gilt bronze globe clock, 1880's, 20in. high. (Sotheby's Belgravia) $935 £450

Gilt bronze mantel clock, 1880's, 16in. high, with porcelain dial. (Sotheby's Belgravia) $644 £310

Dutch gilt travelling clock by Johannes van Ceulen. (Eaton & Hollis) $3,780 £1,750

Fine quality French clock, circa 1850, 10in. high. (Gray's Antique Mews) $845 £375

Unusual Edwardian 'Cycling' mantel timepiece in brass. (Phillips) $280 £130

Early 20th century ivory cased rectangular boudoir clock, probably Swiss, 7cm. high. (Sotheby's Belgravia) $440 £190

Regency mahogany mantel timepiece by Thomas Harlow, London, 15in. high. (Sotheby Humberts) $756 £350

19th century French ormolu mantel clock with porcelain dial. (Hobbs Parker) $649 £320

Gilt spelter mantel clock with glass dome, circa 1880. (Alfie's Antique Market) $326 £145

Edwardian mahogany cased mantel clock with dome top. (Phillips) $61 £30

French Empire clock in bronze and ormolu. (Alfie's Antique Market) $474 £235

Urn-shaped revolving band ormolu clock by Paul Rimbault. (Drewatt, Watson & Barton) $5,400 £2,500

French mantel clock with gilt metal dial, 23in. high, in red tortoiseshell case. (Sotheby Humberts) $1,123 £520

Gilt bronze mantel clock by Rocquet, Paris, 40cm. high. (Leys, Antwerp) $965 £450

Alarm day and night clock by John Hilderson. (Sotheby's) $36,900 £18,000

Mantel clock by Rollin, Paris, in the form of a large snail with a child on its back. (Bracketts) $1,209 £560

Early 18th century gilt metal astronomical travelling clock by Wm. Winrowe, 10in. high. (Christie's) $1,295 £600

Ormolu mantel clock with Meissen fittings. (Smith-Woolley & Perry) $1,372 £610

Mantel clock with white enamel dial by J. W. Beason, London, 11¾in. high. (Sotheby Humberts) $561 £260

English 17th century table clock by Robert Grinkin, London, case 4½in. square. (John D. Fleming & Co.) $34,776 £16,100

17th century Polish brass hexagonal table clock. (Phillips) $7,650 £3,400

Brass timepiece in a floral engraved case by James Muirhead & Son. (Christie's S. Kensington) $2,765 £1,350

19th century French gilt striking mantel clock. (D. M. Nesbit & Co.) $453 £210

French mantel clock in mahogany case, circa 1885, eight-day movement. (Alfie's Antique Market) $312 £120

French Edwardian inlaid mahogany mantel clock. (Alfie's Antique Market) $151 £70

Silver desk clock by Faberge with circular enamel dial, 4¼in. diam. (Heathcote Ball & Co.) $9,504 £4,400

French mantel clock mounted in gilt metal cylinder movement. (Phillips) $174 £85

Augusburg tabernacle clock of 1700, veneered with tortoiseshell and stained horn. (UTO Auktions, Zurich) $172,800 £80,000

French gilt metal clock of Louis XVI design, 11½in. high. (Sotheby Humberts) $560 £260

19th century Dresden cased mantel clock, 11½in. wide. (Woolley & Wallis) $1,620 £750

19th century French marble pillar clock. (J. M. Welch & Son) $388 £180

Good 19th century French mantel clock decorated in the Buhl manner. (Phillips) $246 £120

Mahogany cased clock with tulipwood banding, 25in. high. (Garrod Turner) $2,580 £1,200

Black Forest organ clock in Gothic styled oak case, 34½in. high. (Christie's S. Kensington) $2,590 £1,200

MANTEL CLOCKS

American alarm clock by Jerome, circa 1880. (Alfie's Antique Market) $100 £45

George III ebonised bracket clock by Paterson, Edinburgh. (Phillips) $462 £200

'Enfield' mantel clock in well figured walnut case, 10½in. high, circa 1930. (Christopher Sykes) $185 £80

Fine ornamental brass chiming clock with French Japy movement. (Honiton Galleries) $452 £200

19th century boulle and gilt bronze bracket clock by Martinot a Paris, 32in. high. (Sotheby's Belgravia) $2,000 £950

Liberty & Co. pewter and enamel clock, circa 1905, 20cm. high. (Sotheby's Belgravia) $2,195 £950

Large Goldscheider Art Nouveau terracotta clock, circa 1900, 95cm. high. (Sotheby's Belgravia) $2,080 £900

Fine desk clock in the form of a ship's wheel, circa 1850, 10in. high. (Christopher Sykes) $845 £365

Liberty's 'Tudric' pewter clock with blue enamel face. (Alfie's Antique Market) $145 £65

Early 20th century cast metal clock showing footballers, 18cm. (Sotheby's Belgravia) $165 £75

20th century rococo boulle bracket clock with enamel dial, 40½in. high. (Sotheby's Belgravia) $2,800 £1,350

19th century French brass and glazed mantel clock with porcelain panels and pillars, 16½in. high. (Christie's S. Kensington) $1,500 £680

Black Forest trumpeter clock, circa 1860, 15in. high. (Gray's Antique Mews) $520 £230

Victorian black marble mantel clock with brass fittings. (Phillips) $105 £45

Massive marble clock, 1930's, 29.5cm. high. (Sotheby's Belgravia) $284 £130

Inlaid mantel clock by Barnsdale. (Honiton Galleries) $585 £260

American alarm clock, circa 1890. (Alfie's Antique Market) $160 £70

Large Meissen mantel clock, 23in. high, unmarked. (Neales) $1,800 £800

19th century white marble and ormolu mantel clock, 18in. high. (Christie's S. Kensington) $1,050 £480

Inlaid mantel clock designed by Josef Olbrich, 1902, 35cm. high. (Sotheby's Belgravia) $6,000 £2,600

Victorian brass watchstand, 5½in. high. (Christopher Sykes) $85 £40

Rare 'Hours Clock' by John Bell, 1851, in gilt on repousse copper. (Alfie's Antique Market) $515 £225

Late 19th century Plaue on Havel clockcase, 40.5cm. high. (Sotheby's Belgravia) $680 £300

Red boulle mantel clock, circa 1880, 16¾in. high. (Sotheby's Belgravia) $685 £330

231

MANTEL CLOCKS

Unusual bronze mantel clock on double scroll base, 20in. high, circa 1870. (Sotheby's Belgravia) $335 £150

Charles X gilt bronze mantel clock with outside count wheel, circa 1830, 14in. high. (Sotheby's Belgravia) $860 £400

19th century French ormolu and gros-bleu porcelain mantel clock of Louis XVI design, 24in. wide. (Christie's) $1,800 £800

Bronze mantel clock, dial with Roman numerals, circa 1860, 9½in. high. (Sotheby's Belgravia) $450 £200

Unusual Chinese rosewood table clock and stand, with enamel dial and gilt surround, circa 1800. (Sotheby's) $1,795 £780

Gilt bronze mantel clock with outside count wheel, circa 1870, 25in. high. (Sotheby's Belgravia) $860 £400

Early 19th century mahogany grande sonnerie mantel clock by Dubois & Fils, Jura, 10in. high. (Sotheby's)$3,220 £1,400

Parcel gilt bronze mantel clock, case flanked by winged female sphinxes, circa 1830, 19in. high. (Sotheby's Belgravia) $965 £450

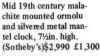

Mid 19th century malachite mounted ormolu and silvered metal mantel clock, 7½in. high. (Sotheby's)$2,990 £1,300

Rare two-faced mahogany ship's clock by Litherland Davies & Co., Liverpool, circa 1840. (Sotheby's) $1,875 £1,250

Viennese gilt wood David and Goliath grande sonnerie mantel clock, 19in. high. (Sotheby's) $2,990 £1,300

Ithaca parlor model calendar clock in walnut case, with double dial.(Robert W. Skinner Inc.) $2,000 £910

Art Nouveau style oak cased mantel clock. (Vernon's) $80 £35

Mid 19th century boulle mantel clock, signed Fearn a Paris, 10½in. high. (Sotheby's Belgravia) $750 £350

Marble mantel clock, dial signed Charles Frodsham & Co., Paris, circa 1880, 14¾in. high. (Sotheby's Belgravia) $630 £280

Mid 19th century gilt bronze mantel clock, dial signed Gudin a Paris, 13½in. high. (Sotheby's Belgravia) $425 £190

Patinated and gilt bronze terrestrial globe clock, stamped G. H. Bte. SGDS, circa 1901, 26½in. high. (Sotheby's Belgravia) $4,730 £2,200

Napoleon III period Louis XV style mantel clock in walnut fire gilt bronze, 94cm. high. (Leys, Antwerp) $1,245 £576

German eight-day striking mantel clock, circa 1900. (Alfie's Antique Market) $425 £185

A Meissen armorial rococo clock case and stand, 54.5cm. high, circa 1735. (Christie's) $4,300 £1,900

Shelf clock by Aaron Willard in inlaid mahogany case, circa 1820. (Sotheby's U.S.A.) $10,000 £4,664

Large Louis XV gilt bronze mantel clock, dial signed Monbro Aine a Paris, circa 1840, 35½in. high. (Sotheby's Belgravia) $5,375 £2,500

Cast metal clock showing a racing cyclist, circa 1900, 18cm. high. (Sotheby's Belgravia) $140 £65

Gilt and patinated bronze globe timepiece, circa 1880, 29¾in. high, movement stamped Chles.(Sotheby's Belgravia) $7,525 £3,500

MANTEL CLOCKS

Ormolu and marble mantel clock, signed Briscard a Paris, circa 1870, 11¼in. high. (Sotheby's Belgravia) $860 £400

Victorian black marble mantel clock with eight-day movement. (Vernon's) $145 £65

Gilt bronze mantel clock, circa 1850, 20¼in. high. (Sotheby's Belgravia) $860 £400

Gilt bronze mantel clock, circa 1880, dial with enamel Roman numerals, 14½in. high. (Sotheby's Belgravia) $1,180 £550

Ormolu and Sevres porcelain mantel clock on gilt wood stand, circa 1880, 19¾in. high. (Sotheby's Belgravia) $1,980 £920

Gilt and patinated bronze mantel clock, dial signed Gille L'Aine, Paris, circa 1870, 21½in. high. (Sotheby's Belgravia) $1,460 £680

Clock from a gilt bronze clock garniture, dial with enamel Roman numerals, circa 1880. (Sotheby's Belgravia) $690 £320

Gilt and silvered bronze mantel clock, circa 1870, movement signed Deniere a Paris, 18¼in. high. (Sotheby's Belgravia) $750 £350

Gilt bronze and Sevres mantel clock, dial signed Lepaute a Paris, circa 1880, 18½in. high. (Sotheby's Belgravia) $1,890 £880

Gilt and patinated bronze mantel clock, circa 1860, 18in. high, surmounted by a group of a Turk and his Horse. (Sotheby's Belgravia) $900 £420

Green boulle mantel clock with sunburst pendulum, 14in. high, circa 1878. (Sotheby's Belgravia) $1,030 £480

Porcelain and ormolu mantel clock, enamel dial with Roman numerals, 15in. high, circa 1880. (Sotheby's Belgravia) $1,460 £680

Gilt brass and champleve enamel mantel clock, dial inscribed Coventry Lever Co., Birmingham, circa 1890, 12in. high. (Sotheby's Belgravia) $690 £320

George III tortoiseshell musical bracket clock for the Turkish market, by Geo. Prior, London, 31in. high. (Sotheby's) $6,900 £3,000

Gilt metal and marble mantel clock, stamped Manning, Worcester, 19in. high, circa 1860. (Sotheby's Belgravia) $360 £160

Gilt bronze and porcelain mantel clock, circa 1880, 20in. high. (Sotheby's Belgravia) $2,365 £1,100

Early 19th century 'Louis XV' gilt bronze mantel clock, dial signed Priqueler A Lure, 16½in. high. (Sotheby's Belgravia) $750 £350

George III mahogany balloon mantel clock by Ellicott, London, circa 1790, 19½in. high. (Sotheby's) $4,370 £1,900

Gilt bronze and enamel mantel clock, movement signed Howell James & Co., Paris, circa 1880, 11½in. high. (Sotheby's Belgravia) $860 £400

Late 19th century parcel gilt bronze lyre timepiece, with sunburst finial, 15½in. high. (Sotheby's Belgravia) $900 £420

White marble and gilt bronze lyre mantel clock, dial signed Leroy Fils, 14in. high, circa 1890. (Sotheby's Belgravia) $1,890 £880

Red boulle bracket clock with outside count wheel, circa 1870, 15¼in. high. (Sotheby's Belgravia) $1,200 £560

Late 19th century American mantel clock with alarm, in mahogany case, 12in. high. (Vernon's) $180 £85

Gilt brass and champleve enamel mantel clock, circa 1880, 13in. high. (Sotheby's Belgravia) $560 £260

MANTEL CLOCKS

Unusual tortoise clock with eight-day French movement, signed Dreyfus. (Sotheby King & Chasemore) $1,245 £580

German hexagonal table clock with movement, signed Michael Fabian Thorn, 11cm. diam. (Christie's) $3,485 £1,550

Ormolu and Sevres porcelain mantel clock, dial signed Raingo Fres., Paris, 12¾in. wide, circa 1880.(Sotheby's Belgravia) $1,115 £520

Good and unusual 19th century Japanese striking screen clock, by Takamura Takesuke, 270mm. high. (Sotheby's) $17,160 £7,800

French mid 20th century painted enamel and gilt metal mantel clock in the form of a screen, signed CSK. (Sotheby's Belgravia) $940 £420

Early French gilt metal pendule de voyage, by Beckera, 8½in. high. (Christie's) $3,920 £1,750

Early 19th century French longcase regulator in ebonised pedestal case, by J. S. Bourdier, Paris, 6ft.2in. high. (Christie's) $12,320 £5,500

9 carat gold cased mantel clock on easel support, Goldsmiths & Silversmiths Co. Ltd., circa 1912, 11.6cm. high. (Sotheby's Belgravia) $1,060 £460

Ornate French 19th century mantel clock. (R. H. Ellis & Sons) $1,290 £600

17th century Flemish musical clock, signed Jean Knaeps, Liege, 2ft.11in. high. (Sotheby's Zurich) $50,850 £22,500

Empire ormolu mantel clock, 22in. high. (Christie's S. Kensington) $1,770 £820

Bronzed brass mantel clock by Shuttleworth, Piccadilly, 16½in. high. (Christie's) $855 £380

Skeleton clock with pierced silver ring, signed Liddell, Liverpool, 18in. high, with a glass dome.(Sotheby's) $3,150 £1,400

Fine brass cathedral skeleton clock signed C. Fiedemann, Liverpool, 24½in. high. (Christie's S. Kensington) $4,860 £2,250

Mid Victorian brass skeleton clock, circa 1860, 15½in. high. (Sotheby's) $925 £400

Fine skeleton clock by James Condliff, Liverpool, 20½in. high, with glass dome. (Sotheby's) $8,740 £3,800

Rare chiming skeleton clock by James Condliff, Liverpool, dated 1860, 2ft. 1in. high, sold with a glass dome. (Sotheby's) $22,500 £10,000

19th century six-pillar fusee skeleton timepiece, in glass shade, 11½in. high. (Vernon's) $785 £350

WALL CLOCKS

Late 19th century mahogany framed wall clock with Roman numerals. (Phillips) $70 £30

Antique rosewood cased wall clock, circa 1840, 23in. high. (Christopher Sykes) $490 £225

Late 19th century mahogany framed wall clock with enamel dial. (Phillips) $110 £50

Gilt bronze cartel clock with outside count wheel, 17in. high, circa 1870. (Sotheby's Belgravia) $900 £420

Custom mahogany weight driven banjo timepiece, dial signed Elmer O. Stennes, Mass. (Robert S. Skinner Inc.) $950 £420

'Louis XV' gilt bronze cartel clock, signed Veuvray Freres, circa 1860, 20in. high. (Sotheby's Belgravia) $1,075 £500

237

WALL CLOCKS

Late 18th/early 19th century French gilt metal repeating wall clock by Perache, Paris, 22in. high. (Lacy Scott) $1,340 £660

19th century mahogany wall clock with enamel dial by Johnson, York. (Phillips) $395 £170

Victorian mahogany framed eight-day wall clock. (Phillips) $115 £50

German Zappler clock, lacking pendulum, 11½in. high. (Christie's) $2,585 £1,150

French gilt wood cartel clock, signed J. Marti et Cie, 39in. high. (Christie's S. Kensington) $4,970 £2,300

Louis XVI ormolu cartel clock, movement, signed Le Nepveu a Paris, 25½in. high. (Christie's) $4,400 £2,000

18th century hooded wall clock in ebonised case, inscribed Ratcliff W. Pool. (Parsons, Welch & Cowell) $755 £350

German telleruhr with concentric calendar ring, 20½in. high. (Christie's) $2,475 £1,100

Tavern wall clock in oak case, circa 1850, 56in. high. (J. M. Welch & Son) $520 £240

Bracket clock by MacKay & Cunningham, Edinburgh, in tortoiseshell veneered brass inlaid case. (P. F. Windibank) $3,885 £1,800

Unusual early 20th century battery driven electric wall timepiece by the Brillie Bros., 18in. high. (Sotheby's) $1,725 £750

Late 19th century American 'Ansonia' wall clock with mahogany case. (Vernon's) $125 £60

Early 19th century Viennese walnut grande sonnerie wall clock, 42in. high. (Sotheby's) $9,200 £4,000

'Louis XVI' gilt bronze cartel clock, dial signed Paris, circa 1870, 33in. high. (Sotheby's Belgravia) $1,765 £820

Early 18th century Dutch Stoelklok with original pendulum and weights, 29in. high. (Boardman's) $3,255 £1,500

19th century walnut cased wall clock with octagonal head. (Phillips) $170 £75

An unusual Sevres gilt metal mounted pendant clock, 46cm. high, circa 1880. (Sotheby's Belgravia) $1,100 £480

George III 'Act of Parliament' clock in black lacquered case, 56in. high. (Olivers) $2,825 £1,250

19th century French wall clock with porcelain face and painted surround. (Vernon's) $510 £220

Victorian Vienna style enamel dialled wall clock with Tunbridgeware style inlay. (Phillips) $165 £80

19th century cuckoo clock in walnut case, 30in. high. (Hy. Duke & Son) $560 £250

19th century American mahogany framed Seth Thomas wall clock. (Vernon's) $140 £60

Gilt bronze cartel clock, circa 1880, 20¾in. high, with white marble dial. (Sotheby's Belgravia) $935 £450

Custom mahogany weight driven banjo timepiece with eagle finial. (Robert W. Skinner Inc.) $1,200 £545

239

Novelty bicycle watch timepiece
(Christie's S. Kensington)
$170 £80

French gold cylinder watch by
Thouret, Paris, 33mm. diam.
(Christie's) $1,530 £680

Gold and pearl set verge watch, in
the form of a basket, by Chevalier
& Cochet, circa 1800, 34mm. long.
(Sotheby's) $7,500 £3,400

18 carat gold pocket watch
by Dent of London with half
hunter case. (Boardman's)
$2,205 £980

Double-sided astronomical gold
watch inscribed J. W. Benson,
London, circa 1870. (Peter
Ineichen, Zurich)
$265,370 £122,857

Rare and interesting engraved silver
gilt skull watch with silver crucifix,
late 18th or early 19th century,
77mm. long. (Sotheby's)
$176,000 £80,000

Gilt metal framed crystal
crucifix watch with silver
dial by D. Oltramare, 60mm.
long. (Sotheby's)
$4,840 £2,200

19th century gold cased two-barrel
lever watch by Breguet, 52mm.
diam. (Sotheby's) $55,000 £25,000

17th century marrow shaped verge
watch with crystal lid and silver
cover, by David du Chemin, Rouen,
47.5mm. long. (Sotheby's)
$15,000 £7,000

18ct. gold chronograph, 1889.
(Manchester Auction Mart)
$518 £240

Watch in a silver case by
Lister of Halifax, dated
1774. (Phillips) $520 £230

Silver cased watch by Abraham
Louis Breguet, circa 1805.
(Shakespear, McTurk &
Graham) $2,160 £1,000

Early 19th century gilt metal mandarin ring watch set with split pearls and garnets, 33mm. diam. (Sotheby's) $6,600 £3,000

Swiss gold and enamel cylinder watch by F. L. Achinard & Nouveau, Geneva, 33mm. diam. (Christie's) $900 £400

Very small gold keyless watch with alarm by Breguet, circa 1836, 13.5mm. diam. (Sotheby's) $58,300 £26,500

Good, rare and important early 17th century silver and gilt metal cruciform watch by Abráham Cusins, 45mm. (Sotheby's) $92,400 £42,000

Gold quarter repeating keyless hunter pocket watch. (Christie's S. Kensington) $16,200 £7,200

Oval silver watch for the Turkish Market, with Turkish numerals and subsidiary lunar dial, 63mm. long. (Sotheby's) $5,500 £2,500

Fine English Lister watch in good condition. (Phillips) $495 £220

Dresden quarter repeating watch. (Christie's S. Kensington) $33,900 £15,000

Gold and tortoiseshell pair-cased verge watch by David Lestourgeon, London, 1694, 52mm. diam. (Sotheby's) $7,920 £3,600

Early 19th century pair-cased key-wound verge watch by Charles Cabrier, London. (Sotheby Bearne)$1,685 £780

French multi-dial silver cased pocket watch. (Phillips) $945 £420

Watch by William Anthony with blue enamel back set with pearls and diamonds, circa 1810, 3½in. high. (Sotheby's) $156,240 £72,000

Gold coin watch formed from a 1902 £4 piece, 36mm. diam. (Christie's) $2,250 £1,000

Gold hunting cased pocket chronometer by Brillman & Co., London, 1863, 52.5mm. diam. (Sotheby's) $3,450 £1,500

Good gold pair-cased cylinder watch by Thos. Grignion, London, 1767, 47mm. diam. (Sotheby's) $2,990 £1,300

Silver pair-cased false pendulum verge watch by Marke Hawkins, 53mm. diam. (Christie's) $1,300 £580

Gold savage two-pin lever watch by G. Cashard, London, 1827, with heavy gold chain and fob seal. (Sotheby's) $1,840 £800

Fine gold keyless lever watch by Charles Frodsham, London, 1884, 50mm. diam. (Christie's) $1,935 £860

Large silver pair-cased verge watch, signed Wm. Smith, 81mm. diam. (Sotheby's Belgravia) $2,760 £1,250

Good gold half-hunting cased minute repeating keyless lever watch by Russells Ltd., Liverpool, 1900. (Sotheby's) $5,750 £2,500

Swiss gold quarter repeating Jacquemart verge watch, 56mm. diam. (Christie's) $4,725 £2,100

Silver pair-cased verge watch, signed Thos. Gorsuch, Salop, 56mm. diam. (Christie's) $900 £400

Fine 9ct. gold self winding wrist watch by Harwood, with luminous numerals and hands, 1924, 29mm. diam. (Sotheby's) $1,035 £450

Good gold open faced fusee keyless watch by Barraud & Lunds, 1902, 52mm. diam. (Sotheby's) $2,645 £1,150

Silver pair-cased verge watch by Edward East, London, 58mm. diam. (Christie's) $1,575 £700

Gold hunting cased minute repeating keyless lever watch by Lange & Sohne, 58mm. diam. (Sotheby's) $34,500 £15,000

Silver pair-cased verge watch signed Corn. Herbert, London, 58mm. diam. (Christie's) $1,350 £600

Swiss silver keyless mystery watch signed A. S. & P. Mysterieuse, Brevete S. G. D. G., 53mm. diam. (Christie's) $1,440 £640

Early French silver verge watch by Estienne Hubert, Rouen, 54mm. diam. (Christie's) $6,100 £2,700

Swiss gold minute repeating keyless lever watch, 47mm. diam. (Christie's) $2,475 £1,100

Early 19th century gold and enamel quarter repeating musical watch for the Chinese market by Bovet, 64mm. diam. (Sotheby's) $19,550 £8,500

Swiss gold hunter cased minute repeating keyless lever calendar chronograph, signed Examined by Webster, 53mm. diam. (Christie's) $5,625 £2,500

Gold quarter repeating automation watch, circa 1820, 55mm. diam. (Sotheby's) $12,650 £5,500

Gold lever watch by D. Glasgow, London, 50mm. diam. (Christie's) $1,800 £800

Early 17th century gold and enamel pair-cased gold watch by Charles Bobinet, 1½in. diam. (Sotheby's) $95,480 £44,000

Good gold open faced Massey crank roller lever watch by Robert Roskell, Liverpool, 1827, 50mm. diam. (Sotheby's) $1,795 £780

Gold hunting cased keyless lever watch by Hasluck Brothers, London, 1893, 48mm. diam., with gold chain and fob. (Sotheby's Belgravia) $450 £200

Good 18th century gold cylinder ring watch set with rose diamonds, 17mm. diam. (Sotheby's) $2,190 £950

Gold hunting cased centre-seconds keyless lever watch, hallmarked 1900, 51mm. diam., with white enamel dial. (Sotheby's Belgravia) $630 £280

Gold and jasper cylinder watch, signed Thomas Hally, London, 50mm. diam. (Christie's) $7,200 £3,200

Small gold and turquoise set verge watch by Moulinie Bautte & Moynier, Geneva, circa 1830, 27mm. diam. (Sotheby's) $2,375 £1,050

Huaut enamel verge watch, signed Huaut. A. Son A. E., 44mm. diam. (Christie's) $13,500 £6,000

Fine gold hunter cased minute repeating keyless lever watch, signed Hamilton & Inches, No. 30046, 55mm. diam. (Christie's) $8,550 £3,800

Gold and enamel open faced lady's verge watch, signed Coeur Pere a Paris, 31mm. diam. (Sotheby's Belgravia) $920 £410

Swiss gold half hunter cased minute repeating keyless lever chronograph, 54mm. diam. (Christie's) $2,475 £1,100

19th century gold quarter repeating independent centre seconds lever watch by Lepine, Paris, 47mm. diam. (Sotheby's) $2,035 £900

Late 18th century gilt metal pair-cased striking cylinder chaise watch by Marriott, London, 132mm. diam. (Sotheby's) $3,840 £1,700

French gold and enamel bridge-cock verge watch, 47mm. diam. (Christie's) $4,275 £1,900

Gold half hunting cased keyless lever Karrusel, 1911, 52mm. diam. (Sotheby's) $6,900 £3,000

Silver hallmarked pair-cased watch by Jno. Robins, London, with enamel dial, 1822. (Sotheby King & Chasemore) $275 £120

Gold half hunter cased minute repeating keyless lever chronograph, London, 1908, 56mm. diam. (Christie's)$8,100 £3,600

Gold half hunting cased centre-seconds keyless lever watch, hallmarked 1901, 51mm. diam., with twist link and interlaced hoop gold chain. (Sotheby's Belgravia) $765 £340

Silver verge calendar watch, circa 1810, 53mm. diam. (Sotheby's) $1,350 £600

Silver cased full plate pocket chronometer by Robert Molyneux, hallmarked 1839, 57mm. diam. (Sotheby's) $4,520 £2,000

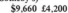

Swiss gold musical keyless lever watch, 56mm. diam. (Christie's) $4,050 £1,800

Silver quarter repeating alarm verge watch, signed Paul Beauvais, London, 55mm. diam. (Christie's) $1,745 £780

Gold hunting cased five minute repeating keyless lever watch by J. Alfred Jurgensen, Copenhagen, 54mm. diam. (Sotheby's) $9,660 £4,200

Silver pair-cased false pendulum verge watch by William Martin, Bristol, 55mm. diam. (Christie's) $1,395 £620

Multi-colour gold verge watch by Horne & Ashe, London, 1809, 47mm. diam. (Sotheby's) $2,215 £980

Gold and enamel duplex watch, signed Ilbery, London, 60mm. diam. (Christie's) $10,800 £4,800

Fine 9ct gold self-winding wrist watch by Harwood, 1929, ex-factory condition, 28mm. diam. (Sotheby's) $1,200 £520

Attractive late 18th century gold, enamel and diamond set ring watch made for the Turkish market by Markwich Markham, London, 19mm. (Sotheby's)
$15,400 £7,000

Silver cased multi-dial calendar watch, 60mm. diam. (Christie's)
$1,600 £725

Gold open faced quarter repeating keyless lever chronograph, dial signed F. A. Chandler, 51mm. diam. (Sotheby's Belgravia) $1,435 £650

Gold hunting cased lever watch by R. H. Goddard, London, 1900, 53mm. diam. (Sotheby's Belgravia) $2,025 £900

Gold open faced keyless lever watch, hallmarked 1909, 53mm. diam. (Sotheby's Belgravia) $495 £220

Gold half hunting cased keyless lever watch, hallmarked 1896, 51mm. diam. (Sotheby's Belgravia) $540 £240

Gold and enamel pair-cased watch and chatelaine. (Sotheby's)
$17,425 £8,500

Gold half hunting cased keyless lever watch by F. Stubbs, hallmarked 1886, 49mm. diam. (Sotheby's Belgravia) $405 £180

Gold hunting cased centre-seconds keyless lever watch by Newsomes & Co., Coventry, 1904, 58mm. diam. (Sotheby's Belgravia)
$1,215 £540

Gold pair-cased verge clockwatch by John Everell, London, 56mm. diam. (Sotheby's) $6,330 £2,800

Silver pair-cased chronometer watch, signed Jessop, Southampton Street, Strand, London, No. 1972, 61mm. diam. (Christie's)
$4,275 £1,900

Silver repousse cased calendar verge watch, signed Langin, London, circa 1730, 54mm. diam. (Christie's)
$3,585 £1,600

Good early 19th century gold and enamel centre-seconds duplex watch for the Chinese market by Ilbery of London, 69mm. diam. (Sotheby's)
$29,900 £13,000

Gold open faced lever watch by James McCabe, London, 1916, 41mm. diam., with gilt metal chain. (Sotheby's Belgravia)
$765 £340

Gold half hunting cased minute repeating lever watch, 51mm. diam. (Sotheby's Belgravia) $2,700 £1,200

Gold minute repeating hunting cased lever watch, hallmarked 1901, 55mm. diam. (Sotheby's Belgravia) $4,160 £1,850

Silver pair-cased false pendulum verge watch, signed William Harrison, London, 60mm. diam. (Christie's) $4,500 £2,000

Gold half hunting cased keyless lever watch by Dent, London, 48mm. diam., hallmarked 1885. (Sotheby's Belgravia) $695 £310

Good gold and split pearl set cylinder watch with gilt pearl set chain, circa 1820, 44mm. diam. (Sotheby's) $14,950 £6,500

Gold half hunting cased keyless lever watch with white enamel dial, 51mm. diam. (Sotheby's Belgravia) $335 £150

Repousse gold pair-cased verge watch by Archambo of London, 1731, 48mm. diam. (Sotheby's)
$4,070 £1,800

Small gold and enamel verge watch, circa 1820, 32mm. diam. (Sotheby's) $1,695 £750

Gold open faced keyless chronograph, hallmarked 1891, 50mm. diam., with gold chain. (Sotheby's Belgravia) $1,350 £600

247

CLOISONNE

One of a pair of late 19th century Chinese cloisonne ewers and covers, 42cm. high. (Sotheby's Belgravia) $1,520 £700

A Qianlong cloisonne wall vase, pear-shaped, with a sealing wax red cloisonne base imitating a wood stand, 25.3cm. (Sotheby's) $290 £130

One of a pair of cloisonne vases, 11½in. high. (Russell, Baldwin & Bright) $540 £250

One of a pair of large early 20th century cloisonne vases with powder blue ground, 24in. high.(Lacy Scott) $530 £260

Small cloisonne pear-shaped vase, turquoise ground, Qianlong period, 4¾in. high. (Christie's)$660 £300

Part of a Qianlong cloisonne enamel altar garniture, each of the five pieces decorated with the Eight Buddhist Emblems on a turquoise ground. (Sotheby's) $13,400 £6,000

One of a pair of large Ming cloisonne vases of archaic gu form, bearing six character Jingtai reignmark, 17th century, 18in. (Sotheby's) $4,460 £2,000

Cloisonne enamel meiping decorated with three bands of a scrolling peony, 11¾in. high. (Christie's)$930 £420

19th century Japanese cloisonne on white metal vase, signed Kyoto Namikawa, 8½in. high.(Christie's S. Kensington) $4,840 £2,200

One of a pair of cloisonne and gilt bronze censers, with domed covers and stands, 18th or early 19th century, 16in. (Christie's) $3,300 £1,500

One of a pair of clois-onne enamel vases, Japanese, 76.5cm. high. (Sotheby King & Chasemore) $4,970 £2,200

A cloisonne tripod censer and cover of archaic ding form and overall turquoise ground, 17th or 18th century, 8in. (Sotheby's) $890 £400

Late 19th century cloisonne pilgrim bottle, 30.5cm. high. (Sotheby's Belgravia) $575 £250

One of a pair of late 19th century cloisonne enamel vases, Japanese, 37cm. high. (Sotheby King & Chasemore)$1,035 £460

A Takahara cloisonne Sake pot and cover, 14.5cm. high, circa 1900. (Sotheby's Belgravia) $440 £190

One of a pair of cloisonne vases, 10½in. high. (Vidler & Co.) $185 £90

Cloisonne circular plaque, 14½in. diam. (James Harrison) $340 £150

Fine 19th century Ming period cloisonne vase, 11½in. high. (Christopher Sykes)$779 £345

One of a pair of Jiaqing cloisonne double gourd vases of rich lapis blue tone, 9in. (Sotheby's) $1,160 £520

unusual Qianlong cloisonne enamel stand modelled as a goose on a circular base of lotus petals, supporting a circular open stand, 8¼in. Sotheby's) $1,560 £700

One of a pair of Qianlong cloisonne urns and covers decorated with the Eight Buddhist Emblems on a turquoise ground, 24in. (Sotheby's) $19,000 £8,500

An unusual Qianlong cloisonne pagoda incense burner enclosing a spinach green jade column, 16¼in. (Sotheby's) $2,000 £900

Mid 19th century cloisonne vase, 69.8cm. high. (Sotheby's Belgravia) $675 £310

Shallow cloisonne dish, 8in. diam., on a hardwood stand. (Vidler & Co.) $92 £45

17th century Chinese cloisonne enamel tripod censer and cover, 12¼in. bronze stand. (Sotheby's) $1,920 £860

Ming dynasty cloisonne box and cover, dated 1426. (Whiteheads) $66,660 £33,000

Qianlong cylindrical cloisonne vase, applied with five small cylindrical vases, 14cm. (Christie's) $2,420 £1,100

One of a pair of Qianlong cloisonne elephants, the body in white, the harness and detachable howdah in colours on a turquoise ground, 19¾in. (Sotheby's) $24,550 £11,000

Cloisonne tripod cauldron of ding shape, 18th or early 19th century, 9½in. high. (Christie's) $1,650 £750

Victorian cloisonne polychrome enamel inkstand in cast brass, 7¾in. long. (Christopher Sykes) $290 £128

One of a pair of rare Qianlong small cloisonne covered koros, decorated with lotus and prunus on a turquoise ground, 6¾in. (Sotheby's) $2,750 £1,250

Late Ming cloisonne bowl decorated with Eight Buddhist Emblems, and a le (joy) character in scrollwork, 4½in (Christie's) $6,600 £3,000

Large 17th century cloisonne vase of archaic hu form with double gilt bronze lion masks with pendant rings, 17½in. (Sotheby's) $935 £420

One of a pair of 19th century cloisonne vases. (Biddle & Webb) $2,480 £1,150

Large Chinese cloisonne vase, circa 1900, 150cm. high, on wooden stand. (Sotheby's Belgravia) $8,680 £4,000

Qianlong cloisonne box and cover, 8in. diam. (Sotheby Humberts) $430 £200

Cloisonne tripod censer, with fruiting vine on turquoise ground, Chenghua reignmark, 17th or 18th century, 4½in. (Christie's) $1,430 £650

A 17th century cloisonne box and cover, the turquoise ground bearing chilong, ruyi heads and shou characters, 5¼in. (Sotheby's) $760 £340

7th century cloisonne bowl decoated with dragons and flowers, 3½in. (Christie's) $1,430 £650

One of a pair of 19th century Chinese cloisonne camels, 41cm. high. (Leys, Antwerp) $3,110 £1,440

One of a pair of late Ming cloisonne saucer dishes, 16th or early 17th century, 4¾in. diam. (Christie's) $575 £260

Qianlong cloisonne tripod censer with domed top, 5½in. (Christie's) $2,090 £950

A pair of large Chinese cloisonne horses, circa 1900. (Gray's Antique Mews) $4,100 £1,800

Qianlong cloisonne mug of European shape, decorated with peony scrolls on a turquoise ground, 4in. high. (Christie's) $2,860 £1,300

quare Qianlong cloisonne vase, ith bats and scrolls on turuoise ground, 5in. (Christie's) $700 £320

A pair of late 19th century Japanese cloisonne enamel vases, 24cm. high. (Sotheby King & Chasemore) $500 £230

One of a pair of 17th century cloisonne pricket candlesticks, with later prickets and wax pans, 20in. (Christie's) $4,180 £1,900

CLOISONNE

Circular silver and shaded cloisonne enamel bowl, Moscow, 1899-1908, 11.6cm. diam. (Sotheby's) $3,650 £1,600

A cloisonne bowl decorated overall with mille fleurs, circa 1880. (Sotheby's Belgravia) $1,200 £520

One of a pair of late 19th century turquoise ground cloisonne wall plates, 30.5cm. diam. (Sotheby's Belgravia) $530 £230

One of a pair of cloisonne vases, circa 1900, 24cm. high. (Sotheby's Belgravia) $1,725 £750

19th century cloisonne vase with flared hexagonal neck, 60cm. high. (Sotheby's Belgravia) $960 £420

Japanese Inaba Nanaho midnight blue ground cloisonne enamel vase, circa 1900, 12cm. high. (Sotheby King & Chasemore) $1,695 £750

COPPER AND BRASS

Late 19th century brass and copper kettle with ebony handle. (Vernon's) $55 £25

Brass and cast iron firegrate on tapering pillared supports, circa 1880. (Sotheby's Belgravia) $450 £200

19th century brass coal box with ring handles and ball feet. (Vernon's) $90 £40

19th century copper samovar with ebony handles. (Vernon's) $265 £120

Late 19th century Oriental brass tray with folding turned wood stand. (Vernon's) $185 £85

Art Nouveau style brass and iron log container. (Vernon's) $120 £55

19th century curved brass snuff box with hinged lid, 75cm. long. (Phillips) $55 £25

One of a pair of unusual brass and copper shaving mugs. (Alfie's Antique Market) $75 £35

17th century brass candle snuffer decorated with Virgin and Child, 7½in. long. (Robert W. Skinner Inc.) $500 £230

Good 19th century copper samovar, 45cm. high.(Phillips) $440 £190

Victorian copper and brass kettle. (Alfie's Antique Market)$100 £45

Large Cromwellian candlestick, circa 1650.(Sotheby's) $2,560 £1,250

One of a pair of mid 19th century English brass milk churns, 17in. high. (Sotheby's Belgravia) $1,380 £600

18th century Swiss nine-branch pricket candlestick on turned stem, incomplete, 29½in. high. (Robert W. Skinner Inc.) $400 £185

18th century German copper grape hod, 1ft.10in. high. (James Harrison) $450 £200

One of a pair of 16th century brass pricket candlesticks, 15½in. high.(Robert W. Skinner Inc.)$1,600 £750

Late 19th century brass desk set of pen tray and two candleholders. (Phillips) $110 £50

One of a pair of early 18th century brass candlesticks on a saucer base, 7¾in. high.(Robert W. Skinner Inc.) $450 £210

COPPER AND BRASS

Set of brass spherical weights from 56lb. to 4oz. (Walker, Barnett & Hill) $1,824 £800

All brass horse hair singer, 13¼in. long, circa 1860. (Christopher Sykes)$108 £48

18th century Dutch brass and copper tobacco box, 6½in. long. (Christopher Sykes) $192 £85

Cast brass letter rack or menu holder, circa 1850, 3in. long. (Christopher Sykes) $85 £38

One of a pair of brass mantel ornaments, circa 1870, 4¼in. wide. (Christopher Sykes) $60 £25

Pair of 18th century brass candle brackets.(Exchange Salerooms) $678 £300

19th century muffin seller's handbell, 10in. high, in perfect condition. (Christopher Sykes) $108 £48

Antique brass loving cup with handles copper riveted to body, circa 1850, 9in. high. (Christopher Sykes) $125 £55

Antique brass door knocker, 8in. high, with circular brass plate. (Christopher Sykes) $108 £48

One of a pair of 19th century gilt brass two-branch wall lights, 17in. high. (Christopher Sykes)$418 £185

Set of four antique copper measures of graduating sizes. (James Harrison) $632 £280

One of a pair of late 18th century American brass andirons, 25in. high. (Robert W. Skinner Inc.) $1,000 £440

Rare Welsh brass tobacco box, circa 1780, 7in. long. (Christopher Sykes) $192 £85

One of a pair of 17th century brass candlesticks, 9½in. high. (Robert W. Skinner Inc.) $600 £260

American copper horse and rider weather-vane, circa 1900, 31in. long. (Robert W. Skinner Inc.) $1,500 £650

Victorian copper tea urn with brass tap and handles. (Alfie's Antique Market) $180 £80

One of a pair of brass mantelpiece ornaments, circa 1810, 4½in. wide. (Christopher Sykes) $83 £37

George III apothecary's brass mortar, circa 1770, 4in. high. (Christopher Sykes) $61 £27

American copper and gold leaf eagle, circa 1900, 20in. high. (Robert W. Skinner Inc.) $450 £200

19th century copper preserve pan with two handles, circa 1840, 13¾in. diam. (Christopher Sykes) $192 £85

Solid brass pipe stopper, circa 1830, 1½in. high. (Christopher Sykes) $65 £29

One of a pair of brass candlesticks, 50cm. high. (Phillips) $135 £60

Set of six copper brass bound checkpump petroleum measures from 5 gallons to ½ gallon. (Walker, Barnett & Hill) $3,192 £1,400

French ormolu hanging scent bottle, 1900. (Alfie's Antique Market) $77 £38

255

English octagonal brass and tortoiseshell snuff box, circa 1700, 3¾in. long. (Sotheby's) $824 £380

Part of a set of ten brass weights graduating from 100gm. to 20kg. (Outhwaite & Litherland) $3,024 £1,400

Brass preserving pan with bronze handles, circa 1830, 12½in. diam. (Christopher Sykes) $128 £57

Dolphin plated brass bell, circa 1860. (Alfie's Antique Market) $270 £120

George III brass and copper urn, 40cm. high. (Phillips) $40 £20

Late 15th century Norwegian gilt copper mounted drinking horn, 9¼in. high. (Sotheby's) $10,850 £5,000

Late 16th/early 17th century mariner's brass astrolabe, 4¾in. diam. (Christie's) $20,520 £9,500

Thick brass flat iron stand, circa 1850, 11in. long. (Christopher Sykes) $63 £28

One of a pair of brass ornamental boots, circa 1835, 3¾in. high. (Christopher Sykes) $65 £30

One of a pair of cast brass candlesticks, circa 1840, 9½in. high. (Christopher Sykes) $153 £68

Lighter made to commemorate the Great War, in the shape of a brass and copper book, 2in. high. (Christopher Sykes) $30 £15

One of a pair of cut glass and gilt brass candelabra, circa 1880, 26in. high. (Sotheby's Belgravia) $915 £440

Lacquer crumb tray and brush painted with chinoiserie scenes. (Phillips)　$71　£35

Copper jelly mould. (Hexton & Cheney) $75　£35

Queen Anne period brass cream pan, circa 1710, 22in. diam., with wrought iron rim. (Christopher Sykes)　$131　£58

Rare circular brass tripod candle reflector, circa 1800, 4½in. diam. (Christopher Sykes) $105　£49

Fine pair of cast brass Bacchanalian figures, 15in. high. (Eadon, Lockwood & Riddle)　$1,080　£500

Adam style fire grate, 34in. wide. (Vost's) $820　£400

One of a pair of late 19th century brass candlesticks, 24cm. high. (Phillips) $71　£35

Magnificent 19th century polished steel and brass fender. (Locke & England) $632　£310

Copper kettle in excellent condition. (Hexton & Cheney)　$112　£52

19th century cast brass bracket with original hanging bell, 14in. high. (Christopher Sykes) $176　£78

17th century Nuremberg brass alms dish. (Leys, Antwerp) $1,036　£480

Antique brass wick lamp. (J. M. Welch & Son) $82　£38

Victorian copper coal helmet with swing handle. (Vernon's) $180 £85

Fine German brass tobacco box, signed Giese, circa 1760, 6½in. long. (Sotheby's) $1,095 £480

19th century copper measure with loop handle, 10in. high. (Vernon's) $95 £45

Oriental brass pot pourri vase with peacock supports. (Vernon's) $105 £50

Fine 19th century copper kettle with brass finial. (Vernon's) $150 £70

Victorian brass letter clip in the form of a hand. (Vernon's) $75 £35

19th century copper log pail with swing handle. (Vernon's) $180 £85

Early 20th century brass smoker's stand. (Vernon's) $75 £35

Large early 19th century copper log container with lion mask handles and paw feet. (Vernon's) $185 £85

Victorian brass watering can. (Vernon's) £75 £35

Victorian two-branch chandelier in solid brass with green glass shades. (Alfie's Antique Market) $450 £200

19th century brass jardiniere with lion mask handles and paw feet. (Vernon's) $105 £50

Early copper tankard with brass rim. (Vernon's) $130 £60

Victorian pierced brass fender on paw feet, 4ft.6in. wide. (Vernon's) $165 £75

Early 19th century two gallon copper measure. (Vernon's) $310 £145

Victorian brass desk lamp. (Vernon's) $65 £30

Late Victorian copper kettle with brass handle. (Vernon's) $60 £30

Victorian bellows with embossed brass facing depicting a domestic scene. (Vernon's) $75 £35

Fine 19th century brass log container with embossed decoration. (Vernon's) $645 £300

Unusual French brass chestnut roaster with embossed lid showing an old man and a young girl. (Vernon's) $215 £100

19th century gun metal ice pail with swing handle. (Vernon's) $105 £50

One of a set of seven late 19th century brass wall lights with scroll supports. (Vernon's) $750 £350

Large 19th century Oriental brass bowl supported on winged mythological figures. (Vernon's) $300 £140

Interesting Victorian combined trivet and companion set. (Vernon's) $115 £55

Late 17th century brass candle-stick on tripod base, 7½in. high. (Robert W. Skinner Inc.) $375 £175

George III paktong firegrate of Adam design, 35in. wide. (Christie's S. Kensington) $4,320 £2,000

19th century copper figure of a dancing faun, 32in. high. (Olivers) $450 £190

German brass alms dish, 15½in. diam., circa 1500. (Sotheby's) $2,625 £1,150

Early gas cigarette lighter, brass, probably English, circa 1880, 20in. high. (Sotheby's Belgravia) $525 £240

16th century octagonal brass candle sconce with repousse decoration, 11in. (Robert W. Skinner Inc.) $425 £200

Early 18th century brass warming pan with pierced front and flat-tened steel handle. (Phillips) $160 £70

One of a set of twelve cylindrical brass measures, from 5 gallons to ¼ gill. (Outhwaite & Litherland) $4,730 £2,200

One of a pair of late 17th century brass candlesticks, 8¾in. high. (Robert W. Skinner Inc.) $4,100 £1,900

French Louis XV brass candle-stick, circa 1715, 10¼in. high. (Robert W. Skinner Inc.) $225 £105

Collection of seven antique brass butcher's bell-shaped weights from 4lb. to 1oz. (Christopher Sykes) $310 £140

One of a pair of early 18th cen-tury brass candlesticks on saucer bases, 7½in. (Robert W. Skinner Inc.) $1,550 £720

Rare corkscrew marked Bonsa. (Christie's) $680 £310

19th century cast iron bar corkscrew with wooden handle, 6in. high. (Christopher Sykes) $200 £90

Wier's patent corkscrew of 1884, single form. (Christie's) $105 £50

Fine 19th century iron corkscrew with brush handle. (Christopher Sykes) $55 £25

Pocket boxwood corkscrew and holder. (Christopher Sykes) $15 £5

Johnnie Walker Scotch advertising corkscrew with brush handle. (Christopher Sykes) $40 £20

Large pocket folding steel corkscrew. (Christopher Sykes) $20 £10

Fine 19th century bar corkscrew, cast iron with round knob wooden handle, 9in. high. (Christopher Sykes)$215 £95

Rare bright steel folding pocket corkscrew, circa 1830. (Christopher Sykes) $100 £45

Wine taster's tap screw with brush handle. (Christopher Sykes) $100 £45

Steel sprung corkscrew. (Christopher Sykes) $65 £30

Lignum vitae corkscrew with brush handle. (Christopher Sykes) $40 £15

Rare direct pressure corkscrew, unmarked. (Christie's) $750 £340

Early steel corkscrew. (Christie's) $395 £180

Excelsior Lever simple corkscrew. (Christie's) $350 £160

19th century iron corkscrew with wooden handle. (Christopher Sykes) $20 £10

19th century cast iron bar corkscrew with round knob wooden handle, 6in. high. (Christopher Sykes) $215 £95

Crown cork remover. (Christopher Sykes) $25 £10

19th century iron corkscrew with ivory handle. (Christopher Sykes) $65 £30

J. H. Perille's patent single side lever corkscrew. (Christie's) $275 £125

Unusual twist spring steel corkscrew. (Christopher Sykes) $20 £10

Georgian pocket steel corkscrew and holder. (Christopher Sykes) $55 £25

Impressive Victorian brass and cast iron bar corkscrew with beechwood handle, 12in. high. (Christopher Sykes) $200 £85

Twisted wire corkscrew. (Christopher Sykes) $12 £5

Fine Hawaiian feather cape, 'ahu'ula, decorated with red and black on a ground of yellow, 39in. wide. (Christie's) $39,600 £18,000

Rare Hawaiian crested helmet, mahiole, of woven 'ie'ie roots, 9in. high. (Christie's)
          $18,700 £8,500

North American Athapaskan Indian beaded velvet cap. (Christie's)
          $330 £150

Edwardian filet panel with hunting scene. (Alfie's Antique Market) $30 £15

Melanesian tunic of woven panels of Job's Tears, probably from New Guinea, 18in. x 13½in. (Christie's) $85 £40

16th century Spanish or Italian needlework fragment in red on natural linen, 34in. wide. (Robert W. Skinner Inc.)
          $425 £195

Two rare Masai warrior's arm-clamps, one of rhinoceros hide, the other of elephant hide, 6in. and 4in. wide. (Christie's)
          $530 £240

Stovepipe bearskin hat belonging to Abraham Lincoln. (Sotheby's N. York) $9,870 £4,590

Rare embroidered white kid lady's hawking glove, mid 18th century, German or Austrian. (Sotheby's)
          $810 £360

North American Athapaskan Indian softskin embroidered jacket. (Christie's) $770 £350

Composite full armour of bright steel, circa 1600. (Christie's & Edmiston's)
          $6,075 £2,700

Santa Cruz tridacna shell pectoral with applied turtleshell fretwork on red cloth cord, 4¾in. diam. (Christie's) $835 £380

Mid 19th century rust ground mandarin's robe with Chinese embroidery. (Sotheby King & Chasemore) $259 £120

19th century Chinese silk hand embroidered skirt. (Alfie's Antique Market) $184 £80

Natural linen corset, boned, lined with linen, circa 1780. (Bonham's) $202 £90

Early 19th century silk brocade jacket. (Alfie's Antique Market) $168 £75

Detail from a late 18th century N. European flounce, 26in. deep. (Alfie's Antique Market) $215 £95

19th century Chinese dragon robe, brilliantly embroidered with dragons and clouds on a chestnut ground. (Sotheby's) $625 £280

Pair of late 18th/early 19th century gent's black leather riding boots, now used as an umbrella stand. (Sotheby's Belgravia) $540 £250

19th century sheet iron articulated helmet of Cromwellian design, circa 1830, 14in. high. (Christopher Sykes) $440 £195

Normandy lace bed cover in whitework and bobbin lace. (Phillips) $388 £180

Early 19th century green silk gown with leg of mutton sleeves, circa 1830.(Phillips) $125 £55

Purple ground Chinese dragon robe, embroidered with dragons and emblems, 19th century. (Sotheby's) $310 £140

18th century ivory silk gown, circa 1750, hand-painted with flowers. (Phillips) $5,250 £2,600

Late 18th century embroidered waistcoat. (Alfie's Antique Market) $90 £42

Late 18th century muff of ivory silk embroidered in coloured silks. (Phillips) $146 £65

Chinese dragon robe. (Parsons, Welch & Cowell) $135 £60

Court suit, circa 1860. (Alfie's Antique Market) $129 £60

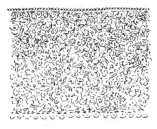

Italian 17th century flounce of point de neige. (Christie's S. Kensington)
$7,750 £3,400

18th century Chinese Kesi dragon robe richly worked with bats and cranes on a blue ground. (Sotheby's)
$535 £240

Scottish regimental sporran of the Argyll and Sutherland Highlanders. (Sotheby's)
$183 £85

Late 19th century officer's dark blue cloth full-dress helmet of the East Surrey Regiment. (Geering & Colyer) $382 £170

Unusual Chinese rank-badge jacket embroidered in gold with quail on a deep indigo ground, circa 1920. (Sotheby's) $360 £160

Green, beaded and sequinned two-piece suit. (Gray's Antique Mews) $756 £350

Blue ground Chinese dragon robe, embroidered with dragons and Buddhist emblems, 19th century. (Sotheby's) $470 £210

French suit of maroon cut velvet, circa 1780. (Christie's S. Kensington)
$4,500 £2,000

265

German shoulder china doll's head with painted features, 5¾in. high, circa 1875. (Sotheby's Belgravia) $685 £310

German shoulder bisque doll's head, impressed 16, circa 1870, 4½in. high. (Sotheby's Belgravia) $375 £170

German shoulder bisque head, circa 1875, 5in. high, with glass eyes and moulded hair. (Sotheby's Belgravia) $330 £150

19th century German bisque headed doll. (Sotheby Bearne) $250 £115

Bisque headed doll with composition body and limbs stamped Thuringa, Germany. (Phillips) $245 £120

'Wendy' bisque doll by Bruno Schmidt of Waltershausen, circa 1900. (Theriault, Pennsylvania) $4,100 £1,900

Jumeau bisque doll, stamped Jumeau in blue, 26in. tall. (Sotheby's Belgravia) $1,015 £460

Attractive French shoulder bisque doll, possibly by Huret, 17½in. tall. (Sotheby's Belgravia) $1,280 £580

Jumeau bisque doll with modern brown wig, 24in. tall, impressed 1907 11. (Sotheby's Belgravia) $885 £400

Fine German shoulder china head doll with kid body, 16in. high, circa 1870. (Sotheby's Belgravia) $1,105 £500

Three Martha Thompson bisque portrait models of The Queen, Prince Charles and Princess Anne. (Sotheby's Belgravia) $665 £300

Huret bisque doll, 17in. high, hands and body repaired, marked Paris 1867. (Sotheby's Belgravia) $2,320 £1,050

Rare German shoulder bisque doll's head, 14in. high, with moulded-on white blouse. (Sotheby's Belgravia) $885 £400

Rare German china head with moulded hair, circa 1860, 3½in. high. (Sotheby's Belgravia) $310 £140

Good German shoulder china head with painted features, 5in. high, circa 1865. (Sotheby's Belgravia) $375 £170

George III carved and painted wooden doll, circa 1770. (Sotheby's Belgravia) $3,935 £1,750

Large Jumeau bisque doll, body marked Jumeau Diplome d'Honneur. (Sotheby's Belgravia) $1,195 £540

Bisque porcelain headed doll by Armand Marseille, Germany, 12in. high. (Christopher Sykes) $215 £95

Rare German shoulder bisque doll with brown hair, 21½in. high, circa 1890, dressed in Norwegian peasant costume. (Sotheby's Belgravia) $685 £310

Good Biedermeier shoulder papier mache doll, 23½in. high, circa 1840. (Sotheby's Belgravia) $1,195 £540

Fine mid 19th century French bisque doll, possibly by Huret, circa 1860, with various items of clothing. (Sotheby's Belgravia) $2,165 £980

Bisque headed walking doll by Simon & Halbig, 42cm. high, with composition body. (Sotheby King & Chasemore) $905 £420

Simon & Halbig bisque headed doll with composite body, 94cm. long. (Phillips) $315 £140

Bisque headed bebe doll by Bru, Paris, 24in. high. (Christie's S. Kensington) $10,800 £5,000

19th century German bisque
headed doll. (Sotheby Bearne)
$130 £60

Simon & Halbig bisque headed
walking doll. (H. Spencer & Sons)
$495 £220

Max Handwerk German doll with
bisque head and ball jointed limbs.
(Sotheby King & Chasemore)
$275 £120

Small bisque headed doll with
stuffed body and composition
arms, 26cm. long. (Phillips)
$80 £35

French bisque headed doll, marked
F. G. (Phillips) $1,355 £600

Bisque headed character child
doll. (Christie's S. Kensington)
$2,590 £1,200

Doll by Simon & Halbig, circa
1900, 13in. high. (Gray's
Antique Mews) $325 £145

French Bru doll. (Theriault,
Pennsylvania) $16,000 £6,925

American 19th century painted
wooden doll, 29cm. high.
(Sotheby King & Chasemore)
$213 £95

19th century German bisque
headed doll. (Sotheby Bearne)
$315 £145

Kammer & Reinhardt 114 doll, 9in. tall,
dressed in original clothes. (Rowland
Gorringe & Co.) $1,190 £550

19th century German bisque
headed baby doll. (Sotheby
Bearne) $215 £100

Well-dressed, neatly coiffed bisque headed Jumeau doll. (Richard W. Withington Inc.) $4,000 £1,755

Ragged cloth-made Izannah Walker doll. (Richard W. Withington Inc.)$2,150 £945

Bru Jne 4 doll, 12½in. high. (Richard W. Withington Inc.) $3,600 £1,580

Bisque head and shoulder dancing doll, 18in. high. (Richard W. Withington Inc.) $850 £375

China headed gentleman doll, 16in. high. (Richard W. Withington Inc.) $270 £120

Bru leather-bodied doll, head, arms and bust of porcelain, 25½in. high. (Loudmer, Poulain's, Paris) $18,245 £8,020

DOLL'S HOUSES

Wooden doll's house in the form of a three-storey building, with nine rooms. (Sotheby's Belgravia) $930 £460

Mid 19th century Noah's Ark with 370 wooden animals, 56cm. long overall. (Sotheby King & Chasemore) $670 £330

Hand-made model of a timber framed house. (Phillips) $1,945 £900

Austrian pre-World War I model Schloss. (Phillips) $140 £70

Good quality mock Tudor doll's house with lift-off top and electric lights, 21in. wide.(Phillips) $570 £250

Early 20th century fully furnished doll's house.(Vernon's)$660 £300

269

Russian silver gilt and enamel teacup and saucer. (Parsons, Welch & Cowell) $240 £120

Late 19th century champleve rat with scroll form ears, 17cm. wide. (Sotheby's Belgravia) $260 £120

Circular Bilston enamel box. (Sotheby King & Chasemore) $151 £75

Enamel bonbonniere in the form of a dog's head. (Sotheby Bearne) $747 £370

Viennese enamel ewer and dish with gilt metal mounts, painted with mythological motifs, circa 1900, unmarked.(Sotheby's Belgravia) $3,360 £1,500

Late 19th century champleve incense burner and cover in the form of a phoenix, 30.5cm. high. (Sotheby's Belgravia) $368 £170

Silver mounted Bilston etui. (Sotheby's) $729 £320

Phoebe Traquair enamel and silver tryptych, early 20th century, 22.2cm. high.(Sotheby's Belgravia) $3,505 £1,600

English Arts & Crafts enamelled folder, 1902, 15.5cm. wide. (Sotheby's Belgravia)$655 £300

Enamelled Swiss snuff box with automata, 8cm. wide, circa 1811-28. (Sotheby's) $60,480 £28,000

Viennese enamel scent bottle. (Christie's S. Kensington) $1,016 £440

Battersea enamel 1759 calendar snuff box. (Bonham's) $462 £200

Circular Bilston enamel
box inscribed 'A Friend's
Gift'. (Sotheby King &
Chasemore) $149 £74

Late 19th century champleve enamel
rat, 20cm. wide. (Sotheby's Belgravia)
$325 £150

Russian silver and
enamel Easter egg.
(H. Dodd & Partn-
ers) $1,912 £850

One of a pair of Viennese
enamel double headed
ostrich cups. (Sotheby's
Belgravia)
$49,680 £23,000

19th century Greek silver and enamel
casket, 13cm. wide. (Sotheby's)
$775 £340

Late 19th century champleve
enamel burner and cover in
the form of a mandarin duck,
26cm. high. (Sotheby's
Belgravia) $325 £150

Enamel plaque made in St.
Paul's Studios, 1901, 12in.
high. (Gray's Antique Mews)
$800 £350

Good German enamel tobacco box, mid
18th century, 12.5cm. wide. (Sotheby's)
$7,810 £3,600

Green marble and champleve
enamel clock, circa 1900,
50in. high. (Sotheby's
Belgravia) $3,950 £1,900

Phoebe Traquair enamel and gilt
copper casket, early 20th century, 19.4cm. high. (Sotheby's
Belgravia) $3,285 £1,500

One of two enamel plaques showing
Christ washing the feet of the Disciples.
(Osmond Tricks) $2,700 £1,200

Bilston enamel plaque transfer
printed with dancing couple.
(Bonham's) $438 £190

271

FABERGE

Reeded gold cigarette case by Faberge, Moscow, 1908-1917, 11cm. wide. (Sotheby's) $2,965 £1,300

Faberge gold and eosite sedan chair, circa 1890. (Sotheby's) $60,000 £27,650

Faberge Imperial presentation box in gold, enamels and diamonds. (Sotheby's U.S.A.) $65,000 £29,955

Faberge rectangular gold cigarette case, St. Petersburg, 1908-1917, 9.6cm. wide. (Sotheby's) $2,965 £1,300

Faberge gold and silver card case, St. Petersburg, 1899-1908, 8.7cm. long. (Sotheby's) $6,155 £2,700

Faberge silver gilt and enamel christening mug. (Harrods Auction Galleries) $1,725 £850

FANS

Historical fan painted with the coronation of Charles of Austria as King of Spain, circa 1703, damaged. (Sotheby's Belgravia) $470 £210

Late 19th century Japanese fan, circa 1890's. (Phillips) $90 £40

George IV period brise fan, circa 1825, 6¼in. high. (Christopher Sykes) $110 £50

Yellow feather fan with floral decoration. (Phillips) $70 £30

Mother-of-pearl fan painted with a garden scene, circa 1740, 29.5cm. long. (Sotheby's Belgravia) $580 £260

Fine English ivory fan painted with pastoral vignettes, with mother-of-pearl backed sticks. (Sotheby's Belgravia) $1,460 £650

Late 18th century pierced ivory fan, gilt and decorated with 'Vernis Martin' vignettes, 25.8cm. long. (Sotheby's Belgravia) $560 £250

Mid 19th century French mother-of-pearl fan with gilt and painted sticks, 29cm. long. (Sotheby's Belgravia) $540 £240

Early 18th century ivory pique fan, damaged, 28cm. long. (Sotheby's Belgravia) $360 £160

18th century ivory fan decorated with classical and chinoiserie scenes, damaged, 30.5cm. long. (Sotheby's Belgravia) $290 £130

Pierced ivory fan with chinoiserie vignettes on blue ground paper mount, circa 1760, 29.5cm. long. (Sotheby's Belgravia) $2,485 £1,110

Tiffany & Co., fan with lace wing, veins of incised mother-of-pearl. (Phillips) $140 £60

Early Victorian lady's fan with rosewood sticks, circa 1840, 9in. high. (Christopher Sykes) $170 £75

Rich black ostrich feather fan, tortoiseshell sticks. (Alfie's Antique Market) $90 £40

BEDS AND CRADLES

Empire mahogany lit en bateau, stamped Jacob D. Rue Meslee, 78in. long. (Christie's) $1,540 £700

19th century Breton style cradle, with turned finials, 90cm. wide. (Phillips) $140 £70

Empire mahogany single bed with panelled head and foot ends, 43¼in. wide. (Christie's) $1,145 £520

19th century mahogany crib with carved end, 97cm. long. (Phillips) $245 £110

Victorian cast iron cradle on castors. (Vernon's) $175 £80

Late Jacobean oak cradle, 37½in. long. (Locke & England) $810 £360

George IV mahogany cradle, 3ft.1in. wide, circa 1825. (Sotheby's) $905 £420

Walnut bedroom suite comprising a bed and a pair of pedestal cupboards, circa 1870. (Sotheby's Belgravia) $1,495 £720

Large walnut bed, circa 1900, 69in. wide. (Sotheby's Belgravia) $1,250 £600

Old English tent bed in fruitwood with ogee shaped canopy, 3ft.3in. wide. (Whiteheads) $1,420 £700

Late 19th century four poster bed with ornate carving. (Lalonde Bros. & Parham) $5,885 £2,900

Victorian mahogany bedstead. (Hy. Duke & Son) $1,580 £680

274

One of a pair of Regency rose-wood bookcases. (Spear & Sons) $4,835 £2,250

Red japanned chinoiserie bookcase, doors applied with gilt tooled book spines, circa 1920. (Sotheby's Belgravia) $1,150 £500

Empire mahogany dwarf bookcase with black marble top, 91in. wide. (Christie's) $3,290 £1,450

Antique oak breakfront book-case, 7ft.6in. wide. (Worsfolds) $2,375 £1,100

William and Mary rosewood pedestal bookcase, 19½in. wide. (Christie's S. Kensington) $4,535 £2,100

Georgian bookcase with astragal glazed doors. (James & Lister Lea) $8,775 £3,900

Georgian mahogany bookcase cupboard, 46in. wide. (J. M. Welch & Son) $2,375 £1,100

Regency mahogany breakfront bookcase with six glazed doors, 155in. wide. (Christie's) $7,390 £3,200

19th century mahogany library bookcase with double glazed doors, 91cm. wide. (Phillips) $740 £320

Walnut bookcase with moulded cornice above two glazed doors, 55in. wide, circa 1870. (Sotheby's Belgravia) $2,400 £1,050

Early 20th century oak sectional bookcase. (Phillips) $150 £65

William IV mahogany library book-case with glazed top, 111cm. wide. (Phillips) $925 £400

Edwardian revolving bookcase of mahogany, 50cm. wide. (Phillips) $452 £200

Oak book cabinet, circa 1859, 37 x 52in. (Sotheby's Belgravia) $3,382 £1,650

Mahogany bookcase with recessed centre cornice, circa 1830, 83¾in. wide. (Christie's) $2,910 £1,300

Victorian mahogany breakfront library bookcase, 6ft.1in. wide. (Parsons, Welch & Cowell) $3,510 £1,560

Victorian burr-walnut library bookcase, 49½in. wide. (Parsons, Welch & Cowell) $2,475 £1,100

Victorian mahogany breakfront bookcase. (Samuel Rains) $3,760 £1,700

Victorian mahogany breakfront library bookcase. (Eadon, Lockwood & Riddle) $4,800 £2,100

Dutch mahogany and marquetry bookcase, circa 1850, 33½in. wide. (Sotheby's Belgravia) $2,800 £1,350

19th century Victorian mahogany bookcase with glazed top, 230cm. high. (Phillips) $360 £160

William IV carved mahogany library bookcase, 84in. wide. (Dacre, Son & Hartley) $2,160 £1,000

William IV carved mahogany library bookcase, 118in. wide. (Dacre, Son & Hartley) $3,460 £1,600

George I style walnut breakfront bookcase, mid 20th century, 220cm. wide. (Sotheby King & Chasemore) $2,590 £1,200

Breakfront library bookcase in strongly marked rosewood, 5ft. 11in. wide. (Phillips)$4,650 £2,300

George IV pollard elm dwarf bookcase with marble top, 72½in. wide. (Christie's) $2,465 £1,100

Mahogany breakfront bookcase of George III design, 101in. wide. (Hy. Duke & Son) $3,075 £1,500

Antique Sheraton design bookcase on cupboard, 4ft.6in. wide. (Worsfolds) $1,910 £850

Victorian walnut bookcase. (Thomas Watson) $6,260 £3,100

George III mahogany bookcase with panelled cupboard to base, 3ft.4½in. wide. (Sotheby King & Chasemore) $2,270 £1,050

Satinwood bookcase by Kerby, London, 8ft.3in. long. (H. C. Wolton & Son) $8,860 £4,100

Mid Victorian heavily carved oak library bookcase, 108in. high. (Dacre, Son & Hartley) $3,460 £1,600

Regency period breakfront bookcase in flame mahogany. (Dennis H. B. Neal) $8,200 £3,800

Early 20th century mahogany breakfront bookcase with a blind fret cornice and bracket feet, 78in. wide. (Sotheby's Belgravia) $2,850 £1,250

19th century Continental oak bookcase. (Sotheby Bearne) $1,400 £650

Edwardian mahogany breakfront bookcase, 72in. wide. (Olivers) $3,620 £1,600

277

Mahogany bureau on bracket feet, 27in. wide, brass period handles. (Worsfolds) $3,160 £1,400

Kingwood and floral marquetry bureau de dame, 2ft.2in. wide, circa 1850. (Sotheby King & Chasemore) $1,470 £650

Dutch marquetry cylinder bureau, circa 1780, 3ft.8½in. wide. (Sotheby's) $6,300 £2,900

George I cylinder bureau in burr yew-wood. (Christie's) $15,960 £7,000

20th century walnut veneered bureau with cabriole legs. (Phillips) $115 £55

George III mahogany and satinwood bureau, circa 1770, 3ft.6in. wide. (Sotheby's) $5,200 £2,300

George III mahogany bureau with brass drop handles, 72cm. wide. (Phillips) $1,730 £750

Early 20th century king-wood parquetry bombe bureau de dame, 30in. wide. (Sotheby's Belgravia) $1,870 £900

Tulipwood and marquetry bureau a cylindre with marble top, circa 1900, 31½in. wide. (Sotheby's Belgravia) $1,455 £700

Late 18th century oak bureau with mahogany banding and brass drop handles. (Phillips) $695 £300

Early 20th century rose-wood and marquetry bureau de dame, 30½in. wide. (Sotheby's Belgravia) $1,455 £700

18th century walnut knee-hole bureau. (Parsons, Welch & Cowell) $3,150 £1,400

19th century floral marquetry cylinder bureau with revolving top, 113cm. wide. (Phillips) $5,080 £2,200

Mid 18th century Louis XV ormolu mounted parquetry cylinder bureau with tambour front, 4ft.3in. wide. (Sotheby's) $4,775 £2,200

Georgian walnut drop-front bureau, 36in. wide. (Honiton Galleries) $3,165 £1,400

19th century Dutch marquetry bureau, 33in. wide. (Olivers) $5,650 £2,500

19th century mahogany writing bureau-cum-chest on bracket feet. (Stanilands) $1,200 £530

Continental oak bureau, carved with cherubs and scrolls, 3ft.5in. wide. (McCartney, Morris & Barker) $1,600 £700

Mid 18th century German ormolu mounted tulip-wood and kingwood bureau, 37in. wide. (Christie's) $103,680 £48,000

18th century Dutch floral marquetry bombe bureau, 114cm. wide. (Phillips) $6,470 £2,800

George I walnut bureau, circa 1720, 2ft.6in. wide, on later bracket feet. (Sotheby's) $3,390 £1,500

Early 18th century oak bureau, 36in. wide. (Olivers) $1,760 £780

Georgian oak bureau with brass drop handles, 37in. wide. (Honiton Galleries) $1,040 £460

South German walnut bureau, circa 1740, 3ft. wide. (Sotheby's) $7,810 £3,600

American Chippendale maple slant top desk, 40in. wide. (Robert W. Skinner Inc.) $5,000 £2,190

Mid 18th century George II provincial oak bureau. (Sotheby Bearne) $1,890 £860

Edwardian mahogany bureau with cross-banded fall flap, 23in. wide. (Hy. Duke & Son) $1,075 £480

18th century style mahogany bureau with four drawers, 90cm. wide. (Phillips) $675 £300

Mid 19th century 'Louis XV' kingwood and mar-quetry bureau de dame with bombe fall-front, 2in. wide. (Sotheby's Belgravia) $10,400 £5,000

18th century walnut writing bureau. (George Comins & Son) $5,335 £2,350

Louis XV style kingwood bureau de dame with brass gallery, 67cm. wide. (Phillips) $875 £380

George III mahogany bureau with burr-walnut and satinwood stringing. (Sotheby Bearne) $1,755 £760

279

Queen Anne walnut
bureau, circa 1710,
2ft.11½in. wide.
(Sotheby's)
$5,184 £2,400

18th century oak bureau,
92cm. wide. (Sotheby,
King & Chasemore)
$1,742 £850

Early 19th century Con-
tinental cylinder desk in
mahogany and marquetry.
(Parsons, Welch & Cowell)
$1,166 £540

'Distressed' finely fig-
ured Georgian maho-
gany bureau, 36in.
wide, on bracket feet.
(T. Bannister & Co.)
$691 £320

George III mahogany
bureau, circa 1770,
4ft. wide. (Sotheby's)
$2,376 £1,100

George I walnut bureau,
33in. wide. (Vost's)
$3,895 £1,900

18th century Dutch mar-
quetry bombe fronted
bureau. (Jackson-Stops &
Staff) $7,128 £3,300

Mid 18th century writ-
ing bureau, 2ft.6in.
wide. (D. M. Nesbit &
Co.) $1,319 £650

Queen Anne walnut and
crossbanded bureau in
two parts, 86cm. wide.
(Sotheby King & Chase-
more) $3,655 £1,800

19th century kingwood
and marquetry bureau
de dame, 29in. wide.
(Christie's S. Kensing-
ton) $1,339 £620

18th century Dutch floral
marquetry bureau with
bombe front, 4ft. wide.
(Russell, Baldwin &
Bright) $7,560 £3,500

Early 18th century red
walnut bureau with fit-
ted interior, 36in. wide.
(J. Francis, T. Jones &
Sons) $1,800 £900

George I walnut bureau,
circa 1725, 3ft.1in. wide.
(Sotheby's)
$5,184 £2,400

Queen Anne walnut bur-
eau, 37½in. wide, on bun
feet. (Lawrence)
$4,050 £1,800

George II mahogany bur-
eau, mid 18th century,
3ft. wide. (Sotheby's)
$2,375 £1,100

Mid 18th century maho-
gany writing bureau
with four drawers. (D.
M. Nesbit & Co.)
$850 £420

South African hardwood bureau made for the Cloets family in Cape Town. (Biddle & Webb) $2,592 £1,200

George I walnut bureau, circa 1725, 2ft.8¾in. wide, restored. (Sotheby's) $2,916 £1,350

Small 18th century fruitwood bureau, 2ft.6in. wide. (Parsons, Welch & Cowell) $1,215 £540

Late 18th century Dutch Louis XV cylinder bureau in marquetry. (Leys, Antwerp) $6,575 £3,044

George I burr-elm bureau, circa 1720, 3ft.1in. wide. (Sotheby's) $8,640 £4,000

Fine 19th century mahogany bureau with four drawers. (Stanilands) $995 £460

18th century German walnut bureau with reconstructed interior and three drawers. (Watson) $4,305 £2,100

18th century oak bureau with four drawers on shaped bracket feet. (Stanilands) $1,145 £530

George I walnut bureau with feather crossbanding, 36in. wide. (Sotheby Humberts) $2,376 £1,100

Late 18th century Dutch bureau with fitted interior and three drawers. (Bradley & Vaughan) $3,890 £1,800

George III satinwood writing table with tambour top, circa 1785, 2ft.6in. wide. (Sotheby's) $6,050 £2,800

Late 18th century oak bureau with fitted interior. (Hobbs Parker) $1,865 £920

Sheraton mahogany and inlaid bureau with four drawers, 39in. wide. (Smith-Woolley & Perry) $1,728 £800

19th century Dutch marquetry and walnut bombeshaped lady's bureau, 90cm. wide. (Sotheby King & Chasemore) $3,045 £1,500

George II walnut bureau with four drawers, 2ft. 11½in. wide, circa 1740. (Sotheby's) $2,700 £1,250

19th century Burmese hardwood bureau with arched and incised legs, 71cm. wide. (Phillips) $450 £220

281

Small late 18th century mahogany bureau on splay feet. (Vernon's) $1,755 £760

Unusual walnut and marquetry double cylinder bureau with two tambour fronts, Italian or Spanish, circa 1780, 6ft. wide.(Sotheby's) $3,795 £1,750

18th century Dutch marquetry bombe bureau. (Jackson-Stops & Staff) $7,095 £3,300

Reproduction Queen Anne style walnut bureau. (J. M. Welch & Son) $585 £270

German parquetry bureau with rectangular top, 29in. wide, on gilt metal mounted cabriole legs. (Christie's) $3,980 £1,800

American 'Wells Fargo' desk by Wootton & Co., 42½in. wide. (Christie's S. Kensington) $6,480 £3,000

Late 19th century American desk by the Wootton Desk Co., Indianapolis.(Sotheby's Belgravia) $3,680 £1,600

Unusual burr-walnut corner bureau on cabriole legs, circa 1920. (Sotheby's) $1,080 £480

Late 19th century satinwood and marquetry cylinder bureau with pull-out writing slide, 42½in. wide. (Sotheby's Belgravia) $5,000 £2,200

Late 19th century kingwood and tulipwood bureau a cylindre with marble top, 34½in. wide. (Sotheby's Belgravia) $2,320 £1,050

Early 19th century flame mahogany bureau on splay feet. (Vernon's) $1,850 £860

19th century French kingwood bureau de dame. (Dickinson, Davy & Markham) $5,015 £2,200

Kingwood cylinder bureau by Oeben, 5ft.2in. wide. (Christie's) $69,700 £34,000

Early Georgian fall-front walnut bureau of five drawers, 3ft.1in. wide. (Coles, Knapp & Kennedy) $2,160 £1,000

George III mahogany tambour top writing desk with side carrying handles, 45in. wide. (Phillips) $2,950 £1,360

Mahogany bureau de dame with pierced gallery and marble top, circa 1900, 32¼in. wide. (Sotheby's Belgravia) $1,370 £620

George I walnut bureau, circa 1725, 2ft.11in. wide, restored. (Sotheby's) $3,135 £1,400

Rare Viennese ormolu mounted mahogany cylinder bureau, circa 1825, 2ft.6in. wide. (Sotheby's) $6,945 £3,200

Antique fall-front bureau in need of restoration. (J. M. Welch & Son) $970 £450

North Italian walnut and marquetry bureau with inlaid flap, late 18th century, 45½in. wide. (Christie's) $5,995 £2,700

Mid 18th century George II walnut bureau, 3ft. wide. (Sotheby's) $3,920 £1,750

Queen Anne cedarwood bureau with sloping hinged lid, 40in. wide. (Christie's) $2,860 £1,250

Rare mid 18th century Dutch colonial padoukwood bureau, 3ft.7½in. wide. (Sotheby's) $1,280 £560

English Queen Anne period oak bureau veneered with walnut, 94cm. wide. (Bonham's) $9,720 £4,300

8th century Dutch marquetry bureau with bombe base, 2in. wide. (Christie's) $4,385 £1,950

Vernis Martin bureau a cylindre, circa 1900, 31½in. wide, with brown marble top. (Sotheby's Belgravia) $1,655 £750

French provincial marquetry bureau, mid 18th century, 39in. wide. (Christie's) $6,525 £2,900

Dutch marquetry cylinder bureau, circa 1775, 3ft. 8in. wide. (Sotheby's) $7,100 £3,100

South German walnut bureau with inverted serpentine lower part, circa 1750, 3ft.4in. wide. (Sotheby's) $3,710 £1,650

Satinwood and marquetry cylinder bureau, late 19th century, 47½in. wide. (Christie's S. Kensington) $4,750 £2,200

Dutch marquetry bureau with shaped flap, on cabriole legs, 33in. wide. (Christie's) $3,630 £1,600

North Italian walnut bureau with fitted interior, 11in. wide. (Christie's) $9,945 £4,400

283

BUREAU BOOKCASES

Good German or Austrian parquetry bureau cabinet, circa 1730, 4ft.3in. wide. (Sotheby's)$18,445 £8,500

George III mahogany cylinder bureau bookcase, circa 1780, 3ft.8in. wide. (Sotheby's) $4,752 £2,200

Georgian mahogany bureau bookcase, 3ft. 6½in. wide, on ogee bracket feet. (Geering & Colyer)
$6,560 £3,200

Regency mahogany cylinder bureau bookcase, circa 1810, 3ft.8in. wide. (Sotheby's) $4,968 £2,300

English scarlet lacquer bureau cabinet, circa 1715-20, 3ft.5in. wide. (Christie's)
$77,760 £36,000

North German mahogany bureau bookcase, circa 1770, 4ft.4in. wide. (Sotheby's)$4,557 £2,100

Early 18th century walnut bureau cabinet with fitted interior, 96cm. wide. (H. Spencer & Sons)
$14,040 £6,500

Fine quality antique mahogany bureau bookcase by Thomas Bradshaw, 3ft.7in. wide. (Worsfolds)
$13,735 £6,700

Late 19th century mahogany bureau bookcase, 30in. wide. (Sotheby King & Chasemore) $2,870 £1,400

Georgian mahogany bureau bookcase, 3ft.5in. wide. (Pearsons)
$3,890 £1,800

Early George III mahogany bureau bookcase by George Speers, 3ft. 5in. wide. (Sotheby's)
$5,876 £2,600

North Italian or South German walnut bureau cabinet, circa 1740, 2ft. 11in. wide. (Sotheby's)
$15,190 £7,000

Early 19th century mahogany and satinwood crossbanded bureau bookcase, 117cm. wide, considerably restored. (Sotheby King & Chasemore)$3,672 £1,700

German walnut bureau cabinet. (Stride's)
$3,672 £1,700

Antique Dutch walnut marquetry bureau cabinet, 4ft. 4in. wide. (Russell, Baldwin & Bright) $6,048 £2,800

George I walnut bureau cabinet, 3ft.2in. wide. (Sotheby King & Chasemore) $12,528 £5,800

Edwardian mahogany bureau bookcase with astragal glazed doors and satinwood inlay, 2ft.9in. wide. (Vernon's) $1,900 £850

Early 18th century South German walnut and mulberry bureau cabinet. (Boardman's)
$14,800 £7,400

Sneezewood estate bureau, early 20th century, made in South Africa. (Walker, Barnett & Hill)
$2,484 £1,150

Fine Victorian walnut cylinder front bureau bookcase. (Biddle & Webb) $3,240 £1,500

Early 19th century mahogany bureau bookcase with astragal glazed doors. (Vernon's) $1,900 £850

George III mahogany bureau bookcase with astragal doors. (Christie's S. Kensington)
$9,072 £4,200

Early 18th century bureau cabinet, circa 1730. (Christie's)
$120,960 £56,000

Good George III mahogany bureau cabinet, circa 1780, 3ft.6½in. wide. (Sotheby's)
$8,640 £4,000

BUREAU BOOKCASES

'Renaissance' walnut and parquetry bureau cabinet stamped Edwards & Roberts, 1880's, 42in. wide. (Sotheby's Belgravia) $2,430 £1,100

Mid Georgian oak bureau cabinet, 44in. wide. (Christie's)
$6,185 £2,700

Dutch walnut and marquetry bureau cabinet with arched cornice, 51in. wide. (Christie's)$14,690 £6,500

Chippendale style bureau cabinet with broken scrolled pediment, 53in. wide. (Christie's)
$5,745 £2,600

18th century mahogany bureau bookcase, carved and rebuilt, circa 1890. (Sotheby's Belgravia)
$2,875 £1,250

Rare George II laburnumwood bureau bookcase, circa 1740, 3ft.6in. wide, doors with original mirror glass panels. (Sotheby's)
$9,340 £4,000

Late George II mahogany bureau bookcase, top with blind Gothic fretwork, circa 1760, 4ft. wide. (Sotheby's)
$3,485 £1,550

18th century Georgian mahogany secretaire cabinet, 42in. wide. (Robert W. Skinner Inc.)
$3,750 £1,705

George III style mahogany bureau bookcase with broken arch cresting, circa 1910. (Sotheby's Belgravia) $2,000 £850

William and Mary double domed bureau bookcase in walnut, 38in. wide. (Boardman's)
$10,850 £5,000

Edwardian mahogany bureau bookcase on cabriole legs. (Vernon's)
$625 £275

Walnut bureau cabinet, circa 1715, with mirrors on the outside of the doors, 47½in. wide. (Christie's)
$21,660 £9,500

Queen Anne walnut bureau cabinet with ogee arched moulded cornice, 41in. wide. (Christie's) $13,260 £6,000

George I red japanned bureau cabinet, 3ft. 4in. wide. (Sotheby's) $7,170 £3,200

Queen Anne burr-walnut bureau bookcase, 26in. wide. (Boardman's) $8,680 £4,000

Georgian mahogany fully fitted bureau bookcase with four graduated drawers. (Frank H. Fellows) $2,260 £1,000

German oak and walnut bureau cabinet with broken scrolled pediment, 47in. wide. (Christie's) $9,280 £4,200

Mahogany bureau bookcase in 18th century style, circa 1890. (McCartney, Morris & Barker) $3,825 £1,700

Early 18th century walnut bureau cabinet with broken scrolled cornice, 43in. wide. (Christie's) $8,085 £3,500

Mid Georgian bureau cabinet in mahogany with triangular broken pediment, 45in. wide. (Christie's)$4,735 £2,050

18th century mahogany bureau cabinet with moulded dentil cornice, 39in. wide. (Christie's) $4,640 £2,000

George I walnut bureau cabinet. (Sotheby King & Chasemore) $13,110 £5,800

George III mahogany bureau bookcase, 42in. wide. (Christie's S. Kensington) $9,070 £4,200

Late 18th century oak bureau bookcase on bracket feet. (Vernon's) $2,770 £1,200

287

CABINETS

Mid 19th century Dutch mahogany and marquetry cabinet, 23in. wide. (Sotheby's Belgravia) $700 £340

Late 17th century Chinese lacquer cabinet, 36in. wide, with ten drawers (McCartney, Morris & Barker) $3,160 £1,400

One of a pair of late 19th century 'Louis XVI' marquetry side cabinets, 33in. wide, with white marble tops. (Sotheby's Belgravia) $3,120 £1,500

19th century marquetry cabinet, 3ft.6in. wide. (Alonzo Dawes & Hoddell) $1,350 £600

17th century oak Flemish cabinet, heavily carved. (Boardman's) $76,230 £33,000

James II red lacquered cabinet on silvered stand. (Locke & England) $14,460 £6,400

18th century style mahogany cabinet on stand on bracket feet, 68cm. wide. (Phillips) $190 £85

'Renaissance' ebony and ivory inlaid breakfront cabinet, Italian, 69in. wide, circa 1870. (Sotheby's Belgravia) $8,320 £4,000

Louis Phillipe marquetry satinwood and kingwood cabinet with ormolu mounts, 3ft.6in. wide. (Phillips) $11,435 £5,060

19th century Continental walnut dentist's cabinet, 64in. high. (J. Francis, T. Jones & Sons) $1,240 £550

Mid 17th century Spanish ebony cabinet on stand, 6ft.2in. high. (Sotheby's) $3,475 £1,680

Ebonised pietra dura side cabinet, circa 1870, 40½in. wide, with black slate top. (Sotheby's Belgravia) $1,870 £900

Ebonised and gilt mahogany wall cabinet, 80cm. wide, circa 1800. (Sotheby's Belgravia) $285 £130

19th century ebony and maple credenza with ormolu mounts. (British Antique Exporters) $1,400 £560

Early 19th century Dutch colonial satinwood, ebony and coromandel-wood cabinet, 4ft.7in. wide. (Sotheby's) $1,735 £800

Late 17th century Indo-Portuguese rosewood and ebony marquetry cabinet on stand, 2ft.2½in. wide. (Sotheby's) $3,365 £1,550

17th century Flemish oak side cabinet. (Phillips) $33,060 £14,500

Late 19th century bamboo music cabinet. (Alfie's Antique Market) $310 £135

Early 18th century Dutch walnut and marquetry cabinet on stand, 46in. wide. (Boardman's) $3,690 £1,700

18th century Italian ebonised and marquetry chest on stand. (Burtenshaw Walker) $3,275 £1,450

17th century Spanish cabinet on stand, veneered in ebony, tortoise-shell and bone. (Harrods Estate Offices) $6,270 £2,800

Edwardian inlaid mahogany music cabinet with fall-front drawers. (Vernon's) $230 £100

Fine 18th century Dutch oak cabinet with shaped pediment. (Boardman's) $6,940 £3,200

Small William and Mary burr-walnut cabinet on chest, 42in. wide. (Boardman's) $5,425 £2,500

289

19th century mahogany apothecary's cabinet. (Christie's S. Kensington) $626 £290

Regency rosewood side cabinet, circa 1810, 3ft.2in. wide, doors faced with pleated green silk. (Sotheby's) $1,945 £900

George III painted side cabinet, circa 1790, 5ft.6in. wide, with white marble top. (Sotheby's) $7,345 £3,400

Edwardian rosewood and ivory music cabinet. (Harrods Auctions) $820 £380

Late George III rosewood writing cabinet, circa 1805, 2ft.6in. wide. (Sotheby's) $6,480 £3,000

17th century Italian cabinet on stand in ebony with pietra dura panels, 1.31m. wide. (Sotheby King & Chasemore) $9,225 £4,100

Japanese black lacquer display cabinet on stand, 77cm. wide. (Phillips) $2,052 £950

Early 18th century French red boulle bureau cabinet, 47in. wide. (Heathcote Ball & Co.) $6,480 £3,000

Victorian inlaid walnut wood cabinet surmounted with oval mirror, 24in. wide. (Churchman's) $350 £155

English mahogany and painted 'Gothic' side cabinet, 1890's, 38in. wide. (Sotheby's Belgravia) $561 £270

17th century Italian cabinet in pine, heavily carved. (H. Spencer & Sons) $10,350 £4,600

Marquetry and oyster veneered cabinet on stand, 1680's, 65in. high. (Parsons, Welch & Cowell) $7,200 £3,600

One of a pair of Regency rosewood and mahogany side cabinets, circa 1815, 3ft.5in. wide. (Sotheby's) $18,575 £8,600

Writing cabinet of dark stained wood by Charles Rennie Mackintosh, 37¼in. wide. (Sotheby's) $172,800 £80,000

Early George III mahogany side cabinet with serpentine top, circa 1765, 4ft. wide. (Sotheby's) $5,400 £2,500

Satinwood and marquetry cabinet on stand. (Christie's) $67,500 £30,000

Early 18th century English lacquer cabinet, 38in. wide. (Heathcote Ball & Co.) $1,705 £840

Antique Chinese glazed cabinet, circa 1830, 44½in. wide. (Christopher Sykes) $2,810 £1,250

18th century North Italian ebonised and Scagliola marble decorated cabinet on stand, 101cm. wide. (Sotheby King & Chasemore) $3,710 £1,650

17th century Flemish carved oak cabinet, 44in. wide. (Parsons, Welch & Cowell) $9,000 £4,000

Victorian black lacquered cabinet in the Chinese manner, 3ft. 1in. wide. (Andrew Grant) $680 £315

19th century Japanese Shibayama cabinet. (Manchester Auction Mart) $7,776 £3,600

Italian ebonised and tortoiseshell cabinet on stand, early 18th century style. (Raymond Inman) $2,640 £1,300

19th century French ebony and marquetry cabinet, 45¼in. wide. (Olivers) $5,537 £2,450

291

English walnut breakfront side cabinet in well figured and burr wood with gilt bronze mounts, circa 1860, 76½in. wide. (Sotheby's Belgravia) $1,980 £860

Dutch marquetry side cabinet, circa 1780, 3ft.10in. wide, on stile feet. (Sotheby's) $2,605 £1,200

Unusual late 19th century English D-shaped satinwood and ebonised side cabinet inlaid with foliage, 61in. wide. (Sotheby's Belgravia) $1,500 £650

One of a pair of English porcelain mounted ebony side cabinets, circa 1880, 93½in. high. (Sotheby's Belgravia) $1,425 £620

Charles II black and gold lacquer cabinet on stand, 50in. wide. (Christie's) $3,480 £1,500

Louis XV provincial oak cabinet, 50in. wide. (Christie's S. Kensington) $4,535 £2,100

Queen Anne walnut cabinet on chest, 41½in. wide. (Christie's) $9,240 £4,000

Late 18th century boulle filing cabinet, sides with Wedgwood plaques, 33½in. wide. (Christie's) $2,420 £1,100

19th century oak and walnut cabinet on chest, heavily carved, 50in. wide. (Christie's) $2,750 £1,200

Ebonised cabinet in the style of Gillow & Co., 104cm. wide, circa 1880. (Sotheby's Belgravia) $350 £160

Good rosewood and marble dental storage cabinet, circa 1915, 5ft.3¼in. high. (Sotheby's Belgravia) $700 £320

Mahogany Art Nouveau side cabinet, inlaid throughout with foliage, 83in. high. (Sotheby's Belgravia) $920 £400

Gilt bronze mounted ebony veneered meuble d'appui, circa 1870, with black slate top, 56½in. wide. (Sotheby's Belgravia) $1,250 £600

Regency bird's eye maple folio cabinet with marble top, 53in. wide. (Christie's) $7,425 £3,200

Good English kingwood side cabinet with crossbanded top and gilt metal mounts, 1860's, 91in. wide. (Sotheby's Belgravia) $4,485 £1,950

German walnut side cabinet in well figured wood, 38½in. wide, 1950's. (Sotheby's Belgravia) $675 £300

Oriental lacquer cabinet on stand. (Parsons, Welch & Cowell) $865 £400

19th century ebonised side cabinet with yew banding, 86cm. wide. (Phillips) $250 £110

English mid Victorian walnut music cabinet in well figured and burr wood, 41in. high. (Sotheby's Belgravia) $830 £360

Satinwood side cabinet, painted with cherubs and portrait medallions, 28in. wide. (Sotheby's Belgravia) $875 £380

An Art Nouveau mahogany cabinet in the Liberty style, 110cm. wide. (Christie's) $1,275 £580

Edwardian Sheraton style music cabinet. (R. L. Lowery & Partners) $280 £130

Oak side cabinet, circa 1905, 152cm. wide, with arched superstructure. (Sotheby's Belgravia) $350 £160

17th century Flemish oak cabinet on stand, dated 1630, 26in. wide. (Boardman's) $3,040 £1,400

Breakfront ebonised, gilt bronze and pietra dura side cabinet, with black slate top, circa 1850, 78in. wide. (Sotheby's Belgravia) $2,100 £950

George III satinwood and marquetry display table on square tapering legs. (Sotheby's Belgravia) $1,500 £650

Early Victorian walnut side cabinet, crossbanded in burr yew-wood, 45in. wide. (Sotheby's Belgravia) $1,250 £550

One of a pair of walnut side cabinets with gilt metal leaf cast mounts, 32½in. wide. (Sotheby's Belgravia) $2,400 £1,050

19th century walnut and tulipwood side cabinet, 33in. wide. (Olivers) $1,245 £550

Boulle side cabinet, inlaid with cut brass strapwork on red tortoiseshell ground, circa 1870, 32½in. wide. (Sotheby's Belgravia) $405 £180

Carved oak side cabinet, with lower part made from a commode, circa 1850-1880, 42in. wide. (Sotheby's Belgravia) $3,205 £1,450

Late 19th century boulle side cabinet, 42in. wide, with restorations. (Sotheby's Belgravia) $1,370 £660

Mid 20th century parquetry side cabinet with marble top, 39in. wide. (Sotheby's Belgravia) $705 £320

Mid 19th century walnut side cabinet with oval porcelain panels to the cupboard doors, 72in. wide. (Sotheby's Belgravia) $1,200 £520

One of a good pair of boulle side cabinets, circa 1860, 28¼in. wide. (Sotheby's Belgravia) $2,035 £920

Walnut breakfront display cabinet with three doors enclosing shelves, 65in. wide. (Sotheby's Belgravia) $950 £420

Finely carved Oriental glass fronted display cabinet with nine shelves. (Worsfolds) $1,730 £800

Ebony and mother-of-pearl serpentine side cabinet with marble top, circa 1870, 48in. wide. (Sotheby's Belgravia) $1,665 £800

William and Mary walnut and floral marquetry cabinet on stand, 36½in. wide. (Christie's) $6,300 £2,800

19th century mahogany display cabinet with single door, 69cm. wide. (Phillips) $740 £320

Kingwood side cabinet with serpentine top, circa 1870, 48in. wide. (Sotheby's Belgravia) $575 £260

19th century ormolu mounted satinwood dwarf cabinet, 33in. wide. (Christie's S. Kensington) $2,270 £1,050

Secretary desk with stepped back drawer and cabinet arrangement, 18th century, 36in. wide. (Robert W. Skinner Inc.) $1,000 £440

18th century Dutch floral marquetry cabinet on chest, 102cm. wide, with gilt metal fittings. (Phillips) $5,080 £2,200

17th century bone and tortoiseshell Spanish cabinet on stand. (Harrods Auctions) $3,550 £2,800

Edwardian mahogany side cabinet. (Biddle & Webb) $910 £400

Walnut side cabinet, doors applied with floral porcelain plaques, 65in. wide, circa 1860. (Sotheby's Belgravia) $2,500 £1,100

French Louis XV style silver display cabinet in marquetry, 158cm. wide. (Leys, Antwerp) $6,920 £3,205

Simple Georgian mahogany canterbury in excellent condition. (Mallams) **$1,480 £640**

Unusual Regency mahogany canterbury with eight divisions, 43in. wide. (Christie's) **$3,365 £1,450**

Regency rosewood canterbury on turned supports, 2ft. high. (Smith-Woolley & Perry) **$405 £180**

Music canterbury made of turned walnut stained pinewood with brass dividing poles, circa 1840, 17in. wide. (Christopher Sykes) **$325 £145**

A fine Victorian mahogany canterbury with fretted partitions. (Vernon's) **$410 £185**

19th century mahogany canterbury on turned legs, 54cm. wide. (May, Whetter & Grose) **$530 £245**

19th century rosewood four division canterbury, 49cm. wide. (Phillips) **$925 £400**

Victorian walnut music canterbury, circa 1850, 4ft.4in. high. (Sotheby King & Chasemore) **$835 £370**

George III mahogany canterbury with three compartments, circa 1800, 1ft.8in. wide. (Sotheby's) **$1,015 £450**

Fine quality Victorian walnut canterbury with drawer, 24in. wide. (Worsfolds) **$830 £370**

Victorian burr-walnut canterbury with shaped oval inlaid table top. (Osmond Tricks) **$735 £340**

Victorian burr-walnut canterbury. (Sotheby Bearne) **$820 £400**

William IV mahogany harp chair with adjustable seat. (Christie's S. Kensington)$480 £210

One of a set of six Regency stained and caned beechwood chairs, circa 1810. (Sotheby's)$2,310 £1,050

One of a set of six Regency ebonised dining chairs, Scottish. (Christie's) $1,165 £520

One of a set of four early 18th century oak chairs with carved top rails. (Phillips) $1,730 £750

One of a set of six Queen Anne style oak dining chairs. (Cobern, Entwistle & Co.) $830 £385

One of a pair of George I walnut dining chairs with slightly curved backs. (Christie's) $2,900 £1,250

One of a set of six early 19th century French provincial cherrywood dining chairs with rush seats. (Vernon's) $1,385 £600

One of a set of six mid 18th century Dutch marquetry dining chairs with serpentine top rails. (Sotheby's) $4,580 £2,000

One of a set of six Queen Anne style oak dining chairs.

English 18th century George II side chair in walnut with solid splat. (Robert W. Skinner Inc.) $375 £170

One of a pair of child's oak Carolean style high back chairs. (Phillips) $165 £80

One of a set of six Edwardian mahogany chairs in Sheraton style. (Phillips) $1,570 £680

One of a set of four 19th century rosewood dining chairs with scrolled balloon backs.(Phillips) $740 £320

One of a set of six William IV rosewood dining chairs, circa 1830. (Sotheby's) $1,810 £800

One of a set of twelve Flemish parcel gilt walnut chairs, circa 1690. (Sotheby's) $9,115 £4,200

One of a set of four Edwardian Art Nouveau oak framed dining chairs with marquetry decoration. (Clevedon Salerooms) $1,015 £440

One of a set of eight Regency simulated rosewood dining chairs with brass inlaid top rails.(Christie's) $9,700 £4,200

297

DINING CHAIRS

One of a set of six 19th century elm Lancashire ladderback chairs with rush seats. (Dacre, Son & Hartley) $1,709 £790

One of a set of four Dutch marquetry dining chairs, circa 1810. (Sotheby's) $1,627 £750

One of a set of four North Italian fruitwood chairs, ivory inlaid, late 18th century. (Christie's S. Kensington) $1,175 £520

One of a set of six mahogany Regency period dining chairs with sabre legs. (Frank R. Marshall & Co.) $2,305 £1,020

One of a set of six Victorian walnut balloon back chairs, circa 1855. (Sotheby King & Chasemore) $1,400 £620

One of a pair of silver gilt and silver veneered throne chairs, circa 1880. (Sotheby's Belgravia) $4,250 £2,050

One of a set of six early 20th century 'Louis XV' side chairs with padded seats and backs. (Sotheby's Belgravia) $500 £240

One of a set of four Edwardian carved mahogany chairs. (Alfie's Antique Market) $270 £120

Cromwellian period high back chair with cane seat and panel back. (Whiteheads) $203 £100

Unusual Bugatti swingback chair, circa 1900, 101cm. high, sides covered in vellum. (Sotheby's Belgravia) $3,927 £1,700

Straight backed chair designed by Frank Lloyd, circa 1910-16, 81.5cm. high. (Sotheby's Belgravia) $6,930 £3,000

One of a set of eight Sheraton style mahogany dining chairs. (West London Auctions) $5,561 £2,450

Fine Indo-Portuguese carved ebony chair, late 17th century. (Sotheby's) $1,128 £520

19th century richly carved baroque chair in oak, covered with silk. (Leys, Antwerp) $1,313 £608

One of a pair of late 17th century oak hall chairs on baluster turned supports. (Sotheby King & Chasemore) $972 £450

One of a pair of rush-seated spindleback country chairs. (Frank R. Marshall & Co.) $456 £202

One of a set of six late 19th century elm Hepplewhite style cottage dining chairs with rush seats. (Sotheby King & Chasemore) $1,310 £580

One of a set of six walnut framed single dining chairs. (D. M. Nesbit & Co.) $1,582 £700

One of a set of four early 19th century mahogany hall chairs with painted crests. (Spear & Sons) $869 £395

One of a set of six George III mahogany chairs, circa 1790. (Sotheby's)$1,853 £820

One of three matching 19th century chairs. (Meads) $346 £150

One of a pair of late 17th century Indo-Portuguese ebony chairs. (Sotheby's) $2,387 £1,100

One of two matching transitional Queen Anne/ Georgian side chairs. (Robert W. Skinner Inc.) $550 £250

One of a set of six George III Hepplewhite dining chairs. (Boardman's) $1,475 £680

One of a set of eight Chippendale style mahogany chairs, American, 20th century. (Robert W. Skinner Inc.) $1,400 £640

Mid 18th century American fan back Windsor side chair, 36in. high. (Robert W. Skinner Inc.)

One of a pair of Queen Anne style side chairs, 41in. high, circa 1730-60. (Robert W. Skinner Inc.) $900 £400

One of a set of six George III mahogany dining chairs, 32½in. high. (Christopher Sykes) $2,929 £1,350

One of a set of eight 18th century Italian oak dining chairs with carved backs. (Boardman's) $2,604 £1,200

One of a pair of oak chairs by Charles Rennie Mackintosh, 1897, 98cm. high. (Sotheby's Belgravia) $7,392 £3,000

17th century English Flemish style side chair in yew and chestnut with cane seat and back. (Robert W. Skinner Inc.) $200 £90

One of a set of six simulated rosewood Regency dining chairs. (Moore, Allen & Innocent) $2,736 £1,200

DINING CHAIRS

Chippendale period mahogany dining chair with pierced splat. (Hobbs Parker) $213 £105

One of two rush-seated spindleback dining chairs. (Frank R. Marshall & Co.) $435 £200

One of a pair of George III mahogany chairs with drop-in seats. (Dacre, Son & Hartley) $302 £140

One of a set of six 19th century carved mahogany dining chairs. (May, Whetter & Grose) $972 £450

One of a set of twelve Chippendale mahogany dining chairs with pierced vase splats. (Messenger May Baverstock) $3,888 £1,800

One of a set of six George III mahogany dining chairs, circa 1780. (Sotheby's) $4,320 £2,000

One of a set of twelve George III mahogany chairs, circa 1785. (Sotheby's) $15,552 £7,200

Late 17th century oak Yorkshire dining chair with swab cushion. (Gray's Antique Mews) $700 £325

One of a pair of Charles II walnut single chairs. (Coles, Knapp & Kennedy) $216 £100

Oak high back chair designed by Charles Rennie Mackintosh, 1897. (Sotheby's Belgravia) $10,370 £4,800

One of a set of seven mahogany William IV chairs of Sheraton design. (Worsfolds) $2,700 £1,200

Carolean walnut chair with carved crest and cane panel back. (Hobbs Parker) $101 £50

One of a pair of late 17th century walnut side chairs. (Hy. Duke & Son) $350 £170

One of a set of six late 19th century elm dining chairs. (Sotheby's) $950 £440

One of a pair of Bettridge & Co. black papier mache boudoir chairs. (D. M. Nesbit & Co.) $505 £250

Mid '80's Art Nouveau oak chair. (Alfie's Antique Market) $191 £85

One of a set of six Victorian mahogany balloon back dining chairs with dralon covered seats. (Hobbs Parker)
$1,015 £500

One of a set of six Regency period mahogany side chairs. (Woolley & Wallis)
$2,073 £960

One of a set of six Chippendale style mahogany dining chairs. (Hobbs Parker)
$1,015 £500

One of a set of six Victorian dining chairs. (Johnsons)
$2,030 £940

Attractive mahogany sabre leg single chair, circa 1810. (Christopher Sykes)
$195 £87

One of a set of six Victorian carved walnut balloon back dining chairs. (Sotheby King & Chasemore)
$1,305 £580

One of a set of six 19th century mahogany dining chairs with shaped top rails. (Phillips)
$451 £220

One of a pair of fine early 19th century Dutch marquetry dining chairs. (Sotheby King & Chasemore)
$1,320 £650

One of a set of six 17th century elm chairs with panel seats. (Chancellor's)
$760 £380

Oak hall chair with back panel carved with hunting scene. (Butler & Hatch Waterman)
$315 £145

One of a set of eight rosewood Victorian balloon back dining chairs with carving to lower rails. (Worsfolds) $2,025 £900

One of a set of twelve Flanders neo-renaissance leather covered chairs. (Leys, Antwerp)
$4,500 £2,100

One of a set of six Victorian balloon back dining chairs in walnut. (Andrew Grant)
$1,332 £650

One of a pair of 18th century oak and walnut Dutch hall chairs. (Hobbs Parker)
$487 £240

One of a set of six George III mahogany dining chairs. (Sotheby Humberts)
$2,160 £1,000

One of a set of nine handsome Victorian carved oak dining chairs with cane seats. (Butler & Hatch Waterman) $1,512 £700

DINING CHAIRS

One of a set of eight English 'William IV' rosewood dining chairs, circa 1840. (Sotheby's Belgravia) $2,070 £900

One of a set of ten George I style dining chairs in mahogany, on ball and claw feet, circa 1900. (Sotheby's Belgravia) $4,750 £2,100

One of a set of four satinwood dining chairs painted with flowers, circa 1900. (Sotheby's Belgravia) $1,350 £580

One of a pair of fine 19th century carved oak hall chairs. (Vernon's) $265 £120

One of a set of six English rosewood drawingroom chairs, circa 1860. (Sotheby's Belgravia) $1,335 £580

One of a set of six late George III mahogany dining chairs, circa 1805. (Sotheby's)$1,550 £680

One of a set of four English walnut side chairs with leaf carved splats, 1860. (Sotheby's Belgravia) $875 £380

One of a set of ten mahogany dining chairs, 18th/19th century, possibly Anglo-Chinese.(Christie's) $1,105 £500

One of a set of six Austrian bentwood dining chairs, stamped Thonet, circa 1920. (Sotheby's Belgravia) $495 £220

Carved oak Welsh spinning stool supported on turned legs. (Phillips) $70 £30

One of a set of six mahogany balloon back dining chairs, circa 1840. (Sotheby's Belgravia) $960 £420

One of a set of eight Victorian rosewood single chairs. (J. M. Welch & Son) $1,730 £800

One of a set of four unusual English mahogany side chairs with carved heads and armorial cartouches, 1870's. (Sotheby's Belgravia) $440 £190

One of a pair of late 19th century Dutch mahogany and marquetry side chairs. (Sotheby's Belgravia) $1,015 £460

One of a set of six painted and gilt wood chairs, late 19th century, partly upholstered in petit-point. (Sotheby's Belgravia) $1,575 £700

One of a set of four early 20th century beechwood chairs on turned legs with H-stretchers. (Vernon's) $130 £60

One of a set of six late 19th century mahogany framed dining chairs. (Vernon's) $520 £225

One of a set of ten late 19th century bentwood dining chairs with wooden seats. (Vernon's) $645 £300

One of a set of six early George III mahogany dining chairs with Gothic pattern splats. (Christie's)$3,315 £1,500

One of a pair of Regency hall chairs with shell backs. (British Antique Exporters) $650 £290

One of a set of six George II mahogany dining chairs, possibly American. (Christie's) $12,150 £5,000

19th century carved oak spinning chair on turned legs. (Vernon's)$65 £30

One of a set of six 19th century French dining chairs with padded backs. (Vernon's) $1,580 £685

One of a set of five mid Georgian mahogany chairs, circa 1760. (Sotheby's) $2,910 £1,300

Mid Georgian mahogany dining chair with waved top rail. (Christie's) $1,575 £700

One of a set of six rose-wood framed cabriole leg dining chairs. (Vernon's)$1,430 £650

One of a set of six German mahogany veneered dining chairs, 1840's. (Sotheby's Belgravia) $1,235 £550

One of a set of eight Regency ebonised and gilded dining chairs. (Christie's) $6,630 £3,000

Fine quality late 18th century carved mahogany Chippendale style dining chair. (British Antique Exporters) $635 £275

One of a set of seven late Victorian carved mahogany chairs, circa 1900.(Sotheby King & Chasemore) $1,600 £740

One of a set of eight George III mahogany dining chairs with comb splats. (Christie's)$5,850 £2,600

One of a set of seven early 19th century elm wheel back kitchen chairs. (Sotheby King & Chasemore) $1,035 £480

303

Two from a set of six Regency rope-back dining chairs. (Spear & Sons) $2,640 £1,300

Two from a set of eight late 19th century oak dining chairs. (Sotheby Humberts) $1,188 £550

Two from an Edwardian drawingroom suite of seven chairs. (Butler & Hatch Waterman) $700 £325

Two from a set of six mahogany dining chairs with square reeded backs. (Dacre, Son & Hartley) $1,835 £850

Two from a set of eight William IV mahogany dining chairs. (Parsons, Welch & Cowell) $365 £180

Two from a set of seven George III mahogany rail-back chairs. (Sotheby King & Chasemore) $1,380 £680

Two from a set of eight mahogany dining chairs on ball and claw feet. (Heathcote Ball & Co.) $4,320 £2,000

Two from a set of twelve George III mahogany dining chairs in Hepplewhite style. (Sotheby King & Chasemore) $16,200 £7,500

Two from a set of eight early 19th century mahogany dining chairs. (Hobbs Parker) $1,258 £620

Two from a set of six late 18th century mahogany dining chairs. (Eadon, Lockwood & Riddle) $950 £440

Two from a set of seven Chippendale period dining chairs. (Parsons, Welch & Cowell) $4,510 £2,200

Pair of children's beechwood folding chairs with Turkey carpet seats. (Phillips) $65 £32

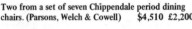

Two from a set of seven Hepplewhite style mahogany dining chairs. (Coles, Knapp & Kennedy) $1,468 £680

Two from a set of eight oak dining chairs in the Sheraton style. (Phillips) $470 £230

Two from a set of eight late 18th century mahogany dining chairs. (Phillips) $8,210 £3,650

Two from a set of eight ebony and boxwood strung mahogany dining chairs in the Hepplewhite style. (Vidler & Co.) $1,805 £880

Two from a set of eight Sheraton period mahogany dining chairs. (Woolley & Wallis) $6,050 £2,800

Two of seven walnut framed Chippendale chairs. (Alfred Mossop & Co.) $1,510 £700

Two from a set of eight 19th century Chippendale style mahogany dining chairs. (Christie's S. Kensington) $5,230 £2,400

Two from a set of eight late 19th century mahogany chairs in the Chippendale style. (Sotheby King & Chasemore) $2,215 £980

Two of a set of six mahogany framed dining chairs on claw and ball feet. (Vernon's) $1,385 £600

Two from a set of six Chippendale style dining chairs with gold brocade seats. (Frank R. Marshall & Co.) $1,695 £750

Two of a set of twelve mahogany dining chairs, 19th century. (Christie's S. Kensington) $11,880 £5,500

Two Edwardian mahogany chairs with inlaid decoration. (Phillips) $215 £95

Victorian oak rocking chair. (Christie's S. Kensington) $1,080 £500

Queen Anne walnut open elbow chair with shaped back. (Coles, Knapp & Kennedy) $355 £165

Italian walnut crinoline chair, circa 1830. (Gray's Antique Mews) $650 £300

Bergere by Jean-Baptiste Sene, circa 1789. (Sotheby's Monaco) $62,735 £29,180

19th century steel framed easy chair with leather upholstery. (Vernon's) $990 £460

One from a set of twelve chairs by George Jacob, 1787. (Sotheby's Monaco) $241,575 £112,360

Edwardian wickerwork easy chair with ribbed seat and back. (Vernon's) $55 £25

Victorian walnut framed nursing chair on turned legs with brass castors. (Vernon's) $165 £75

One of a pair of Hepplewhite armchairs with mahogany frames. (V. & V's) $7,130 £3,300

English walnut armchair with crested back and serpentine seat on cabriole legs, circa 1860. (Sotheby's Belgravia) $760 £330

Pair of early Victorian cabriole leg easy chairs with walnut frames, circa 1860. (Sotheby's Belgravia) $1,000 £450

One of a pair of buffalo horn armchairs by W. Friedrich, Texas. (Christie's S. Kensington) $4,104 £1,900

One of a pair of mid 19th century Indo-Chinese teakwood export armchairs. (Robert W. Skinner Inc.) $1,000 £450

Mid 19th century upholstered armchair with walnut frame.(Phillips)
$370 £180

Lady's Victorian low upholstered chair with walnut frame. (Phillips)
$594 £290

Mid 19th century mahogany armchair with carved cresting rails. (Messenger May & Baverstock) $1,382 £640

George II mahogany armchair with serpentine top back, circa 1750. (Sotheby's)$2,050 £950

Louis XIV oak wing chair with stuffed back, circa 1670. (Sotheby's)
$368 £170

George II mahogany library armchair, circa 1755, back broken. (Sotheby's)
$5,616 £2,600

Rare old open armchair of the George I period with carved paw feet. (Whiteheads) $3,855 £1,900

French Victorian walnut nursing chair. (Alfie's Antique Market)
$540 £240

Mahogany button-back armchair, circa 1850, on moulded cabriole legs. (Sotheby's)
$540 £250

Victorian gentleman's open armchair and a lady's chair with walnut frames upholstered in red velvet. (May, Whetter & Grose) $1,510 £700

One of a pair of George II style mahogany armchairs, 1880's, on cabriole legs. (Sotheby's) $820 £380

Victorian laminated rosewood armchair with carved crest and pierced back. (Robert W. Skinner Inc.) $2,000 £900

One of a pair of George I style wing armchairs. (Harrods Auctions) $1,355 £660

Victorian walnut framed button-back armchair on carved cabriole legs. (Sotheby Bearne) $839 £370

Late George II mahogany armchair with padded arms, circa 1755. (Sotheby's) $2,270 £1,050

Mid Victorian upholstered walnut lady's chair with cabriole legs, 35in. high. (Gray's Antique Mews) $665 £295

One of a pair of Swedish gilt wood bergeres with husk-carved arms, circa 1800. (Sotheby's) $3,038 £1,400

George II red walnut armchair, circa 1755, with stuffed back and seat. (Sotheby's) $4,750 £2,200

One of a pair of 20th century 'Louis XVI' gilt wood fauteuils. (Sotheby's Belgravia) $3,425 £1,550

George III mahogany Gainsborough armchair, circa 1765, with padded arms. (Sotheby's) $2,808 £1,300

A Victorian carved walnut high back armchair on turned legs. (Vernon's) $280 £125

Pair of early 20th century carved and shaped fauteuils with tapestry upholstery. (Lacy Scott) $895 £440

One of a pair of early 19th century coromandelwood open armchairs. (Geering & Colyer) $1,230 £600

18th century framed library chair. (Olivers) $1,580 £700

One of a pair of Victorian deep buttoned tub chairs on turned oak legs. (Phillips) $215 £95

One of a set of four gilt wood fauteuils and a canape, 59in. wide.(Christie's) $6,235 £2,700

Busby's hydraulic-action barber's chair, in chrome and simulated leather, English, circa 1930. (Sotheby's Belgravia) $175 £80

Bent steel rocking chair, 1880's, with brass terminals and padded arms. (Sotheby's Belgravia) $525 £240

Herman Miller lounge chair, 1956, 82cm. high, designed by Charles Eames. (Sotheby's Belgravia) $1,385 £600

George III mahogany armchair, circa 1775. (Sotheby's) $1,415 £620

Mid 19th century English oak X-framed leather upholstered armchair. (Sotheby's Belgravia) $220 £95

One of a pair of Regency mahogany bergeres with padded backs and leather seats, on X-frames. (Christie's) $2,195 £950

Victorian laminated rosewood side chair with carved crest. (Robert W. Skinner Inc.) $400 £181

Two from a set of eight walnut side chairs, mid 19th century, with padded backs. (Sotheby's Belgravia) $4,785 £2,300

One of a pair of armchairs from a ten-piece parcel gilt walnut and canework dining suite, 1930's. (Sotheby's Belgravia) $9,575 £4,200

One of three French or Italian carved beechwood armchairs, circa 1900. (Sotheby's Belgravia) $2,070 £920

One of a pair of Victorian elbow chairs. (Outhwaite & Litherland) $2,260 £1,000

Good George II walnut library armchair, circa 1750, with padded arms. (Sotheby's) $6,695 £3,100

One of a pair of Low Countries Louis XVI walnut fauteuils. (Christie's) $2,940 £1,300

19th century rosewood framed armchair with carved cresting rail.   (Phillips) $460 £200

George III mahogany library armchair of Chippendale style, arm supports carved with foliage. (Christie's) $4,640 £2,000

Late 18th century mahogany framed Gainsborough chair. (Vernon's) $1,200 £520

Fritz Hansens 'egg' chair, 1958, 105.5cm. high, on aluminium base. (Sotheby's Belgravia) $695 £300

English walnut button-back armchair with moulded frame and serpentine seat, circa 1860. (Sotheby's Belgravia) $900 £390

19th century rosewood prie dieu chair with tapestry seat. (Phillips) $145 £65

A pair of 19th century Renaissance style armchairs. (Robert W. Skinner Inc.) $850 £385

George II walnut library armchair on cabriole legs. (Christie's) $1,855 £800

ELBOW CHAIRS

One of a pair of Edwardian inlaid tub chairs. (Alfie's Antique Market) $430 £190

Late 17th century Italian armchair with solid seat. (Sotheby's) $1,128 £520

Late 17th century walnut open-framed armchair. (Drewatt, Watson & Barton) $4,536 £2,100

One of a pair of George II walnut armchairs.(Bruton Knowles)$14,690 £6,800

One of a suite of 'Louis XVI' gilt wood seat furniture, circa 1840. (Sotheby's Belgravia) $1,040 £500

Early 18th century oak carving chair on cabriole front supports. (British Antique Exporters) $575 £250

Early 19th century Regency armchair with crossed sword splat. (Sotheby's) $632 £280

One of a pair of beechwood elbow chairs, circa 1780, hand-painted. (H. C. Wolton & Son) $993 £460

Early 19th century yewwood high hoop back Windsor chair. (Parsons, Welch & Cowell)$542 £250

Queen Anne walnut armchair with solid vase-shaped splat and needlework seat.(Sotheby King & Chasemore) $2,335 £1,150

One of a set of eight mahogany dining chairs, circa 1930, with ball and claw feet. (Sotheby's) $1,339 £620

One of a pair of mid 18th century Venetian painted armchairs with drop-in seats. (Sotheby's) $3,255 £1,500

One of a set of eight 18th/19th century Italian painted dining chairs, including two armchairs. (Sotheby's Belgravia) $915 £440

One of a pair of George I walnut corner chairs standing on pad feet. (Frank R. Marshall & Co.) $7,797 £3,450

French style bergere chair of bucket form on fluted legs. (Phillips) $124 £55

19th century rosewood Savonarola chair with bone and mother-of-pearl inlays. (Neales) $327 £145

One of a pair of Sheraton satinwood and painted armchairs with shield-shaped backs. (Sotheby King & Chasemore) $2,486 £1,100

One of a pair of Italian walnut armchairs, circa 1660, with stuffed backs and seats. (Sotheby's) $4,014 £1,850

Nottingham yew and elm Windsor chair, circa 1830. (Gray's Antique Mews) $632 £280

One of a pair of Empire mahogany armchairs, circa 1810. (Sotheby's) $2,278 £1,050

Anglo-Indian ebony armchair, circa 1830, with caned back and seat. (Sotheby's) $562 £260

One of a set of four Regency simulated rosewood and parcel gilt armchairs. (Christie's S. Kensington) $6,480 £3,000

One of a pair of mid 18th century Venetian painted armchairs. (Sotheby's) $4,123 £1,900

Early 17th century Spanish walnut armchair with leather back and seat. (Sotheby's) $1,041 £480

Dutch child's chair on cabriole legs with pointed club feet. (Worsfolds) $406 £180

One of a set of eight George III mahogany dining chairs, circa 1780. (Sotheby's) $7,344 £3,400

Rare yew-wood and elm seat baby's high chair. (Whiteheads) $1,421 £700

One of a pair of George III mahogany armchairs, circa 1765. (Sotheby's) $5,832 £2,700

One of a set of eight carved mahogany chairs, backs decorated with Prince of Wales feathers. (Sotheby King & Chasemore) $949 £420

George IV caned mahogany library chair, circa 1820. (Sotheby's) $723 £320

Italian style rocking chair with ladder back and leather embossed seat. (Phillips) $339 £150

Satinwood open armchair with cane panels. (Sotheby Humberts) $907 £420

ELBOW CHAIRS

One of a pair of George III painted armchairs, circa 1775.(Sotheby's) $2,160 £1,000

Fine low back Windsor yew-wood armchair in golden yellow colour. (Eadon, Lockwood & Riddle) $650 £300

Victorian mahogany swivel office chair. (Alfie's Antique Market) $173 £77

One of a pair of George III yew-wood Windsor armchairs. (Christie's S. Kensington) $1,537 £750

Oak and elm 19th century spindleback chair with curved arms. (Phillips) $165 £80

One of a pair of Edwardian marquetry inlaid mahogany elbow chairs with spade feet.(Vidler & Co.) $740 £360

One of a set of seven George I walnut dining chairs, circa 1725, including one armchair. (Sotheby's) $20,735 £9,600

17th century oak wainscot chair. (Frank R. Marshall & Co.)$2,810 £1,300

One of a pair of Chinese hardwood armchairs, backs carved with masks. (Sotheby Humberts) $1,080 £500

17th century oak tallback chair. (Hy. Duke & Son) $799 £390

19th century yew-wood smoker's chair. (Dickinson, Davy & Markham) $740 £360

One of a pair of late George III mahogany armchairs, circa 1800. (Sotheby's) $4,536 £2,100

Italian beechwood chair, circa 1740, one of a set of four. (Christie's) $6,910 £3,200

18th century Windsor elbow chair in yew-wood and elm. (Hobbs Parker) $609 £300

One of a set of eight, after Chippendale, Edwardian dining chairs. (Phillips) $1,395 £620

Edwardian mahogany armchair with inlaid decoration.(Phillips) $155 £75

High back yew-wood
Windsor armchair with
crinoline stretcher.
(Eadon, Lockwood &
Riddle) $1,340 £620

17th century oak low
back chair with back
panel carved.(Hy.
Duke & Son)$984 £480

Choice child's chair
in yew-wood and
elm. (Whiteheads)
$2,639 £1,300

18th century Chinese
rosewood open arm-
chair. (Aldridges)
$1,123 £520

One of a set of eight late
Regency mahogany din-
ing chairs. (Vost's)
$5,945 £2,900

17th century style oak
wainscot chair with
carved and panel back.
(Phillips) $450 £220

George III yew-wood
single armchair.
(Christie's S. Kensing-
ton) $820 £400

One of six 1920's walnut
Queen Anne style chairs.
(Stride's) $1,665 £740

One of a set of twelve Windsor chairs of the George III
period, in yew-wood and
elm. (H. Spencer & Sons)
$9,070 £4,200

One of a set of eight
Oriental solid rosewood
dining chairs.(Sotheby's
Belgravia) $1,980 £880

19th century yew-wood
smoker's chair.
(Dickinson, Davy &
Markham) $594 £290

Fine high back, yew-
wood and elm Wind-
sor chair with superb
grain. (Whiteheads)
$1,928 £950

17th century oak North
Country chair with car-
ved back. (R. L. Lowery
& Partners) $325 £150

19th century Continental
carved walnut X-framed
elbow chair in Renais-
sance style. (Alfie's Antique Market) $455 £210

Late 19th century maho-
gany swivel chair with
pierced splat.(Phillips)
$145 £70

Large, old open arm-
chair, heavily carved.
(Butler & Hatch
Waterman)$650 £300

ELBOW CHAIRS

One of two Italian walnut and ivory Savonarola armchairs, circa 1860. (Sotheby's Belgravia) $830 £370

George III mahogany armchair with curved top rail and scrolling splat. (Phillips) $346 £150

German Regency beechwood open armchair with caned back. (Christie's) $2,200 £1,000

One of a set of six George III mahogany chairs, circa 1780. (Sotheby's) $2,735 £1,200

One of a superb set of eight, six singles and two arm, 18th century dining chairs. (British Antique Exporters) $13,000 £5,200

Edwardian inlaid mahogany corner chair. (Phillips) $140 £60

One from a set of six mahogany dining chairs of Chippendale design. (Hy. Duke & Son) $1,525 £680

American William and Mary corner chair, 32in. high, circa 1700-30. (Robert W. Skinner Inc.) $700 £307

Late 18th century yew-wood armchair with H-stretcher. (Vernon's) $845 £365

Early 19th century Yorkshire rocking chair with sea grass seat. (Churchman's) $185 £80

Mid 19th century Windsor armchair in elm and yew-wood, on turned legs with crinoline stretcher. (Sotheby's) $590 £260

Charles II walnut armchair top rail carved with leaves and cherubs, circa 1680. (Sotheby's) $955 £420

One of a set of four elm and yew Windsor chairs. (Christie's) $6,450 £3,000

One of a pair of ebonised armchairs, 1880's, seats lacking. (Sotheby's Belgravia) $370 £170

Bugatti throne armchair in ebonised wood, circa 1895, 140cm. high. (Sotheby's Belgravia) $1,110 £480

Early 17th century oak box seat with scratch-moulded back and shaped sides. (Christie's) $1,190 £520

One of a set of four Chinese mother-of-pearl inlaid rosewood open armchairs. (Christie's) $2,045 £900

Victorian carved oak swivel chair. (Phillips) $185 £80

Late 19th century child's turned beechwood rocking chair. (Churchman's) $210 £95

Late 18th century American writing-arm Windsor chair with saddle seat, 29in. high. (Robert W. Skinner Inc.) $1,800 £790

One of a pair of 17th century Spanish walnut open armchairs with seats upholstered in Turkey-work. (Christie's) $1,260 £550

19th century carver with rush seat. (Meads) $120 £52

George I oak corner commode chair with shaped top rail. (Coles, Knapp & Kennedy) $250 £110

Rocking chair, circa 1870, 3ft.6in. high. (Gray's Antique Mews) $180 £80

Carved oak wainscot chair with panelled back, 17th century. (Hy. Duke & Son) $1,050 £470

Victorian beechwood smoker's chair on turned legs. (Phillips) $85 £38

One of a set of five yew and elm Windsor chairs. (Sotheby's) $5,590 £2,600

One of a set of twelve oak open armchairs of 17th century Spanish design. (Christie's) $3,390 £1,500

One of a pair of Sheraton satinwood armchairs with shield backs, circa 1790. (Sotheby King & Chasemore) $2,365 £1,100

One of a set of six Regency mahogany dining chairs, circa 1815. (Sotheby's) $2,735 £1,200

One of a pair of satinwood caned armchairs, backs with portrait medallions, circa 1900. (Sotheby's Belgravia) $2,300 £1,000

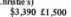

18th century mahogany lattice back armchair with upholstered seat. (Phillips) $695 £300

One of a set of six mahogany dining chairs on square tapering legs, circa 1800. (Sotheby's Belgravia)
$960 £420

American stained beechwood rocking chair with turned legs, circa 1880. (Sotheby's Belgravia)
$365 £160

One of a pair of unusual children's chairs, Russian, 1850's, 26½in. high. (Sotheby's Belgravia)
$195 £90

One of a set of seven George II style mahogany dining chairs with ball and claw feet, circa 1900. (Sotheby's Belgravia)
$1,750 £780

One of a set of six 19th century elm and ash Windsor armchairs. (Christie's S. Kensington)$3,890 £1,800

One of a set of three Regency ebonised and gilded open armchairs.(Christie's)
$4,870 £2,100

Late 19th century Scottish mahogany armchair painted by Rosie Morison, 61in. high. (Sotheby's Belgravia)
$805 £350

Early Louis XV walnut fauteuil with arched back, circa 1730. (Sotheby's)
$2,025 £980

Fine late 18th century Chippendale style elm elbow chair. (British Antique Exporters) $635 £275

One of a set of eight late 19th century mahogany chairs. (Sotheby's)
$2,475 £1,100

Late 17th century Italian walnut armchair with stuffed back and seat. (Sotheby's) $1,530 £680

One of a set of five late 19th century English mahogany dining chairs. (Sotheby's Belgravia) $830 £360

One of a set of six Charles II style oak dining chairs, circa 1900. (Sotheby's Belgravia)
$1,550 £680

One from a set of 19th century Dutch walnut and marquetry chairs. (Sotheby's)
$4,505 £1,950

One of a pair of Regency mahogany bergeres with caned backs, sides and seats. (Christie's)
$5,525 £2,500

One of a set of six mahogany armchairs, circa 1880-1900. (Sotheby's)
$1,910 £850

Superb mahogany Chippendale ribbon back elbow chair on shaped legs. (British Antique Exporters) $1,060 £460

Late 19th century beech-wood and elm stick back elbow chair. (Vernon's) $90 £40

19th century Korean cinnabar lacquer and gilded open arm-chair with leather seat. (Christie's) $1,330 £600

19th century oak framed child's high-chair with rush seat. (Vernon's) $145 £65

Early 19th century Chippendale style mahogany elbow chair on ball and claw feet. (British Antique Exporters) $345 £150

18th century American ladderback armchair, 46in. high. (Robert W. Skinner Inc.) $700 £305

One of an early 20th century suite of George III style draw-ingroom furniture.(Sotheby's Belgravia) $3,220 £1,400

Louis XV gilt wood fau-teuil by J. B. Boulard, 37in. high. (Christie's) $1,655 £750

One of a set of six English mahogany dining chairs, including a pair of armchairs late 1880's. (Sotheby's Belgravia) $1,380 £600

Oak armchair with padded back, down-swept curved arms, circa 1900. (Sotheby's Belgravia) $525 £240

One of a set of nine early 20th century Chippendale style mahogany dining chairs on cabriole legs. (Sotheby's Belgravia) $8,000 £3,500

George I open armchair with arched padded back and bowed seat.(Christie's) $7,070 £3,200

Superb late 18th century Chippendale style mahogany elbow chair on ball and claw feet. (British Antique Exporters) $1,040 £450

One of a set of eight mid 18th century Dutch marquetry chairs.(Sotheby's) $2,250 £1,000

Late 18th century yew-wood stick back elbow chair with elm seat and H-stretcher. (Vernon's) $860 £400

One of a pair of mahogany elbow chairs, probably Continental and early 19th cen-tury, with floral marquetry inlay.(Bonsor Pennington) $3,790 £1,700

319

CHESTS OF DRAWERS

Late 19th century oak chest of drawers with brass handles. (Phillips) $105 £45

Good Charles II walnut chest of drawers, 3ft.2in. wide, circa 1670. (Sotheby's) $1,825 £800

Sheraton period mahogany bow fronted dressing commode. (Woolley & Wallis) $5,830 £2,700

Jacobean oak chest of four long drawers with panelled front. (Worsfolds) $1,470 £650

Oak chest of five drawers with pear drop handles. (Worsfolds) $115 £50

Early George I walnut chest of drawers on later bracket feet, 39½in. wide. (Christie's) $1,900 £820

Early 19th century Dutch walnut and marquetry chest of drawers, 36in. wide. (Christie's) $2,485 £1,100

Late 17th century South German walnut and inlaid chest, decorated with hunting scenes, 142cm. wide. (Sotheby King & Chasemore) $3,130 £1,450

Late George III satinwood chest of drawers, top crossbanded with rosewood, 35½in. wide. (Christie's) $1,740 £750

Mid Georgian mahogany chest of four drawers on bracket feet, 30in. wide. (Christie's) $1,040 £450

Mid 19th century painted chest of seven drawers, with a marble top. (Sotheby's Belgravia) $550 £240

Early Georgian walnut chest with crossbanded quarter top, 38in. wide. (Christie's) $1,790 £800

Oak Jacobean chest of drawers, with pear drop handles. (Worsfolds) $1,015 £450

Early 19th century chest of four drawers on splay feet. (Vernon's) $335 £145

Late 18th century North Italian marquetry chest of three drawers. (Martin & Pole) $6,700 £2,900

William IV bow fronted chest of five drawers on French splay feet, 140cm. wide. (Phillips) $160 £70

Rosewood Wellington chest with a bead and reel border, 30½in. wide, circa 1840. (Sotheby's Belgravia) $1,000 £450

Late George II walnut chest of three drawers, with brushing slide, circa 1760, 2ft.8in. wide. (Sotheby's) $7,750 £3,400

Victorian mahogany campaign chest of two halves with inset brass handles, 40in. wide. (Sotheby's Belgravia) $525 £230

18th century mahogany commode in the form of a chest of four drawers with brass handles, 56cm. wide. (Phillips) $80 £35

George III mahogany chest of six drawers with brass ring handles, 111cm. wide. (Phillips) $115 £50

19th century walnut military chest of drawers, 99cm. wide. (Phillips) $1,385 £600

Early 19th century flame mahogany swept front chest of three drawers with turned wood handles. (Vernon's) $310 £140

Camphorwood chest of nine drawers and secretaire plus galleried decoration. (Eldon E. Worrall) $3,455 £1,600

321

Bow front chest of drawers with fitted toilet drawer, 39in. wide. (Worsfolds) $1,288 £570

Late 17th century oak chest of drawers. (K. Hugh Dodd & Partners) $432 £200

George II yew-wood chest of drawers. (D. M. Nesbit & Co.) $1,977 £875

Inlaid chest of four long drawers, circa 1670, Anglo-Dutch, in oak and softwood, 3ft.6in. wide. (Sotheby's) $1,780 £820

County Federal grain painted chest of drawers, 41in. wide, circa 1795. (Robert W. Skinner Inc.)$2,300 £1,000

George I walnut chest of drawers on bun feet, circa 1720, 32in. wide. (Gray's Antique Mews) $1,135 £525

19th century Eastern inlaid teak chest supported by four mermaids. (Clevedon Salerooms) $1,100 £490

One of a pair of North Italian walnut and marquetry chests, early 18th century, 67in. wide. (Christie's) $19,530 £9,000

Early 19th century marquetry tallboy chest, 3ft.4in. wide. (Pearsons) $1,730 £800

George III mahogany chest of drawers with brass fittings, 124cm. wide. (Phillips) $316 £140

18th century Central European walnut serpentine chest of three drawers. (Locke & England) $13,640 £6,200

George III mahogany chest of five drawers with brass fittings, 106cm. wide. (Phillips) $316 £140

George III mahogany chest of three drawers, 92cm. wide. (Phillips) $646 £280

18th century South German walnut chest. (Langlois Ltd.) $3,146 £1,550

17th century Italian inlaid chest of four drawers, veneered in fruitwood, 4ft.10in. wide. (Sotheby's) $3,580 £1,650

Anglo-Dutch pen-work decorated walnut chest of five drawers, 3ft. 3in. wide, circa 1700. (Sotheby's) $3,146 £1,450

Late 19th century mahogany specimen chest on tapered legs with spade feet. (Phillips) $345 £150

Biedermeier satinwood chest of drawers, circa 1825, 3ft. wide. (Sotheby's) $868 £400

Late 18th century marquetry chest decorated in various woods. (Phillips) $9,550 £4,400

Pine watchmaker's cabinet with brass handles, 17in. high, circa 1880. (Gray's Antique Mews) $97 £43

William and Mary oyster walnut chest of five drawers, 3ft.5in. wide. (Sotheby King & Chasemore) $4,181 £1,850

Late 17th/early 18th century Goanese inlaid chest of drawers, 4ft.3in. wide. (Sotheby's) $4,775 £2,200

Dutch provincial bombe fronted chest on paw feet, circa 1840. (Bradley & Vaughan) $2,050 £900

Jacobean oak chest with a pair of geometrically moulded doors, 3ft.3in. wide. (Sotheby King & Chasemore) $1,039 £460

323

Hepplewhite period bow fronted chest of drawers, 3ft.1½in. wide. (Whiteheads) $3,655 £1,800

George I walnut chest of five drawers, 3ft.3½in. wide, circa 1725. (Sotheby's) $1,035 £480

Attractive oyster veneered olivewood and walnut chest of drawers, circa 1695. (Sotheby's) $5,887 £2,900

Anglo-Dutch chest of two short and three long drawers, circa 1700. (Sotheby's) $8,640 £4,000

French 19th century kingwood and mahogany semainier, 81cm. wide. (Sotheby King & Chasemore) $2,130 £1,050

William and Mary oyster veneered walnut chest of five drawers. (Sotheby's) $5,050 £2,500

Jacobean oak chest of four long drawers, 3ft.6in. wide, on bun feet. (Sotheby King & Chasemore) $3,025 £1,400

Early 18th century walnut chest, decorated with crossbanding and feather-banding, 100cm. wide. (Sotheby King & Chasemore) $810 £400

Mahogany chest of drawers, circa 1810, with original ebony handles and bracket feet, 40in. wide. (Christopher Sykes) $620 £275

Late 18th century George III mahogany serpentine fronted chest, 32in. high. (Sotheby's) $880 £440

Fine small antique walnut Wellington chest of seven drawers, 23in. wide. (Butler & Hatch Waterman) $1,340 £620

Small serpentine fronted chest of drawers in mahogany. (Lawrence) $5,125 £2,500

Jacobean oak chest, 3ft.5in. wide. (Sotheby King & Chasemore) $1,730 £800

17th century oak chest of drawers, 42in. wide. (Hy. Duke & Son) $1,065 £520

Jacobean oak chest of four long drawers, 38in. wide. (Whiteheads) $1,055 £520

James II walnut chest with moulded front embellished with ivory roundels. (Edwards, Bigwood & Bewlay) $5,400 £2,400

Victorian mahogany Wellington chest of seven drawers with turned wood handles, 22in. wide. (Butler & Hatch Waterman) $475 £220

Georgian oak and mahogany military chest, 3ft.1in. wide, with green leather top. (Coles, Knapp & Kennedy) $280 £130

Queen Anne walnut chest of five drawers with oak sides and top, 39in. wide. (Sotheby Humberts) $820 £380

Jacobean yew-wood chest of drawers. (Boardman's) $4,815 £2,350

Early oak chest of four drawers on bun feet, 36in. wide. (Butler & Hatch Waterman) $710 £330

Victorian brass bound camphorwood military chest of five drawers, 2ft.3½in. wide. (D. M. Nesbit & Co.) $1,015 £470

George III mahogany secretaire chest, 76cm. wide. (Sotheby King & Chasemore) $1,035 £460

Early 19th century French mahogany semainier with white marble top, 37in. wide. (Sotheby Humberts) $3,455 £1,600

325

Late 18th century oak tallboy of four long and four short drawers. (Vernon's) $675 £300

Fine 18th century mahogany chest on chest, 45in. wide. (Stanilands) $1,995 £925

Early 18th century walnut, crossbanded and herringbone inlaid tallboy chest, 3ft.5in. wide. (Geering & Colyer) $10,125 £4,500

Queen Anne period walnut crossbanded and herringbone inlay tallboy chest, 3ft.4¼in. wide. (Geering & Colyer) $4,060 £2,000

18th century oak chest on chest with nine drawers, 104cm. wide. (Phillips) $680 £300

George III mahogany tallboy with fluted decoration, circa 1800, 110cm. wide. (Sotheby King & Chasemore) $1,510 £700

William and Mary cabinet on chest fitted with central cupboard. (Worsfolds) $2,810 £1,300

George I walnut tallboy, boxwood inlaid. (Christie's S. Kensington) $4,320 £2,000

George I walnut tallboy. (Lawrence) $2,700 £1,250

George III mahogany tallboy, circa 1780, 3ft.11in. wide. (Sotheby's) $4,520 £2,000

George III mahogany chest on chest with bracket feet and original handles. (Vernon's) $1,100 £475

Late 18th century mahogany chest on chest with brass loop handles. (Vernon's) $1,155 £500

Early 19th century tallboy with nine drawers, 71¾in. high. (Sotheby Bearne) $990 £440

George III mahogany bow fronted tallboy, 104cm. wide. (Sotheby King & Chasemore) $1,100 £510

Mid 19th century mahogany tallboy chest, 40in. wide. (Lacy Scott) $1,015 £500

George III mahogany and crossbanded tallboy, 105cm. wide. (Sotheby King & Chasemore) $1,165 £540

Antique mahogany tallboy, circa 1770, 42in. wide, on original bracket feet. (Christopher Sykes) $1,570 £695

Small reproduction 18th century style mahogany chest on chest. (Phillips) $250 £110

Late 18th century Irish mahogany tallboy on claw feet. (British Antique Exporters)$1,545 £670

Fine George I walnut tallboy, base with secretaire drawer, 42½in. wide. (Christie's) $15,020 £6,800

Early George III mahogany tallboy, 49¼in. wide, on later scrolled feet. (Christie's) $8,400 £3,800

Mid 19th century Georgian design mahogany bow fronted tallboy, 112cm. wide. (Sotheby King & Chasemore) $1,250 £580

George III North Country mahogany tallboy, circa 1780, 3ft.11in. wide. (Sotheby's) $4,560 £2,000

Late George III mahogany tallboy, circa 1805, 3ft.10in. wide. (Sotheby King & Chasemore) $1,470 £650

CHESTS ON STANDS

Fine William and Mary oyster walnut chest on stand, 3ft.5½in. wide. (Geering & Colyer) $4,385 £1,950

George I chest on stand in burr-walnut with brass drop handles, 110cm. wide. (May, Whetter & Grose) $1,080 £500

William and Mary walnut chest on stand, circa 1690, restored, 3ft. wide. (Sotheby's) $3,130 £1,450

William and Mary oyster veneered walnut cabinet on stand, 3ft.2in. wide, circa 1695. (Sotheby's) $4,970 £2,300

18th century amboyna wood chest of five drawers on stand. (Honiton Galleries) $1,130 £500

William and Mary honey coloured chest on stand with bun feet. (Worsfolds) $2,260 £1,000

William and Mary walnut tallboy, 41in. wide. (Sotheby Humberts) $2,160 £1,000

Dutch or Swedish oak chest on stand, circa 1660, 3ft.8in. wide. (Sotheby's) $2,390 £1,100

Walnut Queen Anne chest on stand, circa 1689, 3ft.6in. wide. (Gray's Antique Mews) $4,970 £2,200

George I oak and walnut tallboy. (Sotheby's) $4,070 £1,800

Charles II chest on stand, 3ft.5in. wide, circa 1670. (Sotheby's) $3,080 £1,350

Channel Islands Georgian pale oak chest on stand, 39½in. wide. (Christie's) $2,750 £1,200

William and Mary walnut and crossbanded chest on a later stand, 95cm. wide. (Sotheby King & Chasemore) $820 £400

Early 18th century walnut tallboy with nine drawers, 3ft.4in. wide. (Shakespear, McTurk & Graham) $905 £420

William and Mary oyster veneered walnut chest on stand, 3ft.4½in. wide, circa 1695. (Sotheby's) $6,050 £2,800

Edwardian Sheraton style narrow chest of drawers. (R. L. Lowery & Partners)$605 £280

Walnut and oyster veneered parquetry chest on stand, 3ft.8½in. wide. (Sotheby's) $1,175 £520

William and Mary walnut chest on stand, 55in. high. (Gray's Antique Mews) $7,200 £3,200

17th century Spanish chest on carved stand. (Bradley & Vaughan) $1,185 £520

George I walnut and oak tallboy, circa 1720, later legs, 3ft.4in. wide. (Sotheby's) $4,105 £1,800

Early 18th century chest on stand in oyster walnut veneer inlaid with floral marquetry. (Bradley & Vaughan) $3,435 £1,700

Custom Chippendale mahogany highboy with broken arch top, 36in. wide. (Robert W. Skinner Inc.) $1,300 £590

Queen Anne maple highboy, 38½in. wide, circa 1730-60. (Robert W. Skinner Inc.) $12,000 £5,265

Early 18th century walnut chest on stand, 3ft.2in. wide, decorated with crossbanding and featherbanding. (Sotheby King & Chasemore) $2,215 £980

CHIFFONIERS

Regency rosewood breakfront chiffonier, 72in. wide. (Christie's S. Kensington) $1,835 £850

William IV rosewood chiffonier. (J. M. Welch & Son) $1,945 £900

Late Victorian mahogany chiffonier with arched panel doors. (Vernon's) $190 £85

Late 19th century oak chiffonier with scratch carving. (Phillips) $90 £40

Victorian burr-walnut chiffonier with marble top, 48in. wide. (Harrods Auctions) $680 £340

Regency brass inlaid rosewood chiffonier, 2ft.9in. wide, circa 1810. (Sotheby's) $3,350 £1,550

Late George III mahogany chiffonier, circa 1800, 2ft.3in. wide, with graduated top. (Sotheby's) $4,750 £2,200

Large Edwardian rosewood chiffonier, 8ft.6in. high. (Andrew Grant) $1,080 £480

Mid 19th century rosewood chiffonier with two-tier back, 45in. wide. (T. Bannister & Co.) $865 £400

Early 19th century figured mahogany chiffonier with panelled doors. (Vernon's) $620 £275

Regency rosewood chiffonier with concave outline. (Phillips) $5,150 £2,200

Mahogany secretaire chiffonier with shaped back board, circa 1740, 2ft. 10in. wide.(Sotheby's)$1,695 £750

George III mahogany tray topped commode with inlet handles over double cupboard, 49cm. wide. (Phillips) $645 £280

Victorian mahogany serpentine fronted one step commode with inset carpet top. (Vernon's) $90 £40

George III mahogany tray top commode with tambour front, 52cm. wide. (Phillips) $495 £220

18th century marquetry bedside cupboard, 2ft.6in. high. (Gray's Antique Mews) $735 £325

Early George III mahogany bedside cupboard with shaped gallery, circa 1765, 1ft.8½in. wide. (Sotheby's) $685 £300

Night table of Marie Antoinette, 38in. high, 1784. (Sotheby's Monaco) $62,700 £27,500

Fine unconverted night commode, circa 1800, 28in. high. (Christopher Sykes) $380 £170

Mahogany bedside table, circa 1800, 31in. high, with slatted shelf. (Christopher Sykes) $375 £165

One of a pair of Regency mahogany bedside cupboards, circa 1805, 1ft. 4in. wide. (Sotheby's)$1,595 £700

Late 18th century Chippendale style mahogany night table, 23in. wide, with tray top. (Coles, Knapp & Kennedy) $685 £300

Late 19th century inlaid oak pot cupboard. (Phillips) $115 £55

Edwardian mahogany toilet stand crossbanded in satinwood, 64cm. wide. (Phillips) $100 £45

COMMODE CHESTS

Biedermeier fruitwood commode with panelled ebonised frieze, circa 1820, 4ft. wide. (Sotheby's) $911 £420

One of two Portuguese marquetry commodes, circa 1785, 4ft.1in. wide. (Sotheby's) $7,790 £3,800

Spanish mahogany commode with white marble top, circa 1825, 4ft.1in. wide. (Sotheby's) $1,625 £750

Louis XV commode in marquetry decorated with fire gilt bronze, after Duplessis Pere. (Leys, Antwerp) $13,850 £6,400

Edwardian satinwood commode. (Christie's & Edmiston's) $4,105 £1,900

Louis XV commode in veneerwood, signed Desforges, Paris, circa 1750. (Leys, Antwerp) $11,075 £5,130

German or Austro-Hungarian walnut parquetry commode, circa 1760, 3ft.9¾in. wide. (Sotheby's) $16,275 £7,500

Lombard ivory inlaid walnut commode, circa 1760, 4ft.3in. wide. (Sotheby's) $9,980 £4,600

Louis XV/XVI transitional ormolu mounted marquetry commode, stamped C. Wolff. (Sotheby's) $33,330 £16,500

19th century serpentine fronted tulipwood commode with marble top, 44in. wide. (Worsfolds) $1,010 £450

One of a pair of George III marquetry commodes by William Moore, Dublin, circa 1780, 4ft.5in. wide. (Sotheby's) $66,960 £31,000

18th century Dutch bombe fronted marquetry commode, 36in. wide. (Worsfolds)$3,150 £1,400

18th century Dutch walnut and floral marquetry commode with shaped top. (Sotheby Bearne) $3,670 £1,700

19th century boxwood strung floral marquetry inlaid kingwood commode, 2ft.2in. wide. (Vidler & Co.) $740 £360

Late 18th century Italian commode with marquetry view. (Robert W. Skinner Inc.) $5,500 £2,455

Very important George III ormolu mounted commode by Pierre Langlois, 5ft.1in. wide, circa 1760. (Sotheby's) $259,200 £120,000

Late 18th century Italian rosewood and marquetry commode. (Christie's S. Kensington) $4,920 £2,400

George III mahogany commode, 3ft.4½in. wide, circa 1770. (Sotheby's) $5,615 £2,600

Fine small Leuis XVI commode in walnut and kingwood, 1ft. 9½in. wide. (Buckell & Ballard) $1,890 £875

French provincial walnut commode, circa 1810. (Phillips Ward Price) $2,200 £880

18th century Danish walnut and parcel gilt bombe commode, 78cm. wide. (Phillips) $9,720 £4,500

18th century marquetry commode chest, 49in. wide. (Smith-Woolley & Perry) $4,210 £1,950

One of a pair of ornate French 19th century commodes with ebonised ormolu mounting, (Buckell & Ballard) $6,260 £3,100

North Italian walnut commode, circa 1770, 4ft.7½in. wide. (Sotheby's) $5,210 £2,400

COMMODE CHESTS

18th century Dutch serpentine burr-wood commode, 44in. wide. (Olivers) $1,920 £850

One of a pair of harewood and marquetry commodes with moulded marble tops, circa 1900, 46in. wide. (Sotheby's Belgravia) $17,240 £7,800

Mid 1⁰th century red lacquer serpentine commode, 58in. wide, Italian. (Sotheby's Belgravia) $6,450 £3,100

18th century Italian walnut commode, 42½in. wide. (Christie's) $3,860 £1,700

Louis XIV boulle commode chest. (Christie's) $177,840 £78,000

Kingwood marquetry petit commode, 1870's, 24in. wide, with two drawers. (Sotheby's Belgravia) $1,040 £500

Mid 19th century 'transitional' tulipwood and marquetry commode with marble top, 48in. wide. (Sotheby's Belgravia) $770 £370

Regency boulle commode en tombeau. (Phillips) $20,025 £13,500

'Louis XV' bombe serpentine parquetry commode, circa 1880, 48¼in. wide. (Sotheby's Belgravia) $1,350 £650

Empire mahogany commode with black marble top, 51½in. wide. (Christie's) $2,495 £1,100

Early 19th century French provincial kingwood petite commode, 41cm. high. (Sotheby King & Chasemore) $1,015 £500

Fine Edwards and Roberts mid 19th century marble top Louis XVI style commode in rosewood, 80cm. wide. (Phillips) $3,235 £1,400

19th century Adam style demi-lune commode inlaid and painted with scrolling motifs, by Edwards and Roberts. (Phillips) $1,865 £820

18th century German walnut commode with plank top, 48in. wide. (Boardman's) $1,520 £700

Edwardian semi circular commode inlaid with marquetry, 5ft. wide. (H. C. Wolton & Son) $4,320 £2,000

Sheraton period mahogany bow fronted dressing commode, 3ft. 3in. wide. (Woolley & Wallis) $6,100 £2,700

One of a pair of 18th century Italian semi-elliptical parquetry commodes, veneered in satinwood, walnut and rosewood. 1m. wide. (Phillips) $31,640 £14,000

'Louis XV' kingwood floral marquetry commode with marble top, 126cm. wide. (Phillips) $3,005 £1,300

Vernis Martin bombe commode with marble top, circa 1900, 38in. wide. (Sotheby's Belgravia) $2,705 £1,300

18th century Louis XV provincial walnut commode, 36in. wide. (Robert W. Skinner Inc.) $6,500 £2,950

Kingwood and marquetry demi-lune commode, circa 1900, with grey and orange marble top, 26in. wide. (Sotheby's Belgravia) $1,040 £500

Early 20th century 'Louis XV' rosewood marquetry commode with pink marble top, 50in. wide. (Sotheby's Belgravia) $1,640 £820

19th century kingwood French petite commode with marble top, 18in. wide. (Sotheby Humberts) $905 £420

Louis XV marquetry commode by A. Levesque, 51¼in. wide. (Bonham's) $7,040 £3,200

CORNER CUPBOARDS

19th century mahogany corner cupboard enclosing three shaped shelves. (Vernon's) $85 £35

19th century French kingwood and walnut veneered encoignure, 28½in. wide. (Olivers) $905 £400

18th century style mahogany corner cupboard with lozenge glazed doors, 68cm. wide. (Phillips) $315 £140

One of a pair of ebonised and gilt mahogany corner cupboards, circa 1880, 84cm. high. (Sotheby's Belgravia) $350 £160

Reproduction 18th century mahogany corner cupboard, 66cm. wide. (Phillips) $190 £85

George III oak standing corner cupboard, 3ft.8in. wide. (Sotheby King & Chasemore) $1,920 £850

Late 19th century satin walnut corner cabinet. (Phillips) $300 £130

Dutch walnut and marquetry standing corner cupboard with arched cornice, 51in. wide. (Christie's)
$11,050 £5,000

Sheraton design and period corner display cupboard, 7ft.6in. high. (Worsfolds)
$1,215 £540

Mid 18th century mahogany corner cupboard, 7ft. 5½in. wide. (Sotheby's)
$6,970 £3,400

Early 19th century Georgian design standing mahogany corner cupboard, 120cm. wide. (Sotheby King & Chasemore)
$1,555 £720

Late 18th century stripped pine corner cupboard, 30in. wide.(Dodd)
$495 £220

Ebonised mahogany corner corner cupboard, circa 1880, 115cm. high. (Sotheby's Belgravia) **$165 £75**

Inlaid bow fronted corner display cupboard. (Cobern, Entwistle & Co.) **$280 £130**

Late 18th century bow fronted double door hanging corner cabinet, 3ft.1in. wide. (James Harrison) **$395 £175**

19th century Dutch floral marquetry corner cupboard. (D. M. Nesbit & Co.) **$870 £430**

Carved and painted corner cupboard with pierced cornice, circa 1760, 2ft. 5in. wide. (Sotheby's) **$2,375 £1,100**

Bow fronted pine corner cupboard in two parts, circa 1780, 4ft.7in. wide. (Sotheby's) **$1,370 £600**

18th century Dutch mahogany corner cupboard, 25in. wide. (Phillips) **$6,480 £3,000**

Inlaid corner display cabinet. (D. M. Nesbit & Co.) **$1,410 £625**

18th century standing pine corner cupboard, 108cm. wide. (Sotheby King & Chasemore) **$585 £260**

Georgian fruitwood standing corner cupboard with scrolled broken pediment, 44½in. wide. (Christie's) **$1,365 £620**

Victorian stripped pine hanging corner cupboard with panelled door. (Vernon's) **$220 £100**

French Louis XV period encoignure by Jacques Dubois in ormolu mounted oak, 2.88m. high. (Sotheby's Monaco) **$1,879,210 £835,165**

COURT CUPBOARDS

Queen Anne oak court cupboard. circa 1710, 4ft.3in. wide. (Sotheby's) $2.585 £1.150

Early 18th century oak court cupboard with brass fittings. (Walker, Barnett & Hill) $3,275 £1,400

An 18th century oak court cupboard with fielded panel doors. (Christie's) $2,700 £1,200

Mid 17th century oak court cupboard with carved frieze, 4ft.6in. wide. (Sotheby King & Chasemore) $2,260 £1,000

Commonwealth oak court cupboard with moulded rectangular top, 44½in. wide, inlaid with bone and mother-of-pearl. (Christie's) $4,840 £2,200

17th century oak court cupboard, 41in. wide. (Phillips) $4,455 £1,980

James I oak court cupboard, circa 1620, 5ft. wide. (Sotheby's) $1,395 £620

Early 18th century oak tridarn, 53in. wide, with fielded cupboard doors. (Christie's) $2,925 £1,300

Commonwealth oak court cupboard with moulded cornice, 67in wide. (Christie's) $2,975 £1,300

Oak court cupboard with lunette cornice, baluster supports and heavily carved doors, 64in. wide. (Christie's) $1,830 £800

20th century Jacobean style oak court cupboard with panelled doors. (Vernon's) $950 £425

Continental oak court cupboard heavily carved and of good size. (Russell, Baldwin & Bright) $10,490 £4,600

Victorian walnut breakfront side cabinet, 72in. wide. (Olivers) $3,130 £1,450

Walnut credenza, cupboard door inlaid with a vase and scrolling foliage, 58½in. wide, circa 1870. (Sotheby's Belgravia) $1,100 £480

Victorian burr-walnut breakfront credenza with canted corners, 5ft.7in. wide. (Eadon, Lockwood & Riddle) $1,620 £750

Ebonised porcelain and gilt bronze mounted display cabinet, 1860's, 72in. wide. (Sotheby's Belgravia) $1,830 £880

Marquetry meuble d'appui with breakfront white marble top, 1860's, 78in. wide. (Sotheby's Belgravia) $4,265 £2,050

Boulle side cabinet, 1870's, 78in. wide. (Sotheby's Belgravia) $2,190 £1,400

Victorian walnut and marquetry serpentine side cabinet, 78in. wide. (Olivers) $7,230 £3,200

19th century Flanders carved oak neo-Gothic credenza. (Leys, Antwerp) $4,500 £2,085

Kingwood and marquetry credenza with D-shaped top, 83¾in. long, circa 1870. (Sotheby's Belgravia) $4,180 £1,850

Victorian breakfront walnut credenza, 5ft.7½in. wide, enriched with a Sevres porcelain medallion. (Eadon, Lockwood & Riddle) $2,700 £1,250

Fine mid Victorian walnut and marquetry side cabinet by Gillows. (Christie's) $12,960 £6,000

Fine mid 19th century figured walnut credenza, 6ft. wide. (Heathcote Ball & Co.) $4,975 £2,450

Fine early 18th century oak hall cupboard, 130cm. wide. (Sotheby King & Chasemore) $1,230 £600

Mahogany and oak linen press, 50in. wide. (J. M. Welch & Son) $580 £270

Rare late 17th/early 18th century Dutch colonial aramana wood cupboard, 4ft.5in. wide. (Sotheby's) $1,627 £750

19th century carved padoukwood cupboard, 130cm. wide. (Sotheby King & Chasemore) $1,575 £700

Charles II oak and walnut chest. (Sotheby Humberts) $3,067 £1,420

Early 19th century Yorkshire elmwood and fruitwood cupboard, 42in. wide. (Vost's) $1,435 £700

Walnut marquetry clothes press, 4ft.3in. wide. (Sotheby's) $5,425 £2,500

18th century mahogany clothes press with two drawers. (R. L. Lowery & Partners) $495 £230

French Napoleon III period cupboard inlaid with pewter, brass and red tortoiseshell. (Leys, Antwerp) $19,000 £8,800

17th century carved oak cupboard, 4ft.7in. wide. (Sotheby King & Chasemore) $2,484 £1,150

Late 18th century oak livery cupboard on bracket feet. (Vernon's) $1,150 £500

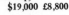

Fine late 18th century Breton oak cupboard, 195cm. wide. (Sotheby King & Chasemore) $1,537 £750

17th century Netherlands renaissance style cupboard in ebony and walnut veneer. (Leys, Antwerp) $6,575 £3,000

17th century German oak standing cupboard with single plank top, 79in. long. (Boardman's) $6,510 £3,000

17th century Flemish carved oak cupboard, 122cm. wide. (Sotheby King & Chasemore) $1,189 £580

Early 18th century oak double wardrobe cupboard, 5ft.6in. wide. (Coles, Knapp & Kennedy) $1,596 £700

Rare English livery cupboard in carved oak with inlaid panels, 3ft.2½in. wide. (Butler & Hatch Waterman) $1,360 £630

Mid 18th century oak cupboard on chest, 186cm. wide. (Sotheby King & Chasemore) $1,530 £680

19th century Flanders carved neo-renaissance cupboard in oak. (Leys, Antwerp) $3,125 £1,450

17th century hall cupboard. (Sotheby King & Chasemore) $4,750 £2,200

18th century American pine step back cupboard, 38in. wide. (Robert W. Skinner Inc.) $1,100 £485

18th century Normandy Regency bridal cupboard in oak. (Leys, Antwerp) $2,750 £1,300

Old carved oak cheese cupboard, heavily carved, 3ft.5in. wide. (Shakespear, McTurk & Graham) $1,123 £520

Dutch mahogany clothes press with stepped pediment, circa 1780, 6ft.10in. wide. (Sotheby's) $6,510 £3,000

341

CUPBOARDS

Regency walnut cupboard with moulded top, circa 1730, 4ft.7in. wide. (Sotheby's) $1,755 £780

One of a pair of 18th century mahogany bedside cupboards. (Parsons, Welch & Cowell) $8,885 £3,950

15th century Gothic oak food cupboard with pierced and carved front, 49in. wide. (Christie's) $6,410 £2,800

Oak cupboard with moulded cornice and double panelled doors, 4ft.3in. wide. (Rye Auction Galleries) $855 £380

Early English livery cupboard in oak with wrought iron hinges, 23½in. wide. (Whiteheads) $1,175 £580

Charles II oak and walnut chest and cupboards, circa 1670, 45½in. high (Sotheby Humberts) $3,195 £1,420

18th century American country pine step back cupboard, 44in. wide. (Robert W. Skinner Inc.) $1,200 £525

Early Louis XV provincial oak cupboard, 3ft.10in. wide, circa 1730. (Sotheby's) $1,875 £820

19th century French provincial cherrywood cupboard with brass fittings. (Vernon's) $2,770 £1,200

Early 19th century French provincial cherrywood cupboard with shaped panel doors. (Vernon's) $4,275 £1,850

Late Victorian carved oak side cupboard with a shaped pediment, 49in. wide. (Sotheby's Belgravia) $640 £280

Early George III mahogany clothes press with moulded cornice, 49½in. wide. (Christie's) $1,160 £500

19th century oak Jacobean style dresser base with carved decoration. (Vernon's) $660 £300

19th century French fruit-wood bedside cupboard. (Phillips) $140 £60

18th century oak food cupboard with moulded top and slatted frieze, 44in. wide. (Christie's) $1,145 £500

Queen Anne oak cupboard in two parts, circa 1710, 4ft.3in. wide. (Sotheby's) $1,665 £720

Massive Dutch oak cupboard, late 17th century. (Christie's & Edmiston's) $13,380 £6,000

Mid 19th century mahogany low press cupboard, 217cm. wide. (Phillips) $345 £150

Early 17th century Flemish or German oak cupboard, 3ft.9in. wide. (Sotheby's) $3,375 £1,500

18th century oak settle with panelled cupboard doors. (British Antique Exporters) $1,480 £640

17th century Italian walnut cupboard with single panel door, 68cm. wide. (Phillips) $300 £130

Fine Dutch walnut and marquetry armoire with moulded cornice, early 18th century, 59½in. wide.(Christie's) $6,100 £2,700

George III mahogany clothes press, 51in. wide. (Christie's) $3,135 £1,400

South German marquetry cupboard on chest, circa 1740, 2ft.11½in. wide. (Sotheby's) $2,860 £1,250

DAVENPORTS

Early 19th century William IV rosewood Davenport desk. (H. C. Chapman & Son) $1,155 £525

Regency burr-walnut Davenport. (Boardman's) $1,580 £700

Late Victorian rosewood and marquetry Davenport. (Christie's S. Kensington) $1,470 £65(

Victorian walnut Davenport. (R. H. Ellis) $1,055 £470

Good rosewood harlequin Davenport with a sliding top, circa 1830. (Sotheby's Belgravia) $1,950 £850

Walnut harlequin Davenport, circa 1860, 59.5cm. wide. (Sotheby's Belgravia) $1,770 £820

19th century walnut Davenport with fretwork panels, 60cm. wide. (Phillips) $1,015 £440

Edwardian inlaid rosewood Davenport with original inkwells. (Alfie's Antique Market) $375 £175

Small late 19th century satinwood Davenport desk. (Gray's Antique Mews) $805 £350

George IV cedar lined mahogany Davenport with pierced brass gallery. (H. C. Wolton & Son) $2,720 £1,260

Regency Davenport of mahogany surmounted by a letter tray, 76cm. wide. (Phillips) $765 £340

Walnut Davenport, circa 1860, 23in. wide, with green leather writing slope. (Sotheby's) $1,080 £500

Boulle Davenport with brass and gilt metal decoration, 21in. wide. (Edwards, Bigwood & Bewlay) $1,610 £750

Walnut Davenport with fitted interior, circa 1870, 22in. wide. (Sotheby's Belgravia) $765 £340

Mahogany Davenport with sloping hinged writing surface, late 1830's, 20in. wide. (Sotheby's Belgravia) $1,170 £520

Mahogany Davenport with pierced brass gallery, 33½in. wide, circa 1830. (Sotheby's) $1,015 £450

Victorian walnut Davenport with satinwood interior, 1ft.10in. wide. (Rye Auction Galleries) $1,010 £450

Marquetry and rosewood Davenport with hinged superstructure, 21in. wide, circa 1900. (Sotheby's Belgravia) $785 £350

Small Victorian walnut Davenport with inset leather to the top. (Vernon's) $725 £325

Olivewood Davenport, top stencilled Jerusalem, circa 1880-1900, 29in. wide. (Sotheby's Belgravia) $1,685 £750

Early Victorian walnut Davenport with maple veneered interior, 21in. wide.(Sotheby's Belgravia) $660 £290

George IV plumbago mahogany Davenport. (Woolley & Wallis) $2,150 £920

Edwardian cedar Davenport inlaid with Irish subjects. (Phillips) $3,860 £1,650

Victorian walnut Davenport with inset leather top. (Dickinson, Davy & Markham) $1,030 £440

Small Edwardian inlaid mahogany bow fronted china cabinet. (Vernon's) $200 £85

Mid 20th century 'Chippendale' mahogany display cabinet on stand with pierced cresting, 51in. wide. (Sotheby's Belgravia) $1,625 £720

Edwardian mahogany china cabinet enclosed by three glazed doors, 4ft.6in. wide. (Vernon's) $285 £125

George III mahogany display cabinet with moulded cornice, 74in. wide. (Christie's) $3,450 £1,500

Fine Dutch marquetry display cabinet with arched moulded cornice, 84½in. wide. (Christie's) $20,610 £9,000

Biedermeier fruitwood display cabinet, 50½in. wide. (Christie's) $1,555 £680

Dutch walnut display cabinet with arched moulded cornice, 57½in. wide. (Christie's) $10,075 £4,400

Fine mahogany Chinese Chippendale chinoiserie display cabinet, circa 1900. (British Antique Exporters) $5,650 £2,500

George III satinwood display cabinet on stand, top crossbanded with rosewood, 28in. wide. (Christie's) $2,250 £950

Walnut and parcel gilt cabinet on stand with glazed top, 40in. wide. (Christie's) $3,165 £1,400

Dutch walnut and marquetry display cabinet with broken triangular pediment, 80in. wide. (Christie's) $4,810 £2,100

Pollard & Co. mahogany 'airtight' display case of circular form, 75in. high, 1920's. (Sotheby's Belgravia) $1,695 £750

Late 19th century mahogany display cabinet. (Phillips) $160 £70

One of a pair of kingwood display cabinets on cabriole legs, circa 1900, 50in. wide. (Sotheby's Belgravia) $17,680 £8,000

19th century brass inlaid mahogany display cabinet, 32½in. wide, with violet marble top. (Neales) $2,375 £1,050

Mahogany display cabinet with broken triangular pediment, 47in. wide, mid 18th century. (Christie's) $6,330 £2,800

Fine Sheraton revival mahogany serpentine display cabinet by Edwards & Roberts, 62in. wide. (Neales) $9,040 £4,000

Art Nouveau mahogany cabinet with marquetry inlay and pewter panel. (Biddle & Webb) $3,645 £1,600

Chippendale mahogany display cabinet on stand with pierced cresting, circa 1890. (Sotheby's Belgravia) $1,300 £580

One of a pair of tulipwood display cabinets with arched upper parts, circa 1900, 31½in. wide. (Sotheby's Belgravia) $12,155 £5,500

Mahogany display cabinet of bow form over base with single drawer. (Phillips) $460 £200

Edwardian Art Nouveau mahogany display cabinet, 54in. wide. (Olivers) $1,040 £460

Late 19th century French kingwood and ormolu mounted marble top breakfront vitrine, 4ft.7in. wide, circa 1880. (Sotheby King & Chasemore) $4,180 £1,850

Late 19th century Continental mahogany display cabinet of polygonal form, 80cm. wide. (Phillips) $875 £380

DISPLAY CABINETS

20th century Chinese open display cabinet in rosewood, 5ft. wide. (Sotheby's) $1,468 £680

George III mahogany book or display case, 4ft.9in. wide, circa 1780. (Sotheby's) $2,916 £1,350

Mahogany and Vernis Martin vitrine with marble top, circa 1900, 24½in. wide. (Sotheby's Belgravia) $1,590 £720

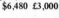

Late 18th century Dutch walnut display cabinet. (Bradley & Vaughan) $6,480 £3,000

Good tulipwood vitrine, circa 1900, with parquetry lower section, 36in. wide. (Sotheby's Belgravia) $3,016 £1,450

18th century Liege carved oak display cabinet. (Leys, Antwerp) $4,838 £2,240

Early 20th century mahogany and glazed display cabinet, 46in. wide, with marble top. (Sotheby's Belgravia) $1,664 £800

Early 20th century mahogany and Vernis Martin vitrine, 40in. wide. (Sotheby's Belgravia) $1,456 £700

Mahogany Chippendale style display cabinet, 4ft.6in. wide. (Geering & Colyer) $2,025 £900

18th century Dutch secretaire silver display cabinet in citronwood marquetry, 120cm. wide. (Leys, Antwerp) $11,767 £5,448

Walnut and simulated rosewood Vernis Martin vitrine, circa 1920, 66in. high. (Sotheby's Belgravia) $1,830 £880

Georgian mahogany china display cabinet, 31½in. wide with glazed doors. (Whiteheads) $2,639 £1,300

Victorian mahogany Chippendale style display cabinet with shaped cornice. (Stanilands)
$1,166 £540

Early 20th century Vernis Martin rosewood vitrine, 27½in. wide. (Sotheby's Belgravia) $2,650 £1,200

Ormolu mounted kingwood vitrine. (Christie's)
$3,240 £1,500

Mid 19th century burr-walnut and ormolu moun-ted display cabinet, 75cm. wide. (Sotheby King & Chasemore) $1,035 £460

Edwardian inlaid and banded mahogany bow-fronted corner display cabinet, 33in. wide. (D. M. Nesbit & Co.)
$1,350 £625

Mid 19th century Dutch marquetry display cabi-net, 4ft.9in. wide. (Sotheby's)
$27,675 £13,500

Satinwood display cabi-net in the Sheraton manner, 61cm. wide. (Sotheby Humberts)
$1,252 £580

Edwardian mahogany framed display cabi-net with shaped mir-rored pediment. (Osmond Tricks)
$984 £480

Kingwood and Vernis Martin serpentine vitrine, circa 1880, 50in. wide. (Sotheby's Belgravia)
$6,240 £3,000

Good kingwood vitrine with breakfront bow fronted gla-zed door, circa 1900, 51in. wide. (Sotheby's Belgravia) $8,400 £3,800

One of a pair of unusual 19th century satinwood china display cabinets, 14in. wide. (Graves, Son & Pilcher)
$6,265 £2,900

Louis XV silver display cabinet with gilt bronze mounts. (Leys, Antwerp)
$6,229 £2,884

349

DISPLAY CABINETS

Dutch marquetry display cabinet, circa 1840, 55in. wide. (Sotheby's Belgravia) $2,430 £1,100

Mid 19th century Flemish carved oak display cabinet, 41½in. wide. (Sotheby's Belgravia) $2,035 £920

Early 19th century mahogany vitrine, frieze with gilt bronze banding, 36in. wide. (Sotheby's Belgravia) $1,590 £720

Bow fronted satinwood display cabinet, inlaid with walnut, possibly German, circa 1910, 70½in. high. (Sotheby's Belgravia) $1,380 £600

Mid 20th century walnut display cabinet in Dutch 18th century style, 58in. wide. (Sotheby's Belgravia) $2,320 £1,050

Small Dutch display cabinet on chest with arched top, circa 1840, 23½in. wide. (Sotheby's Belgravia) $1,880 £850

Dutch walnut and marquetry display cabinet with arched top, circa 1840, 87in. high. (Sotheby's Belgravia) $6,410 £2,900

Mahogany display cabinet with arched mirrored top, 38½in. wide, circa 1900. (Sotheby's Belgravia) $1,850 £800

Chippendale mahogany display cabinet with a blind fret cornice, 57in. wide, circa 1890. (Sotheby's Belgravia) $1,950 £850

Edwardian rosewood and marquetry display cabinet with two drawers. (Alfred Mossop & Co.) $1,965 £910

Dutch mahogany display cabinet with chamfered glazed doors, 44in. wide, circa 1900. (Sotheby's Belgravia) $300 £130

Late 19th century satinwood and inlaid shaped fronted display cabinet, 123cm. wide. (Sotheby King & Chasemore) $2,915 £1,350

French style china closet with curved front and side glasses, 34in. wide. (Robert W. Skinner Inc.) $900 £410

Late 19th century ebonised and ivory inlaid display cabinet, 44in. wide. (Sotheby's Belgravia) $1,370 £620

Early 20th century serpentine marquetry vitrine with brown marble top, 31½in. wide. (Sotheby's Belgravia) $3,315 £1,500

19th century French rosewood and Vernis Martin vitrine, 57in. wide, with ormolu mounts. (Christie's S. Kensington) $4,750 £2,200

Mahogany and marquetry display cabinet on stand with a swan neck pediment, circa 1900. (Sotheby's Belgravia) $3,300 £1,450

George I style walnut display cabinet on bracket feet, 33½in. wide, circa 1900. (Sotheby's Belgravia) $900 £400

Mahogany framed circular display cabinet on stand with scrolling legs, circa 1900. (Sotheby's Belgravia) $7,300 £3,200

Kingwood and marquetry vitrine, circa 1900, 53in. wide. (Sotheby's Belgravia) $6,850 £3,100

19th century boulle display cabinet with a glazed door, 29in. wide. (Sotheby's Belgravia) $875 £380

Bow front satinwood display cabinet painted with flowers, fruit and figures, circa 1900, 77in. high. (Sotheby's Belgravia) $2,420 £1,050

Chinese Chippendale design display cabinet with carved pediment, 37in. wide. (Worsfolds) $1,175 £520

Dutch 18th century marquetry china cabinet, 4ft. 9in. wide, with four drawers beneath. (Elliott & Green) $8,640 £4,000

351

Early oak two drawer dresser and rack with shaped slab legs. (Eadon, Lockwood & Riddle) $1,296 £600

18th century French provincial oak buffet, 124cm. wide. (Phillips)
$330 £160

Early 18th century oak dresser with three-tier rack, 74in. wide. (Smith-Woolley & Perry)
$1,728 £800

Early 18th century oak dresser base with moulded top, 8ft. long. (Heathcote Ball & Co.)
$1,665 £820

18th century oak dresser with pot shelf under, 5ft.8in. wide. (Pearsons) $2,485 £1,150

Early Georgian dresser base in pale oak, 70in. wide.(Christie's)
$5,400 £2,400

18th century oak dresser with mahogany and chequered banding, 6ft.2in. wide. (Russell, Baldwin & Bright)
$3,455 £1,600

18th century French provincial oak buffet, 58¼in. wide. (Olivers)
$2,260 £1,000

18th century oak dresser with shelves. (John D. Fleming) $2,700 £1,250

Late 17th century yew-wood dresser base, 5ft.11in. wide. (Whiteheads)
$10,960 £5,400

English dresser with plate rack above, in good condition. (R. L. Lowery & Partners) $2,375 £1,100

Early 17th century Jacobean dresser base in oak with three drawers, 78¾in. long.(Sotheby King & Chasemore)
$4,500 £2,000

George I oak dresser with later Georgian plate rack, 6ft. wide. (Shakespear, McTurk & Graham) $4,105 £1,900

19th century oak Delft rack, 36½in. wide. (Christopher Sykes) $530 £245

Early 18th century oak dresser with iron hooks in frieze, 4ft. 9in. wide. (Parsons, Welch & Cowell) $3,375 £1,500

Fine late 18th century oak dresser base, 5ft.11in. wide. (Butler & Hatch Waterman) $4,105 £1,900

17th century oak dresser, 56in. wide. (Vost's) $4,305 £2,100

Fine early 18th century oak dresser base, 162cm. wide. (Sotheby King & Chasemore) $2,280 £1,600

German dark oak dresser with three cupboard doors to the base. (Andrew Grant) $2,970 £1,450

Oak dresser base with knob missing, circa 1750. (Nock, Deighton & Son) $1,530 £680

18th century oak dresser, 54in. wide. (Parsons. Welch & Cowell) $2,835 £1,260

Mid Georgian oak dresser base with canopied plate rack, 73in. wide. (Christie's) $2,810 £1,300

Unusual German dresser with two drawers. (Cobern, Entwistle & Co.) $300 £140

18th century Spanish dresser, shelves with original cast iron hooks, 5ft.3in. wide. (Andrew Grant) $2,970 £1,450

353

DRESSERS AND BUFFETS

Small Victorian stripped pine dresser base with shaped brass handles, 4ft. wide. (Vernon's) $305 £140

17th century oak buffet with overhanging frieze on gadrooned baluster supports, 51½in. wide. (Christie's) $1,785 £780

Oak Welsh dresser, probably Caernarvonshire. (K. Hugh Dodd & Partners) $2,590 £1,200

Charles II oak dresser with dentil mounted and pierced cornice, circa 1665, 6ft. 3in. wide. (Sotheby's) $2,050 £900

George III oak dresser with plate racks, 5ft.7in. wide. (Sotheby King & Chasemore) $2,485 £1,100

Georgian oak dresser with three shelves and three drawers, 63in. wide. (Christie's) $3,665 £1,600

George II oak and elm dresser with three drawers, 6ft.10in. wide, circa 1740. (Sotheby's) $1,270 £550

Flemish 17th century oak dresser fitted with three drawers, 7ft. long. (Phillips) $1,900 £880

Small mahogany dresser base with two drawers, 48in. wide. (Christopher Sykes) $620 £275

George II oak and elm dresser with moulded cornice, 4ft.7½in. wide, circa 1750. (Sotheby's) $2,885 £1,250

Florally carved, glass fronted pine Welsh dresser, 7ft.4in. high. (Gray's Antique Mews) $755 £350

Oak dresser with waved frieze and open shelves, 65½in. wide. (Christie's) $1,420 £620

Early 18th century oak dresser base. (West London Auctions) $4,535 £2,100

18th century oak dresser with moulded rectangular top, 84in. wide. (Christie's) $2,420 £1,100

Small Jacobean oak dresser base. (Andrew Grant) $6,155 £2,700

Early 19th century stripped pine dresser with pot cupboard.(Vernon's) $1,350 £600

Oak dresser with moulded cornice above three shelves, circa 1700, 4ft.6½in. wide. (Sotheby's) $2,050 £900

Early 19th century oak dresser with raised plate rack, 5ft.7in. wide. (Lalonde Bros. & Parham) $2,810 £1,300

Mid 18th century oak dresser base, crossbanded with mahogany, 6ft.2in. wide. (Sotheby King & Chasemore) $2,270 £1,050

Early 18th century oak moulded front dresser base, 63in. wide. (Boardman's) $3,365 £1,550

Georgian oak low dresser with moulded rectangular top crossbanded in mahogany, 73½in. wide. (Christie's) $1,870 £850

George II oak dresser with open plate rack, 6ft. wide, circa 1730. (Sotheby's) $2,310 £1,000

Georgian oak Welsh dresser with four plate racks, 6ft. wide. (Geering & Colyer) $2,810 £1,250

Mid 18th century oak dresser, rack with cavetto cornice, 6ft. wide. (Sotheby's) $3,695 £1,600

355

Early Victorian walnut tea table with gilt balustrade. (Hobbs Parker) $955 £470

Sheraton style mahogany dumb waiter. (Honiton Galleries) $225 £100

George II mahogany dumb waiter with two circular tiers, 2ft.2½in. wide, circa 1745. (Sotheby's) $1,620 £720

Regency mahogany dumb waiter with brass gallery and reeded tripod base with claw castors. (Vernon's) $1,350 £600

19th century mahogany three-tier dumb waiter of Georgian design, 118cm. high. (Sotheby King & Chasemore) $710 £350

Good George III mahogany dumb waiter, 3ft.3½in. high, circa 1785. (Sotheby's) $1,945 £900

George III mahogany three-tier dumb waiter, circa 1760, 43in. high. (Christopher Sykes) $1,275 £565

19th century two-tier dumb waiter with turned central column, 68cm. diam. (Phillips) $645 £280

Regency mahogany three-tier dumb waiter with revolving shelves, 29in. wide. (Christie's) $830 £360

George III mahogany dumb waiter, circa 1770, 3ft.6in. high. (Sotheby's) $1,245 £550

19th century two-tier dumb waiter with marquetry and ormolu mounts. (R. H. Ellis) $790 £350

Victorian walnut dumb waiter of two circular tiers, 1ft.8in. diam. (Rye Auction Galleries) $270 £120

Queen Anne mahogany lowboy with shell-carved drawer, 31in. wide. (Robert W. Skinner Inc.) $600 £270

18th century yew-wood lowboy with three drawers, 31in. wide. (Hy. Duke & Son) $2,240 £1,000

Queen Anne oak lowboy with three drawers, 32in. wide. (Morphet's) $905 £400

George I walnut veneered lowboy with original handles and escutcheons. (Buckell & Ballard) $1,675 £825

George II oak lowboy, circa 1775, 31½in. wide. (Christopher Sykes) $635 £295

George II mahogany lowboy with four drawers, circa 1735, 2ft.6in. wide. (Sotheby's) $2,700 £1,250

Mid 18th century oak lowboy on four cabriole legs, 80cm. wide. (Sotheby King & Chasemore) $1,130 £500

Antique walnut lowboy with feather crossbanded top, 3ft. wide. (Vidler & Co.) $900 £440

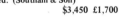

Queen Anne lowboy, with original handles missing and veneer damaged. (Southam & Son) $3,450 £1,700

Late 18th century mahogany lowboy on square cut cabriole legs. (British Antique Exporters) $1,385 £600

Late 18th century mahogany lowboy with original brass fittings. (British Antique Exporters) $635 £275

Early 19th century mahogany lowboy with three drawers and original brass fittings. (British Antique Exporters) $670 £290

357

George II walnut veneered kneehole writing desk, 30in. wide. (Garrod Turner) $7,345 £3,400

Late Georgian mahogany gentleman's kneehole desk, circa 1830, 36in. wide. (Christopher Sykes) $595 £265

Early 20th century Chinese pedestal desk. (Sotheby's Belgravia) $3,130 £1,450

Mid 19th century carved oak pedestal desk, top with outset corners, 62in. wide. (Sotheby's Belgravia) $1,100 £480

Victorian oak pedestal desk by Thomas Knight. (Christie's) $9,070 £4,200

George IV mahogany pedestal desk, circa 1820, with leather top, 5ft. long. (Sotheby's) $4,745 £2,100

Late 19th century shaped front kneehole writing desk on splay feet. (Vernon's) $655 £285

Satinwood kidney shaped kneehole desk with leather top, 124cm. wide. (Sotheby Humberts) $1,340 £620

George III mahogany desk, circa 1765, 6ft.6¾in. wide open. (Sotheby's) $6,480 £3,000

Edwardian Chinese Chippendale style mahogany pedestal desk. (T. Bannister & Co.) $1,145 £530

Early 18th century walnut kneehole desk, 30in. wide. (Boardman's) $3,255 £1,500

20th century Louis XVI style pedestal desk, 72in. wide. (D.M. Nesbit & Co.) $4,405 £1,950

18th century mahogany knee-hole desk, 32in. wide. (Hy. Duke & Son) $920 £450

18th century style mahogany kneehole desk with leatherette top, 125cm. wide. (Phillips) $370 £160

Late 18th century mahogany writing desk with nine drawers, 3ft.6in. wide. (Hobbs Parker) $505 £250

Victorian mahogany cylinder bureau. (Sotheby Bearne) $995 £440

Late 19th century oak pedestal desk with seventeen drawers, 168cm. wide. (Phillips) $615 £300

Rare George II padoukwood knee-hole writing table with leather writing surface, 2ft.11½in. wide. (Sotheby's) $2,915 £1,350

17th century walnut kneehole desk with mirror figured top, 33in. wide. (Christie's) $3,695 £1,600

North Italian rosewood kneehole desk, top crossbanded with tulipwood, 52in. wide. (Christie's) $5,445 £2,400

Queen Anne walnut and cross-banded kneehole dressing table. (Sotheby King & Chasemore) $5,625 £2,500

Oak kneehole desk of five drawers with central inset cupboard. (Worsfolds) $790 £250

Late George III mahogany pedestal desk, circa 1810, 4ft.4in. wide. (Sotheby's) $6,045 £2,800

Early 18th century walnut kneehole desk on bracket feet. (Worsfolds) $2,140 £1,070

359

PEDESTAL AND KNEEHOLE DESKS

George III mahogany kneehole desk with cloth lined top, 47½in. wide. (Christie's) $2,430 £1,200

Unusual carved walnut pedestal desk, 1860's, 46in. wide. (Sotheby's Belgravia) $1,590 £720

Fine George II mahogany kneehole desk with serpentine top, 44½in. wide. (Christie's) $9,945 £4,500

19th century Oriental carved teak writing desk. (V. & V's.) $995 £440

Early 20th century oak kneehole desk with inset leather top. (British Antique Exporters) $460 £200

George II mahogany kneehole desk with leather lined top, 49½in. wide. (Christie's) $20,995 £9,500

'Louis XIV' boulle bureau mazarin, 48in. wide, circa 1850. (Sotheby's Belgravia) $8,400 £3,800

Early 20th century oak roll-top desk with fitted interior. (British Antique Exporters) $1,270 £550

Chinese red hardwood desk, heavily carved and lacquered. (Aldridge) $855 £380

Mahogany pedestal desk of nine drawers with turned wood handles, circa 1880. (Sotheby's Belgravia) $640 £280

Victorian mahogany cylinder top kneehole desk with turned wood handles. (British Antique Exporters) $2,080 £900

Queen Anne style walnut partner's desk with green leather lined top, 3ft.10½in. wide. (Sotheby's) $2,350 £1,050

Black and gold lacquer four-leaf screen, early 18th century, 78½in. high. (Christie's) $735 £320

Kingwood, tulipwood and mahogany three-fold screen, circa 1900, 76in. high. (Sotheby's Belgravia) $1,150 £520

Mid 18th century Dutch leather six-fold screen, 96in. high. (Christie's S. Kensington) $9,070 £4,200

Walnut pole screen with circular embroidered panel, 60in. high, circa 1860. (Sotheby's Belgravia) $415 £180

Ivory applied four-fold low screen, circa 1900, 117.5cm. high. (Sotheby's Belgravia) $690 £300

19th century lithophane screen on turned baluster stem, with Madonna and Child. (Robert W. Skinner Inc.) $100 £45

Late 19th century mother-of-pearl and ivory inlaid lacquer two-fold screen, 191cm. high. (Sotheby's Belgravia) $575 £250

19th century rosewood pole firescreen. (J. M. Welch & Son) $205 £95

18th century Dutch painted leather six-leaf screen, 97in. high.(Christie's)$3,205 £1,400

Mid 19th century oak firescreen with numerous bevel glazed panels. (Sotheby's Belgravia) $550 £240

Late 19th century four-fold lacquer and ivory screen, 189cm. high. (Sotheby's Belgravia) $1,495 £650

19th century padoukwood Oriental screen, heavily carved, 72in. high. (Spear & Sons) $515 £230

361

SCREENS

Late 18th century Chinese soapstone table screen, 17¾in. high. (Sotheby Humberts) $130 £60

Ormolu and enamel three-piece miniature folding screen, 5¼in. high. (Robert W. Skinner Inc.) $550 £250

Small 19th century Oriental screen. (Phillips) $83 £36

One of a pair of 19th century hand-painted heat screens, with ivory handles. (Nottinghill Auction Market) $215 £95

Japanese four-fold lacquer screen. (May, Whetter & Grose) $475 £210

Victorian rosewood pole screen. (Alfie's Antique Market) $250 £110

Fine coromandel four-fold screen with hardstone inlay, 7ft. high. (Russell, Baldwin & Bright) $755 £350

Mid 19th century brass pole with beadwork screen supported on ebonised base. (Phillips) $185 £90

Edwardian mahogany framed sliding firescreen with silkwork panel, 42cm. wide. (Phillips) $70 £30

Chinese lacquer six-fold screen, 6ft. high. (Parsons, Welch & Cowell) $4,160 £1,850

Rosewood pole firescreen. (D. M. Nesbit & Co.) $115 £50

Walnut four-fold screen inset with oval embroidered reserves, 76in. tall, circa 1860. (Sotheby's Belgravia) $3,700 £1,600

362

Rosewood firescreen/
occasional table. (D.
M. Nesbit & Co.)
$340 £150

Chinese firescreen with
mother-of-pearl and silk
needlework panel.
(Honiton Galleries)
$190 £85

William IV mahogany pole screen,
circa 1830, with later tapestry.
(Alfie's Antique Market)
$160 £70

Mahogany framed three-
panel extending screen.
(J. M. Welch & Son)
$205 £95

A rare pair of turned
and carved mahogany
pole firescreens, circa
1790, 59in. high.
(Christopher Sykes)
$1,100 £475

19th century Chinese hardwood screen with red and
black lacquer. (R. H. Ellis)
$1,160 £510

18th century style
mahogany pole
screen with 18th
century sampler.
(Phillips) $130 £55

Chinese Kangxi coromandel
lacquer twelve-leaf screen.
(Christie's) $2,000 £880

Mahogany and lacquered
Oriental draught screen.
(R. H. Ellis)
$1,200 £530

Antique mahogany pole
screen with adjustable
needlework panel, 51in.
high. (Rye Auction
Galleries) $225 £100

Victorian parlour fire-
screen, 4ft. high, in
double-glazed glass case.
(Outhwaite & Litherland)
$670 £310

Good ormolu firescreen,
circa 1860, 26in. wide,
with oval bevelled mirror
plate. (Sotheby's
Belgravia) $1,870 £900

SECRETAIRES AND ESCRITOIRES

William and Mary marquetry secretaire, 3ft.10½in. wide, circa 1695. (Sotheby's) $9,936 £4,600

Oak secretaire by M. H. Baillie-Scott with pewter and marquetry inlay, 46in. high. (Christie's S. Kensington) $4,752 £2,200

Rare satinwood secretaire a abattant, possibly Polish, circa 1820, 2ft.10in. wide. (Sotheby's) $4,340 £2,000

Burr-chestnut secretaire semanier with white marble top, 1870's, 26in. wide. (Sotheby's Belgravia) $995 £450

19th century Continental floral marquetry secretaire abattant. (Phillips) $3,600 £1,600

Fine Queen Anne walnut and featherbanded escritoire, 112cm. wide. (Sotheby King & Chasemore) $3,792 £1,850

Late Georgian mahogany bow front secretaire tallboy, 3ft.9in. wide. (Pearsons) $1,339 £620

A fine 19th century Wootton desk with brass fittings and scroll feet. (Vost's) $4,715 £2,300

20th century mahogany and parquetry secretaire a abattant with red marble top, 29in. wide. (Sotheby's Belgravia) $872 £420

Secretaire a abattant, in flame mahogany. (Frank H. Fellows) $1,808 £800

Small Louis XVI style kingwood secretaire a abattant, 2ft.2in. wide. (Messenger May & Baverstock) $1,339 £620

French secretaire a abattant in oak veneered with tulipwood and kingwood, 58cm. wide, by Jean-Francois Dubot. (Sotheby's) $90,000 £40,000

William and Mary period figured walnut escritoire. (Hobbs Parker)
$2,030 £1,000

Good Liege secretaire cabinet in burr-elm with ebonised and walnut banding, circa 1730, 3ft.11in. wide. (Sotheby's)$10,850 £5,000

William and Mary walnut secretaire with burr-veneered front, circa 1690, 3ft.8½in. wide. (Sotheby's)$6,912 £3,200

Rare George IV mahogany secretaire cabinet, circa 1825, 3ft.6½in. wide. (Sotheby's)
$1,512 £700

Mahogany and trellis parquetry escritoire in the Louis XVI style, 99cm. wide. (Sotheby King & Chasemore)
$4,060 £2,000

19th century Continental walnut secretaire a abattant, 97cm. wide. (Sotheby Humberts)
$864 £400

Early 19th century Dutch marquetry escritoire, 94cm. wide. (Sotheby King & Chasemore) $4,275 £1,900

Early 18th century veneered walnut secretaire chest, 44in. wide and with new feet. (Green & Co.)
$2,250 £1,000

19th century satinwood escritoire, 95cm. wide. (Sotheby King & Chasemore) $6,496 £3,200

Fine Queen Anne walnut and featherbanded escritoire, 97cm. wide. (Sotheby King & Chasemore) $4,305 £2,100

George II period red walnut secretaire, 4ft. 1in. wide. (Geering & Colyer) $852 £420

Early 18th century walnut escritoire with fitted interior. (Sotheby King & Chasemore)
$6,264 £2,900

365

William and Mary escritoire, 39in. wide. (J. M. Welch & Son) $5,615 £2,600

Regency mahogany secretaire chest with ebony stringing. (Hy. Duke & Son) $925 £400

19th century marquetry secretaire with fall front. (Phillips) $3,275 £1,450

Victorian oak secretaire cabinet, 36in. wide. (Hy. Duke & Son) $1,330 £650

Fruitwood secretaire a abattant with marble top, 31¼in. wide. (Christie's) $2,035 £900

Late 17th century Dutch oak secretaire cabinet, 58in. wide. (Heathcote Ball & Co.) $5,400 £2,500

18th century Dutch satinwood and sycamore secretaire, 2ft. wide. (Phillips) $4,555 £2,100

Serpentine kingwood and marquetry secretaire, circa 1870, 27½in. wide. (Sotheby's Belgravia) $5,855 £2,650

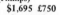

18th century walnut secretaire, 105cm. wide. (Phillips) $1,695 £750

Fine inlaid escritoire. (Burtenshaw Walker) $9,030 £4,200

Mahogany and camphorwood lined campaign secretaire, 40in. wide, circa 1860. (Sotheby's Belgravia) $1,275 £560

Mahogany Wellington secretaire chest of seven graduated drawers, 22in. wide, circa 1880.(Sotheby's Belgravia) $1,250 £550

George III mahogany secretaire bookcase with two Gothic glazed doors, 47in. wide. (Christie's) $5,800 £2,500

George III mahogany library breakfront secretaire bookcase, 68in. wide. (Christie's S. Kensington) $9,935 £4,600

Georgian mahogany secretaire bookcase on shaped bracket feet. (Frank H. Fellows) $1,580 £700

Satinwood and rosewood crossbanded secretaire bookcase on slightly splayed feet, 2ft.9in. wide. (Rye Auction Galleries) $2,925 £1,300

George III style mahogany secretaire breakfront bookcase, 221cm. wide. (Phillips) $3,925 £1,700

American figure mahogany and satinwood lined cylinder secretaire bookcase, 4ft.1in. wide. (Linden Alcock & Co.) $2,665 £1,300

Dutch mahogany secretaire bookcase with carved cresting, late 1840's, 40½in. wide. (Sotheby's Belgravia) $2,165 £980

19th century mahogany breakfront secretaire bookcase, 73in. wide. (Olivers) $6,215 £2,750

Georgian mahogany secretaire bookcase with glazed doors. 3ft.3in. wide. (Worsfolds) $3,505 £1,550

George III mahogany secretaire bookcase with fluted frieze, circa 1775, 3ft.11½in. wide. (Sotheby's) $3,035 £1,350

Early 19th century mahogany secretaire bookcase on splay feet. (Vernon's) $2,000 £900

Late Georgian secretaire bookcase in mahogany with astragal glazed doors. (Worsfolds) $3,535 £1,550

SECRETAIRE BOOKCASES

Late 18th century satin-wood and rosewood banded secretaire bookcase. (Brooks) $11,925 £5,300

George III mahogany secretaire bookcase, 102cm. wide. (Sotheby King & Chasemore) $5,684 £2,800

Georgian mahogany secretaire bookcase with satin-wood and fan inlay, 3ft. 5in. wide. (Messenger May & Baverstock) $3,672 £1,700

George III mahogany small secretaire bookcase, circa 1770, 2ft.7½in. wide. (Sotheby's) $6,048 £2,800

Figured Spanish mahogany Regency breakfront secretaire bookcase. (Kings Auction Rooms) $6,496 £3,200

Secretaire bookcase of late Regency period, with unusually latticed glazed doors. (Buckland & Sons) $3,024 £1,400

George IV mahogany breakfront secretaire bookcase by Gillow. (Tennant) $15,150 £7,500

Georgian mahogany secretaire bookcase on bracket feet, 2ft. 9¼in. wide. (Geering & Colyer) $3,037 £1,350

Mahogany secretaire bookcase, circa 1800, 3ft.5in. wide. (D. M. Nesbit & Co.) $2,034 £900

Late George III secretaire bookcase, circa 1810, 3ft.8in. wide. (Sotheby's) $3,024 £1,400

Kingwood serpentine display secretaire with marble top, circa 1900, 32in. wide. (Sotheby's Belgravia) $1,976 £950

Regency mahogany breakfront secretaire bookcase, 185cm. wide. (Phillips) $4,620 £2,000

Late 18th century mahogany secretaire bookcase, 2ft.10½in. wide. (Geering & Colyer) $2,131 £1,050

Victorian mahogany secretaire bookcase. (Sotheby Bearne) $1,296 £600

Victorian mahogany secretaire bookcase on turned legs. (Andrew Grant) $1,685 £750

Regency mahogany bureau cabinet with tambour cylinder cover, 4ft.4½in. wide. (Christie's) $9,430 £4,600

Queen Anne walnut secretaire cabinet, 2ft.5in. wide, circa 1710, on later bun feet. (Sotheby's) $7,776 £3,600

George III mahogany secretaire bookcase. (Bonham's) $22,220 £11,000

19th century Burmese carved hardwood secretaire cabinet. (Sotheby Bearne) $1,123 £520

George III mahogany library breakfront secretaire bookcase. (Christie's S. Kensington) $9,338 £4,600

Good Georgian secretaire cabinet, 4ft.6in. wide. (Phillips) $4,276 £1,980

Sheraton mahogany secretaire with shell motifs, 57in. wide. (R. Dove) $6,264 £2,900

Georgian mahogany kneehole bookcase/secretaire, 4ft. wide. (Shakespear, McTurk & Graham) $691 £320

Early 19th century mahogany secretaire bookcase with satinwood interior, 3ft.9in. wide. (D. M. Nesbit & Co.) $1,749 £810

18th century French chestnut hall bench with hinged seat, 71in. wide. (Sotheby Humberts) $756 £350

Victorian mahogany framed settee. (Olivers) $1,260 £560

18th century carved oak settle with hinged lid. (Spear & Sons) $1,035 £460

One of a pair of mid 17th century painted beechwood canapes, 72in. wide. (Sotheby's Belgravia) $1,081 £520

Satinwood settee with double panel back and curved arms, 46in. wide. (Heathcote Ball & Co.) $933 £460

George II style upholstered couch on low cabriole legs, 152cm. long. (Phillips) $215 £95

Fine Queen Anne walnut settee, circa 1710, 6ft.8in. wide, worked in wool and silk petit point. (Sotheby's) $4,750 £2,200

Unusual silver and silver veneered throne chair, 45in. wide, circa 1880. (Sotheby's Belgravia) $9,570 £4,600

Mid 19th century Dutch mahogany and marquetry settee of three sections, 65in. wide. (Sotheby's Belgravia) $1,456 £700

16th/17th century French Gothic oak bench, 5ft.11in. wide, with carved front panelling. (Sotheby's) $1,955 £900

Early oak combined settle/bacon cupboard, 5ft.2in. wide. (Butler & Hatch Waterman) $1,512 £700

Large mahogany sofa. (Dacre, Son & Hartley) $1,080 £500

Mahogany framed Hepplewhite design and period settee with fluted arms, 6ft.4in. wide. (Worsfolds) $1,462 £650

Sofa from a three-piece Chinese Chippendale suite. (Phillips) $5,184 £2,400

George II mahogany sofa with triple arched back, circa 1755, 6ft.9in. wide. (Sotheby's) $5,626 £2,600

Walnut framed settee by Constantine & Co., sold with matching lady's easy chair. (Phillips) $3,456 £1,600

19th century carved walnut settee in the Daniel Marot style, 160cm. wide. (King & Chasemore) $675 £300

Victorian walnut and leather upholstered chaise longue, circa 1855, 6ft. 3in. wide. (Sotheby King & Chasemore) $970 £430

Cast iron and wooden slatted garden seat. (Honiton Galleries) $180 £80

Sofa from a Victorian carved walnut renaissance revival suite. (Robert W. Skinner Inc.) $1,900 £860

Mid 17th century box seat settle, 4ft.6in. wide. (Sotheby King & Chasemore) $1,536 £680

19th century Louis XV style gilt wood duchesse en bateau. (Christie's S. Kensington) $1,770 £820

Victorian rosewood and button upholstered triform conversation seat, circa 1850, 125cm. wide. (Sotheby King & Chasemore) $1,401 £620

Queen Anne style walnut settee, 220cm. wide. (Sotheby King & Chasemore) $1,624 £800

371

English walnut chaise longue, with button upholstered end and half back, circa 1860, 74¾in. long. (Sotheby's Belgravia) $1,100 £480

Victorian walnut sofa with grape-carved crest and apron. (Robert W. Skinner Inc.) $400 £180

19th century carved rosewood chaise longue. (V. & V's) $815 £360

Early Louis XV grained beech-wood canape, 77½in. wide, with triple arched back. (Christie's) $3,960 £1,800

Settee from a gilt wood drawingroom suite, circa 1900, 70½in. wide. (Sotheby's Belgravia) $3,315 £1,500

Queen Anne walnut settee on cabriole legs, 59in. wide. (Christie's) $6,525 £2,900

Mid 19th century ebonised settee with button upholstered back and seat, 68in. wide, probably German. (Sotheby's Belgravia) $925 £420

18th century American country pine settle with shaped sides, 75in. long. (Robert W. Skinner Inc.) $1,150 £505

One of a pair of Louis XV white painted and gilded canapes, probably Italian, 57in. wide. (Christie's) $3,110 £1,400

George IV mahogany settee, circa 1820, 6ft.1in. long. (Sotheby's) $1,415 £620

Gilt wood Duchesse, circa 1880, on cabriole legs with scroll feet. (Sotheby's Belgravia)$1,060 £480

19th century American mahogany settee on hairy claw feet, 83½in. wide. (Sotheby's Belgravia) $520 £230

Walnut framed settee with arched back, 71in. wide, circa 1860. (Sotheby's) $720 £320

George I mahogany settee. (W. H. Lane & Son)$2,035 £900

Carved gilt wood day bed with ribbon carved frame, circa 1880, 88in. wide. (Sotheby's Belgravia) $1,435 £650

Scottish 'William IV' chaise longue with moulded frame and overscrolled ends, late 1830's, 78in. (Sotheby's Belgravia) $645 £280

Walnut framed settee of 17th century design with later needlework. (Christie's) $3,390 £1,500

Mahogany inlaid Regency style couch. (Winterton) $1,155 £500

One of a pair of early 20th century 'Louis XV' gilt wood canapes, 72½in. wide. (Sotheby's Belgravia) $1,990 £900

Ash settle designed for Liberty & Co., circa 1900, 51in. wide. (Sotheby's Belgravia) $480 £220

17th century oak settle with high panelled back and open scroll arms, dated 1648. (Outhwaite & Litherland) $3,580 £1,550

18th century Regency style mahogany day bed, 185cm. long. (Phillips) $5,545 £2,400

Italian walnut cassapanca with panelled back on plinth base, 88in. wide. (Christie's) $4,085 £1,800

One of a pair of oak benches in the 18th century style, 54cm. long. (Phillips) $600 £260

Pinewood kitchen mortar rack to hold two mortars, circa 1780, 23½in. wide. (Christopher Sykes) $85 £38

Stained beech and composition corner bracket, 30in. high, circa 1880. (Sotheby's Belgravia) $110 £50

Mahogany Regency set of hanging shelves with carved cresting, circa 1820, 26½in. wide. (Christopher Sykes) $214 £95

Set of stripped pine hanging book-shelves, George III period, 38in. long. (Christopher Sykes)$126 £56

One of a very fine pair of late George III gilt wood eagle wall brackets, circa 1800, 1ft. 3in. high. (Sotheby's) $4,105 £1,900

Mahogany 'Chinese Chippendale' style three-tier wall shelf with fretwork gallery, 56cm. wide. (Phillips) $300 £130

One of a pair of mahogany corner shelves, mid 19th century, 34in. high. (Sotheby's) $630 £280

One of a pair of late 19th century mahogany hanging shelves, 36¼in. wide. (Sotheby's) $720 £320

18th century oak hanging plate rack with shaped top, 57in. wide. (Vernon's) $360 £160

One of a pair of Regency mahogany standing bookshelves, circa 1810, 2ft.6½in. wide. (Sotheby's) $5,175 £2,300

One of a pair of early 20th century gilt wood mirror shelves, 42in. high. (Sotheby's Belgravia) $1,125 £500

One of a pair of yew-wood hanging display cabinets of Queen Anne style, 23in. wide. (Christie's) $790 £350

Late 19th century Sheraton style inlaid mahogany sideboard. (Vernon's) $1,385 £600

Sheraton style sideboard on square tapering legs. (Norton) $3,225 £1,500

Early 19th century mahogany sideboard on tapered legs with spade feet. (Vernon's) $1,120 £485

Olivewood breakfront sideboard with two central cupboard doors, 72in. wide, circa 1930.(Sotheby's Belgravia) $640 £280

George III mahogany sideboard with D-shaped top, 80in. wide. (Christie's) $3,315 £1,500

Custom mahogany Jacobean style sideboard with carved gallery, 58in. wide. (Robert W. Skinner Inc.) $375 £170

Gillow & Co., mahogany sideboard, 190cm. wide, 1880's. (Sotheby's Belgravia) $1,250 • £570

One of a pair of walnut and burr walnut open sideboards, the canted corners held by female caryatids, 58in. wide, circa 1850. (Sotheby's Belgravia)$1,600 £700

Early Victorian mahogany sideboard, mirror back carved with acanthus, fruit and 'C' scrolls, 84½in. wide. (Sotheby's Belgravia) $860 £380

George III mahogany sideboard, circa 1790, 6ft.3in. wide. (Sotheby's) $3,080 £1,350

Georgian style sideboard inlaid with Sheraton design.(Stride's) $4,320 £2,000

Edwardian mahogany sideboard with five drawers. (J. M. Welch & Son) $455 £210

Regency mahogany sideboard, richly veneered, 4ft.9in. wide. (Eadon, Lockwood & Riddle) $756 £350

William IV mahogany and crossbanded bow front sideboard, 155cm. wide. (Sotheby King & Chasemore) $1,218 £600

18th century style mahogany sideboard with five drawers, 173cm. wide. (Phillips)$133 £65

18th century Sheraton revival inlaid mahogany kneehole sideboard. (Neales) $1,665 £740

George III mahogany small sideboard with rectangular top, 34in. wide. (Hy. Duke & Son) $1,599 £780

George III bow fronted mahogany sideboard, 6ft. wide. (Sotheby King & Chasemore) $1,188 £550

18th century Sheraton revival inlaid

George III mahogany serpentine fronted sideboard. (Sotheby's) $5,185 £2,400

Victorian carved oak sideboard with brass fittings. (Phillips) $143 £62

Art Deco mahogany sideboard, circa 1925, 170cm. wide, with twin light fittings at back. (Sotheby's Belgravia)$462 £200

Green lacquered sideboard with two cupboards, 123cm. wide. (Phillips) $214 £95

Walnut sideboard with mirrored superstructure, circa 1900, 108in. wide. (Sotheby's Belgravia) $1,248 £600

Early 19th century mahogany and inlaid sideboard, 51in. long, with brass handles and ivory escutcheons. (Dacre, Son & Hartley) $756 £350

Adam mahogany serving table with concave flanks and bow fronts, 8ft. wide. (Vidler & Co.) $779 £380

Edwardian inlaid mahogany sideboard stamped Edwards & Roberts. (Phillips & Jolly's) $1,260 £560

George III Sheraton design mahogany and satinwood crossbanded bow front sideboard, 7ft. wide, circa 1790. (Sotheby King & Chasemore) $2,034 £900

Regency mahogany breakfronted sideboard, 183cm. wide.(Sotheby King & Chasemore)$2,131 £1,050

Part of a walnut and beechwood seven-piece suite. (Christie's) $49,635 £24,450

Sheraton design sideboard, 6ft. wide. (Stride & Sons) $4,510 £2,200

George III mahogany sideboard with rounded corners, 89in. wide. (Sotheby Humberts)$1,036 £480

George III mahogany sideboard on tapered legs with spade feet. (Phillips) $11,400 £5,000

Regency large crossbanded mahogany sideboard. (Frank H. Fellows) $904 £400

George III semi circular mahogany sideboard, circa 1785, 3ft.6in. wide. (Sotheby's) $6,912 £3,200

Oak sideboard in the style of Bruce Talbert, 1880's, 159cm. wide. (Sotheby's Belgravia) $175 £80

One of a fine pair of George III semi circular painted satinwood sideboards, circa 1790. (Sotheby's) $21,600 £10,000

Unusual inlaid mahogany shaving stand, late 18th century. (K. Hugh Dodd & Partners) $172 £80

Fine quality kidney-shaped gueridon, feather veneered in tulipwood, 19th century. (Eadon, Lockwood & Riddle) $1,015 £470

Carved hardwood umbrella stand in the form of a standing bear. (Gilbert Baitson) $864 £400

Large Royal Worcester majolica umbrella stand, 27¾in. high, circa 1880. (Sotheby's Belgravia) $345 £160

One of a pair of late 18th century George III mahogany candlestands, 51in. high. (Phillips) $2,425 £1,075

Early Victorian mahogany folio rack. (Sotheby Bearne) $1,243 £550

William IV mahogany music stand with hinged top, 58in. high, 1830's. (Sotheby's) $864 £400

George III antique oak steps, circa 1790, 17¼in. wide, original bracket feet. (Christopher Sykes) $214 £95

One of a pair of ebony and pietra dura pedestals, circa 1870's, 18in. wide. (Sotheby's Belgravia) $1,497 £720

Small inlaid two-tier stand with drawer. (Andrew Grant) $495 £230

American country string quartet music stand, 50in. high, circa 1800. (Robert W. Skinner Inc.) $500 £220

19th century inlaid hardwood folding cakestand. (Phillips) $60 £25

1930's tubular chrome tea trolley. (Alfie's Antique Market) $101 £45

19th century rosewood pedestal jardiniere. (J. M. Welch & Son) $291 £135

Turned dark fruitwood 'cat' bowl stand, circa 1870, 15½in. wide. (Christopher Sykes) $131 £58

Very fine 18th century French gueridon in parquetry and inlay, with silk lined drawer. (James Adam & Son) $12,528 £5,800

William and Mary walnut candle stand, late 17th century, 3ft.3in. high. (Sotheby's) $518 £240

French oval gueridon in the Louis XV manner, 19½in. wide. (Geering & Colyer) $1,004 £495

Mid 19th century walnut music stand with double rests. (Phillips) $287 £140

Heavily carved oak hall stand with lifting lidded seat. (Frank H. Fellows) $836 £370

Louis XV style double tier etagere with marble top, 33cm. wide. (Phillips) $410 £200

Victorian brass three-tier cakestand. (Phillips) $46 £20

Fine George III mahogany square toilet stand, circa 1790, 32in. high. (Christopher Sykes) $282 £125

One of two pedestals each with inset marble tops. (Sotheby King & Chasemore) $315 £140

379

Satinwood pedestal of rectangular tapering form, painted with musical trophies, circa 1900. (Sotheby's Belgravia) $785 £340

Large British Faience jardiniere and stand, impressed Burmantofts Faience, England, circa 1882-1904, 41½in. high.(Sotheby's Belgravia) $1,185 £520

19th century oak brass bound circular stick barrel, 53cm. high. (Phillips) $140 £60

William and Mary burrwalnut candle stand, circa 1695, 2ft.11in. high. (Sotheby's) $1,035 £480

Late 19th century bentwood hat stand. (Vernon's) $80 £35

Art Deco wrought iron hall stand, circa 1920. (Sotheby's) $365 £160

Edwardian walnut plant stand with undertier. (Vernon's) $60 £30

Directoire mahogany jardiniere with pierced ormolu bowl, 16¼in. wide (Christie's) $2,310 £1,050

One of a pair of green onyx and champleve enamel mounted torcheres, circa 1900, 47½in. high. (Sotheby's Belgravia) $1,915 £920

18th century style mahogany urn stand with fretwork gallery; 30cm. wide. (Phillips) $195 £85

Set of George III mahogany library steps in the shape of a side table, 29½in. wide. (Christie's) $2,310 £1,000

19th century mahogany music stand with hinged easel, 52cm. wide. (Phillips) $645 £280

One of a pair of circular beadwork stools with mahogany frames. (Phillips) $85 £40

One of a pair of 19th century walnut scroll design footstools. (Vernon's) $195 £75

Footstool from Queen Victoria's royal coach, sold with documents. (Sotheby's Belgravia) $520 £240

Unusual Victorian walnut stool with original castors, circa 1850. (Christopher Sykes) $100 £45

Stool by a 'Master of Buli', West Africa, Luba. (Sotheby's) $518,400 £240,000

Rare late 16th century Italian walnut stool, top with cut-out handle, 1ft.4¼in. wide. (Sotheby's) $1,735 £800

Queen Anne walnut oval stool with cabriole legs and club feet. (H. C. Wolton & Son) $1,685 £780

Ashanti wood stool with upward curving seat, 21¼in. wide. (Sotheby's) $435 £200

Second Empire mahogany stool with drop-in seat, 19½in. square, circa 1870. (Sotheby's Belgravia) $750 £340

Late 19th century mahogany turned leg stool. (Phillips) $35 £15

One of a pair of unusual stools supported by a pair of carved elephants, circa 1900. (Sotheby's Belgravia) $1,425 £620

Regency mahogany and parcel gilt stool, circa 1810, 1ft.10½in. wide. (Sotheby's) $4,970 £2,300

381

Wooden stool from the Austral Islands, probably Tahiti, 22in. wide. (Christie's) $18,360 £8,500

Dutch walnut and marquetry duet stool, upholstered in floral tapestry. (West London Auctions) $475 £220

Egyptian carved walnut stool, circa 1920. (Sotheby's Belgravia) $2,485 £1,150

One of a pair of folding stools by Jean-Baptiste Sene, circa 1786. (Sotheby's) $116,885 £54,115

Queen Anne walnut stool, circa 1710, with moulded cabriole legs. (Sotheby's) $995 £460

Late 19th century Oriental carved teak stool. (Christie's) $70 £30

17th century oak joint stool. (W. H. Lane & Son) $755 £350

Charles I oak joint stool, circa 1630. (Sotheby's) $1,000 £440

George III style dressing stool with needlework top, 45cm. wide. (Phillips) $85 £40

George I walnut stool with drop-in seat, 1ft.9in. wide, circa 1720. (Sotheby's) $775 £360

Early Victorian rosewood, gros point stool. (Gray's Antique Mews) $810 £350

Late 19th century mahogany piano stool on carved cabriole legs. (Phillips) $125 £55

Victorian Eastlake walnut and burl veneer parlour set with cartouche carved crest. (Robert W. Skinner Inc.) $900 £410

Part of a custom mahogany Jacobean-style set of twelve dining chairs. (Robert W. Skinner Inc.)
$725 £330

Victorian carved walnut parlour set of seven pieces. (Robert W. Skinner Inc.) $1,800 £810

A four-piece suite of cast iron garden furniture, late 19th century. (Robert W. Skinner Inc.)$1,200 £525

Lacquered three-piece bergere suite, framework painted with chinoiserie, circa 1920. (Sotheby's Belgravia) $3,500 £1,550

Part of an Edwardian mahogany five-piece suite. (Phillips) $1,060 £460

Art Deco three-piece suite, 1930's, in cut velvet. (Sotheby's Belgravia) $655 £300

Elmwood spindle back cottage suite in excellent condition. (Alfred Mossop & Co.) $570 £265

Liberty & Co., inlaid oak bedroom suite, circa 1900. (Sotheby's Belgravia) $10,165 £4,400

Four chairs from a nine-piece walnut Victorian suite. (Christie's S. Kensington)
$4,105 £1,900

Part of an Edwardian inlaid seven-piece mahogany suite. (J. M. Welch & Son)
$2,160 £1,000

Part of an eight-piece Edwardian Sheraton style inlaid saloon
suite. (T. Bannister & Co.) $1,100 £510

Part of a late Victorian nine-piece walnut framed drawing room suite.
(Manchester Auction Mart) $6,075 £2,700

Part of a late 19th century walnut nine-piece suite with upholstered seats
and backs. (Phillips) $3,235 £1,400

385

Victorian walnut swivel top serpentine card table, 2ft.9in. wide. (Eadon, Lockwood & Riddle) $367 £170

Regency brass inlaid card table, circa 1815, 2ft.11½in. wide, in mahogany with rosewood crossbanding. (Sotheby's) $2,810 £1,300

George III mahogany tea table with turnover top, 35½in. wide. (Christopher Sykes) $663 £295

Late 18th century Irish mahogany folding-top table. (Sotheby Bearne)$1,684 £780

One of a pair of Sheraton style painted satinwood semi circular card tables, 3ft. wide. (Russell, Baldwin & Bright) $2,590 £1,200

Victorian rosewood fold-over card table. (D. M. Nesbit & Co.) $781 £385

Mahogany fold-over card table in the Chippendale style, 89cm. wide. (Phillips) $246 £120

Early 20th century mahogany marquetry card table, 32in. wide, with serpentine sided top. (Sotheby's Belgravia) $1,455 £700

Early Victorian rosewood card table, 36in. wide. (Olivers) $587 £260

George III semi circular marquetry card table, 3ft.1in. wide, circa 1780. (Sotheby's) $5,832 £2,700

Chippendale period padoukwood card and tea table with double fold-over tops, 26¾in. wide. (Geering & Colyer) $2,870 £1,400

18th century mahogany fold-over games table, inset with coin cups, 2ft.7in. wide. (Shakespear, McTurk & Graham) $1,555 £720

Dutch walnut and marquetry inlaid semi circular card table, 2ft.7in. diam. (Geering & Colyer) $527 £260

18th century mahogany fold-over tea table, 3ft. wide. (Hobbs Parker) $730 £360

Mid 18th century Dutch marquetry walnut games table on pad feet. (Sotheby's U.S.A.) $6,000 £2,675

George III mahogany card table, 3ft. wide, circa 1765, with serpentine top. (Sotheby's) $4,968 £2,300

George II mahogany card table, circa 1755, 2ft.10in. wide. (Sotheby's) $1,080 £500

Late George II mahogany card table, circa 1755, 2ft.11½in. wide. (Sotheby's) $2,268 £1,050

Late 18th century satinwood semi circular card table, 29½in. high. (Jackson-Stops & Staff) $2,925 £1,300

Late 18th century George III mahogany tea table with fold-over top. (Edwards, Bigwood & Bewlay) $1,140 £570

One of a pair of Georgian mahogany tea tables. (C. Wesley Haslam & Son) $3,996 £1,850

Regency period rosewood card table, 36in. wide. (Hobbs Parker) $812 £400

Antique oak tea table on cabriole legs, circa 1840, 35in. wide. (Christopher Sykes) $595 £275

George III mahogany card table with serpentine top, 36in. wide. (Sotheby Humberts) $1,405 £650

CARD AND TEA TABLES

William IV mahogany tea table on concave sided base with scroll feet, 40½in. wide, circa 1835. (Sotheby's Belgravia) $540 £240

19th century mahogany fold-over card table, 36in. wide. (J. M. Welch & Son) $885 £410

Kingwood card table with brass bound rim, 31in. square, circa 1880. (Sotheby's Belgravia) $1,550 £700

Boulle card table, circa 1860, inlaid with cut-brass foliage on a red tortoiseshell ground. (Sotheby's Belgravia) $1,550 £700

Edwardian mahogany envelope table with floral marquetry decoration, 57cm. wide. (Phillips) $645 £280

Georgian walnut fold-over card table. (Alfred Mossop & Co.) $840 £390

Dutch marquetry and mahogany serpentine fronted card table, circa 1880, 2ft. 4in. wide. (Sotheby King & Chasemore) $950 £420

Federal mahogany card table, circa 1795, 36in. wide. (Robert W. Skinner Inc.) $700 £305

Late 19th century English walnut card table on moulded cabriole legs, 33¾in. wide. (Sotheby's Belgravia) $715 £310

Haines mahogany card table on four turned and gadrooned supports, circa 1850. (Sotheby's Belgravia) $435 £190

Edwardian inlaid rosewood envelope card table. (Bradley & Vaughan) $775 £340

Sheraton style demi-lune satinwood card table. (Harrods Auction Galleries) $2,050 £900

One of a pair of mid Georgian mahogany card tables, 36in. wide. (Christie's)
$2,320 £1,000

19th century rosewood fold-over card table. (J. M. Welch & Son) $400 £185

William and Mary walnut card table with folding rectangular top, 30½in. wide. (Christie's)
$6,700 £2,900

William IV mahogany fold-over tea table supported on octagonal column, 91cm. wide. (Phillips) $180 £80

George III mahogany fold-over tea table with single drawer, 110cm. wide. (Phillips) $740 £320

Late 18th century Dutch marquetry card table with baize lined top, 2ft.8in. wide. (Sotheby's) $1,330 £580

Boulle card table with swivelling top, circa 1860, 35in. wide. (Sotheby's Belgravia) $1,655 £750

Regency calamanderwood card table with baize lined top, 36in. wide. (Christie's) $3,480 £1,500

Late 19th century walnut envelope card table on cabriole legs. (Vernon's) $320 £145

George III mahogany fold-over table of serpentine form, 94cm. wide. (Phillips) $1,015 £440

Burr walnut fold-over card table on carved cabriole legs, circa 1860. (Sotheby's Belgravia)
$685 £300

Late 18th century walnut card table with baize lined top, legs overlaid with brass, 36in. wide. (Christie's)
$2,155 £950

CONSOL TABLES

Unusual marble top mahogany consol table with D-shaped centre frieze, circa 1900, 70in. wide. (Sotheby's Belgravia) $1,125 £500

Early 19th century marquetry consol table, 33in. wide. (Pearsons) $865 £400

One of a pair of painted D-shaped consol tables with satinwood banding, circa 1870. (Sotheby's Belgravia) $3,200 £1,400

Marble topped consol table with black and grey marble top, 2ft.11in. wide. (Sotheby's) $685 £300

One of a rare pair of Louis XV painted wrought iron consol tables, 35½in. wide. (Christie's) $6,160 £2,800

Mid 19th century rococo style carved and gilded gesso pier glass and consol table, 66in. wide. (Dacre Son & Hartley) $540 £250

Gilt wood consol table of Louis XV style with marble top, legs joined by a shell stretcher, 40in. wide. (Christie's) $1,590 £700

White painted consol table in the manner of William Kent, 5ft. wide, circa 1730. (Sotheby's) $7,390 £3,200

Louis XV gilt wood consol table with brown and white marble top, 40½in. wide. (Christie's) $4,400 £2,000

Fine Regency gilt wood consol table with Sicilian jasper top, 35¼in. wide. (Christie's) $7,070 £3,200

One of a pair of rare George II gilt wood consol tables with brown and white marble tops, 28in. wide. (Christie's) $20,995 £9,500

Gilt wood consol table with marble top, probably Scandinavian, circa 1770, 2ft.8in. wide. (Sotheby's) $1,605 £700

Victorian walnut and marquetry breakfast table, 60in. diam. (Christie's S. Kensington) $5,615 £2,600

Regency rosewood centre table with tip-up top with cut brass band, 53in. diam. (Christie's) $3,810 £1,650

Inlaid Victorian loo table. (Andrew Grant) $1,355 £600

George III mahogany drum table with leather lined top, 50in. diam. (Christie's) $2,910 £1,300

Superb 19th century marquetry table top, no base. (Bradley & Vaughan) $3,190 £1,400

George III mahogany breakfast table with tip-up top, 60in. wide. (Christie's) $6,050 £2,700

Maplewood and parcel gilt centre table with tip-up top, circa 1830, 59in. wide. (Christie's) $1,850 £800

Victorian walnut fold-over card table on quadruple base. (Phillips) $325 £140

Empire mahogany centre table with green marble top, 38½in. diam. (Christie's) $2,155 £950

Victorian burr-walnut loo table of exceptional quality, 4ft.9¾in. wide. (Linden Alcock & Co.) $920 £450

Fine Regency rosewood and amboyna breakfast table, 4ft.6in. diam. (Boardman's) $1,735 £800

Good Regency mahogany circular dining table, 130cm. diam. (Phillips) $1,500 £650

Victorian walnut and marquetry breakfast table, 60in. diam. (Christie's) $5,850 £2,600

Chinese hardwood 3ft. square centre table, deeply carved quadruple angular supports. (H. C. Wolton & Son) $1,620 £750

Circular rosewood Oriental carved table. (R. L. Lowery & Partners) $777 £360

Late Georgian mahogany twin pedestal dining table. (Locke & England) $5,400 £2,500

Walnut, ebony and boxwood strung rosewood centre table with brass bordered edge, 3ft.6in. wide. (Vidler & Co.) $861 £420

Early 19th century circular rosewood dining table, 4ft. diam. (Whiteheads) $1,055 £520

Late George III mahogany breakfast table, 5ft. wide, circa 1810. (Sotheby's) $3,240 £1,500

Regency period rosewood circular snap-top breakfast table, 4ft. diam. (Woolley & Wallis) $3,455 £1,600

Early Victorian dining table with eight section top. (H. Spencer & Sons) $13,275 £5,900

Red boulle centre table, 1870's, 59½in. wide. (Sotheby's Belgravia) $936 £450

Late 18th century mahogany breakfast table on quadruple base. (K. Hugh Dodd & Partners) $1,533 £710

Mahogany extending dining table with circular top, 72in. diam., on Regency turned pillar. (Hy. Duke & Son) $2,870 £1,400

Early 19th century circular mahogany drum table. (Duncan Vincent) $5,278 £2,600

Unusual North German or Russian mahogany centre table, circa 1820, 2ft.6½in. square. (Sotheby's) $1,953 £900

George III rent table, circa 1760. (Sotheby's) $32,000 £15,600

19th century mahogany table with brass claw feet, 36in. diam. (W. H. Lane & Son) $1,414 £700

19th century scarlet boulle and ebonised centre table. (Christie's S. Kensington) $2,050 £950

Mid Victorian walnut loo table with oval top, 58in. wide. (Lacy Scott) $771 £380

Victorian rosewood centre table of serpentine design, 60in. long. (Dacre, Son & Hartley) $907 £420

19th century coromandel breakfast table, 4ft. diam. (Vidler & Co.) $1,476 £720

Oak Jacobean style octagonal table, 104cm. wide. (Phillips) $101 £45

Victorian oval walnut table, finely inlaid. (Andrew Grant) $1,296 £600

Very fine Louis XV drawingroom table in satinwood, 29in. high. (Gray's Antique Mews) $2,475 £1,100

Regency rosewood breakfast table with brass inlaid banding, early 19th century, by John Keene. (Harrods Auction Galleries) $6,380 £2,900

Early 20th century George III style mahogany circular dining table, 72½in. diam. (Sotheby's Belgravia) $2,500 £1,100

Mahogany dining table on four incised legs with white ceramic castors, 53in. diam., circa 1880. (Sotheby's Belgravia) $600 £260

Oriental teak table with round inset variegated marble top and carved apron, 44in. diam. (Robert W. Skinner Inc.) $600 £270

Pitch-pine round tip-top table, 2ft.10½in. diam. (Gray's Antique Mews) $365 £160

Victorian inlaid walnut table with carved scrolled supports and legs. (Dickinson, Davy & Markham) $3,740 £1,700

Late 18th century elm snap-top table on tripod base. (Phillips) $175 £75

Mid 19th century German painted breakfast table, 36½in. diam. (Sotheby's Belgravia) $640 £280

Circular Victorian tilt-top table in walnut marquetry. (Lawrence) $6,050 £2,800

Regency mahogany drum table with circular leather top, 46in. wide. (Christie's) $2,875 £1,300

Mid 19th century marquetry centre table of serpentine outline, 64½in. wide. (Sotheby's Belgravia) $4,000 £1,750

Mid Georgian red walnut gateleg dining table with moulded oval top, 57½in. wide. (Christie's) $4,050 £1,800

Round walnut dining table with carved legs and stretchers, sold with six matching chairs. (Robert W. Skinner Inc.) $650 £295

Edwardian inlaid mahogany kidney-shaped dressing table, 118cm. wide. (Sotheby King & Chasemore) $1,990 £920

Part of an early 20th century bedroom suite, decorated in bleached oak and polychrome. (Woolley & Wallis) $1,780 £780

Queen Anne style walnut and crossbanded kneehole dressing table, 96cm. wide. (Sotheby King & Chasemore) $1,900 £880

George III mahogany dressing table, circa 1780, 2ft.2in. wide. (Sotheby's) $2,590 £1,200

Victorian walnut dressing table. (Phillips) $100 £45

George III mahogany dressing table with real and dummy drawers below. (Hy. Duke & Son) $1,295 £600

Queen Anne black and gold lacquer union suite with bureau base, 21½in. wide. (Christie's) $3,020 £1,300

19th century Sheraton style satinwood veneered dressing table, 21in. wide. (Robert W. Skinner Inc.) $325 £145

Empire mahogany dressing table with arched swing mirror, 30in. wide. (Christie's) $3,960 £1,800

Late 19th century mahogany and marquetry pedestal dressing table, 4ft. long.(Phillips) $2,495 £1,155

Early Victorian bird's eye maple and marquetry kneehole dressing table and matching toilet mirror, 60in. wide. (Christie's S. Kensington) $3,850 £1,750

George III mahogany dressing table by Gillow of Lancaster, circa 1805, 3ft.6in. wide. (Sotheby's) $1,945 £900

395

Solid satinwood and red walnut drop-leaf table, 4ft.10½in. wide open. (Sotheby's)$3,240 £1,500

George II mahogany oval gateleg table, 104cm. wide. (Phillips) $510 £220

Large George II mahogany oval drop-leaf table, circa 1740, 5ft. 11in. wide. (Sotheby's) $2,915 £1,350

George II period red walnut drop-leaf table, 30in. wide, circa 1730. (Christopher Sykes) $645 £285

Queen Anne maple drop-leaf dining table, 36in. diam., on cabriole legs. (Robert W. Skinner Inc.) $5,700 £2,500

American Chippendale mahogany drop-leaf table, 48in. wide, circa 1755. (Robert W. Skinner Inc.) $3,000 £1,315

George II mahogany drop-leaf table with gadrooned moulding on oval top, circa 1740, 4ft.2in. wide. (Sotheby's) $680 £300

George II mahogany drop-leaf oval dining table with scallop carved legs, 5ft.6in. long. (Phillips) $5,715 £2,530

Dutch mahogany and marquetry drop-leaf table, circa 1760, 4ft. wide. (Sotheby's) $975 £450

18th century padoukwood drop-leaf table, 69in. wide. (Hy. Duke & Son) $2,160 £1,000

George II mahogany drop-leaf table, circa 1740, 3ft.11½in. wide. (Sotheby's) $2,160 £1,000

George II mahogany drop-leaf dining table, circa 1740. (Bonham's) $1,845 £820

Early 17th century oak gateleg table. (Phillips) $2,850 £1,250

Late 17th/early 18th century walnut gateleg dining table, 60½in. wide. (Christie's) $4,007 £1,750

17th century oak double gateleg table. (Bradley & Vaughan) $3,890 £1,800

Charles II oak gateleg table on six twist-turned legs, circa 1685, 3ft. 9¼in. wide.   (Sotheby's) $3,305 £1,450

Rare 17th century oak gateleg table, circa 1670, 26½in. diam. (Christopher Sykes) $1,230 £545

Mid 17th century oak gateleg table, 36in. wide. (Sotheby King & Chasemore) $770 £340

18th century style oak drop-leaf table with carved decoration, 90cm. long.(Phillips) $155 £75

17th century oak gateleg table with fitted single drawer. (Worsfolds) $780 £380

Late 17th century oak gateleg table with oval top, circa 1680, 5ft.5½in. wide open.(Sotheby's) $1,640 £720

Small late 17th century oak gateleg table, 32in. wide. (Christopher Sykes) $855 £395

18th century half-round mahogany occasional table, 2ft.6in. wide. (Sotheby King & Chasemore) $1,130 £500

Charles II oak gateleg table on six bobbin-turned legs, circa 1670, 3ft.11½in. wide. (Sotheby's) $1,825 £800

397

Rare 19th century hunt table. (Spear & Sons) $4,500 £1,950

Large Louis XV period French oak refectory table, with wide two-plank top, 9ft.2in. long. (Boardman's) $1,735 £800

Victorian carved oak dining table. (Andrew Grant) $3,735 £1,850

Mid 17th century Emilian walnut table, probably Bologna, 6ft.2½in. long. (Sotheby's) $14,320 £6,600

William IV mahogany two pedestal dining table, circa 1830, 5ft. long. (Sotheby's) $1,555 £720

Early 20th century George III style mahogany dining table, 89in. long. (Sotheby's Belgravia) $600 £260

Regency style mahogany triple pedestal dining table with brass paw feet, 89in. wide. (Dacre, Son & Hartley) $2,920 £1,350

17th century oak refectory table with plank top, 86in. long. (Boardman's) $3,040 £1,400

Fine Thurston full size billiard table, 1907, 151 x 80in. (Sotheby's Belgravia) $21,800 £10,000

Rare George II mahogany two pedestal dining table, circa 1760, 5ft.6in. long. (Sotheby's) $10,800 £5,000

Flemish oak rectangular draw-leaf table with moulded frieze, 27in. wide. (Hy. Duke & Son) $5,825 £2,600

George III mahogany pedestal dining table, circa 1820, 9ft.1in. long extended. (Sotheby's) $7,910 £3,500

Oak draw-leaf refectory table of 16th century design, heavily carved, 78in. long. (Hy Duke & Son) $2,050 £1,000

Oak refectory table with carved frieze, circa 1900, 10ft.7½in. long. (Sotheby's Belgravia) $2,250 £1,000

Rare 17th century Dutch colonial oak refectory table with three-plank top, 4ft.2in. wide. (Sotheby's) $7,380 £3,400

17th century oak draw-leaf refectory table with gadrooned cup and cover baluster legs, 96in. wide. (Christie's) $8,590 £3,800

Elizabethan oak draw-leaf refectory table, 7ft. long, in excellent condition. (H. Spencer & Sons) $18,680 £9,200

Late 16th century English draw-leaf table in oak, 2.67m. long when closed. (Humberts, King & Chasemore) $21,600 £10,000

George III mahogany drop-leaf table, circa 1790, 5ft.9½in. wide. (Sotheby's) $4,750 £2,200

Fine early 17th century oak draw-leaf dining table, 72in. long. (Andrew Sharpe & Partners) $12,640 £5,850

19th century oak refectory table with vine carved frieze, 104in. long. (Dacre, Son & Hartley) $1,675 £775

Fine Jacobean style oak draw-leaf dining table, 7ft. long extended. (Linden Alcock & Co.) $1,065 £520

Single plank oak trestle-end dining table, 8ft.2in. long, with single stretcher. (Coles, Knapp & Kennedy) $3,535 £1,550

Commonwealth design oak refectory dining table, 8ft.3in. long. (Heathcote Ball & Co.) $1,825 £900

18th century carved walnut centre table with marble top, 47in. wide. (Christopher Sykes) $1,695 £750

One half of a tile maker's pottery garden table. (Christie's) $7,560 £3,500

Reproduction French low table, 91cm. wide. (Phillips) $110 £50

Victorian walnut table with round marble top inlaid with intricate patterns. (Robert W. Skinner Inc.) $550 £250

George II style mahogany library table on acanthus carved cabriole legs, circa 1880. (Sotheby's Belgravia) $1,370 £600

Art Nouveau tripod shaped occasional table, inlaid with marquetry. (Robert W. Skinner Inc.) $1,100 £500

Early 19th century German mahogany jardiniere table with marble top, 35cm. diam. (Phillips) $175 £75

Late George II mahogany architect's table with hinged top, circa 1760, 3ft.1½in. wide. (Sotheby's) $3,535 £1,550

One of a pair of early Victorian rosewood and marquetry occasional tables, 28in. high. (Sotheby's Belgravia) $1,000 £450

Good rosewood and parquetry specimen table, circa 1850. (Sotheby's Belgravia) $675 £300

Early Victorian walnut occasional table with triple downswept legs, 27½in. high. (Sotheby's Belgravia) $450 £200

Important Victorian walnut Eastlake style library table with red marble inset, 51in. wide. (Robert W. Skinner Inc.) $3,600 £1,635

Leleu Art Deco games table, circa 1925, 74.5cm. high. (Sotheby's Belgravia) $1,640 £750

Mid 19th century papier mache occasional table, painted with roses and leaves, 26½in. high. (Sotheby's Belgravia) $175 £75

William IV crossbanded mahogany breakfast table on turned centre columns, 110cm. wide. (Phillips) $370 £180

18th century style mahogany tray topped circular tripod table, 45cm. high. (Phillips) $115 £50

English rosewood serpentine top centre table on cabriole legs, circa 1840, 49in. wide. (Sotheby's Belgravia) $415 £180

Ebonised and gilt Regency wine table with brass gallery, 44cm. wide. (Phillips) $230 £100

Late 19th century French marquetry occasional table with two flaps. (Sotheby's Belgravia) $1,400 £620

A Galle beechwood and marquetry occasional table, the oval tray top inlaid with a flowered spray, 71cm. wide. (Christie's) $900 £420

Satinwood circular table, frieze with two drawers, circa 1900, 32in. diam. (Sotheby's Belgravia) $1,150 £500

'Louis XV' oval occasional table in mahogany and parquetry, circa 1900, 23½in. wide. (Sotheby's Belgravia) $1,125 £500

Mid 19th century Italian ebonised blackamoor table with marble top, 20½in. diam. (Sotheby's Belgravia) $1,485. £660

Louis XV style two-tier etagere with floral marquetry, 74cm. wide. (Phillips) $415 £180

Rare late 18th/early 19th century Russian Karelian birch, marquetry and parquetry table a rognon, 3ft. 1in. wide. (Sotheby's) $4,340 £2,000

18th century American pine and maple chair table with circular top, 47in. diam. (Robert W. Skinner Inc.) $1,150 £500

Walnut and marquetry tripod table, 1870's, 36in. wide. (Sotheby's Belgravia) $748 £360

Regency rosewood centre table with circular top, 24in. diam., inset with 18th century Imari dish. (Hy. Duke & Son) $871 £425

Early 20th century 'Louis XIV' gilt wood pier table with red marble top, 50in. wide. (Sotheby's Belgravia) $1,913 £920

Galle fruitwood marquetry table, circa 1900, 75cm. high. (Sotheby's Belgravia) $1,386 £600

Mahogany table a rognon with quarter veneered top, circa 1880, 26½in. wide. (Sotheby's Belgravia) $624 £300

Early 20th century octagonal occasional table in Louis XVI style, with gilt bronze rim, 23½in. wide. (Sotheby's Belgravia) $1,352 £650

'Louis XVI' walnut table a ouvrage, by Henry Dasson, circa 1880, 19½in. wide. (Sotheby's Belgravia) $2,912 £1,400

19th century Regency drum table with marquetry inlay, 25in. diam. (Robert W. Skinner Inc.) $450 £200

George III mahogany supper table with Chinese fretwork at sides and back, 2ft. wide, circa 1770. (Sotheby's) $3,275 £1,450

Late 19th century mahogany and ormolu mounted gueridon, circa 1795. (Sotheby King & Chasemore) $497 £220

Chromed tubular steel table, circa 1935. (Alfie's Antique Market) $101 £45

William and Mary style tavern table, circa 1700-30, 37in. wide. (Robert W. Skinner Inc.) $2,000 £875

Victorian mahogany occasional table on platform base. (Phillips) $150 £65

Small Victorian mahogany display table with shaped top and brass inlay. (Frank H. Fellows) $284 £140

19th century Georgian style mahogany pier table with marble top, 31½in. wide. (Robert W. Skinner Inc.) $1,750 £795

Chippendale cherry tray top candle stand, American, 15 x 14½in. (Robert W. Skinner Inc.) $900 £400

18th century American country pine chair table with circular top, 46in. diam. (Robert W. Skinner Inc.) $1,400 £600

Polished marble and pietra dura occasional table, circa 1879, 21in. diam. (Sotheby's Belgravia) $832 £400

Victorian walnut occasional table with twist support. (Phillips) $103 £45

Regency period mahogany drum top rent table, 27in. diam. (Woolley & Wallis)$4,405 £1,950

Victorian walnut turtle top table with white marble top. (Robert W. Skinner Inc.) $300 £135

18th century mahogany tripod table, 24in. diam. (Dennis H. B. Neal) $1,368 £600

403

Art Deco drawingroom table by Gebroeders Leytens in palisander wood. (Leys, Antwerp) $900 £415

Louis XVI design kingwood and purpleheart centre table by Joubert, 1814, 36½in. wide. (Heathcote Ball & Co.) $5,400 £2,500

Dutch marquetry centre table, circa 1830, with late 17th century panels. (Sotheby's) $9,720 £4,500

Charles II oak games table, 31in. wide, with double opening half-round top. (Boardman's) $1,475 £680

Fine George III satinwood marquetry table with oval top, circa 1780, 2ft. 2in. wide. (Sotheby's) $8,640 £4,000

Ormolu mounted mahogany two-tier table, 1ft.11in. wide, with marble top. (Vidler & Co.) $225 £110

Quartetto of rosewood tables, circa 1920. (Sotheby's) $432 £200

Kingwood and Sevres etagere, top inset with porcelain dish, 1870's, 29in. high. (Sotheby's Belgravia) $4,640 £2,100

Unusual Queen Anne yew-wood table, 2ft.7in. wide, circa 1705. (Sotheby's) $2,485 £1,150

George II mahogany tripod table, circa 1750, 2ft.1in. wide. (Sotheby's) $2,270 £1,050

Flemish 19th century library table inlaid with bone. (Phillips) $2,365 £1,100

Dutch painted tripod table with octagonal top, circa 1740, 2ft.3in. wide. (Sotheby's) $1,450 £620

19th century French ormolu mounted table. (Neales) $1,665 £740

17th century Flemish oak games table, 42in. wide, on three bulbous supports. (Boardman's) $2,170 £1,000

Early George III mahogany tripod silver table, circa 1760, 2ft.2in. diam. (Sotheby's) $4,105 £1,900

Louis XV circular occasional table, veneered in tulipwood and parquetry inlay, 25¾in. diam. (Geering & Colyer) $1,170 £520

19th century mahogany galleried table. (J. M. Welch & Son) $440 £205

Decorative satinwood inlaid mahogany Edwardian occasional table. (Alfie's Antique Market) $360 £160

George III satinwood reading table, circa 1790, 1ft.4½in. wide. (Sotheby's) $2,270 £1,050

18th century marquetry table in two sections, 2ft.3½in. wide. (Sotheby's Monaco) $289,955 £128,870

One of a pair of Regency occasional tripod tables, circa 1810, 1ft.3in. wide. (Sotheby's) $2,810 £1,300

Mid 19th century French marquetry side table of kingwood, 54cm. wide. (Phillips) $245 £120

Rare Anglo-Indian rosewood low table, early 19th century, in Chippendale style, 3ft.3in. wide. (Sotheby's) $3,025 £1,400

Pub table with legs cast to depict ace cricketer W. G. Grace. (Sotheby's Belgravia) $515 £230

405

18th century Portuguese jacaranda tip-up table with trefoil top, 24in. diam. (Christie's) $915 £400

An Oriental rosewood altar table with moulded supports, circa 1900. (Sotheby's Belgravia) $415 £180

A Galle oak and marquetry etagere, the shaped rectangular top inlaid in various printwoods. (Christie's) $630 £290

Chinese export black lacquer centre table, early 19th century, 38½in. wide. (Christie's) $2,785 £1,200

Boulle jardiniere with zinc container on cabriole legs, 1860's, 31½in. wide. (Sotheby's Belgravia) $1,590 £720

Mid Georgian walnut centre table with mottled grey marble top, 48in. wide. (Christie's) $1,390 £600

18th century mahogany circular tray topped table on tripod base. (Phillips) $325 £140

A fruitwood marquetry two-tiered table by Louis Majorelle, 75cm. high. (Christie's) $2,800 £1,300

Victorian walnut circular occasional table on a carved tripod base. (Vernon's) $170 £75

Set of four Regency satinwood quartetto tables with rosewood tops. (Christie's) $6,495 £2,800

Marquetry centre table, stretchers edged with bone and ebony, 45in. wide. (Christie's) $3,390 £1,500

19th century 'Louis XV' oval rosewood rognon decorated with floral marquetry, 62cm. wide.(Phillips) $970 £420

Mahogany Pembroke table in the Chippendale manner, top with gadroon border, 105cm. wide open. (Sotheby Humberts) $400 £185

Fine George III satinwood and marquetry Pembroke table. (Phillips) $6,050 £2,800

George III mahogany Pembroke table, 2ft.8in. wide, circa 1765. (Sotheby's) $1,035 £480

Elegant Pembroke table in mahogany, circa 1830, 26in. high. (Gray's Antique Mews) $400 £185

Early George III mahogany Pembroke dressing table, circa 1760, 1ft.11½in. wide. (Sotheby's) $1,360 £630

Sheraton period mahogany rosewood crossbanded and line inlaid Pembroke table, 3ft.3¼in. wide. (Geering & Colyer) $915 £450

Sheraton painted satinwood Pembroke table. (Messenger May & Baverstock) $1,080 £500

George III mahogany butterfly leaf Pembroke table, circa 1770, 3ft.6½in. high. (Sotheby's) $17,280 £8,000

George III mahogany Pembroke table crossbanded in satinwood, 114cm. wide. (Phillips) $300 £130

George III mahogany Pembroke table, 32in. wide. (Hy. Duke & Son) $2,270 £1,050

George III mahogany Pembroke table crossbanded in satinwood, 100cm. wide. (Phillips) $1,040 £450

George III faded mahogany and crossbanded rectangular Pembroke table, 77cm. wide. (Sotheby King & Chasemore) $755 £350

Art Deco side table, 137cm. wide, 1930's. (Sotheby's Belgravia) $525 £240

19th century French rosewood side table with D-ends. (Worsfolds) $1,350 £600

Regency rosewood and satinwood band inlaid side table. (Geering & Colyer) $2,250 £1,000

One of a pair of late 18th century half circular gilt wood side tables, 32in. wide. (Heathcote Ball & Co.) $1,640 £760

George III solid yew-wood table, circa 1770, 2ft. 6½in. wide. (Sotheby's) $1,404 £650

George II red walnut side table, 24in. wide. (Sotheby Humberts) $1,125 £520

Attractive shagreen-covered side table, 1920's, 40cm. high. (Sotheby's Belgravia) $2,845 £1,300

Bavarian gilt wood side table, Munich, circa 1725, 4ft.2½in. wide, later marble top. (Sotheby's) $2,930 £1,350

Unusual William and Mary oak side or gateleg table. (Sotheby's) $3,485 £1,550

Mid 18th century mahogany side table, 1ft.1½in. wide. (Sotheby King & Chasemore)$1,810 £800

One of a pair of Louis XVI pier tables, 18th century, French, 36in. wide. (Robert W. Skinner Inc.)$1,700 £775

Reproduction French style side table of demi-lune form, 82cm. wide. (Phillips) $145 £65

19th century Dutch floral marquetry walnut side table. (D. M. Nesbit & Co.) $1,625 £800

Early Victorian rosewood side table, 52in. wide. (Olivers) $815 £360

George I walnut side table, top and oak lined drawer crossbanded with feathered inlay. (H. C. Wolton & Son) $12,960 £6,000

Early 19th century black lacquer table, 38in. wide closed. (Christie's S. Kensington) $5,615 £2,600

Queen Anne burr-walnut side table with crossbanded top, 30in. wide. (Christie's) $3,015 £1,300

George I gilt gesso side table, in need of restoration. (Bruton Knowles) $7,560 £3,500

One of a pair of satinwood semi-oval side tables in the Adam manner, 121cm. wide. (Sotheby Humberts) $1,295 £600

Painted satinwood side table with chamfered bowed top, 58½in. wide. (Christie's) $1,350 £600

Mahogany demi-lune side table with single drawer, 130cm. diam. (Phillips) $90 £45

William and Mary oak side table, 33in. wide. (Christie's) $2,375 £1,100

Antique mahogany demi-lune pier table of Adam design, 6ft.6in. wide. (Phillips) $1,100 £500

Mid 18th century Dutch walnut marquetry side table with shaped top. (Sotheby Humberts) $2,700 £1,250

19th century Dutch mahogany
and satinwood crossbanded
sofa table, 42in. wide.
(Phillips) $1,460 £720

George IV mahogany Regency style
sofa table, 20¾in. wide. (Coles, Knapp
& Kennedy) $495 £230

Early 19th century Anglo-
Indian ebony sofa table,
4ft.2in. wide. (Sotheby's)
$1,200 £500

Late George III kingwood veneered sofa table, 4ft.10½in. wide,
circa 1805. (Sotheby's)
$4,750 £2,200

Late 19th century Regency design
mahogany sofa table in poor condition. (Lacy Scott) $610 £300

Regency sofa table, 3ft. long.
(Woolley & Wallis)
$2,810 £1,300

Scottish Regency mahogany sofa
table, top crossbanded in rosewood,
circa 1830, 5ft.7in. wide open.
(Sotheby's) $3,190 £1,400

Regency mahogany pedestal
sofa table, 59in. wide open.
(Lacy Scott) $1,300 £640

Regency rosewood and brass strung
sofa table on four sabre legs on platform base. (Phillips) $3,090 £1,430

Good Regency rosewood sofa
table/games table with satinwood crossbanded top.
(Phillips) $5,225 £2,420

Fine quality Edwardian mahogany sofa
table, 58in. wide. (Butler & Hatch
Waterman) $970 £450

George IV rosewood sofa table
with crossbanded twin-flap top,
64½in. wide open. (Christie's)
$2,085 £900

Regency mahogany sofa table, circa 1810, 2ft.4in. wide, crossbanded in rosewood and satinwood. (Sotheby's) $4,320 £2,000

George III mahogany sofa table with narrow crossbanding, circa 1805, 4ft. 4½in. wide. (Sotheby's) $1,245 £550

Regency mahogany sofa and games table, circa 1815, 4ft. 9in. wide. (Sotheby's) $3,025 £1,400

Regency mahogany sofa table, circa 1820, 5ft. wide open. (Sotheby's) $2,050 £900

Regency period rosewood sofa table on quatrefoil platform base, 36in. closed. (Hobbs Parker) $975 £480

Early 19th century Regency rosewood sofa table, inlaid with brass. (Phillips) $3,875 £1,700

Regency style mahogany sofa table, with top crossbanded in walnut, 104cm. wide. (Phillips) $600 £260

Regency rosewood sofa table inlaid with brass lines, 57½in. wide open. (Christie's) $2,785 £1,200

William IV rosewood sofa table, circa 1830, 4ft.8in. wide open. (Sotheby's) $1,320 £580

Early 19th century Regency mahogany sofa table. (Harrods Auctions) $2,970 £1,350

Early 19th century Regency mahogany sofa table. (Woolley & Wallis) $2,700 £1,200

Early 19th century mahogany sofa table with two end drawers. (Lacy Scott) $770 £380

SUTHERLAND TABLES

20th century oak Sutherland table with canted corners. (Phillips) $45 £20

Small Edwardian mahogany Sutherland table crossbanded in satinwood, 74cm. wide. (Phillips) $255 £110

Late 19th century beechwood Sutherland table on turned legs. (Phillips) $45 £20

Early Victorian burr-walnut Sutherland table with oval flaps and cabriole leg supports. (Vernon's) $515 £225

Edwardian mahogany Sutherland table. (Alfie's Antique Market) $370 £160

19th century solid mahogany Sutherland table on turned legs. (Vernon's) $345 £150

WORKBOXES AND GAMES TABLES

William IV rosewood games table with reversible chess/backgammon board. (Sotheby's) $1,870 £820

Mid Georgian walnut work table with easel top, 27½in. wide. (Christie's) $1,340 £580

Victorian games table, circa 1860, 2ft. wide. (Gray's Antique Mews) $675 £315

Mid 19th century Chinese export lacquer work sewing table on paw feet. (Sotheby's Belgravia) $475 £210

Unusual mahogany and marquetry sewing cabinet with a gallery top, circa 1900. (Sotheby's Belgravia) $730 £320

Walnut card table with four D-shaped flaps, circa 1870.(Sotheby's Belgravia) $1,000 £450

Dutch marquetry semi circular games table with sliding centre leg, 28½in. high. (Worsfolds) $2,250 £1,000

Victorian walnut veneered work table, dated 1889, 22¾in. wide. (Olivers) $405 £180

Marquetry walnut work table with serpentine top, circa 1870, 20¾in. wide, interior with removable tray. (Sotheby's Belgravia) $1,540 £740

George III satinwood work table, 1ft.8in. wide, circa 1790. (Sotheby's) $3,350 £1,550

Victorian walnut games and work table, circa 1850, 61cm. wide. (Sotheby King & Chasemore) $865 £400

William IV rosewood work table. (Gray's Antique Mews) $900 £400

Late 19th century ornately carved padoukwood centre Mahjong table. (Sotheby King & Chasemore) $340 £150

Victorian rosewood and crossbanded chess top work table, inlaid with floral marquetry. (Sotheby King & Chasemore) $990 £440

Floral marquetry Irish yew-wood sewing table. (Messenger May & Baverstock) $755 £350

Walnut work table, circa 1860, 23in. wide, with crossbanded top. (Sotheby's) $390 £180

Russian ebony and boulle games table, late 18th century, 30½in. wide. (Christie's) $43,200 £20,000

Victorian burr-walnut work table. (Sotheby King & Chasemore) $770 £340

Papier mache workbox, unfitted. (J. M. Welch & Son) $820 £380

Victorian rosewood games/ needlework table. (J. M. Welch & Son) $605 £280

19th century burr-walnut work table with diamond inlay top, 61cm. wide. (Phillips) $450 £200

Victorian rosewood needlework table. (J. M. Welch & Son) $625 £290

Ayres mahogany 'racing roulette' games table, circa 1900, 173cm. long. (Sotheby's Belgravia) $1,200 £550

Victorian combined work and games table on a stretcher base. (Vernon's) $700 £310

Victorian burr walnut oval shaped work table, circa 1850, 2ft.1in. wide. (Sotheby King & Chasemore) $770 £340

Victorian papier mache octagonal work table inlaid with mother-of-pearl, 47cm. wide. (Sotheby King & Chasemore) $865 £400

English walnut and marquetry lady's work table, circa 1850, 28in. high. (Sotheby's Belgravia) $830 £360

Mahogany work table with octagonal lid revealing eight lidded compartments, circa 1830. (Sotheby's Belgravia) $620 £270

English walnut combined work and games table with divided swivelling top, 1850's, 28in. high. (Sotheby's Belgravia) $690 £300

George III satinwood oval work table, circa 1790, 1ft.6in. wide. (Sotheby's) $1,185 £520

'Regence' bureau plat with shaped rectangular top, circa 1840, 69in. wide. (Sotheby's Belgravia) $5,305 £2,400

Antique mahogany architect's table with ratchet writing surface. (Worsfolds) $3,455 £1,600

Early 20th century mahogany writing table with outset rounded corners, 56in. wide. (Sotheby's Belgravia) $1,500 £650

Mahogany Carlton House writing desk on square tapering legs with brass castors, 57in. wide, circa 1900. (Sotheby's Belgravia) $3,450 £1,500

English rosewood bonheur du jour inlaid with foliage, circa 1900, 47in. high. (Sotheby's Belgravia) $1,035 £450

Boulle bureau mazarin with brass bordered top, 40in. wide. (Christie's) $12,710 £5,600

Oak library table, top with a blind Gothic frieze, 50½in. wide, circa 1840. (Sotheby's Belgravia) $400 £180

Walnut bonheur du jour with two glazed doors enclosing shelves, 31in. wide. (Sotheby's Belgravia) $1,950 £850

Flemish or German walnut writing desk with crossbanded top, 1880-1890, 40in. wide. (Sotheby's Belgravia) $630 £280

Regency mahogany secretaire writing table, 43in. wide. (Hy. Duke & Son) $1,790 £800

Late 19th century ormolu mounted kingwood bureau plat, 53in. wide. (Christie's S. Kensington) $11,230 £5,200

Edwardian mahogany Carlton House writing desk, inlaid with satinwood stringing, 103cm. wide. (Sotheby King & Chasemore) $2,115 £980

WRITING TABLES AND DESKS

George III mahogany writing table, circa 1780, 5ft. 2in. wide. (Sotheby's) $1,987 £920

Victorian rosewood writing table with sliding red boulle work writing slope, 2ft.8in. wide. (D. M. Nesbit & Co.) $690 £320

Italian parquetry top oak and walnut writing table, 105cm. wide. (Sotheby King & Chasemore) $935 £460

Mahogany Carlton House desk, 1910, with pull-out leather covered writing surface. (Sotheby's Belgravia) $2,250 £1,000

Bonheur du jour in kingwood and Vernis Martin, circa 1900, 45in. wide. (Sotheby's Belgravia) $8,640 £4,000

Regency rosewood library table with plate-glass top, 112cm. wide. (Sotheby King & Chasemore) $955 £470

Satinwood banded and marquetry inlaid mahogany bonheur du jour. (Christie's S. Kensington) $1,010 £500

Burr-walnut and ebonised bonheur du jour, 56in. wide, circa 1870. (Sotheby's Belgravia) $2,360 £1,050

Mid 19th century red boulle bonheur du jour, 81cm. high. (May, Whetter & Grose) $2,050 £950

Walnut bonheur du jour, English, circa 1870, 42½in. wide. (Sotheby's) $2,375 £1,100

George III mahogany and inlaid bonheur du jour, 34in. wide, with D-shaped raised back. (Dacre, Son & Hartley) $3,565 £1,650

Georgian style Carlton House mahogany and inlaid writing desk, 122cm. wide. (Sotheby King & Chasemore) $2,160 £1,000

Early 19th century architect's table with candleslides, on tapered legs. (Worsfolds) $3,455 £1,600

Ormolu mounted mahogany bonheur du jour, circa 1780, 2ft.3½in. wide. (Sotheby's Monaco) $29,000 £13,000

19th century rosewood writing table. (Humberts, King & Chasemore) $1,460 £650

Victorian papier mache and mother-of-pearl writing desk. (Phillips) $891 £395

French Regency writing table and filing cabinet, circa 1720, 5ft. 11½in. wide. (Christie's) $60,480 £28,000

19th century burr-walnut crossbanded and inlaid bonheur du jour, 37in. wide. (Buckell & Ballard) $2,150 £1,075

19th century serpentine front crossbanded bonheur du jour, 3ft.3in. wide. (May, Whetter & Grose) $2,645 £1,225

Very fine Edwardian mahogany escritoire. (R. L. Lowery & Partners) $690 £320

French ebonised bonheur du jour inset with Sevres plaques. (Christie's S. Kensington) $2,828 £1,400

18th century walnut and crossbanded bureau de Mazarin, 110cm. wide. (Sotheby King & Chasemore) $4,725 £2,100

19th century French rosewood and kingwood bureau plat, 3ft.9in. wide. (Messenger May & Baverstock) $1,585 £780

Regency rosewood and cut brass inlay library table, 151cm. wide. (Sotheby King & Chasemore) $8,855 £4,100

417

Regency mahogany writing table, circa 1810, 5ft.0½in. wide, with green leather top. (Sotheby's) $6,264 £2,900

Custom Hepplewhite mahogany tambour desk, 35½in. wide, with satinwood inlay. (Robert W. Skinner Inc.) $1,400 £635

Modern English or French tulipwood bureau plat with brass bound leather top, 70in. wide. (Sotheby's Belgravia) $2,080 £1,000

Small 'Louis XV' kingwood bureau plat, 1840's, 38in. wide. (Sotheby's Belgravia) $2,288 £1,100

Art Deco galuchat and ivory, lady's writing table, circa 1930.(Sotheby's Belgravia) $27,240 £12,000

Late 19th century kingwood and marquetry bureau plat with leather lined top, 59in. wide. (Sotheby's Belgravia) $4,784 £2,300

Early 20th century 'Louis XV' kingwood bureau plat, 49in. wide. (Sotheby's Belgravia) $1,830 £880

Kingwood and Vernis Martin bombe bonheur du jour, circa 1900, 114cm. wide. (Sotheby's Belgravia) $7,130 £3,300

Edwardian walnut desk crossbanded in satinwood, 84cm. wide. (Phillips) $350 £170

Late 19th century marquetry bonheur du jour, 33½in. wide. (Sotheby's Belgravia) $1,664 £800

Fine 19th century Louis XVI bureau plat, 108cm. wide.(Sotheby King & Chasemore) $5,075 £2,500

William IV rosewood writing table, 1ft.5in. wide, circa 1835. (Sotheby's) $1,125 £520

Mid 19th century Louis XV design bureau plat of red boulle and brass, 55in. wide. (Lacy Scott)
$1,948 £960

Carved mahogany library table with leather top, 7ft.2in. wide. (Andrew Grant)
$3,996 £1,850

Louis XV mahogany bureau plat by Christophe Wolff, mid 18th century. (H. Spencer & Sons)
$4,500 £2,000

Late Victorian Carlton House style mahogany desk. (K. Hugh Dodd & Partners)
$1,404 £650

Mahogany writing table with inlaid ebony banded top, circa 1800. (Gray's Antique Mews)
$1,977 £875

Louis XV style bureau in marquetry and gilt bronze. (Leys, Antwerp)
$6,920 £3,200

Genoese walnut parquetry writing table with serpentine top, 5ft. 10in. wide, circa 1760. (Sotheby's)
$13,020 £6,000

19th century French Regency bonheur du jour with tamboured cylinder top, 28½in. wide. (Robert W. Skinner Inc.)
$1,000 £450

Fine Regency burr-elm library table, 4ft.2in. wide, circa 1820. (Sotheby's) $14,688 £6,800

Mid 19th century boulle bonheur du jour, ebonised and ormolu mounted. (Taylor Son & Creber)
$2,675 £775

Victorian oak library table with leather top, American, 19th century, 38in. wide. (Robert W. Skinner Inc.) $775 £350

Late 19th century mahogany and ormolu mounted bonheur du jour, circa 1880, 84cm. wide. (Sotheby King & Chasemore)
$1,468 £680

WRITING TABLES AND DESKS

Dutch mahogany and marquetry partner's desk, circa 1920, 65in. wide. (Sotheby's Belgravia) $1,990 £900

Boulle bonheur du jour on cabriole legs. (Taylor Son & Creber) $1,790 £775

George IV mahogany writing table, circa 1820, 3ft.3in. wide.(Sotheby King & Chasemore)$2,485 £1,100

An Oriental black stained and hardwood writing desk, circa 1900. (Sotheby's Belgravia) $910 £400

Good William IV mahogany library table with green leather top, circa 1830, 5ft. 4in. wide. (Sotheby's) $5,425 £2,400

Early 20th century 'Louis XV' mahogany bureau de dame, 48in. wide, with leather writing surface. (Sotheby's Belgravia) $2,705 £1,300

'Louis XV' kingwood bureau plat of serpentine outline and leather top, circa 1900, 59in. wide. (Sotheby's Belgravia) $5,415 £2,450

Louis XV style rosewood bonheur du jour. (Christie's S. Kensington) $2,145 £950

'Louis XV' ormolu mounted marquetry writing table, circa 1880, 25½in. wide. (Sotheby's Belgravia) $945 £420

Italian ivory inlaid walnut writing desk, circa 1900, 32in. wide. (Sotheby's Belgravia) $585 £260

Edwardian ebony strung satinwood Carlton House desk in immaculate condition. (Clifford Dann & Partners) $4,330 £1,900

Late 19th century Swiss walnut writing desk, superstructure with four small drawers. (Sotheby's Belgravia) $740 £330

George III mahogany architect's table, 35in. wide, with rising top. (Boardman's)
$1,390 £640

'Louis XV' kingwood bureau plat with leather writing surface, circa 1900, 52in. wide. (Sotheby's Belgravia)
$4,310 £1,950

Early 19th century oak slant top school desk on brass cup castors. (British Antique Exporters)
$565 £245

William IV mahogany writing table, circa 1835, 3ft. wide. (Sotheby King & Chasemore)
$815 £360

Late Victorian mahogany writing desk. (Gray's Antique Mews) $785 £345

Edwardian rosewood bonheur du jour, inlaid with satinwood. (Alfie's Antique Market)
$1,105 £490

George III mahogany architect's table, circa 1765, 2ft.11¾in. wide. (Sotheby's) $1,695 £750

Victorian mahogany writing table on turned legs. (Phillips) $205 £90

Small inlaid mahogany writing desk, circa 1900. (Gray's Antique Market) $565 £250

TEAPOYS

Regency simulated rosewood teapoy, lid inlaid with cut brass scrolling, 15in. wide. (Christie's)
$2,090 £900

Attractive William IV mahogany teapoy with octagonal hinged top, 14in. wide. (Coles, Knapp & Kennedy) $420 £195

Early Victorian rosewood teapoy, circa 1840, standing on scroll feet. (Frank R. Marshall & Co.) $440 £195

TRUNKS AND COFFERS

17th century oak coffer with panel-led doors to cupboards. (Hobbs Parker) $570 £280

Oak mule chest, dated 1705, with two side cupboards and two drawers. (Worsfolds) $791 £350

Queen Anne black japanned coffer, circa 1710, 5ft.3in. wide. (Sotheby's) $1,945 £900

Early 18th century oak dower chest with swan neck brass handles, 131cm. long. (Phillips) $615 £300

Late 18th century oak dower chest with iron key plate, 61in. long. (T. Bannister & Co.) $605 £280

16th century oak coffer, fronted by four carved linen fold panels, 3ft. 10in. wide. (Sotheby King & Chasemore) $3,565 £1,650

Early 18th century oak coffer with hinged cover, 64in. wide. (Lacy Scott) $790 £390

Camphorwood chest, heavily carved in the round, 44in. wide. (D. M. Nesbit & Co.) $690 £320

Early 17th century Italian walnut marquetry cassone with moulded lid, 5ft.8in. wide. (Sotheby's) $2,280 £1,050

Early 16th century oak plank chest. (W. H. Lane & Son) $790 £350

Early 18th century oak coffer with interior candle box, 56in. wide. (Lacy Scott) $870 £430

17th century oak mule chest, 47½in. wide. (Christopher Sykes) $1,005 £465

Rare early 16th century North Italian ivory inlaid hardwood cassone, 3ft. 10in. wide. (Sotheby's)
$2,710 £1,250

Small 16th century oak linen fold coffer with plank top, 28½in. wide. (Boardman's) $1,955 £900

Late 16th century oak coffer with iron carrying handles and straps, 159cm. wide. (Sotheby Humberts)
$1,945 £900

Early 17th century carved oak coffer, 4ft.2in. wide. (Sotheby King & Chasemore) $1,730 £800

18th century oak dower chest, dated 1742. (R. L. Lowery & Partners)
$430 £200

Small late 18th century oak coffer with carved front panel, 36in. wide. (T. Bannister & Co.)
$365 £170

Rare 17th century oak domed top ark of plank construction, 97cm. wide. (Sotheby King & Chasemore)
$2,625 £1,280

Mid 17th century oak mule chest with rising top, 4ft.2¾in. wide. (Geering & Colyer) $1,330 £650

Early 18th century panelled carved oak and marquetry coffer, 4ft.3in. wide. (Buckell & Ballard)
$1,165 £575

18th century Indian Indo-Portuguese blanket chest, heavily carved, 58in. long. (Robert W. Skinner Inc.)
$700 £320

George III leather bound trunk, 42in. wide, with brass studs, corners and lockplates. (Christie's S. Kensington)
$1,350 £600

17th century oak coffer, inscribed 'MP 1593', 52in. wide. (Olivers)
$1,310 £580

TRUNKS AND COFFERS

Early 16th century Flemish oak coffer with panelled top and sides, 4ft. wide. (Sotheby's) $1,080 £480

Heavily carved 17th century oak coffer with panelled front. (Turner Fletcher) $1,840 £460

17th century oak coffer with plank top and triple panelled front, 62¼in. wide. (Christie's) $1,145 £500

Early 17th century oak coffer, German or Scandinavian, 3ft.9in. wide. (Sotheby's) $1,260 £560

17th century Italian sacristy chest in walnut, 42in. wide. (Robert W. Skinner Inc.) $650 £295

Queen Anne period small oak mule chest, circa 1720, original wrought iron butterfly hinges, 47in. wide. (Christopher Sykes) $735 £325

Late 18th century oak coffer with panelled front and plank top. (Vernon's) $625 £285

One of a pair of early 19th century Chinese red lacquer leather coffers with brass lock plates, 31in. wide. (Christie's) $6,630 £3,000

Early George II oak coffer with two-plank top, circa 1730, 2ft. 3½in. wide. (Sotheby's) $1,480 £650

17th century ark-top chest, 4ft.9½in. wide. (Lalonde Bros. & Parham) $1,045 £460

19th century Oriental teakwood box, inlaid overall with flowering sprays in various coloured woods, 4ft.6in. wide. (Vernon's) $1,045 £485

Chinese export lacquer green and gold coffer on stand, early 19th century, 36¼in. wide. (Christie's) $3,330 £1,400

Late 17th/early 18th century
leather painted chest with
domed top, 3ft.2in. wide.
(Sotheby's) $1,510 £660

Fine 19th century Oriental inlaid trunk
with brass decoration. (Vernon's)
$925 £400

Late 18th century dark green
leather hide covered coaching
trunk, 36in. long. (Christopher
Sykes) $370 £165

George II walnut and mahogany
chest with hinged lid, circa 1740,
3ft.9in. wide. (Sotheby's)
$3,730 £1,650

Gothic oak coffer with rectangular
top, circa 1520, 4ft.1in. wide.
(Sotheby's) $3,600 £1,600

Carved oak chest, circa 1540,
3ft.4in. wide. (Sotheby's)
$2,250 £1,000

Early 17th century James I oak
chest on stile feet, 3ft.10½in.
wide. (Sotheby's)
$2,810 £1,250

17th century oak and yew small
coffer on gothic arcaded trestle
supports, 30in. wide. (Christie's)
$2,060 £900

George II black japanned chest, mid
18th century, with later stand, 4ft.
1½in. side. (Sotheby's)
$1,185 £520

16th century oak coffer of panelled
construction. (Phillips)
$3,760 £1,650

Painted leather D-shaped coffer
on acanthus carved cabriole legs,
circa 1920. (Sotheby's Belgravia)
$680 £300

Georgian black and gold lacquer
coffer on stand, 50in. wide.
(Christie's) $2,240 £1,000

Early 17th century German marquetry armoire with stepped pediment, 7ft.5in. wide. (Sotheby's)
$5,425   £2,500

19th century Dutch armoire in oak, rosewood and ebony, 6ft. high. (Burtenshaw Walker) $4,715 £2,300

Fine late 18th century French provincial walnut armoire, 4ft.10in. wide. (Sotheby King & Chasemore) $2,375 £1,100

Fine mid 18th century French provincial oak armoire, 172cm. wide. (Sotheby King & Chasemore) $2,870 £1,400

19th century carved oak armoire with four doors, 9ft.8in. wide. (Clevedon Salerooms)
$1,130 £500

Antique mahogany linen wardrobe, 4ft. wide. (Peacock) $574 £260

18th century Spanish oak armoire with doors centred by roundels, 55½in. wide. (Christie's)
$2,155 £950

Dutch walnut and marquetry armoire with arched moulded cornice, 74in. wide. (Christie's)
$18,785 £8,500

Late 18th century North German or Scandinavian elm armoire, 84in. wide. (Christie's)
$1,815 £800

Mid 18th century Dutch walnut armoire, 67½in. wide. (Christie's S. Kensington) $9,070 £4,200

19th century breakfront mahogany wardrobe with satinwood banding, 111in. wide. (Worsfolds)
$2,270 £1,000

Louis XV provincial oak armoire, circa 1765, 4ft.8¾in. wide. (Christie's)
$2,290 £1,000

Good Dutch oak armoire with ebony panels, circa 1660, 6ft.0½in. wide. (Sotheby's) $5,620 £2,600

Large antique oak wardrobe, 63½in. wide, 78in. high. (Butler & Hatch Waterman) $865 £400

18th century Dutch oak kas, 48½in. wide. (Phillips) $5,280 £2,400

Louis XV provincial armoire with two 19th century Japanese lacquer panels. (Sotheby Bearne) $3,240 £1,500

Early 18th century South German walnut armoire, 80in. wide, with carved pediment. (Boardman's) $4,015 £1,850

Good 'Louis XVI' ormolu mounted mahogany armoire stamped A. Beurdeley a Paris, circa 1890, 43in. wide. (Sotheby's Belgravia) $8,320 £4,000

Late 17th century Italian walnut armoire with carved frieze, 46in. wide. (Christie's) $3,405 £1,500

An Art Nouveau marquetry oak wardrobe, 137cm. wide. (Christie's) $610 £280

Early 19th century oak armoire with carved frieze, 4ft.4in. wide. (Sotheby King & Chasemore) $1,580 £700

Ormolu mounted scarlet boulle armoire with arched cornice, 46½in. wide. (Christie's) $2,600 £1,150

Late 19th century mahogany and marquetry breakfront wardrobe, 96in. wide. (Sotheby's Belgravia) $4,100 £1,800

Early 19th century French cherrywood armoire with bra.. fittings. (Vernon's) $1,950 £845

427

WASHSTANDS

19th century rosewood pedestal basin stand. (J. M. Welch & Son) $400 £185

Victorian marble top washstand on a walnut stretcher base. (Vernon's) $170 £75

Victorian mahogany wash cistern complete with bowl. (Vernon's) $277 £120

Early 19th century mahogany combined washstand, pot cupboard and commode. (Vernon's) $740 £320

Edwardian walnut shaving stand with brass framed mirror and marble top. (Vernon's) $170 £75

Sheraton period mahogany toilet stand inlaid with ebony stringing, 22in. wide. (Christopher Sykes) $665 £295

Early 19th century mahogany corner washstand with undershelf. (Vernon's) $450 £200

Late Victorian mahogany washstand with a tiled back and marble top. (Vernon's) $145 £65

Sheraton period corner toilet stand, circa 1790, 43¾in. high. (Christopher Sykes) $665 £295

Early 19th century inlaid mahogany basin stand with hinged cover. (Vernon's) $360 £160

Victorian marble topped washstand on shaped legs. (Phillips) $105 £45

Sheraton mahogany toilet bowl stand, circa 1790, 14in. wide. (Christopher Sykes) $310 £140

428

One of a pair of mahogany oval etageres, each with three tiers, circa 1910. (Sotheby's Belgravia) $1,950 £850

Victorian papier mache whatnot. (Bradley & Vaughan) $1,510 £700

One of a pair of mahogany and burr chestnut etageres, circa 1890, 15in. wide. (Sotheby's Belgravia) $935 £400

Early 19th century mahogany whatnot on turned supports with drawers at the base. (Vernon's) $620 £275

Parquetry three-tier whatnot with lobed upper shelf, stamped Holland & Sons and W. Bassett, 21½in. wide. (Christie's) $2,300 £1,000

Victorian satinwood whatnot of three shelves with spiral supports, 2ft.9in. high. (Vernon's) $450 £200

William IV rosewood whatnot with a three-quarter gallery, circa 1835. (Sotheby's Belgravia) $830 £360

Walnut canterbury/whatnot with pierced three-quarter gallery. (D. M. Nesbit & Co.) $725 £310

Victorian inlaid walnut whatnot with turned supports, 4ft.9in. high. (Sotheby's Belgravia) $810 £360

Victorian carved oak whatnot with 'S' supports and a drawer at the base. (Vernon's) $335 £150

Victorian inlaid walnut three-tier corner whatnot with turned supports. (Vernon's) $280 £125

Edwardian three-tier etagere with gallery top. (J. M. Welch & Son) $185 £85

429

George III mahogany wine cooler. (Christie's & Edmiston's) $4,105 £1,900

Regency mahogany octagonal wine cooler. (Phillips) $1,015 £450

George III brass bound mahogany wine cooler with twin carrying handles, 11in. wide. (Christie's) $2,320 £1,050

George III cellarette with domed lid, 1ft.9in. wide, circa 1785.(Sotheby's) $1,990 £880

Fine Chippendale mahogany cushioned top cellarette with fitted interior and brass carrying handles. (Morphet's) $925 £410

George III mahogany and brass bound octagonal shaped wine cooler, circa 1785. (Sotheby King & Chasemore) $2,810 £1,250

George III serpentine fronted mahogany cellarette, circa 1760, 1ft.6in. wide. (Sotheby's) $3,485 £1,550

George III mahogany wine cooler with brass liner and brass bound body, 23in. wide. (Christie's) $10,160 £4,600

Mid Georgian mahogany cellarette on ogee bracket feet, 17½in. wide. (Christie's) $970 £420

Regency mahogany wine cooler with oval fluted lid, 27½in. wide. (Christie's) $8,150 £3,600

Mid 19th century 'George III' oak wine cooler on stand, 26in. wide. (Sotheby's Belgravia) $485 £210

Fine early 19th century sarcophagus-shaped mahogany wine cooler with original lead lining. (Stride's) $1,075 £460

Newcastle purple and white slag glass beaker. (Vernon's) $35 £15

Pale green glass beaker with slightly convex sides, 1st-2nd century A.D., 2½in. high. (Sotheby's) $350 £160

Cut, stained and engraved 'Ranftbecher', circa 1840, 12cm. high. (Sotheby's) $390 £180

Bohemian enamelled humpen, circa 1590, 11½in. high. $16,200 £7,500

Franconian enamelled glass betrothal humpen and cover, 1615, 41cm. high. (Christie's) $31,320 £14,500

German beaker on three hollow ball feet, engraved with Imperial Arms and artisans' emblems, circa 1730, 10.5cm. high. (Sotheby's) $1,210 £550

Hexagonal Biedermeier drinking glass in ruby red with oval gilt banded green panels, 5in. high. (Vidler & Co.) $165 £80

Biedermeier drinking glass in Bristol blue and pink with etched banded panel, 6in. high. (Vidler & Co.) $155 £75

Pale bluish green glass beaker on hollow folded pad foot, 3rd-4th century A.D., 3¼in. high. (Sotheby's) $330 £150

19th century Mary Gregory beaker depicting a young girl. (Vernon's) $105 £40

North Bohemian lithyalin flared beaker by F. Egermann, circa 1830, 13.5cm. high. (Christie's) $5,850 £2,500

Pale yellowish green glass beaker with straight flaring sides, circa 3rd century A.D., 3¼in. high. (Sotheby's) $400 £180

Engraved beaker of cylindrical form with everted rim, circa 1820, 9.5cm. high. (Sotheby's) $455 £210

Bohemian enamelled overlay beaker with flared bowl, circa 1840, 12.5cm. high. (Sotheby's) $870 £400

Bohemian beaker with waisted cylindrical body, frosted over-all with gilt rim, circa 1835, 11.5cm. high. (Sotheby's) $305 £140

One of a pair of gilt opalescent Ranftbechers, Bohemian, circa 1830, 12.5cm. high.(Sotheby's) $910 £420

Gilt and 'Transparentemail' Ranft-becher by Anton Kothgasser, circa 1820, 11cm. high. (Sotheby's) $2,605 £1,200

Bohemian ruby glass gilt and enamelled spa beaker, circa 1840, 12cm. high. (Sotheby's) $825 £380

Transparent enamelled beaker from the workshop of Samuel Mohn, 1812, 9.8cm. high. (Sotheby's) $17,360 £8,000

Franconian humpen-shaped betro-thal glass and cover, 1615, 16in. high. (Christie's)$31,465 £14,500

One of a pair of Bohemian overlay gilt and enamelled beakers, circa 1840, 12cm. high. (Sotheby's) $1,000 £460

Engraved beaker with waisted bowl, circa 1840, 13cm. high. (Sotheby's) $280 £130

Early 19th century engraved tumbler, probably by Kugler-Graveur, 10cm. high. (Sotheby's) $790 £360

Lithyalin beaker of cylindrical slightly flared section, circa 1830, 11.4cm. high.(Sotheby's) $605 £280

Early sealed wine bottle of gourd type, 1710, 6½in. high. (Sotheby's) $1,040 £480

Sealed and dated wine bottle, inscribed I. Smith, 1706, 6¾in. high. (Sotheby's) $1,625 £750

Sealed and dated wine bottle of dark green metal, inscribed W. Skammell, 1704, 6in. high. (Sotheby's) $1,345 £620

Rare Staffordshire 'enamel' tea bottle, 5½in. high, circa 1760. (Sotheby's) $650 £300

Encrusted bottles. (W. H. Lane & Son) $870 £375

Pair of sealed sherry bottles, 'Dry Sack, Williams and Humber', circa 1880. (Alfie's Antique Market) $75 £40

Attractive Pekin glass bottle of transparent amber coloured metal, Qianlong period, 20.3cm. high. (Sotheby's) $650 £300

Gigantic green glass bottle, mid 17th century, 15in. high. (Christopher Sykes) $85 £40

Sealed and dated wine bottle inscribed Saml. Whittuck, 1751, 9in. high.(Sotheby's) $735 £340

Early globe and shaft wine bottle, circa 1660, 9in. high. (Sotheby's) $3,040 £1,400

Bohemian Zwischengold bottle with silver cap, 12cm. high. (Sotheby's)$1,520 £700

Pear-shaped chemist's shop window display drug bottle, 18in. high, 19th century. (Christopher Sykes) $145 £65

Serving bottle, dark olive green with opaque white inclusions, Shropshire, circa 1800, 12.5cm. high. (Christie's) $435 £190

Pair of 20th century midwife's glass medical bottles, 4¾in. high, in chromium plated holders. (Christopher Sykes) $65 £30

Rare early sealed and dated onion form wine bottle, dated 1699, 13cm. high. (Christie's) $2,300 £1,000

Sealed wine bottle, dark olive green, with kick-in base, circa 1765, 24cm. high.(Christie's)$350 £150

1st century A.D. small blue glass bottle with squat pear-shaped body, 3in. high. (Sotheby's) $1,540 £700

Early English dark green wine bottle, circa 1660, 9½in. high. (Sotheby's) $1,010 £460

Nuremberg wheel engraved glass bottle, circa 1720, 27cm. high. (Sotheby's) $2,200 £1,000

Large pale green glass bottle with indented base, circa 14th century A.D., 15½in. high.(Sotheby's) $880 £400

Good red overlay Pekin glass bottle, with decoration of birds in flowering prunus trees, circa 1800, 19.1cm. high. (Sotheby's) $1,260 £580

Early English dark green wine bottle, circa 1680, 7¾in. high. (Sotheby's) $485 £220

Rare Pekin glass double gourd bottle, clear pink flecked metal with blue overlay, 18th century, 15.5cm. high. (Sotheby's) $1,300 £600

Sealed onion form wine bottle, inscribed Ed. Jones/Burton, 1737, 19cm. high.(Christie's) $415 £180

'L'Homme Lefevre' de Caranza lustre glass bowl, circa 1900, 7.5cm. wide. (Sotheby's Belgravia) $460 £200

Galle cameo glass bowl and cover, circa 1900, 11cm. diam. (Sotheby's Belgravia) $615 £280

One of a set of three Tiffany iridescent glass finger bowls, circa 1900, 12cm. diam. (Sotheby's Belgravia) $440 £200

A Tiffany favrile golden iridescent bowl with globular body, 19cm. high. (Christie's) $875 £400

Palais Royale ormolu mounted translucent red bowl and cover, circa 1830, 16cm. high. (Sotheby's) $870 £400

Cameo glass bride's basket by Mount Washington Glass Co. (Robert W. Skinner Inc.)$750 £340

Blue glass bowl with French silver gilt mounts, circa 1825, 11½in. high. (Sotheby's) $1,075 £480

Lalique glass powder bowl, 6½in. diam. (J. M. Welch & Son) $520 £240

A small Lalique bowl and cover of compressed form, 7cm. diam. (Christie's) $500 £230

Galle enamelled glass bowl, circa 1900, 16.25cm. diam. (Sotheby's Belgravia) $985 £450

Tiffany blue iridescent bowl with swirled blown out body. (Robert W. Skinner Inc.) $450 £205

Galle cameo glass bowl, circa 1900, 20.25cm. diam. (Sotheby's Belgravia) $655 £300

Unusual clear green Pekin glass bowl, decorated in relief with birds and blossom, 16.2cm. diam. (Sotheby's) $325 £150

17th century Venetian glass bowl, 43cm. diam. (Sotheby's) $1,760 £800

Rare Lynn finger bowl of dark emerald green metal, circa 1765, 11.5cm. diam. (Christie's) $415 £180

An Orrefors deep bowl by Edvin Ohrstrom, 18cm. diam. (Christie's) $1,050 £480

18th century latticinio shallow bowl, probably Catalan, 18cm. diam. (Christie's) $390 £170

Galle cameo glass bowl, circa 1900, 11.5cm. wide. (Sotheby's Belgravia) $1,155 £500

A Brocard enamelled Mogul jade bowl, 16.5cm. high. (Christie's) $1,200 £550

Pekin glass bowl of clear carmine metal, decorated with dragons in relief, 19.7cm. wide. (Sotheby's) $825 £380

Islamic green mould blown glass bowl, circa 10th century A.D., 6in. diam. (Sotheby's)$530 £240

Clear yellow Pekin glass bowl, carved with fruit trees and bats, mark of Qianlong, 14.5cm. wide. (Sotheby's) $870 £400

16th or 17th century Facon de Venise latticinio shallow bowl, possibly Venetian, 13.5cm. diam. (Christie's) $5,060 £2,200

Pale bluish green cast glass 'pillar-moulded' bowl, 1st century A.D., 4¼in. diam. (Sotheby's) $570 £260

Late 19th century frosted glass bowl with applied decoration and wavy rim. (Vernon's) $130 £60

Daum cameo glass bowl with quatrefoil rim, circa 1900, 15.5cm. wide. (Sotheby's Belgravia) $990 £440

Fine iridescent Art Glass bowl with wavy rim, 10in. diam. (Vernon's) $105 £50

CANDLESTICKS

Late 18th century free-blown glass pricket candlestick, 9in. high. (Robert W. Skinner Inc.) $275 £130

One of a pair of rare South Staffordshire opaque white glass tapersticks and enamel drip-pans, circa 1760, 18.5cm. high. (Christie's) $920 £400

Early English taperstick, circa 1700, 13.5cm. high. (Phillips) $815 £360

CUPS AND MUGS

Small dark brown Nailsea mug, circa 1870, 6cm. high. (Christie's) $160 £70

Mould blown glass cup of the 1st century A.D., 2½in. high. (Sotheby's) $153,750 £75,000

17th/18th century boot glass, possibly Liege, 15cm. high. (Sotheby's) $910 £420

Bottle glass beer mug with white enamel splatter. (Vernon's) $200 £85

Tiffany gold iridescent loving cup with three handles, 5in. high. (Robert W. Skinner Inc.) $800 £365

New England peachblow punch cup with ribbed handle, 2¼in. high. (Robert W. Skinner Inc.) $175 £80

DECANTERS

Amber glass bottle with shaped stopper and silver neck. (Alfie's Antique Market) $130 £60

Art Deco mallet-shaped decanter. (Alfie's Antique Market) $55 £25

Engraved clear glass and blue overlay decanter and stopper, circa 1929, 28.2cm. high. (Sotheby's Belgravia) $250 £110

Set of four green tinted gilt decanters, stoppers and stand, circa 1790, 9¾in. high.(Sotheby's) $780 £360

One of a pair of late 19th century cut crystal spirit decanters, 9½in. high. (Christopher Sykes) $170 £75

One of a pair of Cork Glass Co. engraved decanters with bull's eye stoppers, circa 1800. (Christie's) $550 £240

Unusual electroplate mounted blue glass decanter, circa 1900, probably English, 29.8cm. high.(Sotheby's Belgravia) $575 £250

One of three English blue tinted decanters, early 19th century, 11¼in. high. (Sotheby's) $615 £280

One of a pair of engraved decanters, 11½in. high, circa 1750, with tapering necks. (Sotheby's) $1,530 £680

Lalique glass decanter of flattened oval section, 27cm. high, 1930's. (Sotheby's Belgravia) $335 £150

Diamond engraved magnum carafe of mallet shape, English, 1822. (Sotheby's) $1,100 £500

One of a pair of Victorian pear-shaped decanters, 22.5cm. high. (Phillips) $80 £40

Late Victorian heavy brass tantalus by Mappin & Webb. (Gray's Antique Mews) $510 £225

Irish cut glass magnum armorial decanter and stopper, circa 1810. (Christie's)$720 £320

Late 19th century blue glass decanter and six glasses, painted, silvered and gilt decorated. (Sotheby's) $590 £260

One of a pair of Irish cut glass decanters and stoppers, circa 1810. (Christie's) $520 £230

Good Bohemian green decanter and stopper, circa 1850, 48cm. high, with triple ringed neck. (Sotheby's Belgravia) $740 £320

Enamelled decanter jug and stopper with flattened body, circa 1870, 31.5cm. high. (Sotheby's Belgravia) $755 £350

One of a pair of English decanters, circa 1820, 9¾in. high. (Sotheby's) $440 £220

One of a pair of late 18th century Venetian glass decanters and stoppers. (Bonham's) $515 £240

One of a pair of cut crystal glass decanters, circa 1890, 9¾in. high. (Christopher Sykes) $190 £85

One of a pair of English decanters and stoppers, circa 1820, 9¼in. high. (Sotheby's) $330 £150

One of a pair of ruby stained octagonal decanters. (Christie's S. Kensington) $130 £60

Ale carafe with cylindrical body and tapering neck, circa 1770, 25.5cm. high. (Christie's) $600 £260

439

DISHES

18th century glass sweetmeat on tripod scroll feet, 6.5cm. high. (Sotheby's) $240 £110

Green glass dish of shallow rounded form, 1st century A.D., 7½in. diam. (Sotheby's) $330 £150

Daum etched and enamelled glass dish with two loop handles, 18.5cm. wide, circa 1900. (Sotheby's Belgravia)$655 £300

Early sweetmeat dish, with shallow bowl and gadrooned base, 3¼in. high, circa 1720. (Sotheby's) $270 £120

Venetian latticinio (vetra di trina) large circular dish, circa 1700, 49.5cm. diam. (Christie's) $1,840 £800

A Lalique circular bowl and cover of matt glass with slightly flared sides, 8cm.diam. (Christie's) $500 £230

A small Mary Gregory amber glass pin tray depicting a boy with a butterfly net. (Vernon's) $200 £85

Smith Brothers powder jar with opal glass body and plated silver top. (Robert W. Skinner Inc.)$225 £100

Small colourless glass dish with rounded sides and twin handles, 2nd-3rd century A.D., 4¼in. (Sotheby's) $660 £300

Gilt and enamelled opaline garniture, circa 1835, 14cm. high. (Sotheby's) $435 £200

Lalique opalescent glass dish and cover, 1920's, 17cm. diam. (Sotheby's Belgravia) $395 £180

Pedestal stemmed stand, circa 1745, 12.5cm. high. (Christie's) $140 £60

440

Colourless glass flask with spherical body, circa 3rd century A.D., 4¾in. high. (Sotheby's)
$330 £150

Bohemian or Franconian tailor's enamelled blue cylindrical flask, dated 1673, 14.5cm. high. (Christie's)
$1,725 £750

Small pale yellowish Islamic glass pilgrim flask, circa 13th century, 3¼in. high.(Sotheby's)$750 £340

Colourless glass flask with dome shaped body, 4th-5th century A.D., 4¾in. high. (Sotheby's)$620 £280

Central European flask with enamelled decoration, circa 1740, 17.5cm. high. (Sotheby's) $840 £380

Manganese purple glass flask of cylindrical form, 3rd-4th century A.D., 4¼in. high. (Sotheby's) $530 £240

GOBLETS

Fine early lead glass coin goblet, 10in. high, probably by Hawley Bishop, circa 1686. (Sotheby's)$4,155 £1,800

Rare baluster goblet with flared cylindrical bowl, circa 1700, 6¾in. high. (Sotheby's) $1,665 £720

Rare goblet, engraved with Frederick the Great and the double eagle of Prussia, circa 1757, 8¼in. high. (Sotheby's) $4,370 £1,900

Baluster goblet with wide flared bowl, circa 1700, 7¼in. high. (Sotheby's) $2,885 £1,250

Early glass-of-lead goblet of Ravenscroft period, circa 1675, 11½in. high. (Sotheby's) $1,110 £480

Fine goblet with pointed round funnel bowl, circa 1700, 7½in. high. (Sotheby's) $1,615 £700

GOBLETS

Dutch engraved goblet of Newcastle type, circa 1750, 8½in. high. (Sotheby's) $1,410 £650

Unrecorded triple-portrait goblet, 1849, 15.5cm. high, engraved by Dominik Biemann. (Sotheby's) $18,445 £8,500

Biedermeier green glass goblet, finely etched with deer, 6¼in. high. (Vidler & Co.) $164 £80

Rare electioneering goblet, the bowl inscribed "Success to Sir Francis Knollys", circa 1745, 19cm. (Christie's) $920 £400

Nuremberg engraved goblet and cover, circa 1680, 39.5cm. (Christie's) $13,350 £5,800

Massive Dutch engraved goblet and cover, circa 1765, 47cm. high. (Christie's) $2,070 £900

Dutch engraved goblet with funnel bowl, circa 1765, 23cm. sold with cover. (Christie's) $735 £320

19th century Bohemian amber overlay glass goblet and cover, 17½in. high. (D. M. Nesbit & Co.) $580 £255

Massive Jacobite air-twist goblet with funnel bowl, circa 1785, 17.5cm. (Christie's) $1,030 £450

Venetian or Anglo-Netherlandish Facon de Venise goblet, circa 1670, 25cm. (Sotheby's) $1,430 £650

Jacobite balustroid goblet with thistle-shaped bowl, circa 1740, 17cm. (Christie's) $780 £340

Netherlandish engraved goblet with flared funnel bowl, circa 1700, 16cm. (Christie's) $920 £400

442

Rare blue goblet, lightly fluted cup and plain stem, circa 1760, 16.5cm. (Christie's) $3,450 £1,500

Unusual blue baluster goblet with funnel bowl, early 18th century, 16cm. (Christie's) $1,265 £550

Anglo-Venetian engraved armorial goblet of soda metal, late 17th century, 16cm. (Christie's) $2,070 £900

Baluster goblet with funnel bowl, circa 1705, 16cm. (Christie's) $1,100 £480

Russian engraved goblet with the cypher of Empress Elizabeth Petrovna, circa 1740, 24cm. (Sotheby's) $990 £450

Fine Bohemian ruby flashed goblet and cover, 52cm. high. (Sotheby King & Chasemore) $1,080 £480

Green goblet with oviform knopped stem with vertical flutes, late 18th century, 16.5cm. high. (Christie's) $435 £190

Composite stemmed goblet with flared straight-sided bowl, circa 1750, 19.5cm. high. (Christie's) $170 £75

Dutch engraved composite stemmed armorial goblet, circa 1750, 19.5cm. high. (Christie's) $2,410 £1,050

Green goblet of bright emerald colour, plain stem on spirally-moulded foot, circa 1760, 13.5cm. (Christie's) $300 £130

Composite stemmed champagne glass with double ogee bowl, circa 1740, 15cm. (Christie's) $210 £90

Large baluster goblet with funnel bowl, circa 1710, 23.5cm. (Christie's) $1,265 £550

17th century Rhenish roemer of light green tint, 14cm. high. (Christie's) $600 £260

Rare Nuremberg Jagd hunting goblet and cover. (Christie's) $2,280 £1,000

17th century Rhenish roemer of light green metal, 14cm. high. (Sotheby's) $925 £420

Engraved glass goblet from Dresden, circa 1730, 11¼in. high. (Sotheby's) $6,050 £2,800

Newcastle Dutch engraved Royal armorial goblet, circa 1745, 21.5cm. high. (Christie's) $4,370 £1,900

Saxon armorial goblet engraved with the Arms of the Duke of Cumberland, circa 1760, 22.5cm. high. (Christie's) $370 £160

Dutch engraved Newcastle goblet with putto and cartouches, circa 1745, 18cm. high. (Christie's) $830 £360

Baluster goblet with flared funnel bowl, circa 1700, 17.5cm. high. (Christie's) $2,760 £1,200

Facon de Venise latticinio goblet, circa 1700. (Christie's) $4,300 £2,000

Bohemian engraved goblet, set on wrythen knop, circa 1730, 17.5cm. high. (Sotheby's) $485 £220

Saxon friendship goblet engraved with conjoined hearts and an inscription, circa 1730, 19.3cm. high. (Sotheby's) $970 £440

Engraved goblet in the manner of David Wolff, inscribed 'Iustitia', circa 1780, 18cm. high. (Christie's) $6,670 £2,900

Nailsea baluster cream jug, clear glass with opaque white decoration, circa 1820, 9cm. high. (Christie's) $275 £120

4th century A.D. pale green glass jug with strap handle, 3¾in. high. (Sotheby's) $240 £110

16th or early 17th century Facon de Venise latticinio ewer, South Netherlands or Venetian, 16.5cm. high. (Christie's)$2,530 £1,100

Cased wheeling peach blow pitcher, 5¼in. high. (Robert W. Skinner Inc.) $650 £295

One of a pair of blue glass ewer ornaments decorated by Mary Gregory, 43cm. high. (May, Whetter & Grose) $205 £95

Large pale green glass jug with ovoid body, 2nd/3rd century A.D., 7½in. high. (Sotheby's) $485 £220

Rainbow satin glass ewer in herringbone pattern with mother-of-pearl finish, 10in. high.(Robert W. Skinner Inc.) $950 £430

Early Victorian claret jug, circa 1840. (Christopher Sykes) $110 £50

Large cut glass ewer in neo-classical style, English, circa 1830, 10½in. high.(Sotheby's) $485 £220

4th century pale green glass pitcher, slightly cracked, 12¾in. high. (Sotheby's) $15,375 £7,500

One of a pair of Waterford cut glass jugs. (Sotheby Humberts) $945 £460

Enamelled milchglas jug, Spanish or Bohemian, circa 1780, 19.3cm. high. (Sotheby's)$165 £75

MISCELLANEOUS

One of a set of seven Victorian glass wine coolers, 14cm. diam. (Phillips) $80 £40

Rare red Pekin glass covered jar, decorated in relief with a dragon among clouds, 12.5cm. high. (Sotheby's) $1,040 £480

Lalique glass powder box and cover, circa 1925, 10.7cm. diam. (Sotheby's Belgravia) $570 £260

One of a pair of blue glass bugles. (Christie's S. Kensington) $225 £100

Four Victorian green fluted glass medicine bottles and stoppers, 24cm. high. (Phillips) $30 £15

Baccarat sulphide glass cameo plaque of Charles X, 10cm. long. (Sotheby's) $340 £150

Daum glass and Brandt wrought iron aquarium, circa 1925, 148cm. high. (Sotheby's Belgravia) $3,065 £1,400

Tiffany bronze and gold iridescent brides basket, 7½in. high. (Robert W. Skinner Inc.) $475 £215

Large glass chemist's jar with armorial transfer, English, circa 1890, 31in. high. (Sotheby's Belgravia) $550 £240

One of a pair of crimson Victorian lustres, circa 1880, 14in. high. (Gray's Antique Mews) $125 £55

Lalique opalescent glass figure 'Suzanne au Bain', 1920's, 23cm. high. (Sotheby's Belgravia) $3,120 £1,350

One of a pair of Bohemian overlay glass lustres, with cranberry glass body, 25cm. high. (Phillips) $150 £70

446

Sulphide glass portrait plaque of George III, 10cm. diam. (Sotheby's) $550 £240

Central European opaque opaline globular teapot and cover, mid 18th century, 16cm. wide. (Christie's) $800 £350

Rare blue overlay Pekin glass waterpot of translucent white metal, 18th century, 5.4cm. high. (Sotheby's) $825 £380

Mt. Washington Royal Flemish covered jar, 7in. high. (Robert W. Skinner Inc.) $2,400 £1,090

Sulphide glass cameo plaque of General Lafayette, 8.5cm. wide. (Sotheby's) $205 £90

Lalique cock's head desk ornament, circa 1925, 20.25cm. high. (Sotheby's Belgravia) $920 £420

Good Loetz iridescent glass 'rose-water sprinkler', 24cm. high, circa 1900. (Sotheby's Belgravia) $2,410 £1,100

Venetian diamond engraved latticinio plate, late 16th century, 16.5cm. diam. (Christie's) $1,840 £800

Stylish Oertel Haida enamelled glass jar and cover, 23cm. high, circa 1905. (Sotheby's Belgravia) $525 £240

Unusual Pekin glass brushpot thinly cased in red, engraved mark of Qianlong, 17.5cm. high. (Sotheby's) $1,085 £500

One of a pair of Lalique dragonfly car mascots mounted as bookends. (Christie's) $2,100 £950

Biemann portrait plaque of oval form, circa 1830, 8cm. long, probably Franzensbad. (Sotheby's) $10,415 £4,800

447

PAPERWEIGHTS

Rare Baccarat flat bouquet weight of two crossed sprays of clematis. (Sotheby's) $11,165 £5,500

Baccarat glass millefiori paperweight signs of zodiac, dated 1847. (Worsfolds) $1,070 £475

Clichy moss ground concentric millefiori paperweight, 6.3cm. diam. (Christie's) $2,925 £1,250

Mid 19th century St. Louis paperweight in clear and coloured glass, 8cm. diam. (Christie's) $108,000 £48,000

Rare Baccarat butterfly and flower weight. (Christie's) $11,110 £5,500

Baccarat faceted translucent blue-flash patterned millefiori paperweight, 7cm. diam. (Christie's) $1,520 £650

Very fine Clichy moss ground paperweight, 8cm. (Sotheby's) $9,600 £4,200

St. Louis cherry paperweight, 8.3cm. (Sotheby's) $2,960 £1,300

Clichy patterned millefiori paperweight, 8.3cm. (Sotheby's) $590 £260

Baccarat butterfly and flower paperweight with star cut base, 7.5cm. diam. (Sotheby's) $3,190 £1,400

St. Louis carpet-ground paperweight, 6cm. (Sotheby's) $3,200 £1,400

Clichy patterned millefiori paperweight with five large setups, 7.5cm. diam. (Christie's) $585 £250

448

Clichy swirl paperweight, 7.5cm. (Sotheby's) $960 £420

Lalique glass frog paperweight, 6.1cm. high, circa 1930. (Sotheby's Belgravia) $1,640 £750

Baccarat close millefiori paperweight, 6.5cm. (Sotheby's) $775 £340

Very rare St. Louis cruciform ground paperweight, 7.5cm. (Sotheby's) $11,500 £5,000

Amber flashed zooglophite paperweight engraved with a stag, 8cm. (Sotheby's) $340 £150

Baccarat double-overlay paperweight, turquoise overlay and millefiori centre, 8cm. (Sotheby's) $3,200 £1,400

Clichy patterned millefiori paperweight, 8cm. diam. (Sotheby's) $2,170 £950

Baccarat primrose paperweight, 6.5cm. (Sotheby's) $590 £260

Clichy Barber's Pole paperweight, signed 'C'. 8.3cm. diam. (Sotheby's) $1,000 £440

Miniature Clichy pansy paperweight, 4.6cm. diam. (Sotheby's) $1,320 £580

Baccarat panelled carpet-ground paperweight, 8cm. (Sotheby's) $3,420 £1,500

St. Louis dahlia paperweight, 8cm. diam. (Sotheby's) $9,100 £4,000

SCENT BOTTLES

One of a pair of gilt enamelled opaline scent bottles and stoppers, circa 1830, 13cm. high. (Sotheby's) $2,385 £1,100

Lalique frosted glass scent bottle, 12cm. high, 1920's. (Sotheby's Belgravia) $260 £120

Lalique glass scent bottle and stopper of swollen cylindrical form, 1930's, 8.7cm. high. (Sotheby's Belgravia) $405 £180

Lalique clear glass scent bottle, 13.5cm. high, 1920's. (Sotheby's Belgravia) $175 £80

Lalique glass scent bottle for Guerlain's 'Shalimar', 17cm. high, circa 1920. (Sotheby's Belgravia) $85 £40

Art Deco pagoda scent bottle, 9in. high. (Nottinghill Auction Market) $145 £65

Lalique glass scent bottle, 1920's, 15.5cm. high, with frosted glass body. (Sotheby's Belgravia) $260 £120

Cameo glass scent bottle with silver cap by Horton & Allday, Chester, 1884, 23.8cm. long. (Sotheby's Belgravia) $1,500 £650

Lalique glass cologne bottle and stopper, 1930's, 17.5cm. high. (Sotheby's Belgravia) $225 £100

Laiique frosted glass scent atomiser, 13cm. high, 1920's (Sotheby's Belgravia) $260 £120

One of a pair of ruby cased scent bottles and stoppers, circa 1850, 19.2cm. high. (Sotheby's Belgravia) $325 £150

Lalique frosted and enamelled glass perfume atomiser, 1930's, 9.5cm. high. (Sotheby's Belgravia) $270 £120

'Ivory cameo' scent bottle in the form of a gourd, circa 1890, with silvered screw cap, 7.5cm. high.(Sotheby's Belgravia) $150 £70

Unusual Lalique glass multiple scent bottle, circa 1920, 22.5cm. long. (Sotheby's Belgravia) $655 £300

Lalique frosted glass scent bottle with metal atomiser fitment, 14cm. high, 1930's. (Sotheby's Belgravia) $355 £150

One of a pair of Lalique frosted glass scent bottles and stoppers, 1920's, 9.2cm. high.(Sotheby's Belgravia) $625 £280

Lalique glass scent bottle, 15.5cm. high, 1920's, with octagonal body. (Sotheby's Belgravia) $185 £85

Unusual gilt metal and plique-a-jour enamel scent phial, 5.8cm. high, circa 1900. (Sotheby's Belgravia) $920 £420

Cut glass perfume bottle with silver screw top by Aspreys, London, 1886. (Christopher Sykes) $65 £30

Cameo glass scent bottle with hinged silver cap, Birmingham, 1886, 12cm. high. (Sotheby's Belgravia) $560 £260

Webb cameo silver mounted scent flask with silver cover, circa 1885, 18cm. long. (Christie's) $1,125 £480

Lalique frosted glass scent atomiser, 15cm. high, 1920's. (Sotheby's Belgravia) $305 £140

Lalique frosted glass scent bottle, 1920's, 12.5cm. high. (Sotheby's Belgravia) $120 £55

Staffordshire opaque glass scent bottle, 1770, 7.5cm. high. (Christie's) $185 £80

STAINED GLASS

Mid 16th century German sepia and yellow stained glass roundel, 9½in. diam, re-leaded. (Sotheby's) $3,690 £1,700

French stained glass panel showing the Risen Christ, dated 1542, 66 x 56cm. (Christie's) $600 £260

15th century English stained glass roundel, 4½in. diam. (Sotheby's) $870 £400

German or Swiss stained glass panel showing a married couple, dated 1597, 33 x 24cm. (Christie's) $530 £230

One of a set of three Victorian stained glass windows, 63in. high. (Vost's) $1,135 £555

One of a pair of German stained glass panels, 16th century, 129.5cm. high. (Christie's) $1,620 £750

TANKARDS

Mid 18th century engraved glass tankard. (Christie's) $950 £425

Enamelled milchglas tankard, Spanish or Bohemian, circa 1780, 13.2cm. high. (Sotheby's) $220 £100

Bohemian cut glass souvenir tankard and cover, circa 1840, 25cm. high. (Christie's) $465 £200

19th century Bohemian silver mounted amber-flashed tankard with strap handle, Birmingham, 1899, 29cm. high. (Sotheby's Belgravia) $540 £250

Central European enamelled glass tankard with pewter lid and foot rim, 18th or 19th century, 24cm. high. (Sotheby's) $750 £340

Large engraved ale tankard with bell bowl, circa 1760, 20cm. high. (Christie's) $735 £320

Ormolu mounted opaline tazza, circa 1830, 13.5cm. high, with scroll handles surmounted by swans. (Sotheby's) $735 £340

16th or 17th century Facon de Venise tazza, 22.5cm. diam. (Sotheby's) $3,100 £1,400

Ormolu mounted amethyst and opaline tazza, circa 1830, 11cm. high. (Sotheby's) $3,255 £1,500

TUMBLERS

Bohemian dated tumbler with leaf-cut base, 1834, 12cm. high. (Sotheby's Belgravia) $585 £270

Bohemian amber-flashed tumbler of thistle shape, circa 1850, 14cm. high. (Sotheby's Belgravia) $475 £220

Bohemian amber-flashed hexagonal tumbler, circa 1850, 14cm. high, with engraved sides. (Christie's) $2,225 £950

Baccarat armorial tumbler with enamelled coat of arms, 9.5cm. high. (Sotheby's) $2,740 £1,200

Bohemian tumbler engraved with Cupids and allegorical scenes, circa 1730, 10.2cm. high. (Sotheby's) $485 £220

Cut glass Baccarat tumbler with enamelled figure of Napoleon, 9.4cm. high. (Sotheby's) $915 £400

Austrian armorial cut glass cylindrical tumbler, circa 1835, 9cm. high. (Christie's) $1,150 £500

Late 17th century Bohemian Jagd flared tumbler, 11cm. high. (Christie's) $920 £400

Bohemian tumbler engraved with Cupids, circa 1730, 10cm. high. (Sotheby's) $750 £340

One of a pair of Art Nouveau silver overlay blue vases. (Alfie's Antique Market) $138 £60

Galle marine cameo glass vase, circa 1900, 23.5cm. high. (Sotheby's Belgravia) $1,752 £800

Galle etched and carved cameo glass vase, circa 1900, 15.5cm. high. (Sotheby's Belgravia) $1,204 £550

One of a pair of Austrian iridescent overlaid glass vases, 23cm. high, circa 1900. (Sotheby's Belgravia) $1,861 £850

Stourbridge cameo glass vase, 5in. high, central band with turquoise 'jewelling'. (McCartney, Morris & Barker) $1,536 £680

Iridescent glass vase by Loetz, circa 1900, 30.75cm. high. (Sotheby's Belgravia) $1,640 £750

Lalique opalescent glass vase of beaker form, 18cm. high, engraved France. (Sotheby King & Chasemore) $739 £320

Edelzinn pewter mounted vase, circa 1900, 25cm. high. (Sotheby's Belgravia) $1,007 £450

Galle enamelled glass vase, circa 1900, 44.25cm. high. (Sotheby's Belgravia) $876 £400

Galle lily-form enamelled glass vase, 1890's, 16.7cm. high. (Sotheby's Belgravia) $3,003 £1,300

Large Galle cameo glass vase, circa 1900, 58.5cm. high. (Sotheby's Belgravia) $2,190 £1,000

Daum etched and gilt 'vase pariant', circa 1900, 26cm. high. (Sotheby's Belgravia) $766 £350

Large Galle cameo glass landscape vase, circa 1900, 63cm. high. (Sotheby's Belgravia) $8,979 £4,100

Large Galle 'blow-out' glass elephant vase, circa 1900, 38cm. high. (Sotheby's Belgravia) $24,090 £11,000

Lalique opalescent Ceylan vase, 1925, 9½in. high. (Gray's Antique Mews) $1,085 £475

Lalique amber glass serpent vase, 1930's, 24.5cm. high. (Sotheby's Belgravia) $9,855 £4,500

Rare and early wood and metal mounted Bakalowits glass vase, 1900, 46.5cm. high. (Sotheby's Belgravia) $20,805 £9,500

Galle cameo glass vase, 12.25cm. high, circa 1900. (Sotheby's Belgravia) $525 £240

Miniature Galle cameo glass solifleur vase, 13cm. high, circa 1900. (Sotheby's Belgravia) $350 £160

Galle cameo glass vase with knopped neck, circa 1900, 40.3cm. high. (Sotheby's Belgravia) $1,270 £550

Galle cameo glass vase, circa 1900, 24.5cm. high. (Sotheby's Belgravia) $646 £280

Unusual carved and internally decorated Christian glass vase, 1890's, 15.25cm. high. (Sotheby's Belgravia) $1,201 £520

Eugene Rousseau glass vase, circa 1885, in shaded bubble brown glass, 18cm. high. (Sotheby's Belgravia) $970 £420

Fine small Galle cameo glass vase, 9cm. high. (Sotheby King & Chasemore) $462 £200

Argy Rousseau pate-de-crystal vase. (Bonham's) $1,296 £600

18th century Pekin glass vase of clear olive green, 5½in. high. (Sotheby's) $4,620 £2,100

Very rare miniature opaque white globular vase, 2½in. high, circa 1770.(Sotheby's) $1,128 £520

Unusual Galle glass vase, circa 1900, 36.7cm. high, in mottled mauve and yellow glass. (Sotheby's Belgravia) $1,848 £800

One of a pair of Bohemian ruby overlay glass vases, 10in. high. (H. Spencer & Sons) $540 £250

Austrian iridescent glass vase by Koloman Moser, circa 1900, 29cm. high. (Sotheby's Belgravia) $1,062 £460

Large Muller Freres cameo glass landscape vase, circa 1900, 55cm. high. (Sotheby's Belgravia) $1,642 £750

Galle cameo glass landscape vase, after 1904, 36cm. high. (Sotheby's Belgravia) $919 £420

Muller Freres carved cameo glass vase, circa 1890, 18.5cm. high. (Sotheby's Belgravia) $919 £420

Lalique barrel-shaped vase, moulded with songbirds perched among leafy branches, 17cm. high. (Sotheby King & Chasemore) $237 £110

Lalique blue glass vase, signed, 6in. high. (Christie's & Edmiston's) $472 £210

Galle cameo glass vase, circa 1900, 15cm. high. (Sotheby's Belgravia) $613 £280

Cameo glass vase by Thomas Webb & Sons, 10.8cm. high. (King & Chasemore) $832 £370

Tiffany flower form vase with green and white flower, 11¾in. high. (Robert W. Skinner Inc.) $1,500 £680

Art Deco vase in pate de verre, signed Muller Freres. (Leys, Antwerp) $1,175 £540

Iridescent glass vase by Loetz with narrow rim, circa 1900, 19.74cm. high. (Sotheby's Belgravia) $985 £450

Muller Freres carved cameo glass vase, 1890's, 40cm. high. (Sotheby's Belgravia) $1,533 £700

Muller Freres cameo glass vase, circa 1900, 19.5cm. high. (Sotheby's) $525 £240

Cameo glass vase by George Woodall, 1885. (Sotheby's Belgravia) $41,040 £19,000

Etched and gilded vase in Orivit gilt metal mount, circa 1900, 25.75cm. high. (Sotheby's Belgravia) $306 £140

Late 19th century cameo glass vase by Galle. (Phillips) $4,086 £1,800

Pate-de-crystal Argy Rousseau vase, 10in. high. (H. Spencer & Sons) $8,362 £3,700

One of a pair of grey glass baluster vases, 18¼in. high.(Christie's S. Kensington) $259 £120

Cristallerie de Pantin cameo glass vase, circa 1900, 16.5cm. high. (Sotheby's Belgravia) $481 £220

VASES

A Galle enamelled three-handled vase in the Persian style, 15cm. high. (Christie's) $1,400 £650

A Lalique vase of flared trumpet shape, 21cm. high. (Christie's) $760 £350

An escalier de cristal ormolu mounted cameo vase, 16.5cm. high. (Christie's) $1,570 £720

Stevens & Williams cameo vase of pale amber ground, with Stourbridge Art Glass marks, circa 1890, 11.5cm. high.(Christie's) $460 £200

Thomas Webb cameo oviform vase by George Woodall, circa 1880, 21cm. high. (Christie's) $1,400 £600

Unusual translucent white Pekin glass vase, carved with landscape panels and two pink dragons, 21.2cm. high. (Sotheby's) $410 £190

An Argy Rousseau pate de verre oviform vase, 14.5cm. high.(Christie's) $5,000 £2,300

A large Galle cameo glass vase of tapering form, 48cm. high. (Christie's) $4,000 £1,800

A Tiffany favrile turquoise iridescent vase with oviform body, 13.5cm. high. (Christie's) $915 £420

Attractive turquoise Pekin glass vase of compressed pear shape, 27.5cm. high. (Sotheby's) $435 £200

J. F. Christy oviform vase designed by Richard Redgrave, 1847, 15cm. high. (Christie's) $970 £420

Well carved Imperial yellow Pekin glass vase of beaker form carved with blossom, 20.5cm. high. (Sotheby's) $1,845 £850

A Lalique globular vase of matt opalescence, 16.5cm. high. (Christie's) $480 £220

Loetz iridescent glass vase, circa 1900, 21.5cm. high. (Sotheby's Belgravia) $165 £280

Lalique vase of duodecagonal section, sided with applied cicada handles, 22.5cm. high. (Sotheby King & Chasemore) $1,080 £500

St. Louis shot glass vase, 11cm. high. (Sotheby's) $2,050 £900

A Galle cameo slender oviform vase with tapering neck, 56.5cm. high. (Christie's) $1,900 £880

A Galle cameo tapering oviform vase with inverted quatrefoil rim, 35cm. high. (Christie's) $2,000 £920

Unusual overlay Pekin glass vase of baluster form, clear metal cased in transparent green, 28cm. high. (Sotheby's) $1,735 £800

A Galle cameo solifleur vase with globular body, 39.5cm. high. (Christie's) $2,200 £1,000

A Lalique flared vase of matt glass and graduated form, 15.5cm. high. (Christie's) $280 £130

Limoges enamel vase decorated with a sea nymph and merman, 18.5cm. high. (Christie's) $550 £240

A Brocard enamelled cylindrical vase with stylised cornflower sprays, 16.5cm. high. (Christie's) $830 £380

A Galle cameo vase of slender tapering oviform on spreading foot, 34cm. high. (Christie's) $825 £380

VASES

Spanish four-handled vase of bluish opalescent glass, early 18th century. (Christie's) $440 £190

Wheeling peach blow rose-bowl, 5½in. high. (Robert W. Skinner Inc.) $300 £135

Galle cameo glass vase of hexagonal design, circa 1900, 21.5cm. high. (Sotheby's Belgravia) $830 £360

Deep red Lalique vase with globular body, slightly damaged. (Robert W. Skinner Inc.) $450 £204

One of a pair of Grecian-style opaque glass vases, 30cm. high. (Phillips) $60 £30

Webb 'ivory cameo' glass vase with tall neck, 31.7cm. high, 1880's. (Sotheby's Belgravia) $905 £420

Rare early 20th century Webb 'rock crystal' engraved vase by William Fritsche, 25cm. high. (Sotheby's Belgravia) $905 £420

Portrait overlay vase with tulip bowl, circa 1850, 45.4cm. high. (Sotheby's Belgravia) $235 £110

One of a pair of yellow ground cameo glass vases, 1880's, 30.1cm. high. (Sotheby's Belgravia) $3,880 £1,800

One of a pair of gilt bronze and glass vases, 11in. high, circa 1880. (Sotheby's Belgravia) $315 £140

One of a pair of Loetz iridescent vases. (Christie's & Edmiston's) $2,165 £950

New England peach blow lily form vase, 18in. high. (Robert W. Skinner Inc.) $600 £270

Engraved wine glass of possible Jacobite significance, circa 1750, 6in. high. (Sotheby's) $540 £240

Baluster wine glass with waisted bowl, circa 1720, 6½in. high. (Sotheby's) $225 £100

Green tinted wine glass with cup shaped bowl, circa 1750, 4¾in. high. (Sotheby's) $450 £200

Unusual wine glass, bell bowl decorated with vertical ribs, 6in. high, circa 1740. (Sotheby's) $215 £95

English baluster wine glass with bell bowl, circa 1720, 6½in. high. (Sotheby's) $330 £150

Wine glass with waisted bucket bowl, circa 1750, 6½in. high. (Sotheby's) $190 £85

Wine glass with double ogee bowl, circa 1780, 6¼in. high. (Sotheby's) $360 £160

Wine glass with flared bucket bowl, circa 1750, 6¼in. high. (Sotheby's) $225 £100

Incised-twist stem wine glass with flared bowl, circa 1750, 6in. high. (Sotheby's) $145 £65

Wine glass with unusual double ogee bowl with moulded vertical ribs, 5¾in. high, circa 1750. (Sotheby's) $360 £160

Wine glass with pan topped bucket bowl, circa 1760, 6in. high. (Sotheby's) $315 £140

Wine glass with wide bell bowl on a stem with single mercury corkscrew, 7in. high, circa 1750. (Sotheby's) $155 £70

WINE GLASSES

18th century dram glass with ogee bowl, 4¼in. high.(Sotheby's) $151 £70

17th century Rhenish roemer of light green metal with concave bowl, 14.8cm. high. (Sotheby's) $607 £280

Dwarf ale glass, circa 1750, 4in. high, bowl with wrythen moulding. (Sotheby's) $260 £120

Baluster wine glass with sturdy conical bowl on solid base, circa 1710, 5in. high. (Sotheby's) $1,041 £480

Engraved ale glass with tall ogee bowl, circa 1765, 7in. high. (Sotheby's) $347 £160

17th century Netherlandish green tinted roemer with cup shaped bowl, 20.5cm. high. (Sotheby's) $5,642 £2,600

Engraved ale glass with tall funnel bowl, circa 1750, 8in. high. (Sotheby's) $434 £200

Colour twist firing glass with small ovoid bowl, circa 1760, 4in. high. (Sotheby's) $2,387 £1,100

Canary twist wine glass with hammer moulded bowl, circa 1760, 6in. high. (Sotheby's) $4,774 £2,200

Engraved wine glass of possible Jacobite significance, with pan-topped bowl, circa 1750, 6in. high. (Sotheby's) $455 £210

Wine glass with ogee bowl and knopped stem, circa 1760, 6½in. high. (Sotheby Bearne) $176 £88

Dutch engraved goblet, circa 1740, 21.5cm. high, with thistle bowl. (Sotheby's) $455 £210

Beilby enamelled wine glass, circa 1770, 5½in. high, with ogee bowl. (Sotheby's) $1,171 £540

Green tinted wine glass with cup bowl, circa 1740, 5½in. high. (Sotheby's) $390 £180

Wine glass with funnel bowl, circa 1745, 6¼in. high. (Sotheby's) $303 £140

Wine glass with ogee bowl on double series opaque twist stem, circa 1760, 4¾in. high. (Sotheby's) $282 £130

Cordial glass with small drawn trumpet bowl, circa 1745, 5¾in. high. (Sotheby's) $195 £90

Baluster goblet with large funnel bowl, circa 1700, 8¾in. high. (Sotheby's) $1,085 £500

Engraved wine or cordial glass, circa 1750, 6¼in. high. (Sotheby's) $195 £90

Wine glass with bell bowl, circa 1730, 6in. high.(Sotheby's) $151 £70

Engraved wine glass with ogee bowl, circa 1760, 6in. high. (Sotheby's) $260 £120

Composite stemmed wine glass of three parts, circa 1750, 7¼in. high. (Sotheby's)$520 £240

Saxon engraved goblet with thistle bowl, 21cm. high, circa 1740. (Sotheby's) $781 £360

Mammoth engraved baluster goblet, circa 1710. (Sotheby's) $1,475 £680

Small baluster wine glass with flared funnel bowl, circa 1710, 13cm. high. (Christie's) $230 £100

Balustroid wine glass of 'Kit Kat' type, of drawn trumpet shape, circa 1730, 16cm. high. (Christie's) $320 £140

Incised twist wine glass with generous funnel bowl, circa 1760, 13.5cm. high. (Christie's) $300 £130

Composite stemmed champagne glass with double ogee bowl, circa 1740, 15cm. high. (Christie's) $210 £90

Air twist Jacobite wine glass with generous bell bowl, circa 1750, 18cm. high. (Christie's) $370 £160

Engraved composite stemmed wine glass with bell bowl, circa 1760, 16.5cm. high. (Christie's) $550 £240

Mixed twist wine glass with waisted bucket bowl, circa 1760, 17cm. high. (Christie's) $485 £210

Large internally decorated glass chalice by Maurice Marinot, late 1920's, 33.5cm. high. (Sotheby's Belgravia) $6,130 £2,800

Light baluster wine glass with flared funnel bowl, circa 1740, 16cm. high. (Christie's) $185 £80

Green wine glass with double ogee bowl, circa 1760, 15cm. high. (Christie's) $735 £320

Composite stemmed wine glass with bell bowl, circa 1750, 16cm. high. (Christie's) $230 £100

Air twist Jacobite wine glass with engraved funnel bowl, circa 1750, 15cm. high. (Christie's) $550 £240

Engraved composite stemmed water glass, circa 1745, 14cm. high. (Christie's) $230 £100

Facet stemmed wine glass, with ogee bowl, cut in the style of James Giles, circa 1780, 15cm. high. (Christie's) $300 £130

Facet stemmed engraved wine glass with ogee bowl, circa 1780, 15.5cm. high. (Christie's) $415 £180

Pedestal stemmed champagne glass with double ogee bowl, circa 1745, 14.5cm. high. (Christie's) $195 £85

Light baluster wine glass of Newcastle type, circa 1750, 16.5cm. high. (Christie's) $255 £110

Newcastle plain stemmed wine glass of slender drawn trumpet shape, circa 1750, 18.5cm. high. (Christie's) $150 £65

Facon de Venise winged wine glass, Low Countries, 17th century, 18cm. high. (Sotheby's) $2,850 £1,300

Jacobite air twist wine glass of drawn trumpet shape, circa 1750, 16cm. high. (Christie's) $575 £250

Balustroid wine glass with flared funnel bowl, circa 1750, 17cm. high. (Christie's) $275 £120

Jacobite air twist wine glass with funnel bowl, circa 1750, 15.5cm. high. (Christie's) $440 £190

Jacobite air twist wine glass of drawn trumpet shape, circa 1750, 15cm. high. (Christie's) $500 £220

Balustroid engraved ale glass with slender funnel bowl, circa 1740, 18cm. high.(Christie's) $440 £190

Inverted baluster wine glass, circa 1710, 7½in. high. (Sotheby King & Chasemore)
$1,695 £750

Jacobite wine glass with funnel bowl, circa 1745, 15cm. high.(Christie's)
$550 £240

Thick walled wine glass, circa 1710, 7½in. high. (Sotheby King & Chasemore)
$1,620 £750

Baluster wine glass with flared funnel bowl, circa 1700, 14.5cm. high. (Christie's)
$1,265 £550

Rare Jacobite opaque twist ratafia glass with ogee bowl, circa 1765, 18cm. high.(Christie's)
$600 £260

Opaque twist ale glass with slender ogee bowl, circa 1770, 19.5cm. high. (Christie's)
$207 £90

Unusual pedestal stemmed wine glass with bell bowl, circa 1730, 18.5cm. high. (Christie's) $690 £300

Engraved air twist ale glass of drawn trumpet shape, circa 1770, 19.5cm. high. (Christie's) $255 £110

Jacobite air twist wine glass with pan-topped bowl, circa 1750, 15.5cm. high. (Christie's)$645 £280

Engraved colour twist wine glass in the Jacobite taste, circa 1770, 14.5cm. high. (Christie's)$690 £300

Opaque twist cordial glass, with funnel bowl, circa 1765, 14.5cm. high. (Christie's)$185 £80

Baluster wine glass with bell bowl, circa 1710, 12.5cm. high. (Christie's)$275 £120

Engraved incised twist wine glass with funnel bowl, circa 1760, 15cm. high. (Christie's)
$415 £180

Baluster wine glass with funnel bowl, circa 1710, 14.5cm. high. (Christie's)
$875 £380

Jacobite opaque twist wine glass with ogee bowl, circa 1770, 14.5cm. high. (Christie's)$460 £200

Baluster wine glass with funnel bowl circa 1710, 14cm. high. (Christie's)
$645 £280

Air twist ale glass with slender funnel bowl, circa 1750, 20.5cm. high. (Christie's)
$255 £110

Balustroid wine glass with trumpet bowl, circa 1750, 17cm. high. (Christie's)
$160 £70

Jacobite air twist wine glass of drawn trumpet shape, circa 1750, 16cm. high. (Christie's)
$690 £300

Engraved air twist wine glass of drawn trumpet shape, circa 1750, 17cm. high. (Christie's)
$800 £350

Opaque twist cordial glass with funnel bowl, circa 1765, 17cm. high. (Christie's) $690 £300

Jacobite air twist wine glass with funnel bowl, circa 1750, 16cm. high. (Christie's) $690 £300

Jacobite wine glass of drawn trumpet shape, circa 1740, 14cm. high. (Christie's) $735 £320

Jacobite air twist wine glass with bell bowl, circa 1750, 16.5cm. high. (Christie's) $800 £350

Gold mounted shell snuffbox, 1774, by Pierre-Francois Mathis de Beaulieu. (Sotheby's) $14,350 £7,000

Antique Irish gold mounted bog oak toothpick box. (Woolley & Wallis) $600 £260

Very fine gold lacquer box of the Meiji period, 5½in. long. (Phillips) $1,945 £900

Early Victorian gold and shell cameo hair ornament. (Bonham's) $1,110 £550

French gold and scarlet lacquer necessaire by Dion, 1771. (Sotheby's) $1,295 £600

9ct. gold rectangular cigar box by Mappin & Webb, 57oz.5dwt., 11¾in. wide. (Sotheby's) $12,585 £5,800

Derby gold cup, 15ct. gold campana-shaped cup and cover, 14¼in. high, 41oz.4dwt. (Sotheby's) $9,115 £4,200

18 carat gold oblong freedom casket applied with enamel vignettes of London, by The Goldsmiths & Silversmiths Co., 1917, 25oz. 2dwt. (Sotheby's) $8,400 £3,600

The Ascot Gold Cup, 18ct. gold cup and cover by Sebastian Garrard, London, 1925, 98oz. 19dwt., 16in. high. (Sotheby's) $32,550 £15,000

Oval gold and enamelled snuffbox by Pierre-Nicolas Quennelle de Romesnil, 1763, 2¾in. wide. (Sotheby's) $86,400 £40,000

Gold mounted box painted with miniatures by Louis-Nicolas van Blarenberghe, Paris, 1765, 3in. wide. (Sotheby's Zurich) $41,685 £20,335

Fine George III 22ct. gold Irish Freedom box, 2¾in. diam., Dublin 1795, 4oz.16dwt. (Sotheby's) $17,920 £8,000

Fine pink tourmaline double vase carved as a bat on a cherry tree, Chinese, probably Qianlong, 7cm. high. (Christie's) $1,320 £600

Chinese aquamarine bamboo pendant carved in relief with a bird on a leafy branch, 3.8cm. long. (Christie's) $660 £300

Ming dynasty steatite circular box and cover carved with phoenix and qilin among foliage, 19cm. diam. (Christie's) $1,210 £550

Serpentine figure of an Eskimo mother carrying her child. (Bonham's) $150 £70

Maori greenstone Hei Tiki neck pendant, 3¼in. long. (Sotheby's) $1,135 £520

Late 19th century agate hard-stone figure of a collie. (Sotheby's) $345 £150

Maori greenstone Hei Tiki neck pendant, cut from an old adze blade, 3½in. long. (Sotheby's) $870 £400

Rare and fine 18th century Chinese lapis lazuli boulder carving of figures in a landscape, 23cm. wide. (Sotheby's) $10,800 £5,000

Maori greenstone Hei Tiki neck pendant, 3¼in. long. (Sotheby's) $1,200 £550

One of a pair of Chinese rose quartz vase groups and covers, 17.2cm. high. (Sotheby's) $690 £320

Late 19th century Russian figure of a collie carved from milky grey agate, 6.4c.n. high. (Sotheby's) $340 £150

Chinese carved hardstone figure of Guanyin, 20in. high, on car-ved hardwood stand.(Heathcote Ball & Co.) $1,640 £760

Chinese pierced coral pendant of two tree shrews each chasing the other's tail, 4.8cm. high. (Sotheby's)$690 £320

Mughal bowl of quartz dyed green, 1613-14, 4¾in. diam. (Sotheby's) $30,750 £15,000

Small pale and deep emerald Chinese carving of figures in a landscape, 5.9cm. high. (Christie's) $3,080 £1,400

Qianlong carnelian carving of a bird, perched on turquoise and lapis blue enamel rockwork, on a cloisonne enamel stand, 7½in. high. (Sotheby's)$1,070 £480

Fine Chinese rock crystal vase and cover carved and pierced with lingzhi fungus, 14cm. high.(Christie's) $1,980 £900

Chinese rock crystal vase and cover, the body carved and pierced, 21.4cm. high. (Christie's) $420 £190

Chinese rose quartz leaping carp vase, the eyes set with tiger-eye cabochons, 23cm. high. (Sotheby's) $1,950 £900

Chinese turquoise matrix group of the Immortal Lan Caihe with two children, 17cm. high. (Sotheby's) $325 £150

A Sino-Tibetan hardstone ewer, extensively mounted in silver, 19th century. (Christie's) $1,100 £480

Rare small deep ruby tourmaline carving of Guanyin seated on rocks, with ivory stand, Chinese, 5.4cm. high. (Christie's) $1,210 £550

Chinese rose quartz vase group carved as a bamboo with flowers and a pheasant, 21.1cm. high. (Sotheby's) $650 £300

Chinese turquoise figure of an immortal maiden holding a mirror and a peony, 11cm. high. (Sotheby's)$4,750 £2,200

One of a pair of rare rhinoceros
horn libation cups, Chinese,
17th or 18th century, 8.8cm.
high. (Sotheby's Hong Kong)
$7,755 £3,525

18th century Chinese rhinoceros horn cup, 2½in. high.
(Robert W. Skinner Inc.)
$650 £295

A rhinoceros horn libation cup,
carved with trees and rocks,
18th century, 4in. high.
(Sotheby's Hong Kong)
$3,685 £1,675

17th or 18th century Chinese
rhinoceros horn cup carved
with dragons and key-patterns,
4½in. wide. (Christie's)
$835 £380

17th or 18th century Chinese
rhinoceros horn libation cup
carved with a flowering
branch and writhing chilong,
9in. high. (Sotheby's)
$715 £320

18th century Chinese rhinoceros
horn libation cup of archaic
inspiration, 5½in. high.
(Sotheby's) $980 £440

17th or 18th century Chinese rhinoceros horn cup of archaic yi form,
cracked, 6in. wide. (Christie's)
$2,420 £1,100

18th century Chinese rhinoceros horn cup, 4in. high.
(Robert W. Skinner Inc.)
$600 £275

18th century Chinese rhinoceros
horn libation cup carved with a
scholar among rocks and pines,
6½in. wide. (Christie's)
$1,650 £750

A good large rhinoceros horn cup
carved inside and out with cliffs
and trees, inscribed on the base
Kangxi, 5½in. high. (Sotheby's
Hong Kong) $6,545 £2,975

Fine rhinoceros horn bowl of
lobed campana shape, 6in.
high. (Sotheby Humberts)
$1,510 £700

17th or 18th century Chinese rhinoceros horn cup carved as an open
hibiscus flower, 5¾in. wide.
(Christie's) $1,050 £480

INROS

17th century Japanese lacquered inro in silver, gold, red and mother-of-pearl. (Robert W. Skinner Inc.) $500 £225

18th century Japanese lacquered inro with mother-of-pearl inlay. (Robert W. Skinner Inc.) $450 £205

18th century Japanese inro, lacquered to simulate bark, inset with ivory, carnelian and jade. (Robert W. Skinner Inc.) $550 £250

18th century four-case inro, unsigned, with unsigned red lacquered wood netsuke. (Christie's) $625 £280

18th century Somada school three-case inro with Chinese agate netsuke. (Christie's) $570 £250

Four-case inro, 18th or 19th century, signed Kajikawa Saku, with 19th century ivory netsuke signed Gyokohosai. (Christie's) $1,120 £500

18th or early 19th century unsigned five-case inro, with unsigned early 19th century ivory netsuke. (Christie's) $1,625 £680

Unsigned 18th or 19th century four-case inro, decorated with storks flying over waves. (Christie's) $1,165 £520

18th century four-case inro decorated in gold and red, unsigned, with unsigned ivory manju netsuke. (Christie's) $850 £380

Late 18th or early 19th century four-case inro, unsigned, with unsigned ivory netsuke. (Christie's) $820 £360

Four-case inro with a coral okime and a wooden manju, unsigned. (Sotheby King & Chasemore) $1,530 £680

Four-case inro, 18th or 19th century, signed Koma Kansai Saku, with unsigned 19th century marine ivory netsuke. (Christie's) $715 £320

472

One-case inro of iron with inlaid decoration and pierced manju. (Sotheby King & Chasemore) $1,015 £450

Fine four-case inro by Shibata Zeshin, decorated with three hozuki and a swarm of ants. (Sotheby's) $13,500 £6,000

19th century Japanese gold lacquered inro with bird, tree, cloud and leaves. (Robert W. Skinner Inc.) $375 £170

18th century Japanese inro inlaid with mother-of-pearl. (Robert W. Skinner Inc.) $350 £160

Japanese black and gold lacquer four-case inro with carved ivory water buffalo netsuke.(Phillips) $800 £350

Four-case inro, finely decorated, signed Shoso, 18th or 19th century, with ivory manju netsuke. (Christie's) $1,120 £500

19th century four-case inro, unsigned, with 19th century wood netsuke signed Raiseki Saku. (Christie's) $785 £350

Three-case inro, inlaid in pewter and mother-of-pearl, inscribed Seisei Korin, with unsigned netsuke. (Christie's) $515 £230

Five-case inro, gold and silver on roiro-nuri ground, signed Kajikawa Saku, with unsigned ivory netsuke, 19th century. (Christie's) $715 £320

Unsigned four-case inro, 18th or 19th century, with unsigned ivory netsuke. (Christie's) $1,120 £500

Five-case inro with carved fruit nut ojime, unsigned. (Sotheby King & Chasemore) $430 £190

Late 19th century unsigned two-case ivory inro, with ivory netsuke by Somei. (Christie's) $775 £340

473

INSTRUMENTS

Unusual 19th century clockmaker's wirepuller in steel, circa 1860. (Christopher Sykes) $55 £25

Steel pocket corkscrew. (Christie's) $75 £35

Large Flemish crossbow, 17th century, with heavy steel bow, 44in. long. (Christie's) $4,275 £1,900

Victorian brass telescope on black lacquered tripod stand, 3in. diam., circa 1850. (Christopher Sykes) $1,050 £465

Georgian mahogany book press, circa 1790, 18in. wide. (Gray's Antique Mews) $345 £150

Late 19th century leather cased surveyor's extending tape rule, 6in. diam. (Christopher Sykes) $55 £25

American stereoscope made of sheet zinc and birchwood, circa 1904, 13in. long. (Sotheby King & Chasemore) $150 £65

Late 19th century brass faced Salter spring balance, up to 41lbs. (Vernon's) $55 £25

2½in. reflecting telescope. (Christie's S. Kensington) $830 £360

Ship's chronometer by W. Weichert, London and Cardiff, in brass bound coromandel case with carrying handles and observation lid. (Phillips) $2,175 £960

Unusual brass spring balance, circa 1870, weighs up to 12lbs. (Christopher Sykes) $85 £40

A ship navigator's star globe by H. Hughes & Son, London. (Christopher Sykes) $890 £385

Brass flake tobacco cutter, 3¼in. long, with small brass handle. (Christopher Sykes) $40 £15

Fountain pen used by King Edward VIII to sign the Abdication Document. (Phillips) $4,500 £2,000

Clock or watchmaker's tool with four punches by L. Hugoniot-Tissot, 6¼in. long. (Christopher Sykes) $45 £20

2½in. reflecting telescope. (Christie's S. Kensington) $1,615 £700

Superb 19th century chronometer by Henry Frodsham. (Bradley & Vaughan) $2,145 £940

Surveyor's fine theodolite by Charles Baker, London, 13in. high. (Christopher Sykes) $1,105 £485

Naval officer's antique brass sextant by D. McGregor & Co., circa 1860, 9½in. long. (Christopher Sykes) $660 £285

Fine pair of Victorian brass letter scales complete with weights. (Vernon's) $75 £35

19th century brass circumferentor with glazed compass rose, on staff-head mounting, 300mm. diam. (Sotheby's) $1,150 £500

Large circular protractor by Chadburn Brothers, Sheffield, 11¾in. diam., in silver. (Christopher Sykes) $180 £80

19th century typewriter. (Sotheby's Belgravia) $2,965 £1,300

Brass sector from HMS Association. (W. H. Lane & Son) $695 £300

One of a pair of 19th century hardwood terrestial and celestial globes on mahogany bases, 103mm. diam. (Sotheby's) $2,760 £1,200

Rare circular plane by Stanley Rule & Level Co., 1877, 10¼in. long. (Christopher Sykes) $175 £80

Copper fire extinguisher with five oval brass plaques, 1930, 29in. high.(Christopher Sykes) $125 £55

Ebony and brass cabinet maker's mortice gauge, 7½in. long, circa 1850. (Christopher Sykes) $65 £25

19th century butcher's bone cutting saw with beechwood handle, circa 1860. (Christopher Sykes) $76 £34

Mahogany and brass apothecary's pill making slab and roller, circa 1850. (Christopher Sykes) $169 £75

Victorian upright stereoscope, 121cm. high, in walnut pedestal case. (Sotheby Humberts) $475 £220

19th century beechwood smoothing plane, 7¼in. long. (Christopher Sykes) $63 £28

Rare late 18th century London pattern cabinet maker's screwdriver with pinewood handle, 17in. long. (Christopher Sykes) $54 £24

Antique brass pastry marker and crimper, circa 1820, 4in. long. (Christopher Sykes) $40 £18

Antique beechwood cabinet maker's smoothing plane, circa 1850, 6¾in. long. (Christopher Sykes) $63 £28

Small 19th century brass sextant by Dolland, London, 115mm. radius. (Sotheby's) $2,070 £900

Late 18th century Dutch brass sextant. (Phillips) $3,118 £1,350

Shipwright's brass and wood rule recovered from the wreck of The Association. (W. H. Lane & Son)
$110 £50

Model of a terrestrial globe in the form of a string box, circa 1890, 4¼in.high. (Christopher Sykes)
$192 £85

Brass monocular microscope by Smith & Beck, plus accessories. (Phillips)
$1,155 £500

A butcher's small 19th century cleaver in steel with oak handle, 13in. long. (Christopher Sykes)
$40 £18

Steel framed wheelbrace with revolving handle in beechwood, 11in. long. (Christopher Sykes)
$63 £28

18th century brass quadrant by J. Sisson, London, 233mm. radius, incomplete. (Sotheby's)
$6,900 £3,000

One of a fine pair of 19th century terrestrial and celestial globes on mahogany stands. (Messenger May & Baverstock)
$5,616 £2,600

Rare brass solar quadrant by Duboia, Paris, circa 1770, in original box. (Sotheby's)
$5,060 £2,200

Mid 19th century plumber's soldering iron, 16in. long, with turned ashwood handle. (Christopher Sykes)
$63 £28

Copper soldering bit with wooden handle, 15in. long. (Christopher Sykes)
$40 £18

A surveyor's fine sighting level in brass, by T. Cooke, York, 9in. wide. (Christopher Sykes)
$488 £225

Victorian mother-of-pearl opera glasses with brass surround. (Christopher Sykes)
$110 £50

Oak based brass postal scales, circa 1870, 7½in. wide. (Christopher Sykes)$108 £48

Mother-of-pearl and decorative enamel opera glasses. (Alfie's Antique Market) $170 £80

19th century brass cased astronomical telescope by J. Lancaster & Sons Ltd., Birmingham. (Geering & Colyer) $1,230 £600

Lambert typewriter no. 5627 by the Gramophone & Typewriter Ltd. (Christie's S. Kensington) $495 £220

Newton's New and Improved Terrestrial Pocket Globe, 1817. (Phillips) $540 £250

Surveyor's brass theodolite by J. Davis, 12¾in. high.(Christopher Sykes) $1,045 £485

Beechwood and brass plough plane by W. Greenslade, Bristol. (Christopher Sykes) $85 £40

Ebony and brass parallel rule, circa 1820. (Christopher Sykes) $58 £27

Steel Scotch pattern brace by F. Soakes (Christopher Sykes) $110 £50

Brass and mahogany three-draw telescope by Dolland, circa 1830. (Christopher Sykes) $205 £95

Universal ring dial by Troughton & Simms, London. (Phillips) $1,510 £700

German gilt metal compendium dial. (Christie's) $7,130 £3,300

18th century boxwood nocturnal dial, inscribed 'Thomas Cooper 1701'. (Phillips) $1,910 £850

Set of 19th century surgical instruments in brass bound mahogany case, 43cm. long. (King & Chasemore) $810 £360

19th century monocular microscope in brass by Smith & Beck, London, sold with glass slides. (Christopher Sykes) $2,700 £1,250

Set of early 19th century grocer's brass scales by Avery, with ten brass weights. (Lacy Scott) $670 £330

Dr. Butcher's saw by Coxeter, circa 1860. (Alfie's Antique Market) $305 £150

Penny-farthing timepiece and aneroid barometer. (Phillips) $302 £140

Beechwood and brass plated brace by Henry Dixon, Sheffield. (Christopher Sykes) $130 £60

Early model of a typewriter by Columbia. (Sotheby's Belgravia) $2,050 £950

Late 15th/early 16th century mariner's astrolabe.(Christie's) $20,520 £9,500

Brass equinoctial dial by Fraser & Sons, London. (Phillips) $1,510 £700

Early 19th century Dutch cucumber slicer, mounted on boxwood. (Phillips) $430 £200

Single draw telescope by Ross of London, 17in. long. (Alfie's Antique Market) $130 £60

Steel and mahogany shoulder plane. (Christopher Sykes) $110 £50

Ebony and brass Naval officer's octant with ivory scales, by Crichton, London, circa 1825. (Christopher Sykes) $830 £385

Early Swiss 'Velograph' typewriter, circa 1887. (Sotheby's Belgravia)$2,375 £1,100

One of a pair of Cruchley's late Cary's terrestrial and celestial globes, 34in. high, 1840's. (Sotheby's) $3,564 £1,650

Patent crimping machine. (J. M. Welch & Son) $135 £60

Brass monocular microscope inscribed Ross. (D. M. Nesbit & Co.) $325 £160

Naval officer's brass sextant by McGregor & Co., circa 1840. (Christopher Sykes) $730 £325

479

Rosewood, brass and steel cabinet maker's set square stamped 'A. Surridge', 7¾in. long, circa 1860. (Christopher Sykes) $31 £14

19th century beechwood coffin-shaped smoothing plane, 8½in. long, by Charles & Co. (Christopher Sykes) $54 £24

Pair of 19th century French brass and iron shop scales. (Vernon's) $80 £35

Mid 18th century South German or Austrian gunmaker's mainspring cramp, 5in. long. (Sotheby's) $1,085 £500

Beechwood egg timing sandglass, 19th century, 6½in. high. (Christopher Sykes) $155 £70

Medical pelvimeter, nickel plated, by Selby of Nottingham. (Christopher Sykes) $40 £18

Antique brass Georgian box lock, circa 1760, with steel key, 6¾in. long. (Christopher Sykes) $130 £60

Opera glasses used by Abraham Lincoln on the night of his assassination. (Sotheby's New York) $23,650 £11,000

17th century wrought iron padlock and key, circa 1680, 5¼in. long. (Christopher Sykes) $101 £45

Fine 18th century English microscope of modified Culpeper type, by Edward Nairne, London, 41cm. (Christie's) $6,270 £2,800

Circular protractor by J. Davies, Derby, 8in. diam., circa 1830. (Christopher Sykes) $130 £60

Victorian magnetic pocket compass in maroon leather case, circa 1850. (Christopher Sykes) $76 £34

19th century French orrery by Delmarche, Paris, brass mounted on mahogany stage. (Phillips) $2,147 £950

Mid 19th century magnetic dry card compass in bronzed brass, 4in. diam. (Christopher Sykes) $153 £68

Sewing machine by Wheeler & Wilson, circa 1854. (Christie's S. Kensington) $561 £260

Optician's sight tester on boxwood measuring arm, 9½in. long, circa 1860. (Christopher Sykes) $176 £78

Light mahogany cased metronome, 9in. high. (Christopher Sykes) $110 £50

Nickel and steel American instrument with ebonite handle, 1905, 4¾in. long. (Christopher Sykes) $40 £18

Armour bright polished set of steelyard scales with cast iron pear-shaped weight. (Christopher Sykes) $79 £35

Monocular compound microscope, circa 1870, 13¼in. high. (Christopher Sykes) $313 £145

Very fine spectroscope, circa 1925, 12in. high. (Christopher Sykes) $169 £75

Late 19th century adjustable hat stretcher of walnut and cast iron, 13in. high. (Christopher Sykes)$108 £48

Good and virtually complete 19th century case of surgeon's instruments by Charriere of Paris. (Sotheby's) $2,760 £1,200

19th century engraved brass sundial, 10in. diam., on oak base plate. (Christopher Sykes) $305 £135

Early 18th century English brass circumferentor by Edmund Culpeper, 32mm. diam. (Christie's) $2,020 £900

Early 19th century brass winding bellows. (Christie's S. Kensington) $430 £200

Simplex typewriter in box. (Phillips) $50 £20

Late 19th century zoetrope, tin on wood, 14in. high. (Sotheby's Belgravia) $525 £240

Good set of mid 19th century Aitken surgical instruments in mahogany case. (Sotheby's Belgravia) $1,100 £500

Teak wood and brass banded ship's wheel, 48½in. diam., circa 1870. (Christopher Sykes) $870 £385

Good English brass binocular microscope, by Baker, London, circa 1870-80, 17in. high. (Sotheby's Belgravia) $830 £380

An English early 19th century surveyor's brass circumferentor. (Sotheby's Belgravia) $920 £400

Table terrestrial telescope in brass with folding tripod brass stand, circa 1830, 42in. long.(Christopher Sykes) $1,017 £450

English zoetrope, tin drum on carved wood stand, circa 1870, 12in. diam.(Sotheby's Belgravia) $300 £130

Goodbrand & Co. revolution counter on mahogany base, circa 1880, 28in. high. (Sotheby's Belgravia) $565 £250

National cash register, chromed brass on wood stand.(Sotheby's Belgravia) $325 £150

Early magic lantern. (Manchester Auction Mart) **$135 £60**

Early 19th century brass and mahogany winding bellows. (Christie's S. Kensington) **$430 £200**

Swiss 'Velograph' typewriter, circa 1887, 6½in. high. (Sotheby's Belgravia) **$2,475 £1,100**

Hall typewriter No. 5380, nickel plated in mahogany case, circa 1887, 15½in. wide. (Sotheby's Belgravia) **$390 £180**

Spencer Browning ebony octant by Cousens & Sons, Swansea, circa 1820, 8½in radius. (Sotheby's Belgravia) **$765 £350**

American Simplex Model D typewriter in original cardboard box, 1930's, 8¾in. wide. (Sotheby's Belgravia) **$85 £40**

American Globe typewriter by the American Typewriter Co., circa 1895. (Sotheby's Belgravia) **$510 £220**

Regency terrestrial globe by Newton, London, 1ft.9in. diam., circa 1820.(Sotheby's) **$4,330 £1,900**

Set of electrical apparatus, including galvanometer, induction coil, wet cell battery, etc., in wooden case, English, 1880-1900. (Sotheby's Belgravia) **$505 £220**

Kinora moving picture viewer with 24 reels, circa 1905, 18½in. long. (Sotheby's Belgravia) **$740 £340**

Mahogany cased stereoscope with ebonised side handles, sold with numerous views. (Phillips) **$145 £65**

Brass candlestick telephone with unusual keyboard dialling unit, circa 1925. (Sotheby's Belgravia) **$370 £170**

Early 17th century painted iron strongbox, covered with strapwork, 2ft.6in. wide. (Sotheby's) $2,929 £1,350

Cast iron 'Gothic' strongbox with hinged lid, 1870's, 13½in. high. (Sotheby's Belgravia) $728 £350

James I iron bound coffer with handles, lock and key, 22in. wide. (Whiteheads) $3,857 £1,900

Victorian cast iron plant stand. (J. M. Welch & Son) $302 £140

Victorian wrought iron and brass fire guard. (Andrew Grant) $902 £440

Unusually shaped cast iron heavy mortar, circa 1740, 6½in. high, 15 lb. in weight. (Christopher Sykes) $79 £35

One of a pair of Edgar Brandt wrought iron fire-dogs, circa 1925, 72cm. high. (Sotheby's Belgravia) $1,000 £480

William IV period cast iron hob grate, circa 1830, 26in. wide. (Christopher Sykes) $192 £85

Fine cast iron figure of a classical woman, circa 1810, on 5½in. square walnut base. (Christopher Sykes) $108 £48

Cast iron and brass dog grate, circa 1890. (Gray's Antique Mews) $292 £110

Antique cast iron front to a hob grate, with brass knobs, apron and side panels, 25½in. wide, circa 1840. (Christopher Sykes) $215 £95

17th century Nuremberg Armada chest with iron clad bindings and ornate lock, 70cm. wide. (Sotheby King & Chasemore) $1,299 £640

Heavy cast iron plaque, circa 1850, 12in. high, polished armour bright. (Christopher Sykes) $101 £45

Austrian life size metal statue of a goat boy playing pipes. (Worsfolds) $1,400 £620

17th century Flemish or German strongbox. (D. M. Nesbit & Co.) $1,695 £750

Twisted wrought iron table rushlight and candleholder on pinewood base, circa 1820, 11in. high. (Christopher Sykes) $131 £58

White enamel bath with chromium plated superstructure, circa 1900. (Christie's S. Kensington) $2,720 £1,200

18th or 19th century Continental iron and brass standing candle-holder, 63in. high. (Robert W. Skinner Inc.) $700 £300

Mid/late Edo period iron tetsubin with rounded sides, signed Ryu-bundo Zukuri. (Sotheby King & Chasemore) $225 £100

One of a pair of Victorian cast iron Warwick style jardinieres, 77cm. high. (Sotheby King & Chasemore) $649 £320

Regency period cast iron grate, circa 1810, 28in. wide. (Christopher Sykes) $170 £85

17th century German painted strongbox, 25in. wide. (Hy. Duke & Son) $1,845 £900

Heavy 16th century iron Armada chest with two period external padlocks and iron locking bar. (Boardman's) $4,340 £2,000

One of a pair of late 19th century cast iron lion passant garden sculptures, 27in. long. (Robert W. Skinner Inc.) $1,500 £650

485

One of two early 19th century tin candle moulds, 13½in. (Robert W. Skinner Inc.) $75 £35

17th century brass and wrought iron skillet on three feet, 23½in. wide. (Christie's) $570 £250

Late 19th century Oriental inlaid and onlaid iron dish, 45.3cm. diam. (Sotheby's Belgravia) $830 £360

Brass cased set of three steel fleams, circa 1820, 3½in. long. (Christopher Sykes) $63 £28

English cast-iron, walnut and marble occasional table with diamond registration mark for June 1845. (Sotheby's Belgravia) $485 £210

Fireside crane with two hinges, 26½in. long, circa 1730, initialled S. W. (Christopher Sykes) $198 £88

17th century iron pan lamp, with ramshorn screw attaching tripod base, 13in. (Robert W. Skinner Inc.) $150 £70

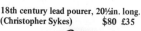

18th century lead pourer, 20½in. long. (Christopher Sykes) $80 £35

Early 18th century Queen Anne steel nutcrackers, 4½in. long, circa 1710. (Christopher Sykes) $31 £14

South German steel casket, circa 1600, with two carrying handles, 8¼in. wide. (Sotheby's) $1,545 £700

Early iron fireback of arched design, dated 1637. (Vernon's) $100 £45

Early 18th century wrought iron chimney crane, 29¼in. long. (Christopher Sykes) $192 £85

17th century Nuremberg rectangular steel casket, 30.5cm. long. (Christie's) $2,592 £1,200

George III serpentine pierced fender in polished steel, circa 1800, 36in. long. (Christopher Sykes) $185 £85

Late 16th century Nuremberg etched steel casket, 9.5cm. wide. (Christie's) $1,123 £520

Early 15th century Swiss iron candlestick with floral decoration, 10½in. (Robert W. Skinner Inc.) $1,150 £535

Steel fire grate in George III manner, 84cm. wide. (Phillips) $460 £200

One of a pair of Komai inlaid iron vases, 13cm. high, late 19th century. (Sotheby's Belgravia) $690 £300

17th century iron birdcage candleholder on tripod base, 14½in. (Robert W. Skinner Inc.) $675 £315

19th century cast iron dog grate, decorated with acanthus leaves and with cast iron fireback. (Vernon's) $345 £160

Queen Anne mechanical iron spit-jack, circa 1700, 13in. high. (Christopher Sykes) $1,073 £475

18th century Germany steel door lock with cut steel key, 18in. long. (Langlois) $570 £260

Very rare three arched cast iron fireback, dated 1630, 23in. wide. (Christopher Sykes) $280 £125

Cast iron Royal Coat of Arms of George III, 19in. x 17in. circa 1810. (Christopher Sykes) $780 £345

Set of seven mid 19th century Indian miniatures on ivory in gilt ribbon frame. (McCartney, Morris & Barker) $685 £300

Late 13th century ivory chess piece, Spanish, 7.9cm. high. (Christie's) $54,000 £25,000

Mid 19th century Meikeisai Hojitsu of Edo, a two-part ivory carved in Shishiabori. (Sotheby King & Chasemore) $474 £210

19th century ivory carving of men dancing. (Alfie's Antique Market) $508 £225

19th century Japanese carved ivory figural group, 4½in. high. (Robert W. Skinner Inc.) $750 £340

Japanese ivory group of a woodsman, circa 1900, signed Seiya, 8.5cm. high. (Sotheby King & Chasemore) $1,039 £460

18th century Bavarian ivory carving. (Phillips) $14,012 £6,200

Carved ivory figure of St. Cecilia after Maderno. (Sotheby's) $907 £420

19th century Japanese ivory carving of Kannon signed Hodo to, and sealed, 18in. high. (Christie's S. Kensington) $1,452 £650

Two German late 18th century ivory beggars, 16cm. high. (Leys, Antwerp) $2,770 £1,280

Ivory warrior and boy, 8in. high, slightly damaged, in the style of Nobuaki. (J. M. Welch & Son) $2,088 £920

Pair of 19th century Chinese ivory figures, 12in. high. (Christie's S. Kensington) $1,231 £570

Fine group of Shoki and Oni by Kano Tomokazu. (Sotheby's) $8,680 £4,000

Japanese ivory goddess, circa 1880, 8in. high. (Gray's Antique Mews) $832 £370

Ivory okimono of two 'go' players, 19th century. (Christie's) $3,825 £1,700

Japanese ivory family group, with Homei seal mark, 10in. high. (Phillips) $1,836 £850

Carved ivory group of a couple staring at a stack of wealth. (Sotheby's Belgravia) $3,075 £1,500

19th century German ivory crucifix on a wooden cross, 24in. high. (Robert W. Skinner Inc.) $700 £320

Burmese or S. Tibetan ivory figure of Sakyamuni, 12th/13th century. (Christie's) $5,850 £2,600

Unusually large 19th century carved ivory Japanese group. (Sotheby's Belgravia) $3,857 £1,900

Two scrimshaw tusks, decorated with warriors and flags, 15cm. and 13cm. high. (Phillips) $24 £12

Two 19th century ivory nudes with putti on ebony pedestal, made in Dieppe. (Leys, Antwerp) $3,100 £1,450

Carved elephant ivory figure of Guanyin and attendant and Fo dog, 19th century, 12¼in. high. (Robert W. Skinner Inc.) $900 £400

Two Dieppe 19th century ivory figures of women. (Leys, Antwerp) $2,950 £1,360

Preiss carved ivory figure of a naked girl, 1930's, 8.75cm. high. (Sotheby's Belgravia) $765 £350

Early Chinese ivory figure of a dromedary, legs missing, Tang or Song dynasty, 4cm. long. (Christie's) $830 £380

English Regency ivory bust of a lady, signed F. M. Jacobs Sc., 13cm. (Christie's) $220 £95

18th century Tibetan ivory amulet plaque, showing the horoscopic Yantra of Bhavacakra Mudra, 10.5cm. high. (Sotheby's) $840 £380

Soviet chess set showing the struggle of communism against capitalism. (Sotheby's New York) $6,875 £3,180

A small carved ivory figure by F. Preiss, 10cm. high. (Christie's) $650 £300

19th century scrimshaw cow horn, 8in. long, circa 1840, inside curve entitled 'Scotland'. (Christopher Sykes) $130 £58

19th century scrimshaw tusk, 20cm. long. (Phillips) $105 £45

19th century Alaskan Eskimo carved walrus tusk, 16¼in. long. (Christopher Sykes) $420 £185

Unusual late 18th/early 19th century Sino-Tibetan ivory figure of the Dhyanibuddha Vairocana, 5 1/8in. high. (Sotheby's) $1,150 £520

18th century Indian ivory swing, probably made for a temple image of Krishna, 33½in. high. (Sotheby's) $2,765 £1,250

17th century ivory statue of Christ at the Column, probably by George Petel. (Phillips) $14,135 £6,200

Ivory okimono of a seated ape and cubs, signed Ichiyusai. (Christie's) $2,150 £1,000

A pair of Chinese ivory figures of geese, Tang or Song dynasty, 2in. and 2½in. high. (Christie's) $2,180 £1,000

A carved ivory figure by F. Preiss, of a seated nude girl, 9cm. high. (Christie's) $915 £420

Fine 16th or 17th century French ivory Virgin and Child, 17.5cm. high. (Christie's) $2,990 £1,300

Antique ivory chess set, coloured in pink and natural, circa 1840. (Christopher Sykes) $85 £38

17th century Goanese ivory and wood figure of St. Francis, 20.5cm. (Christie's) $3,200 £1,400

19th century scrimshaw cow horn, circa 1840, 8½in. long. (Christopher Sykes) $170 £75

Late 19th century French carved ivory hand mirror set with a portrait miniature, 22.3cm. long. (Sotheby's Belgravia) $290 £130

Hound shaped carved ivory needle-case. (Bonham's) $508 £220

Japanese carved ivory figure of a peasant sowing seeds, 13½in. high, on hardwood base. (Bradley & Vaughan) $3,050 £1,350

A pair of 17th century Chinese ivory figures of female musicians, 3¼in. high. (Christie's) $830 £380

17th century Goanese ivory figure of St. John the Baptist, 20cm. (Christie's) $575 £250

491

Eskimo walrus ivory polar bear with
elongated neck, 5in. long.
(Sotheby's) $1,955 £900

Rare late 17th century boxwood
set of Napier's Bones, 10.8 x 8.2cm.
(Christie's) $3,140 £1,400

Eskimo walrus ivory carving of a
sperm whale, inset with walrus
bristle, 2¼in. long. (Sotheby's)
$1,130 £520

Eskimo walrus ivory carving
of a human figure, 3in. high.
(Sotheby's) $520 £240

Unsigned ivory netsuke of a rat carrying her young, their eyes inlaid in
ebony, late 18th or early 19th century.
(Christie's) $540 £240

One of a pair of early 19th
century candlesticks, whale
ivory and baleen overlay on
hollywood, 9in. (Robert W.
Skinner Inc.) $110 £50

Eskimo walrus ivory carving
of a polar bear, 4¾in. long.
(Sotheby's) $1,260 £580

Mid 19th century Kosai ivory Aikuchi
sheath, 46.5cm. long, signed Juroko
Rakanzu. (Sotheby King & Chasemore)
$930 £430

17th century Chinese ivory
seated figure of a lady with
a child, 7½in. high.
(Christie's) $3,270 £1,500

19th century set of ivory dom-
inoes contained in a wooden
box inlaid with a female figure.
(Vernon's) $105 £50

Fine and rare Chinese ivory work-
ing model of a Fuzhou junk under
sail, 59cm. long. (Sotheby's)
$5,575 £2,500

Ivory and silver mounted Austrian tankard, 13½in. high, with
ornately carved body. (H.
Spencer & Son) $5,590 £2,600

Late 18th century Anglo-Indian ivory veneered workbox with octangular lid, 12in. wide. (Christie's) $405 £180

Eskimo walrus ivory carving of a whale, inset with walrus bristle, 4¼in. long. (Sotheby's)
$1,300 £600

Eskimo walrus ivory carving of an artic fox, inset with walrus bristle, 4¼in. long. (Sotheby's)
$955 £440

Carved ivory covered container of basket weave design, 4½in. high. (Robert W. Skinner Inc.)
$320 £145

Eskimo walrus ivory seal head, naturalistically carved, 2¼in. long. (Sotheby's)
$780 £360

Hanging scent bottle with painted ivory and seal, circa 1830-40. (Alfie's Antique Market) $155 £70

Well carved two-cased ivory inro signed Shounsai Yoshimasa, 19th century. (Christie's)
$715 £320

African elephant's tusk carved to depict a procession, 42cm. long. (Phillips) $80 £35

Dieppe carved ivory figure of Queen Marie-Antoinette, skirt opening as a triptych, 8¾in. high. (H. Spencer & Son) $1,035 £480

17th century Chinese ivory figure of a standing scholar, 9in. high. (Christie's) $1,960 £900

Japanese carved ivory box and cover in the form of a swarm of rats, signed. (Phillips) $1,005 £440

One of two carved ivory figures, slightly damaged. (Robert W. Skinner Inc.)
$30 £15

Dark celadon Chinese jade carving of a water buffalo, 17th or 18th century, 14.3cm. long. (Christie's) $1,210 £550

One of a pair of Chinese white jade dishes of shallow form, 5½in. (Sotheby's) $1,550 £720

18th century Chinese pale celadon jade carving of a mythical winged fish, 11.9cm. long.(Christie's) $1,760 £800

Chinese white jade chrysanthemum dish, 19.7cm. (Sotheby's) $1,950 £900

18th century Chinese pale greyish celadon jade rectangular vase with domed cover, 17.1cm. high. (Christie's) $1,100 £500

18th century Chinese celadon green jade brush washer carved as a lotus leaf with chilong, 13.8cm. (Sotheby's) $1,425 £660

Chinese emerald-green jadeite pendant carved with fruiting gourd vine, set with diamonds, 2in. (Sotheby's) $1,300 £600

A spinach green jade set of koro, vase and box, carved with archaic patterns, Chinese. (Sotheby's Hong Kong) $5,720 £2,600

Fine Chinese white jade vase of flattened gu shape, carved in archaic style, 18.9cm. high.(Christie's) $2,100 £950

Good Chinese jadeite pendant carved in archaic style with two chilong, 8cm. (Sotheby's) $865 £400

Chinese pale greyish-white jade carving of three figures in a landscape, 18th or 19th century, 30cm. long. (Christie's) $2,310 £1,050

Green jadeite figure of a bearded sage, holding a shoe, Chinese, 8.4cm. high. (Sotheby's Hong Kong) $1,210 £550

Fine Chinese pale greyish celadon jade carving of two geese holding lotus branches, 18th century, 15.2cm. long. (Christie's) $1,055 £480

Chinese jade set wood sceptre, the jade appliques carved with sages in a landscape, 22in. long. (Sotheby's)$775 £360

Chinese mottled white, beige and greyish celadon jade group of two goats, 18th century, 13.6cm. long.(Christie's) $1,100 £500

One of a pair of Chinese white jade bowls with domed covers, 4¾in. (Sotheby's) $3,000 £1,400

Qianlong spinach green jade vase and cover group. (Sotheby's)$6,050 £2,800

One of a pair of pale greyish celadon jade carvings of storks, on wood stands, Chinese, 16.8cm. high. (Christie's) $1,760 £800

18th century Chinese jade brush pot, rectangular, carved with cranes in a landscape; 18.6cm. high. (Christie's) $1,280 £580

Chinese pale green jade figure of an elephant, with bronze saddle and harness decorated with garnets, 15.2cm. (Sotheby's) $995 £460

Rare Chinese pierced red and white jade pendant showing Zhou Geliang on a mule, 2¼in. (Sotheby's) $1,640 £760

Fine Chinese apple- and emerald-green jade pendant carved and pierced as two coiled chilong, 4.6cm. long. (Christie's) $16,500 £7,500

A pale green jadeite dipper in the shape of a long melon with leaf and a cane basket. (Sotheby's Hong Kong) $4,950 £2,250

Chinese mottled green jade pendant, carved and pierced with birds on flowering and fruiting branches, 4.6cm. long. (Christie's)$1,760 £800

Attractive Chinese yellow-green and russet jade carving of a duck on a lotus leaf, 3½in. (Sotheby's) $520 £240

One of a pair of emerald-green jadeite teabowls with domed covers, Chinese, late 18th or early 19th century, 3½in. high. (Sotheby's Hong Kong) $16,390 £7,450

Late 18th century jade koro and cover. (Woolley & Wallis) $1,560 £720

Chinese soapstone figure of Guanyin, seated and holding a scroll, 18th century, 4¼in. (Sotheby's) $215 £100

Chinese pale green jade figure of a pony, 22cm. (Sotheby's) $775 £360

Well carved white jade rhyton, 17th or 18th century, 4¼in. (Sotheby's Hong Kong) $4,070 £1,850

Chinese jadeite censer and cover of archaic ding form, 29cm. (Sotheby's) $5,185 £2,400

One of a pair of Chinese mottled jade carvings of ladies on rose quartz bases, 17.5cm. high. (Christie's) $1,100 £500

Chinese lapis lazuli group of Guanyin and attendants, on grey-white jade base and carved wood stand, 16.3cm. high. (Christie's) $1,500 £680

Chinese dark celadon and brown jade box and cover, foot restored, 15.9cm. wide. (Christie's) $700 £320

18th century Chinese circular marriage dish, mottled greyish celadon jade, carved with two carp, 22.6cm. wide. (Christie's) $1,540 £700

18th century Chinese spinach green jade incense burner and cover, 17.1cm. high. (Christie's) $5,500 £2,500

Ming dynasty coiled chilong in mutton-fat jade veined with dark brown, 2½in. (Sotheby's) $6,915 £3,200

Chinese lavender jadeite figure of Budai leaning on a bag of wind, 3½in. (Sotheby's) $735 £340

Mottled grey-white Chinese jade pot and cover, carved as a recumbent deer, 9.7cm. long. (Christie's)$835 £380

Chinese white jade carving of two cats, each with lingzhi fungus, 7.3cm. (Sotheby's) $605 £280

Chinese spinach green jade plaque of a foxhunt, on a white jade base, 8in. long. (Sotheby's)$975 £450

Chinese green jade figure of a stag, 28cm. (Sotheby's) $820 £380

Attractive Chinese pale green soapstone figure of Guanyin, seated with an open book, 5¾in. (Sotheby's)$325 £150

A large Imperial jade basin, with incised and gilt Imperial inscription, Qianlong, 10in. long. (Sotheby's Hong Kong) $32,800 £14,000

Qianlong green jade vase carved as hollow trunk with vines and fungus, 16.2cm. (Sotheby's) $5,620 £2,600

18th century Chinese dark celadon jade carving of winged dragon-head fish, 15.2cm. long. (Christie's) $615 £280

Chinese lavender jadeite pendant of rich colour, carved with a shrew on a ball, 1¾in. (Sotheby's) $3,000 £1,400

18th century Chinese white jade brush washer carved as lotus pods with leaves and flowers, 13.7cm. (Sotheby's) $1,840 £850

Diamond set bow brooch, stones pave set. (Sotheby King & Chasemore) $1,575 £700

English silver brooch of racket and ball, Birmingham, 1896, 33mm. high. (Phillips) $45 £20

Jewelled badge from the 1st Queen's Dragoon Guards. (Sotheby's) $3,348 £1,500

Victorian diamond pendant. (Vost's) $2,460 £1,200

Enamel Chinese buckle and earrings. (Alfie's Antique Market) $64 £30

English silver brooch, Birmingham, 1885, 43mm. long.(Phillips) $49 £22

Art Nouveau style brooch set with a diamond. (Christie's S. Kensington) $1,218 £600

Silver brooch circa 1890, English, 56mm. long. (Phillips) $56 £25

Fine Victorian gold, diamond and pearl mounted oval brooch pendant. (Sotheby Bearne)$6,912 £3,200

Gold set sapphire and diamond ring. (Alfie's Antique Market) $140 £65

Linked panel bracelet, signed C. Giuliano. (Christie's S. Kensington) $3,375 £1,500

Crocidolite, garnet and rose diamond brooch, circa 1900. (Sotheby's) $1,012 £450

Silver brooch, circa 1885, of two crossed rackets and tennis shoe, English, 43mm. wide. (Phillips) $63 £28

Viking twisted gold bracelet. (Sotheby's) $13,130 £6,500

A pair of diamond and sapphire mounted ear-clips. (Sotheby Bearne) $2,160 £1,000

Gold racket brooch, circa 1900, 46mm. long. (Phillips) $90 £40

498

Russian niello bracelet, set with turquoise, St. Petersburg, 1884. (Vost's) $266 £130

Brooch in unmarked yellow gold with raised scroll edges. (Sotheby King & Chasemore) $270 £120

Late 19th century gold enamelled butterfly brooch. (Phillips) $7,917 £3,900

Gold and gem set hinged bangle with miniature of Edward VII as Prince of Wales. (Sotheby's) $6,480 £3,000

Victorian gold and gem set serpent necklet, with fitted case. (Sotheby Bearne) $5,400 £2,500

Gold and enamel bangle with detachable miniature of William IV. (Christie's) $4,466 £2,200

Brooch in frog form, set with diamonds and with ruby eyes. (Sotheby King & Chasemore) $1,786 £880

Diamond cluster with 2¼ct. stones set in 18ct. white gold. (Alfie's Antique Market) $843 £375

'Lucky' silver brooch with green stone shamrock, hallmarked Birmingham, 1912, 43mm. high. (Phillips) $101 £45

Important pair of Cartier sapphire and diamond ear-clips. (Sotheby Bearne) $13,500 £6,000

Enamel and gold portrait brooch, 1in. diam., circa 1900. (Gray's Antique Mews) $740 £350

Victorian diamond and turquoise necklace, circa 1830-50. (Frank H. Fellows) $12,600 £5,600

Antique diamond riviere necklace of 58 stones. (Phillips) $34,560 £16,000

Lalique enamelled gold necklace and matching earrings, circa 1900. (Sotheby's Belgravia) $16,400 £8,200

Russian silver gilt and enamel waist belt. (H. Dodd & Partners) $1,912 £850

Pair of Victorian 15ct. gold earrings with coral centre. (Alfie's Antique Market) $151 £70

Art Deco bar brooch, 1920's, 7.5cm. long, in silvered coloured metal set with a band of brilliants. (Sotheby's Belgravia) $186 £85

19th century Japanese locket inlaid with gilt and coloured alloys. (Cubitt & West) $1,188 £550

Diamond brooch of stepped outline. (Sotheby's) $1,085 £500

Liberty & Co. silver and turquoise ring. (Sotheby's Belgravia) $197 £90

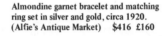

Diamond bandeau of openwork design, millegrain set at intervals with circular cut diamonds. (Sotheby's) $7,810 £3,600

Almondine garnet bracelet and matching ring set in silver and gold, circa 1920. (Alfie's Antique Market) $416 £160

Late 19th century diamond bracelet. (Sotheby's) $1,627 £750

Diamond knot brooch designed as a simple half hitch. (Sotheby's) $3,906 £1,800

Diamond and gold flower brooch, 1½in. diam. (Honiton Galleries) $3,390 £1,500

Gold, ruby and diamond spray brooch, leaves and petals in burnished gold. (Sotheby's Belgravia) $390 £180

One of a pair of diamond pendant earrings, circa 1930. (Sotheby's) $4,123 £1,900

Italian Art Nouveau plique-a-jour enamelled brooch, circa 1900, 8.8cm. wide. (Sotheby's Belgravia) $2,409 £1,100

Sybil Dunlop necklace of quartz and semi-precious stones, circa 1900, 7cm. high. (Sotheby's Belgravia) $1,314 £600

Lalique deep amber glass pendant, 5cm. high, 1920's. (Sotheby's Belgravia) $394 £180

Henri Vever carved horn, gold, opal and turquoise brooch, circa 1900, 8.5cm. high. (Sotheby's Belgravia) $1,052 £480

Victorian diamond cluster set, openwork, stiff hinged bangle. (Christie's S. Kensington) $1,900 £880

Delon gentleman's ring, 1930's, in silvered coloured metal. (Sotheby's Belgravia) $350 £160

Gold, ruby, emerald and diamond brooch in a sunburst design. (Sotheby's) $23,870 £11,000

Oblong shaped diamond plaque brooch pave-set with circular cut diamonds. (Sotheby's) $1,736 £800

Modernist French gold and lacquer bracelet, circa 1930, 19.5cm. long. (Sotheby's Belgravia)$1,642 £750

A diamond and pearl tiara necklace in a design of garlands and ribbon bows, circa 1905. (Sotheby's) $2,200 £1,000

Attractive crystal and diamond bracelet designed as a band of pyramidal crystals topped with diamonds. (Sotheby's) $4,774 £2,200

Georgian enamel suite in silver gilt set with pearls and rubies. (Alfie's Antique Market) $474 £210

Attractive diamond brooch pendant, circa 1905. (Sotheby's) $5,425 £2,500

Liberty & Co. silver and enamel brooch, circa 1905, 3.25cm. wide. (Sotheby's Belgravia) $98 £45

Large Art Nouveau cameo brooch, gold surround set with pearls, circa 1900, 9.75cm. high. (Sotheby's Belgravia) $525 £240

Pearl and diamond brooch, circa 1890, in case. (Sotheby's) $4,340 £2,000

Attractive pearl and rose diamond brooch pendant of upright oval form, circa 1865, French. (Sotheby's) $1,193 £550

Boutet de Monvel gold, opal and enamel ring, 3cm. long, circa 1900. (Sotheby's Belgravia) $1,138 £520

Pearl and diamond neglige, circa 1905. (Sotheby's) $1,736 £800

JEWELLERY

Silver coloured metal brooch, circa 1900, 3.5cm. wide. (Sotheby's Belgravia) $110 £50

Platinum and white gold set diamond and onyx cluster ring. (Sotheby King & Chasemore) $3,670 £1,700

Diamond marquise cluster ring, mounted in all gold. (Christie's) $2,455 £1,050

Diamond fancy pierced rectangular panel and bar link flexible bracelet. (Christie's) $2,225 £950

Bracelet in unmarked white gold with diamond and onyx clusters. (Sotheby King & Chasemore) $4,150 £1,900

Victorian bloodstone-on-agate cameo. (Stride's) $1,355 £600

Diamond double clip brooch, each clip of ribbons and foliate scroll design. (Christie's) $3,745 £1,600

Victorian gold necklace with matching brooch/pendant. (Geering & Colyer) $1,850 £800

Diamond and collet and line flexible bracelet. (Christie's) $3,220 £1,400

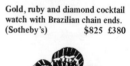

Gold, ruby and diamond cocktail watch with Brazilian chain ends. (Sotheby's) $825 £380

Diamond and rose diamond caduceus brooch. (Christie's) $805 £350

Antique diamond octofoil cluster brooch pendant. (Christie's) $1,495 £650

Gold and plique-a-jour enamel flower and leaf clip brooch with diamond stamen. (Christie's) $980 £420

Lady's Art Deco diamond wrist watch on black silk cord bracelet. (Christie's) $1,450 £620

Antique gold cornelian scarab hinged bangle decorated with applied granulation and filigree work. (Christie's) $1,610 £700

18ct. white gold and platinum
set three-stone diamond ring.
(Sotheby King & Chasemore)
$4,535 £2,100

Diamond and baguette diamond ribbon loop
and floral cluster brooch. (Christie's)
$1,215 £520

Palladium set two diamond and
single emerald ring. (Sotheby
King & Chasemore)
$17,280 £8,000

Art Deco bar brooch, 1920's, 7.5cm. long, in silver
coloured metal set with a band of brilliants.
(Sotheby's Belgravia) $185 £85

Ruby, diamond and enamel flexible bracelet. (Christie's)
$3,975 £1,700

Georg Jensen brooch in silver
coloured metal, 6cm. wide,
1920's. (Sotheby's Belgravia)
$175 £80

Fahrner silver and opal pendant, circa 1900,
4.5cm. high. (Sotheby's Belgravia)
$745 £340

Victorian diamond six-point star
brooch pendant with sapphire
collets between each point.
(Christie's) $1,285 £550

Sapphire and diamond bar
brooch with nine oval
shaped sapphires. (Sotheby's)
$2,385 £1,100

Graduated spectacle set ruby and diamond collet alternate section
bracelet. (Christie's) $2,530 £1,100

One of a pair of diamond pendant earrings. (Christie's)
$4,915 £2,100

Plique-a-jour enamel pendant, circa 1900,
on silver coloured metal, 6.8cm. drop.
(Sotheby's Belgravia) $740 £320

Victorian emerald and diamond
set scroll and festoon brooch with
emerald set runner and twin tassel
drops. (Christie's) $2,225 £950

Antique diamond tiara. (Bonham's) $15,375 £7,500

Diamond pierced ribbon bow brooch. (Christie's)
$1,405 £600

LAMPS

Brass lantern with four glass panels and triple candle-holder, 19in. (Robert W. Skinner Inc.) $800 £370

Early 19th century tin Argand-type outdoor lantern, hexagonal, 30in. (Robert W. Skinner Inc.) $200 £95

Art Deco green patinated bronze figure table lamp on black marble base. (Phillips) $438 £205

19th century Lithophane lamp shade on brass frame, 7¼in. (Robert W. Skinner Inc.) $100 £45

17th century brass standing Sabbath lamp with seven-wick oil pan, 14in. (Robert W. Skinner Inc.) $300 £140

19th century Italian brass lucerna with four wick spouts, 21¼in. (Robert W. Skinner Inc.) $175 £80

Seated figure lamp on marble base. (Alfie's Antique Market) $440 £195

20th century brass floorlamp in Art Nouveau style. (Phillips) $277 £120

Early 19th century Swiss post lantern, tin with horn windows, 18½in. (Robert W. Skinner Inc.) $60 £28

Bronze Art Nouveau Tiffany studio lamp. (Robert W. Skinner Inc.) $1,400 £635

One of a pair of adjustable brass railway table/wall lamps with original shades. (Alfie's Antique Market) $140 £68

Early 19th century brass travelling lantern, sheet brass enclosing a glass cylinder, 7½in. (Robert W. Skinner Inc.) $175 £80

504

Early 19th century free-blown glass whale-oil lamp, 8½in. (Robert W. Skinner Inc.) $350 £160

Early 19th century tin and horn lantern, 15in. (Robert W. Skinner Inc.) $150 £70

Original signed Art Nouveau table lamp. (Alfie's Antique Market) $340 £190

Late 18th century brass travelling lantern with glass bull's eye door and tin top 7½in. (Robert W. Skinner Inc.) $150 £70

Unusual wooden safety lamp by Elwood, White-haven, circa 1795, 10¼in. high. (H. C. Chapman & Son) $555 £245

17th century iron pan lamp with wick support and candle holder, 21in. (Robert W. Skinner Inc.) $350 £165

19th century brass and wood candlestick with fabric lamp shade, 24in. (Robert W. Skinner Inc.) $250 £115

Modernist chromed metal table lamp, French, 1930's, 38cm. high. (Sotheby's Belgravia) $415 £190

Galle cameo glass table lamp with domed shade, circa 1900, 41cm. high. (Sotheby's Belgravia) $4,620 £2,000

Clanny lamp by Laidlaw, circa 1882, 9½in. high. (H. C. Chapman & Son) $165 £72

Art Deco design electric desk lamp, 21in. high, circa 1925. (Christopher Sykes) $305 £135

19th century wooden street lamp, with glass panels. (Robert W. Skinner Inc.) $175 £80

Spelter figure lamp with flame shade. (Alfie's Antique Market) $96 £43

Walter pate de verre and wrought iron table lamp, 1920's, 31cm. high. (Sotheby's Belgravia) $788 £360

One of a pair of cut glass ormolu mounted two light candelabra, probably Irish, 1830. (Christie's) $945 £420

Unusual Barbedienne table lamp, 1930's, 38.5cm. high, of copper sheet in trumpet shape. (Sotheby's Belgravia) $197 £90

Galle cameo glass lamp, circa 1900, 52.5cm. high, in the form of a water-lily. (Sotheby's Belgravia) $30,660 £14,000

Hueck brass and copper oil lamp, circa 1900, 23.5cm. high. (Sotheby's Belgravia) $416 £190

Astral lamp with brass floral Art Nouveau base and frosted shade. (Robert W. Skinner Inc.) $350 £160

19th century French chinoiserie lamp with ormolu base, 14in. high. (Robert W. Skinner Inc.) $350 £160

Le Verre Francais cameo glass lamp with shouldered domed shaped shade, 1920's, 40.5cm. high. (Sotheby's Belgravia) $6,130 £2,800

17th century iron pan lamp. (Robert W. Skinner Inc.) $300 £145

Lithophane desk lamp with five panel shade, 15in. high. (Robert W. Skinner Inc.) $650 £295

Austrian Art Nouveau bronze and ivory table lamp, signed Teraczuk, shade by Galle. (Phillips) $5,443 £2,695

Small Richard cameo glass table lamp base with Galle glass shade, circa 1900, 35cm. high. (Sotheby's Belgravia) $1,642 £750

Rene Lalique's 'L'oiseau de Feu' glass lamp, on a bronze base, 17½in. high. (Phillips) $10,660 £5,200

Signed terracotta figure lamp with hand painted lantern. (Alfie's Antique Market) $399 £185

Webb Burmese fairy lamp with floral decoration, signed. (Robert W. Skinner Inc.) $650 £295

One of a pair of spelter lamps by L. Charles, circa 1900, 91cm. high, fitted for electricity. (Sotheby's Belgravia) $436 £210

Pairpoint desk lamp with Stratford blown-out shade, 8½in. diam. (Robert W. Skinner Inc.) $750 £340

Edwardian brass desk lamp. (Alfie's Antique Market) $146 £68

Chinese hanging lantern. (J. M. Welch & Son) $85 £40

Pairpoint table lamp with reverse painted 'Exeter' shade, 22in. high. (Robert W. Skinner Inc.) $1,300 £590

Pairpoint fairy lamp with blown out pansy shade on wooden base. (Robert W. Skinner Inc.) $325 £145

Cut glass 'Gone with the Wind' lamp, signed L. Straus & Sons, 18½in. high. (Robert W. Skinner Inc.) $6,300 £2,860

Edwardian plated table lamp with shell and metal work spreading shade, 66cm. high. (May, Whetter & Grose) $195 £90

LAMPS

Ruskin table lamp, 1920's-1930's, (Alfie's Antique Market) $190 £85

A pair of Perzel modernist brass wall lights, 37cm. wide, 1930's. (Sotheby's Belgravia)$415 £190

Stephenson safety lamp, circa 1815, 9in. high. (H. C. Chapman & Son) $6800 £300

Daum cameo glass hanging shade in mottled amber and yellow glass, 41.3cm. diam., 1920's. (Sotheby's Belgravia) $2,195 £950

Art Deco Le Faguays gilt bronze lamp, circa 1925, 69cm. high, on marble base. (Sotheby's Belgravia) $3,505 £1,600

Le Verre Francais 'Scarab' cameo glass lamp, 1920's, 49cm. high. (Sotheby's Belgravia) $3,725 £1,700

A bronze and marble table lamp by Aurore Onu modelled as a partially draped nude girl, 80.5cm. high. (Christie's) $3,000 £1,400

One of a pair of bronze cobra table lamps by Edgar Brandt, 51.5cm. high. (Christie's) $7,000 £3,200

Tiffany 'fabrique' table lamp with ten panel amber linen fold glass shade, 20½in. high. (Robert W. Skinner Inc.) $2,300 £1,045

Early 19th century tin folding lantern in book form, 5½in. high. (Robert W. Skinner Inc.) $100 £45

Open tin 'Midgy' lamp with tin shielding, circa 1887, 6in. high. (H. C. Chapman & Son) $40 £20

Crystal lamp with globular shade, 39.5cm. high. (Phillips) $50 £25

Stylish Art Deco solid brass desk lamp. (Alfie's Antique Market) $140 £60

Daum cameo glass lampshade, 31cm. diam., circa 1900. (Sotheby's Belgravia) $2,630 £1,200

French chrome desk lamp with adjustable shade.(Alfie's Antique Market) $70 £30

Heavy silver sanctuary lamp, Birmingham, 1925, 527oz. (Ernest R. de Rome) $11,980 £5,300

Modernist chromed metal standard lamp with strip light, 1930's, 131.5cm. high. (Sotheby's Belgravia) $480 £220

A Tiffany peacock feather leaded glass and gilt metal table lamp, 56cm. high. (Christie's) $2,600 £1,200

One of a pair of Victorian brass oil lamps with cranberry glass bowls and shades, 2ft.3in. high. (Gray's Antique Mews) $340 £150

One of a pair of Anthouard glazed ceramic lamp bases with embroidered shades, French, 1920's. (Sotheby's Belgravia) $1,615 £700

Silver travelling lamp with candleholder and vesta compartments, by Thomas Johnson, London, 1872, 520gm. (Sotheby's Belgravia) $1,300 £580

Desk lamp with swivel shade, 1930's.(Alfie's Antique Market) $70 £30

18th century brass portable lantern with sliding brass door and hinged glass door, 6½in. high. (Robert W. Skinner Inc.) $425 £200

Mid 18th century French lacemaker's lamp, 25.5cm. high. (Christie's) $345 £150

LEAD

Britain's model of a six-horse gun carriage. (Sotheby King & Chasemore) $230 £100

One from a set of eight Britain's Danish Army Life Guards, in original box, No. 2019. (Sotheby's Belgravia) $110 £50

One from a set of Britain's Italian Carabinieri in original box, thirty-two pieces in all. (Sotheby's Belgravia) $245 £110

Lead plaque of Napoleon Bonaparte on horseback, circa 1810, 9½in. high. (Christopher Sykes) $130 £60

Two from a set of fifteen Britain's United States Infantry, including one officer. (Sotheby's Belgravia) $65 £30

Two from a set of sixteen Britain's Mexican Infantry in box, slightly damaged. (Sotheby's Belgravia) $165 £75

Very rare American bridge building unit by Heyde, Germany. (Phillips, N. York) $500 £210

One from a set of sixteen soldiers from Britain's Bulgarian Infantry, in box. (Sotheby's Belgravia) $100 £45

Set of Britain's Civilians, dated 1908, seven pieces in all. (Sotheby's Belgravia) $265 £120

Sundial in the form of a lead blackamoor figure, signed Delander Loudini, 39in. high. (Whiteheads) $11,570 £5,700

510

One of a set of sixteen Britain's Italian Infantry in Colonial Service dress. (Sotheby's Belgravia) $165 £75

Britain's model of the George IV coronation coach and horses, 20¼in. long. (Christopher Sykes) $215 £95

One of a set of sixteen Britain's Dublin Fusiliers, in original Whisstock box No. 109. (Sotheby's Belgravia) $100 £45

Britain's set of French Legion Etrangere Infantry, with mounted officer. (Phillips) $100 £45

Antique cast lead garden flower urn, circa 1750, 14in. diam. (Christopher Sykes) $620 £275

Britain's set of Arabs on horseback. (Phillips) $30 £15

Part of a display of turn-of-the-century firefighters by Mignot, France. (Phillips, N. York) $900 £385

One of a set of eleven Britain's Cossacks, in original Whisstock box No. 136. (Sotheby's Belgravia) $65 £30

Two from a set of ten Britain's Middlesex Yeomanry, dated 1903. (Sotheby's Belgravia) $185 £85

Two from a set of eight Britain's German Infantry, in original box. (Sotheby's Belgravia) $40 £20

511

One of a pair of marble and gilt bronze urns and covers, 17in. high, circa 1870. (Sotheby's Belgravia) $1,870 £900

Tahan gilt bronze and red marble tazza, 1880's, 17in. wide. (Sotheby's Belgravia) $415 £200

One of a pair of statuary marble urns, circa 1900, 31in. high. (Sotheby's Belgravia) $1,455 £700

Cologne Gothic marble figure of the Virgin and Child, circa 1320, 30¼in. high. (Sotheby's) $28,080 £13,000

Large marble urn carved with vine and with inset marble panel, 39in. high, circa 1880. (Sotheby's Belgravia) $995 £450

White marble figure of a woman by Elie Nadelman, 45cm. high. (Bonham's) $12,960 £6,000

Marble portrait bust of William le Marchant by Joseph Nolekens. (Woolley & Wallis) $4,320 £2,000

18th century Netherlandish marble relief of Bacchus, 13in. wide. (Sotheby's) $1,805 £800

12th century Verona marble column with spiral stem, 314cm. high. (Christie's) $3,240 £1,500

Late 13th century Italian marble figure of the Madonna, 72.5cm. high. (Christie's) $8,640 £4,000

White marble group of an Italian greyhound by Joseph Gott, circa 1830, 40¼in. high. (Sotheby's) $3,615 £1,600

18th century English marble bust of a soldier, 77cm. high. (Christie's) $605 £280

Late 17th century Venetian marble head of Winter, 22cm. high. (Christie's) $690 £320

Louis XVI ormolu mounted black and white marble vase with gadrooned oval body, 20in. wide. (Christie's) $17,600 £8,000

Venetian/Byzantine 14th century Verona red marble cistern, 64cm. wide. (Christie's) $2,590 £1,200

Late 19th century English marble bust by MacBride, 82cm. high. (Christie's) $130 £60

19th century Italian coloured marble bust of a young woman, 60cm. (Christie's) $1,610 £700

Late 19th century marble and bronze figure of a seated woman, 26½in. high, Italian. (Christie's N. York) $3,000 £1,400

13th/14th century North Italian pink marble column, 293cm. high. (Christie's) $1,620 £750

Pair of Italian marble statuettes of Cupid and Psyche, signed R. Monti, 1853, 31cm. (Christie's) $875 £380

18th century white marble statuette. (Gray's Antique Mews) $1,130 £500

Mid 19th century English white marble bust of the Duke of Wellington, 59cm. high. (Christie's) $865 £400

Mid 18th century English marble relief of a classical sacrificial scene, 37cm. wide. (Christie's) $650 £300

17th century marble herm, 28.5cm. high. (Christie's) $1,035 £480

Miniature mahogany chest of drawers, circa 1850, 11½in. high. (Christopher Sykes) $195 £85

Late 18th century Dutch miniature walnut cylinder bureau, circa 1770, 1ft.3in. high. (Sotheby's) $675 £300

Late 19th century miniature mahogany chest of three drawers with glass handles. (Vernon's) $65 £30

Rare child's rocking chair in slipware, dated 1868, 8in. high. (Christopher Sykes) $65 £30

Ivory veneered oak miniature bureau, 18th century, probably Russian, 10¼in. wide. (Christie's) $815 £360

Regency period pocket watch stand in the form of a grandfather clock, 13in. high, circa 1825. (Christopher Sykes) $170 £80

Late 17th/early 18th century miniature oak bureau, 1ft.5in. wide. (Sotheby's) $675 £300

Miniature mahogany longcase clock, 14in. high. (Christie's S. Kensington) $690 £320

Walnut and burr-walnut miniature bureau, 13¼in. high. (Christie's S. Kensington) $1,035 £480

19th century apprentice mahogany chest of drawers, 26cm. high. (Phillips) $140 £60

Fine miniature apprentice made settle, Brittany, circa 1850, in oak with hinged lid, 12¾in. long. (Christopher Sykes) $290 £130

French walnut miniature child's berger chair with carved feet. (Worsfolds) $385 £170

Good carved wood Art Nouveau mirror frame, circa 1900, possibly French, 106cm. high. (Sotheby's Belgravia) $1,490 £680

Late 19th century Venetian style wall mirror with bevelled glass. (Vernon's) $110 £50

Early 19th century mahogany framed shield shaped swing mirror. (Vernon's) $65 £30

19th century brass framed wall mirror, 60cm. high. (Phillips) $220 £95

One of a pair of early 20th century Italian gilt wood wall mirrors, 22½in. wide. (Sotheby's Belgravia) $470 £210

Victorian adjustable brass shaving mirror, 45cm. high. (Phillips) $115 £50

Regency parcel gilt and ebonised pier glass, circa 1805, 5ft. 1in. high. (Sotheby's) $1,095 £480

Early 20th century gilt framed convex glass wall mirror, 2ft. diam. (Vernon's) $165 £75

Victorian mahogany framed dressing table mirror with shaped base. (Vernon's) $90 £40

William and Mary japanned dressing toilet mirror with bureau base, circa 1695, 1ft.6in. wide. (Sotheby's) $730 £320

Italian gilt wood wall mirror with two circular plates, circa 1900, 66½in. high. (Sotheby's Belgravia) $1,125 £500

George II walnut toilet mirror with stepped base, circa 1740, 1ft.2in. wide. (Sotheby's) $500 £220

515

MIRRORS

Chippendale period carved gilt wood wall mirror, 51in. high. (Heathcote Ball & Co.) $3,455 £1,600

Rectangular bevelled plate wall mirror, 20in. high. (Hobbs Parker) $131 £65

Sheraton style mahogany framed dressing mirror of shield form. (Phillips) $71 £35

Charles II walnut mirror, circa 1680, 2ft.9in. high. (Sotheby's) $4,750 £2,200

Thuringian kidney-shaped mirror with candle sconces, 58cm. high. (Phillips) $950 £440

Queen Anne walnut toilet mirror, circa 1710, 1ft. 4½in. wide. (Sotheby's) $648 £300

Good Sormani ormolu 'rococo' toilet mirror, circa 1880, 16½in. high. (Sotheby's Belgravia) $1,040 £500

One of a pair of George III gilt wood mirrors. (Christie's) $10,250 £5,000

One of a pair of gilt oval mirrors, 2ft.9in. high. (Vidler & Co.) $225 £110

Queen Anne period carved gilt wood frame landscape mirror, 4ft. wide. (Woolley & Wallis) $1,210 £560

George III gilt wood mirror, circa 1770, 2ft.4in. wide. (Sotheby's) $1,835 £850

Fine German baroque gilt wood frame, 3ft.6in. wide, circa 1690. (Sotheby's) $4,230 £1,950

Bathroom mirror in white vitrolite, surrounded in pink mirror flex, 1940's. (Alfie's Antique Market) $101 £50

One of a pair of Venetian oval wall mirrors, circa 1860, 27in. high. (Sotheby's Belgravia) $582 £280

Late 18th century toilet mirror on box base with three drawers. (Hobbs Parker) $162 £80

One of a pair of George II mahogany mirrors, circa 1740, 2ft.5½in. wide. (Sotheby's) $4,968 £2,300

Late 17th/early 18th century Venetian giltwood mirror, 3ft.5½in. wide. (Sotheby's) $2,061 £950

George II giltwood looking glass, circa 1730, 2ft.7¼in. wide. (Sotheby's) $2,376 £1,100

Late 17th century rare Sicilian baroque painted frame, 5ft.4in. wide. (Sotheby's) $8,680 £4,000

Queen Anne mirror, circa 1710, 5ft.0½in. high. (Sotheby's) $4,752 £2,200

Early George II gilt overmantel mirror, 3ft.6in. wide, circa 1725. (Sotheby's) $2,700 £1,250

Unusual oak and Copeland ceramic wall mirror, circa 1879-80, 122cm. wide. (Sotheby's Belgravia) $1,861 £850

One of a pair of Chippendale mirrors with rococo scrollwork. (Phillips) $14,400 £6,400

Korean hardwood silver mounted dressing case, 19th century, 10in. wide. (Vincent & Vanderpump) $280 £140

517

Early 19th century mahogany mirror stand, 20in. high. (Gray's Antique Mews) $170 £75

Antique satinwood toilet mirror of George III design. (Hy. Duke & Son) $185 £90

18th century style mahogany toilet mirror on trestle supports, 51cm. high. (Phillips) $105 £45

Rare Louis XIV silver mounted toilet mirror, 30in. high. (Christie's) $7,920 £3,600

Hammered copper wall mirror, circa 1900, 76cm. wide. (Sotheby's Belgravia) $350 £160

Charles II wall mirror, with cushion frame, 39in. wide. (Sotheby Humberts) $3,520 £1,600

George I red lacquered mirror surmounted by vellute pediment. (Phillips) $740 £320

Lady's hand mirror in black lacquer and exotic wood case, 15½in. long, circa 1850. (Christopher Sykes) $175 £80

Late 17th century marquetry cushion framed mirror, 141cm. high. (Phillips) $4,340 £1,900

20th century oak framed cheval mirror. (Phillips) $75 £30

18th century Anglo-Indian ivory veneered toilet mirror with bureau base, 21½in. wide. (Christie's) $1,100 £480

Early 20th century mahogany framed cheval mirror with shaped top. (Phillips) $185 £80

George III mahogany dressing mirror strung on boxwood, with three drawers to base. (Phillips) $300 £130

Large Victorian flame mahogany swing mirror. (Gray's Antique Mews) $190 £85

Sheraton mahogany toilet mirror with turned side supports, circa 1800, 18¼in. wide. (Christopher Sykes)$155 £70

Early 19th century Italian carved gilt wood and velvet framed mirror. (Gray's Antique Mews)$270 £120

Victorian mahogany framed toilet mirror on box base. (Phillips) $55 £25

Carved and gilt mirror, circa 1750, 5ft.2in. high.(Bonham's) $5,860 £2,700

Hammered copper mirror, circa 1900, 76cm. wide. (Sotheby's Belgravia) $255 £110

French gilt hall mirror. (Alfie's Antique Market) $575 £265

George III gilt wood overmantel with triple plate, 47in. wide. (Christie's) $1,500 £650

Silver dressing mirror, Chester 1900. (Alfie's Antique Market) $320 £140

One of a pair of Venetian glass mirrors, 160cm. high.(Phillips) $1,385 £600

Victorian cast iron standing or hanging mirror, circa 1850, 14½in. high. (Christopher Sykes) $195 £85

Early George II gilt wood mirror, 3ft.4in. high. (Sotheby's) $3,465 £1,500

A Royal Dux table mirror modelled as a maiden wearing a flowing gown, 43cm. high, circa 1910. (Sotheby's Belgravia) $635 £280

George II gilt wood mirror, circa 1755, 4ft.8in. high. (Sotheby's) $1,615 £700

One of a pair of George III gilt wood mirrors, 49½in. high. (Christie's) $3,580 £1,550

George I gilt wood mirror, circa 1730, 3ft.4½in. high. (Sotheby's) $1,800 £780

Carved gilt wood mirror, circa 1860, 26in. wide. (Sotheby's Belgravia) $885 £400

Fine Queen Anne style walnut framed toilet mirror. (British Antique Exporters)$390 £170

Gilt wood wall mirror with carved frame, circa 1860, 41in. wide. (Sotheby's Belgravia) $1,550 £700

George I walnut toilet mirror, circa 1730, restored, 1ft.6in. wide. (Sotheby's)$910 £400

George II gilt wood wall mirror with swan neck cresting, 2ft. 10in. wide, circa 1740. (Sotheby's) $1,595 £700

19th century Queen Anne style walnut framed mirror. (British Antique Exporters) $205 £90

George I gilt gesso pier glass with divided bevelled plate, 62in. high. (Christie's) $4,860 £2,200

520

Sketches of Ancient and Modern Pugilism, published by Joshua Hudson, 1824. (Gray's Antique Mews) $430 £200

One of a pair of Victorian papier mache letter racks with painted and mother-of-pearl decoration. (Vernon's) $130 £60

One of two cameo carved shells, 6in. wide. (Honiton Galleries) $120 £55

Firemark for the West of England Insurance, 1804- 1894. (Phillips)$180 £80

Two wax figures representing Mrs Peachum and Mrs Trapes, 1921. (Alfie's Antique Market) $95 £45

Card from an extremely rare 17th century pack of Scottish heraldry playing cards. (Stanley Gibbons) $2,925 £1,300

Mid 19th century cigarette lighter, probably French, 18in. high. (Sotheby's Belgravia)$1,960 £900

Pair of desk models of knights in sheet steel armour, 17in. high, circa 1840. (Christopher Sykes) $870 £385

Pale silk parasol, 24in. long, circa 1850. (Christopher Sykes) $35 £15

Oval silhouette by Walter Jordan, circa 1788, 2in. high. (Sotheby's) $1,165 £750

Silver Samorodok evening bag of rect- angular form, St. Petersburg, 1908-17, 18.5cm. wide. (Sotheby's) $2,395 £1,050

17th century Persian blue and white pottery hookah base, 7¼in. long. (Sotheby's) $3,900 £1,750

Scale model of a frigate, 48cm. long. (Sotheby's Belgravia) $5,450 £2,400

Builder's wooden model of the three-masted barque 'Buttermere', 1897, 52in. long. (Christie's) $1,765 £800

Fine live steam-powered wooden model of the paddle steamer 'Brighton Queen', 47½in. long. (Christie's) $1,435 £650

Ship builder's scale model, 37in. long. (Parsons, Welch & Cowell) $785 £350

Model of a three-masted barquentine surrounded by four small boats, 64cm. wide. (Phillips) $155 £75

Accurate 1/24th scale wooden sailing model of the Thames spritsail barge 'Kathleen', 55in. long. (Christie's) $1,545 £700

Modern large scale wooden model of 'The Mayflower', 150cm. high. (Sotheby King & Chasemore) $195 £90

19th century model of a three-masted whaler. (Vernon's) $658 £285

Model of a Victorian tea or wool clipper, circa 1890. (Alfie's Antique Market) $435 £200

Walnut cased model of a herring trawler, circa 1890. (Christopher Sykes) $830 £385

Fine hand made model of an early 19th century whaling boat, 33in. long, circa 1830. (Christopher Sykes) $845 £375

Scale half-model of the steel twin-screw steamer 'Winifred', 116cm. long. (Sotheby King & Chasemore) $820 £360

19th century model of a three-masted man-o-war in wood and ivory. (Vernon's) $750 £340

Rare contemporary mid 19th century dockyard apprentice model of a steam/sail three masted warship, circa 1855, 119in. long. (Christie's) $3,315 £1,500

Napoleonic prisoner-of-war model frigate. (V. & V's) $5,875 £2,600

Contemporary prisoner-of-war fully rigged bone and ebony model of H.M. 16-gun brig 'Pelican', 20in. wide. (Christie's) $7,735 £3,500

Cast metal 'HO' gauge 2-rail electric model of the Italian Railways three coach train set 'Il Settebello' by Conti. (Christie's) $840 £380

7¼in. gauge electric display model of Delaware Lackawana & Western 4-4-0 locomotive. (Lacy Scott) $1,015 £500

Hand-built 'O' gauge electric 2-6-4 L. M. S. tank locomotive, 33cm. long. (Sotheby King & Chasemore) $110 £50

Gauge 'O' 3-rail electric model of the Royal Scot by Bassett-Lowke. (Christie's) $1,435 £650

Gauge 'O' live steam spirit-fired model of an American 2-8-0 locomotive and tender, built by A. Beale, Chelmsford, 1954, 17in. long. (Christie's) $3,535 £1,600

Gauge 'O' clockwork model of a Caledonian Railway 4-4-0 locomotive and tender by Leeds Model Co., for Bassett-Lowke. (Christie's) $930 £420

Part of a Max Handwerk gauge 'O' clockwork train, circa 1930. (Sotheby King & Chasemore) $315 £140

2½in. gauge spirit-fired model of a 4-4-2 locomotive and tender by Bassett-Lowke, 29½in. long. (Christie's) $2,100 £950

Part of a collection of gauge 'I' 3-rail electric Continental railway rolling stock by Marklin. (Christie's)
$1,765 £800

7mm. scale 3-rail electric model of a London and North Eastern Railway Class N2 side tank locomotive, 10½in. long. (Christie's)
$1,060 £480

5in. gauge model of the 0-4-0 Hunslet 'Alice' saddle tank quarry locomotive 'Aileen', 33in. long. (Christie's)
$4,200 £1,900

Early 20th century 2½in. gauge spirit-fired model of a Great Central Railway Robinson Class Express side tank locomotive by Bassett-Lowke, 21½in. long. (Christie's)
$1,435 £650

2½in. gauge model of the Great Western Railway 4-6-0 locomotive and tender 'Purley Grange', 1937, 34in. long. (Christie's)
$1,880 £850

Fine 2½in. gauge model of Stephenson's 'Rocket', built by A. Tyrer, Hastings, 11½in. long. (Christie's)
$3,315 £1,500

Cast metal 'HO' gauge 2-rail electric model of the Italian Railways Express diesel car by Conti. (Christie's)
$265 £120

7mm. finescale 2-rail electric model of a Midland Railway Johnston 2-4-0 locomotive and tender, 14in. long. (Christie's)
$1,765 £800

MODEL TRAINS

Good Basset-Lowke 'O' gauge clockwork Duke of York 4-4-0 locomotive and tender, 37.5cm. long overall. (Sotheby King & Chasemore) $180 £90

Basset-Lowke 'O' gauge electric 4-6-2 Princess Royal locomotive and tender, 51cm. long. (Sotheby King & Chasemore) $990 £440

Fine gauge 'I' live steam spirit-fired 0-2-2-0 side tank locomotive complete with pot boiler, by Bing. (Christie's) $840 £380

Hand-built 4-6-0 gauge 'O' electric locomotive and tender, 41cm. long. (Sotheby King & Chasemore) $170 £75

MODELS

Early 20th century horizontal live steam spirit-fired stationary steam set by Bing, 18½in. high. (Christie's) $330 £150

Rare 20th century small full size triple expansion reversing launch engine, 22in. wide. (Christie's) $2,475 £1,100

Brass and gun metal mid 19th century model of a Maudsley single cylinder four pillar table engine, 12¾in. high. (Christie's) $1,105 £500

Coll et Cie stationary horizontal steam engine, 33cm. wide, together with a saw-bench, 13cm. wide. (Sotheby King & Chasemore) $325 £160

Early 20th century horizontal tinplate hot air engine by Carette, 12¼in. high. (Christie's) $360 £160

Well constructed and detailed copper and brass model Babcock boiler, 31in. high, on metal base. (Christie's) $1,060 £480

526

Model Stuart centre-pillar beam engine, built by R. Wheele, Brighton. (Christie's)
$1,295 £600

Amusing and practical vintage electric Michelin portable tyre pump, circa 1928. (Phillips)
$325 £150

Self-propelled toy steam tricycle. (Sotheby King & Chasemore)
$405 £180

Rare mid 19th century model of a twin cylinder reversing oscillating paddle steamer engine, 20½in. wide. (Christie's)
$2,165 £980

Well built brass model horizontal single cylinder side rod mill engine, 1933, 8¾in. long. (Christie's)
$620 £280

MONEY BANKS

Late 19th century American 'William Tell' mechanical shooting bank, 10¼in. long. (Sotheby's Belgravia)
$450 £200

Victorian varnished pinewood child's money box, circa 1870, 6¼in. high. (Christopher Sykes)
$80 £35

American Leap Frog bank, dated 1891, 5in. high. (Gray's Antique Mews)
$730 £340

Amusing child's money box in the form of a pillar box, circa 1925, 6¼in. high. (Christopher Sykes)
$65 £30

Rare cast iron Victorian money bank in original polychrome paint, 6¾in. high. (Christopher Sykes)
$440 £195

Red and black painted tin money box in the shape of a pillar box, circa 1930, 6½in. high. (Christopher Sykes)
$65 £30

MUSICAL BOXES AND POLYPHONES

Very beautiful late 19th century Swiss 'Roll in Sight' cylinder musical box, 22in. long. (Stanilands) $1,728 £800

Good French Pathe 'Le Gaulois' phonograph with original horn, reproducer and recorder, circa 1905. (Sotheby's Belgravia) $1,035 £450

Czechoslovakian horn gramophone with 10in. turntable and tin horn. (Sotheby's Belgravia) $275 £120

Early 20th century German polyphon disc musical box, 10½in. wide. (Sotheby's Belgravia) $690 £300

19th century Swiss music box on a table stand in burr-walnut veneered case. (Woolley & Wallis) $6,840 £3,000

Swiss 'bells and drum in sight' cylinder musical box, circa 1880, 2ft. wide. (Sotheby's Belgravia) $1,840 £800

Swiss Nicole Freres 'bells in sight' cylinder musical box, circa 1885, 26in. wide. (Sotheby's Belgravia) $2,185 £950

Upright coin-in-slot symphonium in ebonised case, 11¼in. high. (Christie's S. Kensington) $1,728 £800

19th century French musical box in rosewood case. (Harrods Auction Galleries) $868 £430

Late 19th century American concert roller organ in beechwood case, 17in. wide. (Sotheby's Belgravia) $965 £420

English barrel piano mounted on a barrow. (Sotheby's Belgravia) $2,508 £1,100

Fine Swiss musical box in rosewood case inlaid with flowers, 25in. long. (Phillips) $4,060 £2,000

Good English miniature gramophone with 4in. turntable, circa 1920. (Sotheby's Belgravia) $275 £120

Gloriosa musical Christmas tree stand in walnut veneered case, 17½in. wide. (Andrew Grant) $686 £335

Good Pathe Democratic (Zero) phonograph. (Sotheby's Belgravia) $370 £160

19th century polyphon disc musical box. (Olivers) $1,728 £800

English HMV model 132 horn gramophone with 12in. turntable, circa 1929. (Sotheby's Belgravia) $345 £150

Late 19th century German polyphon disc musical box by Schutz in walnut case, 21¾in. wide. (Olivers) $1,808 £800

Late 19th century musical box in rosewood case, 28in. long. (Green's) $1,410 £640

German polyphon disc musical box in walnut veneered case, circa 1904, 21in. wide. (Sotheby's Belgravia) $2,990 £1,300

Mira disc musical box in walnut case, 15¼in. wide, with eighteen discs. (Christie's S. Kensington) $3,240 £1,500

Edison standard phonograph with cylinders, 1904. (Gray's Antique Mews) $475 £220

Edison Bell 'Domestic A' gramophone by Pathe Freres, circa 1901. (Vernon's) $540 £240

Good Gramophone and Typewriter Co., Junior Monarch gramophone, circa 1908. (Sotheby's Belgravia) $735 £320

MUSICAL BOXES AND POLYPHONES

Mid 19th century Swiss Lecoultre key-wound cylinder musical box, 20in. wide. (Sotheby's Belgravia) $800 £350

Columbia Regal Junior horn disc gramophone, circa 1914. (Christie's S. Kensington) $1,245 £550

Rosewood cased lever wind musical box by Berens Blumberg & Co. (Christie's S. Kensington) $7,390 £3,200

Kastenpuck phonograph, 1905. (Gray's Antique Mews) $345 £160

Good Chantel Meteor Music 200 45rpm jukebox with large selection of contemporary discs. (Sotheby's Belgravia) $1,035 £450

German Klingsor gramophone with 10in. turntable, in oak cabinet, circa 1912. (Sotheby's Belgravia) $645 £280

Swiss 19th century music box in rosewood case. (Barber's) $1,035 £460

Gramophone & Typewriter Co., style No. 6, gramophone. (Gray's Antique Mews) $1,055 £450

Gramophone & Typewriter Ltd. New Melba gramophone in mahogany case with mahogany horn. (Christie's S. Kensington) $3,150 £1,400

American Wurlitzer 1100 multiselector jukebox, circa 1947, 4ft.10in. high. (Sotheby's Belgravia) $3,700 £1,600

Ami Continental jukebox in black and chrome finish, 5ft.4in. high.(Sotheby's Belgravia) $690 £300

Swiss 'bells and drum in sight' cylinder musical box, circa 1880, 23½in. wide. (Sotheby's Belgravia) $1,380 £600

Two singing birds in a brass cage. (T. Bannister & Co.) $670 £310

Tanzbaer roll playing concertina. (Christie's S. Kensington) $2,770 £1,200

English Melodia paper roll organette in transfer-printed oak case, circa 1880-1890, 40in. wide. (Sotheby's Belgravia) $230 £100

English barrel piano on wheelbarrow, with ten-tune movement, circa 1900. (Sotheby's Belgravia) $2,530 £1,100

American Wurlitzer 700 78rpm jukebox in cabinet by Paul Fuller, circa 1939, 4ft. high. (Sotheby's Belgravia) $2,760 £1,200

Late 19th century Continental polyphone sold with twenty-two of its original discs. (Sotheby King & Chasemore) $3,025 £1,400

Swiss enamel singing bird box. (Bonham's) $1,010 £500

Edison Fireside Phonograph, circa 1909, in oak case, sold with forty-three cylinders. (Manchester Auction Mart) $650 £300

Musical box by Nicole Freres, 55cm. long. (Sotheby King & Chasemore) $1,210 £560

Victorian rosewood musical box playing seven airs. (Green's) $1,410 £640

New Melba model de-luxe gramophone. (Christie's S. Kensington) $2,710 £1,200

Small late 19th century English barrel organ, playing ten hymns, 19in. high. (Sotheby's Belgravia) $1,265 £550

Italian violin by Stefano Scarampella, Mantua, 1914, length of back 14in. (Sotheby's)$7,006 £3,100

French violin by Honore Derazey, Mirecourt, length of back 14in., sold with four bows. (Sotheby's) $3,164 £1,400

French violin by Paul Bailly, Paris, 1885, length of back 14in., sold with silver mounted bow. (Sotheby's) $1,672 £740

French violin, labelled Vincent Panormo, Paris, 1746, length of back 14in. (Sotheby's)$1,695 £750

Rosewood clarinet with nickel keys, 25½in. long. (Christopher Sykes) $192 £85

Fine rosewood and nickel silver flute by Butler, London, 15in. long. (Christopher Sykes)$85 £38

Clarinet by Hawkes & Son, London, 26in. long. (Christopher Sykes) $168 £78

Fine 19th century rosewood and nickel silver flute, 26in. long. (Christopher Sykes) $196 £87

Composite violoncello labelled Antonius Hieronymus Fr. Amati Cremonen, 1660, length of back 29in. (Sotheby's)$3,616 £1,600

Bavarian violin by Sebastian Kloz, Mittenwald, 1753, length of back 14in. (Sotheby's) $2,736 £1,200

French violin by Charles J. B. Collin-Mezin, Paris, 1879, length of back 14in. (Sotheby's) $1,413 £620

Italian violin by Giovanni Batta Morassi, Cremona, length of back 14in. (Sotheby's)$3,390 £1,500

English viola by Richard Duke, London, sold with a nickel mounted bow, length of back 14¾in. (Sotheby's)$1,322 £580

English violin by George Craske, length of back 14¼in. (Sotheby's) $1,641 £720

Italian violin by J. M. Valenzano, Rome, 1800, length of back 14in. (Sotheby's) $2,034 £900

English violin by John Barrett, London, 1704, length of back 14in. (Sotheby's) $1,185 £520

Late 18th century boxwood and ivory flute by Wm. Henry Potter, London, circa 1770, 21¼in. long. (Christopher Sykes) $214 £95

Unusual finely carved double flute of olivewood, 13½in. long, circa 1820. (Christopher Sykes) $108 £48

Rare Heckelphone by William Heckel.(Sotheby's) $4,320 £2,000

Fine rosewood clarinet by Jerome Thibouville Lamy, circa 1860, 22½in. long. (Christopher Sykes) $196 £87

Italian violin by Rodolfo Fredi, Rome, 1920, length of back 14in. (Sotheby's) $2,736 £1,200

Bohemian violoncello by Johann Ulrich Eberle, Prague, 1746, length of back 29¾in. (Sotheby's) $2,964 £1,300

English violoncello by Thomas Kennedy, London, 1819, length of back 30in. (Sotheby's) $3,420 £1,500

Bavarian violin by Aegidius Kloz, Mittenwald, length of back 13¾in. (Sotheby's) $2,486 £1,100

Gold and tortoiseshell mounted violin bow by W. E. Hill & Sons, 54gm. (Sotheby's) $1,535 £700

French silver mounted violin bow, attributed to Vuillaume, 52gm. (Sotheby's) $2,300 £1,050

Fine eight-keyed ivory flute, circa 1845, unstamped, sounding length 22¾in. (Christie's) $1,435 £650

Late 18th century one-keyed ebony flute with ivory mounts, by Johann Gottlieb Freyer, Potsdam, 21¾in. (Sotheby's) $3,725 £1,700

Four-keyed boxwood flute by Clementi & Co., London, sounding length 21in. (Christie's) $265 £120

Six-keyed boxwood clarinet by C. Gerock, early 19th century, 26in. long. (Christie's) $440 £200

French viola by Nester Audinct, Paris, circa 1891, labelled, length of back 15¾in. (Sotheby's) $1,685 £740

17th century Chittara Battente. (Phillips) $2,235 £1,100

Italian violin by Dante Guastalla, Reggiolo, 1932, length of back 14in. (Sotheby's) $1,370 £600

Regency dital harp, lacquered with gilt badge, 35in. high. (Phillips)$770 £340

Brass military trumpet, circa 1870, 17in. long. (Christopher Sykes) $110 £50

Rare Italian leather covered wooden tenor horn, late 16th century. (Phillips) $7,750 £3,400

Gold mounted violin bow by Percival Wilfred Bryant, London, 60gm. (Sotheby's) $2,015 £920

Silver mounted violin bow by Jas. Tubbs, London, 57gm. (Sotheby's) $1,100 £500

Late 18th century two-keyed stained boxwood oboe by Thos. Cahusac, London, 22¾in. (Sotheby's) $1,535 £700

One-keyed boxwood flute with ivory mounts by Cahusac, London, circa 1800, 20¾in. (Sotheby's) $330 £150

Silver and ivory mounted violin bow attributed to Xavier Tourte, 52gm. (Sotheby's) $1,750 £800

Silver mounted violin bow by Alfred Lamy, Paris, 52gm. (Sotheby's) $1,315 £600

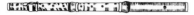

One-keyed boxwood flute with ivory mounts, by M. & H. Oppenheim, London, circa 1800, 20¾in. (Sotheby's) $790 £360

Late 18th century one-keyed boxwood flute by Thos. Cahusac, London, 53.2cm. (Sotheby's) $875 £400

Unusual carved double flute in olivewood, circa 1820. (Christopher Sykes) $110 £50

Czechoslovakian cornet in case, sold with sheet music. (Phillips) $80 £35

Violin by Regnier Stradivari. (Sotheby's) $207,360 £96,000

Rare dancing master's pochette by Robert Cuthbert, London, circa 1650. (Phillips) $1,985 £920

Italian viola by Enrico Politi, labelled, 1945, length of back 16¼in. (Christie's) $4,640 £2,100

Mandoline by Gaetano Figlio di Antonio Vinaccia, dated 1792. (Phillips) $935 £460

Silver bugle with single coil, St. Petersburg, circa 1905, 41cm. long. (Sotheby's) $2,165 £950

Rare Pekin glass flute (Dizi) of translucent milkwhite metal, 48.9cm. (Sotheby's) $910 £420

Violoncello bow by Louis Panormo, London, 73gm. (Sotheby's) $745 £340

Silver mounted violoncello bow, stamped Dodd, 78gm. (Sotheby's) $2,520 £1,150

Fine six-keyed boxwood flute by William Milhouse, London, 23¼in. long. (Christie's) $530 £240

Japanese koto, decorated in gold takamakie, of thirteen strings, the bridges absent, circa 1900. (Sotheby's Belgravia) $505 £220

NETSUKE

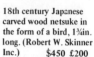

Ivory netsuke of three rats in a basket, signed Ikko. (Christie's S. Kensington) $675 £300

Good ivory netsuke of a reclining goat, with inlaid eyes, Kyoto School, unsigned, late 18th century. (Sotheby's) $1,985 £870

Spirited ivory netsuke of a priest pursuing an oni, unsigned, early 19th century. (Sotheby's) $340 £150

18th century Japanese carved wood netsuke in the form of a bird, 1¾in. long. (Robert W. Skinner Inc.) $450 £200

Ivory netsuke of Kanzan and Jittoku holding a calligraphic scroll, unsigned, early 19th century. (Sotheby's) $390 £170

Goat netsuke by Tomotada. (Sotheby's) $3,650 £1,600

Good okimono style wood netsuke of a monkey tying a rope round a turtle, signed Shomin, Nagoya School. (Sotheby's) $910 £400

Very good and attractive ivory netsuke of a monkey, stained, eyes inlaid in horn, unsigned, early 19th century. (Sotheby's) $960 £420

Wood netsuke of nine masks, some eyes inlaid with ivory, signed Gyokkei, Edo School. (Sotheby's) $480 £210

Wood netsuke of a professional sneezer holding an ivory tickling stick, signed Hokei, Edo School. (Sotheby's) $460 £200

Very good wood netsuke of a reclining stallion, signed Ikko, Nagoya School. (Sotheby's) $1,415 £620

Unusual wood netsuke of an actor with wicker basket containing four masks, each of which fit his face, unsigned, Edo School, 19th century. (Sotheby's) $955 £420

Late 19th century ivory netsuke showing a small boy dressing up. (Christie's) $9,000 £4,200

Fine two part ivory maju netsuke, partly inlaid, signed Kikugawa Saku, Edo School. (Sotheby's) $1,550 £680

Ivory netsuke of a boy trying to climb the Pillar of Nara, signed Karaku, Osaka School. (Sotheby's)$390 £170

Good okimono style ivory netsuke, signed on a red lacquer tablet, Sho, Edo School, late 19th century. (Sotheby's) $1,140 £500

Good and rare ivory netsuke of a tiger and two foxes, stained, unsigned, mid 19th century. (Sotheby's) $1,050 £460

Wood netsuke of a grinning demon mask, boldly carved, unsigned, Edo School, 19th century. (Sotheby's) $275 £120

Good ivory netsuke of a rat on a candle, eyes and candle wick inlaid, unsigned, late 18th century. (Sotheby's) $915 £400

Very good and rare ivory netsuke of a goat, signed Tomochika, Osaka School. (Sotheby's) $1,600 £700

Rare wood and ivory netsuke of a wide hat, showing blind man and long-tongued demon, signed Toun. (Sotheby's) $1,140 £500

Wood netsuke of a man resting, late 19th century, by Ryukei. (Sotheby's Belgravia) $635 £310

Good ivory manju netsuke with sunken panel, carved to show a portrait of Emma-o, signed Gyokuyosai. (Sotheby's) $205 £90

Ivory netsuke of a fishergirl and octopus, lightly stained, eyes inlaid, signed Gyoku, Edo School. (Sotheby's) $480 £210

Fine ivory netsuke of partly burnt chestnut naturalistically stained, signed Ryokusan, contemporary. (Sotheby's) $590 £260

Rare okimono style netsuke of an oni holding a basket, lacquer, ivory and gilt metal, signed Hosai. (Sotheby's) $2,170 £950

Stained wood netsuke of nine comic and dramatic masks, well carved, unsigned, Edo School, 19th century. (Sotheby's) $460 £200

Rare wood and ivory netsuke of Daruma, the robe inlaid with ivory, metal and horn, signed Jugyoku, Edo School. (Sotheby's) $3,300 £1,450

Fine small ivory netsuke of two rabbits with inlaid eyes, School of Hogen Rantei, inscribed Rantei. (Sotheby's) $6,840 £3,000

Fine ivory netsuke of a tigress and three cubs, lightly stained, inlaid eyes, signed Hakuryu, Kyoto School. (Sotheby's) $5,930 £2,600

Fine wood netsuke of a snail emerging from its shell, signed Kokei, Nagoya School. (Sotheby's) $1,390 £610

Good small ivory netsuke of a blind ama struggling to lift a stone, signed Tadatsugu, early 19th century. (Sotheby's) $410 £180

Good and rare ivory netsuke of a mountain cat, with inlaid eye pupils, Kyoto School, unsigned, late 18th or early 19th century. (Sotheby's) $1,255 £550

Large wood netsuke of a dried fish, unsigned, 19th century. (Sotheby's) $660 £290

Finely detailed staghorn netsuke of a bat, unsigned, attributed to Hoshunsai Masayuki, Asakusa School. (Sotheby's) $2,280 £1,000

Marine ivory netsuke of seven masks, engraved and stained detail, signed Kikugawa, Tokyo School, mid 19th century. (Christie's) $490 £220

Early 19th century wood netsuke group, unsigned. (Sotheby King & Chasemore) $360 £160

19th century Shibuichi Kagamibuta netsuke showing Hotei and Fukurokuju, unsigned. (Sotheby's) $255 £110

Well painted mid 19th century netsuke of Fukurojuku, signed Hidechika. (Christie's) $775 £340

Mid 19th century pierced ivory manju, unsigned. (Sotheby King & Chasemore) $450 £200

Rare early ivory netsuke of a Dutchman blowing a trumpet or clarinet, unsigned, 18th century. (Sotheby's) $1,000 £440

Fine ivory netsuke of seven masks, stained red and black and engraved, signed Tadachika, Tokyo School, late 19th century. (Christie's) $540 £240

Unsigned ivory netsuke of a Dutchman holding a cockerel, slightly damaged, late 18th or early 19th century. (Christie's) $715 £320

Finely carved ivory manju netsuke of Seiobo holding a fan, signed Kogetsu, 19th century. (Christie's) $1,455 £650

Ivory netsuke of a Sarumawashi seated on a log, a monkey at his side, engraved and stained brown, signed Yoshiyuki, late 19th century. (Christie's) $630 £280

Boldly carved boxwood netsuke of two wrestlers with inlaid horn eyes, unsigned, 19th century. (Christie's) $1,075 £480

Ivory and wood netsuke of Hotei, signed in seal 'from Meikeisai'. (Phillips) $1,675 £780

Ivory netsuke of a monkey seated among three mushrooms, signed Hompu, early 19th century. (Christie's) $1,010 £450

Late 19th century ivory netsuke of an Oni crouching on a Vajra, signed Hideyuki. (Christie's) $660 £290

18th century Japanese carved wood netsuke, 2in. diam. (Robert W. Skinner Inc.) $375 £70

Good small late 18th century ivory netsuke of a Shishi, unsigned. (Sotheby's) $1,010 £440

Small ivory netsuke of a goat and kid, slightly damaged, signed Tomokazu. (Sotheby's) $1,000 £440

Late 18th century netsuke of a Shishimai dancer, unsigned. (Sotheby's) $645 £280

Unusual 19th century Kagamibuta netsuke showing a peasant and a flying bird, unsigned. (Sotheby's) $440 £190

Mid 19th century ivory netsuke of Gentoku riding the river, unsigned. (Sotheby's) $510 £220

Good late 18th century netsuke group of a Shishi and cub, unsigned. (Sotheby's) $690 £300

Fine stag antler netsuke of bamboo with loose monkey hanging onto one stem, signed Masayuki, Asakusa School, 19th century. (Christie's) $3,360 £1,500

Ivory netsuke of eight masks, engraved and stained red and black, signed Zemin, Tokyo School, 19th century. (Christie's) $715 £320

Ivory netsuke of a snail on a lotus leaf, engraved and stained, slightly damaged, signed Mitsuharu, Kyoto School, 19th century. (Christie's) $380 £170

Ivory netsuke of Shoki and Oni, in the style of Yoshinaga, Kyoto School, unsigned, 18th century. (Sotheby's) $1,185 £520

Rare ivory netsuke group of two toads fighting, by Kiyozumi. (Sotheby's) $600 £260

Small 19th century Kagamibuta netsuke, unsigned. (Sotheby's) $205 £90

Late 18th century ivory netsuke of a Karashishi and cub, unsigned. (Christie's) $775 £340

19th century ivory netsuke of two quail on a millet spray, signed Okatomo. (Christie's) $775 £340

Miniature ribbed pewter chamberstick with bowl shaped drip pan, 2½in. (Robert W. Skinner Inc.) $50 £25

WMF pewter and bronze centrepiece, circa 1900, 25cm. wide. (Sotheby's Belgravia) $645 £280

One of a pair of antique pewter beakers, circa 1820, 4in. high. (Christopher Sykes) $155 £70

Rare Charles II broad rimmed pewter charger, 23½in. diam. (Hy. Duke & Son) $1,525 £680

Unusual German tapered pewter beaker with rococo decoration, circa 1893, 5in. high. (Christopher Sykes) $40 £20

Pewter plate, circa 1790, with touchmarks of a small crowned X, a thistle and a decorative cartouche, 9¾in. diam. (Christopher Sykes) $80 £35

Fine Queen Anne pewter mace and stand, circa 1700, 27in. high. (Christopher Sykes) $620 £275

Large WMF pewter centrepiece, circa 1900, 70cm. high. (Sotheby's Belgravia) $345 £150

WMF pewter mounted green glass claret jug, circa 1900, 41.5cm. high. (Sotheby's Belgravia) $525 £240

18th century Continental pewter plate, 9½in. diam. (Christopher Sykes) $110 £50

Late 18th century Scottish uncrested tappit hen measure, 11in. high. (Christie's) $905 £400

Fine 18th century pewter plate by Joseph and James Speckman, London, 1782, 9¼in. diam. (Christopher Sykes) $130 £55

Miniature pewter chamberstick, 2in. high. (Robert W. Skinner Inc.) $350 £160

Early 19th century pewter half pint tankard in the shape of a tulip. (Christopher Sykes) $65 £30

WMF silvered metal jardiniere with glass liner, circa 1900, 49cm. wide. (Sotheby's Belgravia) $1,015 £440

WMF pewter tazza, circa 1900, 21cm. high. (Sotheby's Belgravia) $700 £320

Mid 18th century pewter candlestick with baluster shaped stem, 6¾in. (Robert W. Skinner Inc.) $110 £50

WMF polished metal centrepiece, circa 1900, 25cm. wide. (Sotheby's Belgravia) $480 £220

Antique pewter belly measure, circa 1820, stamped 'Pint', 5¼in. high. (Christopher Sykes) $125 £55

An unusual pair of 17th century Chinese pewter figures depicting the Hehe Erxian, 8½in. high. (Sotheby's) $1,250 £560

19th century tulip shaped pewter tankard, stamped 'Imperial Pint', circa 1840. (Christopher Sykes) $85 £40

19th century pewter half pint ale tankard, circa 1830, with fish-tail handle. (Christopher Sykes) $80 £35

One of a very fine pair of pewter plates, circa 1720, 9in. diam. (Christopher Sykes) $225 £100

19th century pewter mounted heavy glass jug, 10in. high. (Alfie's Antique Market) $125 £55

William III pewter wrigglework portrait plate, circa 1694-1702. 8½in. diam. (Phillips) $945 £420

Early 18th century two-handled porringer and cover, pewter, 5½in. diam. (Christie's) $3,995 £1,950

One of two pewter chargers by John Home, London, 16½in. diam. (Geering & Colyer) $460 £205

Scottish pewter tappit hen measure, circa 1800, 11in. high overall. (Sotheby's) $800 £370

George III pewter dish with reeded rim, London touchmark, 11.5cm. diam. (Phillips) $15 £8

Fine James I pewter flagon, 15in. high, circa 1610-20. (Sotheby's) $3,690 £1,700

Early 18th century Swiss pewter flagon by Bernard Wick, Basle, 29cm. high. (Sotheby's) $1,520 £700

Octagonal pewter plate in Art Nouveau style, with Tudric hot water jug. (Phillips) $75 £40

Late 17th century relief cast pewter allegorical tankard, 18.3cm. high. (Sotheby's) $1,300 £600

North German pewter guild tankard, 22.3cm. high overall. (Sotheby's) $1,560 £720

One of two 18th century pewter chargers, 15in. diam. (Geering & Colyer) $325 £145

Late 18th century Normandy pewter flagon, 24.5cm. high. (Sotheby's) $1,260 £580

William Brownfield blue glazed
jug with pewter lid, 1868.
(Alfie's Antique Market)$70 £30

18th century pewter inkstand, 9½in. wide.
(Hy. Duke & Son) $710 £330

White metal watch holder in
the Art Nouveau style, 13.5cm.
high. (Phillips) $16 £8

18th century style pewter tappit
hen measure, 14in. high.
(Phillips) $60 £30

'Rare Charles II wrigglework pewter dish,
18¾in. diam., circa 1664. (Sotheby's)
$4,340 £2,000

Good Bernese pewter spouted
wine flagon by Abraham
Ganting, circa 1741, 31cm.
high. (Sotheby's)$4,340 £2,000

Mid 18th century Guernsey pewter pot flagon by Joseph Wingod,
29cm. high. (Sotheby's)
$870 £400

19th century pewter ale tankard, circa
1835. (Christopher Sykes) $85 £40

Scottish pewter crested tappit
hen measure, circa 1880,
12in. high. (Sotheby's)
$825 £380

Very fine pewter covered china
jug by E. Ridgway and Abington
Hanley, dated 1855. (Alfie's
Antique Market) $85 £35

Saxon pretzel baker's guild plate in pewter
by Daniel Gottlob Reinhard, circa 1800,
25cm. diam. (Sotheby's) $1,260 £580

Tudric coffee pot by A. Knox.
(Alfie's Antique Market)
$205 £90

Victorian quart tankard of baluster form with scroll handle and spout, 6½in. high. (Vernon's) $100 £45

Liberty pewter and enamel tobacco box set with blue green enamel cabochons, 4¾in. high. (Vernon's) $250 £110

William III wrigglework pewter tankard, circa 1695, 6½in. high. (Sotheby's) $3,940 £1,750

One of a set of ten wavy-edged pewter plates by Joseph Spackman, London, 9¾in. diam., circa 1760-80. (Sotheby's) $2,140 £950

Swiss pewter Stegkanne with baluster body engraved with flowers, 19th century, 12½in. high. (Christie's) $1,100 £500

Rare twelve-sided pewter dish by Jonas Durrand, Jnr., mid 18th century, 16in. wide. (Sotheby's) $720 £320

Early 18th century English pewter pint measure of 'bud' type, 6in. high. (Christie's) $370 £160

One of a very fine set of six Charles II broad-rimmed plates by William Matthews, London, circa 1675, 9½in. diam. (Sotheby's) $3,615 £1,600

Large 19th century Scottish lidded measure with thumbpiece. (Vernon's) $170 £75

17th century Dutch pewter chandelier with multi-baluster stem, 24in. high. (Christie's) $5,520 £2,400

19th century Swiss pewter Stegkanne with scroll handle, 12½in. high. (Christie's) $840 £380

Rare Charles II candlestick, dated 1670, 7½in. high. (Sotheby's) $5,850 £2,600

Victorian Britannia metal biscuit box on shaped feet. (Vernon's) $63 £28

Early 18th century pewter porringer with domed and footed lid, 8½in. wide. (Christie's)$680 £310

Office ashtray in white metal silver plated, 5in. diam., circa 1900. (Christopher Sykes) $40 £20

James I relief cast wine cup in pewter, 6in. high, circa 1616. (Sotheby's) $9,450 £4,200

Very rare tavern mug in pewter, 4in. high, circa 1690-1700. (Sotheby's)$1,460 £650

William III pewter candlestick, 6½in. high, circa 1690-1700. (Sotheby's) $1,170 £520

18th century pewter flagon with reeded bands and double scroll handle, 13in. high. (Geering & Colyer) $775 £340

WMF pewter liqueur set, 37cm. high, circa 1900. (Sotheby's Belgravia) $450 £200

Early Georgian wrigglework pewter tankard with cover, 7¼in. high, circa 1720. (Sotheby's) $945 £420

Late 18th century Swiss Stegkanne with scroll handle and double volute thumbpiece, 12½in. high.(Christie's) $1,630 £700

Early 18th century pewter charger with moulded rim, 16½in. wide, French. (Christie's) $880 £400

18th/19th century Jersey pewter measure. (Parsons, Welch & Cowell) $530 £230

Late 18th century pewter tankard with scroll handle. (Vernon's) $95 £45

Louis XV decorated pewter porringer and cover, circa 1740-50, 32.3cm. diam. (Sotheby's) $920 £410

Late 17th century Stuart lidless tavern pot, 6in. high. (Sotheby's) $3,840 £1,700

Fine Stuart pewter wrigglework tankard by R. S., 6¾in. high, circa 1675-80. (Sotheby's) $4,050 £1,800

French pewter wall cistern and bowl, dated 1771, by N. J. Schwaller, Lyons. (Sotheby's) $2,165 £950

18th century Swiss pewter tankard by Abraham Hiller, St. Gallen, 19cm. high. (Sotheby's) $675 £300

A W. M. F. plated toilet mirror modelled as a standing girl, 51cm. high. (Christie's) $900 £420

One of a set of three white metal wall scones with five scrolling candle arms, early 20th century. (Sotheby's Belgravia) $475 £210

One of a pair of W. M. F. plated candlesticks on high domed feet, 27.5cm. high. (Christie's) $200 £95

One of a pair of German pricket candleholders, late 17th century, by S. S., Cologne, 24.5cm. high. (Sotheby's) $1,170 £520

18th century Channel Islands pewter litre flagon, 10¾in. high. (Christie's) $815 £360

German guild tankard, circa 1800, 29.2cm. high overall. (Sotheby's) $1,010 £450

Dutch square piano by C. Kadel, Amsterdam, circa 1815, 166.4cm. long. (Sotheby's) $1,640 £750

Victorian rosewood three-quarter grand piano by C. Bechstein, in superb condition. (Frank H. Fellows) $2,710 £1,200

Good square piano by John Broadwood & Sons, London, in mahogany case, circa 1820, 173.3cm. long. (Sotheby's) $1,800 £820

Fine and imposing half grand piano by J. & J. Hopkinson, London, circa 1890. (Messenger May & Baverstock) $17,050 £8,400

Grand pianoforte by John Broadwood & Sons, London, circa 1815, 248.3cm. long. (Sotheby's) $3,950 £1,800

Upright lacquered piano by Spencer, London, in gold Oriental panels and with matching stool.(Worsfolds) $430 £210

Lyraflugel by F. N. Klein, Berlin, circa 1840, 6ft.10in. high. (Sotheby's) $6,570 £3,000

Unusual pianoforte in the form of a sofa table, by John Broadwood & Son, London, 1803, 154.3cm. long. (Sotheby's) $10,000 £4,600

Very rare and important 'Portable Grand Pianoforte' by John Isaac Hawkins, London, circa 1803, 139.1cm. high.(Sotheby's) $16,200 £7,400

Grand piano by Bechstein, circa 1914. (Christie's) $47,740 £22,000

Boudoir grand piano by C. Bechstein, dated 1908. (Hobbs Parker) $3,755 £1,850

Victorian rosewood framed upright pianoforte with brass candle sconces. (Vernon's) $225 £100

Square piano by Johannes Zumpe and Gabriel Buntebart, London, 1770, 4ft. 2½in. long. (Sotheby's) $785 £350

Semi-concert grand pianoforte by Bechstein in cream coloured case. (Christie's) $16,850 £7,800

Square piano by John and Archibald Watsons, Edinburgh, late 18th century, 5ft.3½in. long. (Sotheby's) $630 £280

Fine double-manual harpsichord by William Foster and Edward Fuller, length of case 89in. (Christie's) $5,980 £2,600

Conductor's piano by John Broadwood & Sons, London, circa 1815, 92.1cm. long. (Sotheby's) $2,735 £1,250

Fine two-manual harpsichord by Joseph Kirkman, London, 1798, width 3ft.3½in. (Sotheby's) $39,375 £17,500

Square piano by Longman and Broderip, London, circa 1790, 4ft.10¾in. long. (Sotheby's) $2,025 £900

Parcel gilt and walnut boudoir grand piano by Richard Lipp & Sohn, Stuttgart, circa 1930, 59in. wide. (Sotheby's Belgravia)$4,490 £1,950

Rare mid 17th century Flemish virginals by Cornelius Hagaerts, Antwerp, 4ft.9in. long, on later stand. (Sotheby's) $31,500 £14,000

Grand pianoforte by John Broadwood & Sons, London 1810, 245.6cm. long. (Sotheby's) $2,300 £1,050

Fine Viennese pianoforte by Josef Bohm, circa 1810-15, length of case 88½in. (Christie's) $3,680 £1,600

Grand pianoforte by Joseph Kirkman, London, circa 1800, 227.3cm. long. (Sotheby's) $5,900 £2,700

Eskimo ivory pipe, carved with figures of seals in red and black pigment, 6½in. long. (Sotheby's) $520 £240

Meerschaum pipe of Cecil Rhodes. (Alfie's Antique Market) $430 £165

Eskimo ivory pipe of curving form, 11¾in. long, decorated with red and black pigment. (Sotheby's) $735 £340

Rare Easter Island wood pipe, the bowl carved as a human head, 7¼in. long. (Christie's) $750 £340

Chinese cloisonne opium pipe, circa 1860. (Alfie's Antique Market) $395 £175

18th century wooden pipe with horn and copper lid, 8in. long. (Gray's Antique Market) $215 £95

Late 19th century Meerschaum pipe. (Sotheby's) $370 £165

Late 19th/early 20th century Austrian Meerschaum pipe, 31cm. long. (Sotheby's Belgravia) $950 £420

Meerschaum pipe in case, circa 1880. (Alfie's Antique Market) $240 £110

19th century Oriental pipe. (Phillips) $15 £5

Teke ceremonial pipe with faceted ivory stem and wood bowl, 13in. long. (Sotheby's) $650 £300

German porcelain pipe bowl. (Christie's S. Kensington) $315 £140

Tabriz rug with ivory field, Benlian signature at the corner, 6ft. 7in. x 4ft.7in., circa 1930. (Sotheby's) $2,387 £1,100

Natanz Kashan part silk rug, circa 1930, 6ft.10in. x 4ft.4in., in good condition. (Sotheby's) $3,580 £1,650

Kayseri carpet in silk, 300 x 200cm. (Leys, Antwerp) $15,230 £7,050

Late 19th century Kashan carpet in silk, 316 x 206cm. (Leys, Antwerp) $11,075 £5,125

Carpet designed by Charles Rennie Mackintosh, circa 1902-04, 201 x 271cm. (Sotheby's Belgravia) $925 £400

Yomud Asmalyk rug with attached wool tassels, 3ft.7in. x 2ft. (Robert W. Skinner Inc.) $350 £150

One of a pair of Tabriz rugs, circa 1930, 6ft.3in. x 4ft.6in. (Sotheby's) $2,260 £1,000

Bidjar carpet in tones of rose, celadon and beige, 129 x 89in. (Hy. Duke & Son) $2,912 £1,300

Caucasian rug with dark blue centre field, 4ft.4in. x 3ft.4in. (Robert W. Skinner Inc.) $325 £142

Kazak Oriental rug in red, blue and white, 91½ x 56½in. (Robert W. Skinner Inc.) $3,000 £1,350

Lenkoran Kazak rug, circa 1920, 10ft.8in. x 3ft. 10in. (Sotheby's) $2,500 £1,100

Fine quality Daghestan
rug of prayer design.
(Sotheby Humberts)
$907 £420

One of a pair of fine
Kashan rugs. (Mess-
enger May & Baver-
stock) $1,583 £780

Bokhara carpet, central
reserve formed by six
lines of elephants,
317 x 215cm. (May,
Whetter & Grose)
$1,555 £720

Pakistan Bokhara rug
with crimson ground,
175 x 127cm.
(Phillips) $225 £110

19th century Trans-Caucasian
Kuba Oriental rug, 5ft.5in. x
3ft.6in. (Robert W. Skinner
Inc.) $1,000 £450

Rare Yomut Azmalik rug, 4ft.2in. x 3ft.11in.
(Sotheby's) $13,390 £6,200

Kazak rug, 7ft.4in. x 6ft.2in.
(Woolley & Wallis)
$565 £250

Kashan raised silk prayer
rug, circa 1920, 6ft.5in.
x 4ft.4in. (Sotheby's)
$678 £300

Chinese carpet in good
condition, circa 1920,
9ft. x 6ft.3in.
(Sotheby's)
$1,401 £620

Persian Oriental rug with
central blue field, 81 x
53in. (Robert W. Skinner
Inc.) $2,300 £1,045

Sarouk Oriental rug
with large central
medallion in red, 87
x 53in. (Robert W.
Skinner Inc.)
$2,000 £900

Fine Isfahan carpet with leafy sprays, in good condition, 14ft.4in. x 10ft.7in. (Christie's) $6,050 £2,800

Chondzoresk Kazak rug with cloudband medallions on a madder field, circa 1890, 7ft.10in. x 3ft.11in. (Sotheby's) $4,200 £1,900

Silk Qum rug with birds on branches on an ivory field, 9ft.6in. x 5ft.9in. (Christie's) $8,640 £4,000

Fine Senna rug with blood-red flower heads on a yellow ground, 6ft.5in. x 4ft.6in. (Christie's) $9,075 £4,200

Akstafa Gelim with medallions, peacocks and animals on a madder field, circa 1930, 6ft.8in. x 4ft.9in. (Sotheby's) $775 £350

Fine Yomut carpet with hooked medallions on a nut brown field, 10ft. x 5ft.8in. (Christie's) $3,240 £1,500

Rare Betzellil rug, woven in Jerusalem, in fair condition, circa 1880, 2ft. 7in. x 5ft.2in. (Sotheby's)$1,260 £580

Antique Kashan carpet with vines, willows and bees on an ivory ground, circa 1860, 13ft.9in. x 9ft.8in. (Sotheby's)$10,650 £4,800

Fine Afshar rug with floral sprays on a blood-red field, 6ft.11in. x 5ft. 11in. (Christie's) $1,620 £750

North-West Persian Gelim with bands of guls, circa 1900, 8ft.9in. x 6ft.6in. (Sotheby's) $665 £300

Bergama prayer rug with madder Mehrab, circa 1870, 4ft. x 3ft. (Sotheby's)$775 £350

Fine Kersehir prayer rug with trees and houses on a magenta field, 5ft.6in. x 3ft. 8in. (Christie's) $1,800 £800

Unusual Shirvan pictorial rug with human figures and birds on a red field, 5ft.6in. x 4ft.1in. (Christie's)$4,100 £1,900

North-West Persian rug with Leshgi medallions on a dark blue field, 4ft.9in. x 3ft.11in. (Christie's) $5,185 £2,400

Shiraz Gelim with guls on a panelled field, 8ft. 6in. x 5ft.2in. (Sotheby's)$840 £380

Fine antique Kouba rug with flower heads on a blood-red field, 4ft.8in. x 4ft.1in. (Christie's) $5,620 £2,600

Tabriz rug with animals and foliage on a tan field, 7ft. 5in. x 4ft.5in. (Christie's) $1,620 £750

Fine Serapi runner with five medallions on a camel field, circa 1860, 9ft. x 3ft.4in. (Sotheby's) $1,285 £580

Fine Senna rug with flowering plants on an ivory field, 6ft.8in. x 3ft.9in. (Christie's) $1,190 £800

North-West Persian Kurdish rug with Chelaberd design, circa 1920, 6ft.8in. x 5ft. 3in. (Sotheby's) $1,100 £500

Shirvan Caucasian rug with blue field, 4ft.11in. x 3ft. 1in. (Christie's) $1,300 £600

Fine Kirman portrait relief mat depicting Ahmad Shah, 2ft.7in. x 2ft. (Christie's) $1,300 £600

Fine Central Persian rug with foliage on a rust-red ground, 6ft.11in. x 5ft. 11in. (Christie's) $12,950 £6,000

South Caucasian Gelim with bands of hooked guls, circa 1900, 10ft. 8in. x 6ft.10in. (Sotheby's) $1,550 £700

RUGS

Daghestan rug with trelliswork on an ivory field, circa 1920, 4ft.4in. x 3ft.6in.(Sotheby's) $785 £360

Ghom part silk rug with indigo field, circa 1930, 7ft.6in. x 4ft.7in. (Sotheby's) $5,650 £2,600

Mohtashan Kashan rug with ivory field, circa 1910, 6ft.10in. x 4ft. 5in. (Sotheby's) $2,500 £1,150

Kersehir prayer rug in fair condition, circa 1920, 6ft.2in. x 4ft.3in. (Sotheby's) $700 £320

Shirvan marasali rug, circa 1890-1900, 5ft.4in. x 4ft.5in. (Sotheby King & Chasemore) $3,350 £1,450

Karabagh runner with cherry red field, 11ft. x 3ft.8in., circa 1930. (Sotheby King & Chasemore) $1,295 £560

Persian rug with ivory field, 153cm. x 107cm. (Phillips) $925 £400

Malayer rug with guls and trees on an indigo field, circa 1900, 5ft.4in. x 3ft.6in. (Sotheby's) $650 £300

Rare Royal Hereke silk rug of hunting design, 6ft.1in. x 4ft.4in. (Sotheby King & Chasemore) $18,145 £8,400

Shirvan rug. (Woolley & Wallis)$1,610 £750

Chichaona North African carpet, circa 1930, 9ft.4in. x 6ft.9in. (Sotheby's) $1,410 £650

Fine Tekke Turkman rug with guls on a madder field, circa 1920, 4ft.8in. x 3ft.4in. (Sotheby's) $785 £360

Sampler worked with a house and a verse by Maria Norman, 1832, 16 x 12in. (Hy. Duke & Son) $265 £130

Child's sampler in good condition, 1819. (Manchester Auction Mart) $365 £170

Sampler worked with a house by Caroline Laverstock, 1838, 16 x 11½in. (Hy. Duke & Son) $90 £45

Sampler worked with a verse by Rachel Hill, 1763, 17 x 12in. (Hy. Duke & Son) $265 £130

Late 17th century border-band sampler of bright colouring, 15in. long. (Sotheby's) $495 £230

Sampler by Elizabeth Brook, 1813, 15 x 11½in. (Hy. Duke & Son) $145 £70

SEALS

Very large 18ct. stone set revolving fob seal. (Frank H. Fellows) $305 £135

Brass seal from the Hollandia. (W.H. Lane & Son) $405 £175

Queen Anne seal in gold and gilt. (Alfie's Antique Market) $415 £185

Italian silver and parcel gilt desk seal, 4in. high. (Phillips) $150 £65

Victorian silver sealing set, 1883, 4½in. high. (Sotheby Humberts) $800 £390

Art Nouveau gilt bronze seal, 8.3cm. high, circa 1900. (Sotheby's Belgravia) $395 £180

Shibayama style inlaid silver vessel with dragon feet and handles.
(Phillips) $10,320 £4,800

19th century Japanese Shibayama and ivory brush pot, 5in. high. (Olivers)
$420 £185

One of a pair of Japanese Masayasu Shibayama vases, circa 1900.
(Sotheby's Belgravia) $9,070 £4,200

SIGNS

Chromium plated and enamelled Brooklands Aero Club badge.
(Christie's S. Kensington)
$510 £250

19th century Victorian butcher's shop sign of a carved bull's head, 13in. high, made of oak.
(Christopher Sykes) $645 £285

Fine carved shop sign with original gilt and polychrome colouring, circa 1860, 22in. high. (Christopher Sykes) $620 £285

Etched glass chemist's sign, circa 1870, 40cm. wide. (Christopher Sykes) $215 £95

Sheet metal eagle sign, 42½in. high. (Christopher Sykes)
$160 £75

American kettle advertising sign in metal with iron handle, 22½in. high.
(Robert W. Skinner Inc.)$500 £220

Old English double sided inn sign, 4ft.8½in. high. (Christopher Sykes) $205 £95

Unusual advertising sign for Stephen's Ink, by Jordan-Belston, with domed top 60 x 12in. (Bonham's)$405 £180

Old hand-painted pub sign 'The Bell', on solid wood frame, 34in. wide.
(Christopher Sykes) $215 £95

Enamelled sign advertising Nile Spinning & Doubling Co. Ltd., by Wildman & McGuyer Ltd., Birmingham, 24 x 36in. (Bonham's) $135 £60

Unusual embossed sheet copper insurance firemark from Australia, 8½in. high. (Christopher Sykes) $110 £50

Shaped, printed and enamelled sign for Depot for Oceanic Footwear, 13 x 19in. (Bonham's) $190 £85

Enamelled advertising sign for Spa by Email Belg, 27 x 8½in. (Bonham's) $125 £55

Enamelled sign for Fry's Chocolate by Chromo, Wolverhampton, 30 x 36in. (Bonham's) $765 £340

Enamelled advertising sign for Nut Brown Tobacco in black and white on a red ground, 22½ x 7½in. (Bonham's) $95 £40

Enamelled sign advertising Puritan Soap, on a yellow ground, 24 x 36in. (Bonham's) $235 £105

Enamelled sign advertising Robin Starch, 35½ x 29½in. (Bonham's) $360 £160

Pub mirror with red and gilt lettering in original moulded plaster frame, 26½ x 35in. (Bonham's) $450 £200

Enamelled advertising sign for Strange's A-1 Crystal Oil by Chromo, Wolverhampton, 42 x 20in. (Bonham's) $425 £190

Enamelled sign of an elf in red costume, 30 x 24in. (Bonham's) $180 £80

Enamelled sign advertising Cooper's Sheep Dipping Powder, in the form of a playing card, 30 x 20in. (Bonham's) $585 £260

BASKETS

George III shaped oval cake basket by Alexander Gairdner, Edinburgh, 1778, 14in. wide, 26oz.17dwt. (Sotheby's)
$1,125 £520

Silver gilt fruit basket by Paul Storr. (Bonham's) $5,650 £2,500

George III boat shaped sugar basket, London, 1790, 5oz. (Geering & Colyer) $810 £360

George III boat shaped sweetmeat basket by William Stephenson, London 1782, 6in. wide, 9oz.5dwt. (Sotheby's)
$1,135 £500

George III oblong cake basket by P. & W. Bateman, London, 1811, 13¾in. wide, 35oz.13dwt. (Sotheby's) $2,130 £950

Small George III basket by Hester Bateman, London, 1789, 3in. wide. (Sotheby's)
$760 £340

Henry Wilkinson & Co., shaped circular cake basket, Sheffield, 1844, 612gm., 22.5cm. high. (Sotheby's Belgravia) $480 £230

George III fluted oval cake basket by Solomon Hougham, London, 1803, 14in. long, 27oz.3dwt. (Sotheby's) $1,680 £750

George III boat shaped sweetmeat basket by Hester Bateman, London, 1786, 6¾in. long, 6oz.8dwt. (Sotheby's) $1,475 £650

William IV cake basket by E.E.J. & W. Barnard, London, 1830, 12½in. diam., 47oz.16dwt. (Sotheby's)
$2,060 £920

George III boat shaped silver sweetmeat basket by Peter Podie, London, 1792, 6½oz. (Gray's Antique Mews)
$670 £295

Circular silver basket-weave cakebasket by Howard & Hawksworth, Sheffield, 1856, 1,310gm. (Sotheby's Belgravia) $2,240 £1,000

One of four George III boat shaped sweetmeat baskets by Henry Chawner, 1794, 5½in. long, 16oz.19dwt. (Christie's) $4,640 £2,100

Victorian silver plated cake or fruit basket by Philip Ashberry & Sons, Sheffield, circa 1865. (Alfie's Antique Market) $105 £50

George II oval dessert basket by Robert Brown, London, 1742, 13½in. long, 52oz.1dwt. (Sotheby's) $3,470 £1,550

George II shaped oval cake basket by Edward Wakelin, London, 1752, 15in. wide, 58oz.8dwt. (Sotheby's) $11,200 £5,000

George III oval cake basket by Charles Aldridge and Henry Green, London, 1770, 13½in. long, 26oz.8dwt. (Sotheby's) $2,415 £1,050

Albert Henry Thomson shaped circular cake basket, Sheffield 1892, 26.5cm. diam. 725gm. (Sotheby's Belgravia) $395 £190

Silver pierced boat shaped cake basket in 18th century style, by Walker and Hall, Sheffield, 1906, 856gm. (Sotheby's Belgravia) $940 £420

George III shaped oval cake basket by Emick Romer, 1767, 26oz.14¼in. long. (Christie's) $2,925 £1,300

George III oval cake basket, London, 1802, 14¼in. long, 44oz.2dwt. (Sotheby's Belgravia) $2,495 £1,100

George II shaped oval cake basket by S. Herbert & Co., 1752, 14in. long, 57oz. (Christie's) $5,195 £2,300

Silver cake basket by Paul de Lamerie, 1731. (Christie's) $62,640 £29,000

Sterling silver fruit basket with cast handle, 13½in. wide. (Robert W. Skinner Inc.) $525 £240

BEAKERS

Swedish parcel gilt beaker by Elias Modin, Sundsvall, circa 1770, 7in. high, 14oz.5dwt. (Christie's) $2,520 £1,150

18th century German covered beaker, 6½in. high, circa 1725, 5oz.1dwt. (Sotheby's) $2,015 £900

Commonwealth beaker, York, 1660, 3oz.3dwt., 3½in. high. (Christie's) $900 £400

Dutch beaker on moulded reeded foot, Amsterdam, 1671, 7½in. high, 14oz.13dwt. (Christie's) $8,210 £3,800

George IV silver gilt beaker of Setzbecker form by John Bridge, 1827, 8oz.19dwt. (Christie's) $1,700 £750

One of a matching pair of silver gilt beakers by Edward Barnard & Sons, London, 1862-68, 12.2cm. high, 748gm. (Sotheby's Belgravia) $1,140 £500

Swedish parcel gilt beaker by Lorentz Lindegren, Boras, 1787, 8½in. high, 12oz.7dwt. (Christie's) $1,925 £880

17th century Danish tapering cylindrical beaker by Fridrich Kurz, Copenhagen, 1679, 2¾in. high, 2oz.11dwt. (Sotheby's) $2,495 £1,150

William IV silver gilt cylindrical beaker by Charles Rawlings and William Summers, London, 1834, 3¾in. high, 6oz.19dwt. (Sotheby's) $940 £420

Jensen silver beaker, London, 1929, 15.5cm. high. (Sotheby's Belgravia) $695 £300

17th century Dutch silver beaker. (Phillips) $11,550 £5,000

17th century Hungarian parcel gilt beaker, circa 1650, 5¼in. high, 3oz.17dwt. (Sotheby's) $1,680 £750

One of a pair of straight taper sided beakers. (Andrew Grant) $800 £390

One of a set of six 18ct. gold beakers, 14cm. high, London, 1968, 2,490gm. (Sotheby's Belgravia) $29,380 £13,000

Commonwealth beaker, London, 1658, 3oz.7dwt., 3¼in. high. (Sotheby's) $4,230 £1,950

Swedish parcel gilt beaker by John Wasserman, 1770, 8½in. high, 17oz.17dwt. (Christie's) $3,375 £1,500

German parcel gilt beaker and cover, circa 1680, probably by Thomas Ringler, 4oz. 3dwt., 4¾in. high. (Christie's) $2,810 £1,300

Swedish parcel gilt beaker on fluted domed foot, by Didrik Heitmuller, 1777, 16oz.9dwt., 8½in. high. (Christie's) $2,585 £1,150

Swedish parcel gilt beaker on shaped circular domed foot, 13oz.6dwt., 8½in. high, by Johan Adolf Seseman, 1792. (Christie's) $2,360 £1,050

17th century German parcel gilt beaker by Daniel Manlich, Berlin, 1680, 3oz. 14dwt., 3¾in. high. (Sotheby's) $3,255 £1,500

One of a pair of silver gilt beakers by T. E. Seagars, London, 1849, 13cm. high, 875gm. (Sotheby's Belgravia) $1,040 £500

Fine Dutch beaker on corded foot, by Hotze Swerms, Bolsward, 1707, 6¾in. high, 9oz. 17dwt. (Christie's) $11,230 £5,200

Silver gilt and niello beaker, by E. C., Moscow, 1846, 6.7cm. high. (Sotheby's) $1,255 £550

Swedish parcel gilt beaker by Lorens Stabeus, Stockholm, 1767, 17oz.9dwt., 8¾in. high. (Christie's) $2,300 £1,050

Silver table bell with facetted handle, by Hunt & Roskell, London, 1878, 110gm. (Sotheby's) $650 £290

Good Dutch silver gilt bell by Cornelis de Haan, The Hague, 1775, 5½in. high, 10oz.10dwt. (Sotheby's)$5,265 £2,250

George I plain table bell by Edmund Holaday, 1716, 6oz. 19dwt. (Christie's) $4,500 £2,000

BISCUIT BARRELS

George III silver biscuit box by Benjamin Smith. (Phillips) $855 £395

Silver plated biscuit barrel or cookie jar, circa 1870, 7¼in. diam. (Christopher Sykes) $130 £60

Silver sedan chair biscuit box, by Geo. Edward & Sons, Glasgow, 1899. 684gm. (Sotheby's Belgravia) $1,680 £750

Victorian oak biscuit barrel with plated mounts. (Vernon's) $20 £10

Elkington & Co. electroplated cylindrical biscuit barrel, 22cm. high. (Sotheby's Belgravia) $215 £100

Late 19th century English electroplated circular biscuit box, 18cm. high. (Sotheby's Belgravia) $115 £50

BRANDY SAUCEPANS

George I baluster brandy saucepan by William Fleming, London, 1725, 5½in. wide, 2oz.13dwt. (Sotheby's) $1,520 £700

George III tapering cylindrical brandy saucepan by John Emes, London, 1801, 9in. wide, 7oz.16dwt. (Sotheby's) $1,625 £750

Queen Anne brandy saucepan by Daniel Yerbury, London, 1703, 2¼in. high, 4oz.8dwt.(Sotheby's) $1,735 £800

One of a pair of Indian silver bowls, 5½oz. each. (Gray's Antique Mews) $170 £75

Circular bowl and cover with dragon's head finial, 48oz. (Christie's) $1,370 £620

Early 20th century German oval jardiniere, 49.5cm. wide, 2,400gm. (Sotheby's Belgravia)$1,145 £550

James Ramsay silver two-handled oval flower bowl, Glasgow, 1902, 1,548gm. (Sotheby's) $2,200 £980

Robert Harper & Son silver circular rosebowl with vitruvian scroll border, London, 1882, 838gm. (Sotheby's Belgravia) $985 £440

Two-handled circular silver rosebowl by Wakely & Wheeler, London, 1909, 1,580gm. (Sotheby's Belgravia) $1,610 £720

Artificer's Guild Ltd. electro-plated copper rosebowl and cover, circa 1920, 24.6cm. diam. (Sotheby's Belgravia) $370 £170

Late 19th century Konoike silver bowl. (Sotheby's Belgravia) $1,160 £540

French shaped circular two-handled silver bowl, cover and stand, maker's mark PA/T, circa 1870, 729gm. (Sotheby's Belgravia) $645 £280

Liberty & Co. silver sugar basin and tongs, Birmingham circa 1903-06, 4cm. high. (Sotheby's Belgravia)$555 £240

Circular silver Monteith rosebowl with lion mask handles by Edward Barnard & Sons, 1905, 1,141gm. (Sotheby's Belgravia) $1,210 £540

George II plain circular sugar bowl and cover by Matthew E. Lofthouse, 1730, 13oz. 9dwt. (Christie's) $3,450 £1,500

Atkin Brothers circular rose-bowl, 22.8cm. diam., Sheffield, 1903, 538gm. (Sotheby's Belgravia) $499 £240

Victorian silver rosebowl, London, 1895, by Child & Child. (Vost's) $676 £330

Circular bowl by Joseph Angell, London, 1855, 12.8cm. diam., 258gm. (Sotheby's Belgravia) $374 £180

Jensen silver bowl and spoon, 10cm. high, circa 1947. (Sotheby's Belgravia) $645 £280

Victorian circular standing bowl by Paul Storr, London, 1838, 76oz. 13dwt., 12¾in. diam. (Sotheby's) $5,642 £2,600

Early 19th century Maltese covered sugar bowl, circa 1800, 6¾in. high, 12oz.5dwt. (Sotheby's) $1,085 £500

18th century Maltese circular covered sugar bowl by Gio. Batta Muscat, circa 1790, 5in. high, 6oz.16dwt. (Sotheby's) $911 £420

United States sterling silver punch-bowl with matching ladle and three of the twelve cups, 189oz. (Phillips) $4,870 £2,255

William Mammatt & Sons circular rosebowl, Sheffield, 1899, 31.6cm. diam., 1,826gm. (Sotheby's Belgravia)$1,200 £580

A. D. & C. Houle circular rosebowl, London, 1880, 34.5cm. diam., 1,787gm. (Sotheby's Belgravia) $1,675 £800

Large Chinese silver bowl, 58oz. (Biddle & Webb) $1,200 £580

One of a set of four two-handled bowls and stands by S. Herbert & Co., 1751, 110oz. (Christie's) $34,560 £16,000

George II circular bowl by
John Moore, Junior, Dublin,
1750, 17oz.3dwt., 7¼in. diam.
(Sotheby's) $2,052 £950

Mappin & Webb Ltd., circular three-
handled rosebowl, London, 1918,
30.4cm. diam. (Sotheby's Belgravia)
$1,144 £550

Victorian silver octagonal punch-
bowl with ram's head handles,
London, 1885, 92oz. (Thomas
Watson & Son) $2,808 £1,300

William III Monteith bowl by Robert
Timbrell, London, 1698, 57oz.4dwt.,
11in. diam. (Sotheby's)
            $20,160 £9,000

Large circular two-handled rosebowl
by Richard Hennell, 1864, 17in. diam.,
175oz. (Christie's) $7,425 £3,300

Scottish two-handled flower bowl
on electroplate stand, circa 1882.
(Sotheby's) $907 £420

18th century Maltese covered
sugar bowl by Francesco
Fenech, circa 1780, 5½in. high,
7oz.16dwt. (Sotheby's)
            $1,193 £550

Maltese covered sugar bowl, by
Saverio Cannataci, circa 1820,
6½in. high, 14oz.9dwt.
(Sotheby's) $1,128 £520

French oval dessert bowl by Sixte-Simon
Rion, Paris, circa 1810, 16½in. wide,
61oz.5dwt. (Sotheby's) $3,810 £1,700

Late 17th century Dutch brandy
bowl by Thomas Sibrand Hicht,
Dokkum, 1684, 8½in. wide, 5oz.
14dwt. (Sotheby's)$3,696 £1,650

Atkin Brothers circular rosebowl,
30.7cm. diam., Sheffield, 1911,
1,530gm. (Sotheby's Belgravia)
            $1,310 £580

Japanese Konoike silver bowl,
circa 1895, 28cm. diam.
(Sotheby's Belgravia)$976 £450

Antique silver mounted shell box.
(Woolley & Wallis) $485 £210

Tortoiseshell and silver trinket
box, circa 1912. (Alfie's Antique
Market) $155 £70

Sofid nickel snuff box, circa 1825,
3½in. long. (Christopher Sykes)
                   $60 £25

Large rectangular cigar box,
Birmingham, 1918, 28.2cm.
long. (Sotheby's Belgravia)
$900 £400

Dutch oblong tobacco box, by
Evert Bot, Amsterdam, 1755, 6½in.
long, 7oz. (Christie's)
                $7,560 £3,500

Asprey & Co. Ltd. rectangular
three-section box, London,
1912, 16.4cm. long.(Sotheby's
Belgravia) $585 £260

Rectangular silver casket enamelled
in hues of royal blue, red and
white, 5½in. wide, made in Moscow.
(Neales) $1,500 £750

18th century Dutch oblong tobacco
box by Christoffel Woortman, Amsterdam, 1797, 6oz.6dwt., 6¼in. wide.
(Sotheby's) $1,570 £700

William Comyns rectangular trinket
box, London, 1904, 20.5cm. long.
(Sotheby's Belgravia) $540 £260

German silver rectangular casket,
late 19th/early 20th century,
26.6cm. long, 1,116gm.
(Sotheby's Belgravia) $810 £390

Jewish parcel gilt spice box, mid
18th century, 11¼in. high, 9oz.
5dwt. (Christie's)$3,670 £1,700

Enamelled silver vesta case,
Birmingham, 1888.
(Sotheby's Belgravia)$280 £130

Small Dutch silver coloured metal casket
cast with Egyptian scenes, with pseudo
hallmarks, 1880, 353gm. (Sotheby's
Belgravia) $540 £240

Nutmeg grater by W. J.,
Aberdeen, circa 1830,
1½in. wide. (Christie's &
Edmiston's) $815 £360

Dutch silver gilt circular tobacco box
of bombe form, Middleburg, 1770,
17oz.1dwt.(Christie's)$11,800 £5,200

Walker & Hall oblong soap box, Sheffield, 1901, 19.3cm. long. (Sotheby's Belgravia)$295 £130

Silver and tortoiseshell cigar case with vacant cartouche. (Alfie's Antique Market) $90 £40

Large silver cigar box with hinged cover, 23cm. wide. (Phillips) $215 £100

Good Padgett & Braham Ltd. rectangular silver cigarette box, with gilt and holly-wood interior, 1936, 23cm. long. (Sotheby's Belgravia) $940 £420

Silver filigree patch box. (Alfie's Antique Market) $80 £40

Victorian oblong freedom casket, 1875, 5¼in. long. (Christie's) $11,700 £5,200

William III oval tobacco box by Nathaniel Locke, 1701, 3oz. 12dwt., 3½in. long. (Christie's) $2,800 £1,250

Dutch oblong tobacco box, 1782, 6oz.7dwt., 5½in. long. (Christie's) $4,500 £2,000

Commonwealth silver counter box, circa 1650. (Bonham's) $1,500 £750

18th century German gilt sugar box of shaped oval form, Augsburg, 1735. (Phillips) $9,090 £4,500

George III freedom box by Alex. Ticknell, Dublin, 1797. (Sotheby's) $2,940 £1,450

Victorian oval freedom casket on four swan feet, circa 1875, 22oz., 7¾in. long. (Christie's) $13,500 £6,000

Rectangular shaped card case by Nathaniel Mills & Sons, Birmingham, 1847, 8.7cm. high. (Sotheby's Belgravia)$360 £160

German oval toilet box, probably by Christian Winter or Christoph Warmberger, circa 1700, 8oz. 12dwt. (Christie's)$2,950 £1,300

Unusual Elkington, Mason & Co., electroplated parcel gilt and oxidised electrotype jewel casket, 1852, 22.5cm. long.(Sotheby's Belgravia) $575 £250

567

One of a pair of mid 20th century Italian two-light candelabra, 30.4cm. high. (Sotheby's Belgravia) $995 £440

One of a pair of three-branch filled candelabra in the style of Daniel Marot. (Andrew Grant) $740 £360

One of a pair of 18th century German two-light candelabra, circa 1785, 56oz.2dwt., 14in. high. (Sotheby's) $3,040 £1,400

One of a pair of silver gilt two-light candelabra by John Scofield, 1783, 16½in. high. (Christie's) $56,160 £26,000

One of a pair of Goldsmiths & Silversmiths Co., silver four-light candelabra in 18th century style, 1902, 40.5cm. high. (Sotheby's Belgravia) $4,030 £1,800

One of a pair of WMF silvered metal candelabra, circa 1900, 50.5cm. high. (Sotheby's Belgravia) $3,925 £1,700

One of a pair of silver five-light candelabra by Hawksworth, Eyre & Co., Sheffield, 1901, 44.3cm. high. (Sotheby's Belgravia) $4,030 £1,800

Large Sheffield plate five-light candelabrum table centrepiece by James Dixon & Sons, circa 1835, 72cm. high. (Sotheby's Belgravia) $425 £190

One of a pair of Victorian five-light candelabra by S. Garrard, 1901, 147oz., 16½in. high. (Christie's) $6,525 £2,900

One of a pair of 18th century German candelabra, Augsburg, 1793-95, 17in. high, 70oz.12dwt. (Sotheby's) $6,270 £2,800

One of a pair of early 19th century German candelabra, circa 1825, 28½in. high, 225oz.9dwt. (Sotheby's) $8,065 £3,600

Late 18th century silver plated candelabrum with cast applied leaf decoration, 5in. high. (Robert W. Skinner Inc.) $50 £25

Silver taperstick by Edward Barnet, York, 1713, 2¾oz. (Buckell & Ballard) $1,825 £800

One of a pair of candlesticks by H. Wilkinson & Co., circa 1840, 9¼in. high. (Sotheby's) $390 £180

One of a pair of Victorian silver candlesticks by Walker & Hall, 1897. (Manchester Auction Mart) $805 £365

One of four George II table candlesticks by John Letablere, Dublin, circa 1740, 8¼in. high, 62oz. (Christie's) $7,775 £3,600

One of a pair of 18th century German table candlesticks, circa 1745, 8½in. high, 21oz. 10dwt. (Sotheby's) $3,920 £1,750

One of a pair of George III table candlesticks by John Winter & Co., Sheffield, 1780, 11in. high. (Sotheby's)$1,610 £700

One of a pair of George III candlesticks by John Carter, London, 1762, 10¼in. high, 37oz.1dwt. (Sotheby's)$4,145 £1,850

One of a set of four George III table candlesticks by John Carter, London, 1769, 11¼in. high.(Sotheby's) $4,600 £2,000

One of a pair of George II cast silver candlesticks by John Cafe, London, 1755, 7¾in. high, 32oz. (Geering & Colyer) $2,925 £1,300

One of a set of four George III candlesticks, by Robert Calderwood, Dublin, 1765, 101oz., 14in. high. (Christie's) $7,875 £3,500

One of a pair of George II candlesticks by Thos. Gilpin, London, 1748, 32oz.8dwt., 8¼in. high. (Sotheby's) $4,705 £2,100

One of a pair of early George I table candlesticks by Ambrose Stevenson, London, 1717, 6¼in. high, 14oz. 1dwt. (Sotheby's) $5,825 £2,600

CANDLESTICKS

One of a pair of table candlesticks by J. S. Beresford, London, 1889, 15.3cm. high. (Sotheby's Belgravia)
$520 £250

One of a very fine pair of early 18th century English candlesticks. (Sotheby King & Chasemore)
$3,045 £1,500

One of a set of four late 18th century silver-plated candlesticks, 13in. high. (Phillips)
$795 £368

One of a set of four Dutch table candlesticks, 52oz. (Parsons, Welch & Cowell)
$8,325 £3,700

One of a pair of George III table candlesticks by Alexander MacLeod, Inverness, circa 1815, 10¾in. high.(Sotheby's)
$2,375 £1,100

One of a pair of early George III column candlesticks by Alexander Johnston, London, 1760, 14½in. high, 55oz.5dwt. (Sotheby's)
$2,495 £1,150

One of a pair of 18th century Belgian table candlesticks, Brussels, 1784, 30oz.12dwt., 11½in. high.(Sotheby's)
$3,365 £1,550

One of a pair of William Hutton & Sons Ltd., fluted oval table candlesticks, 28.6cm. high, London, 1897. (Sotheby's Belgravia)
$415 £200

One of a pair of C. S. Harris table candlesticks, London, 1900, loaded, 29.4cm. high. (Sotheby's Belgravia) $790 £380

One of a pair of Wm. Hutton & Sons Ltd., table candlesticks, 28.5cm. high, London, 1910. (Sotheby's Belgravia) $830 £400

One of a set of four early Victorian table candlesticks by R. Garrard, London, 12in. high, 183oz.13dwt. (Sotheby's)$4,560 £2,100

One of a pair of George II table candlesticks by John Preist, London, 1753, 9in. high, 35oz. 5dwt. (Sotheby's)
$2,600 £1,200

570

One of a set of four George III candlesticks by John Roberts & Co., Sheffield, 1805, 8in. high.(Sotheby King & Chasemore) $2,920 £1,350

One of a pair of silver candlesticks by Ramsden & Carr, London, 1904, 8¼in. high, 24¼oz. (Parsons, Welch & Cowell) $1,485 £660

George II taperstick by John Cafe, London, 1743, 4½in. high, 4oz. 7dwt. (Sotheby's) $1,475 £680

One of a set of four George III table candlesticks by William Cafe, 1763, 83oz., 10¾in. high. (Christie's) $9,900 £4,400

One of a set of four George III table candlesticks by John Roberts & Co., Sheffield, 1805, 8in. high. (Sotheby King & Chasemore) $2,915 £1,350

One of a pair of silver candlesticks in Louis XV style, 1774.(Leys, Antwerp) $4,670 £2,165

One of a pair of Belgian table candlesticks, 25cm. high, 1771, 844gm. (Sotheby's Belgravia) $1,205 £580

One of a pair of George II caryatid candlesticks by John Cafe, London, 1749, 49oz.7dwt., 10in. high. (Sotheby's) $3,365 £1,550

One of a pair of Elking-on & Co. Ltd. table candlesticks, 28.5cm. high, Birmingham, 1895. (Sotheby's Belgravia) $770 £370

One of a pair of George I candlesticks by James Gould, London, 1725, 16cm. high, 24oz. (Sotheby King & Chasemore) $3,050 £1,500

One of a pair of early George III table candlesticks by Ebenezer Coker, London, 1763, 10in. high, 37oz.11dwt. (Sotheby's)$2,600 £1,200

One of a pair of Martin, Hall & Co. Ltd. table candlesticks, 23.5cm. high, London, 1893. (Sotheby's Belgravia) $560 £270

CANDLESTICKS

One of a pair of Edwardian Corinthian pillar candlesticks, Sheffield 1905, 6in. tall. (Coles, Knapp & Kennedy) $390 £180

One of four Hamilton & Inches table candlesticks, Edinburgh, 1904, 24.5cm. high. (Sotheby's Belgravia) $1,085 £480

One of a pair of Richard Sibley 17th century style silver table candlesticks, London, 1873, 551gm. (Sotheby's Belgravia) $630 £280

One of a pair of early George III tapersticks by Ebenezer Coker, London, 1760, 6in. high, 14oz.14dwt. (Sotheby's) $4,144 £1,850

One of a pair of 18th century style silver table candlesticks by Hawksworth, Eyre & Co., marked 1895, 21cm. high. (Sotheby's Belgravia) $1,150 £500

One of a pair of Edward Barnard & Sons table candlesticks, in the manner of Rundell, Bridge & Rundell, 1918, 2,360gm. (Sotheby's Belgravia) $2,350 £1,050

One of a set of four late Victorian 18th century style electroplated table candlesticks by Hawksworth, Eyre & Co., 30.8cm. (Sotheby's Belgravia) $735 £320

One of a set of four Queen Anne table candlesticks. (Russell, Baldwin & Bright) $20,905 £9,250

One of a pair of George IV candlesticks by Kitchen & Walker, Sheffield, 1835, 9in. high. (Sotheby's) $2,070 £900

Pair of mid 19th century Portuguese cast silver table candlesticks, maker's mark QAR, 947gm. (Sotheby's Belgravia) $940 £420

One of a pair of silver table candlesticks, maker's mark M. S., London, 1929, 33cm. high. (Sotheby's Belgravia) $850 £380

One of a set of four George III table candlesticks by T. & J. Settle, Sheffield, 1815, 13½in. high. (Sotheby's) $3,255 £1,500

One of a pair of Dutch silver table candlesticks, Delft, 1677, 8½in. high, 29oz. (Christie's N. York) $50,000 £21,740

One of a pair of large Spanish candlesticks, circa 1820, 17in. high. (Christopher Sykes) $890 £395

One of a pair of George I candlesticks on stepped octagonal bases by Richard Bayley, 1724, 17oz.6dwt. (Christie's) $5,675 £2,500

One of a set of four silver table candlesticks by George Wickes, London, 1739, 65oz. (Bonham's) $11,880 £5,500

572

George I plain octagonal pear-shaped caster by Thomas Bamford, 1719, 7½in. high, 9oz.11dwt. (Christie's) $2,260 £1,000

Pair of Queen Anne sugar casters by Stocker & Peacock, 15½oz. (Sotheby King & Chasemore) $5,185 £2,400

George I octagonal kitchen pepper by Glover Johnson, London, 1726, 2oz.16dwt., 3¾in. high. (Sotheby's) $825 £380

George V silver muffineer, London, 1915, 20cm. high, 12oz. (Sotheby Humberts) $300 £140

Set of three George III casters, London, 1817, 15oz. (Sotheby Humberts) $690 £320

One of a pair of Britannia silver Queen Anne lighthouse sugar casters, London, 1706, 13½oz., 6in. high. (Sotheby King & Chasemore) $5,185 £2,400

Vase-shaped sugar caster by F. B. Thomas & Co., London, 1900, 22.2cm. high, 568gm. (Sotheby's Belgravia) $250 £120

Two early silver sugar casters, London, 1726. (Sotheby Humberts) $475 £220

George II sugar caster with pierced lid, by Thomas Wynne, 1759, 19.5cm. high, 7¾oz. (Sotheby Humberts) $625 £290

George II vase-shaped caster by Thomas Bamford, London, 1729, 6in. high, 5oz. 15dwt. (Sotheby's) $1,570 £700

Set of three George I octagonal baluster casters by John Pero, London, 1717, 17oz.3dwt., 6¼in. and 5in. high. (Sotheby's) $3,360 £1,500

George II octagonal caster by Gabriel Sleath, London, 1727, 6¾in. high, 9oz.9dwt. (Sotheby's) $4,320 £2,000

573

Joseph Rodgers & Sons Ltd., epergne, 61cm. wide, Sheffield 1904, 1,352gm. (Sotheby's Belgravia) $1,220 £540

English electroplated table centrepiece, 55cm. high, circa 1860. (Sotheby's Belgravia) $1,340 £650

James Dixon & Sons Ltd., epergne, Sheffield 1904, 38.7cm. high, 2,914gm. (Sotheby's Belgravia) $2,485 £1,100

English electroplated table centrepiece, circa 1861, 56cm. high. (Sotheby's Belgravia) $770 £340

Silver gilt covered sweetmeat bowl by R. & S. Garrard, London, 1839, 24.2cm. high, 2,018gm. (Sotheby's Belgravia) $3,330 £1,600

George V table centrepiece with pierced and moulded decorations, 14in. high. (Russell, Baldwin & Bright) $820 £380

Large silvered metal Art Nouveau centrepiece, circa 1900, 45cm. high. (Sotheby's Belgravia) $740 £320

Fruit dish stand by Henry Wilkinson & Co., Birmingham 1878, 28.3cm. diam., 1,515gm. (Sotheby's Belgravia) $790 £380

Victorian three-branch centrepiece by Henry Wilkinson, Sheffield, 1875, 27¾in. high, 122oz. (Christie's) $2,915 £1,350

George III epergne by Thomas Pitts, 1778, 152oz., 17in. high. (Christie's) $11,700 £5,200

Silver table centrepiece, Birmingham 1866, 48oz., 21in. high. (Sotheby King & Chasemore) $865 £400

Set of three Martin, Hall & Co., Ltd., fruit tazzas, Sheffield 1902-03, 1,656gm. (Sotheby's Belgravia) $935 £450

George II silver gilt epergne by William Cripps, London, 1751, 12in. high, 172oz.8dwt. (Sotheby's) $12,990 £5,800

Continental flower ornament in the form of a swan, Chester, 1899, 8oz.5dwt. (Phillips) $195 £90

Silver fruit stand by I. H., London, 1881, 37oz., 13in. diam. (Sotheby King & Chasemore) $995 £460

WMF electroplated dessert dish stand with cut glass bowl, circa 1900, 42.5cm. high. (Sotheby's Belgravia) $450 £200

John Round & Son silver oval pedestal fruit stand, Sheffield, 1892, 1,140gm. (Sotheby's Belgravia) $1,165 £520

Mappin & Webb Ltd., table centrepiece, London, 1919, 29.5cm. high, 1,466gm. (Sotheby's Belgravia) $1,290 £620

Silver epergne supporting engraved glass vase and dishes, by Elkington & Co., Birmingham, 1907, 1,457gm. of silver. (Sotheby's Belgravia) $1,390 £620

Fine quality epergne. (Alfie's Antique Market) $440 £195

George III four-branch epergne by Matthew Boulton, Birmingham, 1811, 8½in. high, 64oz.2dwt. (Sotheby's) $3,615 £1,600

George IV four-light candelabrum centrepiece by Matt. Boulton, Birmingham, 1825, 123oz. (Christie's) $5,220 £2,300

Victorian centrepiece on shaped triangular base by Barnard & Co., 1840, 259oz., 22¼in. high. (Christie's) $8,550 £3,800

Mid Victorian silver plated centrepiece. (Christie's S. Kensington) $1,130 £500

CHAMBERSTICKS

One of a pair of electroplated chamber candlesticks by Elkington, Mason & Co., 1849, 17cm. diam. (Sotheby's Belgravia) $415 £180

George I chamber candlestick by Sarah Holaday, London, 1721, 4½in. diam., 10oz. (Sotheby's) $820 £350

George II silver gilt chamberstick and snuffers by John Emes, 1801, 6oz.8dwt. (Christie's) $2,385 £1,050

George II chamber candlestick by Paul Crespin, London, 1744, 7in. wide, 11oz.17dwt. (Sotheby's) $4,180 £1,850

William IV silver gilt chamber candlestick by Paul Storr, 1833, 12oz.3dwt. (Christie's) $4,085 £1,800

Naturalistic chamber candlestick by Charles Reily and George Storer, 1828, 6½oz. (Sotheby Bearne) $970 £450

George III chamber candlestick by William Lancester, London, 1774, 8oz.18dwt., 5¾in. diam. (Sotheby's) $1,130 £500

George III shaped circular chamber candlestick, London, 1817, 7¼in. diam., 21oz.18dwt. (Sotheby's) $3,810 £1,700

One of a pair of early George II silver chambersticks by John Hyatt, London, 1761, 17oz.8dwt. (Geering & Colyer) $1,025 £500

CHOCOLATE POTS

Queen Anne plain tapering cylindrical chocolate pot by Joseph Ward, 1706, 27oz., 10½in. high. (Christie's) $11,700 £5,200

French plain pear-shaped chocolate pot by Alexandre de Roussy, Paris, 1779, 6¼in. high, 9oz.2dwt. (Christie's) $2,935 £1,300

Queen Anne tapered cylindrical chocolate pot by Robert Timbrell and Joseph Bell, London, 1711, 25oz.11dwt., 10in. high. (Sotheby's) $8,245 £3,800

French silver cigarette box. (Bonham's) $405 £200

Rectangular Russian silver cigarette box in two compartments. (Sotheby King & Chasemore) $550 £255

German silver cigarette case, inset with sapphires and diamonds. (Bonham's) $315 £140

Russian silver cigarette case enamelled in dark blue, orange, green and claret. (Neales) $650 £300

Early Victorian ladies visiting card case, 4in. high, circa 1840. (Christopher Sykes) $90 £40

Rectangular silver cigarette case by P. J. S., St. Petersburg, 1908-1917, 11.3cm. wide. (Sotheby's Zurich) $1,765 £785

CLARET JUGS

Silver mounted cut-glass claret jug by W. & G. Sissons, Sheffield, 1899, 26cm. high. (Sotheby's Belgravia) $895 £400

Pair of Victorian parcel gilt mounted glass claret jugs by James Franklin, 1853, 28.3cm. high. (Christie's) $2,160 £950

One of a pair of silver gilt mounted engraved glass claret jugs by Robt. Garrard, London, 1856, 28cm. high. (Sotheby's Belgravia) $3,360 £1,500

One of a pair of Jacob Engel cut-glass claret jugs with silver coloured metal mounts, Vienna, circa 1900, 31cm. high. (Sotheby's Belgravia) $875 £420

Silver mounted cut-glass claret jug by Lee & Wigfull, Sheffield, 1895, 27.5cm. high. (Sotheby's Belgravia) $650 £290

Mappin & Webb silver mounted cut-glass claret jug, London, 1902, 28.3cm. high. (Sotheby's Belgravia) $735 £320

CLARET JUGS

German silver mounted clear glass claret jug, by David Kugelmann, late 19th century, 27.5cm. high. (Sotheby's Belgravia)$560 £240

Silver mounted rock crystal engraved clear glass claret jug by William Comyns, London, 1899, 26cm. high. (Sotheby's Belgravia) $490 £210

Joseph Rodgers & Sons silver mounted engraved cranberry flashed glass claret jug, Sheffield, 1875, 28.2cm. high. (Sotheby's Belgravia) $950 £420

Silver mounted plain glass claret jug with rustic handle, by Charles Boyton, London, 1887, 27cm. high. (Sotheby's Belgravia) $465 £200

Silver mounted rock crystal engraved glass claret jug, Birmingham, 1894, 29cm. high. (Sotheby's Belgravia) $725 £310

W. & G. Sissons silver mounted engraved glass claret jug, Sheffield, 1872, 26.2cm. high. (Sotheby's Belgravia) $1,085 £480

COASTERS

Wiener Werkstatte coaster designed by Josef Hoffmann, circa 1920, 9.7cm. diam., in silver coloured metal. (Sotheby's Belgravia) $785 £340

One of a pair of George III circular coasters by Daniel Pontifex, London, 1799, 6¼in. diam. (Sotheby's) $1,015 £450

One of a set of four George IV circular wine coasters by William Eley, London, 1826, 7in. diam. (Sotheby's) $3,905 £1,800

Part of a set of four Sheffield plate wine coasters on wood bases, unmarked, circa 1840, 20.7cm. diam. (Sotheby's Belgravia) $550 £240

One of four Russian shaped circular wine coasters by Nicols & Plinke, 1859. (Christie's) $2,845 £1,300

Pair of Sheffield plate wine coasters on wood bases, unmarked, circa 1850, 19cm. diam. (Sotheby's Belgravia) $275 £120

Heavy tapering cylindrical silver coffee pot by Edward Barnard & Sons, London, 1911, 787gm. (Sotheby's Belgravia) $735 £320

Unusual silver coffee pot, 1903. (McCartney, Morris & Barker) $305 £150

Electroplated shaped oval coffee pot by William Hutton & Sons, circa 1880, 22.9cm. high. (Sotheby's Belgravia) $155 £70

Liberty & Co., silver coffee pot, Birmingham 1906, 21cm. high, with bone handle. (Sotheby's Belgravia) $970 £420

Large pear-shaped plated coffee pot on circular gadrooned foot, probably Irish, circa 1760, 13½in. high. (Christie's) $1,180 £520

Early George II tapered cylindrical coffee pot by Peze Pilleau, London, 1733, 8in. high, 22oz.1dwt. (Sotheby's) $5,150 £2,300

Silver coffee pot by A.S., 1894, 27oz. (Christie's S. Kensington) $1,505 £700

Octagonal 18th century style coffee pot and milk jug by Asprey & Co., London, 1911, 1,109gm., all in. (Sotheby's Belgravia) $1,380 £600

Pear-shaped plated coffee pot on circular foot, circa 1765, 12in. high. (Christie's) $770 £340

A. B. Savory & Sons silver baluster coffee pot, with mark of William Smily, London, 1862, 810gm. (Sotheby's Belgravia) $940 £420

Plain pear-shaped plated coffee pot on circular foot, circa 1760, 13in. high. (Christie's) $815 £360

J. & H. Lias fluted baluster coffee pot with engraved foliate panels, London, 1842, 804gm. (Sotheby's Belgravia) $805 £360

579

George III baluster coffee pot
by William Grundy, London,
1770, 10¾in. high, 31oz.2dwt.
(Sotheby's) $4,774 £2,200

George III baluster coffee pot by
Alice and George Burrows, London,
1817, 26oz.5dwt. (Sotheby's)
$1,080 £500

George III baluster coffee jug by
Henry Greenway, London, 1776,
12¼in. high, 25oz.10dwt.
(Sotheby's) $1,855 £820

Thomas Bradbury & Sons Ltd.
tapering cylindrical coffee jug,
London, 1906, 23.2cm. high,
403gm. (Sotheby's Belgravia)
$452 £200

Maltese coffee pot, circa 1820, 10in.
high, 31oz.11dwt. (Sotheby's)
$2,495 £1,150

18th century baluster shaped
coffee pot, London, 1771,
29oz. (Moore, Allen & Innocent) $3,780 £1,750

George III baluster coffee jug
by William Bruce, London,
1814, 21oz.19dwt., 8¾in. high.
(Sotheby's) $1,265 £550

George III baluster coffee pot by
Richard Morton & Co., Sheffield,
1778, 11½in. high, 23oz.10dwt.
(Sotheby's) $2,800 £1,250

George III silver coffee pot by
William Bayley, London, 1784,
12in. high. (Phillips & Jolly's)
$2,250 £1,000

George II tapering cylindrical coffee
pot by John Hugh Le Sage, London,
1743, 27oz.2dwt., 9½in. high.
(Sotheby's) $2,712 £1,250

William IV coffee pot by Adey
Bellamy Savory, 1834, 31oz.
(Phillips) $1,663 £720

18th century Maltese baluster
coffee pot by Gio. Carlo Cassar,
12¾in. high, 45oz.6dwt.
(Sotheby's) $4,340 £2,000

Edward Barnard & Sons Ltd. tapering octagonal coffee pot, London, 1931, 25.4cm. high. (Sotheby's Belgravia) $768 £340

Goldsmiths & Silversmiths Ltd. baluster coffee pot, 22cm. high, London, 1911, 704gm. (Sotheby's Belgravia) $678 £300

Chased and bellied Victorian coffee pot by J. McKay, Edinburgh, 1859, 10in. high, 27.7oz. (Eadon, Lockwood & Riddle) $1,296 £600

George II baluster coffee pot by Fuller White, London, 1754, 11¼in. high, 41oz.3dwt. (Sotheby's) $5,425 £2,500

George III coffee pot by Henry Chawner, London, 1786, 23oz. (H. Spencer & Sons)$2,622 £1,150

George IV silver coffee pot by Joseph Angell, London, 1823, 11in. high, 34oz. (Gray's Antique Mews) $1,944 £900

George III pear-shaped coffee pot by Hester Bateman, 1782, 31cm. high, 25¾oz. (Sotheby Bearne) $4,104 £1,900

George II tapered cylindrical coffee pot, London, 1729, 28oz. (Andrew Grant) $4,100 £2,000

George III baluster coffee pot by Hester Bateman, London, 1787, 24oz.5dwt., 12¼in. high. (Sotheby's) $5,376 £2,400

George III baluster coffee pot by Daniel Smith and Robert Sharp, London, 1773, 11in. high, 25oz. 9dwt. (Sotheby's) $2,387 £1,100

George II tapered cylindrical coffee pot by John Barbe, London, 1746, 6¼in. high, 12oz.3dwt. (Sotheby's) $5,152 £2,300

George III pear-shaped coffee pot, 11¼in. high, 36oz. (Christie's) $5,616 £2,600

COFFEE POTS AND JUGS

William Hunter compressed circular coffee pot, London, 1841, 28.4oz. (Sotheby's Belgravia) $675 £300

George II plain cylindrical coffee pot by Edward Feline, 1728, 9½in. high, 26oz. (Christie's) $4,420 £2,000

French Empire coffee pot by Jacques-Gabriel-Andre Bompart, Paris, circa 1800, 16oz.12dwt., 8¾in. high. (Sotheby's) $1,695 £750

George III plain pear-shaped coffee pot by David Whyte, 1769, 11in. high, 32oz. (Christie's) $3,680 £1,600

George II fine plain tapering cylindrical coffee pot by Paul de Lamerie, 1730, 7¾in. high, 23oz. (Christie's) $27,625 £12,500

George II coffee pot by Isaac Cookson, Newcastle, 1750, 9in. high, 26oz. (Christie's) $2,990 £1,300

CREAM JUGS

George III helmet shaped milk jug by Robert Sharp, London, 1793, 5in. high, 7oz.8dwt. (Sotheby's) $760 £340

George III cow creamer by John Kentember, London, 1770, 5¾in. long, 4oz. (Sotheby's) $2,810 £1,250

Baluster shaped cream jug and cover, Paris, 1753, 10.5cm. high, 185gm. (Sotheby's Monaco) $5,285 £2,350

George III cream pail by William Vincent, London, 1774, 3¼in. high, 1oz.16dwt. (Sotheby's) $670 £300

Early George III silver gilt cow creamer by John Schuppe, London, 1763, 5½in. long, 3oz.16dwt. (Sotheby's) $5,380 £2,300

Baluster shaped milk jug and cover, stamped on the base, by Jacques-Pierre Marteau, Paris, 1763, 180gm. (Sotheby's Monaco) $2,900 £1,280

Baluster milk jug by E. & J. Barnard, London, 1866, 14.5cm. high, 7oz. (Sotheby's Belgravia) $150 £65

Silver cream jug in the shape of a cow. (Christie's S. Kensington) $680 £300

Fluted baluster milk jug, Exeter, 1850, 15.8cm. high, 251gm. (Sotheby's Belgravia) $205 £100

CRUETS

Early George II two-bottle cruet frame by Paul de Lamerie, London, 1728, 5½in. wide, 14oz. 13dwt. (Sotheby's) $10,850 £5,000

Double oval shaped cruet stand, by Frantz Peter Bunsen, Hanover, circa 1794, 2,120gm., 32.5cm. long. (Sotheby's Monaco) $19,225 £8,545

George III oblong silver gilt egg cruet by John Emes, London, 1806, 37oz.6dwt., 7¼in. wide. (Sotheby's) $2,495 £1,150

Shaped oblong egg cruet by Robert L. Hennell, London, 1860, 26.6oz., 23.8cm. long. (Sotheby's Belgravia) $690 £320

George II two-bottle cruet frame by George Wickes, London, 1742, 12oz., 8¾in. high. (Sotheby's) $5,825 £2,600

George II cruet frame with castors and bottles, by Jabez Daniell, 1749, 55oz. (Christie's) $5,525 £2,500

Table cruet by Paul Storr, London, 1811, 30oz. (Gray's Antique Mews) $3,080 £1,350

One of a pair of Louis XVI two-bottle cruets, 12¾in. wide, by Jacques Favre, Paris, 1778, 51oz.1dwt. (Sotheby's) $3,810 £1,700

Dutch silver cruet frame of waisted oblong form, Amsterdam, 1772, 16oz.19dwt. (Christie's) $1,035 £450

One of a pair of George III wine cups, 6¼in. high, possibly by Charles Hougham, London, 1787, 13oz.7dwt. (Sotheby's)
$2,240 £1,000

George III silver gilt foxhead stirrup cup by Thomas Phipps and Edward Robinson, London, 1807, 2oz.16dwt., 3in. high. (Sotheby's) $3,800 £1,700

George II two-handled cup by Lothian & Robertson, Edinburgh, 1755, 48oz. 5dwt., 8in. high.(Sotheby's)
$1,400 £650

Early 17th century cup and cover by Johan Janes, Hamburg. (Bukowski's, Stockholm)
$11,000 £5,100

Boxed set of liqueur tots in silver and glass, Sheffield, 1909. (Alfie's Antique Market) $250 £110

Solid silver trophy cup, Dublin, 1910, 16oz., 7½in. high. (Christopher Sykes)$280 £125

20th century plated double-handled prize cup, 10in. high. (Vernon's)
$18 £8

George III vase-shaped two-handled cup and cover by Digby Scott and Benjamin Smith, London, 1805, 16½in. high, 99oz.16dwt.(Sotheby's)
$2,600 £1,200

Coconut cup and cover, circa 1632, with mid 18th century additions, 9½in. high. (Sotheby's) $9,075 £4,200

Goldsmiths & Silversmiths Co. Ltd., silver gilt two-handled presentation cup and cover, London, 1902, 22.5cm. high, 1,005gm. (Sotheby's Belgravia)
$835 £370

Liberty silver bowl and cover. (Bonham's) $10,170 £4,500

George III vase-shaped two-handled cup and cover by Benjamin Smith, London, 1807, 120oz. 10dwt. (Sotheby's) $2,495 £1,150

Silver two-handled cup by
John Payne, London, 1762,
12oz. (Frank H. Fellows)
$280 £125

Two-handled silver mounted serpentine cup and cover, circa 1675, 7¼in.
high. (Christie's) $2,590 £1,200

Commonwealth silver gilt caudle
cup and cover by Nicholas
Wollaston, London, 1656, 4½in.
high, 13oz.12dwt. (Sotheby's)
$10,750 £4,800

George III silver gilt two-handled
cup and cover by Smith & Sharp,
London, 1772, 17¾in. high,
121oz.2dwt. (Sotheby's)
$8,510 £3,800

Set of twelve F. Nicoud gilt liqueur
cups and tray, 1880's, in original
fitted case. (Sotheby's Belgravia)
$2,310 £1,000

Silver gilt trophy cup by J.
Barclay Hennell, London,
1878. (Manchester Auction
Mart) $2,360 £1,050

Parcel gilt cup and cover, 12in.
high, Dublin, 1694, 45oz.
(Andrew Grant) $945 £460

Silver replica of a late 17th century flagon, by
Lambert & Co., London, 1908, 1,563gm.
(Sotheby's Belgravia) $1,380 £600

Hunt & Roskell bell-shaped
cup, London, 1856, 16.2cm.
high, 490gm. (Sotheby's
Belgravia) $435 £210

Gold Victorian vase-shaped two-
handled cup and cover by Hunt
& Roskell, 18ct., 17in. high, 97oz.
(Christie's) $43,200 £20,000

Charles Stuart Harris & Son Ltd.
two-handled cup and cover,
London, 1904, 30.7cm. high,
1,924gm. (Sotheby's Belgravia)
$790 £380

George III plain cup and cover by
Francis Crump, 1762, 32oz.
(Phillips) $1,730 £750

CUPS

Silver foxhead stirrup cup with gilt interior, by Hunt & Roskell, London, 1848, 400gm. (Sotheby's Belgravia) $3,140 £1,400

Elizabeth I small communion cup on domed spreading foot, Provincial, unidentified mark, circa 1570, 4oz.12dwt. (Christie's) $1,820 £800

Early 19th century silver wine cup by Paul Storr, 3in. high. (Manchester Auction Mart) $1,080 £480

Joshua Vander silver two-handled presentation cup and cover, London, 1889, 1,512gm. (Sotheby's Belgravia) $1,390 £620

Victorian silver gilt two-handled cup by Elkington & Co., Birmingham, 1897, 15½in. high, 184oz. (Christie's) $4,600 £2,000

George IV silver gilt race cup and cover by Matthew Boulton, Birmingham, 1826, 124oz. (Sotheby's) $3,710 £1,650

DECANTERS

Unusual Saunders and Shepherd silver mounted glass claret jug, London, 1895, 20.4cm. high. (Sotheby's Belgravia) $1,705 £820

English electroplated triform decanter stand, 48cm. high, circa 1860, with three blue glass bottles. (Sotheby's Belgravia) $495 £220

Dutch 19th century decanter with silver mounts. (May, Whetter & Grose) $605 £280

Silver decanter and stopper decorated with pronounced texturing by Christopher Lawrence, London, 1973, 885gm. (Sotheby's Belgravia) $940 £420

One of a pair of silver gilt mounted faceted glass decanters and stoppers, by Reily & Storer, London, 1840, 28cm. high. (Sotheby's Belgravia) $2,250 £1,000

Silver decanter and stopper with fine texturing by Christopher Lawrence, London, 1969, 567gm. (Sotheby's Belgravia) $535 £240

One of a pair of George IV plain
oblong entree dishes and covers
by J. E. Terry, 1821, 12in. long,
140oz. (Christie's) $6,480 £3,000

17th century German sweetmeat
dish, Augsburg, circa 1675,
5¼in. wide, 2oz.9dwt.(Sotheby's)
$1,390 £620

George III entree dish and cover,
London, 1800, 42oz. (D. M.
Nesbit & Co.) $1,595 £700

Silver plated Art Nouveau
sweet dish with glass liner,
circa 1910. (Alfie's Antique
Market) $155 £70

19th century rock crystal, silver gilt and
enamel dish. (Phillips) $13,680 £6,000

Mappin & Webb Ltd. open-
work boat-shaped fruit
dish, 1,323gm., London,
1917, 34.6cm. long.
(Sotheby's Belgravia)
$1,310 £580

One of a pair of Victorian shaped circular vegetable dishes and covers by
Robert Garrard, 1858, 116oz., 11½in.
diam. (Christie's) $9,450 £4,200

Silver wheelbarrow bon-bon
dish, 7½oz. (Honiton
Galleries) $450 £200

George III silver presentation meat
dish, 42.5oz. (Woolley & Wallis)
$1,245 £550

One of a pair of George III oblong entree
dishes and covers by Peter and William
Bateman, London, 1810, 133oz.
(Sotheby's) $4,480 £2,000

Early 19th century Continental silver alms dish, 16¾in.
diam. (Olivers)$1,130 £500

One of a pair of George IV oblong entree
dishes and covers by Edward Barnard &
Sons, London, 1833, 114oz.14dwt.
(Sotheby's) $6,495 £2,900

DISHES

One from a set of four Victorian silver entree dishes by Martin Hall & Co., Sheffield, 1856, 216oz. (Sotheby King & Chasemore) $7,345 £3,400

James Dixon & Sons Ltd., quatrefoil dessert dish, Sheffield, 1894, 29.3cm. long, 630gm. (Sotheby's Belgravia) $705 £340

One of a set of four George IV octagonal entree dishes and covers, 10¾in. wide, by William Eley, London, 1827, 205oz.16dwt.(Sotheby's) $6,295 £2,900

One of a pair of George III vegetable dishes and covers by Paul Storr, 1807, 113oz., 9in. diam. (Christie's) $7,344 £3,400

Shaped oval meat dish with gadroon border, circa 1840, 22in. wide. (Sotheby's) $540 £250

One of a pair of Georgian silver entree dishes, London, 1823, 98oz. (Vost's) $2,970 £1,450

Goldsmiths & Silversmiths Co. Ltd., rectangular breakfast dish, cover and liner, London, 1899, 2,079gm., 34.6cm. wide. (Sotheby's Belgravia) $1,205 £580

Late Victorian silver plated bacon dish. (Alfie's Antique Market) $310 £140

One of a pair of George III entree dishes and covers by Paul Storr, 12in. long, 135oz. (Christie's) $13,000 £6,000

Elkington & Co. Ltd. openwork circular fruit dish, Birmingham, 1907, 25cm. diam., 784gm. (Sotheby's Belgravia) $655 £290

Two Eastern chased silver leaf-shaped dishes. (Phillips) $45 £20

Silver chafing-dish with Belgian hall marks, 1772. (Leys, Antwerp) $620 £290

George IV shaped oval meat dish by William Eley, London, 1826, 14in. wide, 34oz.11dwt. with cover. (Sotheby's) $2,710 £1,250

George IV shaped oval venison dish and cover by William Eley, London, 1826, 20¼in. wide, 86oz.10dwt. (Sotheby's) $5,425 £2,500

One of a set of four George IV oblong entree dishes and covers by William Eley, London, 1826, 258oz., 12¼in. wide. (Sotheby's) $8,030 £3,700

19th century French shaped circular ecuelle with stand and cover by Odiot, Paris, circa 1850, 43oz.13dwt., 10in. diam. (Sotheby's) $1,345 £620

A pair of Victorian silver entree dishes, 30.5cm. wide, 1843, 54oz. (Sotheby Humberts) $605 £280

Goldsmiths & Silversmiths Co. Ltd. octagonal bacon dish, London, 1918, 26.1cm. long, 2,373gm. (Sotheby's Belgravia) $1,920 £850

George III silver oblong entree dish and cover by Paul Storr, London, 1808, 63oz.5dwt. (Geering & Colyer) $1,740 £850

Italian two-handled shaped oval fruit dish, 20th century, 48cm. wide, 1,271gm. (Sotheby's Belgravia) $860 £380

One of a set of four Victorian silver entree dishes, 216oz. (Sotheby King & Chasemore) $7,345 £3,400

William Comyns shaped circular wirework fruit stand, 19.6cm. diam., London, 1908, 439gm. (Sotheby's Belgravia) $415 £200

A pair of dessert stands by E. & J. Barnard, London, 1861, 18cm. high, 1,270gm. (Sotheby's Belgravia) $1,770 £850

18th century Dutch silver gilt tazza by Casparus Janszonius, Haarlem, 4¾in. diam., 3oz.14dwt. (Sotheby's) $1,955 £900

One of a pair of silver shaped oval entree dishes by Hawksworth, Eyre & Co., London, 1911, 2,824gm. (Sotheby's Belgravia) $2,070 £900

One of four George III shaped oblong entree dishes and covers by P. & W. Bateman, 1807, 227oz., 11in. long.. (Christie's) $10,800 £4,800

One of a pair of shaped oval fruit dishes by Elkington & Co., London, 1906, 853gm. (Sotheby's Belgravia)
$970 £420

Oblong silver bread dish with openwork handles, by Christopher Lawrence, London 1969, 1,252gm. (Sotheby's Belgravia) $1,120 £500

Boat-shaped pedestal fruit dish by A. W. & G. Sissons, Sheffield, 1911, 517gm. (Sotheby's Belgravia)
$510 £220

Boat-shaped silver openwork fruit dish by Mappin & Webb, Sheffield, 1913, 752gm. (Sotheby's Belgravia) $1,080 £480

George III silver gilt mounted cut-glass butter dish, stand and cover by Samuel Hennell, 1812, 16.6cm., diam. (Christie's) $2,160 £950

17th century Dutch silver embossed dish, maker's mark H. N., Hague 1666, 82oz. (Phillips) $96,750 £45,000

Martin, Hall & Co., electroplated oval breakfast dish with swivel cover, circa 1890, 36.2cm. wide. (Sotheby's Belgravia) $230 £100

Oblong silver entree dish, cover and handle, by James Deakin & Son, Sheffield, 1898, 2,100 gm. (Sotheby's Belgravia) $2,020 £900

Louis XV plain circular ecuelle and cover with shell-shaped handles, maker's mark FBD, Arras, circa 1750, 17oz.11dwt. (Christie's)
$10,215 £4,500

William Hutton & Sons oval silver entree dish, cover, liner and straining dish, Sheffield, 1898, 2,234gm. (Sotheby's Belgravia)$1,840 £820

Victorian silver ewer by George
Ivory, London 1856, 18in. high,
340gm. (Sotheby's Belgravia)
$4,750 £2,200

A late 19th century Indian silver
ewer, 31cm. high. (Sotheby's
Belgravia) $1,250 £550

George IV compressed baluster wine
ewer by William Eaton, London,
1827, 27oz.9dwt., 8½in. high.
(Sotheby's) $2,280 £1,050

Martin Hall & Co., silver ovoid
ewer, London, 1877, 558gm.
(Sotheby's Belgravia)
$1,075 £480

Late Victorian silver bulbous shaped
wine ewer, London, 1892, 15½in. high,
41oz. (Geering & Colyer)$1,915 £850

Martin, Hall & Co., vase-shaped
silver ewer, London, 1870,
916gm, dented. (Sotheby's
Belgravia) $1,835 £820

One of a pair of George III vase-
shaped wine ewers by Thomas
Holland, London 1807, 14in.
high, 148oz.12dwt. (Sotheby's)
$9,115 £4,200

17th century Italian ewer, Naples, 24oz.
10dwt., 9in. high. (Sotheby's)
$4,340 £2,000

Unusual Australian electroplated
ostrich egg ewer, circa 1880,
34.4cm. high. (Sotheby's
Belgravia) $860 £380

FLAGONS

Large chased and engraved silver
flagon by Robert Hennell, London, 1854, 180gm. (Sotheby's
Belgravia) $3,250 £1,450

Large silver presentation flagon by
Mappin & Webb, London, 1888,
36cm. high, 2,291gm. (Sotheby's
Belgravia) $1,455 £700

Victorian silver beer flagon, London,
1855. (Sotheby King & Chasemore)
$710 £350

One of a pair of Scottish bannock toasters, London, 1871, with antelope horn handles. (McCartney, Morris & Barker) $518 £240

One of six Scandinavian silver tablespoons, 18th century, 11oz. (Robert W. Skinner Inc.) $300 £130

Part of a sixty-three piece Queen's pattern table silver set, 111oz. 2dwt. (Sotheby's) $2,916 £1,350

Part of an eighteen-piece silver gilt dessert service by Martin Hall & Co., Sheffield, 1872, 111oz. (Christie's) $2,916 £1,350

Part of a canteen of Holland, Aldwincle & Slater Old English thread pattern table silver, London, 1900, 5,873gm. (Sotheby's Belgravia) $5,198 £2,300

17th century seal-top spoon of East Anglican origin. (Frank H. Fellows) $587 £260

Heavy Edwardian fiddle and thread silver serving spoon, by W. Hutton, London, 1903, 6oz., 13in. long. (Christopher Sykes) $124 £55

Three-piece electroplated place setting by Charles Rennie Mackintosh, circa 1912. (Sotheby's Belgravia) $554 £240

Inlaid walnut canteen of cutlery. (Harrods Estate Offices) $1,155 £500

Ten coffee spoons and a pair of sugar tongs, in case. (Phillips) $69 £32

Silver apostle spoon showing St. Philip and enlarged London hallmark for 1490. (Woolley & Wallis) $14,688 £6,800

Plain James I seal-top spoon, London, 1606, 6½in. long. (Phillips) $1,155 £500

Georgian silver ladle by George Smith and William Fearn, London, 1790. (Christopher Sykes)$101 £45

Silver tablespoon by Ebenezer Coker. (Frank H. Fellows) $56 £25

Part of an eighty-piece George III Coburg pattern table service by William Eley and William Fearn, London, 1823, 172oz.10dwt. (Sotheby's) $31,360 £14,000

Pair of late 19th century fish servers with bone handles, circa 1880. (Christopher Sykes)$61 £27

Early 17th century Swedish parcel gilt spoon by Peter Povdsen, Va, circa 1610. (Sotheby's) $1,302 £600

20th century Liberty 'Cymric' spoon with enamelled bowl by Archibald Knox. (McCartney, Morris & Barker) $406 £200

Cased set of Norwegian silver gilt and enamel spoons and a pair of tongs. (Honiton Galleries) $339 £150

Late 17th century silver gilt canteen of small size, circa 1690. (Bonham's) $10,912 £4,850

Twelve place canteen of game cutlery with carvers, silver mounts dated 1906. (Alfie's Antique Market) $205 £95

17th century provincial apostle spoon by William Ramsay, Newcastle, circa 1660. (Sotheby's) $1,128 £520

18th century Dutch fish slice by Jan Diederik Pont, 1760, 15in. long, 6oz.15dwt. (Sotheby's) $2,576 £1,150

George III scroll engraved sugar tongs, by Peter and William Bateman, London, 1808. (Christopher Sykes) $100 £45

17th century St. Matthew apostle spoon, Exeter, circa 1650, maker's mark I.P. (Sotheby's)$1,760 £780

One of a set of six late 19th century German decorative spoons, 18.3cm. long, 17.4oz.(Sotheby's Belgravia) $315 £140

James I seal top spoon, circa 1611. (Frank H. Fellows) $565 £250

George III bright cut sugar tongs by George Smith & Thomas Hayter, London, 1798. (Christopher Sykes) $125 £55

Charles II silver spoon with rare boar's head finial. (Phillips) $7,750 £3,400

Part of a set of twelve Goldsmiths & Silversmiths Co., fruit knives and forks, London, 1909, 1,084gm. (Sotheby's Belgravia) $940 £420

Fine set of George III fiddle pattern table cutlery by Robert Peppin, London, 1818, 156oz. (Sotheby King & Chasemore) $3,670 £1,700

Part of a thirty-six piece silver gilt dessert service by Nichols & Plinke, St. Petersburg, 1856. (Sotheby's) $8,210 £3,600

Part of a set of Old English shell and drop pattern table silver, London, 1919, 2,539gm. (Sotheby's Belgravia) $2,800 £1,250

Part of a large lot of early 20th century American flower pattern tableware, mostly silver, by Stieff Co., Baltimore. (Sotheby's Belgravia) $3,450 £1,500

Part of a Reed and Barton extensive canteen of 'Francis I' pattern tableware, 301oz., circa 1949. (Sotheby's Belgravia) $7,380 £3,400

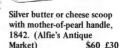

Elizabeth I Maidenhead spoon, London, 1602. (Sotheby's) $2,385 £1,050

Rare pair of Irish provincial serving tongs by Carden Terry, Cork, circa 1765, 5oz. (Phillips) $735 £340

Silver butter or cheese scoop with mother-of-pearl handle, 1842. (Alfie's Antique Market) $60 £30

Pair of silver game skewers, London, 1775, by Hester Bateman. (Frank H. Fellows) $180 £80

Chester silver sugar tongs with claw-like grips, 1914, 4½in. long. (Christopher Sykes) $40 £20

Rare 18th century travelling companion which is also a knife and fork. (Sotheby's) $1,080 £500

One of six Victorian teaspoons sold with sugar tongs by Aldwincle & Slater, London, 1879, 6oz.10dwt. (Sotheby's) $280 £130

Georgian apple corer with turned ivory handle. (Vernon's) $115 £55

One of a set of twelve parcel gilt apostle ice-cream spoons, by Henry Holland & Son, London, 1871, 241gm. (Sotheby's Belgravia) $550 £240

Pair of sugar nips by William Penstone, London, circa 1774, 1oz., engraved with a crest. (Phillips) $120 £55

Edwardian sugar tongs, Sheffield, 1908, ¾oz. (Christopher Sykes) $40 £20

Pair of Georgian silver asparagus servers. (Vost's) $245 £120

Part of a good set of twelve ivory handled silver fruit knives and forks by Elkington & Co., Birmingham, 1899. (Sotheby's Belgravia) $435 £190

Three pieces of silver by Charles Rennie Mackintosh. (Christie's & Edmiston) $7,525 £3,500

Silver composite fruit serving set by Francis Higgins, 1860 and John Gilbert, 1958. (Sotheby's Belgravia) $625 £280

Part of a set of late 19th century Towle Manufacturing Co., tableware, 99.8oz. (Sotheby's Belgravia) $1,845 £850

Part of a 19th century Chawner & Co., beaded Old English pattern table silver, 121oz. (Sotheby's Belgravia) $5,640 £2,600

Part of a set of late 19th century French table silver, maker's mark H. & Cie, 2,419gm. (Sotheby's Belgravia) $1,840 £820

Feather edge caddy spoon by Samuel Pemberton. (Frank H. Fellows)$80 £35

Late Roman/Byzantine silver spoons, 4th-5th century A.D. (Stanley Gibbons Currency Ltd.) $380 £185

One of twelve George II Hanoverian pattern tablespoons by Marmaduke Daintrey, London, 1739, 26oz.19dwt. (Sotheby's) $1,545 £680

Pair of Harrison Brothers & Howson fish servers, Sheffield, 1865, in fitted case. (Sotheby's Belgravia)$475 £210

Pierced silver sugar tongs, 1911, in original box. (Alfie's Antique Market) $55 £25

Silver Harlequin sugar nips, circa 1843. (Alfie's Antique Market) $275 £125

FLATWARE

Part of an one hundred and fifty piece Victorian crested Queen's pattern tableware service by George Adams, London, 1873, 359oz. (Sotheby Beresford Adams) $9,300 £4,000

One of a pair of George II Hanoverian pattern sauce ladles by Elias Cachart, London, 1744, 5oz.5dwt.(Sotheby's) $745 £320

Part of a composite Old English pattern table service, circa 1776-1782. (Christie's) $8,400 £3,800

Part of an extensive service of table silver in Queen Anne style by Francis Higgins, London, 1885, 250oz. (Sotheby's) $22,230 £9,500

Part of an one hundred and twenty-three piece canteen of George IV King's Husk pattern table silver by Paul Storr, W., C. & H. Eley, and Eley & Fearn, 302oz. 14dwt. (Sotheby's) $35,000 £15,000

FRAMES

Gorham Manufacturing Co. rectangular easel mirror, Birmingham, 1912, 43.2cm. high. (Sotheby's Belgravia) $790 £350

Victorian heart mirror, circa 1889. (Alfie's Antique Market) $560 £250

19th century Venetian style mirror, 72cm. high. (Phillips) $60 £30

Liberty & Co. 'Cymric' silver and enamel photograph frame, Birmingham, 1905, 28.5cm. high. (Sotheby's Belgravia) $2,770 £1,200

Art Nouveau style silver framed toilet mirror. (Vernon's) $175 £75

Art Nouveau silver photograph frame, 6in. high. (Vernon's) $85 £40

Silver mounted photograph frame, 16.5cm. high. (Phillips) $55 £25

Two late 19th century German photograph frames in silver coloured metal. (Sotheby's Belgravia) $485 £210

Victorian porcelain photograph frame by C. T. Maling, circa 1875, 19½in. high. (Alfie's Antique Market) $190 £85

GOBLETS AND CHALICES

Stephen Smith & Son lobed bell-shaped wine goblet, London, 1870, 14.3cm. high, 6.5oz. (Sotheby's Belgravia) $90 £40

Holland, Aldwincle & Slater wine goblet, London, 1885, 18.2cm. high, 10oz. (Sotheby's Belgravia) $215 £100

Unusual Charles II wine cup, circa 1675, 3½in. high, 2oz.6dwt. (Sotheby's) $2,690 £1,200

One of a pair of George III wine goblets, London, 1813, 5½in. high, 16oz.18dwt. (Sotheby's) $2,195 £980

Bell-shaped silver goblet, London, 1864, 18.7cm. high, 11.5oz. (Sotheby's Belgravia) $270 £120

18th century Italian chalice and paten by Giovanni Valadier, Rome, 10¼in. high, circa 1775, 24oz.10dwt. (Sotheby's) $1,345 £620

HONEYPOTS

Edwardian silver plated honeypot in the form of a bee. (Vernon's) $195 £85

George III silver gilt honeypot by Paul Storr, London, 1798, 12cm. high, 13oz. (Sotheby Berne) $7,345 £3,400

Silver honeypot by Joseph and John Angell, London, 1836. (Christie's) $1,400 £600

Victorian silver oval shaped inkstand with two cut-glass bottles, London, 1870. (Vernon's) $335 £150

20th century electroplated inkstand with centrepiece of a golfer, 21cm. wide. (Sotheby's Belgravia)
$435 £200

Late Victorian oblong inkstand, 31cm. wide, 33oz.5dwt. (Phillips)$670 £310

C. T. & G. Fox rectangular silver inkstand with two silver mounted glass bottles, London, 1887, 413gm. (Sotheby's Belgravia) $760 £340

Harrods Ltd., two-bottle inkstand on moulded octagonal base, by R. W. Burbridge, London, 1936, 790gm. (Sotheby's Belgravia) $645 £280

Shell inkstand and pot, 11oz., circa 1873. (Alfie's Antique Market) $395 £175

George Angell silver gilt single well inkstand, London, 1860, 21cm. diam. (Sotheby's Belgravia) $455 £220

Guild of Handicrafts Ltd., silver and enamel inkwell, London, 1907, 7.5cm. high.(Sotheby's Belgravia) $370 £170

Late 19th century encrier, ebonised with tortoiseshell and brass decoration. (Vost's)
$615 £300

Oblong two-bottle silver inkstand by Goldsmiths & Silversmiths Co., London, 1927, 719gm. (Sotheby's Belgravia) $670 £300

Oblong two-bottle inkstand by Charles Stuart Harris, London, 1897, 23.8cm. long, 785gm. (Sotheby's Belgravia)
$500 £240

Fine late Victorian inkstand with rococo styled borders, two ink bottles and a silver taper holder, London, 1891, 34oz. (Cooper Hirst) $1,355 £600

Silver inkstand, circa 1914. (Alfie's Antique Market) $170 £75

J. W. Figg two-bottle silver inkstand with silver mounted glass bottles, London, 1882, 288gm.(Sotheby's Belgravia) $540 £240

Unusual Simon Rosenau silver inkstand in the form of a chaise longue, with fitted interior, 1895, 15.4cm. long, 230gm. (Sotheby's Belgravia)
$715 £310

Georgian silver inkstand, London, 1811, 15in. long. (Gray's Antique Mews) $900 £410

Early Victorian inkstand by Paul Storr, London, 1837, 28oz. 16dwt., 11¾in. wide.(Sotheby's) $4,750 £2,200

George III oblong inkstand by John and Thomas Settle, Sheffield, 1815, 11in. long, 36oz.19dwt. (Sotheby's) $4,200 £1,850

Silver inkstand with two bottles, circa 1912, 24oz. (Alfie's Antique Market) $625 £300

Silver encrier by E. & J. Barnard, London, 1852. (Vost's) $965 £470

Silver inkstand, Sheffield, 1882, by M. W. & Co. (Sotheby King & Chasemore) $605 £280

Rectangular silver two-bottle inkstand with marks of W. & J. Barnard and C. J. Hill, London, 1888, 657gm. (Sotheby's Belgravia) $850 £380

Regency silver rectangular shaped standish, Sheffield, 1819, 12oz. (Sotheby Humberts)$345 £160

Stephen Smith & Son rectangular two-bottle inkstand, 34cm. long, London, 1875, 1,093gm., with later bottle holders. (Sotheby's Belgravia)$665 £320

Edward Barnard & Sons beaded oblong silver inkstand with two silver mounted glass bottles, London, 1873, 963gm. (Sotheby's Belgravia) $940 £420

English silver inkstand with watch in lid, 1911. (Gray's Antique Mews) $550 £245

Turner & Simpson Ltd. silver and electroplated inkstand, Birmingham, 1926, 32.8cm. long. (Sotheby's Belgravia) $1,580 £700

Fine papier mache inkstand, the glass inkpots with plated tops. (Vernon's) $120 £55

R. & S. Garrard & Co., silver inkstand in the form of a late 16th century spice box, London, 1903, 497gm. (Sotheby's Belgravia) $760 £340

Simple Queen Anne silver inkstand. (Bonham's) $2,040 £950

Hallmarked silver jug, Chester, 1901. (Frank H. Fellows) $180 £80

Silver topped shaving brush and covered hot water jug by John Holloway, 1788. (Phillips) $3,175 £1,550

Jensen silver jug, London, 1926, 16.5cm. high. (Sotheby's Belgravia) $1,155 £500

Atkin Brothers tapering circular hot water jug on stand, Sheffield, 1878, 33cm. high, 929gm. (Sotheby's Belgravia) $455 £220

George V silver hot water jug, Sheffield, 1914, 6in. wide. (Christopher Sykes) $280 £125

William IV silver water jug, London, 1837. (Alfie's Antique Market) $1,170 £450

Stephen Smith & Son Cellini pattern hot water jug, London, 1870, 27.5cm. high, 1,362gm. (Sotheby's Belgravia) $935 £450

Early George III baluster beer jug by Benjamin Cartwright, London, 1765, 7½in. high, 25oz.7dwt. (Sotheby's) $6,495 £2,900

Martin, Hall & Co. heavy ovoid silver beer jug with armorial engraving, London, 1874, 1,711gm. (Sotheby's Belgravia) $2,240 £1,000

Early Elizabeth I stoneware jug with silver gilt mountings, 7¼in. high, London, 1570. (Phillips) $26,105 £11,500

Heavy and unusual silver water jug in the form of a dozing satyr, by Alexander Macrae, London, 1859, 1,380gm. (Sotheby's Belgravia) $7,170 £3,200

Richard Sawyer silver baluster hot water jug with hinged cover, Dublin, 1845, 391gm. (Sotheby's Belgravia) $670 £300

Victorian army officer's silver whistle. (Phillips) $170 £80

Victorian ear-trumpet with ivory ear-piece and silver trumpet, by Hawkesworth Eyre & Co., Sheffield, 1845. (Christie's S. Kensington) $1,170 £520

One of a pair of Indian silver anklets, 33oz. (Honiton Galleries) $405 £180

Elkington & Co. silver and copper electrotype copy of the plaque 'The Milton Shield', 86cm. high, Birmingham, 1869. (Sotheby's Belgravia) $830 £400

Oak port/brandy dispensing barrel with silver plated bands, circa 1890, 5in. diam. (Christopher Sykes) $195 £85

One of a pair of late 19th century German silver gilt two-light wall sconces, 61cm. high. (Sotheby's Belgravia) $1,920 £850

Wiener Werkstatte bottle cap by Josef Hoffmann, 4.5cm. high, circa 1920. (Sotheby's Belgravia) $415 £180

Silver gilt travelling canteen by Thomas Heming and Robert Garrard, 101oz. (Christie's) $45,000 £20,000

Wiener Werkstatte bottle cap, designed by Josef Hoffmann in silver coloured metal, circa 1920, 4cm. high. (Sotheby's Belgravia) $390 £170

Edwardian plated egg warmer and spirit burner. (Alfie's Antique Market) $70 £30

Unusual Martin, Hall & Co. silver spoon warmer in the shape of a lady's shoe, Sheffield, 1898, 534gm. (Sotheby's Belgravia) $1,230 £550

Cylindrical silver shaving pot with telescopic stand, cover and burner, by R. & S. Garrard & Co., London, 1851, 1,155gm. (Sotheby's Belgravia) $1,615 £720

MISCELLANEOUS

One of a pair of 18th century Sicilian snuffers and stands by Pietro Donia, Messina, 11in. long, 6oz.8dwt. (Sotheby's) $780 £360

19th century Peruvian silver potty, 27½oz. (Sotheby Bearne) $775 £360

Victorian plated dog collar. (Phillips) $405 £180

Victorian silver parcel gilt double spirit measure, 4½in. high. (Christie's S. Kensington) $725 £360

Shaped circular cake stand on short spreading foot, by Atkin Bros., Sheffield, 1933, 936gm.(Sotheby's Belgravia) $965 £420

Rare George III pastille burner by Andrew Fogelberg and Stephen Gilbert, London, 1785, 7¾in. high, 9oz.17dwt. (Sotheby's) $3,040 £1,400

Pilgrim flask by Robert Garrard, London, 1876, 155oz. (Bonham's) $12,530 £5,800

George Unite silver chatelaine, circa 1872. (Alfie's Antique Market) $370 £165

Thomas Bradbury & Sons cylindrical Argyll, in early 19th century style, Sheffield, 1928, 689gm. (Sotheby's Belgravia) $830 £360

William and Mary oval liberty badge by Robert Cooper, 1693. (Sotheby's) $3,655 £1,800

Large Italian hot water stand and cover, by Pietro Spagna, Rome, circa 1830, 445oz. (Christie's) $13,620 £6,000

Silver penny of King Offa's queen, Cynethryth, circa 787-792. (Spink & Son) $21,600 £10,000

602

One of a pair of models of pheasants by Edward Barnard & Sons, London, 1961-62, 1,289gm. (Sotheby's Belgravia)
$1,100 £480

Early 20th century electroplate and antelope horn Welsh dragon table lighter by Walker & Hall, 51.5cm. long. (Sotheby's Belgravia)
$370 £160

One of a pair of models of pheasants, maker's mark LAG, London, 1961. (Sotheby's Belgravia)
$620 £270

Unusual silver model of a water cart with revolving wheels and sprung handle, by E. H. Stockwell, 1885, 176gm. (Sotheby's Belgravia)
$690 £300

Victorian model of a medieval knight on horseback by J. S. Hunt, circa 1840, 6½in. long. (Christie's)
$2,810 £1,250

Charles T. and George Fox owl shaped mustard pot, 11.5cm. high, 9.9oz. (Sotheby's Belgravia)
$840 £360

Silver model of a grouse by Berthold Muller, 13in. high. (Bonham's) $900 £400

Silver model of a running fox by Holland, Aldwincle & Slater, London, 1889, 44.5cm. long. (Sotheby's Belgravia) $1,350 £600

Silver model of a stag. (Graves Son & Pilcher)
$5,185 £2,400

One of a pair of B. Neresheimer & Sohne figures of knights, Hanau, 1911, 2,795gm. (Sotheby's Belgravia) $5,825 £2,800

Two Victorian silver statuettes of jockeys by Barnard & Co., circa 1840, 6¾in. high, 11oz. 11dwt. (Christie's) $855 £380

Silver model of a hunter by L. Wallis Good, 1928, 222oz., 17¾in. long. (Christie's)
$8,100 £3,600

MUGS

G. J. Richards silver spool-shaped child's can, London, 1854, 158gm. (Sotheby's Belgravia) $335 £150

Silver christening mug, Birmingham, 1923, 3in. high. (Christopher Sykes) $65 £30

Christening mug with child's knife, fork and spoon, by Hunt & Roskell and Francis Higgins, 1867-73. (Sotheby's Belgravia) $1,570 £700

Liberty & Co., 'Cymric' silver mug with loop handle, 1901, 7.5cm. high. (Sotheby's Belgravia) $555 £240

Silver christening mug, circa 1858. (Alfie's Antique Market) $130 £60

Charles II baluster mug, London, 1683, 5oz.17dwt. (Sotheby's) $1,680 £750

Edward Barnard & Sons bell-shaped child's can, 6oz.11.7cm. high. (Sotheby's Belgravia) $280 £130

Baluster shaped silver mug, 1752. (McCartney, Morris & Parker) $535 £260

Edward Barnard & Sons child's can, London, 1883, 9.5cm. high, 5.5oz. (Sotheby's Belgravia) $140 £65

MULLS

Scottish Regimental ram's horn snuff mull with silver cover, Edinburgh, 1864. (May, Whetter & Grose) $595 £275

Georgian silver snuff mull. (Alfie's Antique Market) $180 £85

Ram's horn snuff box in the shape of a foot, circa 1790, 4in. high. (Christopher Sykes) $110 £50

George IV baluster mustard pot and spoon by Paul Storr, 1829, 3¼in. high, 6oz.8dwt. (Sotheby's) $1,075 £460

English die-stamped oval mustard pot, Birmingham, 1900. (Sotheby's Belgravia) $195 £90

Italian mustard pot and stand, Naples, 1792, stand 4½in. diam., 7oz.10dwt. (Sotheby's) $385 £170

George III cylindrical mustard pot by Hester Bateman, 1790, with spoon, 3½in. high, 3oz.8dwt. (Sotheby's) $1,015 £450

Silver gilt mustard pot by John Bridge, 1825, 24oz. (Bruton Knowles) $5,535 £2,450

One of a pair of George III vase shaped peppers by Samuel Whitford II, London, 1809, 5oz.8dwt. (Sotheby's) $1,450 £620

George III barrel shaped mustard pot by Robert and David Hennell, London, 1798, 3in. high, 3oz. 13dwt. (Sotheby's) $795 £340

Pair of Victorian silver pepper pots, 1872, with glass eyes, 3½in. high, 5oz.8dwt. (Christie's) $1,810 £800

One of a rare pair of early George III openwork mustard pots by Augustin Le Sage, London, 1765, 7oz.19dwt., 2¾in. high.(Sotheby's) $3,745 £1,600

NEFS

Continental two-masted nef on four wheels, 17½in. high, dated for 1901. (Christie's) $3,615 £1,650

Late 19th century German nef on dolphin stem, with pseudo hallmarks, 732gm. (Sotheby's Belgravia) $1,900 £850

Continental two-masted nef on four wheels, circa 1900, 15¼in. high. (Christie's) $4,380 £2,000

PORRINGERS

Mid 17th century porringer by Nicholas Wollaston, London, 1650. 6in. wide, 7oz.10dwt. (Sotheby's) $4,145 £1,850

Rare Charles II silver gilt porringer and cover, 1670, 29oz. (Christie's) $103,680 £48,000

Commonwealth porringer by Gilbert Shepherd, London, 1656, 2in. high, 2oz.8dwt. (Sotheby's) $1,955 £900

George II silver porringer by Sarah Parr, London, 1731, 10oz. (Sotheby Humberts) $520 £240

Charles II plain silver gilt porringer, 3½in. high, 7oz.7dwt. (Christie's) $1,800 £800

Charles II two-handled porringer, 4½in. high, 13oz.13dwt. (Christie's) $2,375 £1,100

Two-handled circular porringer by Turner Bradbury, London, 1893, 23cm. wide, 16.6oz. (Sotheby's Belgravia) $445 £190

Charles II plain two-handled porringer on rim foot, probably West Country, maker's mark IP, circa 1670, 6oz.3dwt. (Christie's) $3,860 £1,700

William III porringer, by Seth Lofthouse, London, 1700, 6¾in. wide, 7oz.4dwt. (Sotheby's) $1,525 £680

QUAICHS

One of a pair of Indian quaichs, 7oz. (Phillips) $85 £40

Hallmarked silver quaich by Hamilton & Inches. (Frank H. Fellows) $315 £140

Silver mounted wood quaich, 4½in. diam., circa 1720. (Sotheby's) $585 £250

One of a pair of George III oval salt cellars by Paul Storr, London, 1812, 4½in. wide, 18oz.4dwt. (Sotheby's) $2,060 £950

One of two George III oval salts by John Moore and William Abdy, London, 1806, 3½in. wide. (Sotheby King & Chasemore)
$340 £150

One of a pair of oval salt cellars by Paul Storr, London, 1804, 4in. wide, 8oz.15dwt. (Sotheby's) $850 £380

Pair of Edwardian oblong salt cellars and spoons in case. (Phillips) $30 £15

One of a pair of George IV salt cellars by Paul Storr, London, 1827, 3¾in. wide, 7oz.15dwt. (Sotheby's) $3,730 £1,650

Pair of Edwardian circular double-handled salt cellars and two spoons in case, 2oz.15dwt. (Phillips)
$45 £20

One of a set of four late 19th century pedestal salt cellars by B. Weber, 15oz., 12cm. wide. (Sotheby's Belgravia)
$315 £140

Part of a Robert Hennell three-piece condiment set, London, 1842, 542gm. (Sotheby's Belgravia) $580 £260

Silver gilt gem-set table salt by Omar Ramsden, London, 1930. (Parsons, Welch & Cowell)
$1,350 £600

One of a set of four George II circular salt cellars by Peter Taylor, London, 1740, 18oz. 15dwt. (Sotheby's)
$3,050 £1,350

One of a set of six Elkington & Co., cast silver double salt cellars, Birmingham, 1911, 2,964gm. (Sotheby's Belgravia)$8,070 £3,600

One of a set of four George II circular vase shaped salt cellars by Paul Storr, 1804, 21oz. (Christie's) $4,745 £2,100

One of a pair of George III silver sauceboats by W. Quipps, 8in. wide, 22oz. (Eadon, Lockwood & Riddle) $1,730 £800

One of a pair of William IV shell-shaped sauceboats by Charles Fox, 1836, 34oz. (Christie's) $5,175 £2,300

One of a pair of silver sauceboats by Paul de Lamerie, 1748. (Christie's) $6,560 £3,200

One of a pair of George II sauceboats by Fuller White, 1747, 34oz. (Christie's) $5,185 £2,400

Unmarked silver and coconut shell pap boat, circa 1760, 5in. long. (Christopher Sykes) $170 £75

One of a pair of early George III oval sauceboats by William Skeen, London, 1763, 8¼in. wide, 29oz.12dwt. (Sotheby's) $2,280 £1,050

George IV oval sauceboat by E. E. J. & W. Barnard, London, 1829, 7in. wide, 17oz.1dwt. (Sotheby's) $1,970 £880

One of a pair of Victorian shell-form sauceboats by Robert Garrard, London, 1872, 47oz.3dwt., 8¾in. wide. (Sotheby's) $3,145 £1,450

One of a pair of silver sauceboats by Digby Scott and Benjamin Smith, 1806, 115oz. (Phillips) $33,480 £15,500

One of a pair of George IV oval sauceboats by Charles Fox, London, 1823, 9½in. long, 37oz. 1dwt. (Sotheby's)$4,555 £1,100

A pair of silver sauceboats, Birmingham, 1934, 8oz. (Honiton Galleries) $260 £115

One of a pair of George II oval sauceboats by William Cripps, London, 1754, 8in. wide, 28oz. 8dwt. (Sotheby's)$4,230 £1,950

One of a pair of George III plain oval sauceboats by James Young, 1771, 30oz. (Christie's) $5,085 £2,300

One of a pair of George III sauceboats by George Smith, London, 1770, 6¾in. long, 16oz.16dwt. (Sotheby's) $3,135 £1,400

One of a pair of Harrison Brothers & Howson sauceboats, London, 1909, 26oz., 21.5cm. wide. (Sotheby's Belgravia) $630 £290

One of a pair of George II sauceboats by John Pollock, London, 1754, 8¼in. long, 26oz.7dwt. (Sotheby's) $3,390 £1,500

One of a pair of 18th century sauceboats, 8in. wide, circa 1740, 36oz. 12dwt. (Sotheby's) $3,880 £1,800

One of a pair of George II plain oval sauceboats by Thomas Heming, 1756, 23oz. (Christie's) $1,655 £750

SCENT BOTTLES

Silver mounted earthenware scent flask by Sampson Mordan & Co., London, 1885, 5.7cm. long. (Sotheby's Belgravia) $125 £55

Silver mounted porcelain willow pattern scent flask by Sampson Mordan & Co., London, 1885, 5.5cm. long. (Sotheby's Belgravia) $115 £50

Blue overlay scent bottle with silver top, 1890. (Alfie's Antique Market) $80 £40

Silver mounted earthenware scent flask, unmarked, circa 1885, 7cm. long. (Sotheby's Belgravia) $255 £110

Parcel gilt scent flask with hinged lid by Sampson Mordan & Co., London, 1883, 5.4cm. long. (Sotheby's Belgravia) $160 £70

All silver scent bottle, circa 1890-1900. (Alfie's Antique Market) $90 £45

SNUFF BOXES

George III silver gilt oblong snuff box by William Parker, London, 1805, 3in. long. (Sotheby's) $1,520 £650

George IV silver gilt oblong snuff box by Mary Ann and Charles Reily, London, 1828, 6oz.16dwt. (Sotheby's) $1,945 £900

Regency silver gilt snuff box. (Woolley & Wallis) $510 £220

Rectangular silver snuff box with gilt interior, by Nathaniel Mills, Birmingham, 1839, 157gm. (Sotheby's Belgravia) $620 £270

Rare silver gilt 'mask' snuff box, 3in. wide. (Sotheby's) $5,600 £2,500

Small English gilt metal snuff box, mid 18th century, Birmingham, 3.8cm. wide. (Sotheby's) $360 £160

French silver snuff box, Paris, 1730, 6.5cm. wide. (Sotheby's Zurich) $1,820 £810

Silver and niello snuff box with gilt interior, Moscow, circa 1860, 7cm. wide. (Sotheby's) $545 £240

Shaped rectangular silver snuff box with gilt interior by Ed. Smith, Birmingham, 1851, 7.2cm. long. (Sotheby's Belgravia) $435 £190

Victorian papier mache snuff box with metal inlay. (Vernon's) $35 £15

Austro-Hungarian gold rectangular snuff box, Vienna, 1840, 8.2cm. long. (Sotheby's) $2,465 £1,100

George IV silver gilt snuff box with floral decoration. (Vernon's) $360 £165

Attractive Meissen snuff box with silver gilt mounts, circa 1735, 7cm. wide. (Sotheby's) $11,284 £5,200

George II oblong snuff box, London, 1757, 2¾in. wide. (Sotheby's) $1,905 £850

George IV silver gilt musical snuff box by John Brough, London, 1818, 3½in. wide. (Sotheby's)$1,735 £800

George III Irish silver snuff box by Abraham Tuppy, Dublin, 1782, 3¼in. wide. (Christie's S. Kensington) $710 £390

Victorian oblong 'pedlar' snuff box by John Linnet, London, 1838, 3¾in. long. (Sotheby's) $2,340 £1,000

Silver gilt table snuff box, London, 1819, 6oz. (Alonzo Dawes & Hoddell) $1,080 £500

George IV oblong snuff box by Thos. Shaw, Birmingham, 1829, 3¾in. long. (Sotheby's) $980 £420

Unusual silver gilt snuff box in the form of a book, by A. J. Strachan, London. (Sotheby's) $5,480 £2,700

Victorian oblong snuff box by Geo. Unite, Birmingham 1854, 4¼in. long. (Sotheby's) $1,125 £480

Large silver gilt snuff box by Nathaniel Mills, Birmingham, 1835, 206gm. (Sotheby's Belgravia) $1,525 £680

Silver gilt and niello snuff box, Moscow, circa 1850, 8.5cm. wide. (Sotheby's) $1,480 £650

Small English gilt metal snuff box, Birmingham, circa 1750, 4.2cm. wide. (Sotheby's) $290 £130

TANKARDS

Charles II tapering cylindrical tankard, London, 1678, 7¼in. high, 25oz.19dwt. (Sotheby's)
$6,510 £3,000

George II baluster tankard by Fuller White, London, 1759, 26oz.18dwt., 7¾in. high. (Sotheby's)
$4,145 £1,850

Silver quart tankard and cover by Thomas Swift, London, 1789, 29½oz. (Frank H. Fellows)
$1,105 £490

Small silver beer mug, London, 1801, 8½oz. (D. M. Nesbit & Co.)
$390 £170

Queen Anne cylindrical tankard by Nathaniel Locke, London, 1713, 7in. high, 21oz.6dwt. (Sotheby's)
$4,255 £1,900

William and Mary cylindrical tankard, 1691, 24oz. (Christie's)
$2,590 £1,200

Early Charles II tapered cylindrical tankard, London, 1663, 6¼in. high, 23oz.19dwt. (Sotheby's)
$6,050 £2,700

Norwegian cylindrical peg tankard on three pomegranate feet, Oslo, 1684, maker's mark RR or KK, 53oz. (Christie's) $16,350 £7,200

James II tapering cylindrical tankard by John Jackson, London, 1688, 8¾in. high, 39oz.19dwt. (Sotheby's) $7,595 £3,500

George II silver cylindrical quart tankard by Sarah Parr, London, 1731. (Frank H. Fellows) $2,200 £1,000

George III tankard of slight baluster form with domed cover, 24oz.10dwt.(Phillips)
$1,295 £600

George II tapered cylindrical tankard by Thomas Farren, London, 1731, 7¼in. high, 31oz.11dwt.(Sotheby's)
$5,600 £2,500

Massive parcel gilt cylindrical tankard, 9¼in. high, marked Danzig 17th century. (Andrew Grant) $9,840 £4,800

Baluster shaped silver tankard, 1732. (McCartney, Morris & Barker) $560 £260

George III tapering cylindrical tankard, by Peter and Anne Bateman, London, 1797, 7¼in. high, 26oz. 6dwt. (Sotheby's) $1,625 £750

Embossed silver tankard, London, 1674, 38oz. (Phillips) $1,835 £850

Charles II tapering cylindrical tankard, London, 1664, 6¼in. high, 21oz.3dwt. (Sotheby's) $10,850 £5,000

Large tankard of Carolean design, London, 1885, 40oz. (Andrew Grant) $1,845 £900

George III tapered cylindrical tankard by Charles Wright, London, 1778, 8in. high, 26oz.7dwt. (Sotheby's) $2,800 £1,250

Tankard given to Bismarck by Wilhelm I of Prussia, 24½in. high, 1871. (Christie's) $153,680 £68,000

George III gilt lined tankard with lid. (Woolley & Wallis) $1,175 £520

Dutch plain tapering cylindrical tankard on domed foot, maker's mark IF, Groningen, 1705, 8oz. 13dwt. (Christie's) $9,080 £4,000

Queen Anne tapered cylindrical tankard by John Martin Stockar, London, 1712, 16oz.3dwt., 5¾in. high. (Sotheby's) $4,255 £1,900

German cylindrical tankard of silver coloured metal with pseudo-hallmarks, circa 1900, 1,115gm. (Sotheby's Belgravia) $2,350 £1,050

TEA CADDIES

Silver tea caddy, circa 1898, 56mm. wide. (Alfie's Antique Market)
$140 £65

One of a pair of George III square tea caddies by R. & S. Hennell, 1803, 26oz. (Christie's) $4,725 £2,100

Walker & Hall Ltd., bombe tea caddy and cover, Sheffield, 1899, 14.5cm. high, 429gm. (Sotheby's Belgravia)
$355 £170

George III drum-shaped tea caddy by John Vere and Wm. Lutwyche, London, 1768, 4in. high, 15oz. 9dwt. (Sotheby's) $3,470 £1,600

George III silver tea caddy. (Woolley & Wallis) $995 £440

Baluster shaped tea caddy, London, 1897, with repousse panels. (Andrew Grant) $430 £210

Silver tea caddy by Paul de Lamerie, 1724, 13.3cm. high, 15oz.13dwt. (Christie's)
$13,500 £6,000

Set of three George III oblong tea caddies in Chinese silver mounted box. (Christie's) $10,370 £4,800

One of a pair of George II oval tea caddies by John Farnell, London, 1727, 5in. high, 16oz. 10dwt. (Sotheby's)
$3,470 £1,600

George III octagonal tea caddy by George Dowye, London, 1764, 4in. high, 15oz.19dwt.(Sotheby's)
$3,695 £1,650

Square silver tea caddy chased in relief with chinoiserie scenes, by C. T. & G. Fox, London, 1863, 556gm. (Sotheby's Belgravia)
$2,195 £980

George III square tea caddy engraved with imitation Chinese characters, maker's mark AL, 1786, 14oz.7dwt. (Christie's)
$3,400 £1,500

Four-piece tea service by W. G. Sissons, Sheffield, 1928-30, 64oz. (Sotheby King & Chasemore) $1,695 £750

Late 19th century four-piece tea service by Harrison Bros. & Howson, 51oz. (Honiton Galleries) $1,310 £580

William Hutton & Sons Ltd. silver Art Nouveau tea and coffee service with tray, London, 1902-07. (Sotheby's Belgravia) $3,725 £1,700

Six-piece tea and coffee service by Rand W. Wilson, Philadelphia, circa 1825. (Phillips, Ward-Price) $8,815 £3,815

Three-piece silver tea service by Liberty & Co., Birmingham, 1903. (Christie's S. Kensington) $765 £380

A Wang Hing silver coloured metal teaset, circa 1900. (Sotheby's Belgravia) $800 £350

William IV three-piece tea service, London, 1831, 49oz. (Frank H. Fellows) $2,080 £920

George III style three-piece silver tea service, Sheffield, 1934, 46oz. (D. M. Nesbit & Co.) $1,655 £725

TEA AND COFFEE SETS

George Wish four-piece teaset, Sheffield, 1932, 1,995gm. (Sotheby's Belgravia) $977 £470

C. S. Harris teapot and coffee pot, London, 1901-02, 1,314gm. (Sotheby's Belgravia) $707 £340

George IV four-piece tea and coffee service by William Bateman, 77oz. (Christie's) $3,564 £1,650

20th century Chinese silver coloured metal tea service, 1,961gm. (Sotheby's Belgravia) $672 £310

Six-piece Victorian tea and coffee service by Robert Hennell, 1850, 112oz. (Christie's) $4,968 £2,300

Large three-piece silver Dutch tea service, circa 1840. (Leys, Antwerp) $1,450 £675

Elkington & Co. Ltd., four-piece teaset, London, 1901, 2,667gm. (Sotheby's Belgravia) $1,622 £780

Louis XIV pattern three-piece teaset by E. & J. Barnard, London, 1857, 1,720gm. (Sotheby's Belgravia) $1,622 £780

Asprey & Co. Ltd., five-piece teaset and tray, 3,350gm., Birmingham, 1933. (Sotheby's Belgravia) $2,080 £1,000

Three-piece Victorian afternoon teaset, 1893, 13oz. 15dwt. (Phillips) $226 £105

Wire-lined and engraved silver three-piece tea service, Chester, 1911, 26¼oz. (Clifford Dann) $648 £300

Lee & Wigfull Ltd. four-piece teaset, Sheffield, 1935, 1,909gm. (Sotheby's Belgravia) $1,582 £700

Four-piece tea and coffee service, London, 1844, 2,500gm. sold with a pair of sugar tongs. (Sotheby's Belgravia) $2,600 £1,250

Five-piece tea and coffee set with tea kettle by E. & J. Barnard, London, 1866, 4,452gm. (Sotheby's Belgravia) $3,120 £1,500

Hancocks & Co. Ltd., five-piece tea and coffee set, London, 1900-03, 2,274gm. (Sotheby's Belgravia) $1,622 £780

Early 19th century Dutch four-piece teaset, 57oz. 15dwt. (Sotheby's) $2,821 £1,300

TEA AND COFFEE SETS

Part of a four-piece tea and coffee set, 59oz. (Phillips)
$1,166 £540

Good Chinese export silver three-piece bachelor teaset.
(Bonham's)
$305 £150

William IV three-piece teaset with similar coffee pot.
(Woolley & Wallis)
$2,700 £1,250

Victorian silver tea service, London, 1894. (Nottinghill
Antique Market)
$720 £320

Victorian four-piece tea and coffee service by George
Angell, London, 1849, 82oz. (Parsons, Welch &
Cowell)
$2,842 £1,400

Four-piece tea and coffee set, Glasgow, 1909, 61oz.14dwt.
(Sotheby's)
$1,295 £600

Five-piece circular tea and coffee set, 112oz.10dwt.
(Phillips)
$2,030 £940

20th century silver tea and coffee service by Goldsmiths
& Silversmiths Co., 117½oz., with ivory handles.
(Neales)
$2,700 £1,250

George III three-piece oblong silver teaset, London, 1809, 31½oz. (Parsons, Welch & Cowell) $945 £420

George III three-piece teaset by G. McHattie, Edinburgh, 1817, 45oz.7dwt. (Sotheby's) $1,685 £780

Chinese silver three-piece tea service with tray and sugar tongs, circa 1900. (Manchester Auction Mart) $630 £310

Five-piece Edwardian silver tea service, London, 1905-06, 104oz. (Dacre, Son & Hartley) $1,945 £900

Five-piece silver tea and coffee service, London, 1939, 210oz. (Manchester Auction Mart) $3,565 £1,650

Three-piece coffee service by Auguste Dufour, Belgium. (Leys, Antwerp) $965 £450

Four-piece silver tea service by John Angell, London, 1824. (Vosts's) $1,845 £900

Fine Victorian tea and coffee service, London, 1880, 132.5oz., in fitted oak case. (Buckell & Ballard) $2,916 £1,350

619

TEA AND COFFEE SETS

Edwardian silver teaset by Roberts & Belk, Sheffield, 1902, 36½oz. (Olivers) $700 £310

James Dixon & Sons Ltd. three-piece teaset, 1892, Sheffield, 1,303gm. (Sotheby's Belgravia) $1,175 £520

Late 19th century Indian silver teaset of four pieces, 3,778gm. (Sotheby's Belgravia) $1,020 £470

Victorian four-piece tea and coffee service, London, 1851, 80oz.2dwt. (Sotheby's) $3,700 £1,650

Matching four-piece silver tea and coffee set, various makers, London, 1855-57, 2,156gm. (Sotheby's Belgravia) $2,800 £1,250

George IV circular teapot and coffee pot by John Bridge, London, 1823, 47oz.7dwt. (Sotheby's) $1,560 £720

John Edward Terry four-piece silver tea and coffee set, London, 1831, 2,733gm. $4,700 £2,100

Small Edward Barnard & Sons silver three-piece teaset, 1886, with sugar tongs by Francis Higgins, 1886, 646gm. (Sotheby's Belgravia) $1,120 £500

Roberts & Slater silver teapot, hot water jug and sugar basin, en suite, Sheffield, 1852, 1,808gm. (Sotheby's Belgravia) $1,970 £880

Matching three-piece silver teaset, the teapot by W. Hutton & Sons, London, 1907, the jug and basin by J. G. Ltd., Birmingham, 1915, 1,029gm. (Sotheby's Belgravia) $850 £380

Unusual four-piece silver teaset decorated with honeycomb facets, by Joseph and George Angell, 1846, 2,120gm. (Sotheby's Belgravia) $3,920 £1,750

George IV three-piece tea service by Emes & Barnard, London, 1826, 49oz.10dwt. (Sotheby's) $2,240 £1,000

Silver coffee pot and hot water jug, with fibre handles and buttons, maker's mark JW & Co, London, 1936. (Sotheby's Belgravia) $805 £360

Three-piece silver teaset by John Round & Son, Sheffield, 1899, 1,417gm. (Sotheby's Belgravia) $1,230 £550

Matching four-piece silver teaset by various makers, Sheffield, 1882-83, 2,405gm. (Sotheby's Belgravia) $2,350 £1,050

Small Charles Stuart Harris three-piece silver teaset, London, 1878, 77gm. (Sotheby's Belgravia) $830 £370

TEA AND COFFEE SETS

19th century Oriental silver tea service of three pieces with embossed floral design. (Vernon's)
$130 £60

Faceted oval tea pot, kettle and hot water jug by Hamilton & Inches, Edinburgh, 1919-28, 2,368gm. (Sotheby's Belgravia) $2,070 £900

Three-piece George III tea service by W. & P. Cunningham, Edinburgh, 1806, gross 38oz. (Christie's) $3,070 £1,350

R. & S. Garrard & Co., three piece silver teaset, London, 1875, 1,604gm. all in. (Sotheby's Belgravia) $1,835 £820

Reed & Barton sterling silver teaset, Chippendale style, 186 Troy oz. (Robert W. Skinner Inc.)
$4,200 £1,910

Four-piece Victorian tea and coffee service by Barnard & Co., circa 1840, gross 80oz. (Christie's) $6,130 £2,700

Natham & Hayes silver four-piece coffee set, 1901, with P. & W. Bateman sugar tongs, 1806, 1,773gm. all in. (Sotheby's Belgravia) $1,725 £750

Five-piece silver tea service in Egyptian style by Gorham, 90 Troy oz. (Robert W. Skinner Inc.)
$2,000 £910

Small matching electroplated four-piece teaset and tray in Indo-Scottish taste, by Lee & Wigfull, Sheffield, circa 1880. (Sotheby's Belgravia) $335 £150

Sibray, Hall & Co., three-piece silver teaset, maker's mark J. H. London, 1895, 1,256gm. (Sotheby's Belgravia) $1,165 £520

Fine Victorian four-piece silver plate teaset with raised scroll decorations. (James Harrison) $350 £155

Harrison Bros. & Howson silver four-piece teaset, Sheffield & London, 1906-10, 1,066gm. all in. (Sotheby's Belgravia) $1,010 £440

Electroplated four-piece tea and coffee set by Mappin & Webb, circa 1880. (Sotheby's Belgravia) $250 £110

Late Victorian five-piece tea and coffee set by Smith, Sissons & Co., London, 61oz. (Sotheby King & Chasemore) $2,160 £1,000

Early Victorian four-piece silver tea and coffee service by J. Charles Edington, London, 1846, 80oz. (H. C. Wolton & Son) $2,460 £1,140

Five-piece silver teaset by Mark Willis & Sons Ltd., Sheffield, 1905, 3,049gm. all in. (Sotheby's Belgravia) $2,645 £1,150

TEA KETTLES

Late 19th century tea kettle, lampstand and burner, 9¼in. high, in plated silver. (Sotheby's) $345   £160

Art Nouveau silver plated tea kettle and lampstand. (Alfie's Antique Market) $206   £95

George III tea kettle on lampstand by Solomon Hougham, London, 1803, 13¾in. high, 79oz.11dwt. (Sotheby's) $1,510   £700

William IV tea kettle and stand by Paul Storr, London, 1813. (Christie's) $5,500   £2,445

19th century Indian silver teapot with spirit burner, 12in. high. (Gray's Antique Mews) $562   £250

Victorian circular hot water kettle by Hyam Hyams, London, 1858, 50oz.10dwt.(Phillips) $1,080   £500

Edward VII plain bullet shaped tea kettle on stand, London, 1903, 11½in. high, 47oz. (Russell, Baldwin & Bright) $820   £380

Electroplated tea kettle on lampstand by Richard Hodd & Son, circa 1885, 34cm. high. (Sotheby's Belgravia) $220   £95

Marshall & Sons circular tea kettle, Edinburgh, 1840, 25.7cm. high, with later stand. (Sotheby's Belgravia) $1,455   £700

Early George I circular tea kettle and lampstand by Gabriel Sleath, London, 1715, 102oz.8dwt., 15in. high. (Sotheby's) $31,465   £14,500

Thomas Bradbury & Sons Ltd. tea kettle on lampstand, London, 1913, 31.5cm. high, 1,565gm. (Sotheby's Belgravia) $1,355   £600

Victorian plated tea kettle and stand with ebony finial. (Vernon's) $120   £55

Fine Liberty silver tea kettle and stand, Birmingham, 1905, 33cm. high. (H. Spencer & Sons) $3,485   £1,550

Edwardian silver tea kettle on stand, London, 1906, 43¼oz. (Olivers) $610   £270

Early George II tea kettle on lampstand by Thomas Tearle, London, 1728, 13½in. high, 80oz.17dwt. (Sotheby's) $6,945   £3,200

Large electroplated tea kettle on lampstand with burner, by Martin Hall & Co, circa 1870, 41.3cm. high. (Sotheby's Belgravia) $560   £250

Racing trophy modelled as
a teapot. (Phillips)
$1,479 £650

William IV compressed teapot by Paul
Storr, London, 1832, 5¼in. high,
22oz.11dwt. (Sotheby's) $1,680 £750

Part of a tea service by Hunt &
Roskell, 65oz. in all. (Christie's
S. Kensington) $1,320 £650

James Dixon & Son electroplated
teapot, 1880, 10.5cm. high.
(Sotheby's Belgravia)$1,050 £480

George III 'drum' teapot by Parker
& Wakelin, London, 1775,.5in.
high, 15oz.10dwt. (Sotheby's)
$1,520 £700

George III circular teapot by W. &
P. Cunningham, Edinburgh, 1802,
14oz.10dwt. (Phillips) $540 £250

William IV circular flat shaped teapot
by Smith & Gamble, Dublin, 1832,
35oz.10dwt. (Phillips) $540 £250

William IV circular melon teapot by
Paul Storr, London, 1832, 5in. high,
23oz.16dwt. (Sotheby's)
$2,605 £1,200

George II spherical teapot by Johan
Got-helf-Bilsings, Glasgow, circa
1745, 5¾in. high, 16oz.6dwt.
(Sotheby's) $1,525 £680

Early 20th century Chinese silver
coloured metal tea set.
(Sotheby's Belgravia) $440 £190

Silver gilt teapot, 6in. high,
19oz.13dwt. (Sotheby's)
$2,800 £1,250

Dutch melon shaped teapot by I. S.
Busard, The Hague, 1767, 14oz.
18dwt. (Christie's) $6,050 £2,800

TEAPOTS

Early William IV silver teapot. (Osmond Tricks) $605 £260

Henry Wilkinson & Co. compressed melon-shaped silver teapot, Sheffield, 1842, 827gm. (Sotheby's Belgravia) $920 £410

George II bullet-shaped teapot, Edinburgh, 1746, 15oz.9dwt., 5½in. high. (Sotheby's) $905 £420

George III shaped oval teapot by Hester Bateman, London, 1787, 6in. high, 12oz.18dwt. (Sotheby's) $1,300 £600

Oval teapot and stand by John Emes, London, 1804, 21oz. (Phillips) $605 £260

19th century plated teapot with ebony handle and finial. (Vernon's) $55 £25

Lambert & Rawlings fluted circular silver teapot, with mark of Wm. Moulson, London, 1848, 774gm. (Sotheby's Belgravia) $760 £340

George I plain octagonal pear-shaped teapot, 1718, 16oz.19dwt. (Christie's) $11,750 £5,200

George III oval inverted pear-shaped teapot by William Dempster, Edinburgh, 1170, 6½in. high, 24oz.16dwt. (Sotheby's) $1,910 £850

Silver teapot by Peter and Anne Bateman, London, 1832, 14oz. (Biddle & Webb) $855 £370

William IV compressed circular teapot by Robert Hennell, London, 1840, 5½in. high, 22oz.12dwt. (Sotheby's) $1,345 £600

Bullet-shaped silver teapot in early 18th century Scottish style, maker's mark JR, London, 1935, 590gm. (Sotheby's Belgravia) $560 £250

Spherical teapot by William Hunter, London, 1844, 15.7cm. high, 21.2oz. (Sotheby's Belgravia) $340 £145

Circular teapot on four Chinaman feet, circa 1850, 50oz. (Christie's) $1,765 £800

George I bullet-shaped teapot by Humphrey Payne, London, 1725, 5in. high, 14oz.2dwt.(Sotheby's) $4,480 £2,000

George II bullet-shaped teapot by James Kerr, Edinburgh, 1731, 5½in. high, 20oz.4dwt. (Sotheby's) $1,910 £850

George II inverted pear-shaped teapot by James Glen, Glasgow, 6¼in. high, 23oz.10dwt. (Sotheby's) $1,910 £850

Compressed fluted circular teapot by William Moulson, London, 1855, 15cm. high, 25.5oz. (Sotheby's Belgravia) $585 £260

Edward Barnard & Sons spherical teapot, London, 1862, 12.2cm. high, 10oz. (Sotheby's Belgravia) $405 £180

French vase-shaped teapot, Paris, circa 1830, 8in. high, 23oz.12dwt. (Sotheby's) $2,035 £900

Circular teapot by R. & S. Garrard & Co., London, 1897, 16.5cm. high, 26.5oz. (Sotheby's Belgravia) $560 £250

George I bullet-shaped teapot by James Smith, London, 1719, 3¾in. high, 13oz.9dwt. (Sotheby's) $2,820 £1,300

Plain tapering cylindrical teapot by Hunt & Roskell, London, 1866, 14.8cm. high, 23.4oz. (Sotheby's Belgravia) $395 £170

George II bullet-shaped teapot by Gabriel Sleath, London, 1733, 4¼in. high, 13oz.5dwt. (Sotheby's) $2,590 £1,200

TOASTERS

Hukin & Heath silver toast rack, London, 1881, 12cm. wide. (Sotheby's Belgravia) $985 £450

Large Elkington, Mason & Co. seven-bar silver toast rack, Birmingham, 1859, 759gm. (Sotheby's Belgravia) $1,120 £500

Heath & Middleton silver toast rack, 1899, 12.5cm. wide. (Sotheby's Belgravia) $480 £220

TOILET REQUISITES

Lady's five-piece silver mounted dressing table set. (Phillips) $40 £20

19th century Continental silver etui. (Vernon's) $260 £115

Lady's silver mounted dressing table set of six-pieces. (Phillips) $65 £30

Seven-piece dressing table set with silver mounts. (Phillips) $70 £30

Mother-of-pearl and gilt metal necessaire as a musical box. (Sotheby King & Chasemore) $670 £310

Mahogany toilet compendium fitted with mirrors, trays and bottles. (Alfie's Antique Market) $315 £140

Early Victorian dressing case with nine engraved silver fittings, 1841, 11in. wide. (Hy. Duke & Son) $655 £320

19th century French silver gilt crested campaign toilet set, 71oz. (Phillips) $2,785 £1,265

Lady's travelling dressing case by Mappin & Webb, Birmingham, 1918. (Lacy Scott) $465 £230

628

Silver two-handled tray, Birmingham, 1930, 24in. wide. (Green's) $2,250 £1,000

Victorian shaped oblong tray on shell and dolphin feet, maker's mark AC, 1895, 105oz. (Christie's) $4,995 £2,200

Late Victorian silver tray of oval shape by Elkington & Co., Birmingham, 1889, 71oz., 21in. wide. (Sotheby King & Chasemore) $1,730 £800

George II shaped triangular tea kettle stand on hoof feet by Robert Abercromby, 1735, 14oz. 11dwt. (Christie's) $3,630 £1,600

Victorian oak tray with plated mounts. (Phillips) $65 £30

Large English electroplated shaped circular salver, circa 1850, 62cm. diam. (Sotheby's Belgravia) $585 £260

George II plain shaped circular salver on rim foot by William Aytoun, Edinburgh, 1733, 11oz. 14dwt. (Christie's) $1,180 £520

American silver flask-shaped wine ewer and tray by Gorham Mfg. Co., Providence, R. I. 1882, 1,027gm. (Sotheby's Belgravia) $850 £380

Shaped circular salver, 1838. (McCartney, Morris & Barker) $555 £270

George I Irish silver circular salver on domed foot, 1714, 13¼oz., 8½in. diam. (Lalonde Bros. & Parham) $1,945 £900

Two-handled octagonal pierced gallery tea tray by Elkington & Co., London, 1913, 4,700gm. (Sotheby's Belgravia) $4,255 £1,850

Shaped circular salver by A. B. Savory & Sons, London, 1847, 36cm. diam., 43oz. (Sotheby's Belgravia) $495 £220

TRAYS AND SALVERS

George III oval coffee tray by William Burwash and Richard Sibley, London, 1811, 69oz.17dwt. (Sotheby's) $4,340 £2,000

Fine Queen Anne circular salver, on foot, Dublin, 1712-14. (Sotheby's) $3,600 £1,600

Two-handled silver tray, Birmingham, 1930. (Green's) $2,160 £1,000

Charles Fox shaped circular salver, London, 1838, 50cm. diameter, 2,353gm. (Sotheby's Belgravia) $1,289 £620

Victorian oval tea tray by Atkin Brothers, Sheffield, 1875, 29¾in. long, 146oz.19dwt. (Sotheby's) $3,470 £1,600

Magnificent George IV shaped circular salver by Edward Barton, London, 1824, 66cm. diameter, 244oz. (Sotheby Bearne) $8,208 £3,800

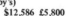

Large, heavy Walker & Hall two-handled rectangular tray, Sheffield, 1901, 75.2cm. wide, 5,086gm. (Sotheby's Belgravia) $2,910 £1,400

Rare Charles II provincial dish by Edward Mangy, Hull, circa 1670, 9¾in. diam., 12oz.17dwt. (Sotheby's) $12,586 £5,800

Atkin Brothers large, two-handled rectangular tray, Sheffield, 1901, 75.5cm. wide, 4,176gm. (Sotheby's Belgravia) $2,600 £1,250

Russian silver tray enamelled in black and turquoise. (Neales) $410 £190

George III two-handled tray by J. Wakelin & R. Garrard, 1796, 80oz., 20in. long. (Christie's) $5,175 £2,300

One of a pair of early Edward VII silver salvers, Sheffield, 1904, 12in. diam., 55oz. (Coles, Knapp & Kennedy) $735 £340

Early 19th century Maltese two-handled tray by Pio Calleja, circa 1800, 10½in. wide, 54oz.10dwt. (Sotheby's) $2,385 £1,100

Queen Anne circular salver, 1705, 22oz., 11in. diam. (Christie's) $3,150 £1,400

Robert Stewart plain oblong two-handled tray, Sheffield, 1904, 76.7cm. wide, 5,045gm. (Sotheby's Belgravia) $2,390 £1,150

George II plain circular salver by John Swift, 1739, 21oz., 10½in. diam. (Christie's) $3,375 £1,500

Silver gilt salver and two waiters, mid 18th century, 79oz. (Christie's) $9,450 £4,200

William and Mary plain circular salver, 1693, 20oz., 11in. diameter. (Christie's) $4,275 £1,900

George III shaped circular salver by Richard Rugg II, London, 1775, 44oz.13dwt., 14¼in. diameter. (Sotheby's) $2,125 £980

Late 17th century Dutch spice tray, Rotterdam, circa 1683, 8½in. wide, 5oz.15dwt. (Sotheby's) $3,690 £1,700

William IV shaped circular salver by Edward Barnard & Sons, London, 1830, 16½in. diameter, 65oz.15dwt. (Sotheby's) $1,955 £900

Harrods Ltd. shaped square salver, 33.5cm., 1,373gm., Sheffield, 1958. (Sotheby's Belgravia) $750 £360

George III shaped snuffers tray by Wm. Stroud, London, 1806, 11in. wide, 11oz. 18dwt. (Sotheby's) $735 £340

Early Victorian silver salver with shaped rim. (McCartney, Morris & Barker) $585 £270

TRAYS AND SALVERS

A circular shaped English salver, Sheffield, 1920, 59cm. diam., 145oz. 6dwt. (Sotheby's Belgravia) $3,505 £1,550

One of a pair of Dutch oval salvers by Diederik Willem Rethmeyer, 1806, 15½in. wide, 38oz.4dwt. (Sotheby's) $6,945 £3,100

Silver gallery tray by Thomas Bradbury & Sons, Sheffield, 1912, 132oz. (Honiton Galleries) $2,940 £1,300

Early George III silver waiter, 12¼oz. (Woolley & Wallis) $1,245 £540

Joseph Rodgers & Sons shaped oval two-handled tea tray, Sheffield, 1903, 72.5cm. wide, 4,258gm. (Sotheby's Belgravia) $3,505 £1,550

One of a set of eighteen silver plates by Edward and John Barnard, 1859, 8in. diam. (Christie's) $13,020 £6,000

George II circular shaped salver by William Peaston, London, 1753, 10¾in. diam., 18oz. 19dwt. (Sotheby's) $1,320 £580

One of a pair of William IV oval meat dishes by Robert Garrard, 18¾in. wide, 138oz.10dwt. (Sotheby's) $6,050 £2,700

George II shaped square salver by Edward Cornock, London, 1728, 13in. square, 44oz.16dwt. (Sotheby's) $21,280 £9,500

One of twelve George II shaped circular dinner plates by John Jacob, 1754, 9½in. diam., 217oz. (Christie's) $11,230 £5,200

An oval shaped silver two-handled tea tray on four hoof supports, by Barker Bros., Birmingham, 1925, 3,722gm. (Sotheby's Belgravia) $3,140 £1,400

French Art Nouveau silvered metal charger, circa 1900, 49.5cm. diam. (Sotheby's Belgravia) $600 £260

Edwardian silver salver by Elkington & Co., Birmingham, 1901, 100oz., 20½in. diam. (Olivers)$1,130 £500

R. & S. Garrard & Co. Georgian style silver gilt dessert dish, by Sebastian Garrard, London, 1911, 946gm. (Sotheby's Belgravia) $900 £400

18th century Maltese salver on foot, by Antonio Pullicino, circa 1745, 10½in. diam., 23oz.3dwt.(Sotheby's) $1,690 £780

Gorham Manufacturing Co. shaped oval two-handled tea tray, 67cm. wide, Birmingham 1920, 4,222gm. (Sotheby's Belgravia)$3,390 £1,500

Victorian shaped circular salver on bracket feet, by J. Mortimer and S. Hunt, 1842, 20¼in. diam., 102oz. (Christie's)$3,565 £1,650

One of a pair of George IV shaped oval meat dishes by Paul Storr, 1828, 16¼in. long, 100oz. (Christie's) $7,775 £3,600

George III oval tea tray by John Crouch and Thomas Hannam, London, 1791, 14¼in. wide, 119oz.6dwt. (Sotheby's) $11,200 £5,000

Antique snuffers and tray in heavy Sheffield plate, circa 1825, 10¾in. long. (Christopher Sykes)$80 £35

Charles Boyton & Sons Ltd. rectangular two-handled tray, London, 1905, 77.5cm. wide, 4,180gm. (Sotheby's Belgravia) $3,165 £1,400

Maltese shaped circular salver, 11¼in. diam., circa 1780, 31oz. (Christie's) $2,520 £1,150

One of six George IV shaped circular dinner plates by Paul Storr, London, 1821, 9¾in. diam., 118oz.9dwt. (Sotheby's) $7,390 £3,300

George II shaped circular salver by William Peaston, London, 1751, 13½in. diam., 37oz.14dwt. (Sotheby's) $2,270 £1,000

TUREENS

One of a pair of George III silver oval sauce tureens and covers, 7in. high, by John Carter, London, 45oz.10dwt. (Geering & Colyer) $2,765 £1,350

Regency plain two-handled soup tureen and cover by J. Cradock and W. Reid, 1817, 113oz. (Christie's) $9,080 £4,000

One of a pair of Sheffield plate sauce tureens, part ivory handles and feet, 6¼in. wide. (Parsons, Welch & Cowell) $440 £205

One of a pair of sauce tureens, covers and stands by Benjamin Smith, 1808, 18.3cm. high, 88oz.10dwt. (Phillips) $15,550 £7,200

George III oval soup tureen and cover by Thomas Heming, London, 1776, 17¾in. wide, 84oz.4dwt. (Sotheby's) $7,615 £3,400

George III circular soup tureen and cover by Digby Scott and Benjamin Smith, London, 1806, 14½in. wide, 148oz.2dwt. (Sotheby's) $3,905 £1,800

Roberts, Smith & Co., Sheffield plate soup tureen and cover, 1845. (Sotheby's Belgravia) $1,305 £580

19th century French silver covered tureen, 12in. high. (Robert W. Skinner Inc.) $1,400 £636

George III shaped oval soup tureen and cover by Butty and Dumee, London, 1769, 16¾in. wide, 107oz.2dwt. (Sotheby's) $12,585 £5,800

Oval soup tureen, circa 1830, 16in. long, engraved with armorials below with gadroon rim. (Sotheby's) $1,625 £850

Silver Victorian sauce tureen by Barnard & Sons, London, 1885, 44oz., 7in. diam. (Sotheby King & Chasemore) $1,035 £480

One of a pair of Gorham sterling silver tureens. (Phillips New York) $4,105 £1,900

Victorian two-handled plain circular soup tureen and cover, by J. McKay, Edinburgh, 1858, 85oz., 10in. diam. (Christie's) $3,670 £1,700

One of a pair of Sheffield plated oval tureens and covers, 16in. wide, circa 1826. (Sotheby's) $1,735 £700

One of a pair of George III oval sauce tureens by Robert Hennell, 1777, 48oz. (Christie's) $4,500 £2,000

George IV compressed circular soup tureen by William Eley, London, 1826, 14½in. high, 155oz.16dwt. (Sotheby's) $7,595 £3,500

George II two-handled soup tureen and cover, Dublin 1745, 164oz., 13¾in. long. (Christie's) $11,500 £5,000

Large Gorham sterling silver tureen. (Phillips New York) $3,240 £1,500

Late Victorian silver soup tureen and cover. (Henry Spencer & Sons) $1,245 £550

German two-handled ecuelle and cover, 5¾in. diam., 15oz.4dwt. (Christie's) $9,000 £4,000

One of a pair of George IV oval sauce tureens and covers by William Eley, London, 1827, 8¼in. wide, 61oz.9dwt. (Sotheby's) $4,015 £1,850

One of a pair of George III silver sauce tureens, by John Carter, London, 1776, 45oz. (Geering & Colyer) $2,915 £1,350

George IV soup tureen and cover by Spooner Clowes & Co., London, 1827, 105oz. (Sotheby's) $5,830 £2,700

French silver circular soup tureen, cover and stand, 5,353gm., circa 1838. (Sotheby's Belgravia) $3,015 £1,450

TUREENS

Italian lobed circular two-handled soup tureen and cover, 68.5oz., 31.5cm. wide. (Sotheby's Belgravia) $1,125 £520

One of a pair of George IV two-handled oblong sauce tureens and covers by T. & J. Settle, Sheffield, 1821, 86oz., 8¾in. long. (Christie's)
$6,075 £2,700

One of a pair of George III two-handled oval sauce tureens and covers by William Holmes, 1778, 43oz. (Christie's)
$4,520 £2,000

URNS

George IV tea urn by Edward Power, Dublin, 1824, 122oz., 15¾in. high. (Sotheby's) $3,130 £1,450

George III two-handled coffee urn by Edward Fernell, 1787, 47oz., 15in. high. (Christie's) $3,600 £1,600

Oblong tea urn, circa 1810, 17in. high, with shaped square base. (Sotheby's) $825 £380

George III vase-shaped coffee urn by Hester Bateman, London 1783, 13½in. high, 35oz.17dwt. (Sotheby's)
$4,480 £2,000

George III two-handled vase-shaped tea urn by Edward Fernell, 1787, 100oz., 23in. high. (Christie's) $4,950 £2,200

George III vase-shaped tea urn by John Denziloe, London, 1789, 110oz.14dwt., 20½in. high. (Sotheby's) $4,105 £1,900

Presentation tea urn by J. McKay, Edinburgh, 1827, 170oz. (Christie's & Edmiston's) $6,550 £2,800

George III two-handled tea urn by A. Fogelberg and S. Gilbert, 1780, 21¾in. high, 122oz. (Christie's)
$6,190 £2,800

Large English Sheffield plate tea urn, circa 1840, 40.5cm. high. (Sotheby's Belgravia) $560 £240

18th century Maltese covered sugar vase by Gio. Cassar, circa 1775, 6¼in. high, 11oz.17dwt. (Sotheby's) $1,955 £900

One of a pair of Fenton Bros. crescent shaped fern vases, Sheffield, 1896, 657gm. (Sotheby's)Belgravia) $670 £300

Austrian covered sugar vase, Vienna, 1794, 7½in. high, 17oz.16dwt. (Sotheby's) $1,345 £600

Liberty & Co. 'Cymric' silver and turquoise matrix vase, 11cm. high, Birmingham, 1903. (Sotheby's Belgravia) $555 £240

Large Victorian silver vase by Messrs. Hancock, 1866, 20¾in. high, 203oz. (Christie's) $5,965 £2,700

One of a pair of C. J. Vander tapering cylindrical flower vases, London, 1901, 33.4cm. high, 84.5oz. (Sotheby's Belgravia) $2,140 £950

One of a pair of large silver baluster vases, engraved Whytock & Sons, Dundee; London, 1896, 3,018gm. (Sotheby's Belgravia) $4,145 £1,850

William IV silver gilt two-handled centrepiece by Paul Storr, 1836, 25½in. high, 513oz. (Christie's) $40,680 £18,000

One of a pair of Goldsmiths & Silversmiths Co. Ltd., flower vases, 20cm. high, 16.3oz. (Sotheby's Belgravia) $325 £150

Late 19th century German decorative posy vase on three openwork supports, 17cm. high, 6.7oz. (Sotheby's Belgravia) $185 £80

Large WMF electroplated electrotype vase, circa 1900, 49cm. high. (Sotheby's Belgravia) $1,060 £460

Victorian two-handled vase and cover by Robert Harper, 1871, 23in. high, 76oz. (Christie's) $2,485 £1,150

637

VINAIGRETTES

George III oblong silver gilt vinaigrette by S. Pemberton, Birmingham, 1813, 1½in. wide. (Sotheby's) $735 £340

Silver vinaigrette in the form of a pocket watch by J. L. Birmingham, 1817. (Sotheby's King & Chasemore) $335 £150

William IV rectangular vinaigrette by J. Wilmore, Birmingham, 1832, 1¾in. wide. (Sotheby's) $560 £260

George III rectangular vinaigrette by M. Linwood, Birmingham, 1812, 1¾in. wide. (Sotheby's) $605 £280

Rare and unusual Victorian vinaigrette by Henry Wilkinson & Co., 1843, 1¼in. wide. (Sotheby's) $625 £290

George III oblong silver gilt vinaigrette by Phipps, Robinson & Phipps, London, 1813, 2in. wide. (Sotheby's) $1,295 £600

Rectangular silver gilt vinaigrette by Gervase Wheeler, Birmingham, 1838, 1¾in. wide. (Sotheby's) $1,250 £580

Oval silver vinaigrette engraved with the Scott Monument, by Nathaniel Mills, 1847, 4.1cm. long. (Sotheby's Belgravia) $575 £250

Rectangular silver gilt vinaigrette, lid decorated with view of Windsor Castle by Nathaniel Mills, Birmingham, 1837, 1¾in. wide. (Sotheby's) $1,250 £580

William IV oblong silver gilt vinaigrette, Birmingham, 1830, 1¼in. wide. (Sotheby's) $410 £190

Good silver gilt vinaigrette posy holder with red hardstone cap, by Thos. Wm. Dee, London, 1866, 155gm. (Sotheby's Belgravia) $2,130 £950

Octagonal hardstone vinaigrette, maker's mark IR, 1½in. wide, circa 1800. (Sotheby's) $215 £100

638

George III oblong vinaigrette
by Matthew Linwood, Birmingham, 1819, 1¼in. wide.
(Sotheby's) $295 £130

George III silver gilt oblong vinaigrette by
William Eley I, London, 1802, 1¼in. wide.
(Sotheby's) $270 £120

George III domed octagonal vinaigrette by Samuel Pemberton,
Birmingham, 1802, 1½in. wide.
(Sotheby's) $315 £140

George III reeded octagonal vinaigrette by Samuel Davis, London,
1808, 2in. wide. (Sotheby's)
     $1,220 £540

George III purse shaped vinaigrette, by William
Eley I, London, 1815, 1½in. wide. (Sotheby's)
     $520 £230

George III oblong vinaigrette,
London, 1806, 1½in. wide.
(Sotheby's) $340 £150

WINE COOLERS

One of a pair of George III gilt
metal wine coolers, early 19th
century, 1ft. high. (Sotheby's)
     $16,850 £7,800

One of a set of four George IV campana shaped
wine coolers by William Eley, London, 1826,
9¾in. high, 331oz.4dwt. (Sotheby's)
     $28,210 £13,000

One of a pair of Sheffield plate
wine coolers, circa 1790, 7in.
high. (Sotheby's)
     $1,640 £700

One of a pair of William IV wine
coolers by Robert Garrard, London, 1835, 120oz. (Phillips)
     $8,600 £4,000

One of a pair of campana shaped wine
coolers, circa 1810, 10¼in. high.
(Sotheby's) $1,085 £500

One of a pair of George III two-handled wine coolers by Wm. Fountain,
1804, 9in. high, 156oz. (Christie's)
     $9,490 £4,200

One of a pair of important French wine coolers by R.-J. Auguste, 1777, on stands by J. J. G. Matthias, Hanover, 1815, 8,095gm. (Sotheby's Monaco) $116,200 £53,400

One of a pair of Warwick vase wine coolers, circa 1820-30, 10in. high. (Sotheby's) $3,565 £1,550

One of a pair of wine coolers with detachable rims and liners, by Jas. Chas. Edington, London, 1838, 8,700gm. (Sotheby's Zurich) $11,850 £5,220

WINE FUNNELS

Silver wine funnel by George Lowe, 1824, 14cm. long. (Vernon's) $400 £175

George III funnel by Thomas Graham, London, 1795, 4¼in. high, 1oz.4dwt. (Sotheby's) $630 £270

Georgian silver wine funnel by E. Morley, London, 1811. (Vost's) $390 £190

WINE LABELS

George IV pierced 'Hollands' wine label by A. W., Edinburgh. (Parsons, Welch & Cowell) $70 £30

Victorian silver wine label by George White, Birmingham, 1867. (Parsons, Welch & Cowell) $60 £25

George III pierced 'Madeira' wine label by Peter and William Bateman, 1824. (Parsons, Welch & Cowell) $155 £70

Victorian wine label, pierced 'Brandy' by Edward and John Barnard, London, 1853. (Parsons, Welch & Cowell) $85 £40

George IV pierced wine label 'Madeira', by Rawlings & Sumner, 1830. (Parsons, Welch & Cowell) $100 £45

One of a pair of William IV labels in vine leaf form by George White, Birmingham, 1838. (Parsons, Welch & Cowell) $180 £80

Unmarked silver wine label, circa 1785, 'Grave'. (Vernon's) $70 £30

Claret label by Mary Binley, London, circa 1765. (Vernon's) $110 £48

George IV pierced 'Madeira' wine label, by RC, London, 1824. (Parsons, Welch & Cowell) $85 £40

SPINNING WHEELS

Early 19th century Flemish painted beech spinning wheel with treadle, 48in. high. (Lacy Scott) $335 £165

18th century stained beechwood spinning wheel. (Vernon's) $290 £125

19th century beechwood spinning wheel. (James & Lister Lea) $110 £50

18th century oak spinning wheel. (Vernon's) $200 £85

Early 19th century spinning wheel in stained beech and fruitwood. (Sotheby's) $585 £260

Stripped pinewood farmhouse spinning wheel, circa 1820, 20in. diam. (Christopher Sykes) $355 £160

Walnut and beechwood spinning wheel, 18th century, with spindle spoke wheel and frame, 23in. wide. (Christie's) $1,150 £500

George III mahogany spinning wheel, early 19th century, made by John Planta, 3ft.1in. high. (Sotheby's) $2,590 £1,200

Superb early 19th century silk spinning wheel. (Bradley & Vaughan) $690 £320

Fine Chinese pale grey and brown agate snuff bottle with white and apple-green jade stopper. (Christie's) $615 £280

Chinese turquoise matrix flattened baluster snuff bottle, with matching stopper. (Christie's) $615 £280

Chinese pale golden amber double snuff bottle, with malachite stoppers. (Christie's) $255 £115

Chinese Mongolian style flattened baluster snuff bottle, set with coral, turquoise and jade. (Christie's) $330 £150

Fine Chinese semi translucent six colour overlay glass snuff bottle with rose quartz stopper. (Christie's) $2,160 £980

Chinese Mongolian style oviform snuff bottle, inset with coral and turquoise, with matching stopper. (Christie's) $375 £170

Well carved Chinese ivory table snuff bottle, carved and pierced, Qianlong seal mark on base. (Christie's) $550 £250

Fine Chinese mottled beige and dark golden amber snuff bottle, with white and apple-green jade stopper. (Christie's) $880 £400

Chinese hornbill snuff bottle carved as Liuhai, with matching stopper. (Christie's) $330 £150

Chinese Mongolian style disc-shaped snuff bottle, set with coral and turquoise. (Christie's) $240 £110

Chinese inside-painted glass snuff bottle, with jade stopper, signed Zhou Leyuan. (Christie's) $530 £240

Fine Chinese mottled brown root amber oviform snuff bottle with silvered metal and jade stopper. (Christie's) $660 £300

Chalcedony snuff bottle with mask-ring handles, mounted in gilt filigree set with turquoise and coral. (Sotheby's Belgravia) $140 £65

Very rare Peking enamel ovoid snuff bottle, from the Peking Palace workshops, Kangxi period. (Sotheby's Belgravia) $8,760 £4,000

Inside-painted glass snuff bottle showing landscape scene, signed Bi Rongjiu, 1907. (Sotheby's Belgravia) $175 £80

Good enamelled glass snuff bottle of double gourd form, with Qianlong mark, probably from the Ye family kilns, circa 1900. (Sotheby's Belgravia) $2,850 £1,300

Fine red cinnabar lacquer flattened oviform snuff bottle, Qianlong mark on base. (Christie's) $1,210 £550

Chinese cloisonne enamel snuff bottle with matching stopper, Qianlong mark on base. (Christie's) $220 £100

Plain Chinese snuff bottle in mottled white, lavender, apple- and emerald-green jade. (Christie's) $880 £400

Chinese hornbill rectangular snuff bottle, carved in relief with figures in a landscape and dragons. (Christie's) $240 £110

Chinese inside-painted glass snuff bottle with jade stopper, signed Yong Shoutian and dated 1924. (Christie's) $220 £100

Chinese ivory snuff bottle, carved with Budai in a tub, Qianlong seal mark on base. (Christie's) $350 £160

Chinese semi translucent overlay glass snuff bottle, red overlay on 'snow-storm' ground. (Christie's) $660 £300

Fine Japanese ivory table snuff bottle, incised with ladies in a landscape. (Christie's) $840 £380

Chinese mottled pale and dark golden amber snuff bottle, carved in low relief, with quartz stopper. (Christie's) $530 £240

Chinese opaque milk-white overlay glass snuff bottle, of blue and red overlay, with agate stopper. (Christie's) $400 £180

Chinese opaque white glass overlay snuff bottle, red overlay, with coral glass and pearl stopper. (Christie's) $210 £95

Fine black jade rectangular Chinese snuff bottle, with gilt metal mounted coral stopper. (Christie's) $570 £260

Fine and rare Peking famille rose enamel snuff bottle with European pastoral scene, from the Peking Palace workshops, Qianlong period. (Sotheby's Belgravia) $230,000 £105,000

Good Canton enamel flattened pear-shape snuff bottle with Qianlong mark, 1770-1830. (Sotheby's Belgravia) $1,360 £620

Pale jade snuff bottle mounted in silver filigree set with turquoise and coral beads. (Sotheby's Belgravia) $155 £70

Chalcedony snuff bottle mounted in gilt filigree set with turquoise and coral. (Sotheby's Belgravia) $110 £50

643

STONE

Aztec frog of banded translucent brown and cream stone,
the eyes set with quartz, 3¼in.
long. (Christie's) $485 £220

Aztec volcanic stone figure, 1300-
1500A.D., 15½in. high.
(Sotheby's) $675 £310

Fine dated octagonal thick slate
sundial, 10in. diam. (Christopher
Sykes) $190 £85

Large sculpture of a pouter pigeon,
1920's, 34.5cm. high, in composition stone. (Sotheby's Belgravia)
$655 £300

Rolls Royce credo, inscribed on
a sandstone plaque. (Phillips)
$215 £95

THE QUALITY REMAINS
LONG AFTER THE PRICE
IS FORGOTTEN......
F. HENRY ROYCE
A.M.I.Mech.E. A.M.I.E.E.

2nd/3rd century A.D. East Roman
basalt head of a horse, 14in long.
(Christie's) $3,390 £1,500

Egyptian black stone figure
of Osiris, 26th dynasty, 9in.
high. (Sotheby's)
$1,275 £580

Chinese grey stone stele with Buddha
and Bodhisattvas, dated 659A.D.,
11½in. high. (Christie's)
$4,360 £2,000

Egyptian limestone Ushabti,
dynasty XVIII, 7½in. high.
(Christie's) $225 £100

Unusual dated incised stone sundial, 12in. high, 1749.
(Christopher Sykes) $440 £195

Chinese grey stone stele with Buddha
and attendants, dated 580A.D., 12in.
high. (Christie's) $1,745 £800

Fine 12th century Pala grey stone
stele carved in high relief with
Surya, 74cm. high. (Christie's)
$4,600 £2,000

644

Stone lamp with wire and iron hinged door, dated 1762, 13in. high. (Robert W. Skinner Inc.) $250 £115

3rd century A.D. Palmyran limestone head of a woman, the eyes inlaid with black glass, 11in. high. (Christie's) $4,750 £2,100

One of two 3rd or 4th century Gandhara grey schist bowls and covers, 11.4cm. high. (Sotheby's) $575 £260

3rd century A.D. Palmyran limestone funerary stele of a woman, 22in. high. (Christie's) $9,490 £4,200

Costa Rican volcanic stone metate of concave oval form, 19½in. wide, 1000-1500 A.D. (Sotheby's) $865 £400

6th century B.C. Cypriot limestone votive figure, 6¼in. high. (Christie's) $435 £190

2nd century B.C. Egyptian painted limestone head of a Ptolemaic pharaoh, 14½in. high. (Christie's) $5,650 £2,500

6th century B.C. Cypriot limestone votive figure holding a tambourine, 9½in. high. (Christie's) $690 £300

Rare New Guinea stone carving of a bird-like form with long face, 4¾in. high. (Christie's) $420 £190

10th century Pala grey stone Stupa base with four arcades of seated Buddhas, 36cm. high. (Christie's) $3,000 £1,300

Mediaeval English red sandstone corbel head with worried expression, 18cm. high. (Christie's) $485 £210

One of a pair of 19th century stone garden jardinieres with baluster supports, 3ft.6in. high. (Vernon's) $400 £185

Belgian Languillier cast iron and ceramic cooking range, circa 1910. (Sotheby's Belgravia) $1,100 £500

French Poel a Bois 'Le Selecte' wood-burning cast iron stove, circa 1910, 22in. high. (Sotheby's Belgravia) $390 £180

French cast iron stove finished in blue-grey vitreous enamel, circa 1920, 22in. high. (Sotheby's Belgravia) $190 £85

Belgian 'Westminster' free-standing stove, circa 1920, 25½in. high. (Sotheby's Belgravia)$765 £350

French Godin 392 cast iron stove, circa 1920, 45in. high. (Sotheby's Belgravia) $570 £260

French Siberia Niledo cast iron bow fronted stove, circa 1910, 28in. high. (Sotheby's Belgravia) $980 £450

Late 19th century French green enamelled cast iron stove by Montherme Lavel-Diel. (Phillips) $205 £90

Late 19th century French cast iron stove supported on cabriole legs. (Vernon's) $145 £65

Late 19th century English grey enamelled cast iron stove in the Art Nouveau style. (Phillips) $170 £75

French Soughland 491 cast iron stove in green vitreous enamel, circa 1900, 30in. high. (Sotheby's Belgravia) $1,300 £600

Pure wood burning stove in cast iron, circa 1880. (Gray's Antique Mews) $595 £275

French 'Monopole' cast iron free-standing stove by Deville & Co., Charleville, circa 1910, 34in. high. (Sotheby's Belgravia)$1,265 £550

Important English Soho 'chinoiseries' tapestry by Joshua Morris, circa 1720, 15ft. wide. (Sotheby's) $18,360 £8,500

Good post-Mortlake mythological tapestry, early 18th century, 17ft. wide. (Sotheby's) $7,775 £3,600

19th century Rescht panel with floral decoration on a madder ground, 9ft.2in. long. (Sotheby's) $2,450 £1,100

'Chinoiseries' tapestry by Joshua Morris, circa 1720, 13ft. wide. (Sotheby's) $15,120 £7,000

Louis XIV Aubusson biblical tapestry, circa 1680, 8 x 6ft. (Sotheby King & Chasemore) $1,835 £850

Long rectangular Rescht panel with seven panels on a pink ground, 15ft. 6in. long. (Sotheby's) $580 £260

'Chinoiseries' tapestry by Joshua Morris, circa 1720, 10ft. wide. (Sotheby's) $5,615 £2,600

Late 17th century Flemish verdure tapestry, 75in. wide. (Robert W. Skinner Inc.) $2,100 £955

Late 19th century Chinese wall hanging with purple silk ground, 172in. wide. (Sotheby's Belgravia) $255 £110

One of a set of eight late 17th century English crewelwork hangings. (Christie's S. Kensington) $19,125 £8,500

Mid 18th century Louis XV Franco-Flemish pastoral tapestry, 8 x 9ft.10in. (Sotheby King & Chasemore) $7,345 £3,400

French tinplate jeu de course, circa 1900, 18in. diam. (Sotheby's Belgravia) $220 £100

Non-flying model of a Fokker Eindekker, 41cm. wingspan. (Phillips) $85 £40

Royal Air Mail Service car by Dinky, slightly worn. (Sotheby's Belgravia) $130 £60

Bryans 'Hidden Treasure' penny-in-the-slot amusement machine, 70cm. high. (Sotheby King & Chasemore) $105 £50

Liverpool Delft miniature tea service. (Christie's) $5,830 £2,700

Bryans '12 Win Clock' penny-in-the-slot amusement machine, 65cm. high. (Sotheby King & Chasemore) $65 £30

Lehmann tinplate clockwork model 'Auto UHU' in original box. (D. M. Nesbit & Co.) $905 £420

American merchantman crane amusement machine by Exhibit Supply Co., circa 1960. (Sotheby's Belgravia) $485 £220

Fine boxed set of graduated pyramid and ABC picture blocks. (Frank H. Fellows) $110 £50

Modern wood model of a trawler, 32in. long, with radio controlled motor. (Olivers) $100 £45

German tinplate photographer toy, circa 1920, 5in. long. (Sotheby's Belgravia) $255 £110

Child's tinplate cooking range, probably French, circa 1900, 18¼in. wide, complete with pans. (Sotheby's Belgravia) $355 £160

Lehmann tinplate toy 'Paddy and the Pig', damaged. (Phillips) $235 £110

Dinky super toy Weetabix Guy van, No.514, in cardboard box, 5¾in. long. (Sotheby's Belgravia) $300 £135

American Louis Marx design tinplate toy, 'Goofy Gardener'. (Phillips) $120 £55

Lehmann Royal Mail 585-tinplate delivery van. (Sotheby's Belgravia) $2,160 £1,000

Carved wooden rocking horse with horsehair mane and tail, 47in. long. (Sotheby's Belgravia) $310 £140

Non-flying model of a Bristol Fighter, 31.5cm. wingspan. (Phillips) $95 £45

Lehmann tinplate clockwork model 'Auto Sisters', in original card box. (D. M. Nesbit & Co.) $735 £340

Carette clockwork tinplate limousine, circa 1910. (Phillips) $2,580 £1,200

French musical automaton. (Phillips)$3,840 £1,700

Lehmann tinplate clockwork model 'Naughty Boy', in original card box. (D. M. Nesbit & Co.) $650 £300

Tinplate clockwork battleship by Ernst Plank, circa 1903. (Bonham's) $2,590 £1,200

Lehmann tinplate clockwork model 'The Bally Mule', in original box. (D. M. Nesbit & Co.) $195 £90

TOYS

German clockwork tinplate toy billiard player, circa 1920. (Gray's Antique Mews) $427 £190

Scale model of a traction engine with a removable canopy, 16in. long. (Stanilands) $2,160 £1,000

Jonet Francais tin model of an Alfa Romeo racing car. (Churchman's) $455 £200

A child's pedal car, early 1930's. (Phillips) $345 £160

Battery operated Japanese automaton, by Alps. (Sotheby King & Chasemore) $125 £55

Model of the Bristol Scout type C, 1915. (Christie's) $370 £180

Shell model of 'Broughton Hall', 26 x 13in. (J. M. Welch & Co.) $140 £65

Material and wire-framed 'Mickey Mouse' family, labelled Deans Rag Book Co. Ltd., London, circa 1930. (Sotheby King & Chasemore) $280 £130

Toy Bentalls removal van. (Phillips) $111 £55

Child's game 'Lamplough's Model Cricket'. (Phillips) $195 £90

1940's Mahjong set in carved wooden cabinet. (Alfie's Antique Market) $145 £65

French faience chess set, made in Gien in the 19th century. (Sotheby's N. York) $5,500 £2,500

1920's clockwork Bing Model T Ford, painted black, 16cm. long. (Sotheby King & Chasemore) $190 £95

Rare biscuit tin modelled as an International Stores van, 32cm. long. (Sotheby King & Chasemore) $225 £110

Rossignal French made clockwork taxi, complete with driver, 14cm. long. (Sotheby King & Chasemore) $135 £60

Good early clockwork fire engine, made in Germany. (Sotheby King & Chasemore) $335 £150

Late 19th century dapple grey rocking horse on fixed boat rockers.(Phillips) $285 £140

German tinplate clockwork fly, circa 1910. (May, Whetter & Grose) $90 £40

Early American tinplate Mickey Mouse clockwork toy, circa 1930. (Sotheby's Belgravia) $1,080 £500

Rare Edwardian Macfarlane Lang tinplate biscuit tin, with hinged roof, 19.5cm. long. (Sotheby's King & Chasemore) $195 £90

Late 19th century French child's rattle. (J. M. Welch & Son) $130 £60

German clockwork toy, circa 1900. (W. H. Lane & Son) $70 £35

Mid Victorian child's shooting range. (Alfie's Antique Market) $110 £50

Tinplate and clockwork clown in a cart by G. & K., 12.5cm. wide. (Sotheby King & Chasemore) $215 £105

Chad Valley clockwork saloon, circa 1947. (Phillips) $760 £330

Meccano motor car construction set no. 2, complete with driver, instruction sheet, key etc. (Sotheby King & Chasemore) $385 £170

Hessmobile car, clockwork. (Christie's S. Kensington) $480 £210

'Bluebird', 1935, made by Britain's Ltd., England. (Alfie's Antique Market) $250 £110

Antique decorated wood 'Pope Joan' game, 10in. diam., circa 1870. (Christopher Sykes) $85 £38

English tinplate novelty toy 'Banana Joe'. (Phillips) $20 £9

Lehmann automobile and driver. (Christie's S. Kensington) $205 £90

Set of six 38-series Dinky sports cars. (Sotheby King & Chasemore) $185 £80

Mickey and Minnie Mouse stuffed dolls. (Sotheby King & Chasemore) $295 £130

Clockwork boat on wheels. (Christie's S. Kensington) $960 £420

Part of F. G. Taylor Zoo series, Chimpanzees' tea party, eighteen-piece in original boxes. (Phillips) $160 £75

Regulation tyre limber, boxed, and a Britains Beetle lorry with driver, boxed. (Phillips) $60 £26

Structo clockwork racing car, 31cm. long. (Sotheby King & Chasemore) $105 £48

Clockwork airship toy. (Christie's S. Kensington) $570 £250

Pre-war Marklin Auto Union Record car. (Alfie's Antique Market) $195 £90

Three little pigs, clockwork, by Schuco. (Christie's S. Kensington) $175 £77

Victorian child's circular musical box with brass winding handle, 3in. diam., circa 1860. (Christopher Sykes) $110 £48

Lehmann bucking mule novelty toy in poor condition, with one leg missing, circa 1910. (Phillips) $80 £35

Doll's wooden teaset, circa 1870. (Christopher Sykes) $85 £38

Victorian child's snakes and ladders game, 16¾in. square, (Christopher Sykes) $40 £18

Ivory and bamboo Mahjong set, circa 1910. (Alfie's Antique Market) $185 £85

Painted pinewood model toy wheelbarrow, circa 1850, 10½in. long. (Christopher Sykes) $80 £35

Clockwork Donald Duck by Schuco. (Christie's Kensington) $95 £40

German clockwork tinplate toy fire engine, 10in. long. (Christopher Sykes) $155 £70

TRANSPORT

Triumph model H solo motorcycle, 1921, 4 h.p. (Sotheby's) $3,205 £1,450

Fine pennyfarthing bicycle, wheel diameter 142cm. (Sotheby King & Chasemore) $1,305 £580

Triumph speed twin 498cc. solo motorcycle, 1960, frame no. H13160. (Sotheby's) $1,990 £900

Rexette De Luxe three-wheeler fore-car, 1904, chassis no. 3529. (Sotheby's) $8,175 £3,700

Governess cart, circa 1900. (Manchester Auction Mart) $1,010 £450

1944 Dodge WC63 6x6 Personnel and Cargo carrier, with winch. (Sotheby King & Chasemore) $7,130 £3,300

Austin Heavy Twelve two-seater open coupe with dickey, 1928, wheelbase 9ft.4in. long. (Sotheby's) $3,755 £1,700

Black painted pennyfarthing bicycle. (Christie's S. Kensington) $1,295 £600

Railton Fairmile 20 h.p. drophead coupe, 1938, wheelbase 9ft.8in. long. (Sotheby's) $2,875 £1,300

Triumph 2H model 249cc. motorcycle, 1937, frame no. TL1301. (Sotheby's) $1,060 £480

Royal Enfield 350cc. G2 model bullet solo trials motorcycle, circa 1953. (Sotheby's) $840 £380

Austin Twelve four-seater tourer, 1934, wheelbase 9ft.4in. long, chassis no. 76505. (Sotheby's) $4,310 £1,950

Panhard et Levasseur 'Paris-Rouen' type dogcart, circa 1893/94, in original condition.
$54,000 £25,000

Matchless G3LS 350cc. solo motorcycle, 1959, with four speed footchange gearbox. (Sotheby's)
$1,325 £600

Fully restored 1942 Ford G.P.W. or Jeep. (Sotheby King & Chasemore)
$4,320 £2,000

Victorian bath chair with original frame and handle. (Coles, Knapp & Kennedy) $100 £45

Corgi 98cc. motor scooter, circa 1950, frame no. 14448. (Sotheby's) $465 £210

Ford Anglia 8 h.p. two-door saloon, 1939, wheelbase 7ft.6in. long. (Sotheby's) $440 £200

B.A.T. solo motorcycle, circa 1901-02, 492cc. (Sotheby's) $4,420 £2,000

James military lightweight 122cc. solo motorcycle, circa 1939-45. (Sotheby's) $840 £380

Fine four-wheel park drag, by Holland & Holland, painted in yellow and black. (J. Francis, T. Jones & Sons)
$14,040 £6,500

Half-scale replica 1922 200 Mile Race winning G. N., unregistered, 5ft.3in. long. (Sotheby's) $1,655 £750

Pennyfarthing bicycle, circa 1870. (Phillips) $1,125 £520

A.J.S. Starmaker special 247cc. racing solo motorcycle, circa 1965-66. (Sotheby's)
$2,760 £1,250

Morgan 4/4 two-seater open
sports, 1957, capacity
1650cc. (Sotheby's)
$5,305 £2,400

Governess cart in good condition.
(Stride's) $860 £400

Humber 14/40 open five-seater tourer,
1929, wheelbase 9ft.8in. long, in good
condition. (Sotheby's) $12,820 £5,800

Morris Minor 8 h.p. saloon, 1933, chassis
no. 26797, wheelbase 7ft.7in. long.
(Sotheby's) $3,755 £1,700

Francis-Barnett 249cc. solo motorcycle, 1933, frame no. CA28094.
(Sotheby's) $995 £450

Austin Seven 'Gordon England'
Cup model two-seater sports,
1927, wheelbase 6ft.3in. long.
(Sotheby's) $7,515 £3,400

M.G. type ZB Magnette saloon, 1958,
wheelbase 8ft.6in. long, capacity 1489cc.
(Sotheby's) $2,210 £1,000

1914 F.N. shaft drive two
speed 250cc. single solo
motorcycle. (Phillips)
$2,915 £1,350

Austin Eight two-door saloon, 1939,
wheelbase 7ft.4½in. long. (Sotheby's)
$1,545 £700

Austin Seven open two-seater, 1935,
wheelbase 6ft.9in. long. (Sotheby's)
$5,745 £2,600

Raleigh 248cc. solo motorcycle,
1928, frame no. 15884.
(Sotheby's) $1,765 £800

Hillman Minx 9.8 h.p. four-seater
tourer, 1933, wheelbase 7ft.8in.
long. (Sotheby's) $2,650 £1,200

Late 19th century rectangular inlaid mahogany tray. (Phillips) $105 £45

Early 19th century oval papier mache tray, 30½in. wide. (Christie's S. Kensington) $755 £350

Victorian inlaid wood serpentine shaped tray. (Alfie's Antique Market) $135 £60

A Galle marquetry rectangular two-handled tray, 37cm. wide. (Christie's) $570 £260

George III papier mache tray, 30½in. wide, with chinoiserie decoration. (Christie's S. Kensington) $865 £400

Early 19th century black papier mache tray, 20¾in. long, with four shades of gilding. (Christopher Sykes) $170 £75

Edwardian mahogany kidney-shaped tray with wavy gallery, 56cm. wide. (Phillips) $65 £30

Victorian papier mache tray with mother-of-pearl surround. (Alfie's Antique Market) $215 £95

Edwardian oval mahogany tray with brass handles, 74cm. long. (Phillips) $115 £50

Pontypool tin bread basket, circa 1860, 12½in. diam. (Christopher Sykes) $105 £45

Pontypool Toleware snuffer tray, circa 1820, 10in. long. (Christopher Sykes) $85 £40

Early 19th century Persian octagonal shaped tray in brass and tin, 11in. wide. (Christopher Sykes) $100 £45

Handsome Soten tsuba, probably by Soten II, late 17th/early 18th century, 7.4cm. diam. (Christie's) $475 £220

18th century Hizen Christian style mokko iron tsuba, 7cm. diam. (Christie's) $325 £150

Fine oval Shakudo-Nanako tsuba decorated with chrysanthemums, signed and dated 1832, 6.8cm. diam. (Christie's) $600 £280

Good iron Sukashi tsuba pierced with a hare beneath the moon, signed Miochin Muneyoshi, 7.6cm. (Sotheby's) $240 £110

Shibuichi tsuba decorated on one side with shishiabori and copper takazogan. (Sotheby King & Chasemore) $360 £160

Good Kinai school iron tsuba showing Mt. Fuji, signed Echizen Ju Kinai, 8.2cm. (Sotheby's) $195 £90

Large armourer's tsuba by Hamano Noriyuki. (Sotheby's) $2,160 £1,000

18th century circular iron tsuba, signed Choshu Hagi Ju Nakai Tomotsune Saku, 8.2cm. diam. (Christie's) $345 £160

Iron Sukashi tsuba, signed Tadatoki, pierced with the signs of the Zodiac. (Sotheby King & Chasemore) $495 £220

Iron Choshu tsuba carved and pierced as a carp, signed Choshu Hagi Ju Toyoaki Saku. (Sotheby's) $410 £190

Shakudo tsuba incised with Takatsuna and Kagesue below Uigawa Bridge, by Hamano Naoyuki, 8.1cm. (Sotheby's) $1,390 £640

Fine Shakudo-Nanako oval tsuba applied with gilded lobsters, signed Eiseisai Mitsuyasu, 7.5cm. (Sotheby's) $1,040 £480

INDEX

666